Encyclopedia of American Business History and Biography

The Automobile Industry, 1896-1920

Encyclopedia of American Business History

Railroads in the Age of Regulation, 1900-1980, edited by Keith Bryant (1988)

Railroads in the Nineteenth Century, edited by Robert L. Frey (1988)

Iron and Steel in the Nineteenth Century, edited by Paul F. Paskoff (1989)

The Automobile Industry, 1920-1980, edited by George S. May (1989)

Banking and Finance to 1913, edited by Larry Schweikart (1990)

The Automobile Industry, 1896-1920, edited by George S. May (1990)

Encyclopedia of American Business History and Biography

The Automobile Industry, 1896-1920

Edited by

George S. May
Eastern Michigan University

A Bruccoli Clark Layman Book

Facts On File
New York • Oxford • Sydney

Encyclopedia of American Business History and Biography: The Automobile Industry, 1896–1920

Facts On File, Inc.
460 Park Avenue South
New York NY 10016
USA

Facts On File Limited
Collins Street
Oxford OX4 1XJ
United Kingdom

Facts On File Pty Ltd
Talavera & Khartoum Rds
North Ryde NSW 2113
Australia

Library of Congress Cataloging-in-Publication Data
The Automobile industry, 1896–1920 / edited by George S. May.
    p. cm. — (Encyclopedia of American business history and
biography)
    "A Bruccoli Clark Layman book."
    Bibliography: p.
    Includes index.
    ISBN 0-8160-2084-1
    1. Automobile industry and trade—United States—History.
I. May, George S. II. Series.
HD9710.U52A815   1989
338.4'76292'097309034—dc20   89-11672
                                              CIP

British and Australian CIP data available on request from Facts On File.

Facts On File books are available at special discounts when purchased
in bulk quantities for businesses, associations, institutions or sales
promotions. Please contact the Special Sales Department of our New York
office at 212/683-2244 (dial 800/322-8755 except in NY, AK, or HI).

Designed by Quentin Fiore
Manufactured by the Maple-Vail Manufacturing Group
Printed in the United States of America   This book is printed on acid-free paper.

10 9 8 7 6 5 4 3 2 1

To the memory of John B. Rae

Contents

Foreword

The Encyclopedia of American Business History and Biography chronicles America's material civilization through its business figures and businesses. It is a record of American aspirations—of success and of failure. It is a history of the impact of business on American life. The volumes have been planned to serve a cross section of users: students, teachers, scholars, researchers, and government and corporate officials. Individual volumes or groups of volumes cover a particular industry during a defined period; thus each *EABH&B* volume is freestanding, providing a history expressed through biographies and buttressed by a wide range of supporting entries. In many cases a single volume is sufficient to treat an industry, but certain industries require two or more volumes. When completed, the *EABH&B* will provide the fullest available history of American enterprise.

The editorial direction of *EABH&B* is provided by the general editor and the editorial board. The general editor appoints volume editors whose duties are to prepare, in consultation with the editorial board, the list of entries for each volume, to assign the entries to contributors, to vet the submitted entries, and to work in close cooperation with the Bruccoli Clark Layman editorial staff so as to maintain consistency of treatment. All entries are written by specialists in their fields, not by staff writers. Volume editors are experienced scholars.

The publishers and editors of *EABH&B* are convinced that timing is crucial to notable careers. Therefore, the biographical entries in each volume of the series place businesses and their leaders in the social, political, and economic contexts of their times. Supplementary background rubrics on companies, inventions, legal decisions, marketing innovations, and other topics are integrated with the biographical entries in alphabetical order.

The general editor and the volume editors determine the space to be allotted to biographies as major entries, standard entries, and short entries.

Major entries, reserved for giants of business and industry (e.g., Henry Ford, J. P. Morgan, Andrew Carnegie, James J. Hill), require approximately 10,000 words. Standard biographical entries are in the range of 3,500-5,000 words. Short entries are reserved for lesser figures who require inclusion and for significant figures about whom little information is available. When appropriate, the biographical entries stress their subjects' roles in shaping the national experience, showing how their activities influenced the way Americans lived. Unattractive or damaging aspects of character and conduct are not suppressed. All biographical entries conform to a basic format.

A significant part of each volume is devoted to concise background entries supporting and elucidating the biographies. These nonbiographical entries provide basic information about the industry or field covered in the volume. Histories of companies are necessarily brief and limited to key events. To establish a context for all entries, each volume includes an overview of the industry treated. These historical introductions are normally written by the volume editors.

We have set for ourselves large tasks and important goals. We aspire to provide a body of work that will help reduce the imbalance in the writing of American history, the study of which too often slights business. Our hope is also to stimulate interest in business leaders, enterprises, and industries that have not been given the scholarly attention they deserve. By setting high standards for accuracy, balanced treatment, original research, and clear writing, we have tried to ensure that these works will commend themselves to those who seek a full account of the development of America.

—William H. Becker
General Editor

Acknowledgments

This book was produced by Bruccoli Clark Layman, Inc. James W. Hipp, series editor for the *Encyclopedia of American Business History and Biography,* and Michael D. Senecal were the in-house editors.

Production coordinator is James W. Hipp. Systems manager is Charles D. Brower. Photography editor is Susan Todd. Permissions editor is Jean W. Ross. Layout and graphics supervisor is Penney L. Haughton. Copyediting supervisor is Bill Adams. Typesetting supervisor is Kathleen M. Flanagan. Typography coordinator is Sheri Beckett Neal. Information systems analyst is George F. Dodge. Charles Lee Egleston and Laura Ingram are editorial associates. The production staff includes Rowena Betts, Anne L. M. Bowman, Teresa Chaney, Patricia Coate, Sarah A. Estes, Mary L. Goodwin, Willie M. Gore, Cynthia Hallman, Susan C. Heath, David Marshall James, Kathy S. Merlette, Laura Garren Moore, John Myrick, Laurrè Sinckler, Maxine K. Smalls, John C. Stone III, Jennifer Toth, and Betsy L. Weinberg.

Walter W. Ross and Parris Boyd did the library research with the assistance of the reference staff at the Thomas Cooper Library of the University of South Carolina: Gwen Baxter, Daniel Boice, Faye Chadwell, Cathy Eckman, Gary Geer, Cathie Gottlieb, David L. Haggard, Jens Holley, Jackie Kinder, Marcia Martin, Laurie Preston, Jean Rhyne, Carol Tobin, and Virginia Weathers.

Introduction

It is generally agreed that commercial production of automobiles began in the United States in 1896, ten years after the first such production had taken place in Europe. Since only a handful of horseless carriages were produced in the early years, and it was not until the 1920s that the automobile assumed the dominant role in American life that it has played ever since, there remain at the end of the twentieth century a great many Americans whose lives have encompassed much if not all of the period covered by that industry's history.

Of course the automobile did not just suddenly appear in the 1890s. Its origins are to be found in humanity's centuries-old dream of mechanized locomotion. Visions of self-propelled vehicles only began to become a reality, however, when the development of the steam engine in the eighteenth century provided the first practical method of powering such vehicles. In 1769 Nicholas-Joseph Cugnot built a cumbersome 3-wheeled steamer that was designed to haul French army artillery pieces. It was rejected as too slow and impractical, but Cugnot nevertheless is regarded as the creator of the first motorized road vehicle. The honor of being the first American to achieve that distinction is usually accorded to Oliver Evans, who, in 1805, constructed a self-propelled steam dredge for the city of Philadelphia. Named the "Oruktor Amphibolos," the ponderous machine moved at such a snail's pace that any hopes Evans may have harbored of winning financial support for a more practical vehicle were effectively ended.

With the development of steam railroads by the late 1820s, interest in self-propelled land vehicles mostly centered on the perfection of this new means of transportation. By the middle of the century, some steam threshing equipment began to be made self-propelled to enable them to be moved more easily from farm to farm during the harvest season. Occasionally, heavy steam-powered road-working machines, known as road locomotives, also were seen lumbering down the highway. These moved under their own power, but it was not until the 1860s that anything that clearly could be regarded as a true ancestor of the automobile appeared in the United States. At that time Sylvester H. Roper, a talented mechanic and inventor living in Roxbury, Massachusetts, tested the first of some ten experimental steam carriages that he built between the 1860s and 1896, when he died while testing a 2-wheeled steamer. One of Roper's steamers, which survives in the Henry Ford Museum in Dearborn, Michigan, is a little 450-pound 2-passenger vehicle built in 1865. The vehicle was demonstrated before audiences throughout the East and Midwest and was billed as a "Family Steam Carriage for the Common Roads."

Many others in addition to Roper were building workable steam-powered horseless carriages in the latter part of the nineteenth century. By the early 1890s two new sources of power had been tested when William Morrison drove an electric vehicle on the streets of Des Moines in 1891 and Frank Duryea made his first test run in Springfield, Massachusetts, in 1893 of a motor wagon designed by him and his brother Charles and employing a gasoline internal combustion engine. Whether Roper, Morrison, and the Duryeas were the first Americans to have success with vehicles using these sources of power has been much debated, but the important point is that the vehicles and those developed by others during these years were all experimental. There was no serious effort made to manufacture any of the vehicles for sale to the public until the very end of the nineteenth century, despite the fact that steam-powered vehicles that worked reasonably well had been around for a good many years.

The delay was in part due to technological factors. It was only in the latter part of the century that the carriage industry, which supplied most of the bodies used by the early vehicles, found ways of building carriages that were strong enough to withstand the greater stress imposed by the attached engines and mechanisms used to power a vehicle originally designed to be pulled by a horse. By that time the larger carriage manufacturers had also developed the means of producing carriages at the rate of one per hour and selling them through networks of franchised dealers—manufacturing and marketing techniques that were to be copied by the automotive industry.

The bicycle industry, which only emerged in the last two decades of the nineteenth century, was probably of greater importance in the rise of the automobile than the long-established carriage industry. The number of carriage manufacturers that enjoyed much success when they converted to the production of motor vehicles was quite small, while the success rate among bicycle companies making the same change in product line was considerably greater. In part this can be attributed to some basic similarities in the products. Ball bearings, cable brake controls, chain- and shaft-drive systems, gearing, tubular frame construction, wire wheels, and pneumatic tires were all an outgrowth of the bicycle industry and were carried over into the design and construction of automobiles.

But the most important contribution made by the bicycle industry was the interest its product aroused in a new means of personal transportation. Until the bicycle achieved its sudden great popularity, beginning in the mid 1880s, the automotive pioneer Hiram Percy Maxim declared that most people had not given much thought "to the possibilities of independent, long-distance travel over the ordinary highway. We thought the railroad was good enough." But one night in 1892 when he was returning by bicycle to Lynn, Massachusetts, after a visit to his girlfriend in nearby Salem, Maxim had a sudden realization of the "revolutionary change in transportation" the bicycle represented. "My bicycle was propelled at a respectable speed by a mechanism operated by my muscles." It enabled him to make the trip in half the time it would have taken in a horse-drawn carriage. The train was faster, but the bicycle enabled him to choose when he was going to depart, the route he would take, and it would deliver him to the door of his home. "If I could build a little engine and use its power to do the pedaling, and if I could use a regular carriage instead of a bicycle, there would be no limit to where I could go. Distances would be halved. Towns would become nearer together. . . . More people would intermingle. It would profoundly influence the course of civilization itself." Although the reasons for the collapse of the bicycle boom in the United States at the turn

of the century are not entirely clear, the fact that the automobile provided its user with even greater mobility and without the physical exertion demanded by the bicycle was no doubt a contributing factor. However, finding and developing the source of power that would replace the foot-driven pedals of the bicycle and that the public would find acceptable were not quite as simple as Maxim and his fellow automotive pioneers at first thought.

New England was the site of the first automobile manufacturing in the country, with Springfield's Duryea company launching commercial automobile production in 1896 with 13 gasoline-powered Duryea motor wagons. But the company was soon out of business, and the other more important companies that arose in that section of the country tended to favor electric or steam power over gasoline. The Pope Manufacturing Company of Hartford, Connecticut, a major bicycle manufacturer, rejected the advice of its chief engineer, Hiram Maxim, that it should emphasize gasoline-powered vehicles when it began automobile production. Instead, nearly all of Pope's industry-leading production of some 500 horseless carriages in 1897-1898 were electrics. The year 1898 also saw the beginnings of the production of steam carriages when the Stanley Brothers Motor Carriage Company produced 100 of the steamers that the twins Francis and Freelan Stanley had developed.

Although electrics and steamers far outnumbered the gasoline cars produced during this early stage of the industry's development, they did not maintain that leadership for long. The number of companies producing electrics and steamers grew, spreading from New England to the Midwest, but well before 1910 it was clear that the gasoline internal combustion engine had won the battle for public acceptance. The ease with which the electric could be started and operated had made it an early favorite, especially among women drivers. But the development of a practical self-starter, introduced in the 1912 Cadillac, which eliminated the difficult job of starting a gasoline car with a crank, also eliminated one of the electric's major selling points and, when combined with limited range imposed by the car's batteries, killed the market for the car. The steamers were better equipped to compete with gasoline cars, but the decision of Cleveland's White company, producers of one of the best steamers, to switch to gasoline car production after 1910 was a clear sign that steamers, like electrics, no longer were regarded as having much of a future.

By 1900-1901 leadership in the new industry was shifting from New England to the Midwest. One reason may have been that much of New England's investment capital was already tied up in that area's well-established industries, whereas the economy in the Midwest was still in a state of flux. But another possible reason is that the automotive producers in New England made the mistake of backing the wrong technology. A good many companies that produced electrics and steamers did arise in the Midwest, but those pioneers, such as Alexander Winton in Cleveland, Elwood Haynes and the Apperson brothers in Kokomo, Indiana, and Thomas B. Jeffery in Kenosha, Wisconsin, who were working on gasoline-powered cars in the 1890s, were more typical of the emphasis that prevailed in that region.

Despite the importance of the automobile manufacturing that developed in Ohio, Indiana, and Wisconsin by the start of the twentieth century, that which was developing in Michigan was far more important and by about 1905 had made that state the worldwide leader of the industry. In Michigan, almost without exception, pioneer developers devoted their attention to gasoline cars. Ransom E. Olds, a manufacturer of steam engines, experimented with a steam car in Lansing in the late 1880s and early 1890s, but his experience convinced him that there were too many problems connected with this power source. He later tinkered with an electric but only because he recognized that the cars had some temporary appeal until problems inherent in the gasoline-powered cars were corrected. Olds was thus unusual in having tried all three methods of powering a horseless carriage, but he left no doubt in a talk he gave in 1897 that he regarded the gasoline engine as by far the best means of powering a road vehicle.

The fact that Olds and many of the other Michigan pioneers, such as Henry Ford, had become thoroughly familiar with the gasoline engine before they moved on to apply it to propelling a vehicle may have given them an advantage over other manufacturers, whose background was based on a knowledge of manufacturing carriages or bicycles. But the biggest advantage they had was in the kind of automobile they decided they wanted to produce. In 1896, when he had built his first gasoline vehicle, Olds declared that his goal was to produce a simple, easy-to-operate, lightweight car with just enough power to meet the average driver's needs. He was by no means alone in having such an objective. Charles E. Duryea had expressed the same ambition two years earlier, but he had little success in achieving it, while Frank Duryea, after the two brothers split up in the late 1890s, went on to design and help build large, powerful, and expensive cars. Larger automobiles came to dominate the production of the companies located in the East and in much of the Midwest. In Michigan, however, the approach outlined by Olds in 1896 was the one that was adopted. Low-priced, high-volume cars became the backbone of the Michigan automobile industry and the lack of such cars proved to be the downfall of production in other parts of the country.

It took Olds several years to get any but a handful of cars on the market. He needed outside financial support, and here again his experience provides a clue as to why Michigan emerged as the leader of the industry. The state's economy had been based on the exploitation of its abundant natural resources, particularly timber and iron and copper ores. As the automobile industry began to emerge, however, the lumber and mining industries had peaked, and individuals who had made fortunes in those areas were looking for new places to invest where their funds would bring a higher return. It was $200,000 of that "old" money that brought about the merger in 1899 of the Olds engine company and the anemic Olds Motor Vehicle Company to form the Olds Motor Works, which survives today as General Motors' (GM) Oldsmobile Division.

With the financial backing he needed and a new factory in Detroit, Olds, after some months of indecision as to what type of car to produce, settled upon a runabout model. With a distinctive front end that led to it being called the curved-dash Oldsmobile, the 600-pound, 1-cylinder car, selling for $650, was, despite production problems resulting from a fire that destroyed the Detroit plant in March 1901, the best-selling car in the country by the end of 1902. A runabout was the name of a standard carriage design, and in choosing it Olds was no innovator. Other American automakers had adopted it earlier when they began to put out the American equivalent of the lightweight car that the French company of DeDion-Bouton had popularized in Europe at the end of the 1890s. The success of the curved-dash Olds had as much to do with the promotional and marketing efforts of the Olds company as it did with the car itself, which was no better than many other runabouts whose makers, however, could not match the breadth of talent assembled in the Olds organization.

The Oldsmobile remained the country's—and the world's—most popular car for several years, with sales by 1904 approaching an annual figure of 5,000, numbers unheard of in the industry before that time. These sales, in turn, stimulated the formation of a host of new companies that hoped to cash in on the proven popularity of the runabout design. Nowhere was the Oldsmobile's influence more important than it was among those who had worked at Olds or who had produced parts for the Oldsmobile. Their successes in establishing new and lasting automobile companies made it certain that Detroit and southern Michigan would achieve dominance in the industry. Jonathan D. Maxwell and Charles B. King, Olds engineers, left in 1902 to design a car for a new Detroit company, Northern, that, through mergers, eventually wound up as part of the Studebaker organization. Maxwell in 1903 designed a new car, named after himself, which was first produced in the East but was brought back to Detroit. In the 1920s the Maxwell company became the foundation of the Chrysler Corporation. Robert Hupp, another Olds employee, left to establish a Detroit company producing the Hupmobile, a car that remained in production until the end of the 1930s. Several other Olds executives, led by Roy D. Chapin and Howard E. Coffin, left to form the Hudson company, for many years one of the most important of the independent automakers. Ransom Olds also left the Olds Motor Works in 1904 as a result of policy disagreements with the majority stockholders. He formed in Lansing the Reo company, whose automobile sales for some years exceeded those of Olds's former company.

Among Oldsmobile parts suppliers, Benjamin Briscoe, whose company made sheet metal parts, provided backing for Jonathan Maxwell that led to the formation of the company producing Maxwell's car. Henry M. Leland, whose Detroit machine shop had made transmissions and engines for the Olds, was principally responsible for the development of the Cadillac company, which, under his leadership, soon progressed from the production of an inexpensive runabout to the high-priced prestige cars for which that Detroit manufacturer became famous. The Dodge brothers, operators of another Detroit

machine shop, who had also produced engines for the Oldsmobile runabout, in 1914 began making their own cars. Dodge cars remain a mainstay of the Chrysler Corporation, which acquired the Dodge company in 1928. But before they had their own car, the Dodges, beginning in 1903, produced engines and other vital parts for another Detroit company, the Ford Motor Company.

Henry Ford had tested his first car in June 1896, more than two months before Olds tested his gasoline car in Lansing. For a variety of reasons, however, it took Ford seven years before any significant number of his cars reached the market. By the time the Ford Motor Company was formed in June 1903, Ransom Olds was well established as the country's most famous automaker. But Olds soon took a back seat to Ford, who emerged as not only the most celebrated automobile manufacturer but probably the most famous industrialist of the century. He did this by building on the foundations laid down by Olds, who had seen that there was a market for a lightweight, low-priced car. But Olds's runabout model proved to be too fragile to withstand the pounding of the notoriously bad roads found throughout the country. By 1904-1905 customer complaints were causing the industry as a whole to turn to the touring car, a bigger and more durable model but also generally about twice as expensive. Olds himself, in his new Reo company, fell in line, giving greater emphasis to the touring car than to the runabout, providing the buyer with increased driving comfort but at a much higher price.

Ford did not follow the industry trend. He remained committed to the low-priced range. The first Fords in 1903 were runabouts, with a more powerful engine than the curved-dash Olds but in other respects much like that industry leader. Ford recognized the defects of the runabout but rather than sacrifice the runabout's major appeal, its low price, through the substitution of a touring car, Ford and his staff concentrated on developing a model that would be much more durable but which could also be sold in the runabout's price range. After a succession of models had been developed, the Ford Model T, introduced in fall 1908, satisfied Ford that he had found the durable, lightweight, easy-to-operate, and easy-to-repair car he had been seeking. More than 15 million Model Ts were produced between 1908 and 1927, and during much of that time the T was the only Ford model manufactured.

The Model T is perhaps the most celebrated car of all time, and it alone would have been sufficient to make its creator famous. But Ford's primary claim to fame as a manufacturer lies in the success of the efforts he instituted to mass-produce the car, an action which made his name synonymous with mass production around the world. Although the Model T was the kind of car Ford had wanted, it cost considerably more to produce than some of Ford's earlier models. He therefore sought to lower the car's price by improving the efficiency of production methods. Earlier, in order to keep up with the demand for the Oldsmobile, Olds had increased output by establishing an early version of a production line, where workers, rather than being involved in building an entire car, were assigned a limited number of tasks, with the parts they needed for such assignments kept close at hand. But while this enabled Oldsmobile production in a year to go from a few hundred to a few thousand cars, the price of the car remained the same. Ford's production reforms went far beyond those that Olds had instituted, with the final step, the development of the moving assembly line in 1913-1914, elevating Ford's production capabilities to annual levels of hundreds of thousands of cars and by the 1920s to millions of units. Unlike Olds, however, an essential part of Ford's goal in introducing these changes was to make it possible progressively to lower the price of the Model T, thereby expanding the number of potential customers for the car and increasing the volume of sales.

Ford's status not only as an industrialist but as a folk hero was further enhanced in 1911 by his victory in the Selden Patent Case, the most famous patent infringement dispute in American history. The case grew out of a patent awarded to George B. Selden in 1895 that claimed to cover all motor vehicles using a gasoline internal combustion engine. In 1899 the Electric Vehicle Company, a New York firm, acquired the rights to Selden's patent and sought to collect royalties from gasoline car companies, which would be licensed to produce cars under the patent. In an effort to stave off costly and prolonged legal conflicts, a group of car manufacturers, led by Detroit's Olds Motor Works and Packard, agreed to recognize the validity of the patent. In 1903 they formed the Association of Licensed Automobile Manufacturers (ALAM), and, in return for saving the Selden patent holders substantial court costs, they were given the right to deter-

mine which companies would be licensed under the patent. The Ford Motor Company was turned down when it applied for admission to the ranks of the ALAM, for reasons that are unclear. The company defiantly went ahead with production, openly challenging the Selden forces to bring it to court. Left with little choice, the ALAM filed suit against Ford in fall 1903, and the case dragged along for more than seven years. Other companies were added to the list of those being sued, but it was Ford that fought the case through to the end. Early in 1911 a federal appeals court agreed with Ford's contention that the terms of the Selden patent applied only to manufacturers using a 2-cycle engine. Since Ford and virtually all other American carmakers used 4-cycle engines, they were not guilty of infringing on the patent-holders' rights.

Aside from the bonanza of free publicity the case generated for Ford, the Selden case had important consequences for the industry. To avoid such legal wranglings in the future, agreements were reached that resulted in a general sharing of patents in the industry. Such agreements were administered by a trade association. The ALAM had been the first such association to have any widespread support in the industry, and although the effect of the 1911 court decision was to wipe out the major reason for the group's existence, it was soon replaced by other organizations. Presently, the Motor Vehicle Manufacturers Association is the recognized voice for the industry's interests.

In addition to representing an industry before the public, the function of a trade association is also to promote greater cooperation and accord among the various elements of the group it represents. The ALAM made great strides in that direction through the leadership it gave to the movement to standardize the size of basic motor vehicle components, such as spark plugs, wheel rims, and nuts and bolts. By eliminating the wasteful and expensive practice of requiring such routine parts to be manufactured according to the differing specifications of each automaker, the ALAM made a contribution that rivaled mass production in promoting greater production efficiency.

The ALAM, however, was often seen as a promoter of discord, not harmony, within the industry because of its power to determine who could or could not be licensed under the Selden patent. It is not clear what goal the association's leadership had in mind in exercising that power. Some, it appears, viewed it as a means of creating a kind of monopoly over the business for a select number of members. "Our Association," Henry B. Joy told James W. Packard shortly after the group was formed, "I hope will be the means of saving the trade to those who are now engaged in the business." Others claimed, however, the goal was to exclude only shoddy, fly-by-night operations and thereby assure the consumer that admission to membership in the ALAM was an indication that the company was a reputable firm producing vehicles of an acceptable nature.

If monopoly were actually its objective, the ALAM leadership could not have taken much satisfaction in the success of its efforts. Whether or not an automobile company was a member of the association seems to have had little or no effect on the public's car-buying habits. During much of the ALAM's life some of the most popular cars on the market were the products of unlicensed companies, with Ford in particular enjoying an almost uninterrupted growth in sales; by 1911 it had become by far the largest producer of cars in the world. However, if the objective of the association was to bring some order to the industry and to provide some guidance as to the quality of the vehicles being produced, it was obvious that despite ALAM's failure to achieve even this, the problem was real.

No one knows how many motor vehicle companies have existed in the United States. One common estimate puts the number at around 1,500, which may or may not include the numerous companies formed to produce trucks, a product that developed side by side with automobiles but that is often overlooked. There is no doubt, however, that this number includes a great many companies that announced their intention to produce a car or truck but never got beyond the construction of a prototype model, if that far. Nevertheless, if these companies are excluded there still remain hundreds of firms, perhaps a thousand, that actually produced something. Most of these arose in the earlier years, with relatively few being formed after 1920. With so many companies vying for attention, market conditions by the beginning of the twentieth century were chaotic. Many companies fell by the wayside due to poor management, inadequate financial resources, or the inferior nature of their product. Others were forced to fold as a result of the normal competitive pressures from the bigger manufacturers. In addition, the panic of 1907 provided an early indication of how sensitive the market for motor vehicles was to any change in the economy. During this brief recession automobile sales dropped sharply, enough to wipe out some manufacturers that did not have sufficient reserves to tide them over until sales recovered. More disturbing, perhaps, was the fact that companies that had supplied parts to these bankrupt firms also suffered and, in some cases, were also faced with the prospect of bankruptcy. The ripple effect, on the economy, of the collapse of an automobile company was already in evidence, foreshadowing the economic consequences that were felt in later periods of recession and depression when the industry had achieved its peak development.

The panic of 1907 helped touch off a wave of interest in cutting down the number of automobile companies. The method most employed in creating more stability in the industry was through merger and consolidation. Although this was a period in which Theodore Roosevelt gained fame as the "Trust Buster," it was also the era in which competition in such industries as steel and farm equipment had been greatly reduced through the merger of several competing firms into the giant U.S. Steel and International Harvester combines. There had been some unsuccessful attempts at merger in the automobile industry prior to 1907, but then in 1907 George W. Perkins of J. P. Morgan & Company raised the subject of consolidation in a discussion with Benjamin Briscoe. Morgan had long been the leading advocate of consolidation as a means of promoting a more stable economy, and he and his company had been the catalyst of the U.S. Steel and International Harvester mergers. Perkins now indicated to Briscoe that Morgan was interested in promoting a merger of leading automobile manufacturers. Briscoe, whose sheet metal company and Maxwell-Briscoe Motor Company had been financed with Morgan's help, took the hint and proceeded later that year to have a meeting with William C. Durant, who was in charge of the highly successful Buick company in Flint, Michigan.

Durant was immediately attracted by Briscoe's suggestion that Buick be a part of the merger. Several years before he had tried unsuccessfully to merge his Durant-Dort Carriage Company with other carriage and wagon manufacturers. Durant had seen that potential merger as a means of strengthening his position in the market for horse-drawn vehicles. Now that he had turned his attention to the automobile industry, Durant saw in Briscoe's idea the means of gaining a greater share of the future market for cars. At a time when total sales in the industry were less than 50,000 units a year, Durant predicted annual sales of at least 1 million within ten years, a prediction that is said to have caused George Perkins to declare in disbelief, "If he has any sense he'll keep those notions to himself." As it turned out, Durant greatly underestimated the demand that actually did develop by 1917, but his reading of the direction in which sales would go convinced him that the manufacturer that offered the public a choice of cars stood a better chance of gaining an increased market share than the one that produced only one model. The latter approach was one that Ford used with enormous success for many years with his Model T, but in the end the diversity that Durant favored would be the marketing strategy that would prevail.

The initial plans to bring about a merger of Buick, Maxwell-Briscoe, Ford, and Reo collapsed in spring 1908 because of differences between Henry Ford and Ransom Olds on the one hand and Durant, Briscoe, and the Morgan interests on the other as to how the merger was to be carried through. After negotiations to bring about a Buick-Maxwell merger likewise had to be called off, Durant and Briscoe went their separate ways. In 1910 Briscoe, with Wall Street backing, was able to organize the United States Motor Company, which ultimately gained control of more than 130 firms. Most of these were small parts manufacturing businesses, and among the automobile manufacturers that were acquired only Briscoe's own Maxwell-Briscoe company was worth very much. Partly as a result of this lack of companies that could help Maxwell-Briscoe cover the losses of other subsidiaries, U.S. Motor was forced into bankruptcy in 1912, with the Maxwell car being about the only thing that survived the collapse.

Durant, meanwhile, in September 1908, had formed the GM Company. It was organized under the laws of New Jersey, but the strength of the company would rest on its operations in Michigan. It was a holding company that technically manufactured nothing but controlled manufacturing companies through its ownership of stock. Durant's Buick was the first GM acquisition, followed later in 1908 by the Olds Motor Works, and in 1909 by a score of other companies including Cadillac and the Oakland Motor Car Company of Pontiac, which,

as part of GM, evolved into Pontiac. Durant also sought to insure his car companies of a supply of parts by acquiring control of several companies producing such components. Like Briscoe, he also picked up some companies that had little or no value. With Buick, Cadillac, and a revitalized Oldsmobile on board, these losing elements within GM did not present as serious a problem as that faced by U.S. Motor. But economic conditions in summer 1910 brought a brief decline in sales and created a severe cash shortage that threatened GM's survival. To save the company, Durant was forced to accept an offer of financial help from an eastern syndicate that included the requirement that he give up his management of the company during the five-year period of the loan. In a spectacular demonstration of his entrepreneurial talents, Durant organized the Chevrolet company, which he then used to regain control of GM in 1916. Durant's second turn at the helm of GM ended in 1920 during another financial crisis, but by that time GM was ready to realize, under new management, its potential for leadership in the industry.

By 1920 the basic patterns that would dictate the future development of the industry had been established. With the development of GM and the parallel expansion of Ford's operations, the giant Michigan-based companies that would dominate the industry were in place. There remained a great many smaller companies, some of them, such as Hudson, Packard, and Hupp, located in Michigan and adding to the already large share of the automobile market held by the Michigan companies. That share amounted to 77.9 percent of the total American motor vehicle output by 1914. Among the non-Michigan companies were such honored names as Pierce-Arrow, Mercer, Peerless, Marmon, Stutz, Franklin, Locomobile, and Auburn, but with the exception of a few companies, such as Willys-Overland in Toledo, which for several years in the second decade of the century was a distant second to Ford in sales, these companies produced small numbers of high-priced luxury cars. They were able to stay in business for a while longer, but eventually their ranks were thinned by competitive advantages possessed by Ford and GM. Only by merging Maxwell and Chalmers, creating a new car bearing his name, and finally purchasing Dodge was Walter Chrysler able to mount a challenge to the leadership of GM and Ford.

Technologically, too, the experimental stage of the automobile's development was largely at an end by 1920. Already by 1910 the automobile had emerged as a vehicle that later generations could recognize as an automobile, in contrast with the primitive, awkward-looking vehicles of only a few years earlier. By 1905 the horseless-carriage school of design was being abandoned, as the engine, which American companies for some reason had thought they had to mount under the carriage, was placed boldly out in front under a hood, a basic feature of a distinctive automotive profile that European manufacturers had adopted years before. The tiller that had been used to steer the first cars had been replaced by the steering wheel, which, from 1908 onward, was more and more likely to be found on the left-hand side of the car. Windshields, running boards, electric horns, and acetylene gas lights were other improvements that had been made by the end of the decade. In the next ten years, the self-starter, introduced on the Cadillac in 1912, the V-8 engine, also introduced by Cadillac in its 1915 model, and the development of the all-steel body were further developments that reduced the possibility of major new breakthroughs occurring in the years after 1920.

By 1920 the automobile had ceased to be a novelty. There were few areas in the country and few individuals that had not been exposed to this means of transportation. For the overwhelming majority of Americans this was a welcome development. Stories of widespread opposition to the automobile have been demonstrated to have been greatly exaggerated if not totally false. The most widely reported source of such opposition was among farmers, but their resentment was not so much directed at the automobile as it was at the manner in which some urban residents, who constituted the bulk of the early car buyers, drove their cars through rural areas with a seeming disregard for the safety of the residents or their livestock. The true attitude of the farmers was soon evident when they adopted it in greater numbers than did urban residents as a whole. To the farmer and his family a car was seen as a liberating force, freeing them from the isolation that horse-drawn conveyances had not been able to eliminate. Most country roads were in wretched condition, but the automobile companies, led by Ford with its Model T, responded by building cars that could operate under those conditions, while at the same time lobbying for the improved roads that would be the long-term solution to this problem in the new automobile age.

Americans cannot be said to have adopted the automobile as readily as they did without some warning of the problems that its widespread adoption would entail. The noise and smell associated with the early gasoline cars were certainly evident to everyone who came in contact with them. One wealthy Detroiter, Barton Peck, abandoned his plans to manufacture cars in the late 1890s because he was convinced that city governments would not for long tolerate their continued presence on their streets. Within a surprisingly short time concerns were being raised regarding the traffic congestion and parking problems that were being created by the growing number of cars in the cities. At least as early as 1912 public health officials were warning of the possible health hazards created by the automobile's exhaust fumes. Motor accidents with resulting injuries or death received extensive attention in the press and by 1917 were leading one insurance spokesman to refer to them as a major crisis.

But through it all sales of cars continued to climb. Early statistics are not as reliable as later ones. In 1900 there are said to have been 8,000 cars in the country. Since no state or local authorities at that time required the registration of motor vehicles, that figure is strictly an estimate, and it probably exaggerates the number. Passenger car sales that year, likewise based on estimates that are not always entirely reliable, have been placed at 4,192. By 1910 sales of cars, trucks, and buses had risen to 187,000, with the total number of cars owned in the country, now based on more reliable registration figures, up to 458,000. By 1920 sales had topped 2 million for the first time, and registrations had passed the 8 million mark.

This growth was fueled by the fact that people were buying something new. It was a seller's market, which enabled the manufacturer to concentrate his efforts on expanding his production facilities to keep up with the demand, knowing that almost any car he produced was likely to find a buyer. By the second decade of the century, however, some were beginning to wonder how much longer these conditions would last before the market was saturated. In 1915 John North Willys made the first major move to begin selling cars on the installment plan. Until then cars had been sold, with only a few exceptions, for cash only. That worked well for as long as there remained a large number of affluent people who were in the market for their first car and who could afford to pay the full price on delivery of the vehicle. But that ultimately restricted the manufacturer from expanding his market to include those for whom the price of even the cheapest car represented an outlay equal to much, if not all, of their annual income. Ford sought to deal with that problem by steadily lowering the price of his car, until by the early 1920s a new Model T could be purchased for just under $300. Even in the 1920s, however, that constituted an amount that the average workingman could not pay in one lump sum without great sacrifice. Thus Ford was finally compelled at the end of that decade to provide his customers with the alternative of a credit plan for the purchase of one of his cars. GM, meanwhile, had set up its General Motors Acceptance Corporation in 1919 to position itself to provide the credit that the changing market conditions of the 1920s would demand.

By 1920, therefore, the motor vehicle and its industry had come an amazingly long way in only some 25 years, but it was only the prelude for what was to come. Ownership of a car had yet, with few exceptions, not trickled down to working-class families. The streetcars and the railroads, at the time referred to as "the poor man's automobile," were flourishing, providing transportation for the masses. The heart of a city's economic life was still centered in its downtown business district, serving a community that was still relatively compact in its dimensions, save for a few narrow suburban enclaves that had developed along interurban commuter lines and were inhabited by upper-middle-class and upper-class families. Most urban residents, however, continued to live close to the places where they worked, as they had done in the past. But all that was about to change as the boom in sales that erupted in the 1920s began to alter these age-old constraints on where one had to live and where business activities had to be carried on. The revolution that Hiram Maxim had seen coming with the automobile age would begin to be felt in the cities, transforming life there as it had already begun to transform life in the rural areas.

This volume deals with the automotive industry from 1896 to 1920. The second volume deals with development from 1920 to 1980. To avoid as much as possible dividing a topic in order to fit it into these two periods, decisions had to be made in the case of topics or individuals that overlapped

these periods as to where they should appear. In the case of GM and Ford, because of the great importance of these companies, it was decided to include historical information on both companies in both volumes. In the case of all other companies, however, the article dealing with each of them appears in the volume covering the period in which that company was founded. A few background entries, such as the one on marketing, have been divided so as to provide information on those subjects in both volumes, but in most cases these articles are to be found in one volume only. The decision as to where to place them may at times seem to have been rather arbitrary, but it is based on an effort to determine in which period the topic under discussion first achieved some importance. This is also the basis for determining where biographical entries should be placed. Here it was felt that in no case should such entries be divided, and thus complete biographies are included in the period in which the individual made his greatest contributions. The biography of Henry Ford is included in this volume because, although Ford remained active in his company almost until his death in 1947, his major contributions are seen as falling into the period before 1920. On the other hand, although Charles Kettering is most famous for developing the self-starter, introduced in 1912, his biography has been included in the second volume because of his post-1920 service as head of research at GM for some three decades.

In a work of this type, it is not possible to cover every topic that many would like to see included. Lack of space, of sufficient information, or of qualified authors to deal with a topic are factors that account for the absence of some entries that might otherwise have been included. With respect to company histories it should be noted that no attempt is made to include entries for all automotive companies. Aside from the fact that any such effort to be all-inclusive would have, because of the sheer number of such companies, made it necessary to drop many worthwhile entries, most of these companies are of interest primarily to automotive specialists. Reference works covering all, or nearly all, these companies are already available. In a more general reference work such as this one, it was felt that it was sufficient to include accounts only of the major companies, plus a representative selection of other companies whose contributions or leaders make them of some importance.

In spite of these and other necessary omissions, however, the editor believes that users of these volumes will find a breadth of information on all aspects of American automotive history that has never before been available either to generalists or specialists.

–George S. May
Eastern Michigan University

Encyclopedia of American Business History and Biography

The Automobile Industry, 1896-1920

AC Spark Plug

by David J. Andrea

University of Michigan

One of the world's largest manufacturers of automotive components, AC Spark Plug produces instrument panels and displays, engine and transmission filters and sensors, spark plugs, emission control devices, fuel pumps, and control systems (cruise controls and electronic pressure and temperature sensors). Once an independent division of General Motors (GM) Corporation, AC Spark Plug merged with GM's Rochester Products Division, a maker of fuel injection components, in 1988 to form a new division, AC-Rochester. This division combines and streamlines within GM electronic engine and transmission controls design, engineering, and manufacturing.

Originally an independent supplier, AC Spark Plug's roots are closely connected to GM's. Albert Champion, a bicycle, motorcycle, and automobile racer, experimented with and produced spark plugs and magnetos in Boston. By fate and good luck, he met William C. Durant, the founder of GM, in 1908. Durant had ambitions to create the world's largest automotive company by combining vehicle manufacturers and supporting component suppliers. Impressed with Champion's Boston shop, Durant purchased the operation for $2,000. Champion moved in 1908 to Flint, Michigan, home of Buick, which Durant controlled and which became GM's first acquisition.

Champion first researched, developed, and produced experimental plugs for Buick high-compression engines. The Champion Ignition Company, incorporated in October 1908, began supplying GM after Champion's initial experiments passed the tests of GM engineers. Durant's expansion plans materialized, and GM bought Oldsmobile, Cadillac, and Oakland (later to become Pontiac) motor companies. By 1910 GM's production reached 31,000 vehicles.

The Champion Ignition Company became a subsidiary of GM in 1909. Albert Champion

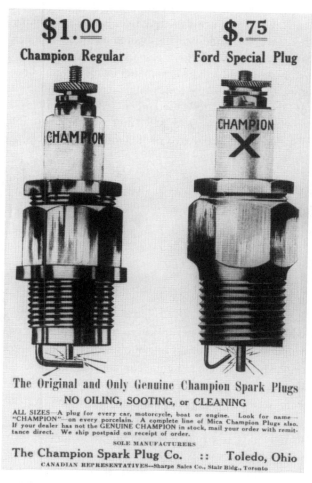

Advertisement for Champion spark plugs, 1911

owned 25 percent of the outstanding stock, Durant controlled 50 percent, and Albert Schmidt, developer of spark plug processing equipment, owned the remaining 25 percent. The company grew rapidly. A separate two-story building soon replaced the original operation on the third floor of the Buick factory, and by 1918 Champion Ignition had three Flint factories.

Albert Champion remained president of the company until his death in 1927. The company's

3

name changed in 1922 to the now-familiar AC Spark Plug Company. Necessary because of another spark plug company bearing Champion's name (the Champion Spark Plug Company headquartered in Toledo, Ohio), litigation resulted in one company keeping the founder's initials, the other his surname. In 1933 GM bought the remaining outstanding stock from Champion's estate (Schmidt sold his shares in 1922), making AC Spark Plug a corporate division.

AC Spark Plug product offerings grew rapidly with many additions centered on its ceramic expertise. Insulators and bearings were natural product extensions. After extensive research and development, AC began producing instruments using ceramic bearings. Known for strong engineering capabilities, AC, still under the leadership of Albert Champion, pioneered oil, air, and fuel filter development. He also led the company to produce the first successful

mechanical fuel pump. A more recent innovation, the catalytic converter, the device that allows motor vehicles to meet current emission control standards, is based substantially on AC's ceramic and internal combustion research.

AC-Rochester Division continues as a major GM automotive component division. It operates six manufacturing complexes in the United States and seven European plants. One of the most customer-diversified GM divisions, AC-Rochester sells components to all major international vehicle manufacturers through overseas sales offices in Europe and Asia.

References:

AC Spark Plug Division Overview (Detroit: General Motors Corporation, 1986);
AC Spark Plug 75th Anniversary 1908-1983 (Detroit: General Motors Corporation, 1983).

Advertisements

by James Wren

Motor Vehicle Manufacturers Association

In the December 1895 issue of *Horseless Age,* which was the first periodical in the United States devoted solely to the automobile industry, there were only three advertisements for motor vehicles. As was the case for the first few years of the American automobile industry, the ads little resembled contemporary ones, in which psychology and sexual desire usually play an equal, if not dominant, role with technical information in selling vehicles. Early advertisements did not extol the virtues of the vehicles they were intended to promote nor did they even actively promote sale of the vehicles. Instead, most of the early ads were mere announcements of new models and featured little more information than the address of the manufacturer. Most did not even reveal the price of the automobile, as the relatively high cost of motor vehicles ensured that those who did purchase the early machines were little concerned with cost.

As the technology of the automobile developed over the course of the first two decades of the twentieth century, the range of style within automo-

bile advertising expanded. While the original goal of automobile manufacturers was to convince a skeptical public that the machines would work and were reliable, once that had been accomplished more-varied purposes for advertising were developed. Luxury cars quickly began to use the now-familiar techniques of associating a particular model with a singular set of cultural values—selling a car by giving it the power to instill status and class.

Advertisements for lower-priced cars, best represented by the evolving Ford Motor Company models, instead emphasized ever-decreasing prices and continuing reliability and durability while trying to sell more and more vehicles to a wider segment of the public. That two-tiered approach to advertising and marketing, between status and price, was the main approach to selling automobiles during the early years of the industry. As the market matured, however, the demands on advertising changed. By the late 1910s and early 1920s most of the cars that were being sold were not being sold to first-time buyers. The market was quickly becoming satu-

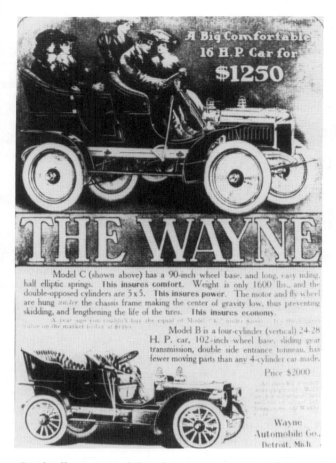

Gradually, automobile advertisements moved from the nuts-and-bolts approach of this 1905 Wayne ad to the imaginative appeal of this 1923 ad for the Jordan Playboy.

rated, as a large percentage of Americans who wanted cars had them. That meant that if these customers kept their vehicles as long as they would probably last, the market for automobiles would be drastically smaller than it might be if the vehicles became more like perishable goods.

This problem was solved to the satisfaction of the manufacturers by Alfred P. Sloan, Jr., of General Motors (GM), who institutionalized a strategy for segmenting markets using nameplate focusing and the annual model change. Sloan's plan, introduced in the early 1920s, was to set up price ranges for each of GM's divisions and to advertise each higher-priced division as a logical step up in status and class. Even if a family could not afford to move up a division, yearly changes in the same division's car, changes that were mainly cosmetic and not technological, could bring renewed esteem, so the ads implied, to the owner.

The new marketing strategy brought about an ironic shift in advertising methods. Luxury cars, which before had concentrated on status messages,

now were the vehicles that claimed mechanical superiority, relying on their known high price tags to convey the former. Many lower-priced cars, however, used status as a selling point, the object being to lure the consumer into the ladder game of climbing nameplates.

Regardless of the methods and intentions of automobile advertising, it has provided many popular cultural icons, one of the most famous being the "Somewhere West of Laramie" ad for the Jordan Playboy. The efforts of advertisers succeeded in making the automobile an integral part of American life and also influenced the way in which an entire culture developed. The marketing and advertising of automobiles were as important as technical innovation to the industry's success.

References:
"Automobile Advertising's Grand Era," *Automobile Quarterly*, 16 (1976): 228-241;

Ralph E. Epstein, *The Automobile Industry: Its Economic and Social Development* (Chicago: Shaw, 1928);

Tim Howley, "Ned Jordan, the Spell He Wove," *Automobile Quarterly*, 13 (1975): 160-167;

John B. Rae, *The American Automobile* (Chicago: University of Chicago Press, 1965).

Archives:

Information on advertising is located in the periodical and sales literature collections of the patent library, Motor Vehicle Manufacturers Association, Detroit, Michigan.

American Motor Car Manufacturers Association

by James Wren

Motor Vehicle Manufacturers Association

The American Motor Car Manufacturers Association (AMCMA) was organized in February 1905 in Detroit by 23 automobile manufacturers as an alternative group of independents opposed to the George Selden internal-combustion-engine patent and to the patent licenser, the Association of Licensed Automobile Manufacturers (ALAM). The new organization attempted to present a united front against the efforts of the ALAM to limit use of the patent.

In 1905 the ALAM, with its determined Selden-patent interests, acquired an exclusive two-year lease on Madison Square Garden for national automobile shows in 1906 and 1907 and announced that they would limit participation to ALAM members. Previously the National Association of Automobile Manufacturers (NAAM) and the Automobile Club of America had conducted the national shows jointly. But as control of NAAM shifted to ALAM member-companies, so too did control of the show committee.

The announcement making the Madison Square Garden show an ALAM exclusive brought forth condemnations from John S. Gray, president of Ford Motor Company, and others, who suggested forming an organization of non-ALAM companies. The National Motor Vehicle Company, the Premier Motor Manufacturing Company, and the St. Louis Car Company joined Ford in organizing the new association.

A meeting was held in Detroit at the Ford plant on February 24, 1905. James Couzens of Ford served as chairman of the steering committee and then as chairman of the management committee when the association was formed. Twenty-three manufacturers became charter members of the new American Motor Car Manufacturers Association. They were: Acme Motor Car Company, Aerocar Company, Ardsley Motor Car Company, Austin Automobile Company, Bartholomew Company, Buckey Manufacturing Company, Crawford Automobile Company, Darris Motor Car Company, Dayton Motor Car Company, Duryea Power Company, Ford Motor Company, Jackson Automobile Company, Knox Motor Truck Company, Marion Motor Car Company, Maxwell-Briscoe Motor Company, Mitchell Motor Car Company, Moline Automobile Company, Moon Motor Car Company, National Motor Vehicle Company, Nordyke and Maroon Company, Premier Motor Manufacturing Company, St. Louis Car Company, and Wayne Automobile Company.

The objectives of the AMCMA were multifaceted: to sponsor auto shows for members, organize races, promote sales of members' products, stimulate public interest in motor vehicles, establish agencies, promote good roads, exchange technical information, and fight anti-auto legislation. The association also disseminated statistics and market data to assist members in determining production and price policies.

One of the first significant decisions of the AMCMA was to secure a lease for the 69th Regiment Armory being constructed near Madison Square Garden. On January 13, 1906, the association opened its first show at the Armory, advertising more vehicles than the ALAM featured.

Alfred E. Reeves, secretary of the New York Automobile Trade Association, was named general manager of the AMCMA in 1906, and he moved the association's offices to New York. Under Reeves's leadership AMCMA membership increased to more than 50. By 1907 the AMCMA auto show moved to Grand Central Palace in New York City.

In 1909 Judge Charles Merrill Hough held that the Selden patent was valid and infringed by those not licensed by the patent holders. Within a short time, under the threat of legal action, 15 AMCMA members left the association and applied to the ALAM for licenses under the Selden patent. By 1910, 30 of the 43 AMCMA members had joined the ALAM. On February 8, 1910, the AMCMA was disbanded in a Chicago meeting.

However, one member of the association, the Ford Motor Company, continued the fight by appealing the Hough decision, and in 1911 the U.S. Circuit Court of Appeals ruled that the Selden patent applied only to cars using a 2-cycle engine, not the 4-cycle engine that Ford and nearly all other auto manufacturers used.

Reference:

William Greenleaf, *Monopoly on Wheels: Henry Ford and the Selden Automobile Patent* (Detroit: Wayne State University Press, 1961).

American Motor League

by James Wren

Motor Vehicle Manufacturers Association

The American Motor League had the distinction of being the first automobile organization in American history. Its effort to represent both trade and consumer interests resulted in its early demise. The league was proposed by Detroit engineer Charles B. King in a letter to the editor of the new magazine *Horseless Age* on October 8, 1895. King wanted a national organization to hold meetings in which enthusiasts could exchange ideas, "where papers could be read and discussions follow as to the respective merits of all points in question."

The league's organizational meeting was held on November 1, 1895, in Chicago. Doctor J. Allen Hornsby was acclaimed chairman. He led a debate involving such automotive pioneers as Charles E. and J. Frank Duryea of Detroit and Elwood Haynes of Kokomo, Indiana, over the structure of the organization. Some wanted to focus on the scientific problems associated with automobiles and to limit membership in the league to appropriate specialists. Others wanted a "broad and liberal" league platform. A committee on organization was appointed and a second meeting planned.

On November 29, 1895, the members of the American Motor League approved a broad constitution for the "advancement of the interests and the use of motor vehicles" by "reports and discussions of mechanical features, by education and agitation, by directing and correcting legislation, by mutual de-

fense of the rights of said vehicles when threatened by adverse judicial decisions, by assisting in the work of constructing better roads, and in any other proper way which will assist to hasten the use and add to the value of motor vehicles as a means of transit."

The league remained in existence for only a few years, probably because its membership was too diverse in the interests it represented to enable the organization to live up to the hopes of its founders that it would be the principal spokesman for the advancement of the automobile. Those who had wanted to restrict membership to automobile manufacturers soon had trade associations that could speak more effectively for the industry. The Society of Automotive Engineers would provide the forum for those who were primarily interested in the mechanical aspects of the automobile, while the American Automobile Association, formed in 1902, quickly became the acknowledged leader in dealing with subjects of interest to motorists.

References:

Horseless Age (November 1895): 8; (December 1895): 27;

George S. May, *A Most Unique Machine: The Michigan Origins of the American Automobile Industry* (Grand Rapids, Mich.: Eerdmans, 1975).

Edgar Apperson

(October 3, 1869-May 12, 1959)

by Ralph D. Gray

Indiana University at Indianapolis

CAREER: Bicycle shop proprietor (1880s-1898); machinist, Riverside Machine Works (1889-1898); engineer, Haynes-Apperson Company (1898-1901); secretary-treasurer (1901-1920), general manager (1917-1920), president, Apperson Brothers Automobile Company (1920-1923).

Edgar Apperson, with his brother Elmer a pioneer in the automobile industry first with the Haynes-Apperson Company and later with the Apperson Brothers Automobile Company, was born near Kokomo, Indiana, on October 3, 1869. He was the youngest of three sons of Elbert S. and Anna Eliza (Landon) Apperson, whose families were among the first settlers in Howard County, Indiana. Little is known about the Apperson boys during their youth. They attended the local schools, worked on the 80-acre homestead their grandfather acquired in 1844, and, in the case of Elmer and Edgar, developed an abiding interest in things mechanical. Edgar's formal education ended with attendance at Kokomo High School, after which time he opened a bicycle shop in Kokomo and built and repaired wheels. While maintaining his own business (into 1898), he also took employment at his brother's Riverside Machine Works, Elmer's second such shop, established in 1889. At the time of his marriage in April 1892 to Laura Pentecost, Edgar was identified in the local press as a "skilled machinist" at the Riverside works. The paper also mentioned that the young couple's first residence was in the home of Mrs. Apperson's mother.

When in late 1893 Elwood Haynes brought his plans (and a gasoline engine) to the Riverside Machine Works and asked for help in building a self-propelled vehicle, Elmer Apperson accepted the job (at the reduced rate of 40 cents per hour because the work was to be done only during "slack time"), but, according to the later testimony of other workmen in the shop, the Appersons considered the proj-

Edgar Apperson (courtesy of the Motor Vehicle Manufacturers Association)

ect absurd. As the work progressed, however, Edgar responded to the challenge and became very much involved in working out the engineering problems associated with the job—as he later stated, everything "had to be worked out from very rough ideas." All three men—Haynes and the Appersons—and others worked many hours on the vehicle, later known as the Haynes "Pioneer." Edgar, perhaps because of his bicycle shop experience, took primary responsibility for the wheels, tires, axles, and steering gear (one of the less-satisfactory features of the first car). Evidently Edgar did not participate in the famous first test drive on July 4, 1894, but he continued to work on improvements for the car—the steering was modified, larger (36-inch rather than 28-inch) wheels were installed, and a more-powerful 2-cylinder engine replaced the 1-cylinder model first used. Edgar also took major responsibility in building the second car to be produced at the Riverside shop, designed and built expressly for the *Chicago Times-Herald* race in November 1895. It featured a 2-cylinder, horizontally opposed engine of his own design. As Edgar remembered the race in 1952, "a front wheel caught in the frog of a streetcar track on the way to the starting line and the rim was smashed. In those days nobody'd ever thought of a spare wheel, or even a spare tire." Consequently, the car did not compete in the race, which was won by J. Frank Duryea, but it was awarded a prize of $150 for its "balanced" and therefore vibration-free engine.

The following year Haynes and the Appersons collaborated on a third automobile, leased to John Robinson for display, with Elmer Apperson as driver, at his circus during the summer of 1896. (In Edgar Apperson's words long after the fact, "The rented-car business isn't so damned new.") Later in the year all three vehicles built by Haynes and the Appersons were displayed together in Indiana and Ohio, and orders were taken for cars to be delivered. It fell to Edgar Apperson to deliver the cars to their new owners and demonstrate driving and maintenance procedures. Fifty percent of the price was payable with the order, with the balance due upon delivery. Thus it was also Edgar's duty to collect the final payment on each car.

His most-publicized early delivery came in 1899, when he and Haynes together motored from Kokomo to Brooklyn, a trip of some 1,050 miles, to fulfill the terms of a conditional purchase by Dr. Ashley A. Webber. Edgar Apperson also recalled a "service" call he made to a Fort Wayne department store, which purchased in 1899 what may have been the first delivery truck in the country. Unable to get the truck started, the company wired for help. Apperson "took a look, put gas in the tank, and off she went."

Apperson proved to be a daring and successful driver in competitions. He won an early speed contest in Boston at the Charles River track in 1897, drove to a perfect score in a 100-mile non-stop contest on Long Island, New York, in 1899, and drove one of the Haynes-Apperson cars that fin-

ished one-two in the New York-Buffalo run across New York State at the time of the Pan-American Exposition in Buffalo (where President McKinley was assassinated) in 1901.

Meanwhile, the Haynes and Apperson collaboration had been formalized through incorporation of the Haynes-Apperson Company in 1898. Edgar was a valued employee of the firm controlled by Haynes and Elmer Apperson, who went their separate ways in the fall of 1901. Edgar then joined with his brother to form their own automobile company, with the younger brother initially controlling one-third of the business. The first Apperson car was sold during the summer of 1902, and perhaps a dozen more sales were made during the year. The business grew steadily, especially after A. G. Seiberling was brought over from the Haynes Automobile Company (the name for Haynes-Apperson after 1905) to supervise production. The company's assets including inventory were valued at $150,000 in 1907, but it was capitalized at $400,000 at the time of its incorporation in 1908, and in 1922 (when refinancing was required) its plant and equipment were valued at $1.4 million. Edgar, never considered to be an effective manager, continued to use his special talents as mechanic, test-and-racing driver, and developmental engineer. "Every car built in the Apperson plant," according to its 1908 catalog, "receives the personal attention of one of the Apperson brothers." More than that, most of the improvements introduced on Apperson cars were first tested on Edgar's personal vehicle, the younger brother spending at least some time behind the wheel virtually every day of the year. In 1930 a newspaper article suggested that Edgar had driven more miles in automobiles than anyone else in the country.

Edgar Apperson did his part to make the Apperson name synonymous with speed and power. With his encouragement the company entered the Vanderbilt Cup races beginning in 1904 using professional drivers, but Edgar Apperson personally defeated Barney Oldfield in a much-publicized hill climb in Pasadena, California, in 1909, trying to repeat for the firm its victory of the previous year. The Apperson Jack Rabbit racer was fitted with a new carburetor Edgar had designed, the first set of cord tires ever made (a B. F. Goodrich development), and extra-strength axles. The last feature permitted Edgar to cross a wooden bridge at full speed while the other drivers had to ease up. A crowd of

THE HAYNES-APPERSON CO.,
KOKOMO, IND.

Are
Actually
Filling
Orders.

They
Have
Got the
Machine
To Sell.

Make the
Haynes-
Apperson
Double
Cylinder
Carriage
Motor

in 4, 6, 8 and 10
horse power.

Motors are
LIGHT, STRONG,
AND RELIABLE.

MOTOR CARRIAGES,   GASOLINE MOTORS,
AND GEARING FOR MOTOR VEHICLES.

PROMPT DELIVERY.   MODERATE PRICES.   PRACTICAL MACHINES.

Haynes-Apperson advertisement dating from 1896, the first year of commercial automobile production in America

20,000 witnessed the Jack Rabbit clear the bridge in one leap of 38 feet and make the 1.1-mile climb in a record time of 1 minute, 24 seconds.

The Apperson company also participated in the first two 500-mile races in Indianapolis, then as now a remarkably effective advertising mechanism. In the first year, 1911, the Apperson car, which had qualified at a speed of 91.83 mph, completed only 82 laps; the second year its racer was hit by a spinning race car while stopped in the pits. Although the Apperson driver, Herb Lytle, and crew were uninjured, the episode persuaded the Appersons to abandon the Indianapolis Motor Speedway. Apperson cars continued to do well at other tracks, and in 1922 an Apperson driven by Charles Basile set several world records on the Beverly Hills 1.25-mile board speedway. The car, sponsored by Pacific Coast Apperson distributor Harris Hansure, set various long-distance records, averaging 83.37 mph during the first 21 hours, more than 80 mph for 24 hours, and completing 2,000 miles in less than 25 hours.

The Apperson company tied much of its advertising to its racing activities. Although the company remained small, never becoming one of the largest producers in Indiana (where scores of automobile manufacturers operated), the Apperson car added to the state's reputation as a producer of fine automobiles. The Apperson image reflected high performance and speed. A 1916 Apperson advertisement for its "Chummy" roadster stated that the car was built for "extremely high speed." The following year its "Roadaplane" advertisement offered this tempting advice: "Open the cut-out—step on the gas—BANG! You're off in a thunder of each cylinder applauding the others. . . . Your judgment of motor car values will never be the same after driving the *famous APPERSON JACK RABBIT.*" There is no evidence, however, that the Appersons, like others connected with the industry—most notably, Carl G. Fisher—did much to support the "good roads" movement in the country. They did participate in a highly publicized tour from Indianapolis to the Pacific Coast sponsored by the Indiana Automobile Manufacturers Association. Some 20 cars and two trucks, including two Haynes and two Apperson automobiles, traveled to San Francisco and Los Angeles in July and August 1913, demonstrating not only the performance of the Indiana-built products but also the need for a transcontinental highway.

In 1917, because of the ill health of his older brother, Edgar took over effective control of the Apperson company, assuming the title of general manager and, upon the death of Elmer Apperson in March 1920, president. Severe financial problems for the company began at that time, too, although such problems were endemic to the industry's small-scale producers, many of whom fell by the wayside in the 1920s, and not the result of mismanagement by the younger brother. The company was forced to obtain a $700,000 bond issue in 1922. The following year a syndicate headed by Don C. McCord and Maurice Rothschild assumed control of the firm and renamed it the Apperson Automobile Company, but its fate was sealed. Production ended early in 1926.

Upon his retirement in 1923, Edgar Apperson moved to Wisconsin, the home of his second wife and where he kept a hunting lodge. He moved again in 1932, with his wife and her foster son, Gilbert Alvord, to Arizona, where he had purchased property in 1917. Many honors came to Apperson during his long retirement. In 1946 he was among the first group to be inducted into the automobile industry's Hall of Fame (along with Henry Ford, Ransom E. Olds, J. Frank Duryea, and others), and he was on hand to cut the ribbon dedicating a Kokomo street—Apperson Way—in his and his brother's honor in October 1955. He also spoke out occasionally on automobile safety matters. The growing number of highway fatalities moved him to favor a national speed limit of 50 mph and severe penalties for both speeders and drunken drivers. His love for the outdoors, for hunting and fishing, also continued, and he made yearly hunting trips to Wyoming long after his eightieth birthday. A warm, gregarious, fun-loving man, a sportsman—he once hit a home run in an Elks Club game off major-league pitcher Christy Mathewson—and an outdoorsman; he traveled all over the United States, Mexico, and Canada on hunting and fishing trips.

Apperson's fun-loving nature is also revealed in an episode involving early Apperson employee Mary Landon. Landon worked for the Haynes-Apperson Company in 1899-1900, and one day in the fall of 1899 Edgar drove her downtown for lunch. Then, telling her he had business elsewhere, he asked her to drive the car back to the factory. Landon, having prepared the lengthy typewritten instructions given to purchasers, knew what to do and covered the distance back without mishap. She had someone crank the motor to start it, "pushed the lever into first speed and with the tiller in my right hand I guided it to the middle of the street . . . and drove into the building and stopped without knocking out a wall as was not uncommon in those days." Much to her surprise, Edgar Apperson was at the factory when she arrived. He had wanted to prove to himself and the country that a woman could drive.

In other matters, Edgar Apperson was, like his brother, Elmer, a Republican, a Presbyterian, a bank director (Howard National Bank, Kokomo), and a member of the Kokomo Country Club. He was also a Mason and an Elk and belonged to several hunting and fishing clubs. He died in Phoenix on May 12, 1959.

References:

J. L. Beardsley, "Apperson Jack Rabbit: America's First Sports Car," *Motor Trend*, 16 (June 1964): 54-57;

Arch Brown, "The Car that Made the Rabbit Famous: [The] 1913 Apperson 'Jack Rabbit,'" *Cars & Parts* (September 1984): 30-33;

Jacob Piatt Dunn, *Indiana and Indianans: A History of Aboriginal and Territorial Indiana and the Century of Statehood*, volume 5 (Chicago & New York: American Historical Society, 1919), p. 2141;

Murray Fahnestock, "The First Woman Drivers," *Antique Automobile* (January-February 1968): 24-27;

Ralph D. Gray, *Alloys and Automobiles: The Life of Elwood Haynes* (Indianapolis: Indiana Historical Society, 1979);

Gray, "Gas Buggy Revisited: A 'Lost' Novel of Kokomo, Indiana," *Indiana Magazine of History*, 70 (March 1974): 24-43;

Wallace Spencer Huffman, "The Apperson Brothers and Their Automobiles," *Indiana History Bulletin*, 41 (January 1964): 195-202;

Clifton J. Phillips, *Indiana in Transition: The Emergence of an Industrial Commonwealth, 1880-1920* (Indianapolis: Indiana Historical Society, 1968), pp. 263-270, 311-316;

Robert E. Pinkerton, "Ed Apperson and the Horseless Carriage," *True: The Man's Magazine*, 30 (March 1952): 20-21, 84-95;

Karl S. Zahm, "Apperson: The Jack Rabbit Car," *Cars & Parts* (January 1984): 42-48.

Elmer Apperson

(August 13, 1861-March 28, 1920)

by Ralph D. Gray

Indiana University at Indianapolis

CAREER: Apprentice, Star Machine Works (1880s); machine shop proprietor (1888); proprietor, Riverside Machine Works (1889-1898); partner, Haynes-Apperson Company (1898-1901); general manager (1901-1917), president, Apperson Brothers Automobile Company (1901-1920).

Elmer Apperson was a pioneer in the American automobile industry. In 1893-1894 he constructed, according to plans prepared by Elwood Haynes (who also supplied a gasoline engine purchased in Michigan), one of the first cars built in the United States. Subsequently he and Haynes built other cars, including one intended for the *Chicago Times-Herald* race in 1895; in 1898 the Haynes-Apperson Company began comparatively large-scale auto production. Apperson withdrew from the company in late 1901 to form the Apperson Brothers Automobile Company with his younger brother, Edgar. Considered the primary force in the company, which produced the famous Apperson "Jack Rabbit" and other fine cars from 1902 until the mid 1920s, Elmer Apperson was a classic self-made man, a farm boy who converted his love for machinery into a prosperous business.

Apperson was born on a Howard County farm about four miles southeast of Kokomo, Indiana, on August 13, 1861, the son of pioneer settlers in the area. His father, Elbert S. Apperson, a native of Virginia, came to Indiana in 1844. His mother, Anna Eliza (Landon) Apperson, was born near Louisville, Kentucky, and came with her family to Howard County in 1852. Married in 1854, the Appersons had three sons: the eldest, Oscar, became a schoolteacher.

Little is known about Elmer Apperson's earliest years except that he lived the life typical of a central Indiana farm lad in the 1860s and 1870s, doing his chores and attending the district schools (one of his teachers was the youthful John W.

Elmer Apperson

Kern, U.S. senator from Indiana from 1911 to 1917). He developed a keen interest in mechanics. He also attended grade school in Kokomo and, briefly, the normal school in Valparaiso, Indiana, but his real joy lay in mechanical work. At some point before coming of age he became a machinist's apprentice at the Star Machine Works in Kokomo, a thriving shop established in 1876 by J. B. Michener where "none but skilled workers" were employed. Michener operated a foundry and general repair business that specialized in producing items used in lumbering and carriage manufacturing—saws, saw guides, and the Star Felloe Machine. It is also known that Apperson earned additional money during the harvest season by working as machinist-in-chief on threshing crews in the vicinity and on sweeps through the Northwest. He once worked briefly in the railroad shops in Peru, Indiana.

In 1888 Elmer Apperson established his own small machine shop in Kokomo: he relocated the business in 1889, moving to larger quarters on the south side of town along Wildcat Creek. That shop, Riverside Machine Works, was destined to become the first automobile manufacturing plant in Indiana. It initially focused, however, on general repair. Apperson also produced items for lumbermen, including saw wedges of the type he patented in 1894. Some ten or twelve men worked in the shop, an unpretentious structure with a dirt floor said to be no larger than a four-anvil blacksmith shop. Among the employees were the youthful Edgar Apperson and his Howard County neighbor, Jonathan D. Maxwell.

The Riverside Machine Shop enjoyed a local reputation for fine workmanship, as did its owner for quality products and probity in business affairs. Consequently, in the fall of 1893 Elwood Haynes approached Elmer Apperson with plans for a self-propelled vehicle he had been developing for several years. The arrangement called for Apperson to construct, during "slack time" and at a rate of 40 cents per hour, the vehicle Haynes had in mind. The figure represented a concession of 10 cents per hour because of the nonpriority terms, but it exceeded by 10 or 15 cents the normal rates then received by employees at the shop. Aside from Elmer Apperson, the employee who took most responsibility for the unusual job was brother Edgar, who was assisted by, among others, Jonathan D. Maxwell and Warren Wrightsman. According to the recollections of E. G. Shortridge, a traveling salesman later employed by the Haynes-Apperson Company, the Appersons initially "ridiculed the idea of a self-propelled car, thought it wholly impractical and openly so expressed themselves." They considered Haynes a wealthy eccentric who was spending his money foolishly. That attitude soon changed, and, in apprentice William Adrian's words, as "the different parts we had made began to take shape" they began "working overtime on the machine." The Appersons designed and fabricated various parts of the chassis, a "double hollow square" made from natural-gas pipes (Haynes was then manager of the local gas company), while Haynes spent many

hours tinkering with the engine (a 1-cylinder marine upright purchased from the Sintz Gas Engine Company of Grand Rapids, Michigan) and calculating gear ratios. The vehicle was fitted with bicycle-type wire-spoke wheels and cushion tires (Edgar Apperson also had a bicycle shop then), and a buggy body (purchased in nearby Peru, Indiana, for $7) topped it off.

By happenstance the machine was completed on the evening of July 3, 1894. The next day, despite the crowds and celebrations attendant to the national holiday, it was brought out for its initial road test. For reasons of safety, since probably no one around had ever seen an automobile before, what was soon called the Haynes "Pioneer" was towed to the outskirts of town and push-started (a starting crank was added later). Three men clambered aboard. Haynes was at the controls; his passengers on that historic occasion were Elmer Apperson and Warren Wrightsman. The vehicle, equipped with only two forward gears and no reverse, no brakes, and no accessories such as lights (in Edgar Apperson's words, "we were doggone lucky when it ran in daylight"), moved off at once at about 7 or 8 mph along Pumpkinvine Pike. About a mile and a half into the country they coasted to a stop, turned around, and drove back all the way to the Riverside shop. When the engine died as the men tried to negotiate an incline into the shop, it marked the end of a promising beginning.

Several problems had to be solved. The engine was too small, the steering was unreliable—as Elwood Haynes testified during Selden patent litigation, it was "positively dangerous"—and its engine was as yet unmuffled. It was, as Edgar Apperson remarked in 1955, "a far cry from the mechanical miracles of today, but it ran. It will run yet."

Evidently at Elmer Apperson's instigation, Haynes and Apperson decided to build a larger, more-powerful vehicle the following year in order to compete in the *Chicago Times-Herald* race in November 1895. That second car, properly labeled a Haynes-Apperson, attracted much attention in Chicago, where both Kokomo cars were exhibited. Unfortunately, en route to the starting line on the morning of the race, the Haynes-Apperson entry was involved in a minor accident—a wheel was caught in streetcar tracks and badly damaged—and could not compete. The race was won by the only other American-built gasoline-powered entrant, the Duryea car built by J. Frank Duryea in Springfield,

Massachusetts, from plans originated by his brother, Charles E. Duryea. The Haynes-Apperson Company had to be content with a prize of $150 for the best-balanced engine, a 2-cylinder "opposed" motor with horizontal pistons designed and built by the Appersons, and with the publicity and interest engendered by America's first automobile race. As a result, Elmer Apperson decided to enter the business of automobile manufacturing. His partner in the enterprise, Haynes, supplied not only some of the necessary capital but, equally important, technical expertise.

The men built a third car in 1896, and that vehicle became, with Elmer Apperson as driver, the feature attraction of the Robinson and Franklin circus during the 1896 season. Apperson also took the car to smaller fairs, to a racecourse in Iowa, to a bicycle show in Minneapolis (where he offered rides for 10 cents a passenger), and to a baseball game in Evansville, Indiana, where his arrival caused the game to be discontinued after the third inning. All three cars built by Haynes and Apperson up to that time were exhibited in Portland, Indiana (Haynes's hometown), and at the Ohio State Fair in Columbus in September 1896.

Soon orders for cars of the type being displayed and demonstrated came in, and full-scale manufacturing began in 1897. The following year, after making the difficult decision to begin what they considered large-scale production (50 cars per year, if the market could support such an outpouring), Elmer Apperson and Elwood Haynes incorporated the Haynes-Apperson Company, capitalized at $25,000. Each man owned just more than 29 percent of the stock, with the remainder taken up by investors in Portland and Kokomo. Using the Riverside Machine Works as their initial factory (although a second, more suitable one was soon occupied), Elmer Apperson served as manager of the manufacturing operations while Elwood Haynes, who continued as Kokomo's gas company manager and as an avid metallurgical researcher in his free moments, assisted in office management and advertising as well as with technical matters. Edgar Apperson gave up his bicycle business to join the automobile company as production supervisor and chief driver, demonstrator, and sales representative. When Dr. Ashley Webber of Brooklyn, New York, agreed to buy a Haynes-Apperson in 1899 if it could be delivered to him under its own power, Haynes joined Edgar Apperson on the cross-

country trip, perhaps the first 1,000-mile automobile tour to be made in the United States.

The Haynes-Apperson Company was one of literally hundreds of automobile companies organized in the latter part of the 1890s. Most of the early companies were small and unsuccessful. Even the Duryea Motor Wagon Company of Springfield, which had initiated volume production of automobiles in 1896, producing 13 that year, failed to survive into the twentieth century. The Haynes-Apperson Company, however, produced nearly 200 automobiles per year by 1900. Production averaged 250 cars per year through 1905. The Appersons withdrew from the company in November 1901 to begin their own Apperson Brothers Automobile Company. Elmer became president and general manager of the family concern while Edgar served as secretary-treasurer and experimental engineer. At that point Haynes gave up his position with the gas company and took over active control of Haynes-Apperson, which he renamed the Haynes Automobile Company in 1905. The Appersons returned to their Riverside building, which they enlarged and modernized, producing their first automobile in July 1902. A conventional car for the time, with a 2-cylinder, front-mounted engine, the 1902 model was priced at $3,500.

Considerable speculation has ensued over the reasons for the break between the Appersons and Haynes, but it appears neither to have been the result of disagreements over the types of cars to build or of personality conflicts between the men. The more likely, but prosaic, reason was simply that the Appersons desired to strike out on their own, and their profits in the joint venture then made it financially feasible. Each partner in the original Haynes-Apperson Company respected the other, and they remained on good personal terms, even during subsequent disputes fueled by aggressive advertising departments in the rival Kokomo firms over who really built what both companies eventually but erroneously termed "America's First Car." It appears that the mistake was an honest one initially. The 1898 demise of the Duryea company brought recognition to Haynes-Apperson as the oldest automobile manufacturing company in operation during the early part of the twentieth century, and the transition from oldest to first was an easy one. Less defensible was the practice, initiated by the advertising departments, of dating the first car from 1893, when work began, rather than 1894, when a success-

Apperson Brothers advertisement, circa 1920, indicating the company's resistance to the practice of the frequent model change

ful test was made. Both Charles Duryea and Henry Ford claimed 1892 dates, later recognized as clearly false, while Haynes and the Appersons invariably and with much documentation gave July 4, 1894, as the date of their initial Pumpkinvine Pike run.

Elmer Apperson served as president of the Apperson Brothers Automobile Company from the time it was organized until his death nearly 19 years later. During that time the Apperson "Jack Rabbit"–a name first used on some models in 1906 and by 1911 applied to all Appersons–became known as one of the best-built cars in America: sleek, sturdy, and fast. Elmer Apperson devoted his life to making his cars better, and better known. As brother Edgar remarked in 1921, the Appersons "have always been conservative," concentrating on only one business and trying to make it a success in terms of quality, not quantity. Apperson car production never exceeded more than a few cars per week, but a wide variety of models was offered, including various custom-made vehicles costing as much as $15,000. It was widely recognized, as designer Burtt Hubbard phrased it in 1970, that Elmer was

the "big spoke" in the company, chiefly responsible for its financial stability. Following Elmer's death in 1920 Edgar directed affairs briefly before selling out to a syndicate headed by Don C. McCord and Maurice Rothschild, but the company failed in 1926.

Although there are no primary records of the Apperson Brothers Automobile Company except for what can be found in published form–in catalogs and advertisements, trade journals, and newspaper notices–a great deal can be pieced together. The first Appersons of 1902 were 2-cylinder, front-engine cars rated at 16 to 25 horsepower. The company's first 4-cylinder engines were produced in 1903 and the first 6-cylinders in 1907, but few 6-cylinder automobiles were produced until 1914. In 1906 an Apperson dealer on the West Coast mounted the figure of a running jackrabbit on the side of his personal car. The name and logo appealed to Elmer Apperson, who began to produce a Jack Rabbit racing model the following year. That was a limited-production automobile, with no more than 15 of the $5,000 machines made the first year, but its speed, power, acceleration, and sleek design made it an instant favorite with the "sporting fraternity." Advertised as being identical to the 96-horsepower racer Edgar Apperson had driven in the Vanderbilt Cup race in 1906 and guaranteed to reach a speed of at least 75 mph (but known to be even faster), the Jack Rabbit was labeled both the nearest thing to a racing car available from a dealer and the fastest stock car in the country.

Within a few years all Apperson models carried the "Jack Rabbit" name and logo, similar in outline to that subsequently used on Greyhound buses. Sweeping new changes were introduced in 1914, when new "light" 4's and 6's–"Elmer Apperson's Greatest Triumph"–were introduced at prices ($1,485 to $1,785) far below previous Apperson models. The following year (for 1916) the Appersons introduced a new 8-cylinder engine designed rapidly but brilliantly by chief designer Burtt Hubbard, a former Reo employee in Detroit who was given the task when Elmer Apperson learned the Cadillac company planned to introduce an 8-cylinder car. Advertised as the "Eight with Eighty Less Parts," Hubbard's mechanical triumph was followed by the popular "Chummy" roadster, for which Elmer Apperson obtained a design patent. The roadster featured divided front seats with an aisle between them for access to the rear. Another notable Apperson design appeared in the Silver Appersons, so designated because of modifications first made by New York dealer C. T. Silver. He had installed an oval radiator, bullet-shaped headlamps mounted low between flat-crowned fenders, a wedge-shaped bumper, and wire wheels. So popular were the new features that the Appersons incorporated the changes into their 1918 models, the so-called Anniversary Appersons.

As early as 1908 the Apperson company began to claim primary responsibility for building what they believed to be America's first car in 1893. Many other "firsts" were also claimed for the company and for the Apperson brothers individually. The 1914 catalog, for example, listed at least 11 such distinctions for Elmer Apperson, whom it labeled "the father of the American automobile." The catalog also contained a "discussion," ostensibly by Elmer Apperson himself, which reviewed his long association with the automobile industry (called one of the seven modern wonders of the world) and his philosophy of automobile manufacturing. "My brother and I," he asserted, "had one

central, dominating thought" from the outset–"to make cars that were mechanically perfect," something they believed they had then achieved. Consequently, he announced an abandonment (temporarily, as it turned out) of "seasons' models"– Apperson cars were "lifetime cars" that did not "go out of date."

The 1914 catalog also stressed a theme that continued in force as long as Elmer Apperson lived– that each Apperson automobile was produced under the personal supervision of the Apperson brothers, who brought their many years of experience to bear upon every car carrying their name. That the claim was at least plausible stems from the limited production schedule of the company– some two cars per week in 1907 up to perhaps 8 or at most 10 per day in the peak years of 1916 and 1919.

Other of the more supportable claims advanced by the Appersons include the invention of the first side-door cars and double ignition (two spark plugs per cylinder, one operated by battery, the other by magneto, an improvement Apperson patented) and firsts in connection with speed contests, hill climbs, and long-distance runs. The controversy between Haynes and Apperson adherents, sometimes referred to as the "Battle of Kokomo," did not reach its peak until after Elmer Apperson's death. Haynes and Apperson had remained above the unseemly barrage of claims and counterclaims emanating from their advertising departments and seemed bemused by them. Even Edgar Apperson issued a statement recognizing Haynes's primary contribution in mid 1920, when the battle raged most openly shortly after his brother's death, but he insisted upon credit for significant practical engineering work provided by the machine shop personnel. Elmer had done much work on the clutches, Edgar on the wheels and bearings.

Much of the Apperson mystique developed from its association with racing, success here coming in large doses early. Both brothers drove in competition, with Edgar the more adventuresome and successful. He defeated Barney Oldfield in a widely publicized hill climb in Pasadena in 1909, and Apperson cars driven by others won important races throughout the country. The company also entered the first two 500-mile races at Indianapolis. In 1911, when a qualifying run between the traps of at least 75 mph was required, Apperson Car No. 35 registered a speed of 91.83. The car, driven by

Herb Lytle, did not finish the race, but the Appersons returned to try again in 1912. That time an accident on the main straightaway sent race cars spinning into the pits. One struck the Apperson car (just after driver Lytle had jumped to safety), heavily damaging both cars and convincing Elmer Apperson that the risks to driver and crew were too great to continue competing at Indianapolis. The Jack Rabbit name, however, continued to be popular, as did other names and slogans adopted by the company.

Although a family-owned enterprise, the Apperson company conducted effective advertising campaigns. In addition to the Jack Rabbit models the Appersons marketed a "Speed Boy," the "Chummy" roadster, and a "Roadaplane Eight" said to float over the road "as an aeroplane floats through space." Additionally, the company employed effective advertising slogans: "The Wizard of the Hills," "Count the Rabbits on the Road," the "Eight with Eighty Less Parts," "Things That Endure" (featuring Apperson cars pictured in front of, for example, the Parthenon), and "Drive an Apperson First, then Decide." The Appersons also stressed that their cars were "95% built in our own shops" under the watchful eyes of the most experienced automobile manufacturers in the country, and they advised customers to "beware of the cars built in factories that turned them out by the thousands and tens of thousands."

In 1917 Elmer Apperson was forced by ill health to relinquish active management of the company. Although Elmer retained the title of president, Edgar took over as general manager. By that time the company, having expanded its production facilities several times at its south-side location, had added a new north-side plant with 500,000 square feet of floor space, doubling the area available for manufacturing. The company continued to prosper during the war years, doing limited work for the government as well as maintaining its automobile production, and it was quick to announce a postwar policy of renewed full production and reduced prices. Company profits during the last years of Elmer Apperson's life continued to average $200,000 annually, but a loss was sustained in 1921, new financing was required in 1922 (through a $700,000 bond issue), and eventually Edgar Apperson lost control of the company.

The Apperson brothers were honored in 1918 by the Press Club of Indiana. The occasion was a din-
ner given by the Apperson company for Kokomo owners of Apperson cars, at which time the brothers were presented with a bronze tablet recognizing "their achievement in building the first practical commercially successful American automobile." Such was the state of automotive history knowledge at the time, although the motivation of the Press Club to perpetuate an awareness of those things for which the Hoosier state was famous is perhaps understandable. It fell to Edgar to accept the tablet because of the impaired health of Elmer; he reviewed events over the past quarter of a century relating to automobile manufacturing and stated that it had been their aim "always to produce the best motor car the state of the art would permit." By that time Elmer was spending considerable time in Chicago, where he maintained a second home and where the Apperson automobile had been enthusiastically received early in his career.

Few other circumstances of Elmer Apperson's life, personality, and character are known. It is known that he was first married sometime before the Chicago race in 1895, but he was widowed by the time the census of 1900 was taken. He married again in October 1900, to Olive Edwards of Kokomo, but that marriage ended in divorce. He got married for the third time to the former Mrs. Catherine Clancy Mitchell of Chicago, who survived her husband. (Some of these matters are aired, with perhaps some basis in fact, in a "novel," actually a roman à clef, by Robert Paterson entitled *Gas Buggy* [1933], which also describes aspects of the early automobile industry in Kokomo.) No personal letters or reminiscences about the elder Apperson have been discovered. Dark-haired, bespectacled, of average height and build, Apperson's serious demeanor in the one photograph of him known to survive indicates a person more likely to be considered a teacher or a banker than a hands-on mechanic, race driver, and automotive pioneer.

Apperson died on March 28, 1920, while attending an automobile race at a track in Los Angeles. His funeral, at his brother's home in Kokomo, was attended by many friends, colleagues, and employees, the latter of whom headed an entourage from the house to Crown Point Cemetery, within earshot of Apperson Plant No. 2. Among the honorary pallbearers was Jonathan D. Maxwell, who helped build the original Apperson car. Apperson had been a man who, according to an obituary written by a boyhood friend, "loved to build cars," and he had few other interests. He was a director of the Curtiss Indiana Company and the Kokomo Trust Company, a member of the Presbyterian church, and a Republican. He also belonged to the Chicago Athletic Club and to country clubs in both Chicago and Kokomo. A later tribute to the Apperson brothers by the city they had helped make famous came in 1955, when a major Kokomo thoroughfare was renamed Apperson Way. That unusual street name recalled an advertising statement, perhaps penned by Elmer himself, that Romans in "days of old traveled along the Appian Way" and that Americans in modern times could travel "the Apperson Way" in comfort and safety. Whether Elwood Haynes or Elmer Apperson deserved the major credit for the gasoline-powered vehicle they produced in 1893-1894, the fact remains that their experiment was successful enough to bring both men into the automobile industry, and both made substantial contributions to it.

References:
J. L. Beardsley, "Apperson Jack Rabbit: America's First Sports Car," *Motor Trend* (June 1964): 54-57;

Arch Brown, "The Car that Made the Rabbit Famous: [The] 1913 Apperson 'Jack Rabbit,' " *Cars & Parts* (September 1984): 30-33;

Jacob Piatt Dunn, *Indiana and Indianans: A History of Aboriginal and Territorial Indiana and the Century of Statehood*, volume 5 (Chicago & New York: American Historical Society, 1919), p. 2141;

Ralph D. Gray, *Alloys and Automobiles: The Life of Elwood Haynes* (Indianapolis: Indiana Historical Society, 1979);

Gray, "Gas Buggy Revisited: A 'Lost' Novel of Kokomo, Indiana," *Indiana Magazine of History*, 70 (March 1974): 24-43;

Wallace Spencer Huffman, "The Apperson Brothers and their Automobiles," *Indiana History Bulletin*, 41 (January 1964): 195-202;

Clifton J. Phillips, *Indiana in Transition: The Emergence of an Industrial Commonwealth, 1880-1920* (Indianapolis: Indiana Historical Society, 1968), pp. 263-270, 311-316;

Karl S. Zahm, "Apperson: The Jack Rabbit Car," *Cars & Parts* (January 1984): 42-48.

Association of Licensed Automobile Manufacturers

by James Wren

Motor Vehicle Manufacturers Association

The Association of Licensed Automobile Manufacturers (ALAM) was an organization of motor vehicle manufacturers who agreed to recognize the validity of the patent granted to inventor George B. Selden on November 5, 1895–U.S. Patent No. 549,160–the master patent on a hydrocarbon gas engine for road or horseless carriage use. The manufacturers agreed to pay royalties and to take licenses under that patent and to join forces for mutual benefit. The association's objective, besides protecting its members' patent rights, was the development and standardization of the automobile industry.

The history of the association is brief, but it was instrumental in stabilizing and standardizing the production of automobiles and auto parts, giving America world leadership in the motor vehicle industry. It was active only from March 5, 1903, to January 9, 1911. During that period it was involved in continuous litigation.

In November 1899 Selden had granted exclusive rights to his patent to the Electric Vehicle Company for $10,000, and $15 on each vehicle sold under the patent. On July 12, 1900, Electric Vehicle brought suit in Federal Court against a parts manufacturer, the Buffalo Gasoline Motor Company, and against the Winton Motor Carriage Company, considered to be the leading maker of gasoline cars at that time, for infringement of the patent. Winton and 20 other automotive firms responded to the suit by forming a defense group called the Hydrocarbon Motor Vehicle Manufacturers Association. Despite the membership of such well-known firms as Duryea, Apperson, and Clarke, the organization was ineffective.

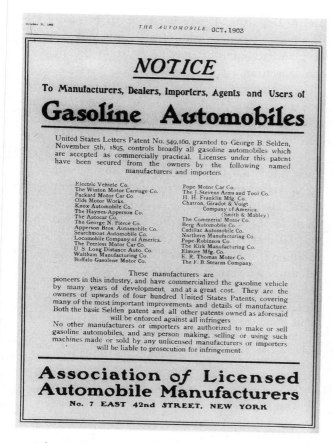

Advertisement in the trade journal Automobile,
October 31, 1903

Winton filed a motion for demurrer but was overruled on November 9, 1900. Then, when two small auto companies—Ranlet and Automobile Forecarriage Company—acknowledged the validity of the Selden patent and other companies joined them, Winton settled with Electric Vehicle on favorable terms, which were soon offered to the other companies. No royalties for prior manufacturing would be collected, and subsequent royalty payments would be used to help defray the costs of previous litigation.

During the course of the settlement George H. Day, president of Electric Vehicle, proposed forming an association of auto manufacturers licensed to use the Selden patent. The idea had been suggested by Henry B. Joy of Packard, who had recognized an opportunity to restrict auto manufacturing. On March 5, 1903, representatives of some 30 auto firms met to consider Day's proposal. Electric Vehicle proposed that licensed manufacturers pay a royalty of 5 percent on the retail price of each car sold. The firms found those terms unacceptable, and each manufacturer mustered $2,500 for ex-

penses in negotiating with Electric Vehicle. A committee of five was appointed for the negotiations. Elihu Cutler of Knox Automobile Company, Charles L. Clifton of Pierce Arrow, Samuel T. Davis of Locomobile, Frederick L. Smith of Olds, and Henry B. Joy of Packard met in New York City early in 1903 with William L. Whitney, electric-vehicle magnate and the power behind the Electric Vehicle Company.

The manufacturers agreed to form an association—the Association of Licensed Automobile Manufacturers—recognizing the validity of the Selden patent (and the Electric Vehicle Company's right to it). Members would pay the association a royalty of 1.25 percent on the catalog price of their cars. One-fifth of that amount would go to Selden (who had agreed to give half of that to George Day), two-fifths would be given to Electric Vehicle, and the remaining two-fifths would be paid to the association. A representative Board of Managers would be created, and an executive committee of five (one of whom was a permanent member from the Electric Vehicle Company) would determine which companies would receive licenses. The executive committee also made decisions concerning litigation. Each member was to contribute $2,500 for general expenses. The agreement was to be effective until November 4, 1912, at which time the Selden patent would expire.

At the meeting one of the officers stated that a major intention of the association other than protection of members' patent rights was to improve American automotive standards and give the public full value for their money by curtailing "wild cat" manufacturers and "get-rich-quick promotions."

Representatives of 18 firms signed the ALAM Articles of Agreement. They were George H. Day of the Electric Vehicle Company, Fred Smith of Olds Motor Works, John S. Clark of Auto Car, Charles Clifton of Pierce Arrow, Henry B. Joy of Packard, Elmer Apperson of Apperson Brothers, Barcley Warbarton of Larchmont Automobile Company, E. H. Cutler of Knox Automobile Company, S. T. Davis, Jr., of Locomobile Company of America, Elwood Haynes of Haynes-Apperson, L. H. Kittredge of Peerless Motor Car Company, George H. Brown of Winton Motor Carriage Company, Lewis Nixon of U.S. Long Distance Automobile Company, Harrison Williams of Waltham Manufacturing Company, Albert A. Pope of International Motor Car Company, J. H. Page of J. Stevens Arms and Tool Company, H. H. Franklin of H. H. Franklin Manufacturing Company, and A. D. Proctor Smith of Charron, Giradot and Voight Company of America. Frederick L. Smith of Olds was elected ALAM president and George Day of the Electric Vehicle Company was appointed general manager.

Several departments of the ALAM were established. The most important was the Mechanical Branch, which provided the first organized American forum in which automotive engineers and factory superintendents could exchange ideas. The Mechanical Branch, which was composed of some 100 engineers and superintendents, was instrumental in the standardization of automobile parts such as spark plugs, screw threads, nuts, bolts, tubing, and rods. The branch also maintained a lab in Hartford, Connecticut, where automotive parts and materials were subjected to rigid tests. Specifications for metals were compiled, which resulted in the use of a stronger and more elastic steel in ALAM products. Steel makers had been ready to furnish a better grade of material if it could be made to uniform specifications superior to the grade of steel used by foreign manufacturers. In 1910 the Mechanical Branch was reorganized as the Society of Automotive Engineers (SAE), and the branch's valuable papers were turned over to the SAE.

Another valuable ALAM department was the Traffic Department, which attempted to secure the best possible transportation rates for ALAM members and to monitor developments in the field of transportation.

During the course of the Selden patent litigation automobile production by ALAM members accounted for 70 to 80 percent of the industry total. But the ALAM was dissolved in 1911 when the U.S. Circuit Court for the Southern District of New York ruled that the Selden patent applied solely to the 2-cycle engine, not to the increasingly dominant 4-cycle Otto engine. The association was reorganized as the Automobile Board of Trade and then the National Automobile Chamber of Commerce to continue efforts to improve the product of the American automotive industry.

References:

James Rood Doolittle, *The Romance of the Automobile Industry* (New York: Klebold, 1916), pp. 174-185;

William Greenleaf, *Monopoly on Wheels* (Detroit: Wayne State University Press, 1961);

"10 Makers of Gasoline Cars Form Association of Licensed Automobile Manufacturers," *Motor World*, 6 (April 2, 1903).

Archives:

Material pertaining to the Association of Licensed Automobile Manufacturers is housed at the Patent Library of the Motor Vehicle Manufacturers Association in Detroit.

Auburn Automobile Company

by Beverly Rae Kimes

New York, New York

In Auburn, Indiana, in 1874, Charles Eckhart, who had worked as a wheelwright for the wagon-building Studebaker brothers, founded the Eckhart Carriage Company. When Eckhart retired in 1893, the firm was among the best known in the Midwest. Sons Frank and Morris Eckhart were then in charge; in 1900 Morris, the most automotively inclined, organized the Auburn Automobile Company with a total capitalization of $2,500. More than two years of experimentation followed. The first production Auburn—a single-cylinder runabout—was displayed at the 1903 Chicago Automobile Show. Fifty were sold in 1904. Auburn produced a 2-cylinder touring car in 1905, followed by a four (with a Rutenber engine) and a six (both Teetors and Continental engines were used) in 1912.

Billed as "The Satisfying Car," the Auburn product enjoyed a good reputation in the Midwest if not stellar sales. Nevertheless, the Eckharts made money until World War I, when hoped-for government contracts remained exactly that—hoped for—and the company shut down operations completely in 1918.

Following the Armistice, a group of Chicago capitalists led by Ralph Bard and including William Wrigley, Jr., decided the Auburn Automobile Company provided a perfect entrée to the automobile industry. Its regional reputation was fine; infused with fresh capital and fresh leadership, the firm could be made profitable on a national basis. Morris Eckhart readily agreed and sold out for a purported $1 million in June 1919. He also agreed to remain as president during the transition period. The new owners gave James I. Farley, Auburn's sales manager since 1908, a position as vice-president. He would remain with the firm until 1926, when he entered politics.

The first product of the new regime was called the Beauty-SIX, which gave unsubtle notice that aesthetic appeal had been added to Auburn auto-

mobiles; its three-tone color scheme was daring if not exactly a creative triumph. By 1922 factory area had expanded to 245,000 square feet in 11 brick-and-concrete buildings on 23 acres of land. Production capacity was more than 10,000 cars annually, but the company produced only six cars a day—more than meeting demand. In four years Auburn sold just 15,717 Beauty-SIXes. Cash surplus in 1920 had been $440,000. In 1923 company income was $10,402. Clearly something was wrong. Ralph Bard and his associates concluded that Auburn needed a new approach.

Bard recruited Errett Lobban Cord to run the company. A super salesman, Cord had no previous experience in running a manufacturing plant. But desperation indicated the wisdom of giving the boy wonder—he had not yet turned thirty—a try. Within months Cord had sold all surplus cars and paid the company debt. He added an 8-cylinder car (with a Lycoming engine) to the line. Gross receipts were $3.5 million in 1924. In three consecutive years Auburn sales doubled. By mid 1926 Cord totally controlled the company. Sales continued to climb: $14.8 million in 1927, $16.5 million in 1928. In 1929 the number of cars sold increased from 12,899 to 23,297, a gain of 80 percent, and Auburn's cash surplus increased 151 percent to $2.2 million.

Cord did it by cleverly marketing a modishly styled automobile that offered more for the money than most car buyers had thought reasonable to expect. Although priced in the medium range, Auburns had high-priced features such as hydraulic brakes and Bijur lubrication. And they were high-performance vehicles. An 8-115 (8 cylinders, 115 horsepower) was once officially timed at 108.46 mph over the measured mile and traveled 2,033 miles for a 24-hour average of 84.7. Stutz's Black Hawk Speedster was slightly faster, but it was a $5,000 car. Auburn's version could be had for

The 1917 Auburn roadster

$2,000. Dealers could not stock the cars fast enough.

The 1929 stock market crash barely slowed Cord down. Sales dipped in 1930 but more than doubled the following year for a profit equaling the previous peak of 1929. One thousand new dealers joined the Auburn bandwagon, abandoning the franchises of other manufacturers to do so. In 1931 Cord focused Auburn production on a single model—an 8-98 that *Fortune* magazine proclaimed "the biggest package in the world for the price." But in the following year Auburn had a V-12 in its lineup for less that $1,000—a price tag far less than any 12-cylinder automobile on the market (then or ever). Many of the speed records put up by the Auburn Twelve stood until World War II.

Then everything fell apart. Sales slumped as the Depression bottomed, but every automobile manufacturer was suffering similarly. More significant to Auburn fortunes than hard times was the fact that the company became merely a cog in the vast Cord empire. The man who had saved Auburn no longer gave it much attention. In addition to the Duesenberg Model J and the all-new automobile he named for himself, Cord diversified into shipbuilding and aviation among numerous other pursuits. Even the people he had selected to run Auburn became involved in the Cord Corporation's far-flung dealings.

In August 1937, under scrutiny by both the Bureau of Internal Revenue and the Securities and Exchange Commission, Cord sold his holdings. Two months later "informed Wall Street sources" reported that the Auburn, Cord, and Duesenberg automobiles would be discontinued. The sources were well informed.

References:

Griffith Borgeson, *Errett Lobban Cord: His Empire, His Motorcars* (Princeton: Princeton Publishing Co., 1984);

Beverly Rae Kimes, "Auburn—From Runabout to Speedster," *Automobile Quarterly*, 5 (Spring 1967): 374-391.

Autocar Company

by George S. May

Eastern Michigan University

Of the numerous motor vehicle companies that sprang up in the late 1890s, Autocar's name appears to be the only one that still is carried by vehicles produced today. (The creators of the Ford and Oldsmobile produced their first experimental vehicles in 1896, but commercial production of vehicles bearing those names did not occur until 1900 or later.) The nature of the vehicles with which the Autocar name has been associated has changed radically over the years, however.

Autocar had its origins in 1897, when Louis S. Clarke founded the Pittsburgh Motor Vehicle Company. Clarke started out producing a handful of small, 3-wheeled vehicles with a 1-cylinder engine mounted between the rear wheels. Three-wheelers had been the first automobiles produced by the European pioneer Benz a decade earlier and were also produced in considerable volume by the French DeDion-Bouton company in the mid 1890s, but by 1898 Clarke turned to what would soon be the dominant 4-wheel format. Exactly when Clarke built his first 4-wheel vehicle is unclear, but the best indications are that he did it sometime in 1899, when he also reorganized his business, forming the Autocar Company on August 28, 1899. Shortly thereafter the company moved from Pittsburgh to Ardmore, Pennsylvania, near Philadelphia, the center of Autocar operations for many decades.

The Autocar was one of the first runabouts on the market. Runabouts were the lightweight adaptation of a standard American carriage style that enjoyed great popularity in the country at the turn of the century. Unlike most of its competitors, the Autocar runabout was powered by a 2-cylinder rather than a 1-cylinder gasoline engine. Shaft-drive and porcelain spark plugs are among the features Autocar is said to have been the first to include. The car also had left-hand steering, but that was abandoned in favor of the right-hand steering ar-

rangement Americans favored in the early years.

The Autocar runabout was hardly a great success. The company produced only 27 in 1900. As Oldsmobiles, Ramblers, Cadillacs, and other runabouts were produced in the thousands in the next several years, the Autocar was transformed into larger models. A 4-cylinder car appeared in 1906. However, Autocar's 1907 entry into the newly developing market for commercial vehicles with a 2-cylinder truck foretold the company's future development. A few automobiles continued to be produced until 1911, but essentially Autocar has been a commercial vehicle manufacturer since 1908.

By 1926, when production of the 2-cylinder model ended, more than 30,000 of the first Autocar commercial vehicles had been turned out. A 4-cylinder truck appeared in 1919 and some electric models in the 1920s. The company began to make conventional trucks in 1926, joining the cabover style of the initial trucks. In the 1930s the company followed the industry trend toward the use of diesel engines, and its trucks became increasingly heavy-duty. Half-tracks were produced for the armed forces during World War II, and in 1946 sales topped 5,000, a company record.

In 1953 the Autocar Company was acquired by White Motor Corporation, the Cleveland truck manufacturer that like Autocar had started out in 1900 as a producer of automobiles but later switched to truck production. Autocar became the heavy-duty truck division of White, and production was moved to Exton, Pennsylvania. The growing competitiveness of the truck business together with generally unfavorable economic conditions in the 1970s, which affected the entire industry, forced White into bankruptcy in 1980 and led to its acquisition by the Swedish manufacturer Volvo in 1981. Volvo has continued producing the Autocar line of heavy-duty trucks at a plant in Ogden, Utah.

References:
Nick Baldwin and others, *The World Guide to Automobile Manufacturers* (New York: Facts on File, 1987);

G. N. Georgano, ed., *The Complete Encyclopedia of Commercial Vehicles* (Osceola, Wis.: Motorbooks International, 1979);

Beverly Rae Kimes and Henry Austin Clark, *Standard Catalog of American Cars, 1805-1942* (Iola, Wis.: Krause Publications, 1985).

Automobile Parts

by George S. May

Eastern Michigan University

In the early stages of the automobile industry most of the manufacturing occurred in the factories that made the various parts. The automobile companies themselves were for the most part assemblers, not manufacturers. They depended on outside firms to supply the wheels, engines, bodies, and other parts they needed. A popular theory that has received support in publications of the Motor Vehicle Manufacturers Association argues that this practice owed its start to a fire that destroyed Detroit's Oldsmobile plant in March 1901. In order to get back into production in a hurry, Olds, it is said, was forced to turn to Detroit companies that could supply parts for the curved-dash Oldsmobile runabout. The method by which that greatly successful car was produced supposedly encouraged other companies to rely on outside suppliers. Parts suppliers have continued to account for as much as 70 percent of the parts used by motor vehicle manufacturers to the present day.

The theory is not supported by the facts. At a time when automobile companies were producing only a handful of cars, it would have been far too great a financial burden for them to attempt to manufacture many of their parts. A year before the Olds fire the trade journal *Motor Age* recommended that companies use the services of firms that were already set up to manufacture parts, thereby enabling the auto companies to devote all their efforts to assembly, "a sufficiently difficult task.... This course requires the least investment, involves the least risk, gives the most rapid turn-over of what money is involved, and finally leads to success by the straightest and easiest road."

Although Olds was not responsible for pioneering the practice, the company provides a good example of the wide range of outside suppliers upon which the industry came to rely. In 1900, as his company was beginning limited production, Ransom Olds placed orders for bodies with Detroit's C. R. Wilson Body Company, a longtime carriage manufacturer that had just turned to producing bodies for horseless carriages. Within a short time, as production increased, Olds also began buying bodies from Detroit's Byron F. Everitt and from H. Jay Hayes of Cleveland. Olds initially ordered wheels from the Weston-Mott Company of Utica, New York, a firm that had earlier made wheels for bicycles and had begun shifting its emphasis to automobile wheels in the late 1890s. By 1902 Olds was buying most of his wheels from Lansing's Prudden Company, and Weston-Mott began supplying axles. Sipe & Sigler of Cleveland received an order for batteries in 1900, and roller bearings were ordered from the Hyatt Roller Bearing Company of Newark. Since Olds manufactured engines, he had originally planned to produce his own engines and some other mechanical parts, but the demand for Olds engines was so great that by 1901 he decided to have the car engines built by the Detroit machine shops operated by the Dodge brothers and Henry M. Leland. Leland's shop had earlier been assigned the job of producing Olds transmissions. Some drop forgings came all the way from Brooklyn, New York, while radiators, fenders, and other sheet metal parts came from a source closer at hand, Detroit's Briscoe Manufacturing Company.

Although there were exceptions, such as the Packard Motor Company, which claimed to make nearly everything that went into its cars, Olds typified the practice followed by most companies. When it started out in 1903 the Ford Motor Company manufactured nothing. It depended on outside suppliers including the Dodge brothers, who gave up the chance to continue their Olds contract and instead supplied "most of the vital parts" for the various Ford models for a decade. Companies sometimes openly boasted that they did nothing but put together parts produced elsewhere. "All the car parts are made by contract with specialists," declared the Wayne Automobile Company, a new Detroit firm, in 1904. "This gives the Wayne Company the advantages of the very best facilities of the best American constructors, far better than any one factory could hope to maintain, and reduces the flat cost to the lowest terms." However, as the larger, more-established companies began to make some of their own parts, companies that continued to rely totally on outside sources came under criticism, and the term "assembled car" came to be used in a derisive and derogatory way.

Solid economic factors lay behind the desire of companies that could afford to do so to reduce the extent to which they were dependent on outside suppliers. With the rapid growth of the industry, suppliers were sometimes hard pressed to keep up with demand. The failure of one key supplier to provide a part when it was needed could cause costly delays. One solution to that problem was to gain control of the parts company. That was the approach taken by General Motors (GM) under William C. Durant, which acquired control of Weston-Mott, Hyatt Roller Bearing, Delco, Remy Electric, AC Spark Plug, and other parts manufacturers in the years from 1909 to 1919. Those subsidiaries could and did sell parts to GM's competitors, but GM's control guaranteed that the corporation's car divisions would have first call on the parts. Ford, the vol-

ume leader in those years, assured itself of the parts it needed by taking the entire production of some of its suppliers, making them virtual subsidiaries. In addition, however, Ford took over the manufacturing of many of its parts, not only for use in the cars coming off the assembly lines but for sale as replacement parts to owners of Ford cars. The sale of spare parts became a lucrative business, and Ford occasionally halted car production to fill the backlog of replacement orders.

The engine was one of the first automotive components that came to be produced in-house in the majority of cases, although companies such as Continental Motor Manufacturing Company of Muskegon, Michigan, would continue to find a market for the sale of its engines to smaller automakers. GM's purchase of an interest in the Fisher Body Company in 1919 and Nash's acquisition of an interest in the Seaman Body Corporation in the same year marked the start of a movement that would see the virtual disappearance of independent body- and coach-building companies within two decades. But predictions that such trends would be extended to all segments of the parts industry were not borne out. The number of motor vehicle manufacturers declined steadily after 1920, but the number of companies supplying producers with parts has remained very large.

References:

George S. May, *R. E. Olds: Auto Industry Pioneer* (Grand Rapids, Mich.: Eerdmans, 1977);

Allan Nevins and Frank Ernest Hill, *Ford: The Times, the Man, the Company* (New York: Scribners, 1954);

John B. Rae, *American Automobile Manufacturers: The First Forty Years* (Philadelphia: Chilton, 1959).

Automobile Shows

by George S. May

Eastern Michigan University

For many years annual trade shows have provided a means by which manufacturers have sought to promote interest in new products. As early as the 1870s carriage makers displayed models they described as improvements over previous years' models, thereby pioneering the practice of the annual model change. The bicycle boom that began in the mid 1880s led bicycle manufacturers to adopt the same practice, and thousands of bicycle enthusiasts attended annual shows in New York, Chicago, and other cities. In the late 1890s automakers began to exhibit at those bicycle shows.

Although a show devoted solely to automobiles was held in Chicago in September 1900, one held in New York's Madison Square Garden in November was touted as the first national automobile trade show. Sponsored by the Automobile Club of America, the week-long event attracted some 48,000 visitors. Vehicles from more than 30 manufacturers were displayed and also demonstrated, on an oval track on the floor of the Garden and on a wooden incline built on the Garden's roof. In subsequent years decorations at the Garden show, which had consisted largely of American flags hung from the ceiling at the inaugural event, became more elaborate. The number of cars on display grew, and the steam and electric cars that had dominated in 1900 gave way to gasoline cars.

Because of the split in auto manufacturer associations caused by the Selden patent fight, two shows were held in New York beginning in January 1906. The Association of Licensed Automobile Manufacturers sponsored the Madison Square Garden event for those companies licensed under the patent, while the American Motor Car Manufacturers Association, representing the manufacturers who produced gasoline cars in defiance of the patent holders, staged its own show at New York's Grand Central Palace. Following the initial victory of the Selden forces in federal district court in 1909, Janu-

ary 1910 was the last time two shows were staged; the unlicensed manufacturers association dissolved, and its members scrambled to be licensed on whatever terms were offered.

Although the New York show was called the National Automobile Show, other cities were soon hosting their own events. For the most part they aspired to only regional significance, but the one held in Chicago came to rival New York's and ultimately supplanted it. In the early years New York continued to be the most popular show for the auto executives who came to discuss business and to enjoy the social opportunities, but Chicago, trade writer Chris Sinsabaugh declared, became "*the* dealers' show, attracting more retailers than New York and affording manufacturers a better opportunity to get in touch with their customers and their prospective customers."

The early shows were indeed places where manufacturers counted on securing orders for their cars. Although stimulating sales continued to be the basic motivation behind the industry's support for the annual show, eventually, with the development of other promotional and advertising techniques, the shows' importance was viewed not in terms of actual orders received but in terms of their indirect influence in stimulating later sales. A survey of those families who attended Detroit's 1987 auto show indicated that 72 percent of them bought a new car before the end of the year. Promoters assumed that it was the sight of the new models that encouraged people to buy a new car after their visit to the exhibition.

The shows have always provided the public a unique opportunity to see many different auto models under one roof. At the first shows manufacturers generally unveiled their latest models for the first time. Excitement grew among industry observers and car enthusiasts as the opening of each show approached. Manufacturers felt great pressure to

View of the inaugural American automobile show, Madison Square Garden, November 3-10, 1900

come in with something new, with the result that they sometimes displayed models that upon close examination could be seen to be only partially finished. For those who were unable to attend auto shows, trade papers, newspapers, and general-circulation magazines carried extensive coverage. Daily papers in cities such as Chicago and Detroit still published massive special sections previewing upcoming shows in the 1980s. But although the auto show continued to provide the only occasion in which new models, both domestic and foreign, could be examined and compared each year, manufacturers no longer waited until the annual event to introduce their new models but sought to get the jump on their competitors by introducing them at press previews and at their dealers well in advance of the shows. Radio and then television provided new methods of arousing public interest, further diluting, but not eliminating, the appeal of the annual extravaganzas.

References:

George S. May, *The Automobile in American Life* (forthcoming, 1990);

Stephen W. Sears, *The Automobile in America* (New York: American Heritage, 1977).

Automotive Trade Publications

by Louis G. Helverson

Free Library of Philadelphia

As any trade or industry develops it leaves behind a trail of written material: letters, shop and experiment notes, catalogs, books, and the like. One of the prominent tracks in this paper trail is the body of trade magazines. These publications inform manufacturers and retailers of new equipment and other items, present general marketing information and company news, and provide a forum for discussion of matters of interest.

In early 1895 there was no automobile industry in the United States, although an imported Daimler vehicle had been exhibited at the World's Columbian Exposition in Chicago in 1893 and several Americans, most notably Charles and Frank Duryea, had made successful cars. Reports of European and American automotive developments had already begun to appear in such publications as *Scientific American*, *Electrical Engineering*, *Power*, and *Iron Age*. In June 1895, stimulated by reports in the French magazine *Le Petite Journal* of an automobile race between Paris and Rouen, H. H. Kohlsaat, publisher of the *Chicago Times-Herald*, offered prizes totaling $5,000 to vehicles that could negotiate a 56-mile course and pass a series of technical tests. Nearly 100 vehicles entered the contest, but on Thanksgiving Day when the race was held, only six were able to make the starting line. Of those six only two, a Duryea and a Benz, successfully completed the snow-covered route. Meanwhile, several American firms began manufacturing cars in earnest. Production totaled 15 units in 1896. As the auto industry coalesced in America, trade publications began to appear. *Motocycle* began publishing in October 1895, and in November 1895 *Horseless Age* appeared. The first issues of *Horseless Age* described the machines entered in the *Times-Herald* race and the results of the race and the technical tests. Early issues also focused on the technology of internal combustion engines.

Motocycle ceased publication in 1897, while *Horseless Age* lasted until 1918.

In June 1896 Philadelphia publisher James Artmen began publishing *Cycle Trade Journal* for the bicycle trade, then at its zenith. In September 1898, Artmen recognized that bicycle manufacturers and dealers were becoming increasingly involved in the automobile trade and expanded the magazine's title to *Cycle and Automobile Trade Journal*. Artmen's editors believed that the motorcycle provided a connecting link between bicycles and automobiles and so reported motorcycle news as well. By 1912 interest in the cycle trade had declined, and the publisher dropped the word *Cycle* from the title. The new *Automobile Trade Journal* ceased publication in 1940.

September 1899 saw the birth of *Automobile* (presently known as *Automotive Industries*), a publication devoted to the owner or prospective owner of an automobile. The magazine provided details of automobile construction and maintenance, accounts of tours and racing events, and other news items of interest to the owner or operator. The weekly *Motor Age* also appeared in September 1899. A companion to *Cycle Age*, it was aimed at the consumer rather than the trade at large. By the end of 1901 the management of the company that published *Cycle Age* and *Motor Age* experienced so much internal dissension that the company was disbanded and the assets sold. *Motor Age* came out in a modified format in January 1902. The new publication's policy was to supply all the news and general information consistent with the best interest of the trade the paper aimed to serve. That change in editorial policy resulted in more emphasis on trade matters and less information for the consumer.

Motor World, "a weekly journal devoted to the automobile and kindred interests," entered the field in October 1900 and ceased publication in 1940. In October 1903 *MoToR* made its appearance. The magazine was tabloid sized, printed on slick paper, and intended for upper-class automobile enthusiasts. Descriptions of touring trips were detailed and well illustrated. Articles detailed the proper costumes to be worn while driving. Lengthy columns described the newest automobile accessories.

The turn-of-the-century automobile faced several obstacles to its acceptance. Public roads were deplorable—most of them outside the urban centers were little more than wagon tracks. The early machines were costly, fragile, and prone to mechanical breakdown, and maintenance and repair was complicated and expensive. Autos were also difficult to operate. Finally, many veterans of horse-and-buggy days resisted the shift to autos. The trade publications naturally tried to promote interest in the new vehicles. Descriptions of new models, components, and accessories were a major part of each publication's content. Lengthy articles on the mechanics of the machines and positive reports from owners were also included, as was information for the automobile tourist. Every race or endurance contest was reported in full. Racing, either on the sands of Daytona and Cape May or at the local horse track, meant money and prestige. The cars proved their reliability (or lack thereof), the builders received publicity for their products, and the public was made aware of the desirability of ownership.

The annual national automobile shows that began in New York in 1900 provided the trade magazines with much of their material. *MoToR* developed that kind of reporting to such a degree that their annual show issues from 1903 through 1940 are highly prized by researchers for their extensive tables of specifications and descriptions of new cars. For years *Cycle and Automobile Trade Journal* issued an annual buying guide accompanying its March issue. It contained illustrations of the vehicles and condensed lists of technical specifications.

By 1910 the automobile industry had matured. Most of the early manufacturers who had entered the trade without sufficient business understanding or who had placed their efforts into machines that went out of favor (such as steam and electric cars) had gone out of business. The public had been educated as to the desirability of owning a car, and civil authorities had been forced to acknowledge the automobile as a legitimate form of transportation. Finally, a great deal of experimental

work had been done and the basic design of the machines had been finalized.

Henry Ford's introduction of the high-quality, low-cost Model T soon put the cost of ownership within the reach of nearly everyone. Efforts of the Society of Automotive Engineers to standardize the size of auto parts helped further reduce the cost of manufacture and repair. Manufacturers' dealer networks were becoming more businesslike, and the manufacturers were better able to distribute and service their products. In 1908, when Ford introduced his Model T, a total of 63,500 vehicles were built. In 1909 the figure jumped to 127,731, and in 1910, 181,000 cars were built.

In the October 1910 issue of *Carriage Monthly* an editorial aimed at the auto trade's advertisers appeared. The editors charged the automotive press with misrepresenting itself and with failing to meet the needs of the trade. The editorial pointed out that trade journals should be circulated among members of the trade only; that they should provide a forum for discussion of problems associated with the trade without the danger of misinterpretation or the negative influence of rumors started by uninitiated readers; and that advertisers in a trade publication were interested in selling to the trade—not to a readership uninterested in their products. The editors concluded that the automotive-trade advertiser needed to develop a better understanding of trade advertising and selling problems.

With the exception of *MoToR* magazine the automobile press began to change. Although details of new car models and accessories continued to be featured, general articles on servicing and repair became more prominent. Business news became more detailed. Plans and layouts for new garages were featured. Increasingly there were stories of successful dealers and service operators. Tips on increasing business and sales were emphasized. As the decade progressed, the need for information on repair of specific cars or components came into demand. The best example of that trend involves the Ford Model T. The sheer number of vehicles needing service and the proliferation of accessories led *Automobile Trade Journal* to devote an entire section of each issue to the Model T.

By the end of the decade the publications, aside from *MoToR*, were set in their editorial content. *Automobile Trade Journal* was the leader in the service area. In addition to monthly charts giving current chassis and model specifications, the publication was regularly including tables of service specifications. *Automobile*, which absorbed *Horseless Age* in 1918, was beginning to direct its contents toward the manufacturer. Articles were beginning to appear explaining manufacturer's shop methods and news items were increasingly aimed at the maker's needs. Sales charts, production stories, and news of trade changes became the norm.

During the 1910s auto manufacturers added many new accessories and gadgets to their products. Probably the most influential accessory was the self-starter introduced by General Motors in 1912. Until the self-starter's introduction the automobile had been a masculine toy—crank-starting was difficult. The self-starter made the automobile a "unisex" machine. Manufacturers recognized the new market segment and began giving thought to aesthetic enhancement. In 1915 less than 2.5 million cars were registered. By 1920 there were more than 9 million. In the midst of that buying spree World War I occurred. Trade publications carried frequent articles on the use of motor vehicles in the war and gave detailed descriptions of how the makers were meeting the needs of both the army and the civilian population. The expense of publishing operations grew sharply after World War I, and publications operating on marginal budgets left the field. Some were sold to financially healthy corporations while others merely stopped publishing.

As the decade came to a close the industry had changed. It was no longer a major function of the trade press to sell the automotive concept. Production methods had been refined during the war and the industry was ready to flood the country with vehicles. The local blacksmith was being replaced as the prime auto repairman by men who had studied the machines and who had received some training in repair by experienced mechanics. The decade of the 1920s would see the trade publications complete their development from magazines that sometimes did not know their readership into the pure trade publications found today.

Axles

by James Wren

Motor Vehicle Manufacturers Association

Two basic types of axles are used in motor vehicles, the dead axle and the live axle. Dead axles are stationary and do not rotate with the wheels, while live axles actually drive the wheels. Some early automobiles used only dead axles, both front and rear, while the wheels were powered by a chain drive connected directly to them from the engine. Even by 1901, however, the rear-wheel-drive live axle was used on a Peerless model, and that configuration was dominant until the 1980s.

The live axle, since it contains a driving shaft from the engine that usually runs perpendicular to the axle itself, contains a differential gear that transfers power from one direction to the other. The live axle also contains driving pinions or connecting gears that reside in a housing. The increasing complexity of axles, differentials, and other elements led manufacturers to replace the original steel tubing with forged tubes of varying sizes to accomplish the separate functions of the axle: wheel support, power transfer, and drive shaft protection.

Early in the industry two types of rear live axles were used: the plain live axle, which performed both the support and drive functions simultaneously, and the fully floating axle, in which the driving shaft was totally enclosed in the outer axle and powered, but did not support, the wheels. While the basic technology of the automobile axle has been unchanged for essentially 100 years, improvements and greater sophistication in gearing, vibration, and noise control continue to change the details of this component.

Walter C. Baker

(June 27, 1867-April 26, 1955)

by Darwin H. Stapleton

Rockefeller Archive Center

CAREER: President, American Ball Bearing Company (1895-1918); vice-president and mechanical engineer, Baker Motor Vehicle Company (1898-1912); director, Peerless Motor Car Company (1900-?).

Walter C. Baker, inventor, entrepreneur, and a pioneer in American automobile development, was born on June 27, 1867, in Hinsdale, New Hampshire. His father, George W. Baker, invented sewing machine devices that were adopted by the White Manufacturing Company (established in 1866) of Cleveland, Ohio. The Baker family moved to Cleveland in 1871. Walter Baker attended Cleveland public schools and studied at Cleveland's Case School of Applied Science from 1888 to 1890. In 1891 he married Frances E. White, daughter of one of the founders of the White Company.

Baker began his professional employment in 1891 with the Cleveland Machine Screw Company, a subsidiary of the White Company and part of the American fastener industry centered in Cleveland. He became particularly interested in ball bearings, a new product at Cleveland Machine Screw, and in 1895 founded a new company, American Ball Bearing Company, to manufacture them. The company's officers included Baker as president, his brother-in-law Fred R. White as vice-president, and Philip Dorn and Frederick C. Dorn as secretary and treasurer. Rollin White and John Grant were also prominent investors. The company's factory was located at Clarkwood Avenue adjacent to the Pennsylvania Railroad on the east side of Cleveland.

With the craze for bicycles at its height, and White and other Cleveland and midwestern firms producing them by the thousands, Baker found a ready market for his product. He sold bearings for electric motors and streetcars, horse-drawn vehicles, and the propellers of Great Lakes freighters. In time the American Ball Bearing Company took or-

ders for axles and other parts from a variety of automobile companies. The company also produced two inventions patented by Baker: a steering knuckle for automobile front wheels and a full-floating rear axle.

In the late 1890s Cleveland was a hotbed of automobile experimentation, and in 1897, with Fred Dorn, Baker developed an electric car. His shop was at the site of the former Brush Electric Company, on Commerce Avenue on the east side of Cleveland near several electrical and mechanical engineering firms that worked closely with one another. Elmer Sperry had his shop adjacent to Baker's and was also developing an electric car and working on various aspects of electric batteries. Rights to the manufacture of Sperry's electric car were purchased by the Cleveland Machine Screw Company, Baker's old firm.

The Baker Motor Vehicle Company was founded in 1898 with Rollin White (of the White Company) as president, Baker as vice-president and mechanical engineer, and Fred White as treasurer. The Baker company established an assembly plant at East 65th Street and Central Avenue, close enough to American Ball Bearing so that Baker and his partners could oversee both enterprises. Like most early automobiles, the Baker was assembled from parts made by other companies. The Baker's motors were manufactured by the Elwell Parker Electric Company of Cleveland.

The Baker company's 1898 model had the form of a buggy, with tiller steering, a .75-horsepower motor, chain drive, and a ten-cell array of batteries. It was similar to other American electrics and most other types of horseless carriages in that it did not vary significantly from the horse-drawn vehicle.

Thomas Edison bought one of the early Baker electrics for use as his personal car. A strong supporter of electric propulsion and devoted to develop-

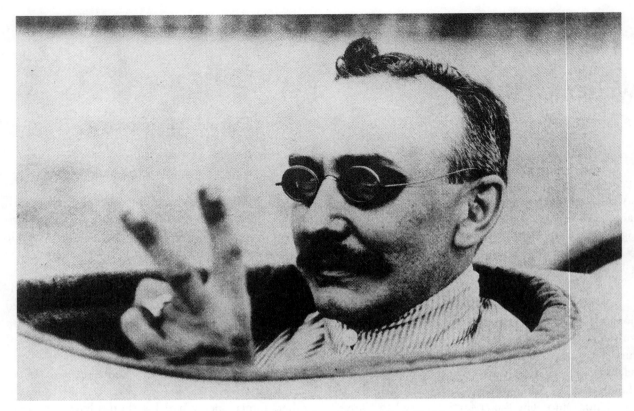

Walter C. Baker, probably in an electric race car of his design called the Torpedo (courtesy of the National Automotive History Collection, Detroit Public Library)

ing a more powerful and durable storage battery, Edison admired Baker's ingenuity. He reportedly told Baker that with Baker's car and Edison batteries, they could put gasoline-engine vehicles out of existence.

Baker was active in designing and developing the Baker automobile during the first eight years of the Baker Motor Vehicle Company's life. He worked on a shaft drive to replace the awkward chain drive common to American automobiles at the time. The Baker exhibited at the New York Automobile Show in 1900 had shaft drive, but shaft drive was standard only on the larger, more expensive models of the Baker line until the 1910 model year.

Baker was an early developer of several other automotive innovations (the rapid evolution of the automobile in its early years makes it difficult to say whether he was "first"), including left-hand steering, the steering wheel, and the thorough adoption of ball bearings. His work was particularly remarkable because American electric-vehicle manufacturers generally lagged behind early gasoline manufacturers in technical innovation.

The most dramatic evidence of Baker's ingenuity was his construction of electric racers. In 1901 he built the "Torpedo" at a reported cost of $10,000. The Torpedo was one of the earliest streamlined racers, with a smooth exterior shell completely covering the frame, seats, engine, and batteries. There were seats for Baker and C.E. Denzer, his assistant. In trials the Torpedo is reported to have reached a speed of 120 mph.

The Torpedo's racing career was limited by a tragedy. On a time trial at Staten Island, New York, on Memorial Day, 1902, the vehicle crashed into a crowd of spectators, killing two. No charges were pressed against Baker. In 1903 he built a similar but smaller racer, the "Torpedo Kid."

After about 1906 Baker was seldom involved in the design of the cars bearing his name. The Baker company retained a reputation for quality, aiming at the market of wealthy women who wanted an elegant, smooth-operating car not needing a starter. In 1915 the company merged with Rauch & Lang, another Cleveland producer of electrics, and under the name of Baker-Raulang the company survived until 1954, when it became a division of Otis Elevator and was renamed Baker Industrial Trucks.

Baker's interests extended to gasoline-engine cars. He was a director and engineering consultant of the Peerless Motor Car Company in Cleveland beginning in 1900. He worked on improving Justin B. Entz's gearless electric transmission and purchased Entz's automobile patents in 1912. In 1915, under license from Baker, the R.M. Owen Company of New York began producing the Owen Magnetic, a car with a gasoline engine that drove an electric generator to supply power to the wheels. Shortly thereafter the Owen company was absorbed by Baker-Raulang, and about 700 Magnetics were produced in Cleveland until 1919.

Baker's most productive efforts were those in the automobile industry, but he was most constantly involved in the ball-bearing business. He served as president of American Ball Bearing from its founding until 1918, when it was merged with 13 other firms to form Standard Parts Company. He then continued with that firm as a consultant.

In his personal life Baker had a lifelong love of the mechanical. He worked on the radio in the early years of its development, flew airplanes, and was active in the Cleveland Engineering Society, the American Society of Mechanical Engineers, and the Society of Automotive Engineers. Shortly before his death on April 26, 1955, Baker told an interviewer that electric automobiles would again become practical when it became possible to transmit energy in the form of electromagnetic waves. He was survived by his wife Fannie, a son, and a daughter.

References:

James J. Flink, *America Adopts the Automobile, 1895-1910* (Cambridge, Mass.: MIT Press, 1970);

The Golden Anniversary Book of the Cleveland Engineering Society (Cleveland: Cleveland Engineering Society, 1930);

David D. Van Tassel and John J. Grabowski, eds., *The Encyclopedia of Cleveland History* (Bloomington: Indiana University Press, 1987);

Richard Wager, *Golden Wheels: The Story of the Automobiles Made in Cleveland and Northeastern Ohio, 1892-1932*, revised edition (Cleveland: Zubal, 1986).

Baker Motor Vehicle Company

by Darwin H. Stapleton

Rockefeller Archive Center

The Baker Motor Vehicle Company was founded in Cleveland, Ohio, in 1898 with Rollin Henry White as president, Walter C. Baker as vice-president and mechanical engineer, and Fred R. White as treasurer. The company's electric passenger automobiles were designed from its founding to 1906 by Baker, who is recognized as one of the most innovative automotive engineers in the early years of the auto industry. The Baker company was perhaps the most successful electric automobile manufacturer in the United States until it merged with the Rausch & Lang Company in 1915.

After experiments in 1897 conducted by Baker and his friend Fred Dorn, the Baker company produced in 1898 an electric buggy weighing 550 pounds. It featured an electric battery of ten cells, a .75-horsepower motor under the seat, a chain drive to the rear axle, and tiller steering on the left-hand side. The Baker was one of the first regularly manufactured automobiles in the United States. It entered the market when electricity, steam, and gasoline were all regarded as appropriate power sources for automobiles.

Because the motors were placed under the seats, the early Baker electrics closely resembled horsedrawn vehicles. But the 1904 line introduced a "motor front" design similar to that of gasoline-engine cars well before most other electric vehicle companies moved away from the more elegant but less functional buggy, surrey, stanhope, and similar forms.

The Baker company generally marketed its passenger cars to the wealthier of the automobile clientele. Prices averaged about $2,000, and decorative elements and accessories were aimed at the fashionable buyers. In 1914 the company announced that

Baker electric at a recharging station, 1908

it had employed a French fashion designer to create special interiors. Like most electrics, the Baker was attractive to women in the cities who had the time and inclination to drive because it did not have to be hand-cranked or fired up to start, and it changed speeds easily.

The company used several publicity techniques to stimulate sales. The Baker was exhibited annually at the Madison Square Garden automobile show beginning with the initial show in 1900. From 1901 to 1903 Walter Baker raced the "Torpedo" and the "Torpedo Kid," streamlined electric-powered cars. The Torpedo was once reportedly clocked at 120 mph. The Baker company also advertised, at first claiming that its product was "The Most Elegant Automobile Made" and later claiming that the Baker was "The Aristocrat of Motordom." Since President William Howard Taft chose a Baker for the White House garage in 1909, those slogans may have seemed particularly apt.

In 1907 the Baker company added a commercial truck to its line and by 1913 had sold trucks, including 50 two-ton trucks to American Express in New York City, to more than 200 companies. The truck line showed steady growth because electrics had advantages over gasoline trucks, where noise, pollution, and the possibility of fire posed problems.

Sales of Baker automobiles were never large. In 1907 the company attempted to expand its contact with the East Coast market by incorporating the Baker Motor Vehicle Company of New York. But one year later the New York company went into bankruptcy. The original firm attempted to carry on through the manufacture of a modestly priced runabout, the Model R, in 1908. The car had a 30-cell battery, a cruising range of 70 miles (with a claimed maximum of 117 miles on a single charge), and a top speed of 22 mph. Innovative engineering features included tubular axles and a pressed-steel frame, the latter adopted at the same time by Henry Ford as a key to mass-producing the Model T. However, the low end of the Baker line could not compete with the cheaper, and usually faster and more powerful, gasoline cars of the time.

Baker automobiles, like all electrics, were severely limited by their reliance on storage batteries, which needed frequent recharging. The power-to-weight ratio of the batteries and motor remained low throughout the developmental phase of the automobile, and the cost of recharging stayed high.

The company's 1915 merger with Rausch & Lang produced the Baker-Raulang Company. The new company displayed Baker automobiles as late as 1918, but it soon focused its attention solely on the manufacture of commercial and industrial trucks. The 1919 U.S. census of manufacturers showed that Baker-Raulang was the only manufacturer of electric vehicles left in Cleveland. That company survived until 1954 when it was absorbed by Otis Elevator and renamed Baker Industrial Trucks.

References:

William G. Rose, *Cleveland: The Making of a City* (Cleveland: World, 1950);

David D. Van Tassel and John J. Grabowski, eds., *The Encyclopedia of Cleveland History* (Bloomington: Indiana University Press, 1987);

Richard Wager, *Golden Wheels: The Story of the Automobiles Made in Cleveland and Northeastern Ohio, 1892-1932*, revised edition (Cleveland: Zubal, 1986).

Oliver E. Barthel

(October 3, 1877-August 28, 1969)

by George S. May

Eastern Michigan University

CAREER: Draftsman, Frontier Iron Works (1894); draftsman (1894), draftsman and assistant, Charles B. King Company (1894-1901); designing engineer, Henry Ford Company (1901-1902); designing engineer, Barthel Motor Company (1903); experimental engineer, Ford Motor Company (1904); experimental engineer, Olds Motor Works (1904-1905); assistant engineer, Great Falls Power Company (1906); consulting engineer (1907-1955).

Although an automotive company bearing his name died in its infancy, Oliver Edward Barthel had a long and varied career as a mechanical engineer and inventor. His work with such pioneering automotive figures as Charles B. King and Henry Ford helped his native Detroit become the center of the American auto industry.

Barthel was born on October 3, 1877, the son of Albrecht Edward and Elizabeth Härter Barthel. The elder Barthel, a native of Augsburg, Germany, had migrated to Detroit, the site of a large German population, to take advantage of that city's demand for men with industrial skills. He was an engineer and took a job with the Michigan Stove Company, one of several companies that made Detroit the world's largest producer of stoves in the late nineteenth century.

Oliver Barthel was educated in the Detroit pub-

Oliver E. Barthel

lic schools, and in schools in Austria, Germany, and France during the four years his father represented the Michigan Stove Company in Europe. He sought to follow in his father's footsteps, but the elder Barthel's death forced the son to cut short his education. At age sixteen he got a job as a draftsman with the Frontier Iron Works of Detroit, producers of marine steam engines. His inexperience, however, quickly led to his dismissal, but that turned out to be fortunate since in November 1894 he was hired by Charles B. King, a move that put him on the ground floor of automotive development in Detroit.

King, an experienced mechanical engineer who had worked for two of Detroit's railroad car manufacturers, formed the Charles B. King Company late in 1893 to produce some of the creations of his inventive mind. Barthel was only his second employee. Barthel and King "got along very well," Barthel recalled. "In fact, we used to work together on the same drawing board, he working righthanded and I working lefthanded." Barthel continued his engineering education through a home-study course and by taking YMCA-sponsored night classes, including one in machine work taught by Henry Ford, but he credited King with providing him with training "that I could not have gotten in any college."

Initially King manufactured a pneumatic hammer that had won a top award at the Chicago World's Fair in 1893 and on which he had been awarded a patent early in 1894. The hammers were manufactured for King in John Lauer's Detroit machine shop. Lauer provided King with office space and allowed him to oversee production. The fact that Barthel spoke German fluently enabled him to relay King's instructions to Lauer's predominantly German work force.

King's arrangement with Lauer permitted him to devote most of his time to developing sales for his hammer and working on new products. King is best known as the builder of the first gasoline automobile to be driven on the streets of Detroit. He had begun preliminary plans for the vehicle in 1893, and Barthel once declared that the car "was practically completed when I came to him in 1894." However, the need to design a better engine and the expense involved in the project delayed King's first test run of what was the second version of the car until March 1896. Barthel worked with King on the project, and he is pictured riding with King in one of the early test drives in the spring of 1896. "Guess it was about the proudest day of my

life," Barthel would assert in later years. Exactly how much he contributed to the design of that pioneering automobile is uncertain. Recalling those developments, he sometimes claimed to have simply "helped Mr. King put that car together," but on other occasions he claimed that he was "instrumental in the creation of the first automobile to run on the streets of Detroit."

King was unable to get the backing he needed to put the car into production, and he had to settle for the manufacture of the engines he had developed. He eventually sold the 1894 version of his horseless carriage to Byron J. Carter of Jackson, Michigan, and Carter hired Barthel to build the engine for the vehicle, since King's engine was not part of the deal. Carter would later produce the Cartercar, the most famous of the friction-drive cars that were on the market for a few years in the early twentieth century. But King's and Barthel's association with Henry Ford attracted far more attention.

Barthel's acquaintanceship with Ford arose not only from the class that he had taken from Ford but also from the fact that Ford was a frequent visitor to John Lauer's machine shop, where Ford brought repair work from the Edison Illuminating Company, where he was chief engineer. "As far as I know," Barthel told a reporter 60 years later, Ford "never had any idea of making a car until I told him about two articles in the American Machinist. One was on how to build a small gas engine with odd pieces. He bought the two issues and told me he was going to build an engine." That was at the end of 1895 or the very first part of 1896, and Barthel declared that he helped Ford by giving him two intake valves out of King's scrap pile. Ford's engine powered the experimental automobile he tested in June 1896. Barthel told this story on numerous occasions, sometimes adding that he was severely reprimanded by King for his unauthorized gift of the valves. King, however, vigorously disputed the accuracy of Barthel's memory, telling an interviewer in 1940: "Oliver Barthel did not give those valves to Ford. I gave them to him. . . . Henry Ford was a friend of mine. . . . I knew Mr. Ford before Barthel did. . . . Barthel was working for me as a general handy man and assistant and I was giving him instruction in drawing. He came to me as a very young fellow."

In their later years both King and Barthel had a natural desire to take credit for having contributed to Ford's emergence as the world's most cele-brated automaker. The limited evidence supports King's version as far as the events of 1895-1896 are concerned, but Barthel's Ford association, unlike King's, was resumed in a far more important man-ner a few years later. Barthel continued with King until 1901, managing the engine and pneumatic tool business for a time in 1898 while King served in the navy during the Spanish-American War, and then taking care of the pneumatic tool business from early 1900—when King sold his engine busi-ness to the Olds Motors and went to work for that company—until May 1901, when King also dis-posed of the pneumatic tool concern. Barthel then sought to set himself up in the automotive business as a consulting engineer. The first to take advan-tage of his services was Henry Ford.

The Detroit Automobile Company, which had been formed in 1899 to produce the car Ford had de-veloped, had been dissolved by the first part of 1901, when the investors became disgusted at Ford's failure to produce. Ford, however, was still able to obtain some money to enable him to con-tinue his experiments, which by May 1901 were cen-tering on the construction of a racing car. Barthel was brought in to work on the racer along with a small group of other men who worked with Ford in those years. In his autobiography Ford took the credit for having designed the car, but Barthel de-clared that he was the one who had been responsi-ble for the racer's design and construction. "I never knew Henry Ford to design a car," he testified in 1952. "There was no possibility of Henry Ford sit-ting down and detailing a car." That statement must stand as one of the most negative assessments of Ford's abilities on record.

The racing car, nicknamed "Sweepstakes," was completed by mid summer, and in one half-mile run Barthel claimed that he achieved a speed of 72 mph. Since there were no observers the re-sults remained unofficial. In October Ford drove the car to victory in the featured event at the first auto races held in Michigan, at a dirt track in Grosse Pointe. The victory persuaded new investors to organize the Henry Ford Company to take advan-tage of Ford's newly won fame. Ford hired Barthel to work full-time for the new firm, but Barthel dis-covered that rather than discussing the design of a passenger car Ford "talked mostly about wanting to build a larger and faster racing car." It was Ford's concentration on racing rather than on pro-ducing a marketable automobile that led his latest group of backers to dismiss him in March 1902.

After Ford's departure Barthel took over his du-ties, and he came up with a 4-passenger car using a 2-cylinder engine he said he had designed, although there is some evidence that Ford contributed to the design while he was still with the Henry Ford Com-pany. However, Henry M. Leland, the operator of Detroit's best-known machine shop, who was con-sulted later that year for advice on what should be done with the Ford-less company, rejected Barthel's 2-cylinder engine in favor of a 1-cylinder design be-cause of the great success the Olds Motor Works was having with its 1-cylinder curved-dash Olds-mobile. Leland's suggestion was accepted, and the company was reorganized late in 1902 as the Cadil-lac Automobile Company. The first 1-cylinder Cadil-lacs appeared early in 1903.

In later years Barthel would claim he had held the position of chief engineer for Cadillac, but if he was with the company after the old Henry Ford Com-pany had acquired that famous name it could not have been for long, since by 1903 he was with the Barthel Motor Company. Barthel's name had ac-quired enough renown that the founders of the com-pany thought it would attract enough money to bring success. But although Alex Groesbeck, rising Detroit attorney and future three-term governor of Michigan, was among the investors, the Barthel com-pany failed to get off the ground, producing noth-ing except the prototype automobile Barthel designed. Understandably, Barthel had little to say in his old age about the company that bore his name and that was out of business in less than a year. Its failure may have had something to do with his later harsh assessment of Henry Ford, a man who may indeed have had no more ability than Barthel but who had made it big while Barthel failed. There were rumors that Barthel had a chance to obtain stock in the Ford Motor Company when it was organized in 1903 but that he rejected the offer. On at least one occasion he told a re-porter that both he and his brother, Otto, a patent at-torney, could have bought Ford stock for "next to nothing. . . . I never think about it." he said. "That is, not too regretfully. I could have bought a lot of stocks. They were all shaky, including Ford. You might say I was too close to the picture. . . . I had tre-mendous faith in the automobile's future, but I couldn't know which firm would succeed."

Barthel (left) and Charles B. King testing King's first experimental car, March 6, 1896

After the collapse of the Barthel Motor Company, Barthel worked for a short while on experimental projects for the Ford Motor Company and then for Olds Motor Works, where his activity seems to have centered not on automobiles but on marine engines. He would claim he designed the first outboard motor in 1906. That same year he became assistant engineer for the Great Falls Power Company and worked on a hydroelectrical power survey in Tennessee. From that time until ill health forced his retirement in 1955 Barthel operated a consulting business in Detroit. The 34 patents he was awarded over those years included patents for devices relating to elevated railways, laundry machinery, airplane propellers, and color lamps used in the treatment of diseases, but it was his work in the automotive field for which he remained best remembered in Detroit. His claims, such as that he designed and built the first streamlined automobile body, in 1912, the first car with an instrument board and concealed dashboard, and, in 1917, the first all-steel automobile body must be taken with a grain of salt, but his contributions were undoubtedly substantial. By the 1950s he was affectionately viewed as one of the elder statesmen of Detroit's motor industry.

Barthel had many interests. He was an avid yachtsman and was credited with having given the great Gar Wood his first lessons in powerboat racing. Like Henry Ford, Barthel was interested in reviving old-fashioned early American dances, and he had a passionate interest in gardening, keeping huge potted tropical trees in his Detroit office that obscured the view of the Detroit skyline. He married Adele Gertrude Vargason in 1906, and they had one son, Oliver Edward Barthel, Jr., who survived his father. Barthel died on August 28, 1969, a few weeks short of his ninety-second birthday.

Reference:

George S. May, *A Most Unique Machine: The Michigan Origins of the American Automobile Industry* (Grand Rapids, Mich.: Eerdmans, 1975).

Archives:

Material relating to Oliver E. Barthel may be found in the biographical files of the National Automotive History Collection at the Detroit Public Library and at the Ford Archives at the Henry Ford Museum, Dearborn, Michigan, which includes a transcript of an interview with Barthel made in 1952.

Vincent Bendix

(August 12, 1881-March 27, 1945)

by George S. May

Eastern Michigan University

CAREER: Sales manager, Holsman Automobile Company (1907); president, Bendix Company (1907-1910); self-employed inventor and developer of automotive parts (1910-1923); co-founder, Perrot Brake Company (1923); president, Bendix Corporation (1924-1929); president (1929-1942), chairman, Bendix Aviation Corporation (1942); president, Bendix Helicopters (1944-1945).

Vincent Bendix, prominent in the auto industry but identified more with the aviation and home appliance industries, was born in Moline, Illinois, on August 12, 1881, the son of John and Alma Danielson Bendix. John Bendix was a minister in the Swedish Methodist Episcopal Church, and the family's Swedish background led to the decoration of his son by the king of Sweden for his financial support of the work of Swedish archaeologist Sven Hedin.

The Bendix family left Moline for Chicago while Vincent was still a boy. In Chicago young Bendix first began to demonstrate talent in mechanics. That encouraged him to leave for New York when he was sixteen to continue to add to his knowledge while supporting himself with a variety of odd jobs.

Sometime around 1907 Bendix returned to Chicago, where he became sales manager of the Holsman Automobile Company. Holsman produced one of the "high-wheeler" motor buggies popular among midwestern farmers because their outsize wheels enabled them to be driven on the area's deeply rutted dirt roads. Bendix then took over the Triumph Motor Car Company, reorganized it as the Bendix Company, and put out his own high-wheeler, the Bendix 30, with a 4-cylinder, 30-horsepower engine. Bendix reportedly produced 7,000 of the cars between 1907 and 1910, a substantial figure for a small automaker at that stage of the industry's development. But the appeal of the

high-wheeler was short-lived. The buggy-type construction could not compete with that of Ford's sturdy Model T, and the Model T's price was significantly less than that of the high-wheelers by 1910.

The demise of the Bendix Company typified the fate of most early automobile companies, but Bendix used the knowledge he had gained to turn from the production of the entire car to that of some of its parts. In 1914 he received a patent, one of 150 patents he would be granted, for a device that greatly improved the performance of the electric starters that had begun to replace hand cranks. The Eclipse Machine Company of Chicago, which he had licensed in 1913 to produce a triple-thread screw needed in his device, was licensed to manufacture the Bendix starter drive. Its adoption in the popular Chevrolet Baby Grand touring car led to its widespread use in the industry.

The royalties Bendix received from the production of his starter drive (1.5 million units were produced by 1919) enabled him to acquire the Winkler-Crimm Wagon Company of South Bend, Indiana, manufacturers of utility vehicles such as fire engines. South Bend became the base of his manufacturing operations, which were extended into a new segment of the automotive parts field in 1923 when he met French automotive engineer Henri Perrot while on a trip to Europe. Perrot had received patents on a linkage system for 4-wheel brakes and on a brake shoe. That November Bendix and Perrot established the Perrot Brake Company in South Bend to produce Perrot's brake shoe and also to assume Perrot's interest in the linkage system, which General Motors had been licensed to produce.

To finance the expansion of that business the brake company was reorganized on December 18, 1924, as the Bendix Corporation. Its stock was sold to the public at an initial price of $26 a share. By 1928 Bendix controlled about 25 percent of the market for brakes, and the price of its stock shot

Advertisement for the Bendix Company's high-wheeler. Bendix produced about 7,000 of the cars between 1907 and 1910.

up. That same year Bendix gained majority control of the Eclipse Machine Company, producers of the Bendix starter drive. The purchase was carried through with financial support from General Motors, the major purchaser of the Bendix device.

On April 13, 1929, Vincent Bendix, who had begun to diversify into the production of aircraft components following the upsurge of interest in aviation resulting from Charles Lindbergh's trans-Atlantic flight in 1927, reorganized his business as the Bendix Aviation Corporation. General Motors purchased a 24 percent stake in the company and put two of its most promising executives, Charles E. Wilson and Albert Bradley, on the board of directors.

Aviation products comprised only 8 percent of the new company's business, which continued to be centered on automotive parts and expanded in 1929 with the acquisition of the Stromberg Carburetor Company. Nevertheless, even though Bendix reportedly did not like to fly, his establishment of the Transcontinental Air Race caused the public to asso-

ciate his name with aviation far more than it did with the automotive industry, where his contributions were far less visible. Further obscuring the major focus of his business was the development in the mid 1930s of an automatic washing machine by two engineers employed by a Bendix subsidiary, the Hydraulic Brake Company. The Bendix Home Appliance Company was formed in 1936, but aside from allowing the use of his name, Vincent Bendix had very little connection with the popular washer, and the Bendix Aviation Corporation sold its interest in the company in 1940.

That sale occurred during a period of great change at Bendix. The company had been hard hit by the Depression. Its stock, which had sold for as much as $420 in 1929, plummeted to a mere $4.37 in 1933. However, as the auto industry began to bounce back and as Bendix extended its parts production into such new areas as power brakes and power steering, business picked up. By 1935 dividend payments, which had been suspended in 1932, were resumed.

Meanwhile, Vincent Bendix was getting into serious financial difficulties unrelated to his parts business. In the 1920s he had made large real estate investments in Chicago. He purchased the great Potter Palmer mansion, where he established the Bendix Galleries to exhibit an art collection that included some Rembrandts. On June 7, 1939, after holders of real estate bonds Bendix had guaranteed went to court and demanded payment, Bendix was forced to declare bankruptcy. Assets of some $2 million were offset by liabilities of $14 million. Bendix resigned the presidency of Bendix Aviation on February 24, 1942, even though the company was not involved in his personal financial problems. After a token period as chairman, his official ties with the company he founded in 1924 were ended on March 18. Ever alert to possible future developments, he organized Bendix Helicopters in 1944 with the idea that there would be a postwar market for 4-passenger family helicopters. But before Bendix could test the idea, he died, on March 27, 1945, of a coronary thrombosis.

Bendix was married once, to Elizabeth Channon, on April 6, 1922. They had no children, and she divorced him after ten years. Bendix was survived only by the corporation he had founded and by the devices he had patented.

Even before he resigned from Bendix Aviation his influence in the automotive industry had declined as General Motors began to assert itself. Ernest R. Breech, one of two GM executives who took seats on the board in 1937 to replace Wilson and Bradley, who had been promoted to higher positions at GM, began installing some of the managerial system for which GM would be noted. Bendix, which essentially had been a holding company, was converted to an operating company. When Bendix resigned as president in 1942 he was succeeded by Breech, who soon moved the company's headquarters to Detroit. Following the war, which had brought Bendix huge contracts, Breech moved on to the Ford Motor Company to help Henry Ford II revitalize that business. In 1948 General Motors, which had considered taking over Bendix and making it one of its divisions, sold its interest as part of its policy to give up its minority interests in other businesses. Breech was replaced by Malcolm P. Ferguson, who had been general manager of Bendix's South Bend auto parts plant. Despite the continuing importance of defense contracts and the production of aviation components, the company's

auto parts business, which boomed in the postwar years, was the largest contributor of profits. In recognition of the diversity of its product lines, the company name was changed back to Bendix Corporation in 1960.

While defense contracts assumed much more importance in the 1960s, Bendix enhanced its presence in the automotive area with its acquisition of the Fram Corporation, makers of air and oil filters, and of Autolite, the spark plug company Ford was forced by a court order to sell. But Bendix is best remembered for the bizarre events following the naming of William A. Agee as chairman in 1976, succeeding W. Michael Blumenthal, who resigned to become secretary of the treasury in the Carter administration.

Agee, an aggressive administrator, continued the policy of diversification in the late 1970s, but his 1979 appointment of Mary Cunningham, a Harvard Business School graduate, as his executive assistant aroused rumors concerning their personal involvement. The rumors seemed to have had some basis in fact because Agee suddenly divorced his wife in 1980 and married Cunningham a few months later in 1981. The controversy triggered internal dissensions and the resignation of top officials. When Agee promoted Cunningham to fill one of the vacancies, his defense of the action was so ineffectual that she was forced to resign.

Before she left, however, she and Agee had been laying out plans to use the company's huge cash reserves to finance large-scale acquisitions. After failing in a bid to gain a large share of RCA stock, Bendix announced its intention of acquiring the Martin-Marietta Corporation in August 1982. In response, Martin-Marietta unveiled its own plans to take over Bendix. By the latter part of September both companies succeeded in acquiring a majority interest in the other. Legal impasse was averted on September 24, 1982, when the Allied Corporation took over Bendix for $1.9 billion. Martin-Marietta surrendered its interest in Bendix in return for its survival as an independent company.

William Agee was named president of Allied but was forced out in February 1983. Bendix was a subsidiary of Allied until September 1985 when it became a division of what was by then the Allied-Signal Corporation. A sale in 1986 eliminated many former Bendix products, and Bendix ceased to be the name of a manufacturing operation. However, Allied-Signal retained the Bendix name on some of the products of its Automotive Group.

References:
Peter F. Aartz, *Merger* (New York: Morrow, 1985);

Thomas Derdak, ed., *International Directory of Company Histories*, volume 1 (Chicago & London: St. James, 1988);

Hope Lampert, *Till Death Do Us Part* (New York: Harcourt Brace Jovanovich, 1983);

Alfred P. Sloan, Jr., *My Years With General Motors* (Garden City, N. Y.: Doubleday, 1964).

Bodies

by George S. May

Eastern Michigan University

It was their bodies as much as their means of propulsion that caused early American automobiles to be referred to as horseless carriages. While French automakers as early as 1891 were creating a look that was unique to the new form of transportation, their American counterparts with rare exceptions sought to adapt their self-propelling mechanisms to the variety of carriages designed to be pulled by horses. Some changes in design had to be made, causing one carriage trade journal to observe in 1899 that none of the horseless carriages bore "a fair resemblance to the type after which they were supposed to be fashioned." Nevertheless, part of the reasoning of early American producers seems to have been that their vehicles would be more readily accepted if they came wrapped in a familiar package.

Because of the nature of their mechanical requirements, the speeds at which they normally could be operated, and the necessity of restricting their use to urban areas, electric vehicles were best suited to the traditional designs of the carriage builders. Steamers and gasoline-powered vehicles were a different matter. Not only was it more difficult to attach their complicated mechanisms to the carriage frame, the owners' expectations that they could operate such automobiles at higher speeds and over much greater distances also required major changes in body construction. The most obvious change was in the placement of the engine. In the experimental steamer he built in 1887, Ransom E. Olds placed the engine under the seat of the vehicle in the belief that he had to "get the machinery out of sight, never thinking that we do not try to get the horse or locomotive out of sight." Five years later, the more powerful energy unit Olds used in his second steamer loomed at the rear of the fringe-covered carriage, but later in the decade when he switched to gasoline power, he again tucked the engine beneath the body. When Hiram Maxim proposed to place the engine of the Pope Manufacturing Company's first gasoline car out in front under a hood as French designers were doing, some company officials objected. "Who ever saw a horse carriage with a big box in front of the dash?" Although Maxim won that argument, it was not until about 1905, as the increasingly dominant gasoline cars moved from small 1- or 2-cylinder engines to more powerful units, that designers moved the engine from what one writer described as its "ignominious position under the body and placed [it] forward under a protecting bonnet." At the same time, changes in the construction of the body and chassis to accommodate an increase in the car's load-carrying capacity forced further modifications of standard carriage-building practices. By 1907 William Frederick Dix declared that the automobile had emerged triumphantly "as an engine of locomotion. Today it no longer sails under false colors; it looks the world in the face, an enfranchised motor car."

In the early stages of automobile development companies were primarily concerned with solving the engineering problems that continually emerged. Construction of car bodies was left to companies or individuals who had earlier built carriages. Carriage manufacturers that sought to become manufacturers of automobiles had little success; those who confined themselves to the more familiar field of body production did much better. Studebaker of South Bend, the largest of the carriage and wagon manufacturers, was the only firm to make a successful long-term transition to automobile production, but even

Pre-assembly-line body construction, early 1900s (courtesy of the Motor Vehicle Manufacturers Association)

it began by making only bodies. Detroit's C. R. Wilson Carriage Company was in on the ground floor of that city's automotive development, supplying bodies to the Olds Motor Works as early as 1900. Connecticut's New Haven Carriage Company, whose designer, William Hooker Atwood, designed the bodies of the first cars produced by the Pope Manufacturing Company in 1896-1897, began by 1902 to supply bodies that emphasized elegant coach work tailored to the individual wishes of purchasers of high-priced luxury models. That was the kind of business that attracted many carriage builders, including Brewster & Company of Long Island, one of America's most prestigious carriage builders since 1810. Around the time of World War I Brewster briefly produced its own car, but it was best known for the bodies it mounted on Marmons, Packards, Lanchesters, and, especially, Rolls-Royces.

In 1908 Frederic J. Fisher, the eldest of six brothers who learned the carriage and wagon building trade in Norwalk, Ohio, from their father, formed the Fisher Body Company to meet the needs of large-volume car producers. The Briggs Manufac-

turing Company, formed in 1909 by Walter O. Briggs, supplied bodies to Ford Motor Company and became for a time the world's largest manufacturer of automobile bodies.

Both Briggs and Fisher Body were pioneers in the production of closed bodies, with Fisher organizing the separate Fisher Closed Body Company in 1910 to handle an order from Cadillac for 150 units. Open bodies had been constructed of wood in accordance with the traditions of carriage-building practices, but wood did not provide the strength needed for closed body construction. The problem was partially remedied by attaching sheet metal panels over parts of the wood body, but the most satisfactory solution came with the development of all-steel construction. Edward G. Budd, whose background was in sheet metal, not carriage building, pioneered that development, establishing the Edward G. Budd Manufacturing Company in 1912 to produce all-steel bodies for Oakland and an increasing number of other companies. Opposition arose from established coach builders, who continued to favor metal-covered wooden bodies, but the performance of motor vehicles using all-steel bodies provided convincing proof of the superiority of that type of construction. It was quicker and cheaper to stamp out steel bodies, and metal construction gave a new generation of designers greater design flexibility. Soon rounded, graceful body lines replaced the square, often awkward-appearing lines dictated by the conventions of carriage-building style and the nature of wood construction.

By the 1920s the advocates of the all-steel body had prevailed, and by the mid 1920s production of closed cars surpassed that of open cars. But despite the radical construction changes that had

taken place, style names such as brougham, runabout, sedan, coupè, and landaulet, all carryovers from carriage terminology, continued to be used, even though the automotive body styles bearing those names barely resembled the carriage styles the terms originally described.

References:

Automotive Industry of America (Southfield, Mich.: Prestige, 1979);

George S. May, *The Automobile and American Life* (forthcoming 1990).

Borg-Warner Corporation

by George S. May

Eastern Michigan University

Borg-Warner Corporation was founded in 1928 by banking interests that wished to create a stable automotive parts company by combining several companies making a variety of different parts. Through those companies the origins of the auto-parts giant extend back to the industry's earliest days.

The first part of the corporate name derives from the firm of Borg and Beck, formed in 1904 in Moline, Illinois, by Charles W. Borg and Marshall Beck. Borg, a Swedish immigrant, had worked for Deere and Mansur, the Moline farm equipment manufacturer. Later, Borg's son, George W. Borg, who had also worked at Deere and Mansur and had graduated from Augustana College, joined the firm. Borg and Beck produced woodworking machines, including one Charles Borg had invented that shaped wagon poles. As the demand for wagon and carriage parts began to decline, the company branched into the production of small parts for automobiles.

In 1908 the Velie Motor Vehicle Company was formed. William Velie, the founder, was John Deere's grandson, and the Deere company handled sales of the Velie cars. When the company encountered difficulties with the clutch used in its cars, it was natural that it turned to the Borgs, former Deere employees. That led to the product for which the Borg and Beck division of Borg-Warner is still famous—an improved disk clutch. George Borg and Gus Nelson, Borg and Beck's chief mechanical assis-

tant, are most commonly credited with the clutch's development, although others claim that the inventor was Charles Borg. Regardless, the clutch, which was first used in Jeffrey trucks and passenger cars just prior to World War I, became the company's principal product and standard equipment on millions of vehicles.

In 1921 the Borg and Beck partnership was purchased by a bank, and George Borg became president of the company. Borg directed an expansion, seeking to avoid having to depend exclusively on one product. He established the Standard Parts Company and opened a chain of auto parts stores. In the latter part of the 1920s he played a key role in the merger activities that led to Borg-Warner's formation, and he served as the corporation's first president. He left Borg-Warner in 1940 to give his full attention to the George W. Borg Corporation, which had started out making automobile clocks before moving into other areas, such as precision instruments, and particularly textiles, for which Borg would be best known in his later years.

The other part of Borg-Warner's name comes from the Warner Gear Company, which was formed in Muncie, Indiana, in 1901. An order from the Olds Motor Works for 4,000 differentials got the company off to an auspicious start. Rear axles, steering gears, and clutches were also produced by Warner Gear. At the start of the 1920s the company developed a standardized transmission, known as the T-64. It was first adopted as standard equipment on Paige and Chalmers cars, and by the time the company became part of Borg-Warner in 1928 the transmission had also been used on Chrysler, Reo, Jordan, Locomobile, Gardner, Auburn, Moon, Graham Brothers, Marmon, Rickenbacker, Velie, and Paige cars and trucks. Charles S. Davis, secretary-treasurer of Warner Gear, would help bring the company into the Borg-Warner combine and would later serve as president and chairman of the corporation.

The two other charter members of Borg-Warner were the Marvel Carburetor Company and the Mechanics Universal Joint Company. The former originated in Indianapolis in the early years of the century, when B. N. Pierce and George Schebler developed two advanced types of carburetors. After producing those for several years they dissolved their partnership. Schebler stayed in Indianapolis, where he produced the Schebler Model B Carburetor that came to be used in many cars and tractors and in nearly all fire engines. Pierce moved to Flint, Michigan, and formed the Marvel Carburetor Company, which supplied that part in the early 1920s to various General Motors vehicles as well as to Nash and Hudson. Schebler rejoined Pierce later in the decade, and the Marvel company was located in Detroit at the time it became part of Borg-Warner.

The Mechanics Universal Joint Company, a Rockford, Illinois, business, had started out as the Mechanics Machine Company. That company began producing transmissions in 1911. It also did some work with axles and differentials. It had supplied some transmissions to Chevrolet in 1914, and when the company developed a "block type" universal joint in a malleable iron housing it became standard equipment on all Chevrolets. An improved model with sealed-in lubricant was brought out on 1921 models.

In 1929 four more parts manufacturers became part of Borg-Warner. Two of those were producers of clutches. The Rockford Drilling Machine Company produced clutches for tractor and farm implement manufacturers, but the Long Manufacturing Company of Detroit, although it had started out making radiators for cars, began making clutches in 1922 and soon became Borg and Beck's principal competitor. The Galesburg Coulter-Disc Company, another of the 1929 acquisitions, sup-

plied disks to both Long and Borg and Beck. The fourth of the 1929 companies was the Morse Chain Company, whose origins date back to the 1880s, when it produced bicycle chains. With the coming of automobiles the company developed the Morse Silent Chain, which was installed in the 1912 Cadillac. By the late 1920s that automotive timing chain was reportedly used in about 40 percent of American cars.

In the years that followed Borg-Warner expanded into other industries, including stoves, refrigerators, plastics, hydraulics, health services, and protective services. Automotive parts, both original and replacement parts, remained the corporation's largest volume operation. The management staff of the auto group was moved in 1975 from the corporate headquarters in Chicago to the Detroit area. It was the diversity of Borg-Warner's product lines, however, that helped to make it a prime takeover target by the mid 1980s. On March 31, 1987, Samuel J. Heyman, chairman of GAF Corporation, tendered a bid of $3.2 billion to take over the company. At $46 a share, Heyman's offer was more than twice the book value of Borg-Warner stock, but Borg-Warner's billion-dollar chemicals and plastics operation made an attractive addition to GAF's specialty chemicals division. Although the bid was couched in friendly terms, with a promise that the Borg-Warner name would be retained in the merged company and places would be found for senior Borg-Warner executives, Borg-Warner, led by its chief executive, Clarence E. Johnson, rejected GAF's offer. To stave off renewed takeover attempts, Borg-Warner, through Merrill Lynch Capital Markets, the brokerage company's investment banking unit, had carried out a $4.23 billion leveraged buyout (LBO) by May 1987. In return for taking the company private, the LBO, which was at that time the third largest on record, left Borg-Warner with a $3.7 billion debt, $2 billion of which was due in 1988. After the market crash in October 1987, the 12.75 percent junk bonds that were issued to finance the deal slipped in value from 93 to 84. But although 1988 sales of $3.218 billion, down from $3.554 billion in 1987, dropped Borg-Warner from 119th to 142nd on the *Fortune* 500 list, signs indicated that Borg-Warner would come through the ordeal safely.

References:

Automotive Industry of America (Southfield, Mich.: Prestige, 1979);

"Cash, Flash, and Dash: Can this be Merrill?," *Business Week*, no. 2998 (May 11, 1987): 124, 126;

"Cornering Borg-Warner," *Business Week*, no. 2993 (April 13, 1987): 39;

"Will GAF Cash in its Borg-Warner Chips—Or up the ante?," *Business Week*, no. 2996 (April 27, 1987): 34-35.

Brakes

by James Wren

Motor Vehicle Manufacturers Association

One of the obvious problems associated with motor vehicles during their early development was the need to slow or to stop them as desired. Early brakes were adaptations of wagon and carriage brakes, ranging from snubbing devices—steel wires or chains pulled against the axle—to spoon brakes—blocks of wood pressed directly against a wheel by means of a lever. The obvious disadvantages of those primitive devices soon resulted in the development of various new braking systems.

One of the first was the external contracting, or band, brake, which used a metal or wooden drum wrapped around the wheel to apply stopping pressure. Most automobiles at the beginning of the twentieth century used that type of device. A problem with that type of brake was that it was constantly exposed to the environment, and the concomitant snow, rain, and mud adversely affected the brake's performance. The logical development was invention of an internal brake, but that required a reversal of the principle upon which the brake operated.

In 1901 William Maybach, the brilliant German automotive engineer, designed an internal expanding brake, which, when activated, pressed shoes against the interior of the wheel or the drive shaft. That design solved many of the problems associated with the external brakes and remained the basis for most braking systems until the widespread adoption of the disc brake in the 1970s. But of course certain problems persisted.

Three of the most severe were the lack of durability of the drum system, the build-up of heat and friction, and the equal application of sufficient braking power. The first two were solved by turning away from the light, heat-resistant sheet steel that was used in most early drum brakes to stronger, heat-dissipating aluminum and iron. The last problem was solved, or at least mitigated, by the adoption of 4-wheel, hydraulically operated systems based on Blaise Pascal's theorem that pressure applied to a fluid in an enclosed body is transmitted equally in all directions. Although the fundamental modern concept of a brake based on that idea was devised in 1908 and installed in several French models in 1911, the first American production cars to use the system were the 1921 Duesenbergs. Chrysler followed suit in 1924, and soon the hydraulic brake system was generally adopted on larger vehicles.

Brayton Engines

by James Wren

Motor Vehicle Manufacturers Association

George Baily Brayton was an American pioneer in the development and manufacture of the internal combustion gas engine. The Brayton 2-stroke continuous-compression-cycle liquid petroleum engine was patented in 1872 in America and Great Britain. The engine was used in trains and boats and in industrial applications. Although Brayton's engines proved unacceptable for automobiles because they could not achieve sufficient thermal efficiency, the Brayton thermodynamic cycle is still used in the modern continuous-cycle gas engine. Brayton's engines are also significant for their role in the Selden patent fight of the early twentieth century.

Brayton was born in East Greenwich, Rhode Island, in 1839, at a time when invention in mechanical power was just gaining momentum in America. He was strongly influenced by his father, a superintendent for a cotton textile mill who also invented machinery attachments for looms to supplement the family income. Following his father's footsteps, young Brayton's love of machines and mechanics caused him to forgo a high-school education for machinist's training in Providence. At an early age he developed a breech-loading gun and a tank riveter and experimented with combustion engines and fuels.

Brayton's machinist training gained him employment at the Exeter Machine Works in New Hampshire. At Exeter he developed a steam generator for home heating, which soon became the company's major product. The boiler's success inspired Brayton to devote full time to the development of a gasoline engine. Fortunately, Exeter owner William Burlingame was so impressed with Brayton that he financed the engine's development and provided laboratory space at the Exeter factory for Brayton's experiments. Upon completion of the first continuous-compression-cycle model in 1872

(the first engine to use liquid petroleum for fuel), Brayton constructed an oil engine (the first to use crude petroleum) that has been cited as an anticipation of Rudolph Diesel's rational heat engine. A Brayton Petroleum Engine was cited for its speed in motorboat use in the March 1, 1878, issue of *Scientific News*. The thermodynamic cycle of Brayton's engines was composed of two adiabotic and two isobaric changes in alternate order with energy transfer in turbojets and is sometimes called the Joules cycle.

Although Brayton engines were never widely accepted, they became among the most widely discussed in history because of a patent issued to George B. Selden in 1895 for a "road engine" equipped with an engine of the Brayton type. The Selden litigation lasted until 1911, when the U.S. Circuit Court of Appeals ruled the patent "valid but not infringed" by most auto manufacturers, who by then had overwhelmingly adopted the Otto 4-cycle combustion system.

Brayton was married in October 1864 in Providence, Rhode Island, and had one son, Harry. He died in 1892. His wife, Rhoda, and son were witnesses in the Selden lawsuit and testified as to Brayton's unremitting labor in the design and construction of gas engines.

References:

"The Brayton Engine," *Scientific American*, 36 (January 13, 1877): 19-20;

"Brayton's Hydro-Carbon Engine," *Engineer* (July 19, 1878): 48;

Dugald Clerk, *The Gas and Oil Engine*, seventh edition (New York: Wiley, 1896);

Lyle B. Cummins, *Internal Fire* (Lake Oswego, Oreg.: Carnot, 1975), pp. 184-186.

Benjamin Briscoe

(May 24, 1867-June 27, 1945)

by George S. May

Eastern Michigan University

CAREER: Operator of sheet metal companies (1885-1900); president, Briscoe Manufacturing Company (1900-1903); president, Maxwell-Briscoe Manufacturing Company (1903-1910); president, United States Motor Company (1910-1912); partner, cyclecar companies (1913-1916); president, Briscoe Motor Corporation (1914-1921); lieutenant-commander, U.S. Navy (1917-1919); actively involved in oil, gold mining, and agricultural pursuits (1919-1945).

Benjamin Briscoe, a major figure in the early period of the auto industry and the promoter of one of the two greatest efforts to consolidate automobile companies, was born in Detroit on May 24, 1867, the son of Joseph A. and Sarah Smith Briscoe. Briscoe's paternal grandfather settled in Detroit in 1837, and both he and Briscoe's father contributed significantly to the development of railroads in Michigan through inventions that improved railroad rolling stock. Unlike his younger brother Frank, who was born in 1875 and spent eight years in undergraduate and graduate work at the University of Michigan and in Europe before entering the business world, Benjamin Briscoe skipped college and went directly into business, first as a clerk at a Detroit wholesale firm and then, in 1885, as the owner of his own firm, Benjamin Briscoe and Company.

That company, which Briscoe formed with a capital of only $472, produced sheet metal goods such as tubs, pails, and sprinkler cans. The company was subsequently purchased by the American Can Company. Briscoe went on to organize the Detroit Galvanizing and Sheet Metal Works. Corrugated pipe, made with a machine he had invented, was one of its products. Briscoe also produced sheet metal parts for stoves, a major industry in Detroit. In 1900, when Frank Briscoe joined the business, the company was reorganized as the Briscoe

Benjamin Briscoe (courtesy of the Motor Vehicle Manufacturers Association)

Manufacturing Company. A bank failure in 1901 brought the firm to the brink of collapse, and, although he got some temporary help locally, Benjamin Briscoe said he decided to get the money he needed "where money was." He went to the very top–J. P. Morgan & Company, where he claimed to have persuaded Morgan himself to put up $100,000. As a result, "Mr. Morgan and myself became . . . the main owners of the Briscoe Manufacturing Co." That Wall Street connection would be of crucial importance in Briscoe's automotive career.

That career had its beginning in 1902 when Ransom E. Olds, accompanied by Jonathan Maxwell, one of his engineers, came into the Briscoe shop with one of the radiators for the curved-dash Oldsmobile runabout. The Olds Motor Works had been making its own radiator, which it called a "cooler," but it was not satisfactory. Briscoe, who said he first thought that Olds had brought in some kind of "antiquated band instrument," solved the problem by having his staff design a watertight cooler. The Briscoe company received a contract to build 4,400 of them, and in a short time the company, which was already one of Detroit's largest sheet metal operations, was also producing fenders, tanks, toolboxes, and other items and was said to have become the country's largest supplier of sheet metal parts to the auto industry.

Profitable as the parts business may have been, however, the success that Olds and some of the other Detroit automakers were beginning to enjoy aroused in the Briscoes, as Frank picturesquely phrased it, "an itch to get into the big tent." They had been providing some parts and financial assistance to David D. Buick, with whom Benjamin Briscoe may have become acquainted because of Buick's earlier plumbing supply business, in support of Buick's experimental automotive work. In September 1902 they entered into an agreement with Buick to cancel his debt to them and to furnish him an additional $650 in return for the car he was building. By the spring of 1903 the car had been completed and tested, but although the Briscoes allowed Buick to use it to help him raise the money to put it into production, he had had no luck. The two brothers then agreed to loan him more money, in return for which Buick's business was reorganized as the Buick Manufacturing Company with a capitalization of $100,000. The Briscoes took $99,700 of that, leaving Buick only $300 but with the understanding that if he paid off his debt to them by September they would give him all of their stock. Otherwise, they would take control of the company.

Before long it was obvious to the Briscoes that David Buick was not going to come up with the money to pay them off. On a visit to Flint that summer one of the brothers learned that the directors of the Flint Wagon Works were interested in acquiring an automobile company as a hedge against the effects that car sales would have on the carriage trade. After a meeting between Benjamin Briscoe and Flint head James Whiting and an inspection of the one Buick that had been built, in early September 1903 the Flint businessmen paid the Briscoes $10,000 for their interest in the Buick Manufacturing Company, which they moved to Flint—with re-

sults that would have spectacular consequences for that city's economy.

Benjamin Briscoe was anxious to unload his interest in Buick's unpromising company because in the meantime he had become involved with a car being developed by Jonathan Maxwell, the veteran automotive engineer whom he had met in 1902. At that time, Maxwell had been employed by the Olds Motor Works, but he left to design a car for a new Detroit company, Northern. Then, on July 4, 1903, Briscoe, together with another businessman, C. W. Althouse, agreed to furnish Maxwell with $3,000 to build the prototype of another new car. Althouse had to withdraw because of ill health, and it was left to Briscoe to witness the successful Christmas-day test of Maxwell's car.

Briscoe then turned the presidency of the sheet metal company over to his brother and formed the Maxwell-Briscoe Motor Company to produce Maxwell's car. Briscoe was careful, however, to maintain control of the company. He could not get the financial backing he needed in Detroit, where, he said, "there was a feeling on the part of capitalists that the [auto industry] was growing too fast, and that the automobile had then reached the limit of its possibilities." Briscoe's opinion runs counter to the usual view that Detroit bankers were generous in the help they provided, one reason cited for that city's rise to leadership in the industry. However, it may well have been that the emergence of the Olds Motor Works, Northern, Cadillac, Ford, and other companies all within a short period of time caused the city's financial leaders to conclude it was time to stand back and allow the city's economy to adjust before proceeding with more development.

Rebuffed at home, Briscoe called upon his Wall Street contacts and got $100,000 from the banking firm of Richard Irvin & Company, while J. P. Morgan & Company handled the sale of $250,000 in Maxwell-Briscoe bonds. The support was dependent upon Briscoe's ability to lease the Tarrytown, New York, plant that had been used by the defunct Mobile Steam Car Company. The lease was obtained, and by June 1904 operations of the new company were underway. After a slow start, by 1906 Maxwells were the only car produced in the East that seriously challenged the volume leadership of the Michigan companies.

While Jonathan Maxwell handled the production end of the business, Benjamin Briscoe busily pushed the company's expansion, adding plants in Pawtucket, Rhode Island, and Newcastle, Indiana, to the leased quarters in Tarrytown that Briscoe purchased in 1906. He probably expanded too fast, as he himself may have begun to recognize by March 1907, when he expressed to fellow members of the American Motor Car Manufacturers Association his concern that the industry production was dangerously close to outstripping the demands of the market. Those fears seemed to have been realized late in 1907 when a financial panic briefly sent sales plummeting. Briscoe, according to Alfred Reeves, an industry insider and later an associate of Briscoe's, carried his company through the crisis "by selling participating debentures to the dealers who were given a more favorable cost price to themselves on cars and trucks," a practice, Reeves observed in 1945, that would not have appealed to the Securities and Exchange Commission had it been in existence.

Reeves said Briscoe was forced to resort to such unusual financial arrangements because the Morgans' interest in the automobile was rumored to have declined when they felt it was becoming a threat to their dominant interest in railroads. However, it would probably be more accurate to say that J. P. Morgan & Company, which Briscoe said was earning 20 percent on the money it had loaned to Maxwell-Briscoe, had not lost interest in the automobile as much as it had lost faith in the ability of the industry to remain profitable as it was then organized. Morgan had long sought to bring order out of chaos by consolidating competing companies into one large corporation. According to William C. Durant it was the suggestion of George W. Perkins, a Morgan partner, that Briscoe seek to bring about such a consolidation in the auto industry to provide the stability the industry needed and its Wall Street backers demanded.

Sometime in the latter part of 1907 Briscoe telephoned Durant, who, ironically, had made the Buick company, which Briscoe had eagerly gotten rid of four years before, into one of the two biggest auto producers in the country. "Billy," he said, "I have a most important matter to discuss with you. . . . It's the biggest thing in the country. There's millions in it." Durant was too busy to come to Chicago, where Briscoe was staying, and so Briscoe came to Flint, and the two men discussed the Morgans' and Briscoe's ideas for a consolidation of leading auto companies. The financial

problems that Maxwell-Briscoe was suffering through no doubt accounted for much of his interest in making that company part of a merger. "I believe the history of almost every combination," he later observed, "will show that the principal motive comes from being hard up." However, although Buick also had problems paying its bills because of declining sales during the 1907-1908 panic, Durant was far more optimistic about future growth possibilities than Briscoe, and he quickly endorsed the idea of a combination of producers as a means of gaining a greater share of that expanding market. But he felt that Briscoe's plan to approach some 20 companies, including those that produced such high-priced models as Packard, Peerless, Pierce-Arrow, and Thomas, was impractical because the product of those companies did not have enough in common with the kinds of cars Buick and Maxwell-Briscoe produced. Instead, he suggested that Briscoe talk with Henry Ford and Ransom Olds, whose Fords and Reos were, with Buicks and Maxwells, the industry's low-price volume leaders. "I suggested he first see Henry Ford," Durant said, since Ford "was in the limelight, liked publicity and unless he could lead the procession would not play."

Briscoe accepted Durant's suggestion, and he shortly met with Olds in Lansing and Ford in Detroit and found both were willing to discuss a consolidation. A meeting was held in Detroit on January 17, 1908, in which Ford, Olds, Durant, and Briscoe tried to put together a preliminary plan for consolidation they could present to the Morgan company, which would handle the financial arrangements. According to the notes that Ford's business manager, James Couzens, had taken (apparently at the time Briscoe first broached the subject of a merger to Ford), the new company would be capitalized at about $35 million, with Ford, Reo, and Buick each to be valued at $7,125,000 and Maxwell-Briscoe at $6,125,000. The remainder of the stock in the new company, after the stockholders in the four companies had received their share based on those valuations, was to be sold or distributed as bonuses to the participating companies. Durant indicates, however, that at the January meeting of the four executives in Detroit there was considerable argument over the valuations. Briscoe was never happy with the fact that his company was given a value less than that of the three Michigan companies. In addition, he and Durant did not agree on the nature of the corporation that would result from the merger.

Durant wanted a holding company, which would control the four companies through its ownership of the stock but would allow the management of each company to operate without central control. Briscoe favored consolidating purchasing, engineering, sales, and advertising for all four companies and creating a central committee that would set overall operating policies. As Briscoe put it, "Durant is for states' rights. I am for a union."

A week later the four men met in New York to continue their talks in the office of Herbert L. Satterlee, J. P. Morgan's son-in-law and a member of the Wall Street law firm of Ward, Hayden and Satterlee. There were other discussions in New York in the next several months, although how many is uncertain. At one of them, probably in May, the talks ran into unresolvable problems. It was discovered that there was a fundamental disagreement over how the consolidation was to be accomplished. Durant and Briscoe both had in mind an arrangement whereby stockholders in the four companies would exchange their shares for shares in the new corporation, with little or no money changing hands. But at some point either Ford or Couzens said it would take at least $3 million, in addition to stock, to bring the Ford company into the merger. Olds then declared that if Ford got that kind of money, Reo would demand a similar amount for its participation. That was upsetting enough to Satterlee, who had also been led to believe that the four executives would buy some of the stock in the new corporation, thereby helping to finance its formation. However, when Satterlee asked Ford how much stock he planned to buy, Ford replied that he did not intend to buy any. The astonished Satterlee called Durant and Briscoe into an adjoining office and demanded to know what was going on. Durant said he was as surprised as Satterlee since he had assumed that Ford and Olds agreed with the plan to bring their companies into the merger through an exchange of stock. Briscoe then had to admit that Ford had stated that he wanted money for his company when Briscoe had first talked with him. Since Ford had not raised the issue when negotiations had begun, Briscoe had thought Ford had decided to go along with the other approach.

Satterlee, who felt he had been misled by Briscoe, returned to the other office and informed Ford and Olds "that there had been a misunderstanding, that the matter of finance was entirely up to the bankers, and when they had perfected their plan, another meeting would be called." But no more meetings were held at which Ford or Olds was present, for the amount of money they were asking, extremely modest as it would now seem to have been, was much more than the amount the Morgan company was willing to commit itself to raising.

The possibility of a merger between Buick and Maxwell-Briscoe was still very much alive, however, and on June 29 Briscoe provided the newspapers with the first concrete confirmation that rumors of a merger were "not altogether without foundation." There had been, he said, "a series of conferences in which was discussed the feasibility of the proposition in its many phases, financial and physical, all with the end in view to place the business of making and selling moderate-priced motor cars on a basis that will be attractive to the average buyer." Briscoe indicated that he still favored a centralization of some of the activities of the companies involved, without, however, eliminating "the individualities" of the cars the companies produced.

It was Briscoe's willingness to open up to the press, in contrast with Durant's refusal to confirm or deny the rumors that circulated, that brought an end to the talks of a merger between their companies. A detailed discussion of the proposed merger that appeared in the *New York Times* on July 31 (probably based on information supplied by Briscoe) angered the Morgan officials, who were already unhappy at Durant's handling of the authority the Buick stockholders had given him the previous spring to arrange an exchange of stock on whatever terms he thought were satisfactory. As a result, the Morgan company refused to cooperate with further plans for a Buick-Maxwell merger. Briscoe wrote to Durant on August 4 that he could not understand why "the people on the 'corner'" were so upset by the *Times* article, but in any event the two of them ought to be able to handle the financing of the merger themselves. "We have both concluded that a million dollars in cash would be enough to finance the proposition and I will eat my shoes if we can't raise a million dollars between us." But on second thought Briscoe recognized that he was too closely tied to the Morgans to proceed with a merger without their approval. Before the end of the month prospects of a consolidation of Durant's and Briscoe's companies had come to an end.

Durant, unwilling to surrender the power he held to commit the Buick stock to a consolidation, went ahead on his own in September to form the General Motors Company. According to one story, possibly apocryphal, Durant chose the name one day when Briscoe was in his office and had told him that George Perkins would not allow him to use the name International Motors Company, the name Perkins had reserved for the earlier Ford-Reo-Buick-Maxwell combination. Durant then took a piece of paper, crossed out the word "International" and wrote "General." "How does that look?" he asked Briscoe. "You mean you'll call your organization the 'General Motors Company'?" Briscoe inquired. "Yes," Durant replied. However the famous name may have originated, Durant acquired control of some two dozen companies during the next year. Many were of little enduring importance, but his own Buick plus the companies that would produce the Pontiacs, the Oldsmobiles, and the Cadillacs provided the basis for the dominance General Motors (GM) would eventually achieve.

Meanwhile, Briscoe was pursuing his own takeover plans. A lack of solid documentary material makes it impossible to piece together a satisfactory account of what was behind Briscoe's or, for that matter, Durant's actions. Certainly Briscoe, like Durant, was driven by his ambition, which made him unwilling to be content with the success of his own company, whose production in 1909 fell just short of 10,000 units, more than twice the previous year's totals. But it is equally certain that Briscoe was not acting alone. The sharp rebound in automobile sales after the panic of 1907 intensified Wall Street's interest in moves toward greater consolidation. Not only was the House of Morgan, Briscoe's long-time partner, involved, so was Anthony Brady, a Wall Street veteran who had made a fortune through earlier utility and traction line mergers. The panic had caused him to put on hold an auto industry consolidation he had been seeking to put together, but he now turned his attention back to that area and would become perhaps the principal backer of Briscoe's activities. To confuse matters, however, he also was involved with General Motors, serving as a director of that company from 1910 to 1915.

Briscoe's first attempt to find a new partner in a consolidation after the collapse of the Buick-Maxwell talks came in November 1908, when he was given an option to purchase 60 percent of Cadillac's stock for $150 per share. His inability to find the money to exercise that option and gain control of one of the industry's most solid companies did not bode well for his future success.

During the following months, as the list of General Motors' acquisitions lengthened, Briscoe reopened negotiations with Durant. In July they worked out a deal whereby GM would acquire not only Maxwell-Briscoe but also the Briscoe sheet metal company and the Brush Runabout Company that Frank Briscoe had organized in 1907—all for $5 million in General Motors stock. Twelve years later Briscoe reflected that the stock by that time would have been worth in excess of $100 million, but the Morgan interests vetoed the deal, insisting that Durant come up with an additional $2 million in cash. That was too much for Durant, who was having a hard enough time finding the more than $4 million he needed to acquire Cadillac that summer, and Briscoe's latest merger plans collapsed.

Later that summer, as rumors of a GM acquisition of his company continued to circulate, Briscoe declared that it was more likely that Maxwell-Briscoe would be the one doing the acquiring. Thus, in the latter part of September, Briscoe and Alfred Reeves, who was now working with Briscoe, met with Ransom Olds to seek to bring Reo into their proposed new combination. However, Olds's continued insistence on cash, not stock, as the basis for his company's participation ended these negotiations. In the same period Briscoe said Ford offered him the same deal Ford had offered Durant, but Ford's $8 million asking price, even though it could be spread out in several installments, was as much beyond Briscoe's reach as it was Durant's, and the chance to acquire Ford again slipped away.

Finally, in January 1910 the United States Motor Company, which was to be Briscoe's answer to Durant's General Motors, was formed. In addition to backing from Anthony Brady, the Morgan interests were also deeply involved along with the investment banker Eugene Meyer. Briscoe's own company was of course U.S. Motor's first acquisition, but unfortunately it would be the only one of the company's numerous acquisitions that could contribute significantly to its profitability. There were widespread reports in the spring of 1910 that E-M-F, a major Detroit company, was about to be acquired, but instead it fell into the hands of Studebaker. Reo was another reported takeover candidate, but although some U.S. Motor backers did acquire some Reo stock, Ransom Olds's demand for $7 million in cash for a controlling stock interest killed Briscoe's chances of getting the Lansing company, which could have given U.S. Motor a car whose volume would have been second only to Maxwell's.

Frank Briscoe's Brush Runabout failed to live up to the promise offered by its excellent initial sales, in part because the runabout's design, when compared with other low-priced cars of the day, was perceived as outmoded. The Columbia Motor Car Company, one of Anthony Brady's interests, was another early acquisition. As the successor to the Electric Vehicle Company, Columbia controlled the Selden Patent, which, because it was claimed to apply to all gasoline cars, had had great potential value. But a court decision early in 1911 so severely limited the validity of that claim as to make the patent virtually worthless, a judgment that could also apply to the cars Columbia produced. Thomas and Stoddard-Dayton, producers of high-priced, low-volume cars, and the truck manufacturers Alden-Sampson and Grabowsky were other vehicle companies included among the 130 companies, most of them small firms making auto parts, that joined the fold by 1912.

By the end of 1912 U.S. Motor had gone bankrupt and was out of business. There are several explanations. One holds that Briscoe, true to his "unionist" concept of consolidation, moved too fast in trying to centralize authority. In the process he had destroyed the ability of the managers of the various units to maintain the individual character of the companies. Another view is that U.S. Motor failed because the Maxwell car was the only one buyers were interested in, and its sales were not enough to offset the losses sustained by other company divisions. However, according to the automotive journalist Chris Sinsabaugh, Briscoe and a good many others believed that U.S. Motor fell victim to outside financial manipulation over which management had no control. In 1910 U.S. Motor, with the help of George Perkins and Eugene Meyer, had obtained $6 million through a bond issue that stipulated that if the company's assets were ever appraised below a certain amount the entire issue would be called in. When an appraisal was made in 1912 Sinsabaugh implies that there was some kind of conspiracy to make sure that the appraisers reported a net worth that was less than the required percentage. In actual-

ity, it was claimed, U.S. Motor was well within the permitted limit and Maxwell-Briscoe, with a net profit of over $600,000, might still have been able to carry the company along. But the company was put through receivership, and the only survivor was Maxwell, which was reorganized by Walter Flanders—without Briscoe and shortly without Jonathan Maxwell. Maxwell continued until the 1920s, when new financial problems brought it under the control of Walter Chrysler, who made it the stepping stone for the organization of the Chrysler Corporation in 1925.

Benjamin Briscoe's post-1912 career is something of an anticlimax, but it provides evidence of a remarkable ability to bounce back and move into new and different ventures, which leads one to hope that a full-scale biography of this unusual man will sometime appear. Following the collapse of U.S. Motor, Briscoe and his brother went to France in 1913. There they formed Briscoe Frères to produce a cyclecar designed by French engineers, which they called the Ajax. Returning to the United States, they formed the Argo Motor Company in March 1914 to produce the American version of the car, which appeared for a couple of years before the cyclecar fad had ended. Meantime, late in 1913, Briscoe formed the Briscoe Motor Corporation, located in Jackson, Michigan, which began production in 1914 of the Briscoe, a 4-cylinder car distinguished by a body made of material similar to papier-mâché and particularly by its single headlight. By 1916 the famous cyclops headlight had been replaced by more-standard twin headlights. With the addition of an 8-cylinder engine that year production totaled 7,100 and increased to 8,100 the following year.

With the entry of the United States into World War I, Briscoe entered government service, first in Washington and then as a lieutenant commander in the navy directing naval aircraft work in Italy and southern France. In 1919 Briscoe was promoted to commander and was awarded the Navy Cross for his wartime service. After the war, although the Briscoe Motor Corporation continued in business for several years, control of the company passed into other hands, with the car's name being changed to Earl in 1921, after Clarence A. Earl, the new vice-president. Briscoe meanwhile turned to the oil business, going to Montreal, Canada, for a time to manage the Frontenac Oil Company, which employed an improved method that Briscoe helped develop for refining crude oil. Subsequently Briscoe became involved in gold mining in Alma, Colorado, and ore milling in Idaho Springs in the same state.

In 1938 Briscoe suffered a slight stroke. Early that same year his wife, Lewis Snyder Briscoe, died in Denver, where they were then residing. Briscoe retired to Florida, where he purchased 3,000 acres in Dunnellon. There he carried on experiments with tung trees and varieties of hay until his death on June 27, 1945. He was survived by his second wife, Ellen Lustig Briscoe, and a son and two daughters by his first wife. Frank Briscoe, who was involved in a variety of manufacturing activities in later years, died in 1954.

Benjamin Briscoe was possessed of considerable talents as a promoter and organizer. The Maxwell car was his major legacy and one that in a sense survives in the Chrysler Corporation. Circum-

stances beyond his control probably caused the failure of what he had hoped would be his major achievement, but, as Chris Sinsabaugh observes, "a somewhat different shuffling of the cards of fate could have produced results from which the motor industry might have drawn no little benefit. Who knows?"

References:

Nick Baldwin and others, *The World Guide to Automobile Manufacturers* (New York: Facts on File, 1987);

George S. May, *A Most Unique Machine: The Michigan Origins of the American Automobile Industry* (Grand Rapids, Mich: Eerdmans, 1975);

May, *R. E. Olds: Auto Industry Pioneer* (Grand Rapids, Mich: Eerdmans, 1977);

Alfred Reeves, "Benjamin Briscoe, 1867-1945," *Old-Timers News*, 3 (July 1945): 31-33;

Chris Sinsabaugh, *Who Me? Forty Years of Automobile History* (Detroit: Arnold-Powers, 1940).

Alanson Partridge Brush

(February 10, 1878-March 6, 1952)

by George S. May

Eastern Michigan University

CAREER: Engineer, Leland & Faulconer Manufacturing Company (1899-1904); chief engineer, Cadillac Motor Car Company (1904-1905); independent experimental automotive work (1905-1907); co-founder and chief engineer, Oakland Motor Car Company (1907-1909); acting chief engineer, Buick Motor Company (1909-1913); general automobile consultant and consultant in patent litigation (1913-1952).

Although Alanson P. Brush is remembered as the designer of the Brush Runabout, his importance in the early development of the auto industry lies in his work on the Oldsmobile, the Cadillac, the Oakland, the Buick, the Marmon, and other cars of greater lasting significance. Brush was born in Detroit on February 10, 1878, the son of Hannah Matilda Brush and Charles Allen Brush, who was a teacher. He attended school in Detroit and the suburb of Birmingham, and upon the outbreak of the Spanish-American War in 1898 he enlisted in the 31st Michigan Volunteer Regiment and served as ar-

tificer in Company I. The regiment was stationed in Cuba for some months after the conclusion of fighting in the summer of 1898.

As a boy Brush demonstrated a natural bent for mechanics. He and an older brother built a tiny steam engine of their own design. In the 1960s it was owned by one of his sisters and was still operational. Upon his return to Detroit in 1899 it was natural for him to go to work for the Leland & Faulconer Manufacturing Company, perhaps Detroit's best-known machine shop, where he could gain more practical experience. His first important assignment at Leland & Faulconer came in 1901 in connection with a contract the company had received to produce 2,000 engines and transmissions for the curved-dash Oldsmobile runabout. Brush designed some of the gear-cutting tools needed for the job, which was threatened with cancellation when problems developed with the production of the engines. Henry M. Leland, head of the company, called him in. "You are a good mechanic," he told Brush. "Can't you think of some way out of this diffi-

Alanson Partridge Brush

culty?" Brush thought he might know a solution, but it would take several days to try it out. "All right," Leland told him. "Go to it, boy! The shop is yours to command. Just get that machine to working right." Brush overcame the problem, and Leland's staff was soon able to deliver the engines so quickly, Leland declared, "that Mr. Olds said we must have a motor incubator at our place."

Greatly impressed with Brush's work, Leland was heard to remark to a business acquaintance, "I've got a young fellow in my shop, in fact, I have a contract with him, who knows more about internal combustion engines than any one else in the United States." Leland gave Brush permission to devote some of his time to experimental work. An improved carburetor Brush developed led Charles Strelinger, a Detroit tool and hardware wholesaler who had helped set Leland up in business in 1890, to commission Brush to design an inexpensive engine that could be used in small boats. The $1,000 he received from Strelinger for the job encouraged Brush to marry his girlfriend, Jane Marsh, on March 29, 1902. She was the daughter of Augustus

Marsh of Grand Rapids, Michigan, a Presbyterian minister. The Brushes would have two daughters, both of whom died in infancy.

Although there is some uncertainty about who in the Leland organization was responsible, the best evidence indicates that it was Brush who decided that the Oldsmobile engine they were building could be improved, with the result that he was able to update it from a 3-horsepower to a 10-horsepower rating by the summer of 1902. The Olds company did not want to use the more powerful unit because of the expense that would have been involved in redesigning the runabout to handle the new engine. At that same time Leland was approached by the officers of the Henry Ford Company, who had dismissed Ford in March 1902 because he was spending all of his time developing a racing car, not a passenger car. They came to Leland a few months later to ask for advice. One report says that they wanted to know how much money they could get if they sold the company's plant and equipment. Brush, however, in a letter he wrote in 1950 to Frank Briscoe, declares that the Ford officials sought Leland's advice concerning a car that would be powered by a 2-cylinder engine Brush said had been designed by Ford but which Ford's assistant and successor at the Henry Ford Company, Oliver E. Barthel, apparently also had a hand in developing. Leland persuaded them to abandon that engine on the grounds, Brush said, "that the Olds Company had demonstrated the saleability of a car using the less expensive single-cylinder engine."

Brush was given the job of designing a single-cylinder engine and transmission, which he did, adapting the improved Olds engine he had already designed. When the superintendent at the Cadillac Automobile Company (new name for the Henry Ford Company) proved unable to handle the task of putting together a car with the engine Brush had designed, the Cadillac officials asked Leland to assign Brush to take the superintendent's place. Brush and other Leland workers quickly assembled a prototype in the Leland & Faulconer shop. Brush took it on a test run on October 20, 1902, with Wilfred Leland, Henry Leland's son, as his passenger. The Cadillac Model A, as it was named, went on public exhibition in Detroit four days later and "evoked much favorable comment. It is a handsome vehicle, substantial and yet trim looking, runs with absolutely no noise or vibration, starts without any grind-

Alanson Brush aboard a Brush Model D Runabout equipped for winter driving, 1911

ing or noise of clutch engaging, and at the rumored price of $750 is likely to prove a sensation in the trade."

The writer of that glowing report was undoubtedly guilty of some exaggeration in his assessment of the performance of the first Cadillac, but it did indeed, as he had predicted, become a sensation when it was introduced in 1903. The heads of the Cadillac company came to rely increasingly on Leland & Faulconer, and when other suppliers did not provide as prompt and high-quality service as Leland they were able to persuade him to take over the management of the automobile company in 1904 and to merge his machine shop and the auto company in 1905 as the Cadillac Motor Car Company. In the process, Brush became Cadillac's chief engineer, designing the Cadillac Model B, a single-cylinder car with improved frame and body construction, and in 1905 a 4-cylinder model that manifested Leland's desire to transform Cadillac into one of the industry's higher-priced ranges.

By 1905 Brush was receiving a salary of around $10,000 per year, big money for that day. He and his wife lived in a house on Harper Avenue in Detroit that they rented for $35 per month.

Across the alley behind them lived Henry Ford, and Brush and Ford sometimes played ball in the alley with Ford's son, Edsel. Brush had replaced Ford as the designer of automobiles for the businessmen who had invested in the old Henry Ford Company, but Brush was not to remain for long with the Cadillac company. His departure was not due to a falling out with the investors who had dumped Ford but because he could no longer work for Henry Leland.

Leland, it is clear, was never an easy man to work for, and he became more difficult after he took over the management of Cadillac. He regarded Brush as his protégé who was always to be grateful for the boost Leland had given to his career. Brush did not like Leland's labor ideas. "Labor is a commodity, like any other commodity, to be bought in the cheapest market," Brush said Leland had once told him. "In order to achieve this, we need, and should have at all times, a *pool of unemployment*." Jane Brush declared that the sharp difference between Leland's views, which led him to become a prime mover of the antiunion policy fostered by Detroit's Employers' Association, and those of Brush, who believed that a worker had the right to work and to be paid a just salary in proportion to the work he did, was an important cause of the friction that developed between the two.

More important than such philosophical differences, however, was Brush's resentment at Leland's efforts to tell him what to do. He was especially piqued at Leland's efforts to control Brush's patents, the ultimate cause of the break that occurred in 1905. Although Leland would seem to have been rather generous in allowing Brush to take out in his own name patents on inventions and improvements he had developed as an employee of Leland & Faulconer and Cadillac, Brush objected to Leland's use of those patents. With the aid of Charles Strelinger, Brush hired a leading Detroit attorney, Alexis C. Angell, to negotiate a settlement whereby Cadillac would pay Brush $40,000 for the use of his patents and designs for two years, during which time Brush was prohibited from entering into any business that would be competitive to Cadillac. After two years, Cadillac would pay Brush royalties on any of his patents it still wished to use.

Leland, Brush's widow said, told the Cadillac directors, "with great confidence, that inside of two years he would 'eliminate all the Brush' there was in their cars, thus relieving them from the necessity of paying royalties." But Leland was unable to do that, and as a result Cadillac paid Brush royalties for the remaining life of some of his patents.

From 1905 to 1907 Brush busied himself with experiments in a shop he built near his home in Detroit. He designed a small car in which he could test ideas he had for features such as coil springs that could provide a more comfortable ride. When he had completed the car and pushed it out, he and Frank Briscoe, who with his brother Benjamin produced automobile parts at their Briscoe Manufacturing Company, took a ride, and Briscoe said, "Al, I think there is a future for this little car—*just as it stands—and I want to build it*!" Briscoe, whose brother had become one of the country's leading auto magnates by backing a car designed by Jonathan Maxwell, had "an itch to get into the big tent," and Brush agreed to license Briscoe to produce the car. Jane Brush says she was dismayed when she learned that Briscoe planned to call the car the Brush Runabout. "Oh no, Al," she said. "Do not let them tie your name to the smallest car you ever designed!" But Brush did not raise objections to the use of his name and Briscoe went ahead.

At $500 the Brush Runabout was a bargain, and production rose from about 500 in 1907 to an estimated 10,000 runabouts (and delivery vans of a similar design) by 1910. The latter production figure equaled the 1910 output of Benjamin Briscoe's Maxwell-Briscoe Company. The two companies were joined that year in the United States Motor consolidation that Benjamin Briscoe organized. The collapse of that combine in 1912 brought an end to the Brush Runabout, although the automobile continued to be produced until the summer of 1913. The car would probably not have survived by itself in any event. It contained some advantageous features, such as a left-hand drive, employed a year before the Ford Model T in 1908 started an industrywide trend away from the right-hand position that had been a carryover from horse-drawn carriage practices. But the lightweight wooden buggy construction of the Brush Runabout was not suited to the wear and tear of that day's roads. A popular refrain that the Brush had a "wooden body, wooden axles, wooden wheels, and wooden run" was unfair, but Jane Brush was understandably upset that her husband was remembered for that car and not for his more important work.

Brush benefited financially from the Brush Runabout's brief popularity, but he was not involved with its production. Instead, in 1907 he became a cofounder with Edward W. Murphy of the Oakland Motor Car Company, a business that survives today as the Pontiac division of General Motors (GM). Murphy was the head of the Pontiac Buggy Company, which he had founded in 1890, and like a good many carriage manufacturers he was beginning to think a switch to automobiles would be a wise move. He liked the Brush Runabout when he saw it, and he asked Brush if he could design a car that Murphy's proposed company could produce. Since the two-year period of the agreement he had made with Cadillac was expiring, Brush was eager to get back into an active manufacturing position, and he agreed to join Murphy. He brought with him the design for a 2-cylinder automobile he had prepared when he was with Cadillac but which that company had not used. It became the initial Oakland offering.

The Brushes moved to Pontiac, and, according to Jane Brush, Brush was looking forward to the opportunity to introduce new models for Oakland free of the restraints he had worked under at Cadillac. In 1908 the first of those new models appeared, a 4-cylinder car, the Oakland Model K, which attracted attention by its success in hill-climbing competitions. But it would be the last Oakland model Brush would design, for in 1909 control of the company passed into the hands of William C. Durant's GM.

Durant's interest in acquiring Oakland had less to do with its worth, which was not a great deal since at the end of 1908 it had produced only 278 cars, than it did with his desire to arouse more interest in GM by adding to the roster of companies it had acquired. In his unpublished memoirs, prepared years later, Durant said he had one of his associates approach Edward Murphy and the other Oakland investors to warn them of the danger of relying on the company's engineer, Brush, to design successful cars. If he misjudged the public's tastes at any time, the company could face financial disaster. They would be wise, therefore, to exchange their Oakland stock for stock in General Motors, where their investment would be backed by several cars and a variety of engineering talent. The other stockholders were sold on the idea and exchanged their stock, but Murphy refused, leaving Durant without the controlling interest he sought. Only by applying his fabled persuasive powers did Durant break down Murphy's resistance and get his stock, a few days before Murphy died.

Jane Brush's account of the Oakland takeover, which she likewise wrote many years later, differs somewhat from Durant's. According to her version, it was Brush, who owned the largest block of Oakland stock, who was opposed to turning the control of the company over to GM, but he was out-voted by the other stockholders and forced to go along with the deal.

Brush did not stay with Oakland under the new GM regime. Instead, Durant got him to become acting chief engineer at Buick, replacing Walter Marr, who had contracted tuberculosis. The Brushes packed up and moved to Flint, where they lived until 1913. They developed close friendships with some of the automobile men and their families who had been drawn to Flint by the explosive growth of Buick under Durant's direction. Among those new friends was Charles Stewart Mott, head of the parts manufacturer Weston-Mott, whom Brush found not only shared his love of automobiles but also his liking for the outdoors and boating. A lasting friendship resulted. "Many a vacation period," Jane Brush recalled, "found the Motts and

the Brushes exploring Georgian Bay in our boat the Voyager, or later, the Agawa, or down in Florida waters in the Ibis or some similar craft."

At Buick, Brush was able to overcome the opposition to relocating the car's steering position from the right- to the left-hand side. He introduced the use of steel-alloy transmission gears in place of case-hardened soft-steel gears, which had been a source of considerable problems in Buicks. He also designed an improved steering gear and secured the adoption of 4-door, cowl-dash bodies. But it would appear that he was not entirely happy in Flint, finding it hard to adjust to Durant's style of management. Jane Brush does not provide a clear account of exactly what caused Brush to leave Flint in 1913. She says that he had been acting under Durant's orders in his job at Buick but that he had also been acting as a consultant for the General Motors organization. However, by the terms of the loan Durant had negotiated in 1910 to bail out GM, he was not directly involved in the management of Buick or GM from the fall of 1910. In any event, when Brush learned that Walter Marr "had made an almost miraculous recovery from tuberculosis and would soon be back in Flint," he decided that it was an opportune time to leave.

Brush had somehow lost the General Motors stock he had acquired in exchange for his Oakland stock—another detail on which Jane Brush's memory failed her in later years—but the royalties that he continued to receive on his patents (he would ultimately receive 150 patents) provided the Brushes with a comfortable income. They moved back to Detroit, where Brush continued to serve as a consultant to General Motors. In 1915 he established a consulting firm, the Brush Engineering Association, with his brother, William A. Brush, as the business manager. The firm was quite successful for several years, working with companies such as the American Ball Bearing Company but primarily concentrating on automotive work. His most important work in that early period was with Marmon, with whom he was associated from 1913 to 1919, designing the Marmon Model 34, an advanced car that provided the company with the best sales it had yet enjoyed. Later, in the 1920s, Brush designed a car for Albert Champion, the spark plug manufacturer, who had plans to produce a medium-priced car with features previously found only in high-priced models. Brush completed construction of the car, but Champion's death put an end to the plans for

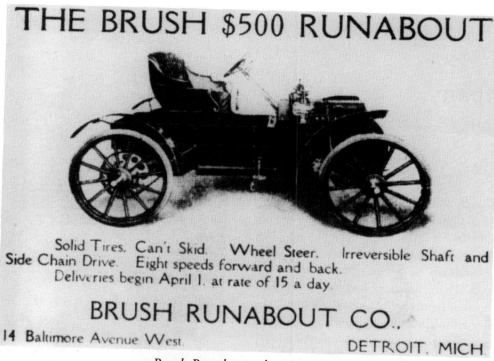

Brush Runabout advertisement

its production. It was, Jane Brush said, in many respects "the hardest knock Alanson had ever had to take."

By the end of the 1920s the call for Brush's services had greatly declined. Most automotive companies had built up their own engineering staffs. He closed down his consulting business and during the last 20 years of his life carried on in a new career as one of the best-known and most widely employed consultants to lawyers engaged in patent litigation. He was active in the Society of Automotive Engineers, the American Society of Mechanical Engineers, the Masonic lodge, and in a variety of country clubs and yacht clubs.

Brush died in Detroit on March 6, 1952. A few weeks later Frank Briscoe wrote to Jane Brush that he felt that Brush ranked with Henry Ford and Ransom Olds as the three who had "produced the first three practical automobiles to be built anywhere in the world. . . . These first three successes were the work of men who had had no college training or in fact any regular engineering training except what they picked up by themselves." Briscoe was no doubt prejudiced in favor of the man who had enabled him to have a short stay in the "big tent" of auto production, but he may have given Jane Brush an idea for the biography of her husband that she would later write. "Without Benefit

of College" was the title for her account of one of the last of the self-taught mechanics and engineers who dominated the auto industry in its early period but who, by the time of his death, had been replaced by college graduates.

References:

Nick Baldwin and others, *The World Guide to Automobile Manufacturers* (New York: Facts on File, 1987);

Lawrence R. Gustin, *Billy Durant: Creator of General Motors* (Grand Rapids, Mich.: Eerdmans, 1973);

George S. May, *A Most Unique Machine: The Michigan Origins of the American Automobile Industry* (Grand Rapids, Mich: Eerdmans, 1975);

John B. Rae, *The American Automobile: A Brief History* (Chicago: University of Chicago Press, 1963);

Bernard A. Weisberger, *The Dream Maker: William C. Durant, Founder of General Motors* (Boston: Little, Brown, 1979).

Archives:

The present writer consulted the manuscript of Jane Brush's biography of Alanson Brush, entitled "Without Benefit of College," in the early 1970s at the offices of the Michigan Historical Commission in Lansing. That agency received the manuscript some years before and had it under consideration for publication. Jane Brush had died, and her brother, Harry Marsh, had assumed control of the manuscript. He, too, died by the mid 1970s. What has become of the manuscript since then is not known.

Budd Company

by Robert J. Kothe

Atlanta, Georgia

The Budd Company, a major supplier of automotive parts, was founded by Edward Gowan Budd, who was born in 1870 in Smyrna, Delaware. His early training was as a machinist with the G. W. & S. Taylor Company of Smyrna before he moved to Philadelphia. There he continued his apprenticeship in the shops of Bement, Miles and Company, advancing to the job of drafting office foreman of the hydraulic press design group. In addition to that practical training, Budd took correspondence courses from the Franklin Institute and evening courses at the University of Pennsylvania.

In 1899 Budd was hired as shop superintendent for the American Pulley Company, where he was involved in the first commercial manufacture of sheet metal pulleys. Developing new methods of fabricating metal would be the central theme in Budd's career and in the early history of the Budd Company. In 1902 he became general manager of the Hale and Kilburn Company in Philadelphia, a company that produced seats and trim for railway cars. His earlier experience with sheet metal led him to substitute pressed sheet metal parts for the castings the company had previously used in its production.

Budd's contacts with the auto industry began in 1909, when he supervised the production of welded pressed steel panels to cover the wood framework of Hupp Motor Car bodies. In 1910 he constructed an all-steel automobile body in the Hale and Kilburn plant. The first all-steel body may date from as early as 1905, but it was not commercially important, and Budd's efforts to persuade his company to produce the body he had developed were likewise unsuccessful.

In 1912 Budd left Hale and Kilburn and formed the Edward G. Budd Manufacturing Company to produce all-steel bodies. The initial capitalization was $100,000, most of it supplied by Budd, although there were two other investors. At the out-

Edward Gowan Budd

set the company was so small that it had to store its supply of steel and one large press in a circus tent outside its rented shop in northeast Philadelphia. Budd also had to overcome the tradition that auto bodies should be made of wood, a carry-over from the carriage industry. Budd had discussed his new all-steel bodies with Charles W. Nash, who became president of General Motors (GM) in 1912. As a result, Budd received an order for 2,000 all-steel touring car bodies from the Oakland Motor Company, one of the companies controlled by GM. That opened the door to other orders, the most important of which came in 1914, when John and Horace Dodge ordered 5,000 bodies for the new car they were putting out. That order followed in 1915 by an order for 50,000 bodies, and although Buick, Ford, Studebaker, and Willys-Overland were ordering bodies from Budd by 1917, Dodge would be the company's largest customer over the next decade.

The durability of Dodge all-steel bodies led the army to make Dodge cars standard transportation during World War I. The demands of war conditions also led Budd in 1916 to move into the production of steel wheels, replacing wooden spoke wheels. The Budd Wheel Company, which he formed to produce the wheels, was an entirely separate business from the Edward G. Budd Manufacturing Company, and the two remained separate until 1946 when, shortly before Budd's death, they were merged to form the Budd Company.

Budd was more than a manufacturer of steel bodies. He was an enthusiastic advocate of steel. The company sponsored stunts to demonstrate the superiority of steel bodies. They had an elephant sit on one and sent others off steep inclines to illustrate their strength. The body that was introduced on the 1923 Dodge helped to increase the growing demand for closed, as opposed to open, cars. Budd chose to share the patent rights he held on his steel bodies with other American body companies, but although that benefited those competitors, Budd's promotions, which gained him new business from Ford and Chrysler, led him in 1925 to open a body plant in Detroit, where he also moved the wheel company. The volume of business it conducted with the auto industry eventually led the company to move its headquarters from Philadelphia to the Detroit area, where it remains, in the suburban community of Troy. Budd was also active on the international market. He was deeply involved with the French automaker Citroën, and Budd plants also operated in Europe and Canada.

In the 1920s Budd also became a leader in the fabrication of stainless steel, a material that was difficult to form and weld. A process invented by the company and trade named "Shotweld" became standard in the industry. To promote the use of stainless steel, Budd resorted to one of his more flamboyant advertising efforts. In 1931 his company built the Pioneer, a stainless-steel airplane, which was flown all over the United States and Eu-

rope and was later donated to the Franklin Institute.

Of more practical importance was its production of stainless-steel railroad vehicles. In 1934 Budd built the Pioneer Zephyr, a self-contained three-car stainless-steel train, which was also the nation's first diesel-powered train. It built many of the great streamlined trains of the 1930s, such as the Super Chief, the Flying Yankee, and the Chicagoan. It also built models of individual rail cars it called Zephyrs, Rockets, Silver Meteors, Champions, and El Capitans.

Budd's auto body division became somewhat less important as the large manufacturers became more vertically integrated and absorbed some of the larger independent body companies, although a market still existed and continues to exist for the production of specialty models that were difficult to integrate completely in the assembly line. Budd also produced subassemblies such as the frames. During World War II Budd produced a variety of armaments, including the original bazookas.

Edward G. Budd died in 1946, but his family remained involved in the business. His son, Edward G. Budd, Jr., succeeded him as company president. He held that post until 1965. He then served as chairman until he retired in 1967.

After the end of World War II the Budd Company continued in the railroad car business. Much of the business was in parts, such as the disc brake systems it successfully promoted, rather than complete cars. Parts for the auto companies, broadened to include plastic and electronic components, continued to be a major part of the company's business.

As the American railroad system declined the heavy rail car business became less important to Budd. Transit cars became increasingly important as many American cities upgraded their urban transportation systems.

Budd built the Metroliner cars for the New York-Washington shuttle run and was a major supplier of cars for the Long Island railroad and landed a $130-million contract for the Chicago system. However, competition in the production of rail and subway passenger cars was intense and highly political as foreign manufacturers entered the American market. Budd's attempts to influence decisions in that area caused the company some embarrassments, as senior executives were charged with bribery.

The company enjoyed some success in international railroad markets with its futuristic high-speed SPV-2000, but Budd became less active in that area as the 1970s drew to a close. It did make an effort to compete for a major order in the New York City subway system in the early 1980s. That effort was abandoned after a bitter struggle in which Budd claimed that consideration of a bid from a government-subsidized Canadian company made it impossible for a domestic company to compete.

In the mid 1970s Budd had financial difficulties. The Metroliner project, while successful in an engineering sense, was a financial disaster. In addition, 40 percent of its automotive output was sold to a single customer, Ford. That left the company vulnerable not only to the auto market in general but the health of Ford in particular. Other potential monetary disasters were the lawsuits against the company's wheel division charging that the unexpected separation of its two-piece truck and bus wheel rims had caused serious injuries and several deaths, primarily to servicemen who were inflating the tires.

In 1978 Budd was purchased for about $300 million by Thyssen A.G., a West German firm best known as a steel maker. Budd continued to lose money until the mid 1980s, when it once again started to turn profits.

Budd is currently a $1.4 billion firm that produces a variety of parts for transportation companies. It is still active as a body builder, turning out station wagon bodies for Ford Taurus automobiles. Of particular interest to old-car enthusiasts is the fact it still has the body dies for the original Ford Thunderbirds.

David Dunbar Buick

(September 17, 1854-March 6, 1929)

by George S. May

Eastern Michigan University

CAREER: Cofounder and president, Buick & Sherwood Plumbing and Supply Company (1882-1901); president, Buick Auto-Vim and Power Company (1900-1902); president, Buick Manufacturing Company (1902-1903); secretary, general manager, and director (1903-1904), secretary and director (1904-1906?), director, Buick Motor Company (1906?-1908).

David Dunbar Buick, who long before his death had been living proof that fortune does not necessarily accompany a famous name, was born in Arbroath, Scotland, on September 17, 1854. When he was two years old his parents, Alexander and Jane Buick, brought him to the United States, where they settled in Detroit. Three years later Alexander Buick died, and by the time David Buick was eleven he had been forced to leave school to work on a farm.

In 1869 Buick got a job with the Alexander Manufacturing Company, a Detroit firm that produced enameled iron toilet bowls and wooden closet tanks. He was eventually named foreman of the shop, his advancement aided by the knowledge of the machinist's trade that he gained while at the James Flower & Brothers Machine Shop sometime in that period. Henry Ford was an apprentice machinist at Flower & Brothers in 1880. In 1878 Buick married Catherine Schwinck. They would have four children. The oldest, Thomas D. Buick, was closely involved in some of Buick's later business activities.

When the Alexander company failed in 1882, Buick and William S. Sherwood joined forces to take over the business, which they proceeded to develop into a successful plumbing-supply company. The fact that Buick showed no managerial abilities in his later automotive career suggests that that aspect of the plumbing business was handled by Sherwood while Buick contributed his talents as a machinist and inventor. Between 1881 and 1899 Buick received 13 patents, all but one related to plumbing. He was best known for developing a new method for fixing porcelain onto metal, a process that contributed greatly to the company's success in a period in which indoor plumbing facilities

David Dunbar Buick (courtesy of the General Motors Institute Alumni Foundation Collection of Industrial History)

were being rapidly incorporated in the nation's urban areas. In December 1899, however, the plumbing company was sold for $100,000 to the Standard Sanitary Manufacturing Company. Buick & Sherwood continued to exist in name at least, and David Buick retained the title of president until sometime in 1901, despite the fact that he held only one share of stock in the firm. At the same time he was serving as the president of a new company he organized from his share of the $100,000, the Buick Auto-Vim and Power Company. By 1902 he no longer had any connection with the plumbing business and was devoting his attention entirely to his new interest.

That interest was not initially focused strictly on the automobiles with which his name would shortly be associated. Instead, the Buick Auto-Vim and Power Company was set up to manufacture marine and stationary engines as well as to continue work that Buick had been doing in trying to adapt a marine engine for use in powering a carriage. The latter effort proved unsuccessful, and Buick's engine company instead developed the "valve-in-head" gasoline engine that would be used with great success in the early Buick cars. Although Buick no doubt played a part in the development of that engine, major credit for its design is given to Walter L. Marr and Eugene C. Richard. Marr, who is said to have designed an engine that powered a car he built in 1898, was the general manager of Buick's company, but he and Buick, a difficult person to deal with, got into a fight, and Marr quit. Richard, a Frenchman who is said to have done some work for the Olds Motor Works before coming to work for Buick, apparently took over the work on the engine and completed the job.

In 1902 Buick reorganized his business as the Buick Manufacturing Company. He now concentrated on using the "valve-in-head" engine in an automobile. At least as early as April 1901 Buick began devoting most of his attention to automotive work, for at that time he offered to sell Walter Marr "the Automobile, known as the Buick Automobile, for the sum of $300." For $1,500 more he was also willing to sell Marr some of his engines, the patterns for those engines, a "delivery wagon body, two new carriage bodies, and runabout body." There is no evidence that a completed automobile had been built and tested by that time, but the fact that Buick was willing to sell those items for such a small amount of money suggests that he was already running short of the funds needed to continue his experimental work. Finally, in September 1902 he persuaded Benjamin and Frank Briscoe, operators of a Detroit sheet metal company that had become a major supplier of auto parts to write off the debt Buick had incurred with them and to provide him with an additional $650 in return for the car Buick was working on. The car was completed and successfully tested by early 1903, and the Briscoes allowed Buick to use it in his efforts to secure the financing he would need to put it into production.

In the spring of 1903 Buick (who had had no luck in recruiting investors) and the Briscoes came to a new agreement. The Buick Manufacturing Company was succeeded by the Buick Motor Company, with a capitalization of $100,000. The Briscoes increased to about $3,500 the amount they loaned Buick, and in return they received $99,700 of the new company's stock. Buick, who continued as president, had only $300 of the stock, but he was given the option of acquiring all the stock if he repaid his debt by September 1903. If he did not, the Briscoes would assume direct control of the company.

By the summer it was becoming clear to the Briscoes that Buick was not going to come through, and not wanting to be stuck with a company whose future seemed highly uncertain, they looked for another way out. They found it in the persons of James H. Whiting and his fellow directors of the Flint Wagon Works, Flint's second largest carriage and wagon manufacturer. For some time Whiting had been interested in entering the auto industry to protect the carriage company from the declining sales that were bound to result from the increasing popularity of the new means of transportation. Whiting and the other directors went to Detroit, saw a demonstration of the one Buick that had been built, and proceeded to buy the Briscoe brothers' interest in the Buick Motor Company for $10,000. The Buick company was moved to Flint, and Whiting succeeded David Buick as president. Buick and his son Thomas were assigned 1,500 shares in the recapitalized company, but they would not actually own them until Buick's debts, which the Flint investors had paid, had been repaid from the dividends the stock would earn.

David Buick was named to the board of directors and was appointed secretary and, in effect, general manager. Further work on the Buick automobile was undertaken, and by July 1904 a stripped-down 2-cylinder model was driven from Flint to Detroit and back by Walter Marr, who had rejoined Buick in 1903, and Tom Buick. By August the first production Buick came out of the plant in Flint, but long before then Whiting and his fellow directors from the wagon works had concluded that there was no chance the company could succeed under David Buick's management. Whiting therefore approached William C. Durant, the guiding genius of Flint's largest carriage manufacturer, the Durant-Dort Carriage Company, to see if he would agree to apply his legendary promotional talents to saving Whiting and the other investors from a financial disaster. Durant was ready for a new challenge, and, after giving the Buick automobile a rigorous series of road tests to determine its merits, he agreed to the suggestion. On November 1, 1904, he assumed the management of Buick Motor.

David Buick's days with the company were now numbered. Durant kept him on as secretary and as a director, and he resisted suggestions that the car should be renamed the Durant. Durant liked the name Buick, although he wondered if people would know how to pronounce it. "Would they call it Booick?," he asked. He seems to have made an effort to find some way in which Buick's talents could be put to use in the company, and in 1908 a news story told of the "experimental room" that Buick and Marr ran. By that time, however, Buick was no longer the company's secretary and his financial status, which had forced him to put off for many months in 1905 and 1906 the payment of an attorney's bill of $92.58 because he did not have that kind of money, had benefited only modestly from the prosperity of the Buick company under Durant's management.

Sometime in the latter part of 1908, David Buick resigned from the company. Since he had never repaid the money he owed to the Whiting interests, he had to surrender all of the stock held in his name. Durant, however, saw that the man after whom the company was named would be taken care of. Buick was given $100,000 or possibly more—the exact figure is not known for certain—but he managed the money no more wisely than the money he had gotten from the sale of the plumbing business. Oil and gold mining ventures in California, an effort with his son Tom to manufacture carburetors, and another automotive try in Grand Rapids all proved to be failures, and by the latter part of the 1920s David Buick was teaching mechanics at a YMCA school in Detroit. At that time he told Bruce Catton, the future Pulitzer Prize historian who was then a young newspaper reporter, that everyday he saw many cars on the streets that carried his name but he did not have the money needed to buy one. Virtually penniless, he died at Detroit's Harper Hospital on March 6, 1929.

References:

Lawrence R. Gustin, *Billy Durant: Creator of General Motors* (Grand Rapids, Mich.: Eerdmans, 1973);

George Humphrey Maines, *Men, A City, and A Buick, 1903-1953* (Flint, Mich.: Advertisers Press, 1953);

George S. May, *A Most Unique Machine: The Michigan Origins of the American Automobile Industry* (Grand Rapids, Mich.: Eerdmans, 1975).

Buick Motor Company

by Richard P. Scharchburg

GMI Engineering & Management Institute

The origins of the Buick Motor Division of General Motors Corporation begin with its predecessor, the Buick Motor Company, and its founder, David Dunbar Buick. David Buick was born in Arbroath, Scotland, on September 17, 1854. Two years later his parents immigrated to the United States, eventually settling in Detroit. Little is known about his childhood and schooling. It is generally agreed that he delivered papers for the *Detroit Free Press and Daily Union* and apprenticed at the James Flower & Brothers Machine Shop. A short time later he was employed by the Alexander Manufacturing Company in the plumbing supply business. In 1882 he formed a partnership with former schoolmate William S. Sherwood to take over the faltering company. Renamed Buick & Sherwood Plumbing and Supply Company, the firm prospered. It was in the Buick & Sherwood shop that David Buick began to indulge his love of mechanics and engineering.

By most accounts Buick was a man of progressive ideas and native mechanical ability but little business interest or caution. Finances did not concern or interest him. He was regarded as impulsive and impractical, unable to sit still unless his thoughts were concentrated on some mechanical problem. The record shows that he was granted 13 patents on devices including a lawn sprinkler and a process for affixing porcelain to cast iron. The porcelain fixing process made possible white bathtubs and related items. Buick could have stayed in the plumbing business and become a millionaire, but to him a bathtub must have been a silent and uninteresting object in contrast with gasoline engines being developed throughout the country. He and Sherwood sold their business in 1899, and Buick began experimenting with engines.

In 1901 Buick set up the Buick Auto-Vim and Power Company to manufacture his experimental "L-head" engine for marine and stationary use. The company also tried to adapt the L-head for road use, but that proved impractical. Still, Buick had his mind set on making automobiles. In April 1901 he offered to sell to Auto-Vim designer Walter L. Marr "the Automobile, known as the Buick Automobile, for the sum of $300." He offered several engines, patterns, and bodies to Marr for $1,500 more. On August 16 Buick sold Marr "All my right, title, and interest in the Automobile known as the Buick Automobile" for $225. The sale furnishes more evidence of Buick's capital needs than it does of his progress in outfitting a functional car. As 1902 approached, Buick and his engineers set about designing an automotive engine, and Buick looked around for new funds. In 1902 he reorganized his business as the Buick Manufacturing Company. By then the Buick "valve-in-head" automobile engine was taking shape.

In September 1902 Buick found additional financing from the Briscoe brothers of Detroit. The Briscoes were in the metal stamping business, manufacturing mud guards (fenders), coolers (radiators), and other metal parts for Michigan's incipient auto industry. The Briscoes continued to express interest and provide modest financial backing. As the amount of money they supplied increased, however, they demanded more security, through a reorganization of the company. On May 19, 1903, the Buick Motor Company was incorporated with a capitalization of $100,000. The Briscoes were to receive $99,700 of the stock and Buick $300. Buick was given the option to purchase the company stock, provided he repay his debt to the Briscoes, which then stood at $3,500, before September of that year.

In the summer, when it became clear that Buick would not be able to repay his debt, the Briscoes began to search for a buyer for the Buick company. They had met Jonathan Maxwell, who already had a car nearly ready for production. They heard of an enterprising Flint wagon maker, James H. Whiting, who had some interest in engines. A

Buick Model G, 1906, with a 2-cylinder engine and a retractable steering wheel (courtesy of Rick Lenz)

deal was struck, and the Flint Wagon Works, of which Whiting was manager, bought out the Briscoe interest. The Buick company had still not marketed its first car. Announcement of the purchase appeared in the *Flint Journal* of September 11, 1903, and specified the new enterprise would manufacture "stationary and marine engines, automobile engines, transmissions, carburetors, spark plugs, etc." When Whiting was asked about rumors of automobile manufacture, "he smiled pleasantly and suggested that for the present the engines and accessories would be built by the new factory and that the broader opportunity was one for further consideration." In September construction began on a Buick plant in Flint, and engine production began there three months later.

The new Buick Motor Company was incorporated on January 19, 1904, at a $75,000 capitalization. David Buick and his son Thomas received 1,500 shares of stock between them, contingent upon the repayment of Buick's debt, which the Briscoes transferred to Flint, from dividends. Buick was also appointed company secretary.

Probably at Buick's or Walter L. Marr's urging, Whiting soon put a few of the Flint Wagon Works "eggs in the tool box" of the first Flint-built

Buick car. The first valve-in-head double-opposed engine was ready for installation on May 27, 1904. The automobile followed soon after. Several Flint workers recalled seeing the first Buick chugging around the Wagon Works early in July 1904. Whiting then called for a test run to Detroit and back. Walter Marr and Thomas Buick drove the car from the Buick plant on Kearsley Street on July 9 and returned there on July 12.

The *Flint Journal* of July 13 reported that in spite of some minor problems, such as getting lost and returning to Flint by way of Lapeer, the Buick made the trip home in the remarkable time of 3 hours and 37 minutes, at a rate of slightly less than 30 mph. "The machine made the run without a skip and reached here [Flint] in the best of condition. We took hills handily with our high speed gear and the machine sounded like a locomotive. It simply climbed. In one place we raced with an electric car and showed them the way. We went so fast at another time that we could not see the village six-mile-an-hour sign."

Gradually production began at the Buick Motor Company plant near the Wagon Works. The first car, a Model B, was delivered to Dr. Herbert Hills of Flint on August 13, 1904. Orders for an-

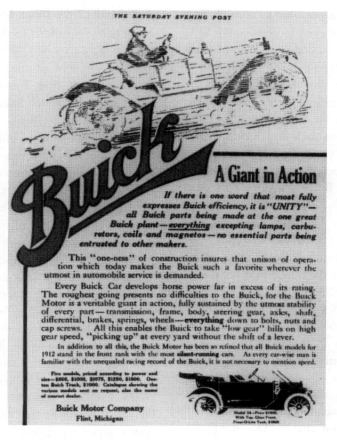

Buick advertisement stressing the company's independence from parts suppliers, 1912

other 16 Buicks had also come in, and by the middle of September 1904 the cars were delivered. Yet another 11 Buicks were on order by that time.

Still, Whiting was not pleased with the situation. He had a lot to worry about. He had brought the Buick company to Flint hoping to help the city. But Buick was deep in debt to several Flint banks, and the Association of Licensed Automobile Manufacturers, the holder of the Selden internal combustion engine "road engine" patent, was threatening to stop production of the Buick as they had with the Hardy Flint roadster a year earlier. Moreover, Whiting was personally concerned because it had been at his encouragement that Flint Wagon Works had purchased Buick, and he had approved the move into motorcars. He began to search for a way to reinforce his investment.

On the suggestion of Fred Aldrich, secretary of the Durant-Dort Carriage Company, Whiting approached company head William C. Durant with an investment offer. Durant was initially reticent, but soon the idea of moving into automobile production began to appeal to him. He agreed to recapi-

talize the Buick Motor Company at $300,000. On November 1, 1904, the deal was completed. Durant assumed control of the company, and David Buick gradually fell from influence. By September 1905 he held only 110 shares of Buick stock and had been relegated to an "experimental room" engineering role.

Buick production increased from 37 in 1904 to 750 in 1905 to 1,400 in 1906. For the 1908 model year Buick released its famous Model 10, a low-priced car with a planetary transmission that became the sensation of the industry. Although it is difficult to make comparisons between companies because of the lack of uniformity in recording production figures, it would appear that Buick had become the industry's leading producer. Its output of 8,820 cars for the 1908 model year was more than the combined production of Ford and Cadillac.

Meanwhile, Durant had attracted to Flint various parts manufacturers, many of whom were later absorbed by Buick. Durant also hired such able men as Louis Chevrolet and Albert Champion, and brought Charles Stewart Mott and the Weston-Mott Axle Company to Flint. At the same time he began devoting more and more time to formulating an auto combine to produce even more cars. On September 16, 1908, he founded General Motors (GM) Company, a New Jersey corporation with a capital stock of $2,000. Twelve days later the stock was increased to $12.5 million, to be used to enable GM to gain control of car companies. On October 1 Buick became the first such acquisition, when nearly all of its common stock was exchanged for GM preferred common stock.

From that time on, Buick's history was part of the history of GM, but for nearly ten years Buick remained a separate company. General Motors, a holding company, controlled the Buick voting stock and could influence Buick operations through its ability to choose the Buick board of directors.

Durant continued to keep a close watch on Buick, and the company continued to prosper, with production of 30,525 cars in the 1910 model year keeping the company firmly in first place among car manufacturers. Durant relied on Buick sales to support his ambitious expansion plans. By 1910 he no longer had time to manage the company, and leadership at Buick passed into the capable hands of Charles W. Nash and then Walter P. Chrysler. Chrysler made major improvements in the assembly operations that pushed production over the 100,000 mark in 1916. Although Buick did not keep pace with the rapid gains made by Ford with its low-priced Model T, Buick did maintain leadership in its price range and continued to be the strongest unit in the GM combine.

In 1917-1918 the GM holding company was transformed into the General Motors Corporation, and the companies it had controlled then became manufacturing divisions of the corporation. In the 1920s Alfred P. Sloan, Jr., who took charge of GM when circumstances forced Durant to leave late in 1920, differentiated between the company's car divisions by assigning each a price range in which its products would be sold. Buick became the second most expensive of the lines GM offered, behind only Cadillac. With production exceeding 200,000 cars a year by the mid 1920s, Buick remained a major source of the strength that enabled GM to replace Ford as the industry's volume leader.

In 1929 the Buick Division came out with the Marquette, a lower-priced car designed to bridge the gap between the Oldsmobile and the Buick, but the new car was dropped after only a year. That year also saw new Buicks appear with a slight bulge beneath the belt line, which led to them being dubbed "pregnant Buicks." As a result of the design error, subsequent Buicks gained notoriety for their conservative, uninspired styling, which, together with the economic effects of the Depression, caused sales to drop to their lowest level in nearly two decades in 1932. When Harlow Curtice took over the management of the division in 1933, however, the outlook quickly changed. Models were given names rather than numbers, and by 1936 exciting new styling was introduced.

The Buicks of the years after World War II were big, powerful cars with styling features that sometimes bordered on the outlandish. In the mid 1950s Buick sales pushed it to the number-three spot behind Chevrolet and Ford. A sharp drop in sales in the late 1950s led to a return to more restrained styling. The 1963 Buick Riviera in particular has been hailed for the elegance of its appearance. Its success helped Buick reassert its claim to prestige and to continue to be one of the most dependable contributors to GM's success.

References:

Terry B. Dunham and Lawrence R. Gustin, *The Buick: A Complete History* (Princeton: Princeton Publishing Co., 1985);

Margery Durant, *My Father* (New York: Putnam's, 1929);

George Humphrey Maines, *Men, a City, and a Buick, 1903-1953* (Flint, Mich.: Advertisers Press, 1953);

Frank M. Rodolph, *Industrial History of Flint*, 2 volumes (Flint, Mich.: Flint Journal, 1949);

Bernard A. Weisberger, *The Dream Maker: William C. Durant, Founder of General Motors* (Boston: Little, Brown, 1979).

Archives:

Material on David Dunbar Buick can be found in the William C. Durant Papers and the Daniel Wilkerson Files in the GMI Alumni Foundation Collection of Industrial History, GMI Engineering and Management Institute, Flint, Michigan.

Bumpers

by James Wren

Motor Vehicle Manufacturers Association

Automobile bumpers were introduced soon after the turn of the century. Most were added for appearance rather than safety and consisted of metal bars attached to the front of the car with long bolts. Those offered little in the way of protection, and in 1902 Frederick Simms and the Simms Company, an accessory dealer, offered spring mounted pneumatic bumpers as a safety option.

Most bumpers in the early years were intended merely to knock movable objects out of the way. But they were extremely rigid pieces of metal, which upon impact with another car or a wall caused a tremendous transfer of energy to the occupants of a vehicle. Even the addition of spring mount-ing failed to make a substantial improvement.

By the mid 1910s several automobile manufacturers switched to spring bar bumpers, which were designed to yield gradually upon impact. They featured a weak, but reinforced impact center and two elongated steel loops at each end of the bumper. In a minor crash the weak center would bend, but the springs and reinforcement would allow it to return to its original shape and position. In slightly more serious contact, the bumper might permanently bend and crease, but the car would be protected to a degree. Although speeds and destructive power increased greatly, bumper technology did not seriously advance until the 1960s.

Rigid bumper on a 1918 Detroit Electric coupe (courtesy of the Henry Ford Museum, Dearborn, Michigan)

Cadillac Automobile Company

by George S. May

Eastern Michigan University

The Cadillac Automobile Company was the successor firm to the Henry Ford Company, which had been organized on November 30, 1901, to produce a car designed by Henry Ford. William Murphy, the principal backer of the Detroit firm, and his associates had been among the investors in the earlier Detroit Automobile Company, which had been dissolved early in 1901 after Ford failed to provide a car he was willing to put on the market. The Murphy group hoped it would have better luck with Ford in the new company, particularly because the publicity Ford had received from his victory in an automobile race in October 1901 would give a car bearing his name increased commercial appeal. However, Ford was so enamored of racing that he spent his time developing a powerful new racing vehicle, not a passenger car, and on March 10, 1902, he was fired.

There are conflicting accounts concerning the events that led to the transformation of the Henry Ford Company into the Cadillac company later in 1902. However, they all agree that the company's backers had sought the advice of Henry M. Leland, the highly respected head of Detroit's Leland and Faulconer machine shop. That shop was a prime supplier of parts for the Oldsmobile runabout, which, by 1902, had become the country's top-selling car. Murphy and his associates, therefore, turned to Leland in hopes that he would suggest how their company might achieve a similar degree of success or at least how they might avoid losing their investment.

Leland persuaded Murphy and his associates to stay in the business, promising them that with the advice of his staff a successful car could be built. On August 27, 1902, Ford's name was dropped and the company was reorganized as the Cadillac Automobile Company, adopting the name of the founder of the city of Detroit. Leland was given a small amount of stock in the company and was named to its board of directors. Oliver E. Barthel, who had been Henry Ford's assistant, continued on with the company after Ford's departure and designed a 4-passenger, 2-cylinder car, using an engine that he and probably Ford had worked on. Leland, however, advised that this model be dropped in favor of one using an improved version of the Oldsmobile's 1-cylinder engine that Leland's staff had designed.

At the request of the Cadillac officials, Alanson P. Brush of Leland's staff was assigned the task of designing this 1-cylinder car. By October 20, 1902, Brush was able to give the car its first test-drive. A slightly heavier version of the runabout style Oldsmobile had made popular, the Cadillac Model A, as it was called, attracted favorable attention, enabling William E. Metzger, Cadillac's sales manager, to line up dealers and obtain more than 1,000 orders before production began in March 1903. By the end of the year about 1,700 Cadillacs had been produced. With production rising to about 2,500 in 1904 despite delays caused by a fire that virtually wiped out the factory on April 13, Cadillac helped solidify Detroit's reputation as a center of the automobile industry.

Henry Leland's primary role during this period was to supply engines and transmissions produced in his shop. Late in 1904, at the urgings of William Murphy and Lem Bowen, another Cadillac investor, Leland agreed to become president and general manager of Cadillac, with his son Wilfred becoming assistant treasurer. The following year Cadillac and Leland's company, Leland & Faulconer, merged under the new name of the Cadillac Motor Car Company. Under Leland's direction, Cadillac sales continued to rise, and although Leland followed the industrywide trend of introducing bigger, heavier models, including several 4-cylinder models priced at more than $2,000, he

Cadillac chief engineer Alanson P. Brush (behind the wheel) and Wilfred Leland, son of future company president, Henry M. Leland, test-driving the prototype of the Model A, Cadillac's first production car, in October 1902 (courtesy of Automobile Quarterly *Archives)*

did not abandon the $750 1-cylinder runabout, keeping it in production until 1908.

Leland's main contribution to the creation of Cadillac's image as one of the most respected cars on the road lay in his insistence that a high level of workmanship and precision must be applied to the production of the cars. Upon becoming general manager of Cadillac, Leland is said to have ordered "that emery cloth and file should never be used in the assembly room for the Cadillac." In a celebrated demonstration of the success he had in achieving his goal of complete interchangeability of the car's parts, three Cadillac runabouts, taken from the stock of the company's agent in England, were put through a Standardization Test, sponsored by the Royal Automobile Club at the Brooklands racetrack near London on February 29, 1908. The cars were completely disassembled and the parts mixed up. Club observers then replaced 89 parts with identical parts from a stock supplied by the English agent. The cars were then reassembled by workers who were permitted to use nothing but a wrench,

hammer, screwdriver, and pliers. The cars were test-driven, and all three were still working perfectly after 500 miles around the track. In 1909, therefore, Cadillac received the Dewar Trophy, the industry's highest award, "in recognition of the most noteworthy performance of the year."

It was the excellence of the car, as well as the sales figures, that made Cadillac a prime target of those who sought to put together a merger of the leading automobile companies. In November 1908 Benjamin Briscoe, whose plans to merge his Maxwell-Briscoe company with Buick, Ford and Reo had fallen through earlier that year, obtained an option to acquire 60 percent of Cadillac's stock at $150 a share. He was unable to get the backing needed to exercise this option, however, leaving the way open for Buick's William C. Durant to make his own bid for control of Cadillac, adding it to those already acquired by the General Motors (GM) Company which Durant had organized in September 1908. Durant, who was able to pick up most of GM's acquisitions through an exchange of

The 1912 Cadillac, the first car to be equipped with a self-starter and a battery-generator lighting system (courtesy of General Motors Corporation)

stock, with little cash changing hands, soon learned that the Lelands wanted cash, not stock, for Cadillac. After much difficulty, Durant was finally able to meet the Lelands' asking price of $4.5 million in cash, plus $275,000 in GM preferred stock. A contract was signed on July 1, 1909, to make Cadillac one of the firms controlled by the GM holding company.

On July 29, 1909, the Cadillac stockholders received their payments at the rate of about $300 a share, and William Murphy, the largest shareholder with 3,055 shares, Lem Bowen, and the other investors who are reported to have invested a total of only $327,000 in cash in the company, earned a handsome profit. Durant, however, asked the Lelands, who each held 1,340 shares of Cadillac stock, to continue to run the business. They agreed to do so if they were left free to run it according to their high standards. "That is exactly what I want," Durant said. "I want you to continue to run the Cadillac exactly as though it were still your own. You will receive no directions from anyone."

Although it would not be until August 1917 that Cadillac became an operating division of the newly formed GM Corporation, its existence as an independent company actually ended in 1909 when the GM holding company gained its controlling stock interest in the company. Cadillac, together with Buick, was the most profitable of GM's acquisitions, and its profits helped to carry the company along during its often troubled early years.

Under Leland's direction, Cadillac's reputation as a high-priced prestige car continued to be grounded on respect for its technical excellence. The 1912 Cadillac was instantly famous as the first car to employ the self-starter that had been developed by Charles B. Kettering with Leland's encouragement. "The car without a crank" earned Cadillac its second Dewar Trophy. Three years later Cadillac won further fame as an innovator when the 1915 model-year cars were the first American automobiles produced in quantity to have an 8-cylinder engine. The Leland era ended in 1917, however, when he and his son were removed from

Cadillac, apparently because the directors felt they were operating too independently.

Under the new order at GM that emerged by the early 1920s greater efforts were made to promote Cadillac's luxury car status by emphasizing the look of the car. This was in keeping with the view of Alfred P. Sloan, Jr., GM's head, that cosmetic changes in a car's appearance were the way to attract buyers in a time of market saturation. In 1925 Lawrence P. Fisher, one of the brothers who ran the Fisher Body Company, now controlled by GM, was named general manager of Cadillac. The following year Fisher hired Harley J. Earl, a brilliant automotive stylist, to design a new car that would be priced between Cadillac and Buick, GM's next most expensive car. So as not to damage the prestige value of owning a Cadillac, the new car was given a different name, LaSalle. Earl's graceful design made the LaSalle, when it first appeared in 1927, one of the most acclaimed cars of that classic automotive era. It was too late to make major alterations in the 1927 Cadillac, which was already in the works when Earl arrived, but by taking advantage of the new, fast-drying Duco paints, he was able to create the illusion of change by offering that year's Cadillac models in a variety of colors.

Later in 1927 Earl was placed in charge of styling for all of GM's divisions, but it is his work for Cadillac for which he is most famous. The LaSalle continued to be an elegant, fondly remembered car, but it was finally dropped in 1940 when it was decided that smaller cars carrying the Cadillac name sold better. Of the Cadillacs of this period, the 1938 Sixty-Special is famous as the production car in which Earl and his staff for the first time did away with the running board.

In the 1950s Cadillac came to dominate the American luxury car field, with annual sales usually well over the 100,000 figure, far surpassing those of Ford's Lincoln or Chrysler's Imperial and also those of Packard, long the premier American luxury carmaker. In the 1960s Cadillac styling reflected the more restrained approach that was adopted in response to the criticisms leveled at the excesses of the 1950s, but Cadillac production soared to more than 200,000 by mid decade and to 266,798 units in 1969. Cadillac sales figures, like those of all big cars, were hard hit by the economic recessions of the 1970s and early 1980s, and GM's decision in the late 1970s to produce smaller, more fuel-efficient Cadillacs was greeted less than enthusiastically by those who loved this quintessential gas-guzzler. Although European luxury cars were, by the 1980s, the favored models of the affluent younger generation, ownership of a Cadillac continued to be regarded by most Americans as the preferred status symbol, and by 1985, as times got better and gas prices stabilized, Cadillac production rose to more than 368,000.

References:

Nick Baldwin and others, *The World Guide to Automobile Manufacturers* (New York: Facts on File, 1987);

Stephen Bayley, *Harley Earl and the Dream Machine* (New York: Knopf, 1983);

Ed Cray, *Chrome Colossus: General Motors and Its Times* (New York: McGraw-Hill, 1980);

Maurice D. Hendry, *Cadillac, Standard of the World: The Complete Seventy-five Year History* (Princeton: Princeton Publishing Co., 1973);

Beverly Rae Kimes and Henry Austin Clark, *Standard Catalog of American Cars, 1805-1942* (Iola, Wis.: Krause, 1985);

Mrs. Wilfred C. Leland and M. D. Millbrook, *Master of Precision: Henry M. Leland* (Detroit: Wayne State University Press, 1966);

George S. May, *A Most Unique Machine: The Michigan Origins of the American Automobile Industry* (Grand Rapids, Mich.: Eerdmans, 1975).

Cartercar

by George S. May

Eastern Michigan University

The best known of the friction-drive cars, the Cartercar was developed by Byron J. Carter, who was born in 1863 near Jackson, Michigan. Beginning in 1885 Carter operated a print shop in Jackson, adding a bicycle shop a decade later. By the latter part of the 1890s, however, Carter's primary interest turned to the automobile. In June 1899 he paid Charles B. King of Detroit $616.75 for one of King's experimental motor carriages minus the engine. With help from Oliver Barthel, King's assistant, Carter built an engine for the carriage, but although he said it worked satisfactorily, he turned his attention away from gasoline-powered to steam-powered vehicles. By the summer of 1901 he had built two steamers, which he and a friend drove as far as Painesville, Ohio, on their way to the Pan-American Exposition in Buffalo, before road and weather conditions forced them to return to Jackson.

A year later Carter and two other Jackson businessmen formed the Jackson Automobile Company. By the end of the year work had started on a 3-cylinder steamer named the Jaxon, which the company exhibited at the Detroit and Chicago auto shows early in 1903. A few of the steamers were sold, but Carter reported that the 1-cylinder gasoline runabout he also exhibited "seemed to be preferred." Gasoline-powered cars, called Jacksons, were all the company would produce during the nearly 20 years it remained in business after 1904.

Byron Carter, however, was not a part of that later history. In 1903 he had completed a lightweight runabout employing the friction-drive transmission on which he was said to have begun working in 1901 and which he would patent in 1904. As a local paper explained, Carter used "friction discs, instead of gears, so arranged as to be instantly changed to any desired speed. The discs also change to forward or backward movement, and can be used as a brake to stop [the] machine by revers-

ing lever." The paper promised that friction drive would "revolutionize automobile building."

Carter built several other cars using friction-drive transmission in addition to the prototype that appeared in the summer of 1903, but his partners were apparently not interested in his innovative, if not revolutionary, mechanism. It was announced in May 1904 that he had "severed his connection with the Jackson Automobile Co." Late in 1905 he got the backing he needed in Detroit, where the Motorcar Company was formed. Carter served as manager and second vice-president. The first Cartercars appeared in 1906, and production for that year totaled 101. At the seventh annual New York auto show that year the Lambert and the Simplicity were two other friction-drive cars, besides the Cartercar, on display. "In none of the three," *Motor Age* reported, "did the friction members look as if they could readily be protected from mud and splashed water, and there was no opportunity to test the claims of the makers regarding the efficiency of the device under adverse weather conditions."

Although *Scientific American* reported in 1910 that Carter's original car, after seven years and more than 25,000 miles on the road, was still in operating condition, suspicions regarding potential problems with the friction-drive, whether justified or not, no doubt affected sales of the Cartercar. Production rose to 264 in 1907 and 325 in 1908, but the totals scarcely evidenced a significant move on the part of buyers away from cars employing standard transmissions. Nevertheless, in 1909 William C. Durant added the Cartercar to the list of cars whose production his new General Motors (GM) holding company controlled. "They say I shouldn't have bought Cartercar," Durant later said to his longtime associate, A. B. C. Hardy. "Well, how was any one to know that Cartercar wasn't to be the thing? It had the friction drive and

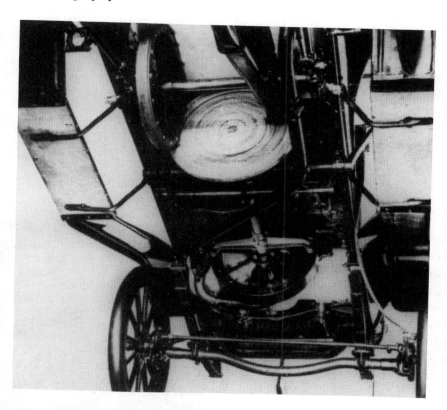

The Cartercar friction-drive mechanism (courtesy of the Henry Ford Museum, Dearborn, Michigan)

no other had it [Durant was mistaken there, of course]. How could I tell what these engineers would say next? Maybe friction drive would be the thing. . . . I was for getting every car in sight, playing safe all along the line."

Like so many of Durant's acquisitions, however, Cartercar did not prove worth keeping. The car's friction drive did not prove to be "the thing," and in 1915 production came to an end. The entire operation was closed out in February 1917. The Motorcar Company had merged in 1908 with the Pontiac Spring and Wagon Company of Pontiac, and the cars after that time had been produced in that city. Now the abandoned Pontiac plant was transferred to GM's more successful Oakland car division.

By that time Byron Carter was dead, and although his friction-drive had not had a dramatic impact, his death is alleged to have led to an automotive development of obvious importance—the self-starter. According to the story, Carter died in 1910 as a result of an accident that occurred when he stopped on Belle Isle in Detroit to help a woman whose car had stalled. When Carter tried to crank the car, the motor backfired and the crank inflicted severe injuries on him. Two officials of the Cadillac company who were passing by stopped and rushed Carter to the hospital, but he contracted pneumonia and died. When Henry Leland, head of Cadillac, heard of what had happened, he exclaimed, "Those vicious cranks!" He promptly had Charles Kettering invent the electric self-starter, which first appeared on the 1912 Cadillac. Before long cranking a car was a thing of the past. However, although Carter did die of pneumonia, his death occurred at home on April 6, 1908, and accounts of his death contain no references to an accident. If there was an accident involving a crank that made Leland encourage Kettering to proceed with his work on a self-starter, it was apparently some other unfortunate Good Samaritan, not Carter, who was the victim.

References:

Nick Baldwin and others, *The World Guide to Automobile Manufacturers* (New York: Facts on File, 1987);

George S. May, *A Most Unique Machine: The Michigan Origins of the American Automobile Industry* (Grand Rapids, Mich.: Eerdmans, 1975).

Hugh Chalmers

(October 3, 1873-June 2, 1932)

by George S. May

Eastern Michigan University

CAREER: Office boy (1887-1891), salesman (1891-1897), district sales manager (1897-1898), assistant general sales manager (1898-1900), vice-president and general manager, National Cash Register Company (1900-1907); president, Chalmers-Detroit Company (1908-1910); president, Chalmers Motor Company (1910-1916); chairman, Chalmers Motor Corporation (1916-1922); president, Chalkis Manufacturing Company (1917-1919).

Hugh Chalmers, whose company was one of two on which the Chrysler Corporation was founded, was born in Dayton, Ohio, on October 3, 1873. He was the son of Jeanette Bell and Thomas Chalmers, a stonecutter who came to America from his native Scotland in 1865. Young Chalmers left school when he was fourteen to become an office boy at Dayton's National Cash Register Company (NCR).

When he joined NCR in the late 1880s, that company was beginning a period of phenomenal growth resulting from John H. Patterson's innovative sales practices. Patterson's highly trained sales staff became a breeding ground for future automobile executives. With training in shorthand and bookkeeping that he picked up at an evening school, Chalmers had advanced to the position of salesman by the time he was eighteen. Two years later he was out on the road with his own district to cover, and by 1897 he was Patterson's sales manager for the state of Ohio, supervising 24 agents and salesmen. Within a year he had been promoted to assistant general sales manager and by 1900, at the age of twenty-seven, he had become vice-president and general manager of a company employing 5,500 workers and salesmen.

In 1907 Chalmers gave up that job, which reportedly paid $72,000 per year. Roy D. Chapin of

Hugh Chalmers

the E. R. Thomas-Detroit Company persuaded him to invest in that automobile manufacturing firm. Chalmers bought part of the interest of the principal stockholder, Edwin R. Thomas, and the company was reorganized as the Chalmers-Detroit Company with Chalmers as president. The Chalmers 30, a 4-cylinder, 30-horsepower car designed by Howard E. Coffin, the company's chief engineer, was introduced in 1908 for the 1909 model year. It carried a price tag of $1,500, well below the price at which the earlier Thomas-Detroit had been sold. Chalmers declared in an advertising brochure that the company could make a profit for the year at that price level if 2,500 cars were sold. By the end of fiscal 1909 on June 30, 1909, Chalmers-Detroit had invoiced 2,476 Chalmers 30s and 611 of the more expensive Chalmers 40s, for a total of 3,007 cars. Sales of $4,589,422 resulted in total profits of $1,015,822. A 100 percent cash dividend was declared, and the mortgage on the company's factory was paid off, further signs that Chalmers had made no mistake in leaving the National Cash Register Company. Sales of more than 6,000 in 1910 were added confirmation of the arrival of Chalmers as a major automaker.

Hugh Chalmers's time in the limelight did not last for long, however. Although the car he first sold represented a sharp reduction in price from those the company he had taken over previously marketed, Chalmers soon set his sights on the higher priced market. To be sure, early in 1909 he, Chapin, Coffin, and several others formed the Hudson Motor Car Company to produce a car that would be less expensive than the Chalmers 30, but by the end of the year Chalmers had severed his ties with Hudson, selling his stock to Chapin, Coffin, and Frederick Bezner for $80,000. At the same time he bought their holdings in Chalmers-Detroit for $788,000 and renamed the company Chalmers Motor Company. The Chalmers models that followed got bigger, and their prices kept going up. Chris Sinsabaugh, a veteran automotive journalist of the era, believed that Chalmers "wanted to build the type of car—the big one—that he himself would like to drive." However, besides satisfying his own ego, Chalmers was well aware that bigger cars were more profitable to produce. By 1911, when he felt that the market was beginning to reach a saturation point, he may have decided that it was wiser to concentrate on the wealthier classes, who could afford to pay cash for the more expensive cars, rather than continue to try to appeal to the less-affluent consumers with cheaper cars. At a time when credit for an auto purchase was rarely available, few people of average means could afford to buy a car. In 1913 Chalmers was one of the backers of a new company that produced the Saxon, the cheapest car on the market. But he sold his stock two years later, wisely enough in view of the impossible task that Saxon faced in competing with the Ford Model T in the low-priced field.

The problem faced by Chalmers's own cars was that they faced equally stiff competition in the high-priced field. In 1913 Chalmers began offering 6-cylinder models to go along with his 4-cylinder cars, but, as he ruefully remarked to Roy Chapin late in 1913, "it doesn't seem to make much difference to our good friends, the Cadillac, how much six-cylinder 'hollering' we do, because they seem to be able to ship in the neighborhood of 2000 of their Four's a month." In October 1913, Chalmers said, "We thought we were doing pretty well to ship 1111," but when Cadillac reported shipments of 2,016 of its 4-cylinder cars for that same month "they certainly dimmed our shining lights." By 1915 all Chalmers cars came with a 6-cylinder engine, but by then Cadillac had broken new ground with America's first 8-cylinder engines in cars produced in any quantity.

The Chalmers company's peak year came in 1916 with 21,408 cars produced. Thirty years later, Eugene Lewis, a fellow auto industry executive, recalled how Chalmers had sold 13,000 of those cars in three hours to his assembled distributors. Chalmers, Lewis declared, "was a super salesman. . . . If Hugh had been as fine a manufacturer as he was a salesman, his cars would probably be well known today." Instead, it was all downhill for the company after 1916.

In 1916 the company was reorganized as the Chalmers Motor Corporation, with Hugh Chalmers moving up to be chairman of the board. Walter E. Flanders, a production man who had been with Ford, E-M-F, Studebaker, his own Flanders company, and Maxwell, was brought in as company president. Chalmers and Maxwell entered into a business alliance that fell just short of a merger. With 15 manufacturing buildings and 36 acres of floor space in Detroit, Chalmers was overexpanded and space was leased to the Maxwell company to produce its autos. During World War I Maxwell produced army tractors in those leased quarters. After the war, efforts to formalize the merger were hampered by bickering between the staffs of the two firms. The onset of a depression in the last half of 1920 added to the companies' problems. Maxwell was particularly hard hit since it had gone heavily into debt to finance postwar expansion programs. In a complicated series of moves, the financial institutions to whom the two companies owed money brought in Walter P. Chrysler, who succeeded in guiding Maxwell and Chalmers through liquidation processes that ended with Chalmers being taken over by Maxwell in 1922. Under Chrysler's direc-

The 1914 Chalmers Six

tion, Chalmers cars were produced by the new Maxwell corporation until the end of the 1923 model year, after which all production centered on Maxwell until Chrysler was able to get his namesake car on the market.

Hugh Chalmers was only marginally involved with those developments after he became chairman of Chalmers. During the war he was head of Chalkis Manufacturing Company, which produced antiaircraft guns. On behalf of the National Automobile Chamber of Commerce he was also active at the nation's capital helping to coordinate the military and naval production work of the auto industry. By the summer of 1921, as prospects for the Chalmers company grew even gloomier, Chalmers was talking to Roy Chapin about a position with the National Automobile Chamber of Commerce "that he could assume," as Chapin informed Chamber president Charles Clifton, "on the basis, of course, of remuneration."

Chalmers and his wife, Frances Houser Chalmers, whom he married on August 22, 1901, had five children. With the two older children going to school in the East, Chalmers told Chapin and Clifton he was thinking of moving to New York, where it would be easy for him to travel to Washington to carry on the same kind of lobbying activities he had carried out during the war. At first there was some interest in Chalmers's proposal. Chapin told an industry colleague that he had "great respect for Chalmers' ability, and possibly in certain special instances he might be of great value." But the negotiations soon bogged down, as other officials expressed fears that Chalmers's appointment would create friction with key members of the chamber's staff. In addition, doubts were expressed as to whether Chalmers would be as effective in Washington as an employee of the chamber as he had been earlier as an active manufacturer.

No job seems to have been offered to Chalmers, who wrote to Clifton in August 1921 asking him not to spread the word around of his interest since "I don't want the idea to get out that I am looking for a job, as such is not the case." Significantly, however, he told Clifton that he and his wife felt they should move East to be closer to their children, "especially as I haven't anything now which compels me to live in Detroit."

The dissolution of the Chalmers company severed Hugh Chalmers's ties with the auto industry.

He retired to the East, where he died on June 2, 1932, in Beacon, New York. Chris Sinsabaugh said he always thought that if Chalmers had stuck with the light car and had "refined it as he went along, he instead of Ford might have become the mass-production manufacturer of the industry." But Chalmers's ambitions led him in the other direction. Sinsabaugh thought it was appropriate that at Chalmers's funeral there "was a long wheel-base hearse awaiting" outside the church. "Chalmers took his last ride in the big car he˙always had wanted to build!"

References:

Nick Baldwin and others, *The World Guide to Automo-*

bile Manufacturers (New York: Facts on File, 1987);

Eugene W. Lewis, *Motor Memories: A Saga of Whirling Gears* (Detroit: Alved, 1947);

John B. Rae, *American Automobile Manufacturers: The First Forty Years* (Philadelphia: Chilton, 1959);

Chris Sinsabaugh, *Who, Me? Forty Years of Automobile History* (Detroit: Arnold-Powers, 1940).

Archives:

The Roy D. Chapin Papers in the Michigan Historical Collections, Bentley Library, University of Michigan, contain correspondence between Chapin and Chalmers and a few records relating to the Chalmers-Detroit Company.

Albert Champion

(April 2, 1878-October 27, 1927)

by Richard P. Scharchburg

GMI Engineering & Management Institute

CAREER: Bicycle, motorcycle, and automobile racer, France and the United States (1894-1904); co-founder and director, Albert Champion Company (1905-1908); founder and president, Champion Ignition Company [later AC Spark Plug Company] (1908-1927).

Albert Champion is one of a dozen or so of the early auto pioneers whose contribution to industrial and commercial development is often overlooked. Champion was founder of two manufacturing companies in the United States and manager of two concerns in Europe that manufactured components for the automobile. There is a distinct element of the romantic in his career, for the same spirit and flair that gained him international fame as a bicycle racer in his youth marked his progressive and constructive activities in the industrial world and his colorful private life.

Champion, best known as founder of the AC Division of General Motors (GM) Corporation, was born in Paris, France, on April 2, 1878, and there he must have received his early education. Sources reveal little about his family or his early life, but at about age twelve he obtained employ-

ment as an errand and office boy for M. Clement, a leading bicycle manufacturer in France.

In 1894 Champion, with Clement's encouragement and backing, began entering his employer's product in racing events. He did very well, eventually becoming middle-distance champion of France. As the first representative of France to compete with cyclists in the United States, Champion came to America in 1899 for a series of races. He brought with him bicycles, tricycles, motorcycles, and motor magnetos. He capped his French bicycle championship with the American championship and then the world championship. He also took part in automobile and motorcycle races.

Champion returned to France convinced that the automobile was the wave of the future. He studied and worked on automobile manufacture with the idea of becoming an accessories salesman in the United States. He returned to the United States in 1900 still interested in cycling. In a race at Waltham, Massachusetts, that year he fell at high speed. Two other riders, following behind, crashed into a pole and were killed. But Champion, grabbing another bicycle, remounted and rode on, coming from behind to win the race anyway.

Albert Champion (courtesy of the General Motors Institute Alumni Foundation Collection of Industrial History)

About that time Champion drove the "Gray Wolf," one of Packard Motor Car Company's first racing cars, at Brighton Beach. In fact, he drove it through a fence and smashed himself up. In spite of the crash he received an offer to drive 18 races in France. His leg had been fractured and doctors warned him it might have to be amputated. But he went back to France and won every race. On top of that he studied automobile mechanics in his spare time.

Returning to the United States again, Champion was hailed as an authority on automobiles. In the winter of 1904 he decided to stop trying to make speed records and instead build equipment to enable others to make them. In 1905, with others, he started the Albert Champion Company in Boston for the manufacture of spark plugs and the importation of magnetos. The Boston plant flourished, and as demand increased a second plant was opened in Toledo, Ohio.

In 1908 GM founder William C. Durant began searching for a dependable and cost-effective supply of spark plugs and other electrical equipment for Buick cars, which at that time were the best-selling in the United States, exceeding the combined production of Ford and Cadillac. Durant struck a deal with Champion to sever his connection with the Boston and Toledo firms and come to Flint to establish an independent firm to manufacture ignition devices under the name Champion Ignition Company. The company's name was later changed to AC Spark Plug Company to avoid confusion with Champion's earlier firm, which continues in business today as the Champion Spark Plug Company.

To meet GM's immediate demand for spark plugs, Champion established production facilities in a third-floor room in the Buick Plant in Flint. One of his associates, fellow Frenchman Albert Schmidt, designed the company's early processing machines, which gave its spark plugs a quality advantage. Champion Ignition began production with only 15 employees to machine thread the steel shells and gland nuts, then assemble fired clay insulators between the two metal parts. The clay used in the plugs was imported from France. The method of firing clay insulators to assure proper strength and size was a closely guarded company secret. In the beginning Champion Ignition had but one kiln man, and not even Champion himself could enter the kiln room when he was at work for fear his methods would be exposed.

In 1910 Buick purchased control of Champion Ignition, and it began to operate as a GM subsidiary. AC's first home of its own, a two-story structure located on the southeast corner of Industrial Avenue and Harriet Street in Flint, was completed in 1912. The building provided more than 33,000 square feet of floor space and gave AC the capability to increase production.

By the mid 1920s AC was not only supplying GM's needs but was also supplying spark plugs to more than 200 independent manufacturers, reaching a production capacity in excess of 200,000 plugs daily. Company records also indicate that AC was the world's largest manufacturer of speedometers, with a daily output of more than 7,000. The speedometers constituted original equipment in such famed cars as Buick, Cadillac, Chevrolet, Chrysler, Gray, Maxwell, Oakland, and Oldsmobile, as well as in GMC trucks. The company also developed a substantial business manufacturing the AC Air Cleaner.

AC's reputation for reliable and dependable spark plugs gained national attention in May 1927, when Col. Charles A. Lindbergh stated after his historic landing at LeBourget Airfield, Paris, that "AC Spark Plugs functioned perfectly during the entire flight" across the Atlantic. In succeeding years Lindbergh and other aviation pioneers promoted AC aviation spark plugs.

During Champion's tenure as company president AC purchased one of the oldest established spark plug manufactories operating in England and France. In England the business of the corporation was conducted under the name AC-Sphinx Sparking Plug Company, out of Birmingham, and in France under the name AC-Oleo Company, with a well-equipped factory at Levailois-Perret.

Employment increased steadily as the fast-developing automotive industry demanded more spark plugs and other AC products as they were developed. In 1925 the company purchased an unused factory building located in the green meadowland on the east side of Flint along the Dort Highway. The structure had been originally erected for the manufacture of Dort automobiles, but those plans were abandoned following the death of the founder, J. Dallas Dort. Unfortunately, Albert Champion was never to see or occupy the new facilities. The lead article in the November 5, 1927, issue of *Automotive Industries* proclaimed: "Flowers Deck Office Champion Never Saw." The new building had been rushed to completion, and all the executives moved into the new quarters, while Champion was on his annual trip to Europe to attend the London and Paris automobile shows and to inspect AC operations in England and France. He died under unusual circumstances in Paris on October 27.

On October 1 Champion and his second wife, Edna, set sail from New York to Europe. They attended the London and Paris automobile shows, and Champion inspected his new factory, which was completed in Paris during the previous summer. He was apparently in good health, although one of his associates, Pierre Tournier, told officials that Champion mentioned feeling ill at the Paris show. According to a 1937 news article in the possession of Champion's brother's widow, Irene Champion, on the day of his death Champion got in a fistfight with Charles L. Brazelle, an ex-prizefighter and later the common-law husband of Edna Champion. The article reported that the fight started when Champion met his wife and Brazelle in a Paris hotel. Battling a claim on the Champion estate made later by Brazelle, family lawyers told a New York probate court that "Albert Champion died an hour after Brazelle struck him in a barroom brawl." Irene Champion believed that the fight took place in a private room in which Champion confronted Brazelle. Other American newspapers told a different story. One stated: "Albert Champion left his rooms in Paris the afternoon of October 27, 1927. Dinner and friends waited for him at the Hotel Maurice. . . . As Albert stepped into the hotel's banquet room at 5 p.m., he collapsed into the arms of a business friend, Pierre Tournier. In a moment, the 49-year old Champion was dead." The account also states that "doctors said he was struck by an embolism, the sudden clotting of an artery." Paris police never suggested that the death was violent.

Whatever the truth about the unusual circumstances of Albert Champion's death, the fact remains that during his life he began the foundations of a great industry that still bears his initials. Champion lived to see his plans grandly realized and to see the city in which he had determined to make his fortune emerge as one of the industrial centers of the world. He died without departing from his stern, self-imposed regimen of work, which he would have no doubt wanted.

Reference:
Bernard A. Weisberger, *The Dream Maker: William C. Durant, Founder of General Motors* (Boston: Little, Brown, 1979).

Chandler Motor Company

by George S. May

Eastern Michigan University

The Chandler Motor Company, organized early in 1913, joined such earlier firms as Winton, White, Baker, Peerless, and Rauch and Lang that had made Cleveland, Ohio, the Midwest's first major center of the auto industry. Frederick S. Chandler and the other founders of the company were industry veterans, all former executives of the H. A. Lozier Company. It was not surprising, therefore, that their car bore a close resemblance to the Lozier, but the 6-cylinder Chandler's price tag of $1,785 stood in marked contrast with that of the Lozier, which had ranged from $6,000 to $8,000.

The new company did very well at the outset, with sales increasing from 550 the first year to 15,000 by 1916, which made Chandler the city's largest volume producer of cars. The figures impressed investors, who eagerly oversubscribed the company's stock offerings, but the company recognized that a lower-priced entry was also needed if Chandler was to compete with some of the medium-sized firms in Michigan and elsewhere in the Midwest. A subsidiary, the Cleveland Automobile Company, was organized in 1919 to produce a smaller 6-cylinder car starting at $1,385. The Cleveland was not intended to compete with cars such as Ford or Chevrolet in the low-priced range but instead with cars such as the Essex, which was introduced at the same time by Hudson.

Combined Chandler and Cleveland sales in 1920 totaled 40,000, which proved to be the company's high-water mark. The depression that began in the last half of 1920 and continued for the next two years led to a decline from which the company never fully recovered. In 1923, when sales moved back up to 25,500 from the previous year's

20,500, the Cleveland outsold the Chandler, but three years later, as the company struggled to survive, it was the Cleveland, not the higher-priced Chandler, that it decided to abandon. Efforts to increase the Chandler's appeal by adding an 8-cylinder model in 1927 were to no avail. Hudson, the Detroit company with whom Chandler's sales had been comparable in the previous decade, was now far ahead of the Cleveland company, and in 1928 the Hupp Motor Car Company, another Detroit company of medium-size that was still doing well while many were languishing, acquired control of Chandler. It continued the production of the Chandler car until mid 1929, after which it used the old Chandler and Cleveland plants to produce one of its Hupmobile models for three years.

The Chandler's end came in the same period in which the other Cleveland companies were also being forced out of business. The only exception was White, which had wisely switched from passenger car to truck production. Lacking the resources of their contemporaries in Michigan, where the importance of a broad diversity of models, including strong entries in the high-volume, low-priced field, had long been recognized, the Cleveland companies were doomed to fail.

References:

Nick Baldwin and others, *The World Guide to Automobile Manufacturers* (New York: Facts on File, 1987);

Beverly Rae Kimes and Henry Austin Clark, *Standard Catalog of American Cars, 1805-1942* (Iola, Wis.: Krause, 1985).

Roy Dikeman Chapin

(February 23, 1880-February 16, 1936)

by Alec Kirby

George Washington University

CAREER: Photographer and test driver (1901); sales department (1902-1903), sales manager, Olds Motor Works (1904-1906); general manager, E. R. Thomas-Detroit (1906-1908); treasurer and general manager, Chalmers-Detroit Company (1908-1909); president (1909-1923, 1933-1936), chairman, Hudson Motor Car Company (1923-1933); president, Essex Motor Car Company (1918-1922); U.S. secretary of commerce (1932-1933).

Roy Dikeman Chapin, pioneer automotive executive and U.S. secretary of commerce from 1932 to 1933, was born on February 23, 1880, in Lansing, Michigan. The second of three children born to Edward Cornelius and Ella King Chapin, he came from a family of comfortable means. His father was a respected lawyer, known for his honesty, kindliness, wit, and judgment. Chapin would later be known for some of the same qualities.

Chapin later looked upon his youth as a time of tranquil happiness. The only serious matter he could recall was his uncertain health. He suffered several early attacks of pneumonia, and doctors warned his parents to keep him from playing sports. That prohibition freed him to pursue other interests, usually involving science. A member of his high school science club, he was particularly intrigued with electricity. Lansing had recently adopted electric streetlights, and Chapin assisted his father in equipping their house for electricity. Another favorite hobby was photography. In his early teens Chapin constructed his own camera, a square box with a pinhole in front, a finder on top, and glass plates onto which the pictures were exposed. Photography quickly became more than a hobby. Charging up to 25 cents for a print, he earned a reasonable income when not busy with after-school activities. He also worked as business manager for his high school paper and as manager of the junior

Roy Dikeman Chapin

class fund, which helped students from poorer families finance their school activities.

After graduating from high school in June 1897 Chapin drifted for a brief period. In an era when men such as Jay Gould and Andrew Carnegie acquired riches without a college education, Chapin was not convinced that university training would be a good use of his time. For more than a year he held low-level jobs in such fields as advertising sales and rent collection. His biggest hope was that his friend George Field, who had gone to work in a New York investment firm, would find him a job on Wall Street. As the months passed Chapin began to reconsider college. In February 1899 he entered the University of Michigan at Ann Arbor. Because he still harbored a suspicion that a liberal arts education was impractical, he began to sit in on law classes to acquire what he thought were useful skills.

As in high school, Chapin spent his extracurricular time in business-related activities. In his sophomore year his fraternity appointed him steward, a post normally reserved for a senior. The fraternity had fallen heavily into debt, and no upperclassman would accept the responsibility. Chapin promptly worked out a payment schedule with local merchants and slashed fraternity expenditures. He was initially unpopular for cutting the food budget, but his brothers eventually praised him as a disciplined and shrewd manager.

Although Chapin would later be awarded an honorary M.A. by the University of Michigan, he never completed his undergraduate program, dropping out in the spring of 1901 to take a job with the Olds Motor Works in Detroit, where the Olds automobile operation had been moved when it was refinanced in 1899. Horace Loomis, a friend of Chapin's who was an engineer for the Olds company, took Chapin for a test drive in the little curved-dash Oldsmobile runabout Loomis had helped design. As Loomis and Chapin sped along at as much as 18 mph, Chapin exclaimed: "Wonderful, this is the stuff for me. I'm going to quit school and join up."

Olds needed extra help to make up lost production time resulting from a fire that destroyed the plant in March 1901, so Chapin was quickly hired at a salary of $35 per month. Initially, his photography skills were used to provide illustrations for promotional literature on the runabout. He worked at a variety of assignments when a machinists' strike in May 1901 forced company head Ransom E. Olds to keep the plant going with nonstriking workers. But Chapin's major responsibility came to be test driving, a job he enjoyed so much that as head of the Hudson Motor Car Company years later, he would sometimes take out one of the new cars for a trial run across southern Michigan.

In October 1901 Chapin drove an Oldsmobile to second place in a ten-mile race for lightweight cars, one of the events making up the first auto races held in the Detroit area. That was a prelude to the most celebrated event in Chapin's life, his drive from Detroit to New York in late October

and early November in a curved-dash Oldsmobile. Although Ransom Olds later claimed credit for the stunt, the idea may have originated with Chapin, who always displayed a keen sense of what was needed to sell a product. In this case there was the desire to demonstrate that a car weighing less than 600 pounds and costing only $650 was still durable enough to withstand the bad roads of the period.

Chapin's departure was timed so that he would arrive in New York for the second annual Madison Square Garden automobile show. He completed the 820 miles in seven and a half days. During the trip he had to make several detours to find passable roads. The effort also highlighted several difficulties with the car. The cylinder gaskets tended to blow out when the runabout was going uphill, and the combination of poor roads and crude tires necessitated stopping every few miles to reinflate the tires with a bicycle pump. Yet only one serious breakdown occurred. When Chapin pulled off the road to avoid a team of horses, the mainspring of the car snapped, and Chapin was obliged to wait until a new one arrived from Detroit. On November 5 he pulled into New York City and headed toward the Waldorf-Astoria Hotel, where Olds and other company executives waited. Covered with mud, he looked so disreputable that the Waldorf doorman insisted that he enter through the service entrance. The car was cleaned up and placed on display at the auto show.

Over the years the automotive press has tended to overstate the significance of Chapin's Detroit-to-New York run. Chapin has been credited with smashing American long-distance driving records, but several previous drivers posted better numbers. Far from creating a press sensation at the time, the trip was ignored in Detroit's two daily papers. The Olds company did make effective use of the trip in its advertisements, which drew additional attention to a car that was already doing well, and the run increased Chapin's stature in the company.

In 1902 Chapin received a top assignment in the Olds sales department. He owed his advancement to Fred Smith, the company's secretary-treasurer and the son of the principal Olds investor. Smith took a liking to the young man, writing to Chapin's mother in June 1902 that "of all the young men we have around us in a similar capacity, he promises to be the best, and I have great confidence in his good sense and sound judgment."

Surprisingly, Ransom Olds did not share Smith's enthusiasm, apparently feeling that a man more knowledgeable about a car's workings should be in charge of sales. Smith defended Chapin, telling Olds that "Chapin does *good* work in the office. You don't perhaps realize it, but he is posted thoroughly on the business being done in the various agencies. I don't think you do the boy justice, quite." Smith went on to predict that Chapin would "make a tip top strong man anywhere before he gets through."

Chapin enjoyed the personal side of selling. He approached the job in a low-key manner. Never a desk-pounder, he prepared for sales campaigns with intensive investigation and relied on facts to persuade customers. He mastered automotive technology and established contacts across the country. But despite rapidly rising sales that made the Olds Motor Works the top-selling company in the industry, Ransom Olds and Fred Smith clashed over basic policies. With Smith, his father, and several friends controlling a large majority of the company stock, Olds found his influence rapidly deteriorating, and in January 1904 he resigned as general manager. A few months later, having sold his stock, he resigned as a director of the company.

Although Fred Smith, now in undisputed control, named him sales manager, Chapin did not feel comfortable with the new management. In 1905 he was offered a job with the New-York based U.S. Long Distance Auto Company. He accepted the position on the condition that he could bring with him two fellow Olds employees. When that demand was rejected he unhappily returned to Detroit.

Seeking a new line of opportunity, Chapin and three of his Olds associates, Howard E. Coffin, Frederick O. Bezner, and James J. Brady, planned to abandon Olds and establish their own automobile company. Chapin conceived the original plan. He proposed they market a runabout designed by Coffin but rejected by the Smiths. The problem was raising the necessary $150,000 to $200,000 to start the new company. The four could muster only about $2,000 each. Nevertheless, in April 1906 Chapin submitted his resignation to the Olds Motor Works. He traveled to California to see a friend, E. P. Brinegar, an Olds dealer who also sold the Thomas Flyer, a high-priced automobile produced by wealthy Buffalo industrialist Edwin R. Thomas. Brinegar encouraged Chapin to approach Thomas about investing in the new company. Not only did Thomas have the financial resources, he commanded a dealer organization. Chapin, remembering his difficulties with the backers of Olds Motor Works, also noted that Thomas was too busy managing his own company to interfere with Chapin's.

Meeting Thomas in San Francisco, Chapin reported that he and his associates had a car designed and ready to manufacture. A light runabout, it would not compete with the Thomas Flyer. He proposed that a new company, E. R. Thomas-Detroit, manufacture 500 of the automobiles in the first year, to be purchased by E. R. Thomas-Buffalo—manufacturer of the Flyer—and marketed through its dealers. Thomas stood to benefit both as an investor and as a distributor. Impressed, he accepted. The next day Chapin and Thomas departed, for Chicago, where the other three associates waited. Only hours after their train departed, San Francisco was reduced to rubble by the earthquake and fire of April 18.

In Chicago Thomas and the Chapin group formalized the arrangement. The new company was to be capitalized for $300,000, of which $150,000 was to be invested immediately. Thomas was to pay $100,000 and the four others $50,000 among them. Also, Thomas was elected president, Chapin general manager, Bezner secretary, Coffin vice-president, and Brady second vice-president. The Chapin group found raising the necessary $50,000 for their share of the capitalization an immense problem. Chapin was able to muster $3,000 with the help of his father. Coffin was able to equal that while Bezner and Brady remained at $2,000 each. Chapin traveled to New York to court investors, but he was unsuccessful. The partners vowed to proceed anyway.

The new Thomas-Detroit Company rented a building owned by Modern Match Company with 20,000 feet of floor space. The Coffin-designed car, like most automobiles of the era, was assembled from component parts manufactured by other companies. To test the reliability of the car the firm initially ordered three complete sets of components. Aware that many automobile firms had been reduced to bankruptcy because parts-suppliers had not produced equipment that met specifications, Thomas-Detroit insisted on tightly drawn contracts with suppliers who guaranteed satisfactory performance. Workers completed the first car in August,

Chapin behind the wheel of the curved-dash Oldsmobile runabout he drove from Detroit to New York City in October-November 1901 (courtesy of Chrysler Corporation)

and the two others were completed shortly thereafter.

The cars operated perfectly. Thomas-Detroit immediately ordered parts for the 500 they had contracted with Thomas to produce. Attention to quality control surely figured prominently in enabling the company to meet its production schedule, something few newly established automobile firms had been able to accomplish. But the company remained on shaky financial ground. Thomas had produced his $100,000, but by the autumn of 1906 the four others still lacked the $40,000 necessary to complete their part of the deal. Desperate for capital, Chapin approached Alexander McPherson of the First and Old Detroit National Bank. With no more collateral than promises he urged McPherson to lend the required sum. Drawing on his considerable sales skills, Chapin emphasized the experience of the company's founders and their access to the sales organization of the Thomas-Buffalo Company. Chapin succeeded in winning the loan. With its capital assured, Thomas-Detroit completed its initial

500-car contract by the end of June 1907 with no surplus inventory and no cars returned by dissatisfied customers. Demand for the automobile was brisk, and Thomas-Detroit was able to pay an 80 percent dividend. Thomas received $80,000, and the other four were able to repay their bank loan.

With great optimism, the partners began to plan for the future, engaging an architect to design a large factory. Meanwhile, Chapin was looking for ways to enhance the reputation of the fledgling company. Recalling his promotional trek from Detroit to New York for Olds, he decided in July 1907 to pilot a Thomas-Detroit car in the annual Glidden Tour—a 1,000-mile event designed to test automotive reliability. On the tour in Mishawaka, Indiana, Chapin was arrested for speeding. His arrest was covered widely by amused newspapers and generated good publicity for Thomas-Detroit. An accident forced Chapin to withdraw from the competition at the end of the second day.

The prosperity of Thomas-Detroit allowed Chapin, Coffin, Bezner, and Brady to recover their original funds and to realize a sizable income. But it also led to a reexamination of their arrangement with Thomas. Without its own dealer organization, Thomas-Detroit was vulnerable. It could produce only as many cars as Thomas-Buffalo was able to distribute. Chapin worried that Thomas at any time could discontinue marketing the light cars. He decided to reduce Thomas's influence by finding another investor to buy part of Thomas's holdings. Thomas was receptive to an offer for part of his stock.

Chapin found the perfect investor in Hugh Chalmers. Chalmers, aged thirty-four, had just resigned from the National Cash Register Company, where he was earning a salary of $72,000 per year. He agreed to buy half of the Thomas interest and to work full-time developing a sales organization for the renamed Chalmers-Detroit Company. After the transaction Chalmers and Thomas each owned one-third of the stock, and Chapin, Coffin, Bezner, and Brady shared the remaining one-third. By acting together, the Chapin group could reasonably hope to swing the Chalmers or Thomas vote on any issue that might arise.

Under the new arrangement Chapin became treasurer and general manager, exceeded in authority only by Chalmers. Chapin's duties included production supervision, handling dealer complaints, and ensuring customer satisfaction. As a lieutenant to Chalmers, he received $24,000 per year. He and his associates augmented their income by forming the Metal Products Company, which sold automobile axles to Chalmers-Detroit. Each of the investors soon received $23,000 per year from that venture.

The new Chalmers-Detroit model sold well, although the firm did not experience the explosive growth the founders had envisioned. While the company's sales were respectable, every dollar the firm made had to be divided equally between Chalmers, Thomas, and the total interest of the other partners. Chapin was making only one-eighth of the profit of Chalmers and drawing less than half his salary. Quickly Chapin, Coffin, Brady, and Bezner became restless. In October 1908 the group sponsored two former Olds colleagues, R. B. Jackson and George W. Dunham, in developing a car designed by Coffin (known as the Model 20) and two other models designed by Jackson and Dunham. Under the arrangement the original quartet provided the salaries of Jackson and Dunham and work-

shop expenses. Additional funding was provided by the uncle of Jackson's wife—Joseph L. Hudson, the head of Detroit's largest department store. The new firm was named the Hudson Motor Car Company. Chapin and his partners were optimistic about the prospects of the new company, and they gradually disassociated themselves from Chalmers, who in 1909 bought out their interest in Chalmers-Detroit for $700,000.

Throwing his considerable energies into the Hudson Company, Chapin drew up extensive advertising to emphasize that an automobile was not a wasteful luxury but a practical tool that would allow professionals to conduct business with greater speed and efficiency. The promotion worked. In the fall of 1910 Hudson built a huge new factory to meet increasing demand. At the end of 1910 the firm's sales had reached $4,878,600 with profits of approximately $500,000. Holding 20 percent of the company's stock, Chapin—at age thirty—had become a millionaire.

Having achieved what had long been a financial goal, Chapin began to consider retiring from business. In the winter of 1911 he and his partners held a dinner conference with other Hudson officials. Like Chapin, Coffin and Bezner were also contemplating retirement, but no one wanted to turn over the company to strangers. As a result they presented the other executives with an opportunity to acquire more stock and assume control. The junior partners were reluctant to take the financial risk, and the deal never materialized. Still, the Chapin group managed to reduce their work load. Chapin and Coffin took repeated European vacations, and Bezner never returned to a full-time role. But Chapin continued to act as policymaker for Hudson. He devoted particular attention to cutting costs. He also toyed with the idea—which he ultimately rejected—of engaging Hudson in the manufacture of trucks, taxicabs, and airplanes. Aviation was a special interest: Chapin had attended air shows in France in 1909. He was cautious, though, about undertaking such a risky venture. In a newspaper interview in 1909 he remarked that "the airplane is interesting from a scientific and a sporting standpoint. As a business proposition I do not think it is likely to take a prominent position for several years."

In addition to his work with his own companies, Chapin had been active in industry trade associations since his days with Olds, and he would

Four of the founders of the Hudson Motor Car Company in a 1910 Hudson Model 21: left to right, R. B. Jackson, Frederick O. Bezner, Howard E. Coffin, and Chapin (courtesy of General Motors Corporation)

eventually become one of the most widely respected spokesmen for the industry. He was especially active in the promotion of good roads, an interest he claimed originated from his experience on the 1901 drive from Detroit to New York, where the only good roads "were a few miles of macadam near Rhinecliff, on the Hudson." By 1905 Chapin was serving on the good roads committees of the National Association of Automobile Manufacturers and the American Motor League and was lobbying in Lansing to try to get the state legislature to provide improvement funds.

In 1913 Chapin and fellow auto executive Henry B. Joy of Packard became the most active forces in the Lincoln Highway Association, founded that year by Carl G. Fisher of Indianapolis. The association made its chief goal the establishment of a coast-to-coast through route, made "of concrete wherever possible." Chapin saw the project as a way to advance safety and efficiency in automotive travel. At the time there was no central authority to lay out a roadway beyond local jurisdictions. State highway bureaus were rare, and there was no federal legislation providing for the coordination of state roads. The Lincoln Highway Association lob-

bied individual jurisdictions to improve their part of the proposed highway.

Chapin's wealth and industrial prominence along with his relative youth made him one of America's most eligible bachelors. He enjoyed a full social life until 1914, when he abruptly changed his lifestyle, marrying Inez Tiedeman, daughter of the mayor of Savannah, to whom Chapin was introduced by his friend Howard Coffin, who had close ties with the area.

Meanwhile the Hudson Motor Car Company was apparently prospering; the company achieved its first 10,000-car year in 1914. But Hudson's increasing sales were misleading. In May 1915 the directors voted a $3 dividend based on a $2.5 million gain in total sales from the year before. An analysis of the figures, though, revealed that the company's profits had been only $250,000. Without the careful guidance of Chapin, Coffin, and Bezner, Hudson's costs had risen dramatically. Refocusing his attention on the firm, Chapin agreed in June 1916 to a proposal from the head of General Motors, William C. Durant, to include Hudson in a merger of automobile companies and parts manufacturers Durant was trying to put together. When that plan collapsed, Chapin took the dramatic step of involving Hudson in parts manufacture, even though none of Hudson's executives had experience in large-scale manufacturing. For a time the enterprise was a nightmare of alternating shortages and wasteful surpluses.

As Chapin was grappling with those problems, the national business climate was thrown into turmoil with the entrance of the United States into the European war in April 1917. Six months later Secretary of War Newton Baker appointed Chapin to serve on the Highway Transport Committee of the Council on National Defense. One of the purposes of the committee was to facilitate orderly military transportation by advising railroad and highway officials. As a way of lessening the wartime burden on the railway system he successfully convinced manufacturers to have army-purchased trucks driven from their midwestern factories to ports in the East. Thousands of vehicles moved overland from Michigan, Illinois, Indiana, and Ohio to Boston, New York, and other seaboard cities. Shortly after the commencement of the project the Railroad Administration reported that 20,000 freight cars were being released to perform other services.

The committee lacked enforcement power and had only a modest budget. Chapin's salesmanship skills were put to a test when he tried to sell the notion of gasless Sundays to the public. The committee did mobilize the cooperation of the American Automobile Association and other groups in facilitating the war effort and pushed for increased motor truck production and development. More than 20,000 volunteers were trained to answer questions about highways and highway transportation and to encourage the operation of truck traffic to relieve railroad congestion. The latter was a particularly urgent task. As the war progressed certain cities were declared to be embargo points: no goods were to be shipped there until existing congestion had been relieved. Working with railroad executives, Chapin mapped out a strategy to create trucking centers near the embargo points to haul goods to their destinations.

During the war Chapin developed a long-term strategy for highway development to protect the United States against future transportation emergencies. Within the National Automobile Chamber of Commerce he created a highway committee and served as its chairman. In that capacity he met with

government leaders, including the secretaries of war, interior, and commerce, to stress that the Federal Office of Public Roads was hopelessly small and should be expanded. He also arranged meetings with state governors and local road officials in his continuing campaign to win greater appropriations for highway construction.

While Chapin devoted his energies to national service the financial situation of his business continued to decline. Chapin had scrupulously avoided using his Washington position to seek war contracts for his firm, and Hudson did not receive a major war contract until August 1918—three months before the armistice and too late to compensate for loss of civilian sales. In 1918 Chapin and his associates established a separate company, Essex Motors, to experiment with marketing lower-priced cars without risking the Hudson name. But the war increased the costs of producing an automobile, and when the first Essex was completed in the spring of 1918, at $1,395 it was much too expensive. Returning from Washington in December, Chapin faced the prospect of costly factory reconversion in an era of tightening automotive competition.

Challenged, Chapin plunged back into the automobile business. He hoped the Essex would appeal to consumers despite its high cost. In January 1919 he contracted for $1 million worth of new machinery and equipment, adding 75,000 square feet of factory floor space. He was gambling on selling a total of 40,000 Hudson and Essex cars—70 percent more than Hudson's best prior year. The enormous risk paid off: the Hudson and Essex companies delivered 41,566 automobiles in 1919, including over 20,000 of the Essex. Profits almost doubled from 1918, reaching $2,287,104. In one year Chapin had stabilized his interests.

In 1920-1921, however, the United States suffered a serious economic downturn, and Hudson and Essex suffered proportionately. Production in 1921 dropped to less than two-thirds of the preceding year, while profits shrank to $915,000. Hudson had no reserve capital, and for the first time in a decade Chapin and his associates slashed prices and voted to suspend dividends. In 1922 the independent Essex Company was absorbed by Hudson, although the company continued to sell cars under both names.

Chapin again responded with a gamble. For years he had studied the feasibility of manufacturing a low-priced, closed-body automobile, again influenced, he claimed, by the experience of driving the open Oldsmobile in the cold of the late fall of 1901. He noted that in Europe moderately priced closed cars had won approval, but American manufacturers—concentrating on volume—emphasized open touring cars and charged high prices for sedan or limousine bodies. The cost obstacle was difficult to overcome since closed bodies were almost wholly handmade—large stamping presses for steel body sheets were unknown. Chapin believed that an inexpensive steel body would sell even if it lacked detailed workmanship. Early in 1922 Hudson offered closed body Hudson and Essex models for only $100 more than the company's open models—reducing the retail price below the cost of manufacture unless the cars were sold in extraordinary volume. Fortunately the closed bodies were an immediate success. Indeed, in the first third of 1922 closed models accounted for 55 percent of Hudson and Essex sales.

The success with closed bodies made Hudson attractive to Wall Street. Early in 1922 the financial house of Hornblower & Weeks, supported by the Bankers Trust Company of New York, began negotiating with Chapin with the idea of putting Hudson shares on the New York Stock Exchange. That appealed to Chapin, Coffin, Bezner, and the other partners, who recognized that going public would make whatever shares they retained convertible to cash. Chapin conducted the negotiations and secured a settlement that left his control of the company undisturbed. The stock issue, offered on the New York Exchange on April 8, 1922, was an immediate success, with Hudson's original stockholders receiving $7 million in cash and $16 million in the new stock. Seven months later Chapin resigned the presidency of Hudson and assumed the less demanding post of chairman of the board.

Chapin lessened his involvement with Hudson to spend more time with his family. By 1926 he and his wife had three sons and two daughters. Working with architect John Russell Pope, they constructed a large home in the Detroit suburb of Grosse Pointe Farms, which was featured in a 1932 issue of *Town and Country*. Meanwhile Chapin continued his efforts on behalf of the transportation industry. In 1924 he served on the executive committee of the Pan American Confederation for Highway Education. In 1927 he was elected president of the National Automobile Chamber of Commerce. He also served as president of the Sixth Interna-

tional Roads Congress, held in Washington, D.C., in 1930. He was active in local civic affairs and served on the boards of many companies.

The following year friends urged him to seek election to the U.S. Senate. He refused, insisting that he had no ambitions for elective office. President Herbert Hoover had great respect for him, however, and in February 1930—hours after Chapin's sixth child, a girl, was born—the president telephoned to offer him the post of undersecretary of war. The next day Chapin wired his refusal, explaining that he felt he should devote more time to Hudson. Hoover persisted. He finally persuaded Chapin to join his cabinet as secretary of commerce in June 1932.

Chapin's tenure at the Commerce Department, though brief, received widespread praise. He pushed hard for an expansive export trade and called for federal and state cooperation in port development and in the expansion of overland transportation. He also unsuccessfully pressed Hoover to soften his support for prohibition. In February 1933, shortly before leaving office following Hoover's defeat in his bid for a second term, Chapin became involved in an effort to forestall the collapse of one of Detroit's two major banking groups, the Guardian Detroit Union Group. One of the components of that group had requested funds from the federal Reconstruction Finance Corporation (RFC), which it said it needed to survive. The RFC refused to loan any money unless the group's largest depositors, the automotive Big Three (GM, Chrysler, and Ford), provided substantial funds of their own. GM and Chrysler agreed, but Henry Ford refused. Chapin went to Detroit to plead with Ford, whom he had known for more than 30 years, but Ford refused to change his mind. With no relief available, Michigan's governor ordered a state bank holiday in mid February.

Returning to Detroit after the inauguration of President Franklin Delano Roosevelt, Chapin again confronted a financially threatened Hudson Motor Car Company. Battered by falling sales, the company had lost nearly $2 million in 1931 and almost $5.5 million in 1932 and appeared headed for greater losses in 1933. Chapin resumed the Hudson presidency in May 1933. He ordered the redesign of the 1934 models at a cost of hundreds of thousands of dollars in retooling. He also authorized a vigorous advertising campaign, and Hudson became one of the first automobile companies to

Chapin testing a curved-dash Oldsmobile in 1901 (courtesy of Michigan Historical Collections)

make consistent use of radio. After Chapin successfully acquired new capital, Hudson's fortunes gradually improved. A profit of nearly $600,000 was posted in 1935–Hudson's first profit in five years.

In addition to placing Hudson on a solid footing once again, Chapin labored long and hard as the industry's foremost spokesman in the drafting of the automotive code of the New Deal's National Industrial Recovery Act, legislation that Chapin and most of his fellow executives strongly opposed. He was, however, much in favor of Roosevelt's Reciprocal Trade program, and he corresponded extensively with Michigan senator Arthur H. Vandenberg to secure his support for the legislation. He continued working busily through 1935 and into 1936.

Late in January 1936 Chapin, although suffering from a bad cold, went to Washington for a conference on highway traffic. He had not shaken the cold when he returned. Still, he kept a date to play indoor tennis with Edsel Ford and others, thinking the exercise might be helpful. But he contracted pneumonia and died in Detroit's Henry Ford Hospital on February 16. He was survived by his wife and six children, the eldest of whom, Roy Dikeman Chapin, Jr., would ultimately serve as the chairman of American Motors Corporation, the 1954 successor to Chapin's Hudson Motor Car Company.

Few have gained as much respect in the automotive industry as Chapin, both for what he accomplished on his own and for his work for the industry as a whole. As Frank W. Roche, publisher of automotive trade journals, has observed, Chapin was always a man who "carefully plotted out what he intended to do and how he was going to do it. . . . Beneath the surface of a smiling, genial personality there was a drive and determination that swept aside all obstacles and made him an outstanding figure in the automobile industry."

References:

John C. Long, *Roy D. Chapin* (N.p.: Privately published, 1945);

George S. May, "The Detroit-New York Odyssey of Roy D. Chapin," *Detroit in Perspective*, 2 (August 1973): 5-25;

May, *A Most Unique Machine: The Michigan Origins of the American Automobile Industry* (Grand Rapids, Mich.: Eerdmans, 1975).

Archives:

The papers of Roy D. Chapin are in the Michigan Historical Collections, Bentley Historical Library, University of Michigan, Ann Arbor.

Louis Chevrolet

(December 25, 1878-June 6, 1941)

by Richard P. Scharchburg

GMI Engineering & Management Institute

CAREER: Mechanic, Mors Auto Company, France (1898-1900); mechanic, engineer, and race driver, United States (1900-1907); race driver and engine designer, Buick Motor Car Company (1907-1910); chief engineer, Chevrolet Motor Car Company (1911-1913); president and general manager, Frontenac Motor Company (1916-1926).

Louis Joseph Chevrolet, pioneer automobile racer and designer, was born on December 25, 1878, in La Chaux-de-Fonds, Switzerland, the second son of clockmaker Joseph Felicien Chevrolet and Angelena Marie Chevrolet. When Louis was six the family immigrated to France and settled in the Burgundian town of Beaune. All seven Chevrolet children had to leave school early to help support the family. Joseph Chevrolet tried to teach his boys about machinery and how to do detailed work with their hands. Apparently some of Joseph's teaching rubbed off on Louis and his two brothers Arthur and Gaston, because all three pursued careers that utilized their mechanical abilities.

After completing his education Louis Chevrolet ventured into bicycle building and sold his bicycles under the trade name Frontenac. That trade name was to be identified with the Chevrolet brothers for the rest of their lives. Meanwhile Louis Chevrolet began to show an interest in motorcars. He found employment with the Mors Auto Company in 1898.

Chevrolet came to America in 1900, lived for a short time in Montreal, Canada, and eventually settled in Brooklyn, New York, where he got a job as a mechanic for the local DeDion Bouton car agency. The job eventually brought an opportunity to drive as a substitute in a racing contest. The amount of time he devoted to racing increased. He drove Fiat cars to victory at Sheepshead Bay and in other major contests in 1905. He even bested the leg-

Louis Chevrolet

endary Barney Oldfield three times that year, making Chevrolet one of motor racing's elite.

In the spring of 1905 Chevrolet married Suzanne Treyvoux, a French girl he probably met at an auto race. Accounts of the romance suggest that Treyvoux, like the rest of his racing fans, was enamored of Chevrolet's reckless style. Their wedding trip to Niagara Falls was timed not to conflict with the husband's participation in a race in Morris Park, New York.

In 1906 Chevrolet began to make attempts to branch out on his own. He attempted to set up a general automobile business in New York under the name Chevrolet-Kenen Auto Company, and he also met with Walter Christie to plan a front drive V-8 racer. But neither venture panned out. Sometime in 1907 William C. Durant, who had recently consolidated the Buick Motor Car Company in Flint, sized up the attention generated by Chevrolet's racing exploits and invited Louis and his brother Arthur to audition for a job as his chauffeur. Reportedly Durant took them to the dirt track behind the Buick plant in Flint and challenged them to a race. Louis won and was surprised when Durant announced that the chauffeur's job was Arthur's. Louis had been faster, yes, but Arthur had taken fewer chances. There was a consolation: Durant asked Louis to join the Buick racing team. He even offered Chevrolet a free hand in the design of automobile engines. Chevrolet was expected to do one thing only—win races.

As part of the Buick racing team, the Chevrolet brothers found themselves in the company of such well-known drivers as "Bullet Bob" Burman and Louis Strang. Louis Chevrolet pushed the Buick machines to the limit and beyond and earned a reputation as the man to beat. He also won recognition as a sensitive engine mechanic.

By any standard the Buick racing effort was extraordinary. The company entered more than one car in almost every event. The Buick racers christened "Bugs" because their aerodynamic shape resembled a June bug were especially successful. In the car's first-ever run, Bob Burman drove a Bug to a time trial record of 105.7 mph at the Grand Circuit Speedway at Indianapolis. That record was only one of five firsts and three seconds accumulated that day by the team. The Bug records were only the beginning. In 1907 Walter L. Marr took a Model F Buick to Eagle Rock, New Jersey, and won a hill climb in 2 minutes, 18.75 seconds. Marr then went on to victory in the Mount Washington Hill Climb. H. J. Koehler, who had won the Wilkes-Barre Hill Climb in a Buick the previous year, drove to a 47.8-mph victory in the Empire City 100-mile race in October 1906. Buicks did not, of course, win every race they entered. Occasionally they crashed or retired. But Burman's third place in the 1910 Grand Prize race at Savannah, Georgia, was the best showing of the American entries there. The more than 500 trophies Buick cars captured by 1911 were unsurpassed in American motordom.

Simultaneously with the departure of Durant from active management of General Motors (GM)

Company in 1910, Buick began to phase out its aggressive participation in racing. The conservative Charles Nash, Buick president and later president of GM, cut costs to ensure the success of the company. Beginning sometime in 1909 Louis Chevrolet began to spend his spare time working in a garage at 3939 Grand River Avenue in Detroit, where he developed both a 4- and a 6-cylinder engine. After Durant lost control of GM he let Chevrolet know he was in the market for a new product and a new name. In October 1911 Durant and Chevrolet decided to put the 6-cylinder model Chevrolet had been working on into production. Chevrolet's version of the planning is succinct. Durant told him they needed a car. "So I build one." Chevrolet became chief engineer for a company incorporated under his own name.

In 1912 a few 6-cylinder Chevrolets were produced at a Detroit plant on Grand Boulevard. Simultaneously, at the Little Motor Company (another Durant-financed enterprise) location in Flint, progress was being made toward the introduction of an automobile that was lighter and lower-priced than the 6-cylinder Chevrolet. Within a year Durant consolidated production in Flint under the Chevrolet banner. The 6-cylinder model was soon dropped from the line. The next year the 4-cylinder Baby Grand touring car went into production, to be followed shortly by a sports roadster called the Royal Mail. Later still came the Chevrolet 490, which was supposed to sell for $490, in competition with the Ford Model T.

Louis Chevrolet got lost in the shuffle between Detroit and Flint. He departed from the company bearing his name in 1913, shortly after the move to Flint. Probably Chevrolet could not reconcile himself to the move from high-performance cars to smaller, mass-market cars. His interests still ran to high-performance, high-priced automobiles. Durant and Chevrolet also clashed personally. Durant did not approve of Chevrolet's cigarette habit. He thought Chevrolet should smoke cigars because they created a better image. With the split Durant had control of both the Chevrolet name and the company, just as he had with David Buick and the Buick car.

Chevrolet had played no part in the production effort in either Detroit or Flint. He was in no way expected to be involved in actual manufacturing operations, for the good reason that he had neither the liking nor the aptitude for it. After the

Chevrolet (left) and Bob Burman in their record-setting Buick "Bug" racers, circa 1909

opening of the Indianapolis Speedway in 1911 he spent most of his time there. In 1914 and 1915 he sold his Chevrolet stock. Except for short interludes of work for the Blood Brothers of Allegan, Michigan, and on the American Beauty-SIX for the American Motors Company of Plainfield, New Jersey, his attention centered on racing through 1921. He organized the Frontenac Motor Company in 1916 to market a racing car under that name. A major change of location came in 1919, when William Small of Monroe Motor Company induced Louis and Arthur Chevrolet to occupy quarters in Indianapolis and build Monroe-Frontenac racing cars.

Louis and Arthur Chevrolet continued on the racing circuit, often breaking records. Louis was making good money, and, unlike most race drivers, whose winnings were consumed in the fast life around the circuit, he invested in solid and potentially profitable ventures. One involved manufacturing an advanced-design straight 8-cylinder engine with C. W. Van Ranst, who had been part of the Duesenberg effort to produce aircraft engines in World War I. The two produced two engines that featured an aluminum barrel-type crankcase, dual overhead camshafts driven by spur gears, and four valves per cylinder. The two prototypes were installed in cars entered in the 1920 Indianapolis 500. The engines developed problems when accelerated to more than 3,000 rpm, but the one driven

by Tommy Milton edged out a victory, through skillful driving more than anything else. An oil leak, the cause of the problem under racing conditions, was easily corrected, and subsequent wins on the same course later in 1920 and in 1921 (in a new Chevrolet-built car) appeared to confirm Chevrolet and Van Ranst's judgment of the superiority of their design.

Chevrolet managed to get Alan A. Ryan and his associates at the Stutz Motorcar Company to raise $1 million to finance the manufacture of a sports car using the new V-8 engine. But too much up-front money was used on facilities, machinery, and materials, and when sales did not meet expectations there was nothing in reserve to sustain the venture.

Louis Chevrolet came out of the Van Ranst venture broke, but he soon found new success. In 1923, with Arthur Chevrolet as production manager, Louis built an 8-valve push-rod Frontenac cylinder head that could be mounted on the block of a Model-T Ford, giving a remarkable increase in engine performance. Souped-up "Fronty Fords" became numerous, especially at racing events. At the peak the Chevrolet brothers were building Frontenac heads at the rate of about 60 per day. Interest did not last long, however, and estimates indicate that no more than 10,000 were ever produced. But the venture was profitable as long as it lasted, and the income no doubt helped Louis Chevrolet offset

Chevrolet driving a 1914 Buick

some of the losses from the Stutz-backed sports car. An attempt to build still another Frontenac car, this time around an Argyll single-sleeve-valve engine, likewise came to nothing.

In 1926 Louis and Arthur Chevrolet designed a light aircraft engine called the Chevrolair 333. With help from industrialist Glenn Martin, Louis Chevrolet started the Chevrolet Aircraft Corporation to build and market the Chevrolair engine. As it turned out, the Chevrolair 333 was of little interest to anyone beyond Martin, and it was not until years later that it reappeared as the Martin 4-333.

Louis Chevrolet traveled a rocky road the last years of his life. During the Depression he was forced by dwindling financial circumstances to sell his interest in the Chevrolair engine. Accounts suggest that whenever his health permitted he continued to tinker with engines. During his later years he did design work on a helicopter and on a 10-cylinder aircraft engine.

In 1933, his money gone, Chevrolet returned to Detroit. He was able to find work as a mechanic with the Chevrolet Division of General Motors. Later events were even more unkind. His health was of increasing concern. In the late 1930s he suffered a cerebral hemorrhage and several increasingly severe paralytic strokes. The loss of his brother Gaston and his second son combined with his poor health was too much for the aging Chevrolet to bear. He died on June 6, 1941.

Today Chevrolet is chiefly remembered because his name is on Chevrolet cars. But appropriately, he is buried at Holy Cross Cemetery in Indianapolis, close to the scene of his past glories on the racing circuit. Records at the Indianapolis Speedway Museum recall Chevrolet's exploits on the old brick track.

References:

Griffith Borgeson, *The Golden Age of the American Racing Car* (New York: Norton, 1966);

Daniel Dolan, "Chevrolet was the Name, Car Racing Was His Game," *Flint Journal*, August 30, 1970;

Terry B. Dunham and Lawrence R. Gustin, *The Buick: A Complete History* (Princeton: Princeton Publishing Co., 1985);

Frank B. Rodolf, "Louis Chevrolet, With His Flowing Mustachios, Was Prominent in Flint in Pioneer Auto Days," *Flint Journal*, June 6, 1941;

Walter W. Ruch, "A Great Chevrolet Named Louis," *Friends* (July 1971);

Richard P. Scharchburg, *W. C. Durant: the Boss* (Flint, Mich.: GMI Press, 1973).

Chevrolet Motor Car Company

by George S. May

Eastern Michigan University

A year after he had been forced to give up his control of General Motors (GM) to obtain the financial help that company needed, William C. Durant organized the Chevrolet Motor Car Company on November 3, 1911. The company was named after Louis Chevrolet, who had been one of the team of race car drivers whose great success driving Buicks had helped publicize the cars of Durant's first automobile company. Chevrolet had gone on to design a 6-cylinder car the new company produced and that Durant hoped would have special appeal because of its designer's racing fame. The initial production of 2,999 Chevrolets in 1912 was handled by a plant in Detroit, but by 1913 Durant had moved operations to Flint, where he had a larger plant available. The company also acquired a plant in Tarrytown, New York, that had been vacated by Maxwell-Briscoe.

By the end of 1913 Louis Chevrolet had left the company. Until his death in 1941 he and the company that bore his name had no connection, save for a brief period in the 1930s when financial reverses led him to take a menial job at what was by then the General Motors Chevrolet Division. Chevrolet's 1913 departure was at least partly due to his displeasure at Durant's decision to drop the former race car driver's automobile in favor of a smaller, lower-priced 4-cylinder car. The decision to concentrate on the low-priced market with which Chevrolet would from then on be associated was a wise one. The 4-cylinder Baby Grand and Royal Mail models pushed production to more than 13,000 by 1915. The Chevrolet 490, a name that supposedly referred to the car's selling price, sent production for 1916 soaring to nearly 63,000 units.

Such figures represented no serious threat to the dominance of the low-priced Ford Model T, whose 1916 production figures topped 730,000, but they were nevertheless further indication that the new company was doing well. For Durant,

Chevrolet's success would be the means by which he regained control of General Motors. He had been playing upon the dissatisfaction of some GM stockholders with the conservative management style of the bankers who controlled the company by offering to buy up their stock. By the end of the five-year term of the loan the bankers had made to GM, Durant had acquired stock that about equaled the amount held by the bankers. A deadlock between the two factions was broken in the fall of 1915 when they agreed to allow three directors named by Pierre S. du Pont, representing a neutral group of stockholders, to be the swing votes on the board between the equal number of delegates representing the Durant and bankers' groups. Determined to gain undisputed control of GM, Durant then reorganized Chevrolet under the lenient corporation laws of the state of Delaware to allow him to offer to trade five shares of Chevrolet stock for one GM share. Although the bidding for GM stock in 1914 and 1915 had driven the stock's price well over $500, the market's interest in Chevrolet made the combined value of five of its shares much more than the price of one GM share, and there was a rush to take Durant up on his offer. By early spring 1916 Durant clearly had in his possession the majority stock interest he needed to oust the bankers and to reinstall himself as GM's president on June 1, 1916.

In the fall of 1916 the General Motors Corporation was organized, and by August 1917 the earlier GM holding company had been dissolved, and the manufacturing companies it controlled had been converted into operating divisions of the new corporation. Shortly thereafter Chevrolet, too, became one of General Motors' manufacturing units, along with Buick, Cadillac, Oakland, Olds, and the other automotive divisions. However, since Chevrolet, because of Durant's 5-for-1 stock deal, was GM's majority stockholder, it was several

The 1912 Little Four, Chevrolet Motor Car Company's first production car (courtesy of Automobile Quarterly *Archives)*

years before the complicated process of transforming it from a completely separate and independent firm into an operating division was completed.

For a time, however, it was somewhat doubtful whether GM would continue with the production of Chevrolets. At the start of the 1920s Chevrolets were the best-selling of the corporation's cars, but in the managerial shake-up that followed the forced departure of Durant at the end of 1920, there were some who felt that the Chevrolet lines should be abandoned. The Chevrolet 490, which now sold for from $795 to $1,375, could not compete with the Ford Model T either in price or quality, and the higher-priced Chevrolet FB model sold for virtually the same price as some of GM's Oakland and Oldsmobile models. But Alfred P. Sloan, Jr., who emerged as GM's top executive, kept Chevrolet as part of a revamped approach to the marketing of GM's several car lines. He assigned each of the car divisions a particular price range in which they would operate, and the higher-priced Chevrolets were dumped. Cadillac was designated

as the corporation's top-of-the-line automobile, and at the other end Chevrolet would be the bottom-of-the-line, given the unenviable task of competing with the Model T for the mass market.

By the latter part of the 1920s the gap between Chevrolet and Ford had been closed. From that time on Chevrolet would generally be out in front as the industry's volume leader. Three factors account for what most observers in 1920 would have felt was a most unlikely development. First was Sloan's decision that Chevrolet would not try to compete directly with the Model T in terms of price. Instead, by offering a car that included features such as a self-starter and demountable rims, features not found on the Model T, Sloan sought to attract buyers from the upper ranges of those who were considering a low-priced car and who would feel that the added convenience and comfort of the Chevrolet was worth a price about $90 more than Ford's. Second was the hiring of Ford's William S. Knudsen in 1922 to be in charge of Chevrolet operations. It was Knudsen's aggressive and effective man-

*A 1914 Chevrolet Baby Grand sporting the Chevrolet company's familiar "bow-tie" trademark
(courtesy of the Library of the Campbell-Ewald Company, Detroit, Michigan)*

agement that enabled Chevrolet to draw closer to Ford in the next few years. It was Henry Ford's failure to retain such capable executives as Knudsen (and even more his refusal to listen to those who were advising him in the early 1920s that the public's tastes were changing) that was responsible for the declining sales of the Model T by the middle of the decade. More than anything else, that gave Chevrolet the opportunity to unseat the longtime volume leader. Finally even Ford recognized the need for change, and six months after abandoning the Model T in 1927 the company began producing the Model A. That was an outstanding car, fully in tune with what buyers now wanted, and it enabled Ford to retake first position, but not for long. At the end of 1928, a year in which total Chevrolet production since 1912 passed the 5-million mark, Knudsen introduced a 6-cylinder Chevrolet that, in combination with Henry Ford's increasingly outdated management style, soon brought Chevrolet back to the top.

Throughout the 1930s and on up to the halt of passenger car production during World War II Chevrolet was almost always out in front, and it picked up where it had left off when car production resumed after the war. But by the early 1950s the new management that had been installed at Ford after Henry Ford II succeeded his grandfather was making a determined bid to regain its leadership in the low-priced field. Chevrolet sales remained excellent, but among automobile enthusiasts the car, still powered by Knudsen's 6-cylinder engine (dubbed the "cast-iron wonder"), was referred to as "an old lady's car." The 1953 introduction of the expensive Corvette sports car was the first move by Chevrolet and GM management to change the division's image. After a shaky start the Corvette developed into an enormous success. Far more important in enabling Chevrolet to hold off Ford's challenge in the high-volume, low-priced car range was the introduction in 1955 of models powered by Ed Cole's 8-cylinder engine. That engine, in souped-

Chevrolet Classic Six, 1912 or 1913

up versions, soon made Chevrolet models such as the 1957 Bel Air some of the all-time favorites among a younger generation of car buyers.

By the 1960s Chevrolet led the industry not only in total production but in the variety that it offered. Customers had a choice of models, body styles, engines, transmissions, colors, and a wide range of other features virtually guaranteeing that no two Chevrolets were exactly the same. Some models were more successful than others. The Corvair, introduced in the 1960 model year in response to the demand for smaller, more fuel efficient cars, was an innovative, air-cooled, rear-engine model that faded from the scene a decade later, in part because of contentions that early versions had been unsafe to drive. The Chevy II and the Chevelle, introduced later in the 1960s, were more traditional and more successful entries in the market for somewhat smaller cars, while the Camaro, introduced in 1967, was a strong competitor to the Ford Mustang, introduced three years earlier, among sportier models referred to as "pony cars." Packed with options that most buyers wanted, the Camaro, like many other Chevrolet models besides the Corvette, was no longer a cheap car.

In 1970, as a response to the alarming increase in sales of small imports, GM introduced the much-heralded subcompact Vega. It would prove to be an even greater source of embarrassment than Chevrolet's earlier Corvair. But the Chevette, essentially a copy of a car produced by GM's German subsidiary, was a more successful and longer-lasting entry in the scramble to produce fuel efficient models following the escalation of gas prices in the mid 1970s. Ford's subcompact Escort became the best-selling car in the world in the 1980s, but Chevrolet's overall variety of models enabled it to retain its leadership in total volume. In addition to automobiles, Chevrolet pickup trucks, part of the commercial vehicle production that had been an important element in the division since the early days, had now become popular alternatives to the standard passenger car and were the best-selling Chevrolet vehicles. They competed vigorously with the Ford pickup for the distinction of being the most popular motor vehicle on the market.

References:
Ed Cray, *Chrome Colossus: General Motors and Its Times* (New York: McGraw-Hill, 1980);

George S. May, *The Automobile in American Life* (forthcoming, 1990);

Alfred P. Sloan, Jr., *My Years with General Motors* (Garden City, N.Y.: Doubleday, 1964);

Bernard Weisberger, *The Dream Maker: William C. Durant, Founder of General Motors* (Boston: Little, Brown, 1979).

Louis Semple Clarke

(August 23, 1866-January 6, 1957)

by Genevieve Wren

Motor Vehicle Research Services

CAREER: Partner, Pittsburgh Motor Vehicle Company (1897-1899); president and chief engineer (1899-1918), vice-president and consulting engineer, Autocar Company (1918-1929).

Louis Semple Clarke is best known as president of the Autocar Company of Ardmore, Pennsylvania, the company that introduced the cab-over-engine concept in truck design in 1908. In 1901 Clarke built the first shaft-driven automobile in the United States, and he is also credited with the development of the double-reduction axle-drive system and the circulating-oil lubrication system. His first company, Pittsburgh Motor Vehicle Company, marketed automobiles as early as 1897.

Clarke was born in Pittsburgh on August 23, 1866, the son of businessman Charles John Clarke and Louisa Semple Clarke. He received a private-school education and attended West University. Mechanically inclined from an early age, he had his own workshop by the time he was fifteen. He designed and built a camera when he was sixteen. After leaving school he worked for a time on the production of an Edison "talking machine." Later he worked for the Western Pennsylvania Phonograph Company, and then he became a partner in a wholesale machine supplies and hardware firm, Somers, Fitter & Clarke. He left that firm in 1895 to conduct automotive research.

Early in 1896 Clarke developed a spark plug for use in gasoline engines. In partnership with William Morgan he built his first three-wheeled vehicle later that year. With Morgan and several others he incorporated the Pittsburgh Motor Vehicle Company in 1897. Clarke served as president and chief engineer of the firm, which produced and sold several four-passenger cars in 1897 and 1898. In 1898 Clarke designed a phaeton, or touring car, that featured a 2-cylinder engine and a then-novel left-hand-drive arrangement. The car proved so popular that

Louis Semple Clarke

in 1899 Clarke and his associates increased the company's capitalization and renamed it the Autocar Company. The following year Autocar moved to larger facilities in Ardmore, Pennsylvania. The 2-cylinder phaeton remained the company's major product until about 1908.

At Ardmore, Clarke continued to develop new concepts in automotive engineering. Aside from the 1901 shaft-driven automobile and the axle and oil-lubrication systems, he designed improved porcelain spark plugs and an efficient disk-type clutch mechanism. Autocar also began to move into truck production. The company marketed a "delivery wagon" available in a variety of sizes beginning in 1899 and introduced the 2-ton model XVII, probably the first American-built shaft-driven truck, in 1907. The company began to phase out car production in 1908.

Autocar also introduced the 2-cylinder model XXI truck in 1908. The truck had a short 97-inch wheelbase, and the engine was mounted under the driver's seat, which swung out of the way to give access. Over the next 12 years the company produced more than 30,000 of the cab-over-engine model XXIs, which grew more popular as more states restricted the length of trucks permitted on the highways.

Clarke designed an armored car that Autocar produced for a Canadian army regiment during World War I. He later developed an aerial "depth-bomb" used in antisubmarine warfare by the U.S. Navy. Sometime after the war Clarke reduced his role in the Autocar Company, becoming vice-

president and consulting engineer. He sold his interest in the company in 1929 and retired. During World War II he returned to Autocar on a volunteer basis to supervise the production of military vehicles. But after retirement he spent most of his time in Palm Beach, Florida, where he had maintained a home since 1892, painting, sculpting, carving, and taking photographs. He died in Palm Beach on January 6, 1957.

References:
"The Autocar Story," *Dana Digest*, 2 (Fall 1961);
Cycle and Automobile Trade Journal (December 1, 1924);
James Wren and Genevieve Wren, *Motor Trucks of America* (Ann Arbor: University of Michigan Press, 1979).

Archives:
Material on Louis Semple Clarke is located at the Motor Vehicle Manufacturers Association, Detroit, Michigan.

Charles Clifton

(September 20, 1853-June 21, 1928)

by Genevieve Wren

Motor Vehicle Research Services

CAREER: Clerk, Sidney Shepard & Company (1871-1876); passenger department, Erie Railroad (1876-1878); clerk, Buffalo Grape Sugar Company (1878); general manager, Colgate Gilbert (1878-1880); treasurer, Bell, Lewis & Yates Coal Mining Company (1880-1897); secretary-treasurer, George N. Pierce Company (1897-1909); director and treasurer (1909-1916), president (1916-1919), chairman, Pierce-Arrow Motor Car Company (1919-1928).

Charles Clifton, most prominent in the automobile industry as president and then chairman of Pierce-Arrow Motor Car Company, was born in Buffalo, New York, on September 20, 1853, the son of Henry Clifton and Elizabeth Dorsheimer Clifton. He was educated in Buffalo public schools and at the Highland Military Academy and began his career in 1871 as a clerk for the hardware firm of Sidney Shepard & Company. In 1876 he moved to the passenger department of the Erie Railroad at Buf-

falo. Two years later he accepted a clerkship at the Buffalo Grape Sugar Company, but he left soon after to become general manager for Buffalo starch manufacturer Colgate Gilbert. In 1880 he found a lasting position, as treasurer for the Bell, Lewis & Yates Coal Mining Company.

By the time Clifton married Buffalo native Grace Gorham on January 22, 1891, he had achieved a leading position in his community. He was in his tenth year of service in the New York National Guard (he would serve until 1893) and served as a director of several Buffalo companies. The Cliftons had a son, Gorham, and a daughter, Alice.

In 1897 Clifton left the coal company to take a position as a secretary and treasurer of the George N. Pierce Company of Buffalo, a bicycle manufacturer. Soon the Pierce Company started to manufacture automobiles, and from his position as secretary Pierce helped lead the organizational development of the automotive industry. The Pierce firm

Charles Clifton

joined the National Association of Automobile Manufacturers, and Clifton was serving as vice-president of the organization when it dissolved in 1904. In 1905 he became president of the Association of Licensed Automobile Manufacturers (ALAM) and helped lead the effort to control automobile production by confining it to those firms licensed by the ALAM under the terms of the Selden internal combustion engine patent. He remained ALAM president until 1912, after the association lost its suit against the Ford Motor Company for infringement of the patent.

Meanwhile in 1909 the Pierce firm was reorganized as the Pierce-Arrow Motor Company, and Clifton became a director and the company's treasurer. Under his energetic and wise leadership, Pierce-Arrow cars quickly attained recognition as outstanding examples of design and craftsmanship. After the Selden patent loss Clifton turned in the direction of parts standardization as president of the National Automobile Chamber of Commerce. He was instrumental in originating the 1915 cross-licensing agreement among chamber members that allowed free use of all patented designs and methods in the industry. The agreement made automotive parts standardization possible and aided in the development of mass-production techniques.

In 1916 Clifton achieved the presidency of Pierce-Arrow, but he served in the position only a short while, resigning to become chairman of the company board in 1919. During Clifton's tenure as company president World War I diverted some of his attention from business. He directed the Buffalo effort for Allied war relief and worked on behalf of French war orphans. In his later years Clifton devoted himself to community service. He constructed an addition to the Buffalo General Hospital known as Clifton Memorial Hall and funded restoration of the community's Episcopal church. Clifton died in Buffalo on June 21, 1928.

References:

James Rood Doolittle, *The Romance of the Automobile Industry* (New York: Klebold, 1916);

Motor Vehicle Manufacturers Association, *Automobiles of America* (Detroit: Wayne State University Press, 1974).

Howard E. Coffin

(September 6, 1873-November 21, 1937)

by Robert J. Kothe

Atlanta, Georgia

CAREER: Chief experimental engineer (1902-1905), chief engineer, Olds Motor Works (1905-1906); vice-president and chief engineer, E. R. Thomas-Detroit Company (1906-1908); vice-president and chief engineer, Chalmers-Detroit Company (1908-1909); vice-president, chief engineer, consulting engineer, Hudson Motor Car Company (1909-1930); president, National Air Transport (1925-1930).

Howard Earle Coffin was born in West Militia, Ohio, on September 6, 1873, to Julius Coffin and Sarah Jones Coffin, emigrants from England. He spent his youth in West Militia and then went to boarding school in Maryville, Tennessee. Later, after his mother moved the family to Ann Arbor, Michigan, to administer a boardinghouse, he attended public high school. Coffin studied engineering at the University of Michigan from 1893 to 1896 but then was forced because of lack of funds to take a part-time position at the post office in Ann Arbor. He continued his education part-time and also developed a single-cylinder 2-cycle gasoline engine. After that he constructed a steam car, which he later claimed provided transportation on his mail route for several years. The vehicle is presently housed in the collections of the Henry Ford Museum in Dearborn, Michigan.

In 1900 Coffin returned to full-time study at the University of Michigan, but prior to graduation he accepted a position as chief experimental engineer with the Olds Motor Works, the Detroit-based producer of the single-cylinder curved-dash Oldsmobile runabout. He began to establish a reputation as an outstanding designer and was named the company's chief engineer in 1905.

The success of the curved-dash Oldsmobile contributed to the rise of several future automotive industry leaders. The Dodge brothers, Horace and

Howard E. Coffin

John, originally were major Olds contractors, as was Henry Leland, who later founded both the Cadillac and Lincoln companies. Coffin's exposure to the atmosphere of entrepreneurship surrounding the Olds operation no doubt influenced him to decide to become more than an employee. In February 1906 he joined with Olds colleagues Roy Dikeman Chapin, Frederick O. Bezner, and James Brady to form the E. R. Thomas-Detroit Company in partnership with Buffalo, New York, automaker Edwin R. Thomas. The firm used the established dealer network of Thomas's Buffalo company, makers of several upper-market cars, but it marketed a smaller, less-expensive vehicle.

Coffin served as vice-president and chief engineer of the firm and was responsible with his three Olds partners for securing $50,000 of the company's $150,000 of paid-in capital. The group fell far short of that goal and failed to attract further investors, so Thomas agreed to increase his investment. Coffin designed the 2-cylinder Thomas Detroit automobile, 500 of which were assembled in a former match factory in the first year. In 1908 Thomas agreed to sell his interest in the company to Hugh Chalmers, recently retired administrator of National Cash Register Company. The company reorganized as Chalmers-Detroit with Chalmers as president and produced an essentially unchanged car. Later in the year the company marketed a 4-cylinder, 30-horsepower model selling for $1,500.

Chalmers's capital and increasing public appreciation of the performance of Chalmers-Detroit cars on the racing circuit contributed to growing sales for the company. Coffin began to involve himself in other ventures. In 1909 he, Chapin, Bezner, and Chalmers became interested in a small, 4-cylinder car designed by two other former Olds employees, Roscoe B. Jackson and George W. Durham. That group solicited financial backing from J. L. Hudson, owner of Detroit's largest department store, to organize the Hudson Motor Car Company and produce the car as a low-priced companion to the Chalmers-Detroit. Before the end of 1909, however, Chalmers sold his interest to Coffin, Chapin, and Bezner for $80,000. They in turn sold their Chalmers-Detroit holdings to Chalmers for $788,000.

Hudson left the management of the company bearing his name to Chapin, company president, and Coffin, who continued in his role as vice-president and chief engineer. The company produced 1,100 Hudsons in 1909 and 4,556 in 1910. While Chapin provided the managerial drive, Coffin headed the design effort. The company continued to produce better cars. By 1912, when Hudson announced a 6-cylinder model for 1913, the automotive press touted Coffin as the industry's "foremost engineer," responsible for more "successful" automobiles than any other. The source of his success was his realization that the appearance of automobiles played a part in marketing strategy. In an analysis of the industry's 1914 models he noted that makers were presenting fewer mechanical improve-

ments as new features. Mechanical features such as the self-starter that distinguished the 1912 Cadillac were quickly adopted by all carmakers, and as a matter of course the possibility of achieving major new technological breakthroughs declined over time. Chapin recommended, therefore, that Hudson distinguish its new models through "annual changes in body styles." He noted a streamlining trend in competitors' makes and suggested making "comfort—even luxury—combined with convenience and utility" the chief design objective. The company went in that direction. Advertisements for the 1916 Hudson emphasized the car's "Yacht-like Body," its "Ever-Lustre Finish," and its "Roomier Tonneau."

Coffin became deeply involved in the organizational side of the automobile industry. He was a founding member of the Society of Automobile (later Automotive) Engineers (SAE) and served as its president in 1910. He was active in the Association of Licensed Automobile Manufacturers and served as that group's chairman for the committee on tests. He was also interested in racing and helped found the Manufacturers Contest Association, which attempted unsuccessfully to regulate the sport for a time. In the SAE Coffin was a leader in the effort to standardize automotive parts and materials. As a result of his efforts, for example, 800 types of lock washers were reduced to 16 standard sizes. Those kinds of reductions lowered manufacturing costs and increased the efficiency of parts procurement, making mass production more viable.

As a member of the National Automotive Chamber of Commerce, Coffin was also a leader in the instigation of a cross-licensing pool of automotive patent holders. Under the arrangement any member of the pool could use the patented designs of the others. If someone developed a superior transmission or carburetor, everyone was supposed to benefit. But the pool was not entirely successful, because not all the major patent holders joined.

Coffin withdrew from active involvement in the management of Hudson as his wealth and influence grew. He retained the title of vice-president but retreated to a consultative engineering role. Involvement in government service took up much of his time during World War I. He became deeply involved in the industrial effort to equip the military, taking a position in 1915 as chairman of the committee on production, organization, manufacture, and standardization of the Naval Consulting Board. His responsibilities included taking an inventory of the nation's industrial capacity. The following year President Woodrow Wilson appointed Coffin to a commission to advise the Council of National Defense, created to direct the preparedness program. In 1917 Coffin was made chairman of the Aircraft Production Board, where he standardized the designs and materials in military aircraft. One of the achievements of that board was the design of the Liberty engine, but the war ended before Chapin could exert much influence on aircraft production.

The wartime aircraft experience stimulated Coffin's interest in airplanes after the war. In 1919 he went to Europe to study aviation as a member of an American research group. In 1922 he helped organize and served as the first president of the National Aeronautical Association. Then, in 1925 he became president of a pioneering airline company, National Air Transport. The company, woefully undercapitalized at $2 million, concentrated on the mail-carrying business. It resisted expanding into passenger transport long after other airlines realized the potential in that market. Coffin ceased his association with the firm in 1930.

In the 1920s Coffin also became a real estate investor through the Detroit Realty Investment Company and the Coffin Realty Investment Company. The firms had large holdings in the developing Grosse Pointe area of Detroit as well as on Long Island and the Sea Island region. Coffin's interest in the Sea Islands dated back to his attendance at the 1911 Vanderbilt Cup automobile races, held annually in Savannah, Georgia, in those years. He went hunting on nearby Sapeloe Island and was so enchanted he bought 20,000 acres for $150,000.

In the years that followed Coffin spent more and more time on the island, which had supported a cotton plantation owned by Thomas Spaulding that was raided by Union troops during the Civil War. He built a massive home, later made the property of the state of Georgia, on the ruins of the Spaulding home and lived there in baronial fashion. The house boasted indoor and outdoor swimming pools and more than 60 rooms furnished with antiques. Guests such as Calvin Coolidge, Herbert Hoover, and Charles Lindbergh had to fly or take a boat to get to the place. Coffin was determined to reform the economy of the Sapeloe area. He introduced purebred cattle to the island, repaired its century-old drainage system, and reopened a cannery on the mainland. He experimented, with lim-

ited success, with oyster farming, but he could not prevent area oystermen from raiding his beds. He also funded efforts to preserve the fragile ecology of the Sea Island region. Most important, through his chairmanship of the Sea Island Company he provided the driving force in the development of the Sea Island Resort and Golf Club, today one of Georgia's most elegant vacation retreats.

The Depression placed a great strain on Coffin's fortune. Although many of his properties remained valuable, his income, estimated at $800,000 per year in the mid 1920s, dropped dramatically. In 1930 Coffin gave up his position at Hudson, and he started a new career as chairman of Southeastern Cotton, a textile marketing firm. To raise operating funds for the new venture he sold his Sapeloe holdings. He also experienced tragedy in his personal life in the 1930s. His first wife, Matilda, whom he had married in 1907, died in 1932 after an extended illness. The couple had no children. He married Gladys Baker in 1937, but by that time his health had deteriorated precariously. Coffin died on November 21, 1937, at his nephew's Sea Island home from an apparently self-inflicted gunshot wound.

Coffin was an extraordinary engineer and entrepreneur who contributed to the development of the automobile industry both as a designer and an organizer. He went on to pioneer in the development of the American airline and tourist industries. He was a history scholar and received honorary degrees in history from Mercer and Oglethorpe Universities as well as an honorary engineering degree from the University of Michigan. Throughout his career he found motivation in the desire to go beyond personal interest to influence the American business world as a whole.

References:

Eugene W. Lewis, *Motor Memories: A Saga of Whirling Gears* (Detroit: Alved, 1947);

George S. May, *The Automobile in American Life* (forthcoming, 1990);

John B. Rae, *American Automobile Manufacturers: The First Forty Years* (Philadelphia: Chilton, 1959).

Archives:

Material on Howard E. Coffin can be found in the Roy Dikeman Chapin papers in the Michigan Historical Collections, Bentley Historical Library, University of Michigan, Ann Arbor.

Cole Motor Car Company

by Beverly Rae Kimes

New York, New York

The Panic of 1907 convinced Joseph J. Cole to become an automobile manufacturer. Although the "business failure" columns of the automotive trade press ominously suggested the risks involved, he was confident of success. An Indiana farm boy who had parlayed a year in business school and a good head for business into top management posts at two major carriage-making concerns, Cole had saved the considerable sum of $25,000 by 1904 and purchased half interest in the Gates-Osborn Carriage Company of Indianapolis. Thirteen months later the firm became the Cole Carriage Company, and Cole carried it to new levels of prosperity. Profits in 1906 totaled $11,065.57, with a stock dividend of $7,500. Cole expanded the product line to 49 different varieties of horse-drawn vehicles.

A prudent man, Cole entered the automobile business gingerly. First, he hired a graduate engineer, Charles S. Crawford, who would later become famous with the Stutz Motor Car Company. Second, he borrowed the barn of a neighbor in which to build a prototype. Given Cole's background in carriage making, that first automobile was, not surprisingly, a high wheeler. Introduced in October 1908, the Cole Solid Tire Automobile was well received, with 170 units sold in less than a year. But Cole quickly recognized, before most motor buggy makers, that the high wheeler was a dead-end design.

By June 1909 the Cole Motor Car Company had superseded the Cole Carriage Company and a line of standard cars was introduced. By year's end more than 100 4-cylinder Cole Model 30's had been sold. All of them, no doubt, were equipped with Firestone tires, since Harvey S. Firestone had been gracious enough to lend Cole the money necessary to launch production of the line.

To publicize his new car Cole went racing. In 1910, at the Vanderbilt Cup on Long Island, "Wild Bill" Endicott drove a Model 30 Flyer to victory in

Advertisement for Cole Motor Car Company's top-selling 8-cylinder car, introduced in 1918

the 126.4-mile Massapequa Trophy event, averaging 55 mph and defeating cars twice its $1,500 price. The Cole name was aggressively promoted—on land with sponsorship of a baseball team and booster club as well as a Cole cigar, and in the air with a huge gas-filled balloon and a Wright Biplane. In the latter a Cole automobile engine was installed, and the plane was entered in the *New York American*'s coast-to-coast flying contest. Alas, the Cole-powered Wright finished second, but the publicity accrued was first-class.

By the end of 1910 Cole output had reached 783 vehicles. Capital stock was increased from $100,000 to $300,000, and a 30,000-square-foot

The 1918 Cole Model 871 Roadster (courtesy of Automobile Quarterly)

factory addition increased production capacity to 2,000 cars annually. Sales in 1912 totaled 1,991 cars. In 1913 the model range was expanded to two 4-cylinders and a new 6-cylinder car, with a price range of $1,685 to $3,000, plus a berline limousine at a hefty $4,250. Two years later a V-8 was introduced, which soon displaced all previous models.

By then racing had been discontinued. Cole had found the niche for his company—as a competitor to Cadillac. Indeed, General Motors' Northway Division, which produced Cadillac's V-8, built Cole's as well. Earlier Cole had dispatched Crawford to Detroit to assist in its design.

The Cole was an "assembled" car and therefore was derided by the giant automakers, who could afford to produce most components in-house. Cole preferred the designation "Standardized Car" for his product, which also provided a sly counterpoint to Cadillac's celebrated "Standard of the World" slogan. Amusingly, an early brochure stoutly declared that "Cole motorcars do not bloom once a year like Easter lilies"—a slap at the industry practice of annual model revisions—but Cole began "blooming" new cars by the calendar soon after.

Although Cole flatly turned down several offers from William C. Durant to become part of General Motors, he did give consideration for awhile to joining other Hoosier manufacturers in a "GM of In-

diana." Ultimately he elected to remain independent. In 1918 Cole's new Aero-Eight, a design pacesetter, was enthusiastically received by both press and public. The company would also pioneer the use of balloon tires.

Early in 1919 Cole announced a major expansion program. The existing factory could not accommodate the demand for the new Aero-Eight. Two new buildings increased factory space to nearly 600,000 square feet. The Cole Company's 1919 output of 6,225 automobiles was second only to Cadillac among America's high-priced automakers. The expansion promised to raise Cole's annual business from $14 million to more than $30 million. But what Cole did not foresee was the post-World War I depression (few manufacturers did)—and it hit his company at the worst possible time—as it expanded. Only 1,722 cars left the Cole factory in 1922, just 1,522 in 1923.

Automobile company failures were rife during the early 1920s. J. J. Cole chose not to fail—nor to jeopardize his personal fortune. The process of liquidating the Cole Motor Car Company began early in 1925. Ten months later J. J. Cole died suddenly of an infection at the age of fifty-six.

Reference:

Dave Emanuel, "Cole: The Pride of Indianapolis," *Automobile Quarterly*, 22 (Second Quarter 1984): 206-215.

Cooling Systems

by James Wren

Motor Vehicle Manufacturers Association

One of the many early problems associated with the use of the internal combustion engine to power automobiles was the need to control the large amount of heat produced by its operation. Some of the particular problems accompanying excessive heat were premature ignition, engine knock, and lubricant burn-off, the last raising the danger of engine lockup. While excessive heat caused problems, excessive cooling also brought its own difficulties, including poor fuel economy, power loss, and direct interference with combustion itself.

Manufacturers had available to them only two alternative cooling systems: air cooling and water cooling. At first, most opted for a passive air cooling system, as this involved little extra design work at a time when more central technological issues were still being resolved. By adding radiating fins to the engine block, the manufacturers hoped enough heat could be transferred to the fins and therefore to the surrounding air. Unfortunately, most of these early engines were rather large 1- or 2-cylinder machines which were located under the driver's seat or very low in the engine frame. The location of the engines made it impractical that passive cooling could be used, raising the necessity that an active system be devised. Even the alternative, the front-mounting of engines, did not solve the prob-

lem because of the slow speeds of the vehicle.

Obviously, water cooled systems required a much more complex design, and despite one being introduced in 1885 in Carl Benz's first car, it was several years before water cooled systems using radiators became dominant. As the water systems were more efficient at cooling, a means of limiting the lowering of temperatures became necessary. The thermostat was the answer. One of the first, a thermostat used to restrict water flow during ignition, was introduced on a Cadillac in 1914 and is still used in vehicles today.

Another early problem with water systems was that there was no means of preventing the water from evaporating. Some motorists used alcohol to raise boiling points, but it was not until the invention of ethylene glycol, or antifreeze, that driving became possible in all types of weather. Before the development of this preventative, it might take 40 gallons of water to complete a 100-mile journey.

Because of the complexity and added mechanical weight of water cooled systems many manufacturers bucked the trend and continued to use air cooled systems. Although water devices dominated, the Volkswagen Beetle, one of the most popular models of the mid to late twentieth century, proved that air cooled systems were not completely anachronistic.

James Couzens

(August 26, 1872-October 22, 1936)

by Alec Kirby

George Washington University

CAREER: Car-checker (1890-1893), manager, freight office, Michigan Central Railroad (1893-1895); bookkeeper and general assistant, Malcomson Fuel Company (1895-1903); business manager, secretary, sales manager, vice-president, treasurer, general manager, Ford Motor Company (1903-1915); chairman, Detroit Street Railway Commission (1913-1915); police commissioner, Detroit (1916-1918); mayor, Detroit (1918-1922); U.S. senator (1922-1936).

James Couzens, Ford Motor Company executive and U.S. senator from Michigan, was the eldest of the five children of James Joseph and Emma Clift Couzens. Chatham, Ontario, where Couzens was born, had not been the settlement of choice for his father, who at age twenty-one had left his native London, England, for Detroit, Michigan. A shortage of funds, however, forced him to make his home in Chatham, 50 miles short of his original destination. A year later he sent for his wife after saving a small sum as a grocer's clerk. Their son, who was born on August 26, 1872, was christened James Joseph Couzens, Jr., but at a young age he began calling himself simply James Couzens, declaring that he would not "be junior to anyone."

While Couzens was still a small child, his father abandoned the grocery trade and became a laborer in a soap factory, and the fortunes of the family steadily improved. James Joseph Couzens became a salesman for the soap company before establishing "Chatham Steam Soap Works, James J. Couzens, Prop." in 1881. Four years later he became a dealer in coal and ice as well as soap. Finally he became a manufacturer of cement paving blocks. The financial success of the family ensured a respectable social position for Couzens, yet he was continually reminded of the value of thrift and hard work. A practical and driven man, the elder Couzens would brook no idle behavior in any mem-

James Couzens

ber of his family. To a remarkable degree, Couzens came to emulate his father. By age nine he was earning ten cents per week by pumping the organ at a local church. He augmented this income by selling soap door-to-door before obtaining a job as a lamptender. James proved to be more adept at earning money than earning good grades in school; at age twelve he resolved that he would not go to high school, dismissing it as a waste of time. However, he changed his mind after losing a bookkeeping job on the grounds that he was too inexperienced. He failed the entrance exam, and his irate father sent him to the unpleasant work of manufacturing soap as punishment. Learning his lesson, the newly studious Couzens passed a second exam. Successfully completing high school, Couzens enrolled in the Canada Business College in Chatham for a two-year course in bookkeeping.

Yet Chatham was too confining for Couzens, and in 1890 he left for Detroit, obtaining a job as a car-checker for the Michigan Central Railroad. He remained in this position for three years, performing his work diligently. His good performance paid off in 1893, when he was promoted to manager of the yard's freight office, a position in which he was in contact with shippers from many industries. He demonstrated his loyalty to his employer by his refusal to buckle under to the complaints businessmen lodged regarding freight charges. "The way Jim Couzens talked with these patrons on the telephone, giving them holy hell, was just astounding," a colleague recalled. When a coal dealer, Alexander Y. Malcomson, one day protested the railroad rates, Couzens won the respect of the businessman by the manner in which he defended the railroad's policies. In 1895 Malcomson offered Couzens a job as a bookkeeper and general assistant for the Malcomson Fuel Company, at a salary of $75 per month. Couzens accepted, and with this advancement he made Detroit his permanent home. Two years later, in 1897, he became a naturalized citizen of the United States. The following year he married Margaret Manning, who came from a middle-class Detroit family.

For Couzens, these early years in Detroit as a rising executive and, before long, a young father, were to be the happiest of his life, but the most prosperous years were yet to come. In 1902 Malcomson entered into a financial partnership with the cash-strapped Henry Ford. At the time Ford had already endured two dismal failures in the automotive trade. His first effort, the Detroit Automobile Company, ended when Ford's financial backers became exasperated with his perfectionism and his resulting refusal to settle upon a marketable car. In November 1901 the Henry Ford Company was formed. But after a few months, when Ford again showed no signs of putting a car into production, his backers dismissed him. At this point, Malcomson, who knew Ford and as an automobile enthusiast had followed Ford's success in automobile racing, approached him about financing a third commercial venture. When a partnership agreement was signed on August 20, 1902, Couzens was placed in charge of keeping track of the expenditures incurred as Ford worked on the development of a car, using funds provided by Malcomson.

By the early part of 1903 enough progress had been made so that Malcomson and Ford, who had converted their partnership agreement into a corporation, went ahead with efforts to raise the funds needed to put a car into production by the sale of stock. Although Ford approached some potential investors, nearly all of those who did invest in the company were brought in through the efforts of Malcomson. One of them was James Couzens, who, although he knew nothing about cars, had become convinced that the proposed company had the potential to be a money-maker. The problem was that Couzens had only $400 in savings. His mother-in-law would have been willing to loan him money, but when he decided that would not be a wise move, he approached his father, who quickly rejected his son's appeal for money. Couzens's sister, Rosetta, a schoolteacher in Chatham, gave him $100, and then Malcomson advanced Couzens $500 from a bonus Couzens was due to receive and also agreed to accept his employee's promissory note for $1,500. Thus when the Ford Motor Company was incorporated on June 16, 1903, with a capitalization of $100,000, Couzens had a $2,500 interest in the new firm.

When the stockholders held their first meeting two days later, Henry Ford, who together with Malcomson had been awarded 51 percent of the stock, divided equally between the two men, was elected vice-president and general manager in charge of production. Malcomson did not receive the positions he had expected to receive. Instead of the post of president going to Malcomson it was given to John S. Gray, a Detroit banker and businessman who had invested $10,500 in the company—more than anyone else. Gray was also Malcomson's uncle and had helped his nephew secure the loan he needed to finance an expansion of his coal business the previous winter. Malcomson wanted to devote his full time to the automobile company, handling the business side while Ford supervised production. But Gray insisted that he concentrate on the coal company to make certain its bank loans were paid off. When Malcomson protested that Couzens could handle the coal business very capably, Gray responded: "If Couzens is so good, then you can send him to the automobile business. He can watch that for you." As a result, Couzens was named secretary and business manager, while Malcomson had to be satisfied with the less-important position of treasurer.

From 1903 until he resigned in 1915, James Couzens was at least as responsible for the success of the Ford Motor Company as Henry Ford himself. At various times other titles were added to those he had been given in 1903, but they simply reinforced the control he had been assigned over the business and financial side of the operations. For Alexander Malcomson this meant further frustration in his hopes of becoming the dominant force in the company. Instead of watching after Malcomson's interests, Couzens soon demonstrated that his loyalties were to the company, not to his former employer. When Malcomson, who was on the board of directors, attempted to remove Couzens as business manager and to take his place, only one other director supported him. Faced with opposition from both Ford and Couzens, Malcomson finally gave up in 1906, selling his stock to Ford, who thus gained control of a majority of the company's stock. Couzens took over the job of treasurer, previously held by Malcomson.

Although Ford, who also became president in 1906 upon the death of John Gray, now had the power to do whatever he wanted, he continued to rely heavily on Couzens. Their relations at the outset had been somewhat strained. In July 1903, when the first Ford models were ready to be shipped out, Ford discovered some problem which he said had to be corrected before the cars could be sold. Couzens, however, insisted that the cars must be sent on their way, regardless of defects. The company's cash reserves were practically exhausted, and unless money came in quickly from car sales Ford would be unable to pay its workers or its suppliers and would be forced out of business. Couzens had his way, the cars were shipped, and the resulting income had placed the company on solid financial ground, where it remained throughout his tenure with the firm.

Sales were one of Couzens's responsibilities, and even when a separate sales manager was appointed the position remained under his supervision. At the outset he was busy lining up dealers, including such big names as John Wanamaker, the department store magnate, who for a time had the franchise to sell Fords in New York and Philadelphia.

Innovation, however, would be the hallmark of Couzens's sales strategy. Key regions were staffed not by independent agents but by salaried employees, giving Couzens greater control over operations. To provide the incentive lost in this novel arrangement, Couzens paid top salaries and instituted a then-unique bonus system, arranging a cash reward for managers whose sales topped certain figures. Despite his creativity in managing sales, Couzens was an extremely cautious financial administrator. Setting the company's credit policy, he was adamant that any proposed expansion be paid out of profits rather than through borrowing.

This financial conservatism was matched by exacting professional conduct. Cold and aloof, Couzens spent his workdays, often 18 hours long, immersed in detail. Determined that contracts entered into by Ford were to be carried out completely, he demanded the same performance of other contract parties. Ford employees suspected of engaging in anything but sober, meticulous work quickly learned about Couzens's infamous temper. When one branch manager wrote to Couzens requesting a large bonus, Couzens tartly replied: "I had put you down for $21,000. . . . Your letter has cost you $5,000, because it showed that you did not trust me to treat you fairly. I have now put you down for $16,000."

Couzens also handled Ford's advertising, writing the copy for the first Ford ads and continuing to keep a close eye on this aspect of the business after advertising managers were hired in 1907. In addition to emphasizing supposedly superior qualities that made the company's cars such a good buy, Couzens's advertisements kept the spotlight on Henry Ford, who was referred to as America's foremost automotive designer. For more than a decade Couzens continued to make this the central theme in the company's advertising. When Hudson advertisements for its 1912 models featured the company's chief engineer, Howard E. Coffin, whom the company hailed as the leading automotive designer, Couzens wrote to Hudson's president, Roy D. Chapin, demanding a retraction, arguing that everyone acknowledged Ford to be the automotive design leader. Chapin's response that this was "a matter of opinion" touched off a spirited exchange that reflected the importance Couzens attached to maintaining the preeminence of Henry Ford among automotive figures.

Many automotive companies in this period followed a similar strategy in crediting their success to the efforts of one person. But Couzens saw this strategy as a way of fighting the suit brought against the company in fall 1903 for infringing on the rights of those who controlled the patent awarded to George B. Selden in 1895. The Selden patent claimed to cover all gasoline-propelled cars, thereby making any company manufacturing such cars without a license from the Selden patent holders subject to legal action. Ford had applied for a license from the Association of Licensed Automobile Manufacturers (ALAM) when the company was being organized, but the application was turned down for reasons that are still unclear. Couzens was adamant that they should go ahead with the production of cars regardless of the legal consequences. When the ALAM published advertisements warning that anyone who sold or purchased unlicensed cars would be subject to prosecution, Couzens countered with ads that promised to protect from any lawsuit those who sold or bought Fords. To buttress the company's case, the ads asserted that Ford had built his first gasoline car in 1893, two years before the issuance of the Selden patent, and that "Our Mr. Ford made the first Gasoline Automobile in Detroit and the third in the United States." All three assertions were incorrect but even if Couzens knew this, and it is possible he did not, he probably viewed it as a justifiable tactic in combating the efforts of the ALAM, or "The Trust," as he called it. By directly challenging the Selden forces rather than simply ignoring them as did other unlicensed producers, Couzens left the ALAM no choice but to file a suit against the Ford company. Otherwise, the ALAM and the Selden patent would become a laughingstock in the industry. Henry Ford benefited enormously by the company's victory in 1911, but Couzens, David Lewis contends, "perhaps deserves equal credit with Ford in pressing the Selden suit to a victorious conclusion."

Couzens was in fact if not in name Henry Ford's partner during the early years of the company. He was a junior partner, to be sure, but one whose authority was far more independent from the control of Ford than would be true of officials in later years when Ford demanded complete subservience. Couzens's special status was most clearly demonstrated when he appeared with Ford in the negotiations between 1907 and 1909 that proposed the merger of Ford with several other automakers.

Notes Couzens kept in his journal for 1907 provide detailed information on the proposed merger of Ford with Buick, Reo, and Maxwell-Briscoe. When meetings were held in the first half of 1908 to discuss the merger, Couzens accompanied Ford, but there is no mention that anyone but William C. Durant of Buick, Ransom Olds of Reo, and Benjamin Briscoe of Maxwell-Briscoe represented those companies in the talks. There is some evidence that Ford had become bored by the routine of running an established company. On one occasion he told Couzens that perhaps he should step down and turn the presidency over to Couzens. He may well have been looking to retire from the business, but in a way that would have generated cash. When it became clear in the talks that Durant and Briscoe had in mind an exchange of stock with very little money involved, there is some evidence that it was Couzens who spoke up and indicated that the Ford company would have to be given at least $3 million in addition to stock to become part of the consolidated firm. Other reports have Ford making this demand, which, when Ransom Olds proceeded to ask for a similar amount for control of Reo, brought an end to these merger talks.

Both Durant and Briscoe went on to pursue new merger ideas, and both tried in fall 1909 to draw Ford into their companies. Durant had created General Motors (GM) in September 1908, and a year later, when he broached the subject of a merger to Couzens, he was advised that Ford might agree to a new offer to acquire his company. The Ford Motor Company had just lost the first round in the Selden patent case, and Ford's discouragement at this defeat left him open to a suggested merger. Durant went to New York on October 5, 1909, and held negotiations with Couzens. Ford was described by Couzens as "sick in body and disturbed in mind," and he left it up to the business manager to handle the face-to-face talks with Durant. In the plan that Couzens worked out with Durant, the company was to be sold for $8 million. Henry Ford would retire from the business, but Couzens planned to acquire 25 percent of the Ford stock and remain actively involved in managing the company when it came under the control of GM.

When Couzens brought the details of the plan to Ford's room, he found him lying on the floor seeking relief from an attack of lumbago. When Couzens told him of Durant's offer of $8 million for the company, Ford said, "All right. But—*gold on the table*!" "How do you mean that?" Couzens asked. "I mean cash," Ford replied.

GM board minutes indicate that Durant received an option on October 5 to buy all the Ford stock for $8 million with a down payment of $2 million in cash and the remainder to be paid over two years. It is not clear if the plan to allow Couzens to increase his Ford stock ownership and to remain with the company was a part of this agreement. On October 24 Ford and Couzens took Durant on a secret Sunday tour of the company's Detroit plant and checked the company's inventory. However, although GM directors two days later formally approved the purchase agreement, the New York bankers to whom Durant went to get the needed funds turned down the loan request, and he, for a second time, lost the chance to gain control of Ford.

Couzens again represented Ford when the company was approached by Benjamin Briscoe, who sought to make Ford part of his proposed United States Motor consolidation. As in Durant's case, Couzens told Briscoe's representative that $8 million would be an acceptable figure, but he said, skeptically, "Let's see the color of your money." As Couzens may have suspected, Briscoe was unable to raise the money, and the merger fell through. Rumors that Ford would be or had been part of a merger continued to circulate, however, until Couzens in September 1910 issued a statement that the company had "no intention of . . . being connected with any combination."

By this time Couzens had become a wealthy man. His starting salary of $200 a month had by 1906 been increased to $10,000 a year plus a bonus for every car sold. Meanwhile, the dividends the company paid its shareholders had quickly enabled Couzens to pay off the $1,500 note he had given as part payment for his original stock and had also enabled him to increase his holdings until his approximately 11 percent of the stock was second only to that of Henry Ford.

In 1904 Couzens moved his growing family into a new home in Detroit, and six years later they moved into a still-larger Detroit home while also acquiring a farm in Bloomfield Hills, a community that soon became the fashionable address for younger Detroit automotive executives. Couzens's rising economic status was matched by a newfound social and corporate prominence. He was received as a member of the prestigious Detroit Club and the Detroit Athletic Club and became active in the Detroit Chamber of Commerce, being elected president of that organization in 1913.

But his increasing wealth did not entirely satisfy Couzens. Partly this was due to the workaholic's disdain for leisure. But it also resulted from his growing social consciousness. Couzens had been deeply influenced in the 1890s by the legendary Detroit reform mayor, Hazen S. Pingree, who had expanded the city's social and welfare services. Although Couzens had buried his admiration for Pingree in his striving for economic advancement, the ideal of public service remained within him. In 1913, at the age of forty-one, Couzens, now a multimillionaire, came to the realization that his life's activities were not personally fulfilling now that his material well-being was assured. Looking back on this period, Couzens reflected that "I seemed to have no interest in life for a while. I had achieved what I started out to do." In July 1913 he tendered his resignation from the Ford Motor Company, yet he remained with the company when he was offered the chairmanship of the Detroit Street Railway Commission, recently created by the city. Municipal control of streetcar lines had been an elusive goal of Pingree's, and Couzens jumped at this chance for part-time public service, thinking he could find personal fulfillment while remaining with Ford.

His social awareness, however, had changed his attitude toward company affairs. He began to view the company as a social instrument, a vehicle for solving "the labor problem." He increasingly objected to the exploitation of workers through sweatshop conditions and low wages. To ensure greater job security he stripped foremen of the power to fire workers and insisted that workers could not be fired until they had been tried out in other departments. Also, the working day was cut from ten hours to nine. In January 1914 it was Couzens who successfully pressed Ford to institute the famous $5 daily wage for his workers, an increase of more than $2.50, although in typical Couzens fashion the credit for the wage increase was publicly bestowed on Ford.

To Couzens's increasing social awareness was added, after the summer of 1914, bitter disagreement with Henry Ford over the proper relationship of the United States to the war in Europe. Ford, immediately upon the outbreak of the conflict, issued statements denouncing the war and declaring that his factory would never produce war materiel. By

*Couzens with Henry Ford in 1915, the year Couzens left the Ford Motor Company
(courtesy of the Henry Ford Museum, Dearborn, Michigan)*

this time Couzens was serving as vice-president, treasurer, and general manager of the company, from which he exercised a veto power over virtually all of the firm's operations—including the contents of the company organ, the *Ford Times*. Scrutinizing the page proofs of the magazine on October 11, 1915, Couzens read an article which referred to Henry Ford's opposition to the government's preparedness program. The next morning Couzens informed Ford that he had withheld the article on the grounds that the views expressed were personal and not those of the company. In fact, Couzens vehemently disagreed with Ford's isolationist worldview and was an ardent supporter of American rearmament. Ford was furious with the decision, and in his anger told Couzens to print the article or resign. "Well, then," Couzens replied, "I will quit."

Couzens's resignation probably was welcomed by both men. Ford had reached the stage in his career when he no longer was willing to share authority in the company. "The friendly relations that have existed between us for years have been changed of late," Couzens declared in a statement is-

sued to the press, "our disagreements daily becoming more violent." Couzens declared that it "was through my efforts that the Ford Motor Company was built up around one man—Henry Ford. I have never in my life worked for any man. . . . I will be willing to work with Henry Ford, but I refuse to work for him." Thus, he explained, he had felt compelled to resign. Ford issued a brief statement, declaring that it was Couzens's privilege to explain the reasons behind his resignation. "Mr. Couzens' resignation was not entirely unexpected. I have seen that there was a possibility of it for a week, or more."

Couzens retained his stock in the Ford Motor Company and also his seat on the board of directors, but after his departure Henry Ford was the only stockholder involved in the day-to-day administering of the company. In 1919 Ford, angered by action taken by John and Horace Dodge, who retained their Ford stock but also started their own automobile company, decided to eliminate the minority stockholders entirely. Working through emissaries, he bought their stock, with Couzens receiving $29,308,858 more per share than other stockholders. For the $100 his sister Rosetta had given him, which he had converted into stock in her name, she received $260,000 (her stock had already earned her $95,000 in dividends since 1903).

The paths of Couzens and Henry Ford crossed on occasion thereafter in ways that caused public notice. In 1923, when there was a grass-roots movement promoting Henry Ford for president, Couzens helped torpedo the idea by declaring that the notion of Ford in the White House was "ridiculous." In 1933 Couzens and Ford again clashed over the issue of federal aid to failing Detroit banks. The positions of both men were the result of misunderstandings of the other's views. Both were essentially in agreement that such assistance at that time was unwarranted. However, despite such disagreements, the two continued to have respect for one another. Couzens told the Detroit Republican Club on one occasion, "I never loved a man and thought so much of a man in his place as I do Henry Ford. . . .There never was a man who was kinder and more thoughtful and respectful to me than Henry Ford." On Ford's part his feelings for his one-time partner were revealed when he served as a pallbearer at Couzens's funeral in 1936.

When Couzens resigned as Ford's business manager in 1915, he was worth anywhere from $40 million to $60 million. Recognized as alert and energetic, it was inconceivable that he would simply retire. In addition to remaining as a director of Ford until 1919, he also retained the presidency of a bank in Highland Park that he had helped found. Yet his interest was focused on public affairs. In September 1916 Detroit Mayor Oscar B. Marx, engaged in a tight reelection struggle and desperate to surround himself with prominent and respected individuals, appointed Couzens to serve as police commissioner. Accepting the offer, Couzens's service won him widespread praise. Attempting to master his new professional environment, Couzens vowed to conduct a personal study of police conditions in Detroit. Not revealing his identity, he personally walked the streets talking to policemen, bartenders, and virtually anyone else with an opinion on crime. Shocked at the extent of lawlessness in his home city, he issued an ultimatum that all police officers were to enforce the laws even when off duty. His striving to build a "disciplined city" sometimes led him to conflict with other officials. His relations with local politicians, including the reelected Mayor

Marx, were strained. Early in 1918 Couzens left Detroit for Washington, D.C., to serve as head of a motor-truck division within the War Department.

By the spring of that year Couzens had tentatively decided to enter national affairs by running for the seat of retiring Michigan senator William Alden Smith. Couzens had been on the periphery of the Republican party for several years, including serving as an elector for Charles Evans Hughes in the presidential election of 1916. Yet the announcement that Henry Ford would be a senatorial candidate caused Couzens to reconsider, and he once again set his sights on local issues in Detroit. In late spring Couzens announced that he would run for mayor of his adopted hometown. In the November elections he swept to victory—as Ford, running as a Democrat, went down to defeat.

As mayor, Couzens, taking advantage of a city charter granting large amounts of authority to the Detroit executive, wielded power with little subtlety. He even took to sending the police department every morning a list of the license numbers of automobiles he had observed breaking traffic laws on his way to work. Despite his occasional eccentricities, Couzens was credited with restoring sound management to city administration, and restoring a sense of professionalism in government service. By far his greatest accomplishment was in 1922, when he successfully persuaded voters to approve the purchase of streetcar lines.

Couzens's attention was suddenly redirected toward national politics on November 29, 1922, when he received a telephone call from Michigan governor Alex Groesbeck, appointing him to the U.S. Senate, to replace Senator Truman Newberry, who had resigned 11 days earlier. Ironically, Couzens thus took the senatorial position Ford had sought in 1918, since it was Newberry who had defeated Ford in that election.

Within a week of taking his seat in the Senate, Couzens earned the stamp of Republican insurgent. He voted against a subsidy of private merchant ships—a measure President Harding had made a personal appearance before Congress to promote. Progressive Senate leaders Robert La Follette, Sr., and George Norris revealed the proximity of Couzens's view to their own by supporting him for chairman of the Senate Committee on Interstate Commerce, despite Couzens's lowly first-term status. Much of their respect for the freshman senator centered on Couzens's proud independence. Such independence was prominently displayed when Harding appointed James G. McNary to the office of comptroller of the currency. Like Couzens, McNary had served as a bank president; unlike Couzens, McNary had frequently borrowed bank funds for his personal use. Appalled by the appointment, Couzens went to the White House to demand that Harding rescind. The president, however, was furious that Couzens had made public his findings on McNary's background. The senator remained adamant and threatened to pursue a one-man filibuster unless McNary's name was withdrawn. Harding relented and submitted another name for nomination.

This incident created nationwide attention for the new legislator, and his name was instantly associated with insurgency and progressivism. To one reporter Couzens said, "I'm radical as hell when I see an evil that ought to be ended."

Perhaps the most significant battle of his senate career involved the efforts of Treasury Secretary Andrew Mellon to cut taxes for the wealthy. In December 1923 Couzens, who had expressed a degree of sympathy for the idea in earlier speeches, wrote the secretary seeking a rationale for the cuts. In his letter he noted the frequently cited reasons: high rates were stifling business activity; the government would collect more revenue—not less—from lowered rates; and high taxes were driving funds into tax-exempt securities rather than into capital investment. Mellon's reply noted that Couzens's own considerable fortune was invested in tax-exempt securities, thus sheltering the senator from income tax. Couzens was enraged. In a return letter he demanded to know Mellon's net worth, and to what extent the treasury secretary would benefit by his proposed tax reduction.

In February 1924 Couzens, seeking to discredit Mellon, introduced a resolution calling for an investigation of the Bureau of Internal Revenue, an arm of the Treasury Department. Passed by a coalition of Republicans and Democrats, the investigation obtained from the bureau its files on 38 corporations in which Mellon was, or had been, financially interested. Several of these firms, it was learned, had received large tax rebates. Mellon argued that the rebates were merely routine and professed not to be concerned. Yet Mellon surely wanted Couzens out of the Senate. In 1925 President Calvin Coolidge offered Couzens the position of ambassador to the Court of St. James's. Couzens coolly refused. Still, Mellon had other resources.

On March 5, 1925, the Treasury Department brought a tax action against Couzens charging that he had underpaid approximately $10 million in taxes on the sale of his Ford Motor Company stock in 1919. Other former Ford stockholders were included in the suit, but there seemed little question that Couzens was the chief target. After three years of court battles the matter was dropped when the government's own files revealed that Couzens had not paid too little income tax; he had in fact paid too much and was entitled to a $900,000 refund.

During the lengthy fight over this case, Couzens had promised that if he won he would donate the $10 million in question to charity. In 1929 he used the money, along with $1,880,700 added in 1934, to establish a fund to "promote the health, welfare, happiness, and development of the children of the state of Michigan." Not anxious for external monuments to his generosity, he stipulated that all the money must be spent within 25 years after the date of the fund's establishment. Further, he refused to call the fund the "Couzens Foundation" or to otherwise call attention to his role in establishing it. Instead, it was called simply the Children's Fund. Although it was the best known of his philanthropies, by the time of his death in 1936 the total of his philanthropic contributions had reached about $30 million—or slightly more than the amount he had received in 1919 in the sale of his Ford stock.

In 1924 Couzens faced election for the first time, and his prospects—given his progressive record—did not seem particularly bright. Politically powerful organizations eagerly lined up to oppose him: the Anti-Saloon League; the Chamber of Commerce; the manufacturers associations; and (because his wife was a Catholic) the Ku Klux Klan. Conservative Michigan Republicans rallied behind Hal Smith, an attorney for the Michigan Manufacturers Association (he later withdrew from the race), and federal judge Arthur J. Tuttle. Yet it was not strictly Couzens's voting record that was at the center of his bid for the GOP nomination. Rather, it was his refusal to disavow the presidential candidacy of Robert La Follette, running as a Progressive. Under pressure from Michigan newspaper editors (including his friend, the conservative Grand Rapids editor Arthur Vandenburg) to denounce La Follette, Couzens would only say that he personally would vote for Coolidge. This was not sufficient for stalwart GOP leaders; yet in the primary election Couzens–boosted by many Democrats who crossed over into the Republican primary to vote for him–coasted to a comfortable victory. In the November election he received the support of La Follette Progressives, Socialists, many Democrats, and conservative Republicans who had no other choice. With this support he easily won election to his first full term.

Also elected for his first full term in 1924 was Calvin Coolidge. For the next four years Couzens was to be a particularly bitter opponent of the conservative president. The animosity erupted almost immediately after the election, when Coolidge appointed Charles B. Warren of Detroit as attorney general. Warren, a major contributor to the GOP, had been associated as a lawyer and stockholder with a large sugar company prosecuted under the antitrust laws. He was under indictment in the antitrust suit, which was still pending as Warren's name was sent to Capitol Hill. Critics noted that Warren, if confirmed, conceivably could dispose of his own antitrust case. As a Michigan senator, however, Couzens was under severe pressure to support the nomination. Nevertheless he announced his opposition and led the senate fight against Warren. After one close vote rejecting the nomination, Coolidge angrily submitted the name again only to see it disapproved a second time by a larger margin. Throughout the years 1924-1928 Couzens fought Coolidge's efforts to block salary increases for postal employees, criticized the administration's ouster of General "Billy" Mitchell from the Army, and expressed contempt for the State Department for its refusal to allow a British Communist to visit the United States.

The compassion that prompted Couzens's philanthropy was evident during the Depression. For years the former businessman had warned that the wild financial speculation of the 1920s carried with it the danger of a stock market crash. Four months before the crash occurred, Couzens bitterly criticized the Federal Reserve Board for encouraging speculation, which he vigorously insisted would only lead to disaster. After the crash the senator fixed the blame squarely on businessmen who had paid inadequate wages while constructing paper fortunes. In the face of the Depression Couzens demanded that the unemployed be given immediate relief. In summer 1931 Couzens, having handily won reelection the year before, joined with a group of senators urging President Hoover to call a spe-

cial session of Congress to enact legislation allowing federal relief funds to be distributed by municipal governments. Couzens was acting with the knowledge that Mayor Frank Murphy of Detroit had warned him that Detroit would require an additional $10 million to provide relief through the winter. When Hoover rejected the proposal, Couzens announced that he personally would contribute $1 million for Detroit's relief rolls, if other wealthy residents of the city would contribute an additional $9 million. However, this sum could not be raised. Also in summer 1931 Couzens called for a massive government program to construct libraries, museums, highways, bridges, and other public assets in an effort to combat unemployment, even if the program would triple the national debt. President Hoover rejected the proposal out of hand.

Couzens had by this time already incurred the wrath of the president by frequently identifying himself with the president's legislative opposition. Their first break occurred over Couzens's support for a government-run power facility at Muscle Shoals, Alabama. Hoover, in his first message to Congress, criticized the idea. Later disputes with the administration included Hoover's opposition to the early payment of veterans' bonuses. During the 1932 presidential election Couzens refused to publicly support Hoover and was pleased at the victory of the New York governor Franklin Roosevelt.

Yet as a notoriously independent senator Couzens did not always agree with the new president. Early in the new administration Couzens expressed exasperation at FDR's Economy Bill of 1933, which proposed reducing, among other things, veterans' benefits. Couzens, remembering the bitter conflict between Hoover and the Bonus Army, saw the act as evidence that the Old Guard Wall Street interests were still in control. Taking to the Senate floor in a futile effort to stop the measure, Couzens delivered one of the longest speeches of his career. Yet the New Deal proved to be largely suited to Couzens's vision of an activist, centralist government. Years earlier the Michigan senator had proposed a federal program for young men, which would give them housing on available army bases while the government provided them with work aimed at environmental conservation. Thus Couzens was delighted with FDR's Civilian Conservation Corps, which closely followed the Couzens proposal. He was equally pleased when the president–like Couzens years before–called for the repeal of the Volstead Act, which enforced the prohibition amendment, and advocated new banking laws, such as the compulsory separation of investment activities from commercial banking. Couzens was especially pleased when the president called for the creation of the Tennessee Valley Authority, thus establishing the public-power project at Muscle Shoals that Couzens had advocated for years. Still, the senator did not automatically approve of all New Deal measures. For example, Couzens was convinced that public housing was less a subsidy for the needy than a handout to private contractors, and he voted against the bill establishing the United States Housing Authority. His occasional opposition to FDR did not always stem from conservative impulses: he criticized the Works Progress Administration (WPA) for paying its employees wages that the senator believed were wholly inadequate; Couzens successfully pressed for an amendment to the WPA appropriations to increase wage rates.

Generally, though, Couzens took pride in being associated with the New Deal. But support for a Democratic president presented him with obvious difficulties as he approached reelection in 1936. As he had refused to push for the reelection of President Hoover in 1932, so now he defied pleas from his supporters that he campaign against Roosevelt in 1936. In the Michigan Republican senatorial primary, this refusal clearly endangered his chances for renomination. In his two previous bids for renomination he had been supported by Democrats who had crossed over to vote for him in the GOP primary; yet the state's Democratic party had recently experienced a surge of growth, and it was expected that there would be little cross-party voting in 1936. One potential solution was for Couzens to switch parties and run as a Democrat. Former Detroit mayor Frank Murphy and other leading state Democrats urged him to do so. After toying with the idea for some months Couzens announced he would remain a Republican. To do otherwise, he believed, would be to open himself to charges that he had abandoned his party. His decision resulted in a heated primary contest. Wilbur J. Brucker, a former governor and later secretary of the army in the Eisenhower administration, announced that he would be a candidate for the GOP senatorial nomination, and the state party organization quickly rallied around him.

Despite the challenge Couzens remained virtually inactive in the primary campaign. He had never

taken the time to build a grass roots political organization. Being bitterly opposed to the practice of patronage, moreover, he was bereft of support among prominent state officials and party professionals. This was worsened by his refusal to embark on a speaking tour of the state, largely because he was barraged during personal appearances with questions about which presidential candidate he supported. When he finally announced publicly what had been obvious for some time, that he favored FDR's reelection, he was inundated with criticism by state party loyalists. Couzens was aware that he was committing political suicide and expressed neither surprise nor regret when the primary results were tabulated. In a landslide victory, Brucker had garnered 328,560 votes to Couzens's 199,204.

Days after the primary, Roosevelt wrote Couzens to express his regret over the senator's defeat. He also asked Couzens to accept the chairmanship of the newly created Maritime Commission. Although intrigued with the offer, Couzens hesitated. He did not have experience in shipping matters and was reluctant to be dependent on lower-level commission experts. He promised that he would inform Roosevelt of his decision after the November election.

Yet Couzens's health, slowly failing for years, took a turn for the worse one month after his defeat in the senatorial primary. On September 18, while working at his office in Birmingham, he felt weak and feverish and went home to bed. Five days later he was admitted to Detroit's Harper Hospital for jaundice and diabetes. Despite his weak health, Couzens refused to remain hospitalized and left one week later. On October 14, however, he was again hospitalized for a stomach disorder. Yet the next day he insisted on a strenuous day of campaigning in Detroit for Roosevelt. Readmitted to the hospital the following day, his condition deteriorated rapidly following an operation for uremic poisoning. He died on October 22, 1936, and was buried in Detroit's Woodlawn Cemetery. He was survived by his wife and four of their six children.

Harry Barnard, author of the one full-scale biography of Couzens, aptly titled it *Independent Man.* From his youth, when he refused to be called James Couzens, Jr., his life had been a constant demonstration of his determination to be his own man, no matter what the cost. In politics his independence ultimately led to his rejection by the party with which he was nominally affiliated, but not before he amassed an extensive record of accomplishments. In business, his refusal to take orders from Henry Ford caused his resignation from the Ford Motor Company, but only after his more than 12 years of brilliant service enabled that company to survive at a time when many others were succumbing to the fierce competition of an emerging industry.

References:

Harry Barnard, *Independent Man: The Life of Senator James Couzens* (New York: Scribners, 1958);

David L. Lewis, *The Public Image of Henry Ford: An American Folk Hero and His Company* (Detroit: Wayne State University Press, 1976);

George S. May, *A Most Unique Machine: The Michigan Origins of the American Automobile Industry* (Grand Rapids, Mich.: Eerdmans, 1975);

Allan Nevins and Frank Ernest Hill, *Ford: The Times, The Man, The Company* (New York: Scribners, 1954);

William Adams Simonds, *Henry Ford: His Life, His Work, His Genius* (Indianapolis: Bobbs-Merrill, 1943);

Keith Sward, *The Legend of Henry Ford* (New York: Rinehart, 1948).

Archives:

The papers of James Couzens are in the Manuscript Division of the Library of Congress, Washington, D.C. In addition, a vast amount of material relating to Couzens's service with the Ford Motor Company is found in the Ford Archives in the Henry Ford Museum, Dearborn, Michigan.

Dana Corporation

by David J. Andrea

University of Michigan

The Dana Corporation, an international company, supplies the automotive and on- and off-road heavy truck industries in the original equipment and replacement markets. Dana also serves the industrial equipment and financial services markets. Its principal products are organized into five major groups: drivetrain systems, engine parts, chassis products, fluid power systems, and industrial power transmission products.

The company originated as the Spicer Manufacturing Company in 1904. Founded by Clarence Spicer, the inventor of the first practical motor vehicle universal joint and driveshaft, the company provided the infant U.S. automotive industry with innovative power transmission solutions. Early motor vehicles were conceived by combining existing transportation methods (horse carriages and bicycles) to mobile power sources (internal combustion or steam engines and electric storage batteries). Many early vehicles used bicycle chains to transmit engine power to the drive wheels. Chains broke easily in the harsh operating conditions of early motoring. Solid drive shafts, more durable than chains, did not offer enough flexibility to power drive wheels moving up and down on rough roads.

Spicer's universal joint invention provided needed flexibility and durability.

Like many automotive suppliers of this era, the founder of Spicer Manufacturing had mechanical flair but not a particularly keen interest in business. As the automobile industry grew, Spicer Manufacturing's business activities quickly expanded beyond the financial and planning abilities of Spicer. In 1914 Charles Dana, a Toledo, Ohio, lawyer, politician, and businessman, took control of Spicer Manufacturing. Renamed in 1946 the Dana Corporation, the company recognized Mr. Dana's contribution and its expansion into other mechanical components.

Known for a commitment to superior human relations and customer satisfaction, Dana's organization, policies, and strategic planning process are often studied by American business school students. The company prides itself on "The Dana Style," the beliefs of Dana employees. The current corporate philosophy that people are Dana's most important asset stems from Charles Dana's leadership. Mr. Dana initiated this core principle by stating: "The one thing really worthwhile about an organization is its men and women. No one knows better than I the value of advice direct from the workman." This belief forms the basis of Dana's corporate culture.

Vehicle manufacturers view Dana as an innovative supplier providing design, engineering, and manufacturing expertise. The Toledo, Ohio, firm has grown to be in 1988 a $5 billion enterprise employing 40,000 people. It operates approximately 470 facilities in 26 countries. A responsive supplier, Dana restructured its organization in 1983 and 1988 to meet changing customer needs. Built from the company's original universal and driveshaft products, Dana is a worldwide leader in transmission and engine components, chassis and suspension parts, and hydraulic control equipment. Beginning

in the 1970s Dana diversified into financial services operating personal and corporate savings and loan institutions, leasing and corporate finance activities, and real estate development.

References:

Dana Corporation 1987 Annual Report (Toledo, Ohio: Dana Corporation, 1988);

Dana Corporation 1988 Annual Report (Toledo, Ohio: Dana Corporation, 1989);

The Dana Style (Toledo, Ohio: Dana Corporation, 1987);

Products, Systems, and Services (Toledo, Ohio: Dana Corporation, 1987).

George H. Day

(April 3, 1851-November 21, 1907)

by James Wren

Motor Vehicle Manufacturers Association

CAREER: Clerk, Charter Oak Life Insurance Company (1870-1877); secretary, vice-president, president, Weed Sewing Machine Company (1877-1890); vice-president and general manager, Pope Manufacturing Company (1890-1899); president, Columbia & Electric Vehicle Company (1899-1900); president, Electric Vehicle Company (1900-1907); president, Association of Licensed Automobile Manufacturers (1903-1907).

George Herbert Day, president of the Electric Vehicle Company when that group sought to license car producers under the terms of the Selden internal combustion engine patent, was born on April 3, 1851, in Brooklyn, Connecticut, the son of fourth-generation residents of the area. He received his education in the public schools of his village and beginning in 1869 at Hobart College in Geneva, New York. About a year later he left college to take a clerk's position at the Charter Oak Life Insurance Company in Hartford.

In 1877 Day left the insurance job to join the administration of the Weed Sewing Machine Company. He married Katherine Beach, daughter of the Weed company's president, J. Watson Beach, that same year. Within two years Day accepted the posi-

George H. Day

tion of vice-president of the company. As vice-president he arranged for his firm to build an experimental bicycle for Albert A. Pope, later esteemed as the "father of the American bicycle." The company's work impressed Pope, and he licensed it to produce the model for sale by his firm, the Pope Manufacturing Company. Under Day's direction Weed shifted quickly to bicycle production, in the process demonstrating the adaptability of techniques of mass manufacture. Soon Day assumed the Weed firm's presidency. He became Pope's trusted colleague, and the bicycles, especially the Columbia safety and chainless model, attained leadership in the industry.

In 1890 the Pope Manufacturing Company absorbed the Weed Sewing Machine Company, and Day became vice-president and general manager of the enlarged organization. By then the Pope company had formed subsidiaries to make tires, steel tubing, and small parts and had become Hartford's leading industrial firm. Eventually the firm moved into automobile production. In 1895 Day learned that a Pope official had rebuffed the suggestion of Hiram P. Maxim, factory superintendent of the American Projectile Company of Lynn, Massachusetts, that Pope manufacture a gasoline-powered tricycle of his design (on the grounds that a motorized vehicle offered no calisthenic benefit to the user). After receiving favorable reports of Maxim's work, Day invited him to become engineer for a new Pope motor carriage department, and Maxim set to work.

Maxim soon realized that Day and other Pope officials lacked enthusiasm for gasoline power, the medium Maxim favored. Even after Maxim constructed an improved gasoline car in 1898, Day remained unimpressed, believing that the electric would eventually dominate. The company had tested its first electric six months earlier, and after that the designers, except Maxim and a few others, directed most of their attention in that direction. In 1897-1898 Pope produced some 500 automobiles, most of them electrics.

The decision of the Pope company to concentrate on the production of electric vehicles was partially bound up in the patent controversies of the time. William Greenleaf states that "between 1895 and 1899 no other American company was so well posted as the Pope firm on developments in the automotive art." Initially only a minority in the Pope company believed the patent George B. Selden received in 1895 for a "road engine" he designed in 1879 could exert a restraining effect on the gaso-

line segment of the industry. Then, in 1899, during negotiations between William C. Whitney and Albert Pope arranging the purchase of the automotive assets of the Pope firm by Whitney's organization, the Electric Vehicle Company, Whitney asked if any of the company's potential products violated existing patents and if a patent existed that presented the opportunity to achieve control of a part of the industry. When Whitney found out that the Selden patent could be construed as having a basic character (in terms of gasoline engine production only) and that certain financiers had already approached Selden about a sale, he made control of the patent a contingency for his firm's purchase of Pope.

The Pope-Whitney automotive holdings were incorporated as the Columbia Automobile Company in April 1899, and Day became vice-president of the new firm. A few weeks later it was consolidated with the other Whitney holdings to become the Columbia & Electric Vehicle Company, and Day assumed the presidency. The Electric Vehicle Company continued to exist as a public transportation concern, and it contracted to purchase the entire output of Columbia & Electric. Selden granted Columbia & Electric exclusive license to his patent on November 4, 1899. In June 1900 Columbia & Electric merged into the Electric Vehicle Company, and the latter took control over the patent.

Soon the error in the decision to concentrate on electric vehicle production appeared obvious. Before the end of 1900 Electric Vehicle Company fell under debt pressure and stockholders' accusations of mismanagement. So the company decided to use the Selden patent to compel royalty payments on every gasoline car made and started filing infringement suits in court, including an action against the Winton Motor Carriage Company of Cleveland, a leading gasoline car manufacturer of the day. The threatened gasoline firms formed an association, the Hydro-Carbon Motor Vehicle Manufacturers' Association, to fight back. Litigation dragged on. The Electric Vehicle Company won a significant tactical victory against Winton in 1901, but Day doubted the patent could withstand continued assault.

Meanwhile engineers made improvements in gasoline engine technology, and manufacturers tried to dilute the influence of the Electric Vehicle Company. Two of them, Henry Joy of Packard and Fred Smith of Olds Motor Works, proposed to Day the creation of an association of manufacturers licensed to make gasoline cars under the Selden patent. By then the Electric Vehicle Company had almost ceased production, and Day saw that gasoline was the fuel of the future. A series of organizational meetings held in late 1902 and early 1903 brought the Association of Licensed Automobile Manufacturers (ALAM) into existence. Day was named president of the group. The ALAM continued the fight for control of the auto industry through the Selden patent and also helped rationalize the industry, by restrict-

ing manufacture to "reputable" firms and standardizing parts. Day served in the association until he died suddenly of a heart attack on November 21, 1907. He left his wife, five children, and a legacy of industrial achievement and advocacy.

Reference:

William Greenleaf, *Monopoly on Wheels: Henry Ford and the Selden Automobile Patent* (Detroit: Wayne State University Press, 1961).

Delco

by George S. May

Eastern Michigan University

One of the most familiar of all auto parts names, Delco is an acronym derived from the name of a company founded in 1909 by Charles F. Kettering and Edward A. Deeds, the Dayton Engineering Laboratories Company. Kettering, who had degrees in electrical and mechanical engineering from Ohio State University, had been head of research at Dayton's National Cash Register Company, developing many devices that improved the performance of cash registers. He resigned from the company in 1909 and, together with Deeds, who had been the works manager at National Cash Register, established the company that a few years later would be officially renamed Delco.

Originally a research and experimental operation where Kettering turned his inventive talents to developing improved electrical equipment for automobiles, Delco also became a manufacturer in order to meet the demand for the electric self-starter, Kettering's most famous invention, which was introduced in the 1912 Cadillacs. Delco's starters and its other electrical equipment were available to any auto manufacturer who wanted to use them. There was always the possibility, therefore, that the demand at any time might exceed the company's supply, leaving one or more customers short of a part and causing delays in production. Thus in 1916, when William C. Durant regained control of General Motors (GM), he moved to make certain that GM's car producing units would have first call on

the output of Delco and certain other parts manufacturers.

In May of that year Durant formed the United Motors Corporation, pulling five companies together into one organization. One, the Perlman Rim Corporation of Jackson, Michigan, produced wheels. Two others, the Hyatt Roller Bearing Company of Newark and the New Departure Manufacturing Company of Bristol, Connecticut, produced bearings. The other two were the Remy Electric Company of Anderson, Indiana, and Delco, both producers of electrical equipment. Durant acquired Delco by paying Kettering and Deeds $5 million in cash and $3 million in United Motors stock.

Two years later, in June 1918, United Motors was absorbed by GM, largely through an exchange of stock. That brought Delco into the GM organization, and a year later the corporation also acquired several other Dayton companies Kettering had formed, including his Domestic Engineering Company, producers of a home-lighting system that Kettering had developed. Later, the Delco name would also be applied to that company, which became the Delco-Light Company but remained separate from the earlier Delco company.

It has often been said that the major significance of these acquisitions for GM was that they enabled the corporation to acquire the services of Kettering. Certainly Kettering's contributions as head of the GM research organization, which was a direct product of his earlier Dayton research operation, were of major consequence in the corporation's rise to dominance in the industry, but the acquisition of Delco itself was of no little significance. Long after Kettering, the Delco name continues to be carried on batteries, generators, electric motors, horns, switches, and a wide variety of other equipment produced at plants in and around Dayton, Rochester, New York, and Anderson, Indiana, where the Delco-Remy Division combines the once-competing companies that were acquired by the United Motors consolidation in 1916.

References:
Stuart W. Leslie, *Boss Kettering* (New York: Columbia University Press, 1983);
Alfred P. Sloan, Jr., *My Years with General Motors* (Garden City, N.Y.: Doubleday, 1964);
Bernard A. Weisberger, *The Dream Maker: William C. Durant, Founder of General Motors* (Boston: Little, Brown, 1979).

Detroit Electric Car Company

by George S. May

Eastern Michigan University

Although Detroit is world famous for its gasoline-powered cars, the city was also the home of America's most successful battery-powered car, the Detroit Electric. The car originated with the Anderson Carriage Manufacturing Company, which was founded in 1884 and produced some 160,000 carriages by the early part of the twentieth century. At that time the Detroit firm decided to abandon carriages in favor of automobiles. Rather than trying to produce the gasoline cars that had already emerged as the most popular type of automobiles, as many carriage manufacturers did with limited success, Anderson wisely chose to produce electrics. Traditional carriage styles were most easily adapted to electrics, which, because their batteries constantly had to be recharged, were confined to use in cities where they were close to charging stations. They could only be driven at slow speeds, approximating the speeds of the horse-drawn traffic for which the carriages were originally designed.

The Anderson company made a clean break with its past and hired an automotive engineer, George W. Bacon, to design an electric that would establish a new distance record. It was claimed that Bacon's prototype went 140 miles before its batteries needed recharging, but if so, that performance, twice the normal range of an electric, was not repeated in the production models that began to appear in June 1907. That first year 125 Detroit Electrics were produced. Production rose to 400 in 1908 and 650 in 1909. By 1910, when production

Mrs. William K. Vanderbilt, Jr., in her Detroit Electric Model D, 1910 (courtesy of the Motor Vehicle Manufacturers Association, Lazarnick Collection)

reached the 1,600 range, there were nine models available. On some models certain features, such as an artificial radiator in front, were designed to make them resemble gasoline cars, but on the whole the Detroit Electrics retained the high, bulky look of the true carriage, not the sharply modified designs that gasoline car designers were being forced

General Electric engineer C. P. Steinmetz and the 1914 Detroit Electric

to adopt because of the far greater speeds and range possible in such cars.

In 1911 the Anderson carriage company was reorganized as the Anderson Electric Car Company with backing from Detroit's Book family, which had earlier been involved with Detroit's E-M-F gasoline automobile company. Later, in 1919, the company was again renamed, this time the Detroit Electric Car Company. At the time it was the country's leading electric car manufacturer. Its customers, it liked to boast, included 14 manufacturers of gasoline cars, including Henry Ford, but its major clientele was women who found electric cars easier to drive than gasoline cars, which had to be cranked to be started. However, with the introduction of a practical self-starter in 1912, electrics ceased to have that advantage, although Mrs. Henry B. Joy, wife of a former Packard president, drove her Detroit Electric until her death in 1957. By the post-World War I period, as electric sales declined, Detroit Electric gave more emphasis to commercial vehicle production, since electric delivery vehicles still had an appeal to some businesses.

In 1927 the Detroit Electric Company was forced into receivership. Alfred O. Dunk a Detroiter who had made a career of taking over bankrupt auto companies, was appointed receiver. When orders for Detroit Electrics continued to come in, Dunk, rather than closing out the business, filled them. Without any advertising or sales force, by 1930 Dunk was turning out from ten to twelve electrics each month, modernized to look not like horseless carriages but like other automobiles of the day. They sold for from $2,800 to $4,200. Limited production continued after Dunk's death in 1936 and, according to the automotive journalist Chris Sinsabaugh, still continued in 1940, by which time the company was the country's sole surviving electric car producer. Sinsabaugh was told that by 1940 Detroit Electric had built 13,862 of the total of about 50,000 electrics that manufacturers had turned out. It was apparently about that time, however, that the company finally closed its doors, bringing to an end the production of a type of car that had been the auto industry's early leader.

References:

Nick Baldwin and others, *The World Guide to Automobile Manufacturers* (New York: Facts on File, 1987);
Chris Sinsabaugh, *Who, Me? Forty Years of Automobile History* (Detroit: Arnold-Powers, 1940).

Horace Elgin Dodge

(May 17, 1868-December 10, 1920)

by Charles K. Hyde

Wayne State University

CAREER: Partner, Evans & Dodge Bicycle Company (1897-1900); vice-president and general manager (1900-1920), president, Dodge Brothers Company (1920).

Horace Elgin Dodge, automobile manufacturer, was born on May 17, 1868, in the village of Niles, Michigan, located on the St. Joseph River, in the southwest corner of the state. He was one of three children born to Daniel Rugg Dodge and Maria Casto Dodge. His sister Delphine was five years older than Horace, while his brother John Francis, who became his lifelong business partner, was four years older. Daniel Rugg Dodge and his two brothers, Edwin and Caleb, operated a foundry and machine shop in Niles, but their business never prospered. They were among the impoverished of this community, with the Dodge children going barefoot even in the winter months.

In addition to bearing the burdens of poverty, Horace had to struggle with peers who teased him unmercifully over his name. Horace grew up without many friends and tried to hide his sensitivity about his name by becoming belligerent and temperamental. He went by the name of Elgin Dodge in Niles, and after the Dodge family left Niles, he variously called himself Delbert, Dellie, H. E., and Ed. Horace finally put this embarrassment over his name behind him when he named his first boy, born in 1900, Horace Elgin Dodge, Jr.

Many of Horace's later interests emerged during his youthful years in Niles. His mechanical abilities developed quickly, in part because he was encouraged to tinker in his father's machine shop. He and John Dodge often played with Fred Bonine, the son of a wealthy Niles family and the first boy in the village to own an expensive high-wheel bicycle. Motivated largely by envy, the Dodge brothers, with thirteen-year-old Horace doing the bulk of the work, built their own functional high-wheel bi-

Horace Elgin Dodge

cycle from scrap materials and proudly rode it down Main Street. Horace was fascinated by the boats that plied the St. Joseph River and dreamed of owning the biggest, fastest boat in the world. He also spent much time at the large, elaborate house of John S. Tuttle, the richest man in Niles. Tuttle encouraged Horace to play his piano, and the boy soon developed a love of music that would continue for the rest of his life. Horace vowed to someday own a house as beautiful as Tuttle's, complete with piano.

The village of Niles and the Dodge family machine shop fell on hard times as traffic on the St. Joseph River declined in the late 1870s. After the deaths of his two brothers in 1882, Daniel Rugg Dodge moved his family to Port Huron, Michigan, a busy maritime center at the southern end of Lake Huron, some sixty miles north of Detroit. There he established a machine shop specializing in internal combustion marine engines. Daniel Dodge and his two sons worked for the Upton Manufacturing Company, an agricultural implements firm owned by James S. Upton, a distant relative of the Dodges. Despite his mother's objections, Horace never returned to high school to complete his education.

In 1886 the Dodge family moved to Detroit, where the eighteen-year-old Horace and his brother John found work at the Murphy Boiler Works. John Dodge soon became a foreman and earned the respectable salary of $20 per week. He and Horace remained there for six years and gained valuable experience working under the direction of Thomas Murphy, a noted marine engineer. In 1894 the Dodge brothers began working as machinists for the Dominion Typograph Company in Windsor, Ontario, where they each earned $150 per month. They remained in Detroit but crossed the Detroit River each day by ferryboat. While working for Dominion Typograph, Horace designed new machines to cut the matrices for the letters, achieving greater accuracy than was previously possible. He also invented a four-point, dirt-proof, adjustable bicycle ball bearing, and in 1897 the Dodge brothers, with Fred Evans, founded the Evans & Dodge Bicycle Company, leased the Dominion Typograph plant, and manufactured their machine, the E & D bicycle.

At the time the Dodge brothers began working at Dominion Typograph, Horace began courting the Scottish-born Christina Anna Thomson, whose father was a sailmaker in Detroit's shipbuilding industry. She had worked for the Morton Baking Company, packing cookies, and held several other factory jobs before she started teaching piano in 1896. Horace was attracted to Anna, as she called herself, in part because she was an accomplished pianist with formal music training. They were married in 1896, but had no money for a honeymoon, and initially lived with Horace's parents. Anna saved for a belated honeymoon trip to Niagara Falls but gave Horace the $200 she had accumulated so that he and John could lease the Dominion Typograph Company buildings in 1897. Horace and Anna remained married throughout his life,

with the marriage resulting in two children, Delphine Ione in 1899 and Horace Elgin, Jr., in 1900. As the Dodge brothers prospered, Anna enjoyed the benefits of affluence, including living in larger and more elaborate houses, but she fondly recalled the early days with Horace and once commented, "The happiest years of my life were when I was packing Horace's lunch pail."

When John and Horace Dodge established their own machine shop in Detroit in 1900, they rented space in the Boydell Building but soon built a large, three-story machine shop at Hastings and Monroe Avenue, which they occupied in 1902. Their early success came from supplying Ransom Olds with automobile components. They won a contract to build 2,000 engines for Olds in 1901, and in the following year Olds awarded them a contract for 3,000 transmissions, making the Dodges the largest parts suppliers in the early automobile industry. John Dodge usually negotiated these contracts and took care of the financial arrangements, while Horace designed the machinery needed for production.

The mechanical genius of Horace Dodge was critical in establishing the alliance that emerged in 1903 between Henry Ford and the Dodges. In 1902 Ford approached the Dodge brothers with sketches of a new automobile he planned to produce, which included a new gasoline engine that C. Harold Wills and Ford had designed. Ford had convinced coal dealers Alexander Malcomson and James Couzens to back his enterprise but needed a commitment from a reputable machine shop to produce the needed components. Horace studied the plans and then redesigned the engine and rear axle to improve their operating efficiency. Horace's modifications to the original design helped make this first Ford automobile, the Model A, a mechanical and marketing success. In February 1903 the Dodges agreed to supply Ford with 650 chassis (including engines, transmissions, and axles), and because Ford was chronically short of funds, the Dodges agreed in June 1903 to accept 10 percent of the Ford Motor Company stock in lieu of payments owed them. They went on to work exclusively on Ford contracts until 1914, and they remained major stockholders in the Ford Motor Company until 1919.

The Horace Dodge family, especially Anna Dodge, enjoyed the affluence that the Dodges had achieved within three years after their initial contract with Ford. In summer 1906 Horace applied for membership in the Country Club of Detroit, located in Grosse Pointe. When his application was rejected, the humiliated Horace bought a parcel of land next to the club and vowed to build a house so extravagant that it would make the Country Club "look like a shanty." He hired the young Detroit architect Albert Kahn to design an elaborate red sandstone English Renaissance-style residence, which was completed in 1910. This was a larger, more palatial house than John Dodge's Boston Boulevard home and included a great pipe organ and elaborate formal rose gardens extending down to the banks of the Detroit River. The Horace Dodges chose the name "Rose Terrace" for their new home. After Horace's death and her subsequent remarriage, Anna Dodge bought the adjacent Country Club of Detroit property, demolished the original Rose Terrace, and built an even more elaborate mansion, also called Rose Terrace, completed in 1934.

Anna Dodge enjoyed the trappings of wealth, hosted elaborate formal dinner parties at Rose Terrace, and made great efforts to fit into the Grosse Pointe social scene. She enrolled her children in the finest private schools Grosse Pointe offered and planned to send them to prestigious eastern finishing schools when they reached adolescence. Horace and John Dodge continued to visit the saloons of Detroit, including many tough, working-class establishments. Horace kept the same friends he had known when he was poor, although they were never really welcome at Rose Terrace. Horace preferred to spend quiet, private evenings at home playing his organ rather than socializing with the Grosse Pointe elite. In a biographical sketch following the younger Dodge's death in 1920, F. W. Hersey observed, "Sitting at his magnificent pipe organ, Horace E. Dodge forgot for the time being the mechanical side of life and the cross-fires of commerce."

Horace and John Dodge enjoyed very little leisure in 1913-1914, when they introduced their own automobile and vastly changed their manufacturing operations. They had remained Henry Ford's chief supplier of engines, transmissions, and chassis since 1903, and as Ford's production increased dramatically with the introduction of the Model T in 1908, the Dodges were nearly overwhelmed with work. In a move that paralleled Ford's opening of his Highland Park plant in 1910, the Dodges built a new manufacturing facility on a 30-acre site in nearby Hamtramck the same year. In 1912 alone, they supplied Ford with 180,000 transmission-axle sets,

with future prospects for even larger orders. Increasingly wary of their dependence on Ford contracts and wanting to build a car of their own, the Dodge brothers gave Ford the required one year's notice in July 1913 that they would stop making components for him.

The design of the Dodge automobile, introduced in late 1914, was perhaps Horace Dodge's greatest achievement. Like everything the Dodge brothers did, this was a joint effort, but Horace was chiefly responsible. He did much of the design work during periods of seclusion in a cottage on John Dodge's Meadow Brook estate. Horace Dodge also made improvements in existing machines used to build the new car, or in many cases designed new machinery from scratch. For example, he studied the enameling ovens used to paint car bodies and designed an improved oven that reduced heat loss from nearly 40 percent to about 4 percent.

The first Dodge automobile was a five-passenger touring car with a wheelbase of 110 inches, powered by a 35-horsepower, 4-cylinder "L-head" head engine of Horace's own design. The engine proved so reliable and efficient that it was the only one used in Dodge automobiles for many years. Innovative design features included an electric starting/ignition system that made stalling the engine nearly impossible, a cone clutch, pressurized fuel system, and an all-steel body fabricated by the Edward G. Budd Manufacturing Company. *Automobile Topics*, which offered a "sneak preview" of the new car, described it as "a handsome, comfortable, medium-sized car for five people, with plenty of room and plenty of power, and built to run for years."

During World War I the United States government asked the Dodge brothers to produce a delicate recoil mechanism used in the French 155 mm artillery piece. This device had been fabricated entirely by manual production methods, and as a result French factories produced only five a day. Horace Dodge devised an entirely new manufacturing scheme to make the mechanism by machine, and in the course of four months designed 129 specialized machines previously unknown to American industry. He also made several improvements to the recoil mechanism itself, besides designing the new manufacturing plant to make them. The new plant never reached the production level of 50 mechanisms per day that John Dodge had promised, but it did make 30 per day, all of the finest quality.

John and Horace Dodge (front row center) with a group of Dodge Brothers executives in front of Horace's Grosse Pointe, Michigan, home (courtesy of the Chrysler Historical Collection)

Horace was, above all else, a thorough, painstaking, and gifted designer and inventor. He remained the "inside man" in the Dodge partnership and never lost touch with the machinery, processes, or workmen in their plants. He was able to operate every piece of machinery in the sprawling Dodge manufacturing plants. One of the countless obituary notices that appeared at his death noted, "His office was literally a museum of parts, past, present, and prospective, for Dodge Brothers cars. He was constantly scheming improved details, new processes, new methods and was always building new machinery. He never lost the touch of a craftsman, could never let machinery alone."

Horace was by far a more quiet, taciturn, and generally shy character than his brother John. Although not as quick-tempered as his brother, once aroused he could become just as belligerent. Following an evening at a local saloon, Horace was struggling to crank his Model A Ford when a passerby stopped to watch him curse his uncooperative auto-

mobile. When the man snickered, Horace stopped momentarily, knocked the man to the pavement, and then resumed cranking. Horace's temper tantrums were often short-lived but were followed by long periods of withdrawal and sulking. He preferred to avoid direct personal confrontations, even with his wife Anna. Although she often disapproved of much of John Dodge's conduct, she learned that criticizing him would only result in Horace offering an angry defense of his brother.

Horace Dodge's abiding interests in life, in addition to machines, were music and powerboats. He was a self-taught pianist beginning in his youth in Niles, and he also learned to play the violin before he married Anna. The Horace Dodges were regular visitors to the Detroit Opera House during the early years of their marriage, despite the financial sacrifices such visits required. After he achieved great wealth, Horace could pursue his interest in music without limits. This was a side of his personality generally hidden from public view. Horace Dodge did occasionally play the organ at Rose Terrace for his most intimate friends, and even less frequently he would play the violin.

When several Detroit society women were promoting a new symphony orchestra for the city shortly after the turn of the century, Anna Dodge made a contribution of $1,000 for this effort, beginning a long-term relationship between the Horace Dodge family and the Detroit Symphony Orchestra. Following a concert in January 1918, the Detroit Symphony manager discussed the orchestra's financial difficulties with Horace, including the difficulty of getting commitments for financial support when the orchestra did not have a permanent resident conductor. Horace briefly considered buying the orchestra but instead financed the search for an outstanding conductor. He was instrumental in bringing the brilliant Russian pianist Ossip Salomonowitsch Gabrilowitsch to serve as conductor of the Detroit Symphony. The new conductor insisted that the symphony should have its own auditorium, and Horace led the campaign to raise funds for the project.

The new auditorium, Orchestra Hall, opened in October 1919 and was the home of the Detroit Symphony through 1939. Soon after Orchestra Hall opened, Horace Dodge was hunting with friends in northern Michigan and remembered that he was about to miss the performance of a favorite concerto. He chartered a special train to Detroit and arrived at Orchestra Hall shortly before the program began. He sat in the back of the auditorium, still in his hunting clothes, became totally immersed in the music, and then left to rejoin his hunting party in the north woods. The Detroit Symphony Orchestra has held special performances at Orchestra Hall for many years and made it its permanent home in the 1989-1990 concert season.

Horace Dodge's other great interest can also be traced to his childhood in Niles, when he watched the powerboats on the St. Joseph River. He first indulged this interest in a serious way in 1904, when he ordered a steam-powered launch from the Studer Boat Works in Detroit, at a cost of $1,800, but an explosion and fire destroyed his expensive toy just as it was nearly finished. He rebuilt this 40-foot launch as the *Lotus* and soon thereafter designed and built another craft, the *Hornet*.

Although John Dodge did not share Horace's enthusiasm for boats and yachts of all sizes and styles, the two often owned and operated the boats

jointly. In 1910 he and John took delivery on a 100-foot diesel-powered yacht, the *Hornet II*, which Horace had designed. Equipped with two 1,000-horsepower engines, it was able to cruise along the Detroit River at thirty knots, or twice the speed of the next fastest boat. At one point John and Horace had a drunken argument in Churchill's saloon over where they would take their next cruise, and they agreed to flip a coin for sole ownership of the boat. Horace won the coin toss but then noted that since John would be his guest on the planned cruise, the older brother could choose the destination.

As he became wealthy, Horace pursued this expensive hobby more seriously. His yacht, the *Nokomis*, launched in 1914, was 180 feet long and had all the features of a small, luxurious house. Appropriately, Horace was named commodore of the Detroit Boat Club in December 1913. He then commissioned the naval architects Gielow and Orr to design an even larger vessel, the *Nokomis II*, launched in 1917. It measured 243 feet in length, with a 32-foot beam, and was easily the largest private yacht on the Great Lakes. With patriotic resignation, Horace Dodge saw both *Nokomis I* and *II* pressed into wartime service in spring 1917. When the *Nokomis II* was returned at the end of the war, Horace renamed it the *Delphine*, after his daughter. At the time of his death a new yacht, the *Delphine II*, was nearly completed. He had planned to take this steel vessel, measuring 257 feet in length, on a world cruise.

Anna Dodge showed much more interest in penetrating upper-crust social circles both in and outside of Detroit than Horace. They began wintering in Palm Beach, Florida, where Anna hoped to launch her daughter Delphine into more exclusive social circles than were available in Detroit. Delphine's social debut in Detroit, held in December 1919 in the Statler Hotel, was the most elaborate that Detroit had witnessed. After the death of John Dodge in mid January 1920, Anna Dodge convinced Horace to return to Florida in late February. There Delphine met James H. R. Cromwell, from a prominent Philadelphia family, and planned a brief engagement followed by a June wedding. Horace was shocked by his daughter's plans to marry someone she had known for only a month and to have the wedding less than six months after John's death, but he reluctantly gave in to the wishes of Delphine and Anna. Delphine's wedding took place at the Jefferson Avenue Presbyterian Church in Detroit on June 16, 1920. The ceremony was followed by an elaborate reception at Rose Terrace. It easily ranked as one of the major social events of the year, with nearly 3,000 in attendance, virtually all of Detroit's *Blue Book* aristocracy. Ostentatious displays of the Dodge wealth could be found everywhere. Horace presented Anna with a five-strand pearl necklace worth $1.5 million for the occasion, while giving his daughter, among many gifts, a more modest single strand of pearls that cost $100,000. At the reception that followed, guests could enjoy music from a 100-piece band that played on a terrace near the Detroit River, or they could listen to the Detroit Symphony Orchestra, which played special numbers prepared in recognition of their benefactor, Horace Dodge. John Dodge's widow, Matilda, who reluctantly agreed to attend, wore mourning clothes.

Horace was also interested in Detroit politics but never became involved in the prominent way that John Dodge had. Horace's friend John Stein became county sheriff in December 1916, and he immediately named Horace Dodge one of his twenty-five undersheriffs. This became a serious side interest for Horace, who visited the county jail regularly, distributed gifts to the inmates, and often gave them jobs after their release. He often wore his diamond-studded gold deputy's badge on official business. Horace once helped the sheriff's department transfer prisoners from the Wayne County jail to the state prison at Marquette, some 500 miles away, and rented a private railroad car for the occasion, so the entire party made the trip in style. After Stein unexpectedly lost the sheriff's election in December 1918, Horace gave him a large house worth more than $20,000 as a token of his appreciation.

In addition to making charitable gifts to old friends and acquaintances, Horace Dodge engaged in several other philanthropic efforts. He supported the Dodge Brothers Company paternalistic programs for its employees and remained a major supporter of the Detroit Museum of Art and the Detroit Symphony Orchestra. Shortly after Horace Dodge's death in December 1920, Victor Herbert wrote the Dodge Brothers March, "dedicated by Mr. Herbert to Mr. Horace E. Dodge in respectful appreciation of his efforts toward the advancement of American Music." The Dodge Brothers Company had 100,000 phonograph records of the march produced and distributed.

Horace Dodge also contributed a total of $80,000 to the Protestant Orphan Asylum, one of Anna Dodge's favorite charities, and paid most of the costs of building a new Jefferson Avenue Presbyterian Church. During the early part of 1920, a doctor at the Good Samaritan Hospital in Palm Beach, Florida, had treated Horace, who then donated $50,000 to the hospital for the construction of an isolation wing for patients with contagious diseases. Following Horace's death, Dodge Brothers, Inc. donated 627 acres of Oakland County real estate in eleven parcels to the State of Michigan, to be used as public parks and to serve as a memorial to the Dodge brothers.

Most of Horace Dodge's last year of life was extremely difficult, for he was chronically ill the entire time, suffering in part from the heartbreak of John's death. Initially, when the two were stricken with influenza while attending the National Automobile Show in New York City in January 1920, Horace was the sicker of the two, but he survived, while John died on January 14 at the Ritz-Carlton Hotel. Horace did not attend John's funeral and did not even return to Detroit until the second week of February. Then he visited the huge, white stone mausoleum where John was interred to view the body before the casket was permanently sealed. Horace, still weakened from his bout with influenza, then left for Florida with his family, hoping that the warmer climate would help his recovery. Horace's physical and mental health seemed to improve right through Delphine's wedding in June 1920, but then he suffered several relapses.

The younger Dodge seemed physically and emotionally drained by his brother's death as much as by his own illness. He rarely visited the Dodge Brothers manufacturing plant, leaving the operation of the firm to trusted lieutenants. The few times he went to the plant, he became withdrawn and melancholy for weeks afterward. Following his daughter's wedding, he attended the Republican National Convention in Chicago but retreated to his bed upon his return. Horace had always dressed impeccably, but following John's death he completely ignored his wardrobe, much to Anna's dismay.

In late fall 1920 he began to show interest in the new Dodge yacht, the *Delphine II*, which was under construction, and even visited the factory a few times. When Horace Elgin Dodge, Jr., became engaged to Lois Knowlson, from a prominent Detroit family, Horace, Sr., was pleased, but he again became ill after the engagement party held in Detroit in November. Amidst Horace's plans to return to Florida the Detroit Symphony Orchestra performed a private concert for him at Rose Terrace, and he had his attorneys prepare a new will before he left Detroit in late November. He seemed to improve slightly after arriving in Florida, but began hemorrhaging on December 7. Horace Dodge died on Sunday, December 10, 1920, at age fifty-two, less than eleven months after his brother.

Horace Dodge's body was returned to Detroit on a special funeral train, which was met at the Michigan Central Railroad Depot by several hundred friends and acquaintances. Veteran Dodge factory workers served as pallbearers, moving the enormous bronze casket to the hearse. Horace's remains were first brought to Blake Chapel on Peterboro Street, chosen because it was located close to downtown Detroit and was therefore more accessible to Dodge employees. More than 23,000 Dodge workers and business associates viewed Horace Dodge for the last time at this chapel. The body was then moved to Rose Terrace and placed on a bier in the music room, surrounded by roses. The funeral, held on Wednesday afternoon at Rose Terrace, featured an organist who played Horace's favorite songs, with a concluding dirge by the Detroit Symphony Orchestra. The Presbyterian minister, Reverend Forrer, eulogized Horace Dodge as "a man with a passion for music . . . a mechanic with the soul of a poet." The funeral procession, in an eerie replay of the events of the previous January, including nearly the same cast of characters, went past the silent Dodge factory in Hamtramck and on to the Dodge mausoleum at Woodlawn Cemetery, where the coffin was placed inside the vault.

Horace Dodge was one of the most important figures in the early development of the automobile industry in Detroit. Because he and John Dodge were lifelong partners in business, their contributions were often inseparable. Horace Dodge was the mechanical genius behind their success. He was responsible for the design of the E & D bicycle, most of the components that Dodge Brothers manufactured for Henry Ford, the Dodge automobile itself, and the machinery used to produce all of those products and many more. It was Horace Dodge's talents that allowed Dodge Brothers to successfully manufacture the recoil mechanism for the French 155 mm artillery during the First World War. He was one of a handful of vital innovators who revolutionized the mechanical side of Detroit's early automobile industry, and who have seldom received recognition for their contributions. While lacking the outgoing, aggressive style of his brother, Horace Dodge probably made more lasting contributions to the Detroit community, especially through his support of the Detroit Symphony Orchestra.

References:

Clarence M. Burton, *The City of Detroit, Michigan, 1701-1922* (Detroit: Clarke, 1922);

Caroline Latham and David Agresta, *Dodge Dynasty: The Car and the Family that Rocked Detroit* (San Diego: Harcourt Brace Jovanovich, 1985);

George S. May, *R. E. Olds: Auto Industry Pioneer* (Grand Rapids, Mich.: Eerdmans, 1977);

Allan Nevins, *Ford: The Times, the Man, the Company* (New York: Scribners, 1954);

Jean Maddern Pitrone, *Tangled Web: Legacy of Auto Pioneer John F. Dodge* (Hamtramck, Mich.: Avenue, 1989);

Pitrone and Joan Potter Elwart, *The Dodges: The Auto Family Fortune and Misfortune* (South Bend, Ind.: Icarus, 1981).

Archives:

Material concerning Horace Dodge is located in the Dodge Papers at Burton Historical Collections, Detroit Public Library; and in the John Dodge Papers at Meadow Brook Hall Historical Archives, Rochester, Michigan.

John Francis Dodge

(October 25, 1864-January 14, 1920)

by Charles K. Hyde

Wayne State University

CAREER: Partner, Evans & Dodge Bicycle Company (1897-1900); president and treasurer, Dodge Brothers Company (1900-1920); director (1903-1913), vice-president, Ford Motor Company (1906-1913); vice-president, Ford Manufacturing Company (1905-1907).

John Francis Dodge, automobile manufacturer, was born on October 25, 1864, in the village of Niles, Michigan, located on the St. Joseph River in the southwest corner of the state. He was one of three children born to Daniel Rugg Dodge and Maria Casto Dodge. His sister Delphine was a year older than John, while his brother Horace Elgin, who became his lifelong business partner, was four years younger. Daniel Rugg Dodge and his two brothers, Edwin and Caleb, operated a foundry and machine shop in Niles, but their business never prospered. They were among the impoverished of the community, with the Dodge children going barefoot even in the winter months.

The combined effects of growing up poor in Niles and the influence of Maria Dodge made John Dodge and his siblings ambitious, persistent, and resilient. John received an award for punctuality from the Union Grammar School in Niles in 1877 for not being absent or late for school in three years. His first job consisted of driving a cow three miles per day, for which he earned 50 cents per month. As a teenager, he lugged sacks of bran out of railroad cars for 50 cents per day. John graduated from Niles High School in 1882, a considerable achievement for an impoverished youth of that era.

As traffic on the St. Joseph River declined in the late 1870s, so did the village of Niles and the Dodge machine shop. With the deaths of his brothers in 1882, Daniel Dodge moved his family to Port Huron, Michigan, a busy maritime center at the juncture of Lake Huron and the St. Clair River, some

John Francis Dodge

60 miles north of Detroit. There, Daniel Dodge and his two sons worked for the Upton Manufacturing Company, an agricultural implements firm owned by James S. Upton, a distant relative by marriage. The Dodge family lived in Uptonville, just south of Port Huron, in a house next to the manufacturing plant. In Uptonville, Daniel Dodge established a machine shop specializing in internal combustion marine engines. His two sons worked in their father's shop and for a local agricultural implements manufacturer.

In 1886 the Dodge family moved to Detroit, where the twenty-two-year-old John and his brother Horace found work at the Murphy Boiler Works, which made marine boilers. John Dodge soon became a foreman and earned the respectable salary of $20 per week. He and Horace remained there for six years and gained valuable experience working under the direction of Thomas Murphy, a noted marine engineer. In 1894 the Dodge brothers began working as machinists for the Dominion Typograph Company in Windsor, Ontario, where they each earned $150 per month. They remained in Detroit but crossed the Detroit River each day by ferryboat.

John married Ivy Hawkins, a Canadian-born dressmaker, in September 1892, and the couple produced three children–Winifred, born in 1894, Isabel Cleves, born in 1896, and John Duval, born in 1898. John became superintendent of the Dominion Typograph plant in 1897 but stopped working for a time because of severe respiratory problems, apparently tuberculosis. He stayed at home in bed, unable to work at age thirty-two, and took medications to regain his strength. John treated his chronic cough with a Parke-Davis compound known as *131* and increasingly supplemented it with whiskey.

Horace had invented an improved bicycle ball bearing, and in 1897 the two brothers founded the Evans & Dodge Bicycle Company with Fred S. Evans, leased the Typograph Company plant, and manufactured their product, the E & D bicycle. They dissolved their Canadian venture in 1900 and received cash and machinery with a combined value of about $10,000 as their share of the firm's equity. John and Horace started their own machine shop with 12 employees in Detroit in 1900. Their venture was a great success, and they soon built a large, three-story machine shop at Hastings Street and Monroe Avenue, which they occupied in early 1902.

This was a time of triumph for John Dodge, but it was also a time of defeat and personal loss. Ivy Hawkins Dodge, chronically ill with tuberculosis since August 1898, died in September 1901, leaving John with the twin burdens of managing the machine shop and raising three young children. He was so poor at the time of Ivy's death that he had to borrow from relatives to pay for her funeral and burial plot. This was also a pivotal period for the two Dodge brothers, because it marked their entry into the nascent automobile industry.

Ransom E. Olds built the first automobile factory in Detroit in 1899 and by 1901 became the largest producer in the industry, concentrating exclusively on one model, the "Curved-Dash Olds." Like other early automakers, Olds was primarily an assembler of parts and components built by others rather than a manufacturer of automobiles. The Dodge brothers began building engines for Olds in early 1901 and in June of that year signed a contract to supply him with 2,000 engines. The following year Olds awarded the Dodges a contract for 3,000 transmissions, making them the largest parts suppliers in the industry. In February 1903 the Dodge brothers agreed to supply Henry Ford with 650 chassis (including engines, transmissions, and axles), and in June 1903 they became substantial stockholders in the newly incorporated Ford Motor Company. The Dodge brothers worked exclusively on Ford contracts from 1903 until 1914, and they were major stockholders in the Ford Motor Company until 1919.

John Dodge's success was the result of hard work and enormous sacrifice. During the time the brothers supplied Ransom Olds with engines and transmissions, they practically lived at their Boydell Building shop, working in stretches of 20 hours or more and seldom spending any time at home, except on weekends. John's respiratory problems returned during this period, and the combined pressures of his failing health, excessive work, and Ivy's death led him to drink to excess during his free time, with Horace serving as his loyal companion. Both were boisterous and unruly, but John's behavior was legendary. One Saturday night he ordered a saloon keeper to dance on a tabletop, and when the man refused, John threatened him with a revolver. When the frightened man danced, John applauded his efforts by smashing dozens of glasses against the bar mirrors. John Dodge returned to the saloon a few days later and generously compensated the owner for the damages and inconvenience. He and Horace, however, never allowed these sprees to interfere with their success as automobile parts manufacturers.

John also sought out female companionship after Ivy's death. In 1902 he hired a stenographer, Matilda Rausch, the daughter of a saloon keeper and a graduate of Gorsline Business College. John quickly became her sole escort and typically spent two or three evenings a week with her, despite the fact that she was nearly 20 years younger. John also hired a housekeeper, Isabelle Smith, to take care of his three children and his aged mother, who lived with them. In an impetuous move, John quietly married Isabelle in Canada in December 1903, with only Horace and his wife Anna as witnesses. No Detroit newspaper carried an announcement of the marriage, and John always referred to his second wife only as "my housekeeper." This was a marriage of convenience, and John continued his relationship with Matilda, the woman he loved. He insisted that his marriage be kept secret, and within a year, Isabelle left him. John's mother died in August 1907, and on October 29, 1907, he and Isabelle were divorced, in a small Michigan town several hundred miles from Detroit, without a whisper of publicity. Six weeks later John Dodge married his beloved Matilda, with only Horace and Anna Dodge present. He did not invite Matilda's parents to the wedding ceremony or to an elaborate dinner that followed. His third marriage produced three additional children—Frances Matilda in 1914, Daniel George in 1917, and Anna Margaret in 1919.

As Dodge Brothers Company flourished, John began to accumulate the symbols of wealth. Shortly before he married Matilda, he built an elaborate home in the fashionable Boston Boulevard neighborhood of Detroit. He moved from his modest house, valued at about $4,000 and located in a working-class neighborhood, to his mansion, which cost $250,000. John also bought a 320-acre farm in Rochester, Michigan, north of Detroit, for $50,000, the first of several parcels that eventually became his Meadow Brook estate. In an act of reconciliation, John asked Matilda's parents to move to Rochester and manage his new property. He built numerous guest houses at Meadow Brook and began spending most of his spare time there, particularly weekends, when he relaxed by wandering through the estate.

John's marriage to Matilda coincided with the start of a long period of unqualified business triumphs. The Dodge brothers remained Henry Ford's major suppliers of engines and transmissions, and their business expanded and prospered, particularly when Ford's output jumped dramatically after the introduction of the Model T in 1908. In a move that paralleled Ford's opening of his Highland Park plant in 1910, the Dodges built a new plant on a 30-acre site in nearby Hamtramck the same year. In 1912 alone, they supplied Ford with 180,000 transmission-axle sets, with future prospects for even larger orders.

Wary of their total dependence on Ford contracts and wanting to build an automobile of their own, in July 1913 they gave Ford the required 1-year notice that they would stop making components for him. John resigned his post of vice-president of the Ford Motor Company, and the Dodge brothers began designing their new automobile and expanding the Hamtramck plant to build it. They produced the first Dodge car in November 1914 and quickly became one of the major Detroit automakers. The Dodge brothers retained their 10 percent share of Ford Motor Company stock, which Henry Ford eventually bought from them in 1919 for $25 million, after the Dodges had successfully forced Ford to pay substantial dividends to all the stockholders. With the sale of their Ford stock, plus the stock dividends and profits from Ford contracts over the years, the Dodge brothers earned about $32 million from their original 1903 investment of $10,000. The fates of the Dodges and Henry Ford were inextricably intertwined for more than 15 years, with each contributing substantially to the other's success.

John Dodge's personality reflected his background of poverty, his difficult and often tragic personal life, and his enormous success. Of the two imposing, broad-shouldered, red-haired brothers, John was clearly the more outgoing, fun-loving, articulate, and aggressive, while simultaneously being strong-willed, quick-tempered, and occasionally prone to violence. He was hardworking, earthy, practical, and ingenious, but he was also generous and public-spirited. John was not diplomatic, genteel, or refined in his manners, and on more than one occasion was simply a boor. In most respects he never adjusted very well to his success, particularly to his enormous wealth and the social status that accompanied it.

The often contradictory facets of John's personality can be seen throughout his life. He had always kept a strong attachment to his hometown of Niles, and in 1913 the Dodge brothers offered a gift of $100,000 to the town, to be used as the citizens saw fit. John promised to double the gift if the townspeople could prove they would spend the money wisely but arrogantly pointed out to them that this gift was a minor one since he and Horace were worth $50 million. The manner in which the offer was made resulted in a backlash from the people of Niles, who rejected the proposal. After the sale of

John and Horace Dodge in the back seat of the first Dodge car, produced at the brothers' factory in Hamtramck, Michigan, in November 1914 (courtesy of Chrysler Corporation)

his Ford stock, John decided that his Boston Boulevard residence, hardly a modest house, was inappropriate for a man of his wealth. He began building an enormous residence in Grosse Pointe in 1919, one that would dwarf anything previously built in Michigan. The house would have 110 rooms and 24 baths, enclose more than two acres of floor space, and cost more than $4 million. Only partially completed at the time of John's death in 1920, the house was left vacant until Matilda Dodge had it demolished in 1941.

John was not known for his diplomacy. In the middle of World War I, the U.S. secretary of war, Newton Baker, wanted to find an American manufacturer to help produce a delicate recoil mechanism for several types of French artillery. John went to Washington to meet with Baker and a delegation of French manufacturers who were already making the mechanism. They offered to send their skilled craftsmen to Detroit to show the Dodges how to make the device, but John abruptly told them that all he needed to begin mass production was a blueprint. He warned them in earthy language that they would have to comply with his wishes if they wanted the mechanism built. Baker complained

that he was not accustomed to having visitors speak to him in that type of language, and John's only response was "The war would be a hell of a lot better off if you were!" After conferring with Horace, John returned to Washington, asked how many of the mechanisms the government wanted, and promised to begin deliveries in four months. To the astonishment of the French and American officials, John lived up to his promises.

John's relationship with his son John Duval Dodge is a good example of the elder Dodge's impetuous nature. After the younger Dodge married, at age nineteen, an eighteen-year-old Detroit girl, and the elder Dodge read about it in the newspapers, he pledged to disown his son. John Dodge's last will, made public after his death in January 1920, showed his continued anger, for he left John Duval Dodge only $150 a month for life from the large estate. John Dodge's quick temper often ended in violence. He read an article critical of him and one of his political cronies in the *Detroit Times* in September 1916. He rushed to the home of James Schermerhorn, owner of the *Times*, punched him in the jaw, and threatened to beat him severely the next time he printed any stories critical of Dodge's friends.

Perhaps the ugliest example of John's temper occurred in January 1911 in Schneider's Saloon in downtown Detroit. Dodge and his friend Robert Oakman, both drunk, provoked an argument with a prominent Detroit attorney, Thomas J. Mahon, a cripple with two wooden legs, and his friend, Edmund Joncas. Dodge and Oakman beat Mahon unmercifully, with both men taking turns kicking him. But Dodge became even more angry when Mahon refused his offer to help him to a cab, and nearly resumed kicking the crippled man in the face. Mahon, who was severely injured in this unprovoked, vicious attack, filed a damage suit for $25,000 and had Dodge and Oakman arrested. Mahon eventually dropped the suit after Dodge made a generous out-of-court settlement.

Typical of many of Detroit's new automotive millionaires from modest backgrounds, John tried to gain the acceptance of established society with extraordinary displays of spending on traditional social functions. Largely at the insistence of Matilda, the debut party for John's eldest daughter, Winifred, held in December 1913, rivaled any that Detroit society had ever seen. They presented Winifred at a dinner dance at the elegant Pontchartrain Hotel, in an elaborate English garden setting complete with hedges, shrubbery, and songbirds discreetly hidden in the greenery. The local society paper, *Detroit Saturday Night*, judged the event a great success.

John became a powerful figure in Detroit politics in the 1910s. He had become active in local elections, and Detroit's mayor appointed him to the Board of Water Commissioners in 1905. Dodge made substantial contributions of money and influence to the successful 1912 mayoral campaign of Oscar B. Marx, who then appointed him to the newly created Board of Street Railway Commissioners. Dodge, Marx, and Robert Oakman dominated the local Republican party organization during the 1910s.

Dodge served as a delegate to the Republican National Convention in Chicago in 1916 and was frequently mentioned as a replacement for the retiring senator from Michigan, William Alden Smith, but he refused to run. Dodge developed an interest in the life of Alexander Hamilton and researched the subject so intensely that he became an authority on Hamilton's life. When Arthur S. Vandenberg, later a U.S. senator, began research on Hamilton, he consulted Dodge, who provided him with materi-

als he later used in two books he wrote on the early American statesman.

Politics and public service often went hand in hand for Dodge. He served on Detroit's Board of Water Commissioners from 1905 to 1910 and was instrumental in having a new pumping station built that vastly improved water pressure throughout the city. When he left the Water Department, Detroit had one of the most modern city water systems in the United States, along with some of the lowest water rates. Mayor Marx appointed Dodge to the newly created Detroit Street Railway Commission in July 1913, when the city was trying to acquire the privately owned Detroit United Railway (DUR), which operated the streetcar system. The commission had ordered reduced streetcar fares, to take effect on August 7, 1913. The DUR instructed its conductors to refuse to accept the lower fare, but the Detroit police commissioner threatened to have policemen seize the streetcars and force the motormen to operate them. The Detroit newspapers predicted civil unrest when the reduced fare was supposed to go into effect. Dodge and fellow commissioner James Couzens, a powerful figure in the Ford Motor Company, offered the city the use of more than 1,000 automobiles to replace the streetcars, and this threat forced the DUR to agree to a compromise fare schedule, thus avoiding a potentially dangerous confrontation.

Both Dodge brothers respected their employees and made special efforts to keep in touch with the shop floor. They used a piece-rate pay system but did not set unreasonably high work quotas. The Dodge brothers provided free beer and sandwiches to foundry and forge workers at 9 a.m. and 3 p.m. daily and voluntarily established a hospital/clinic in the Hamtramck plant for the employees and their families. The Dodges set aside a special $5 million fund to provide for needy workers and the widows of former employees. One of their paternalistic practices was the creation of a workshop known as the "Playpen," which provided space, materials, and tools for retirees who wanted to do craft work. Once, when Horace and John returned from a long trip, they discovered that the plant superintendent had closed the "Playpen" as an economy measure. They not only ordered it reopened but then drove around to the retirees' homes and personally invited them all back.

John Dodge also used a combination of paternalism and a genuine understanding of his employees to avoid labor unrest or unionization in his manufacturing plants. He did, however, occasionally receive threats against himself or his family from disgruntled employees. Both Dodge brothers began to carry guns and to urge other family members to do the same. Given their paternalistic treatment of their workers, John could never understand why his employees might find labor unions appealing. He seemed willing to do whatever was necessary to keep unionists out of his factory. In July 1913, while John was vacationing in Europe, he received reports from labor spies he had hired to investigate the activities of labor organizers from the Industrial Workers of the World (IWW), active in the Detroit automobile plants at that time. When the IWW sought a permit to speak in front of the Dodge plant in Hamtramck, Dodge used his political influence to squelch their request.

Dodge also made several charitable contributions of note before his death in 1920. He gave a clubhouse worth about $100,000 to the Detroit Federation of Women's Clubs, a donation of $135,000 to the Salvation Army Auxiliary to retire the mortgage on its hospital, and a gift of $250,000 to the First Presbyterian Church in Detroit. In 1922 Dodge Brothers, Inc. donated 627 acres of Oakland County real estate in 11 different locations to the State of Michigan, to be used as public parks and to serve as a memorial to John and Horace Dodge.

In early January 1920 John and Horace Dodge attended the National Automobile Show in New York City. Both contracted influenza on January 7, and initially Horace was by far the sicker of the two. As Horace began to recover, John's condition steadily worsened, despite the help of the best doctors the family could summon to his suite at the Ritz-Carlton Hotel. Their efforts to counteract his infection were unsuccessful, and he lapsed into unconsciousness. His tuberculosis-damaged lungs filled with fluid, and John Dodge died on Wednesday, January 14, at age fifty-five.

His body was returned to Detroit aboard a baggage car draped in black on the *Wolverine*, one of the finest trains of the day. The train arrived in Detroit Friday afternoon, where a delegation of 16 shopmen from the Dodge factory carried the coffin from the baggage car to a hearse, walking between lines of plant workers who had waited for 6 hours in the cold. The following day a throng of people, ranging from the widows of Dodge factory workers to Detroit's elite, passed through the Boston Boulevard home of John Dodge to view the body and pay their respects. The funeral took place at the Dodge home, with burial at Woodlawn Cemetery in Detroit. Many prominent Detroiters attended the funeral, including Henry Ford and James Couzens, then the city's mayor. Those most notably absent included Matilda Dodge and Horace Dodge, both too ill with influenza to attend, and John Duval Dodge, the estranged son, who had not arrived from Texas.

John Dodge was one of perhaps a dozen important figures in the early development of the automobile industry of Detroit. Because he and Horace Dodge were lifelong partners in business, their contributions were often inseparable. John clearly provided their enterprises with visionary, dynamic leadership, especially in terms of their relationships with outsiders. John also contributed in substantial ways to the ultimate success of Henry Ford, not only as a key early supplier and stockholder in the Ford Motor Company, but also as an independent voice within Ford's circle of advisers. John demonstrated through his management style and labor relations practices that large-scale production of automobiles could be profitably undertaken without the degradation of workers that took place at Ford's Highland Park plant and elsewhere in the automobile industry. He was a distinctive character among the Detroit automakers of his time because of his active involvement in politics and public service. At the time of his death, the *Detroit Free Press* noted:

> This community can ill afford to lose John Dodge. He was a citizen who counted. He was one of the big forces in the making of modern Detroit and there is every reason to believe that if he had lived, the next ten-year period would have been the time of his greatest accomplishment.

References:

Clarence M. Burton, *The City of Detroit, Michigan, 1701-1922* (Detroit: Clarke, 1922);

Caroline Latham and David Agresta, *Dodge Dynasty: The Car and the Family that Rocked Detroit* (San Diego: Harcourt Brace Jovanovich, 1989);

George S. May, *R. E. Olds: Auto Industry Pioneer* (Grand Rapids, Mich.: Eerdmans, 1977);

Allan Nevins, *Ford: The Times, the Man, the Company* (New York: Scribners, 1954);

Jean Maddern Pitrone, *Tangled Web: Legacy of Auto Pioneer John F. Dodge* (Hamtramck, Mich.: Avenue, 1989);

Pitrone and Joan Potter Elwart, *The Dodges: The Auto Family Fortune and Misfortune* (South Bend, Ind.: Icarus, 1981).

Archives:

Material concerning John F. Dodge is contained in the Dodge Papers at Burton Historical Collections, Detroit Public Library; and in the John Dodge Papers at Meadow Brook Hall Historical Archives, Rochester, Michigan.

Dodge Brothers Company

by Charles K. Hyde

Wayne State University

John Francis Dodge and Horace Elgin Dodge, with Fred S. Evans, established the Evans & Dodge Bicycle Company in 1897 to manufacture a bicycle based on an improved ball bearing that Horace Dodge developed. The two brothers, both experienced machinists, produced the E & D bicycle in Windsor, Ontario, directly across the Detroit River from Detroit, Michigan, in factory space they had leased from the Canadian Typograph Company. Their initial venture had become part of the Canadian Cycle & Motor Company by 1900, when the Dodge brothers decided to leave the bicycle industry to establish their own business in Detroit.

The Dodges received a total of $10,000 in cash and machinery as their share of the Canadian venture and used those resources to open a machine shop, operating as Dodge Brothers Company. The firm began with only 12 employees working in rented space in the Boydell Building in Detroit. Initially, John Dodge scoured the city, looking for business from any source. For the first year Dodge Brothers performed a wide variety of tasks for Detroit's stove manufacturers, shipbuilders, and carriage makers.

In the early part of 1901 John and Horace Dodge began producing components for Detroit's nascent automobile industry, and by the end of the year they were making nothing else. They initially worked on contracts for Ransom E. Olds, who built the first automobile factory in Detroit in 1899 and beginning in 1901 became the largest producer in the industry by concentrating exclusively on one model, a curved-dash runabout. Like other early automakers, Olds was primarily an assembler of parts and components made by others rather than a manufacturer of whole automobiles. Dodge Brothers

The Dodge Brothers Company's answer to the no-frills Ford Model T, 1914

began supplying Olds with engines in early 1901 and in June 1901 signed a contract to build 2,000 engines for him. When Olds awarded Dodge Brothers a contract for 3,000 transmissions the following year, the firm had become the most important parts supplier in the Detroit automobile industry. To accommodate the enormous volume of new work,

Dodge Brothers moved to a new three-story plant on Monroe Avenue at Hastings Street in 1902. The Monroe Avenue plant was Detroit's largest and best-equipped machine shop, with more than 150 employees working exclusively on automobile parts and components.

In early 1903 Dodge Brothers Company and Henry Ford established an alliance that had profound effects on all the parties involved for the next 15 years. Henry Ford approached the Dodge brothers in 1902 with sketches of an automobile he planned to produce, which included a new gasoline engine C. Harold Wills and Ford had designed. Ford convinced coal dealers Alexander Malcomson and James Couzens to back his enterprise but needed a commitment from a reputable machine shop to produce the needed components. Horace Dodge studied the plans and then redesigned the engine and rear axle to improve their efficiency. Those modifications to the original design helped make this first Ford automobile, the Model A, a mechanical and marketing success.

On February 23, 1903, Dodge Brothers Company agreed to supply Henry Ford with 650 chassis (including engines, transmissions, and axles) for $250 each. The agreement was a courageous move by the Dodges, because they gave up their lucrative contracts with Olds and simultaneously linked their fate with Henry Ford, who was penniless and a proven failure as an automobile manufacturer. Ford, like Ransom Olds, was little more than an assembler of components at the time, and the Dodges were building a nearly complete automobile that lacked only wheels and a body.

Because Ford was chronically short of funds, the Dodges agreed to accept 10 percent of the capital stock of the Ford Motor Company, incorporated on June 16, 1903, in lieu of payments owed them. Dodge Brothers in effect invested in Henry Ford's future, by providing him with about $10,000 worth of capital, consisting of about $7,000 in components and a $3,000 bank note. Dodge Brothers delivered its first chassis to Ford's Mack Avenue assembly plant in July on horse-drawn hayracks.

Dodge Brothers Company and the Ford Motor Company grew and prospered together for more than a decade. Henry Ford complained in the early years that Dodge workers produced shoddy components because they were paid by the piece, but his criticisms faded as Ford Motor Company

sales and profits soared. The Dodges began to receive substantial dividends from their Ford stock beginning in June 1904, a reflection of their contribution to Ford's success. In those early years the Dodges had more money invested in machinery and equipment than the Ford Motor Company. At the end of 1904, for example, Ford had less than $10,000 in factory equipment while Dodge Brothers Company had spent more than $60,000 on machinery used in manufacturing the Ford automobile. During the first three or four years of the Ford Motor Company the Dodges had considerably more money at risk in the venture than Henry Ford or any of the other stockholders.

When Ford moved into his new Piquette Avenue assembly plant in spring 1905, Dodge Brothers supplied 400 "rigs" (engines and transmissions) per month. Later that year Ford established the Ford Manufacturing Company as a separate entity in order to manufacture components on his own for the low-priced Model N. That move was part of Ford's plan to rid himself of one of his major stockholders, Alexander Malcomson, rather than an effort to undercut the Dodges. While the Dodges were his major supplier of components, Ford remained essentially an assembler until 1913. Over the course of the decade from 1903 to 1913, Dodge Brothers made about 60 percent of the entire Ford automobile, including all the major components except for bodies, wheels, and tires.

Ford production soared with the introduction of the Model T in 1908 and continued to climb after the company moved into its Highland Park plant two years later. By that time the Dodge brothers had nearly 500 employees at the Monroe Avenue plant, which was clearly too cramped for the volume of work they were producing. In the spring of 1910, Dodge Brothers Company began construction of a new plant on a 30-acre parcel the firm had purchased in Hamtramck, a largely rural area on Detroit's northern outskirts. There is no solid evidence that the Dodges were already planning to build their own automobile, for the first set of buildings provided them only with the capability to produce gears, other machined products, forgings, and castings.

Dodge Brothers Company broke ground for the first new building, the forge shop, on June 2, 1910, and began moving into the plant in late November. Albert Kahn, who also served as Ford's architect for the Highland Park plant, designed the first set of buildings, including a four-story concrete machine shop, powerhouse, forge shop, blacksmith shop, and office structure. The Detroit architectural firm of Smith, Hinchman & Grylls designed a foundry in 1912 and a heat treat building in 1913, completing the initial wave of construction at the site.

John Dodge's 1910 diary affords a rare look at the relationship between a Detroit industrialist, his architect, and building contractors during a time of almost frantic expansion of the automobile industry. Dodge noted on April 26th, "Gave Albert Kahn the first sketches for (the) new factory in Hamtramick [*sic*]." After several additional meetings John Dodge approved final building plans on June 3, they were put out for bid on June 7, and contracts were awarded on June 21. The basic structural steel, concrete, and masonry work was completed by mid October, and by the end of November Dodge Brothers Company began production in the new plant. In slightly more than seven months they had turned preliminary plans into completed buildings.

The move to the Hamtramck plant marked the beginning of a series of changes in the management style and personal lives of the Dodge brothers. Each had his own office located at opposite ends of the second floor of the new office building, farther removed from the shop floor than ever before. At about this time they began the practice of not responding to mail addressed to Dodge Brothers unless the "B" in Brothers was capitalized. They convinced an old friend, Frederick J. Haynes, to join the firm in 1912, and Haynes quickly became the trusted lieutenant with day-to-day managerial responsibilities. John and Horace Dodge began to take lengthy trips to Florida and Europe, leaving Haynes in charge. Since the Hamtramck plant was located far from the downtown saloons the Dodges had frequented for lunch, they began a habit of going to John Dodge's Boston Boulevard home for their midday break.

Even before the Dodges began to produce their own automobile, their Hamtramck factory was one of the most impressive manufacturing plants in the Detroit area. By mid 1914 the 5,000 men who worked there daily cut 34,000 gears, turned 25 tons of brass and 75 tons of grey iron into castings, and consumed 150 tons of steel for forgings. The annual production of components was impressive–transmissions, rear axles, drive shafts, front axles, and crankshafts, all in quantities of 200,000 or greater; 855,000 connecting rods; 412,000 universal joints; and an additional two dozen major parts or assemblies, including steering gears, in numbers exceeding 200,000. Two lengthy descriptions of the Dodge plant, which appeared in the *Michigan Manufacturer and Financial Record* and in *Automobile Topics* in 1914, listed dozens of examples of modern, innovative equipment and processes used there.

John and Horace Dodge respected their employees and made special efforts to keep in touch with the shop floor. They used a piece-rate pay system but did not set unreasonably high work quotas. The Dodge brothers provided free beer and sandwiches to foundry and forge workers at 9 A.M. and 3 P.M. daily and voluntarily established a hospital/clinic in the Hamtramck plant for the employees and their families. The Dodges created a special $5 million fund to provide for needy workers and the widows of former employees. One of their paternalistic practices was the creation of a workshop known as the "Playpen," which provided space, materials, and tools for retirees who wanted to do craft work. Once, when the brothers returned from a long trip, they discovered that the plant superintendent had closed the Playpen as an economy measure. They not only ordered it reopened but then drove around to the retirees' homes and personally invited them all back.

The Dodge brothers used a combination of paternalism and a genuine understanding of their employees to avoid labor unrest or unionization in their manufacturing plants. Given their paternalistic treatment of their workers, John and Horace Dodge could never understand why their employees might find labor unions appealing. John Dodge was especially willing to do whatever was necessary to keep unionists out of the factory. In July 1913, while he was vacationing in Europe, John received reports from labor spies he had hired to investigate the activities of labor organizers from the Industrial Workers of the World (IWW), active in the Detroit automobile plants at that time. When the IWW sought a permit to speak to the work force at the Dodge plant in Hamtramck, Dodge used his political influence to deny their request.

Because they had wanted to build their own automobile for some time and feared their dependence on Henry Ford, in July 1913 the Dodge brothers gave Ford the required one year's notice that they would stop making components for him.

*Proving grounds at the Dodge Brothers Hamtramck, Michigan, factory, constructed in 1915
(courtesy of Chrysler Corporation)*

John Dodge resigned as director and vice-president of the Ford Motor Company, but he and Horace retained the Ford stock they had held since 1903. Following several efforts to force Ford to distribute dividends to his stockholders, which culminated in a successful Dodge lawsuit, Henry Ford bought the Dodge shares for $25 million in 1919. During the course of their business relationship with the Ford Motor Company, John and Horace Dodge earned $1.7 million in profits on their Ford contracts and $5.4 million in dividends from their Ford stock, which, combined with the sale of the stock, yielded a return of about $32 million on their 1903 investment of $10,000.

Once the Dodges had decided to manufacture their own automobile, they had to enlarge substantially the Hamtramck plant, while reorganizing the existing facilities and equipment. Virtually all of the plant expansion and retooling took place in 1914. Major new buildings, including a massive four-story concrete assembly building, a large four-story press shop, carpenter and die shops, testing facilities, and an addition to the office building, were constructed. The plant nearly tripled in size, from about 500,000 square feet in 1913 to nearly 1.4 million in 1915.

Dodge Brothers spent more than $1 million on new buildings and at least $500,000 on retooling. In ceasing production of Ford components and preparing to make the Dodge automobile, the firm had to scrap and replace most of the existing tools and equipment. The retooling overwhelmed Dodge's force of 180 tool-and-die makers, so Dodge Brothers hired four other Detroit firms to produce the required fixtures and jigs. The firm formally incorporated on July 1, 1914, with capital stock of $5 million divided equally between the two brothers. The firm enlarged its capital stock on November 1, 1917, to $10 million, still tightly controlled by John and Horace Dodge. Plant expansion continued in the late 1910s, with the construction of nearly 2 million square feet of additional floor space from 1916 to 1920.

While the Dodge brothers prepared their manufacturing complex to start production, public interest in the Dodge car was enormous. The Dodge reputation for high-quality work practically guaranteed them a ready market. In August 1914 the *Michigan Manufacturer and Financial Record* declared, "When the Dodge Bros. new car comes out, there is no question that it will be the best thing on the market for the money." Their reasoning was simple—"The Dodge brothers are the two best mechanics in Michigan." In fact, before anyone had seen the new car, more than 13,000 individuals had asked to become Dodge dealers, including several Ford agents who wanted to add the Dodge line to their existing offerings.

Dodge Brothers also used advertising effectively in promoting the new automobile. They ran a series of billboard advertisements that began with only the words *Dodge Brothers* for several weeks. They added *Motor Car*, which ran for several more weeks, and, finally, *Reliable, Dependable, Sound*. The formal announcement of the new car, with no illustrations, appeared in the *Saturday Evening Post* on August 19, 1914–"Dodge Brothers, Detroit, who have manufactured the vital parts for more than 500,000 motor cars, will this fall market a car bearing their own name." One of their early ads read, "Think of all the Ford owners who would like to own an automobile."

The first Dodge automobile was an enormous success both in terms of sales and design. While both brothers worked together to develop the car, Horace Dodge was chiefly responsible for the final result. He did much of the design work during periods of seclusion in a cottage on John Dodge's Meadow Brook estate. Together the brothers conducted extensive and innovative tests of materials and components. For instance, they decided the brand of tires they would put on the car by dropping the products of each of the competitors from the roof of one of their buildings, in a crude endurance test. John Dodge devised his own test of crashworthiness by driving one of their prototypes into a brick wall at a speed of about 15 mph. Horace Dodge made numerous improvements in existing machines used to build the new car, or in many cases, designed new machinery from scratch. For example, he studied the enameling ovens used to dry painted car bodies and designed an improved oven that reduced heat loss from nearly 40 percent to about 4 percent.

The first model was a five-passenger touring car with a wheelbase of 110 inches, powered by a 35-horsepower, 4-cylinder L-head engine of Horace's design. The engine proved so reliable and efficient that it was the only one used in Dodge automobiles for many years. Innovative design features included an electric starting/ignition system that made stalling nearly impossible, a cone clutch, a pressurized fuel system, and an all-steel body fabricated by the Edward G. Budd Manufacturing Company. *Automobile Topics*, which offered a "sneak preview" of the new car, described it as "a handsome, comfortable, medium-sized car for five peo-

ple, with plenty of room and plenty of power, and built to run for years." The solid, dependable, and plain-looking automobile weighed 2,200 pounds and sold for $785, placing it about midway between the Model T and more-expensive luxury models.

The first Dodge automobile, subsequently named "Old Betsy," came off the assembly line on November 14, 1914. John and Horace Dodge, wearing dark overcoats and bowlers, rode in the first car to John's Boston Boulevard house, where they posed for pictures. Production in 1914 was limited to only 249 touring cars, as the Dodge brothers slowly brought the new plant into full-scale production. The demand for the Dodge automobile was so great that Dodge Brothers had to ration deliveries carefully to their dealers for more than a year. Dodge introduced a two-passenger roadster, which also sold for $785, in August 1915 and produced slightly more than 45,000 cars in 1915 at the Hamtramck plant, where the labor force had grown to more than 7,000 by the end of the year. Dodge Brothers adopted several practices that allowed them to concentrate on improving manufacturing efficiency. Like Ford, they produced only a single chassis, offered with several bodies. Dodge maintained the policy of "constant improvements but no yearly model change" over the entire period from 1914 to 1928.

The Dodge car developed a reputation for dependable service, which contributed greatly to its success. During the 1916 American expedition against the Mexican bandit Pancho Villa, war correspondent A. H. E. Beckett published several reports in *Motor Age* on the use of Dodge cars in the campaign. After Lt. George S. Patton led a daring surprise raid against a bandit headquarters, using three Dodges, Gen. John J. "Blackjack" Pershing, the commander of the expeditionary force, ordered his staff to use Dodge cars exclusively. Pershing ordered 250 more Dodges for his staff, and they continued to drive them on the battlefields of France.

The firm enjoyed steady growth and prosperity in the late 1910s. Production climbed from 70,000 cars in 1916 to 124,000 in 1917, leveled off briefly, and then reached a new peak of 145,000 units in 1920, when the Hamtramck plant employed 20,000. Dodge was consistently the fourth-largest automobile manufacturer in the late 1910s, behind Ford, Chevrolet, and Buick.

Dodge Brothers Company was best known for its automobiles, but the firm achieved several other noteworthy feats of product design and production. In the midst of World War I, the U.S. secretary of war, Newton Baker, wanted to find an American manufacturer to produce a delicate recoil mechanism for several types of French artillery. John Dodge went to Washington to meet with Baker and a delegation of French manufacturers, who were able to produce only five per day because of the manual production methods employed. They offered to send their skilled craftsmen to Detroit to show the Dodges how to make the device, but John Dodge abruptly told them that all he needed to begin machine production was a blueprint. He warned them in earthy language that they would have to comply with his wishes if they wanted the mechanism built. The secretary of war complained that he was not accustomed to having visitors speak to him in that type of language, and John Dodge's only response was, "the war would be a hell of a lot better off if you were."

The War Department provided Dodge with a model of the recoil mechanism, which he brought back to Detroit. After conferring with Horace, John Dodge returned to Washington, committed Dodge Brothers to make 50 recoil mechanisms per day, and promised to begin deliveries in four months. However, the Dodges insisted that they be allowed to build their own plant and equipment without government interference, and they agreed to supply the mechanisms at cost. The American government, which had no options, accepted the Dodges' offer on October 27, 1917. Dodge Brothers immediately began building a $10 million munitions plant measuring 600 feet by 800 feet and had 1,800 men working at the site throughout the winter months.

Horace Dodge devised an entirely new manufacturing scheme to produce the recoil mechanism by machine, and in the course of four months he designed 129 specialized machines previously unknown to American industry. He also made several improvements to the recoil mechanism itself. In their final agreement with the government, the Dodges agreed to take a profit of 10 percent of costs, largely to allow for the payment of taxes. To the astonishment of French and American officials, Dodge Brothers Company made the first deliveries of the much-needed devices, all of perfect quality, as promised. They never reached the production level of 50 mechanisms per day that John Dodge had promised but did make 30 per day, six times the French output. Dodge Brothers Company also

contributed to the war effort by producing two lightweight delivery trucks, with one of the models used for ambulances. The Dodge plant was also the scene of several major Liberty Loan drives.

The deaths of both Dodge Brothers Company founders in 1920 disrupted the firm's operations and the recession of 1921 added to the problems. None of the Dodge children had much interest in managing the firm, in part because their fathers had excluded them. John's son, John Duval Dodge, enjoyed the life of a playboy, while Horace E. Dodge, Jr., had no managerial or mechanical talents. Following Horace Dodge's death in December 1920, the plant was idle for nearly four months, and then it reopened under the direction of Frederick J. Haynes, who served as company president through 1925. Production in 1921 was only 91,000 vehicles, but output rebounded to 164,000 in 1922. Dodge Brothers continued to grow during the early 1920s, with production reaching a plateau of about 250,000 cars in 1924-1925. Dodge sales were firmly in third place in the industry in 1925, behind Ford (nearly 1.7 million) and Chevrolet (470,000). The firm's normal labor force in the mid 1920s was 20,000.

The excellent reputation of the Dodge automobile continued untarnished throughout the 1920s and greatly aided sales. The Dodge used more drop forgings and vanadium steel than any of its competitors, regardless of price. In the 1925 Dodge, for example, 64 percent of all the steel was vanadium, while the Ford had 48 percent, and the Buick only 11 percent. Dodge maintained high quality by making 5,200 different inspections at their Hamtramck plant and by sending teams of inspectors to monitor its suppliers.

The Dodge car continued to get a lot of free publicity. When the American explorer Roy Chapman Andrews led the American Museum of Natural History's Central Asiatic expeditions from 1924 to 1928, traveling over thousands of miles of rugged terrain, he insisted on using Dodges exclusively and widely publicized their toughness. Overall statistics on automobile usage seemed to support the Dodge reputation for durability as well. Dodge Brothers boasted that in March 1925 more than 90 percent of the 1.3 million cars it had sold since 1914 were still in use, and that nearly two-thirds of Dodge sales were to previous owners of Dodge automobiles. Furthermore, the firm could marshall a good deal of evidence that its cars were preferred by doctors, traveling salesmen, and others who prized reliability, and that the Dodge retained more of its value as a used car than other makes.

The Dodge factory complex, already one of the largest in the industry in 1920, with 3.3 million square feet of floor space, expanded by another 1.2 million square feet in the 1920s. All the major elements of the Dodge car were manufactured and assembled there by 1925, including castings, forgings, bodies, engines, transmissions, and other major components. The complex was largely self-sufficient, producing its own electricity, compressed air, and steam, as well as most of its own machinery and tools. It was a fully integrated manufacturing and assembly plant by the mid 1920s. By 1925 Dodge operated five major plants in the Detroit area. To avoid confusion, the Hamtramck plant became known as "Main Plant" or simply "Dodge Main," the name it kept for the rest of the life of the complex.

The widows of John and Horace Dodge became increasingly interested in withdrawing entirely from Dodge Brothers, in part because there was no prospect that any of their children would manage the firm. On May 1, 1925, the Dodge heirs announced the sale of Dodge Brothers to the New York investment bank Dillon, Read & Company for $146 million, including $50 million for goodwill. The sale was reported to be the largest single cash business transaction that had occurred in the United States up to that time. The firm was reincorporated in Maryland, and new Dodge stock was offered to the public. Dillon, Read also acquired Graham Brothers, a large truck manufacturer, in 1925 and merged the two firms. Raymond Graham became the general manager of Dodge from 1925 to 1928, while Edward J. Wilmer, a Wisconsin utility executive, served as president.

Dillon, Read was not familiar with the automobile industry and made a series of marketing blunders that weakened Dodge considerably. The Dodge automobile had been a sales success because it had a reputation for quality and durability, but cost only about $100 more than a Model T. Dillon, Read made Dodge into a luxury line, with appropriate prices. In 1928, when the Model A sold for $495, the lowest-priced Dodge had a price tag of $895, while the more expensive models sold for nearly $2,000. Dodge sales nose-dived from 332,000 units in 1926 to only 205,000 vehicles in 1927.

Dillon, Read turned Dodge Brothers into a failing business that barely met its payrolls in early 1928. When Walter P. Chrysler made overtures to the investment bankers for the purchase of Dodge Brothers, they were amenable to an offer. Chrysler acquired Dodge on May 29, 1928, for $170 million, and Dodge Brothers became the Dodge Division of the Chrysler Corporation. Walter Chrysler's purchase of Dodge, described by one observer as "the minnow swallowing the whale," was the key element of his plan to challenge General Motors and Ford as major automakers.

During its 28 years of independent life Dodge Brothers Company was a significant element in the American automobile industry. The firm was the premier supplier of parts and components to the Detroit automobile industry through 1913. It was a key contributor to the growth and success of the Ford Motor Company through 1913 as well. Dodge Brothers Company became the largest and most significant independent producer of mid-priced automobiles during the years from 1914 to 1928. Finally, the firm was the most important single element in the Chrysler Corporation's emergence as the last of the Big Three automakers of the late 1920s.

References:

Clarence M. Burton, *The City of Detroit, Michigan, 1701-1922* (Detroit: Clarke, 1922);

Dave Chambers, "1914-1964: Dodge Brothers First 50 Years," *Antique Automobile* (November 1964): 4-35;

Walter P. Chrysler and Boyden Sparkes, *Life of an American Workman* (New York: Curtis, 1937);

Dodge Brothers, *Acquisition of the Assets and Business of Dodge Brothers, A Michigan Corporation* (N.p., 1925);

"Dodge Brothers as Quality Producers of Cars," *Automobile Topics*, 34 (June 13, 1914): 377-389;

"Dodge Brothers Reveal the Car They Will Make," *Automobile Topics*, 35 (November 7, 1914): 905-911;

H. Cole Estep, "How the Dodge Brothers Plant Was Reorganized," *Iron Trade Review*, 56 (May 6, 1915): 909-916;

George S. May, *R. E. Olds: Auto Industry Pioneer* (Grand Rapids, Mich.: Eerdmans, 1977);

Allan Nevins, *Ford: The Times, The Man, The Company* (New York: Scribners, 1954);

Jean Madden Pitrose and Joan Potter Elwart, *The Dodges: The Auto Family Fortune and Misfortune* (South Bend, Ind.: Icarus, 1981).

Archives:

Material concerning Dodge Brothers is located in the Chrysler Historical Collection at Chrysler Corporation

World Headquarters, Highland Park, Michigan; the Dodge Papers at Burton Historical Collections, Detroit Public Library; the John Dodge Papers at Meadow Brook Hall Historical Archives, Rochester, Michigan; the Henry Ford Archives at the Edison Institute, Dearborn, Michigan; and in the National Automotive History Collection at Detroit Public Library, Detroit, Michigan.

Josiah Dallas Dort

(February 2, 1861-May 17, 1924)

by Richard P. Scharchburg

GMI Engineering & Management Institute

CAREER: Salesman (1876-1886); president and co-founder, Durant-Dort Carriage Company (1886-1917); president, Dort Motor Car Company (1915-1924).

Josiah Dallas Dort, always known as Dallas, was cofounder of the Durant-Dort Carriage Company, later guiding the carriage company into production of trucks, and finally cars, when the name was changed to Dort Motor Car Company. Dort was also instrumental in providing early financing for Buick, General Motors (GM), and Chevrolet from the surplus cash in the treasury of the Durant-Dort Carriage Company. He was an outstanding example of a businessman who felt a strong sense of duty to his community and provided civic leadership, even though he never sought political office.

A little more than a month before Abraham Lincoln was inaugurated as the sixteenth president of the United States, Josiah Dallas Dort was born February 2, 1861, in Inkster, Michigan, son of Josiah and Marcy Dort. He was educated in the public schools and graduated from Wayne High School. He later attended Michigan State Normal School in nearby Ypsilanti.

After his father's death in 1871, Dort began working with his mother in the family general store. When he was sixteen—and already a college student—he was offered a job in a crockery store in Ypsilanti, a job he took because his mother was gradually closing out her husband's store. At the end of two years' employment with the crockery firm, he had passed through the errand-boy stage and had been promoted to a position that combined the duties of clerk and janitor—duties that found him sweeping the store long before the first customers arrived and helping to unpack merchandise long after the last buyer had departed. In 1876, when his employer opened a similar store in Jackson, Michigan, Dort followed.

By 1879 Dort was not only the highest-paid retail crockery salesman in Jackson (earning $600 a year), but he was also thoroughly dissatisfied with his job and disillusioned as to his future. He left the crockery business and, with the help of relatives in Flint, Michigan, secured a job at Whiting & Richards Hardware. While selling building hardware, he met and became friends with another young man, William C. Durant, who was to have a considerable impact on his future. The friendship of Dort and Durant became close, and there developed from this early meeting an eventual business association.

Later Dort took a job in Saginaw, Michigan, with yet another hardware firm, where his work attracted the attention of one of Michigan's larger hardware jobbers. They offered to double his pay if he would come to work as a traveling sales representative. But the life of a "drummer"—a common name for a traveling salesman—was not to his liking, and a business opportunity drew him back to Flint.

The hardware store, now owned by Dort's former boss at Whiting & Richards, where he was first hired, was experiencing financial difficulties. In 1885 the new owner offered to employ Dort in order to utilize his considerable retailing experience in resurrecting the dying business. When asked by his new employer about the best and quickest way to shake the business loose from its downward slide, Dort's answer was quick and short: specialize and advertise.

After some careful thought, it was decided that the business would specialize in bronze hardware, cathedral glass, and plate glass, using these specialized lines to attract a steady clientele. The shift to a specialty store proved more profitable than

Flint, Michigan, office of the Durant-Dort Carriage Company, 1898 (left to right): Josiah Dallas Dort, William Crapo Durant, sales manager Charles Bonbright, an unidentified secretary, and secretary Fred A. Aldrich (courtesy of Carl Bonbright)

even Dort had imagined. Dort was aggressive in his sales technique, and his persuasive presentations to prospective buyers were usually convincing. His employer was pleased with his work, but as Dort was not working for himself, his prospects were still limited.

In summer 1886 Dort and Durant were introduced to a new generation of horse-drawn carts. As they spoke together one day outside Dort's place of employment, they noticed a group of young men admiring a new road cart owned by a mutual acquaintance, Johnny Alger. Alger offered Durant a ride to a meeting, and without much hesitation Durant climbed on. There was hardly room for the two men on the narrow seat, and Durant, recalling the incident later, said he was prepared for a rough ride, expecting to be jarred off at the next rut or bump in the dirt streets.

But the cart had its seat attached with an unusual stirrup-shaped, spring-loaded device mounted under the shafts of the cart. Durant was impressed

with the ride and instantly recognized the vehicle as a "self seller." He found the local outlet that was selling the carts and discovered they were made in Coldwater, Michigan.

He took the first train to Coldwater and went to the shop where the carts were being manufactured. Inquiring about the business, he learned the manufacturers, William H. Schmedlen and Thomas O'Brien, were not as enthusiastic as he was about the carts. Durant asked if they were interested in expanding the business and even offered to invest some money or help raise additional capital if required. Schmedlen and O'Brien instead offered him the entire cart business, with accompanying patent, for $2,000, including all the finished carts on hand—everything but their tools.

Durant quickly found an attorney, had a contract drawn, and was on his way back to Flint to raise the necessary money to pay for the patent and business he had bought. He convinced a local banker to loan him the money, and on September

28, 1886, the Flint Road Cart Company came into being. Durant went to see his friend Dort and asked him if he wanted to form a partnership—and, more important, add a little operating capital to the company. Dort recalled in 1924 that they each put in $1,500 at the start, and soon afterward each invested another $3,500, making a total actual capital of $10,000. It was agreed that Dort would handle the management and production end of the business and Durant would handle sales and promotion. But 1886 was a risky time to start a new carriage business in Flint. There were already several established carriage makers there, and in addition, the economy was in transition following a lumbering boom that had ended. But Durant and Dort both had a flair for salesmanship. Additionally, Dort was anxious to start his own business, they had a unique product, and they were both young and willing to work hard. The new business partners rented a small building, and true to his word, Schmedlen came to Flint and set up the shop to manufacture road carts.

A sample cart was assembled and hurriedly shipped to the Tri-State Fair in Madison, Wisconsin. The cart was entered in competition for horse-drawn vehicles of its class and was awarded a blue ribbon. The prize stimulated demand for the carts.

However, Durant's orders for carts came in faster than the small shop could manufacture them, and Dort contracted with an established carriage manufacturer, W. A. Paterson, to produce 3,200 carts at $12.50 (plus 3 cents for delivery). The carts then retailed for $22.50 each.

Before fulfilling his contract with Dort and Durant's firm, Paterson saw the sales appeal of the cart business and devised a cart of his own that he sold for $15—undercutting the Flint Road Cart Company's price by $7.50. To meet Paterson's price, Dort decided that they quickly had to expand manufacturing facilities themselves.

Dort found an empty factory and leased half of it. But the machinery that was needed called for cash—which they did not have. Dort resorted to some creative financing. No doubt still stinging from the lesson taught by Paterson's muscling his way into the road cart market, Dort recommended that they buy 200 Paterson carriages, change the nameplates, and rush them onto the market as Blue Ribbon carriages. This method not only raised the necessary capital for expansion but also launched the road cart company into the carriage business.

In 1895 the Flint Road Cart Company changed its name to Durant-Dort Carriage Company and on September 9 recapitalized at $150,000. In just seven years the original $2,000 had multiplied 75 times. Several particularly successful years saw dividends of 30, 60, 90, and even 100 percent. The sole owners were Dort, president; Durant, treasurer; and Fred A. Aldrich, secretary, and the dividends were paid only to those three men in the first years of the company's operations.

Under Dort's management the carriage company's production steadily increased. The company soon added other carriages to the original Blue Ribbon Line. First, in 1892, was the Webster, followed by the Victoria in 1894, and the Diamond in 1896. The business associates also founded several subsidiaries. The Flint Gear & Top Company and the Imperial Wheel Company marked the beginning of the company's production of component parts to cut still further the prices of Durant-Dort carriages. There soon followed, after Imperial Wheel, the Flint Axle Company and the Flint Varnish & Color Works. The ventures into axles and paint brought the entire Durant-Dort production operations into Flint for the first time in the company's history. Dort was president of all eight Flint divisions of Durant-Dort, and the pressure-cooker pace of operations must have been staggering.

Peak production for Durant-Dort was reached in 1906 when 50,600 vehicles were made. From that high point production fell steadily until 1917 when the last shipment of Durant-Dort carriages left for Port Huron. One era for Dallas Dort was ending, but another had already begun.

Some Flint carriage manufacturers refused to take automobiles seriously during the first few years of the twentieth century. In fact, Durant-Dort Carriage Company carried on its greatest expansion while the first automobiles were being made. Dort's partner, Durant, and a former Durant-Dort vice-president, A. B. C. Hardy, were among the carriage makers who were beginning new careers in the automobile business. Hardy came back from vacation in Europe in 1901 and formed the Flint Automobile Company, and Durant joined the Buick Motor Company in 1904, one year after its founding in Detroit by David D. Buick.

By 1904 Dort was well aware of the impending downfall of the horse and buggy as the major means of personal transport. He looked at the prospects for the future of Durant-Dort, and instead of

Factory of the Durant-Dort Carriage Company, 1905

liquidating assets as production declined, Dort increased capitalization in 1900 and again in 1901, and finally in 1907 boosted the capital stock to $2 million. Even though carriage production, and thus profits, were declining, the Durant-Dort bank account continued to grow.

With the increased capitalization, Durant-Dort began to diversify. The company entered the real estate business on a gigantic scale, originating Flint's first planned neighborhood–Civic Park–as a model of industrial, residential, educational, and recreational development. More important for the beginnings of automobile production, Dort led the company in the purchase of millions of dollars in automobile company shares. Gradually the Durant-Dort company itself began to build motor trucks and finally turned completely to automobile production.

The company's first contact with the infant automobile industry was thrust upon it by a gift from Durant. When Durant received $202,000 in Buick stock as a bonus, he turned the stock over to the Durant-Dort treasury, insisting it really belonged to the company. When various Flint business leaders were seeking the return of Buick assembly operations from Jackson in 1905, Durant-Dort sub-

scribed to another $100,000 worth of Buick stock. Durant-Dort also made the old Imperial Wheel plant on Hamilton Avenue available to Buick at a reasonable price and in lieu of cash was prepared to take additional Buick stock in payment. Dort was quite instrumental in persuading C. S. Mott to move his Weston-Mott Axle Company to Flint to provide Buick with a dependable supply of wheels and axles. Durant-Dort was a major subscriber to the stock issue that was required to induce the Weston-Mott company to relocate in Flint.

When Durant organized GM in 1908, Durant-Dort, like many other Buick shareholders, gave Durant full authority over its Buick shares, estimated by one source to be as much as one-third of Buick stock outstanding. In order to provide still more cash for the fledgling GM while not depleting its own cash reserves, the Durant-Dort Company borrowed from banks in Chicago, pledging as collateral 2,000 shares of GM stock. By 1909 the Durant-Dort treasury held about $2 million in GM shares. Canceled notes among Durant's papers in GMI's Alumni Historical Collection show that Dort personally signed notes for Durant's loans made in order to consummate GM's purchase of the Cadillac Motor Car Company in 1909. In 1910 a large bloc of stock was loaned from Durant-Dort's holdings to GM when it was needed for a $15 million loan from eastern bankers to save GM from receivership. Obviously Durant-Dort was a major financial asset in the early development of Buick and GM.

In fall 1912 Durant-Dort authorized subscriptions to $1.225 million in Chevrolet stock, exactly half of the original Chevrolet capitalization. It again made the Imperial Wheel plant on Hamilton Avenue available for production, this time for Chevrolet, when the decision was made in 1913 to move operations from Detroit to Flint. On October 11, 1912, Durant-Dort subscribed to 759 shares (worth $79,900) of Sterling Motor Company stock. Durant had organized Sterling to build engines for the Little automobile. The incorporation of Sterling Motors had been announced on August 9, 1912, by "the same interests who are identified with Republic Motors." Durant was elected president; Dort, vice-president; Curtis R. Hathaway, secretary; Edwin R. Campbell, treasurer; and Fred Aldrich, assistant secretary-treasurer. Thus, there were three prominent members of the Durant-Dort board at the head of the new Durant automobile endeavor. Again, plans demonstrated a close collaboration between Durant-Dort and Flint's emerging automobile industry. The Sterling factory was to have been located in Flint but eventually opened in the plant vacated by Chevrolet when it moved from Detroit.

The *Flint Journal* announced on August 9, 1912, that Durant, Dort, "and allied interests" had recently brought about organization of Republic Motors of Delaware, "which will be the holding company for the Chevrolet, Little, Mason and others already organized." Holding company headquarters were planned for New York, "but the industries would be centered in Flint and possibly Detroit." Under Dort's leadership the carriage company also invested in several automobile-related ventures, usually organized by Durant, including the Little and Mason companies.

In the final days of carriage production Dort recognized the inevitable and announced in July 1912 the purchase of materials to build 100 experimental automobiles. His annual report to the Durant-Dort stockholders for 1912 was otherwise bleak. He explained the decrease in sales was due to the competition of automobiles, streetcars, and motorcycles, and to the disastrous crop failures in the West, Northeast, and South. He reported profits had dropped 90 percent that year, from $227,584

to $22,733. This was also the same meeting when he recommended subscribing to 50 percent of the capitalization of Chevrolet; Dort's actions would suggest that he was leading the carriage company cautiously, but correctly, into automobile-related ventures.

Early in 1913 Dort announced, under the name of the Flint Motor Wagon Company, the manufacture of two models of motor delivery wagons, the Flint and the Best. They were sent to the New York automobile show, and after subsequent display of the trucks in Chicago, the federal government ordered ten trucks—hardly a spectacular beginning, but a beginning nonetheless.

On September 10, 1913, Dort recommended organization of an independent automobile company to produce a car of medium size priced from $1,000 to $1,200, and on January 1, 1915, the Dort Motor Car Company was incorporated. Dort was elected president; David M. Averill, vice-president; Fred A. Aldrich, secretary-treasurer; and John D. Mansfield, general manager; all of these were former Durant-Dort employees. The Durant-Dort treasury bought a large bloc of the new stock, and Dort himself initially invested $300,000 of his own money.

The former carriage plants were turned into automobile plants, paid for with Dort Motor shares. All that remained of the carriage business was an immense capitalization and a stock of horse-drawn vehicles. Most Durant-Dort stockholders invested in Dort Motor, some trading their carriage shares for Dort Motor stock. Dort Motor operations started very promisingly and grew swiftly. A Canadian division, Gray-Dort Motors, Ltd., of Chatham, Ontario, was formed in 1917.

In 1913 the first Dort automobiles were offered to the public—a roadster at $495 and a touring model at $680. During the firm's first several years, output was plagued with numerous mechanical problems, but by 1916 most of these had been solved, and production reached 10,225 vehicles.

Production climbed again in 1917 when the company introduced two new models. To provide for the expansion of the product line, capitalization was increased to $1.5 million. In 1918 production began to lag because of the entry of the United States into World War I. Dort spent a considerable part of his time raising funds for the Liberty Loan drives, leaving vice-president David Averill and the other officers of the company in charge of production. Capitalization was again increased in 1918, this time to $2 million. Following World War I the company's books posted their best years in 1919 and 1920. Vehicle production reached 26,700 units in 1920, and profits exceeded $1 million.

In 1920 a $3.5 million plant was built on Flint's east side with an annual production capacity of 12,000 cars. During that same year facilities were purchased in Kalamazoo, Michigan, to make closed Dort automobile bodies. Dort Motor's production schedule was projected for 40,000 vehicles in 1921.

By 1921, however, the post-World War I recession had set in, and even Dort's old partner, Durant, and GM were soon in financial difficulty. The effects of the recession on a small company such as Dort Motors were fatal. Dort Motors could not sell enough cars to operate the plants profitably. Output of 750 cars a month was necessary to break even, and production never reached one-third of that requirement. A loss of $280,000 was posted for 1923, and liquidation began in 1924. The last meeting of the Dort stockholders was held October 5, 1926, and the company joined the ranks of many early automobile companies whose names and products were never heard from or seen again.

Durant-Dort had about $1.225 million invested in the Dort Motor Company when it collapsed. To help build the Dort highway plant, the Durant-Dort company had bought $1.5 million of Dort Motor first-mortgage bonds. Two years later it returned to Dort Motor 50,000 preferred motor shares, so that Dort Motor could resell them as a 50 percent dividend on Dort Motor common shares. The carriage firm sacrificed heavily but in vain to try to save its motor venture. The legal end of Durant-Dort came on September 9, 1923. According to records of the company in the Sloan Museum, the stockholders decided to spread its dissolution over four years with one quarter of its assets to be distributed to its stockholders—now just Dort and Aldrich—in annual payments. In August 1924 its capital was reduced from $1 million to $5,000.

The stress of a failing business venture took its toll on Dort, and on May 17, 1924, he suffered a fatal heart attack on a Flint golf course. The whole city mourned, and businesses, industries, and schools shut down to honor his passing.

But Dort's impact on Flint had not been merely as leading industrialist and financier of the early automobile industry. He was a proponent of city planning and Flint's park system, a leader in benefits for workers, founder of the Community Music Association, promotor of Flint's east side industrial corridor, a director of Citizen's Bank, and a founder of the Flint Golf and Country Club. Tributes at the time of his death proclaimed that "he had given more money and time to civic service than any other individual in the city. He was the most beloved citizen in Flint's history."

His business success should be credited to hard work and his ability to inspire the loyalty of workers and surround himself with capable people. He then sought to make the most of their abilities while at the same time rewarding productivity and hard work by instituting a Dort-designed program of profit sharing. He is reported as saying one should give a man "all the rope he wanted" on the theory he would "either hang himself or build a ladder to success." Dort's willingness to place faith in his associates made him an object of respect and affection in both Flint and the entire automobile industry.

References:

Lawrence R. Gustin, *Billy Durant* (Grand Rapids, Mich.: Eerdmans, 1973);

George S. May, *A Most Unique Machine* (Grand Rapids, Mich.: Eerdmans, 1975);

John B. Rae, *American Automobile Manufacturers* (Philadelphia: Chilton, 1959);

Robert G. Schafer, *J. Dallas Dort* (Flint, Mich.: University of Michigan Archives Occasional Paper, 1975);

Bernard A. Weisberger, *The Dream Maker* (Boston: Little, Brown, 1979).

Archives:

The minute books of the Durant-Dort Carriage Company and the Dort Motor Company are located in the Perry Archives of the Sloan Museum in Flint. The Dort family has most generously permitted use of their considerable collections as well as those deposited in the GMI Alumni Foundation collection of Industrial History at GMI Engineering & Management Institute in Flint.

William Crapo Durant

(December 8, 1861-March 18, 1947)

by Bernard A. Weisberger

Chatham, New York

CAREER: Salesman, (1879-1886); founder and treasurer, Durant-Dort Carriage Company, (1886-1919); treasurer, Buick Motor Company, (1904-1919); founder and director, (1908-1910), president, General Motors Corporation, (1915-1920); founder and treasurer, Chevrolet Motor Company, (1911-1917); founder and president, Durant Motor Company, (1920-1931).

Put simply, William Crapo Durant was one of the handful of men responsible for the phenomenally swift rise of the American automobile industry, and through it the transformation of American life and culture. As a founding father of General Motors (GM) and some of its most important constituent companies, as the man who recruited or trained some of the most famous men in the automobile business, and above all as a visionary who foresaw and acted on the potentialities of the automobile revolution during its early unpromising years, Durant stands in the front rank of American business history. He fell from power and into obscurity because he had more charm than administrative awareness and had a compulsion for stock market and other gambles that were spectacular when they paid off and fatal when they did not. But his achievements, fairly regarded, far outweigh his flaws.

Though he was associated in the public mind with Michigan and Wall Street, Durant was a New Englander by birth and ancestry. He was born in Boston on December 8, 1861, to William Clark and Rebecca Crapo Durant. His father was an obscure bank clerk originally from New Hampshire. His mother was the daughter of Henry Howland Crapo, a New Bedford, Massachusetts, native, who had speculated in western pine lands, moved west in 1858, and, by 1861 had become a rich and notable citizen of the sawmill town of Flint, Michigan. In 1864 he was elected governor of the state and served two terms.

William Crapo Durant (courtesy of the General Motors Institute Alumni Foundation Collection of Industrial History)

Durant inherited his maternal grandfather's ambition and enterprise. From his father he derived a reputed charm and an ultimately fatal weakness for stock speculation. The senior Durant left banking for stockbrokering, failed at it, failed at any other enterprise, quarreled with his wife, scandalized in-laws, and simply vanished from the scene in 1872—allegedly addicted to alcohol. At that time Rebecca moved, with her ten-year-old son and a slightly older daughter, back "home" to Flint.

Durant grew up in a close-knit smalltown atmosphere that respected and rewarded enterprise. Flint capitalists and artisans adapted well to the slow dwindling of its lumber industry as the Michigan forests were exhausted. They turned to the manufacture of flour, woodenware, textiles, paper, farm implements, and especially wagons and carriages. Durant plunged into this world of doers willingly and eagerly. He left Flint's high school in his senior year, prior to graduation, and went to work at an array of clerical and sales jobs. He quickly showed a talent for selling. He sold cigars, patent medicines, and insurance so successfully that by the time of his marriage to Clara Pitt in June 1885, he was marked as a young man with a bright future. In the following year he took the step that would lift him far beyond local horizons when he became, overnight, a carriage maker.

His entrepreneurial career began in a chance meeting in September 1886 with a friend who was driving a light and unusually comfortable 2-wheel cart. Durant was so enthused over the vehicle, which was manufactured in Coldwater, some 75 miles from Flint, that he promptly traveled there and persuaded the two-partner concern that had made the cart to sell him the company for $1,500. Durant raised the money through a bank loan and by initiating a partnership with a young Flint neighbor, Josiah Dallas Dort, who was likewise seeking a chance for growth and independence. Hardly was the ink dry on the incorporation papers of the Flint Road Cart (FRC) Company when Durant rushed by train to several county fairs and returned inside of two weeks with orders for 600 carts. The FRC Company could only produce some two a day at best, but the impetuous and optimistic Durant subcontracted his orders to a local wagon-making competitor, William Paterson (who was happy to find a use for his idle plant capacity), and soon Durant and Dort were launched on a two-decade-long rise to the peak of the horse-drawn vehicle business. The FRC Company was recapitalized at $150,000 in 1892 and reorganized with Durant as treasurer. It was reincorporated in 1895 as the Durant-Dort Carriage Company, at which time it already had two subsidiaries; by 1901 it was capitalized at $1.5 million, owned eight factories in Flint alone, was producing tens of thousands of horse-drawn vehicles annually (its peak of 56,000 was reached in 1906), and was one reason why Flint, then numbering 15,000 in pop-

ulation and ranked tenth in manufacturing in Michigan, proudly dubbed itself "The Vehicle City."

In this early venture, Durant found and refined some of the principles—both good and bad—that would shape his career. One was to preserve freedom of maneuver by achieving, as fully as possible, independence from suppliers and subcontractors through vertical integration. (He learned this the hard way when Paterson, as a producer of carts under the FRC label, twice acquired lists of Durant's customers and wooed them away with cheaper models of his own.) Eventually Durant tried to bring the manufacture of all his components—wheels, subassemblies, paint, varnish, and even minor parts such as whip sockets—under direct ownership or that of Flint friends and neighbors. "Our plan," he later wrote, "was to manufacture practically every important part of a buggy. . . . This gave us control of the business in that line as long as carriages were in demand." He created the Flint Gear & Top Company in 1897, bought the Imperial Wheel Company in 1898, started the Flint Axle Works in 1900, and added the Flint Varnish Works in 1901.

A second Durant hallmark was product diversification, both in style and price. In 1892 he added the Webster Vehicle Company, which made light spring wagons, and in 1894 the Victoria Vehicle Company, responsible for production of 4-wheel buggies. In 1896 a low-priced line, Diamond Buggy, was joined to the company, and eventually Durant-Dort itself manufactured components and even complete vehicles (under other labels) for chain distributors. Durant was the catalyst for all this growth, achieving his results not merely through advertising but also by constant travel and the creation of a nationwide network of dealers and distributors linked to him not only through self-interest but also through personal loyalty. His charm and warmth were invincible; joined to his imaginativeness they spelled success.

Yet it became evident early that Durant's management style was essentially personal, collegial, and inconsistent. He surrounded himself with a network of close associates to whom he delegated freely but planlessly during his frequent absences. His joy was in building, not administering, and though he worked relentlessly at the schemes that consumed his days and nights, he either avoided details or became temporarily lost in them. His primary Durant-Dort colleagues were Dort himself,

Fred Aldrich, Fred Hohensee, Charles Bonbright, Alex B. C. Hardy, and Charles M. Nash (who began work in the Durant-Dort blacksmith shop and rapidly rose to a supervisory production position). At its peak Durant-Dort remained a family concern, with Durant the unquestioned paternal figure. This role suited his temperamental need for approval and liberated him for great deeds, but would make for a difficult later transition into a period of truly large-scale industrial organization.

These flaws, however, were not to be evident for a long time to come. In 1904 Durant, forty-two years old, was a successful millionaire whose personal life was slipping but who was professionally ripe to conquer new worlds. A growing estrangement from his wife led him to spend more and more time in New York, where he apparently began to play the stock market. From this vantage point he may or may not have heard the rumble of the approaching combustion-engine revolution that would soon make his carriage empire an antiquity. There is no clue to what he thought of automobiles before 1904, but in that year, called back to Flint, he jumped into the "game" as a full-time and dazzling player.

The initial spark was provided by Flint neighbors who found themselves stuck with a dying enterprise called the Buick Motor Company and wanted Durant to help them revive it. The challenge seemed formidable even for his talents. In 1899 David Buick, a successful Detroit manufacturer of bathtubs, had joined the ranks of those trying to produce a commercially viable automobile. In collaboration with Walter Marr and Eugene Richard, he created an excellent engine, but it took him until 1902 to complete a first production model (Buick Model A), by which time he had exhausted all $100,000 of his own money. He sold his enterprise and his services to Frank and Benjamin Briscoe, already engaged in the manufacture of radiators, fenders, and gas tanks for Ransom Olds and other carmakers. They in turn resold the company for a mere $10,000 to James Whiting, director of the Flint Wagon Works, who moved the entire concern to Flint. Whiting and other local investors in Buick wisely planned a gradual shift of their base from carriages to cars, but their early hopes waned as a struggling Buick and Marr could produce no more than forty cars (Buick Model B) in 1904. The $75,000 put up by Flint banks was in serious danger late in the year, and it was at that point that an appeal to

Durant was made. After a long period of thoughtful test drives he agreed to take direction—insisting on a free hand—and on November 1, 1904, he became treasurer and chairman of the board.

In the prime of life, Durant demonstrated his inimitable plunger's style. He promptly recapitalized Buick Motor Company at $300,000 (soon after raised to $500,000), and he traveled to the New York Automobile Show in January 1905, returning with orders in hand for 1,108 Buicks. He had instantly grasped the essentials of the new business. Capital must be raised in genuinely significant amounts to sustain a production process far more complicated than wagons had required. A high-quality (but medium-to-low-cost) product must be the engineering goal, in order to overcome public hesitation about the difficulties and costs of automobile ownership, and to tap a potentially gigantic market. As clearly as Henry Ford, Durant saw that the automobile could only flourish if it lost its image as a luxury; it had to be sold first to practical professional and business men, and eventually to farmers and workers. And Durant quickly realized that a broad network of sales and service agencies would be necessary to reach customers in the heartland and guarantee them maintenance support. He took to heart the words of a service executive whom he hired: "You aren't selling cars to mechanics."

During 1905 Durant deftly disposed of the many new shares of Buick in such a way as to raise working cash, and in addition to involve Flint ever more deeply in Buick's future. He had plenty of shares to work with; the company was recapitalized yet again in September at $1.5 million. Though such increases looked suspiciously like stock watering, the actual value of the assets increased quickly enough to keep up with the paper capitalization. Durant's optimism was justified by solid and steady improvement.

He hired talented designers, like Flint's Arthur Mason, to give him engine improvements that were translated into speed and power, two qualities that he exalted in his advertisements and made the basis for mass sales. "When better automobiles are made," Durant proclaimed, "Buick will build them." And the Buick Company did—though David Buick himself left in 1908 and drifted into obscurity. In that year 1,400 cars bearing his name were sold; the next year the total rose to 4,641, and in 1908 sales hit 8,487. Demand for Buicks was unflag-

Durant with Josiah Dallas Dort in 1908, four years after Durant left active management of the Durant-Dort Carriage Company to revitalize the Buick Motor Company

ging, and so was Durant's faith in them. During a brief money panic and business slump in 1907, he somehow found money to keep his production lines running and to replenish inventories, and when recovery came he was ahead of the competition with cars ready to sell.

In 1908, the year in which Ford produced the Model T, the Buick Model 10, known as the White Streak, appeared, offering a 4-cylinder, 18-horsepower 2- or 3-seater to buyers at a price of $1,000. It was hugely successful and helped push Buick toward a record 30,525 sales in 1910. Durant kept expanding production facilities, and in 1907 he scored a vertical integration coup by bringing the Weston-Mott Axle Company from Utica, New York, to Flint. With it came its owner, Charles S. Mott, thereafter a constant figure in Flint. Durant also maintained Buick's technological edge and public visibility by fielding a race team whose stars were Lewis Strang, Bob Burman, and the Chevrolet brothers, Arthur and Louis. Increasingly Flint was known as the home of Buick, and its 30,000 citizens, as of 1910, almost universally looked to Durant as the father of all blessings.

Only four years after taking over Buick, he had proven to be a Napoleon of the new industry. His personal life also underwent restructuring. In 1906, when his daughter Margery married Dr. Edwin Campbell of Flint, Durant moved in with the young couple. In spring 1908 he divorced Clara Pitt Durant, and on the day after the decree became final, married nineteen-year-old Catherine Lederer of Jackson, Michigan.

With this chapter of his past closed, he was receptive when Ben Briscoe telephoned him, asking for a meeting to discuss a proposal described with the words: "There's millions in it." At a quickly arranged breakfast conference in Flint, Briscoe explained what was on his mind: nothing less than a plan to unite the major firms in the automobile industry in one company. The seed of GM was planted.

After his failed venture with Buick in 1903, Briscoe had joined with Jonathan D. Maxwell to produce the Maxwell-Briscoe automobile, which was enjoying respectable sales in 1908. But Briscoe, like others in the business, feared the destabilizing effects of unregulated competition among the hundreds of companies in production in 1907. He saw a future of continued price wars, unpredictable swings on the securities market, sudden failures that wiped out jobs and savings, and bitter struggles over limited supplies of materials and components. If it were possible to have "one big concern of such dominating influence in the automobile industry as . . . the United States Steel Corporation exercise[d] in steel," its mere presence, he believed, "would prevent many of the abuses that we believed existed."

Briscoe asked Durant to join him in creating such a combination. Durant would bring the greater reputation and proven skills to the task, but Briscoe had an asset in a connection to J. P. Morgan & Company, which had expressed tentative willingness to undertake the financing that would be required. Durant accepted the proposal, and at his suggestion, negotiations began among four manufacturers: himself and Briscoe, Henry Ford, and Ransom E. Olds. Olds had parted with his original backers in 1904, leaving them the right to use the name of "Oldsmobile," while he himself (with new partners) created the line known as the Reo (from his initials). These four makes together accounted for a substantial share of the 43,300 cars sold in 1907 and offered a firm base for the proposed consolidation. Discussions, which included a representative of Morgan, began in spring 1908 but almost immediately hit a snag. Durant envisaged a holding company, issuing $35 million in stock, which the constituent firms would take in exchange for their own, while they continued to operate under their existing managements. But Ford, and then Olds, made it clear that they simply wanted to sell out for cash, at least temporarily. Morgan was not interested on those terms and said so. Thereupon Ford and Olds, both sturdy individualists, pulled out, leaving Briscoe and Durant, in the latter's words, to "go it alone."

But that proved no easy task. Negotiations continued through the summer but were marked by increasing discord between Durant and the house of Morgan. Durant, for his part, was impatient with the legally cautious and secretive Morgan style of operation, and above all with the Morgan insistence on a large share of control in any combination they helped to engineer. In turn the great investment bank was wary not only of the still fragile automobile business, but especially of a man who, despite his success with Buick, struck them as a plunger and careless risk taker. By the end of August the deal had collapsed.

Then Durant, forsaking Briscoe's participation and Morgan's blessing, sprang one of the surprises he enjoyed by running ahead on his own. He had quietly bought an option on the Oldsmobile Company. So he now had two companies to consolidate, and he effected this on September 16, 1908, by chartering the General Motors Corporation in New Jersey. The new company issued $12.5 million in stock and then "bought" Buick and Oldsmobile for stock and a pittance of cash. Though he took no title at the time—he was simply one of the directors—GM was undeniably what he proudly called it later— "my baby."

In the ensuing twenty-four months he embarked on a breathtaking course of expansion. It created the foundation of the modern GM, but both the financing and organization were so fragile that the new corporation was bound to undergo a crisis before long. Durant purchased the Oakland Motor Company (later renamed Pontiac), and then, to give the corporation a high-priced quality car, the Cadillac Motor Company, already renowned for engineering precision. The owners, Wilfred and Henry Leland, drove a hard bargain, demanding $4.5 million in cash, which Durant raised by heavily milk-

ing the treasury of his chief cash producer, the Buick Company.

Cadillac and Oakland were merely preliminary acquisitions. Durant went on to buy vehicles now long forgotten—the Marquette, the Cartercar, the Welch, the Elmore, and the Reliance truck. His strategy was to cover a market almost indiscriminately because no one could yet know just what combination of size, motive power, appointments, and safety features would best sell. "I was for getting every car in sight, playing it safe all along the line," he was later to explain. He even had a second chance to bid on the Ford Motor Company in 1909, when Ford once again was in a mood to sell. This time the asking price was $8 million in cash. Durant was willing, but the sum was beyond his power to raise internally, and no bank was forthcoming with a loan to effect the merger. So the deal withered, leaving behind only enticing speculations on what might have been.

Durant also continued his farsighted pattern of securing control of components. He discovered Albert Champion and his company, which manufactured spark plugs in Boston, and he convinced the Frenchman to move to Flint to set up a new enterprise, later to become the AC division of GM. (Like Olds, Champion left his name as a trademark to his original backers and conferred his initials on a new line). But while the Champion story seemed to duplicate Durant's success with Mott, some of his other vertical integration efforts proved far less shrewd. He gave up millions in GM shares for the Heany Lamp Company, which was a total failure in providing electric lights for autos. He also bought factories of uneven soundness to produce engines, castings, electrical apparatus, and other automotive parts.

By 1910 GM included twenty-five firms, valued at $54 million dollars, scattered in Michigan, Ontario, and New York. They had been acquired for a total outlay of some $33 million, of which only $6.2 million had been in cash. The glitter of the performance obscured deep problems. There was no unified system of accounting, purchasing, marketing, or engineering research. There were simply twenty-five independent firms, loosely run by Durant, who was a power unto himself. GM had no cash reserves, little working cash, and no prudent voices to cut costs and cancel failing projects. Inevitably, any contraction in sales or credit—any widespread economic slump—would put the corpora-

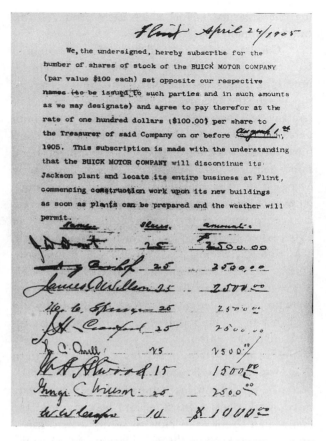

One of the stock subscriptions through which Durant raised working capital at Buick

tion in deep trouble. And such a crunch came in spring and summer 1910, when fully eighteen auto firms alone foundered. GM staggered under rapidly accumulating debts—the exact figures unknown but changing for the worse month by month. Finally, in September a syndicate of Boston and New York bankers saved GM from bankruptcy with a loan of $15 million, on terms that the founder considered extortion—a $4.25 million commission, plus a $6 million bonus of stock. Moreover, all of GM's voting stock was to go into a five-year voting trust on which Durant would sit as a single impotent director, outnumbered by bank representatives added to the board. But he had no choice other than to capitulate to save his company. Durant seethed inwardly as he watched the new, conservative leadership liquidate relentlessly and devote receipts to debt retirement instead of to dividends and growth.

In retrospect Durant's impatience is understandable. His vision of the long-run future was far ahead of the bankers'. He predicted, in 1910, when fewer than 100,000 automobiles were in use, that some day 90 million Americans would be automo-

bile drivers, and that there would be 2 million cars on the road as early as 1920 (a total actually reached in 1916). But he was unconcerned with the short run, and in fact GM needed the tightening that the bankers gave it. Durant's problem, as it was later described by Alfred P. Sloan, was that he could create but he could not administer.

His creativity within GM was temporarily thwarted by the bankers in 1910. But he promptly exercised it outside the corporation, with astounding luck and success. He decided to introduce another make of automobile on his own. His first move, in 1911, was again to ask his old Flint associates for the local support that nourished him. He went to Louis Chevrolet, of his Buick racing team, and announced: "We're going to need a car."

Durant set Chevrolet to work in a rented Detroit shop designing the new vehicle, the funds coming from the sale of stock in a newly created Chevrolet Motor Company. But it was not Durant's style to leave matters at so simple a level. He also set up a second company and a second designer—William Little—in Flint to produce another low-priced car, and yet a third corporation, Mason Motors, to build power plants for both Littles and Chevrolets.

His timing was excellent. Flint's horse-drawn vehicle builders were ready for the final phaseout of their operations. The Flint Wagon Works readily sold him its facilities, and Durant-Dort likewise furnished its founder with work space and operating cash in return for stock in Durant's three new companies. Flint was unshaken in its faith that Durant would in time turn these certificates into cash.

Success took some time but it arrived. In 1912 and 1913, two contentious years, Durant juggled both his corporate and personal lives in search of the right combination. The car known as the Little, produced largely through the dedicated supervisory efforts of A. B. C. Hardy, enjoyed modest sales despite its unpromising name. But Louis Chevrolet's first production, a large, 6-cylinder model selling at $2,151, was a failure. Some time after its appearance Chevrolet departed in a huff, leaving his name to immortality. Durant moved the Chevrolet operation to New York City in a bid to increase its visibility to eastern bankers. The transfer coincided with his own personal transfer from Flint. He settled in an apartment on New York's Park Avenue, not far from where daughter Margery, nearing the end of the first of her four marriages, had taken up residence. He also brought his aging mother to live in New York. Finally, in 1913, he resigned all of his posts in the Durant-Dort Company. There would always be emotional and financial links with Flint, but Durant had at last become one more midwesterner whom success finally brought to settle in New York.

In 1913 Durant put all of his eggs in the Chevrolet basket, folding both Little Motors and Mason Motors into an enlarged Chevrolet Company. In 1914 the breakthrough came, the reward for many months of hard work by the competent technical associates whom Durant chose, whom he backed with money produced by his persuasiveness, and to whom he allowed free rein to produce a quality car at an attractive price. Two Chevrolet models displayed at that year's auto show—the Royal Mail at $750 and the Baby Grand at $875—were spectacular successes. In 1915 the line was enlarged by the addition of the Chevrolet 490, which, at $550, offered serious competition to Ford's hugely popular Model T. Five thousand cars with the familiar Chevrolet bow-tie logo (designed by Durant) were sold in 1914. By the end of 1916, 70,701 Chevrolets—each earning profits between $78 and $112—had been sold. It was far short of the 308,213 Model Ts then in service, but a year later Chevrolet's total of cars on the road reached 125,882. They poured out of parts and assembly factories in Texas, California, Ontario, New York, and Michigan and were sold through a national network of dealerships.

In 1915 and 1916 the automobile revolution was reaching a stage of technological stability. A more-or-less standard car was making its appearance, featuring front-mounted engines, H-slot gear shifts, and demountable wheel rims to ease tire changes. Closed bodies and electric lighting—and self-starting—would soon become common. "Humanity had never wanted any machine as much as it wanted this one," Sloan said afterwards, and in America his statement was proven by the leap in the number of in-service automobiles—1 million in 1916, double that only six years later. A proven success at last, the automobile now had little trouble attracting banker interest.

Durant was riding the wave, and with Chevrolet triumphant in 1915, he revealed the ambitious plan that may have motivated him all along—to use his winnings to reclaim his former company. For months prior to the annual meeting of GM directors slated for September, he collected proxies and

bought GM shares. At the time of the meeting he had enough of them to force a deadlock in the vote for a new board. The impasse was broken by the board's enlargement to include three new "neutral" directors, acceptable both to Durant and to the leader of the opposing faction, James J. Storrow, head of the Boston investment house of Lee, Higginson & Company. The three were named by a relative newcomer to the board, and to the automobile business. He was Pierre S. du Pont, and the men he chose were associates from his own Du Pont Corporation, an important organization in GM's future.

There was still some doubt as to the extent of Durant's control of GM in September 1915, but the following six months saw him put the matter beyond question through a complicated maneuver, namely the takeover of "big" GM by "little" Chevrolet. This was achieved through a public offer to exchange Chevrolet stock for GM stock at a ratio of 5 to 1 (later reduced to 4 to 1). So attractive did this trade offer prove that by May 1916 the treasury of Chevrolet Motor Company owned or controlled 450,000 of 826,000 GM shares then outstanding.

Two factors made the trade-in so successful. Chevrolet stock was plentiful, and its price was rising. Durant had increased Chevrolet capitalization to $20 million in 1915 and then to $80 million, enabling him to finance expansion with his favored "currency." (Significantly, however, he was finally obliged to go beyond Flint for money on this scale, still another step in his "easternization." He became closely associated with Louis G. Kaufman of the Chatham and Phoenix National Bank, who became a Chevrolet director and a conduit to the New York financial community.) In contrast to the surge in Chevrolet stock prices, GM stock remained relatively unalluring, due to the retrenchment policies of the voting trust. Hence the 5-for-1 and 4-for-1 trades produced varying but measurable profits on each share of GM yielded. (At one point in 1915, for example, a single GM share was worth $558, while five Chevrolet shares brought $700.)

Actually GM's prospects were excellent. The Storrow supervision had laid important foundations for the future, especially in the matter of personnel. Storrow had promoted Charles Nash from the presidency of Buick to the presidency of GM. Storrow claimed later that Nash's management turned the concern from a "wreck" into one with $25 million in the bank. Moreover, Storrow and Nash had

*Durant during his tenure as president of the Durant Motor Company
(courtesy of Catherine L. Durant)*

hired Walter Chrysler to take over at Buick, luring him from the American Locomotive Company. Chrysler, a brilliant railroad production expert, came (at an initial reduction in salary) because he was eager to get into the automobile business, even though he had never driven a car until 1908. He proved an almost immediate success. Nevertheless, GM's hesitation about entering the low-priced market was costly in competitive terms; even its sales of 76,078 units in 1915 left it far short of a commanding market share. That weakness had depressed its stock prices and provided Durant with his opportunity.

Storrow's group made last-minute efforts to have GM shareholders elect a new three-year voting trust, but they were doomed to fail, even though they enlisted the support of Mott and Nash himself—to the latter's ultimate discomfort. In May 1916 Durant, in full control, forced both Storrow and Nash to resign. But Durant shrewdly lured Chrysler into remaining at GM for at least three years more, with a characteristically bold offer of $500,000 a year in salary—cash or stock—which was a tenfold in-

crease for Chrysler. The aftermath for Nash was a new start, as Storrow set him up in Kenosha, Wisconsin, to produce an automobile known as the Rambler. And the sequel for Durant was the sweet taste of success. On the night of June 1, 1916, he told his wife over dinner: "I took General Motors back from the bankers today." He had no idea how difficult it would be to keep it.

He began his second reign at GM with much success. His annual personal income from 1916 through 1918 was on the order of $3 million, and in 1917 he bought an expensive home called "Raymere" in Deal, New Jersey. In business he continued to be a risk taker. He organized a separate combination of components manufacturers. These included the Delco, Remy Electric, Perlman Rim, New Departure Ball Bearing, and Hyatt Roller Bearing companies, which he grouped together with several other parts-making establishments under the rubric of United Motors Corporation. The purchases were, as usual, financed largely with stock. The most important acquisitions of United Motors, however, were human rather than material. With

Hyatt Roller Bearing came its co-owner and chairman,. Alfred P. Sloan, Jr., and with Delco (Dayton Engineering Laboratories Company) came one of its founders, Charles F. Kettering. Sloan had administrative genius equal to that of Kettering in engineering. Sloan eventually became president and board chairman of GM and Kettering its director of research, and their distinguished careers proved that Durant had struck a bargain in adding them to the team at $13.5 million for the Hyatt firm and $8 million for Delco.

Durant was now the guiding figure and major stockholder in three companies—United Motors, Chevrolet, and GM. Despite suggestions that he merge the three, he held back, particularly because he cherished Chevrolet's independence. He did, however, assist in the transformation of GM from a holding into an operating company through a rechartering in Delaware in 1916 and a new and enlarged issue of stock. Thus, except for Chevrolet, the various car and parts companies under the GM umbrella became divisions—a first, tentative consolidating step.

Meanwhile, du Pont was elected chairman of GM's board of directors late in 1916. He was a man wholly unlike Durant. Du Pont was fully attuned to organization on the scale demanded by the twentieth century. Along with two cousins, Coleman and Alfred du Pont, he had bought out his family's long-established blasting powder company, E. I. du Pont de Nemours, Inc., in 1902, and was slowly transforming it into a broad-based organization for making and marketing chemicals and synthetics. He had set up a model management staff system, with separate offices for personnel, legal work, purchasing, reporting, development, manufacturing and the like—all reporting to and supervised by an executive committee and a finance committee at the top. During this modernization, however, the Du Pont corporation went on with its manufacture of munitions and was piling up enormous wartime profits from 1914 through 1918.

Du Pont's chief assistant for development, John J. Raskob, was a self-made success, the son of an immigrant cigar maker in upstate New York. Raskob was somewhat like Durant in that he was imaginative and optimistic, and constantly crackling with bold schemes. On the other hand, he had a sense of restraint that Durant lacked.

It was inevitable that there should be eventual friction between Durant and the du Pont-Raskob team. Du Pont took his chairmanship seriously and believed that he could bring financial and administrative order to GM while Durant, as president, could focus on the operations side that he appeared to handle so successfully. This, needless to say, was far from Durant's pattern. Still, in the first year, relations among the three men were courteous and even good-natured.

But in 1917 changes began to take place. Du Pont insisted that the GM board name a finance committee to prepare budgets and to approve large capital outlays and won his point with the directors. Raskob continued to press, against Durant's resistance, for the merging of United Motors and Chevrolet into the GM structure. Events in the stock market played into Raskob's hands. GM stock dropped from 200 in January 1917 to 75 in October. Durant had made heavy purchases of the stock on margin and repeated margin calls as the price dropped forced him to ask the finance committee of the board for a loan of $1 million, on the grounds that his buying had been necessary to maintain public confidence in the stock and help the company. The committee turned down the loan, finding it a bad precedent, but it "gave" Durant his money by voting him an annual salary—something he had not previously requested—of $500,000 retroactive to January 1, 1916. Technically he had received what he wanted but in the process had become more dependent on the board.

Nor did the matter end there. The depression in GM stock prices (angrily credited by Durant to bearish speculators on Wall Street) was making it hard to raise needed expansion capital through sale of new shares. Raskob now made a momentous suggestion. The Du Pont Corporation had a surplus of more than $50 million in its treasury and could wisely invest $25 million of it in GM and Chevrolet stock to raise and stabilize the price. Durant was sufficiently hard-pressed to accept the proposition even though it came with two strings attached. One was that the GM-United Motors-Chevrolet merger must be approved, and the other was that GM directors responsible to the Du Pont Corporation must thereafter play a controlling financial role.

It then remained for Raskob to sell the idea to the Du Pont Corporation board in December 1917, by means of a paper that came to be known as the Raskob Memorandum. In it he painted a bright future for the automobile industry, stressed the value of diversified investments for the Du Pont exchequer, and noted that there would be excellent prospects for attaining an exclusive right to supply the great quantities of paint, varnish, and synthetic fabrics required by GM. He even said it was his belief that "ultimately the Du Pont Company will absolutely control and dominate the whole General Motors situation with the entire approval of Mr. Durant," a statement that would undoubtedly have stunned Durant, who was not present and never saw the memorandum. (Raskob was most probably stating only personal opinions and overselling his case, but the memorandum came back to haunt the du Ponts in 1949 when the government brought—and ultimately won—an antitrust suit to force the Du Pont Corporation, by then a majority stockholder in GM, to divest itself of the motor combine.)

Raskob, with Pierre du Pont's clear support, won his point. The Du Pont board authorized the $25 million purchase of some 98,000 GM and 134,000 Chevrolet shares, making the Wilmington-based corporation the second largest holder of GM stock and deeply affecting Durant's future.

Outwardly unperturbed, Durant continued his expansionism, with uneven results. He discovered a small, nearly bankrupt Detroit company known as Guardian Frigerator that was struggling to market a new invention, an electric cooler to replace kitchen iceboxes. Excited by its potential, he financed a reorganization from his personal funds, set up a production and marketing staff and facilities, and rechristened the company as Frigidaire. In March 1919 he sold it for $56,366 to GM, where it became in time a major and fruitful division. But he chose losers as well as winners. In 1918 he persuaded the board to buy the Samson Sieve-Grip Tractor Company in California and the Janesville Machine Company in Wisconsin. His purpose was to generate a line of trucks, large automobiles, and tractors to compete with Henry Ford for the American farm market. He particularly wanted the Samson line to include yet another new invention, this one called the Iron Horse—a small tractor guided by reins in the hands of an operator walking behind. Throughout 1919 the Iron Horse gobbled development money and ended, like the whole Samson venture, as a costly failure. The entire division was written off in 1920 as a loss of $33 million, recouped in part by the sale of inventory and reconversion of the Janesville plant into a Chevrolet factory.

In 1919 Durant's appetite for growth created no problems with the GM board, which was also in a feverishly acquisitive mood. From 1918 to 1920 it went on a buying binge equal to that from 1908 to 1910, except that the expenditures were now in multimillions instead of millions. The modern era of gigantic enterprise had made its mark on GM. Newly created divisions included the General Motors Acceptance Corporation (GMAC), to finance installment buying of GM cars, the GM Export Division, and GM of Canada. Companies that were bought either in whole or in part (through purchases of a controlling interest) included Fisher Body, Scripps-Booth, Interstate Motors, T. W. Warner (gear-makers), and Dayton-Wright Airplane. In addition blocks of shares were purchased in the Goodyear and Dunlop rubber tire enterprises, and in other companies making parts and subassemblies. Millions were appropriated to begin construction of a huge new office building in Detroit, slated to carry Durant's name. This last project was initiated over his determined opposition. He was not only uninterested in having his name blazoned, but the whole idea of sheltering a centralized bureaucratic and administrative complex for his company was alien to him. He was hard put to adjust to the needs of a GM which, in December 1918, employed 49,118 people, had $370 million in outstanding stock, and totaled $270 million of annual gross receipts based on sales of 246,834 "units"—including military transportation and hardware produced for the United States armed forces.

In 1919 there was no change in the growth pattern. More stock was issued to raise capital, bringing GM to a position where it shared the distinction with United States Steel of being a billion-dollar corporation. The year's net sales were nearly $510 million; there were $60 million in earnings, of which $22 million were paid out in dividends. Two and a half years after GM had been reclaimed by Durant, its net assets showed an eightfold increase—to $452 million. It was a multi-state supercorporation, with nearly 86,000 people on its payroll. It was also economically vulnerable, since it had gigantic fixed investments and their relentless costs, and a high burden of service charges on its outstanding debts.

Even Durant was becoming concerned with what he believed to be an overly generous manner of handling the requests of production managers in the different divisions, each one striving to stockpile supplies and personnel and boost production targets. Even the supposedly conservative finance committee rarely said "no." Sloan worried about "management by crony." Du Pont, the soul of rationality, injected a comptroller, a personnel consultant, and a development team into the top management structure, trying to move toward control. And du Pont approvingly read and filed a reorganization plan submitted by Sloan to Durant and genially ignored.

One of the Du Pont experts sent to "help" Durant, John Lee Pratt, discovered the founder still ahead of his contemporaries in long-range vision, worrying about future supplies of petroleum, plate glass, and batteries, and curious about the automotive possibilities of new metals such as aluminum. But Durant was still an unstructured short-term "boss." He sometimes immersed himself for hours in small details like the makeup of an advertisement. He kept important executives waiting while he personally dealt with calls from a bank of ten phones in his office. Many of these were to his numerous stockbrokers. Worst of all he impulsively, and with the best intentions in the world, often interfered with the decisions of his appointees. This habit finally lost the company Walter Chrysler. After Durant had hired away good men from Buick, created unnecessary subsidiaries, and announced the building and purchasing of plants without consulting with Chrysler, the tough ex-railroad mechanic announced: "Now, Billy, I'm through," and walked out in March 1920. Sloan, too, thought about departing at the end of that year but was overtaken by dramatic events that led to Durant's ouster.

The beginning of the end came early in 1920. More capital was needed, and Raskob wanted to cast a wider net for stock purchasers. One step was to join Durant in organizing syndicates to prop the price and salability of GM. But that was not enough to bring in the $50 million or $60 million required. Nothing less than banker participation would do, and so in 1920 J. P. Morgan & Company was enlisted to subscribe for 1.8 million shares. As a condition, six new directors had to be added to the board, including Morgan vice-president Edward R. Stettinius, plus two other bankers, plus three finance directors from other corporations. Twelve years after Morgan had first spurned Durant, and four years after he had boasted of recapturing GM from the bankers,

Durant's company was tied tightly to Wall Street. In a final spectacular denouement, he now brought his own numbered days to an end.

In mid 1920, a postwar economic slump shattered automobile business expectations. GM had targeted the production and sale of 876,000 units for 1920, an average of nearly 75,000 a month. But June sales were only 47,000. November's fell to 12,700, and those for January 1921 were a mere 6,150. Unused inventory piled up in the plants despite emergency freezing of purchases. Commitments devoured cash reserves. And GM stock toppled from a midyear price somewhat in the vicinity of $50 a share to $14 a share by the first week in November.

The collapse in stock prices destroyed Durant. During the long slump he used his personal fortune to buy GM shares. He always maintained that he did it for the future of the company, but it is also likely that he was thinking of the many friends he had advised to become GM shareholders. He could not bear to acknowledge that his wizardry was no longer able to enrich them. Whatever the reason, the steady decline and the inexorable calls for more margin and collateral had driven him, by November, to the end of his resources. This fact was revealed in a characteristic way. Durant, pursuing a long-favored scheme, announced a new personal venture, the creation of the Durant Company, which would buy stocks in quantity and then resell them in small blocks, on the installment plan if necessary, to people of modest incomes. The theoretical idea was to democratically disperse stock ownership and discourage large-scale speculation. But one immediate purpose was disclosed when Durant offered to *sell* GM shares to prospective enrollees. In retrospect it seems clear that he needed to unload some stock to raise cash.

This immediately brought sharp questions from Stettinius and du Pont. Durant was president of GM and a member of buying syndicates to hold the price up. What on earth did he mean by selling? A meeting was arranged on November 10, and it began a ten-day crisis during which Durant's position unraveled completely, leaving him, at its end, in financial tatters and expelled from GM's leadership. Durant was forced to admit that he owed a sum of unknown dimensions—it turned out to be some $27 million—to his brokers, secured by 4.5 million shares of GM stock, some Durant's, some borrowed. If he could not come up with money quickly, the entire mass of stock would be dumped upon the market, which would be catastrophic for the corporation.

The Morgan and du Pont interests were angry but could not avoid the necessity of bailing out Durant in some fashion. Dwight Morrow, Morgan's representative, was particularly hostile at what he perceived as secretiveness and disloyalty on Durant's part. It was the ultimate clash between the points of view of the corporate banker and small-town individualist. The banker was fated to win. Raskob finally crafted a plan that all parties, Durant included, accepted. In essence, a special holding company was created and funded by the Du Pont and Morgan firms. It bought more than 2.5 million GM shares from Durant at a price of $9.50 a share—4.5 points below the market price—thus giving him the cash to pay the brokers. When he had done so, he had some $7,000 left from the sale of stock that he had bought for millions, and the du Ponts were the majority holders in GM. In addition the stock was kept off the market. Durant was allowed to keep a 40 percent interest in the holding company, but he had no voting rights, and it was made clear to him that he was to resign. On December 1, 1920, he left GM's Broadway offices permanently, bravely joking with his long-faced personal office staff.

From this point on, Durant's career becomes less important from a business standpoint and can be summarized fairly swiftly. Fifty-nine years old at the time of his resignation, he could have retired, but he chose to make one more comeback attempt in the automotive industry. This time, however, the Chevrolet magic was not there. It was a different business that he faced, he himself was a changed man, and when obstacles arose he took refuge in the dangerous allurements of the stock market.

Before he had been out of office a month, Durant announced plans to build what he would later describe to a friend as "a real good car." Before 1921 was over he was hard at work assembling a new large-scale organization. Raising some $5 million in seed money for a new start was no problem. He procured part of it by selling his 40 percent interest in the company that had taken over his GM shares. The rest came mainly from the sale of stock in his new enterprise, to be known as Durant Motors. It was not hard to find subscribers. His name still carried weight, and he had kept the network of friends earned by his winning ways over

the years—from office workers and elevator operators whom he had sometimes called in for a quick, relaxing game of checkers, to dealers and suppliers whom he had treated well and who were willing to help him liberally in hopes of future rewards. He still had the power that Walter Chrysler described, to "coax a bird right down from a tree." Finally he drew on a general reservoir of sympathy for a perceived underdog, since it was a widespread belief, especially around Flint, that he had been done in by Morgan and the eastern financial aristocracy.

At first it did seem that the old tale would be repeated; 1921 and 1922 were full of well-publicized activity. Durant acquired factories for production of 4- and 6-cylinder cars in Long Island City, Elizabeth, Lansing, Muncie, and Flint. He claimed 30,000 orders in hand before a single Durant rolled off the line. He unveiled a $348 competitor for Model T in the form of the Star, a more civilized automobile for the money. He also purchased the Locomobile Company of Bridgeport in order to acquire a luxury line. He attached a cluster of parts-making plants to his enterprise.

By mid 1923 Durant Motors controlled 10 factories with a 650,000-car-a-year capacity and 4,000 dealers lined up to sell them. On paper it was a formidable entry into the unforgiving field of automotive competition. But appearances were deceiving. The elements of Durant Motors had not been bought, like those of GM in its first days, by payments in stock. Sellers now required cash, and Durant's initial supply was heavily depleted. Moreover, after the opening flurry of enthusiasm, the stock of Durant Motors never performed well enough to raise capital. Traded on the New York Curb Exchange, it peaked at 84 in 1923 and thereafter slid downward.

Most importantly, Durant himself was a different man. He had come to believe in his own legend, a change marked by the use of his own name, for the first time, on the automobiles he sold. He showed a new streak of defensive querulousness, too. Whereas in the old days he had rarely had time to air quarrels or losses, he now gave several interviews accusing his onetime GM partners of bad faith and bad dealing. Most of all he was easily distracted by nonautomotive pet projects. To carry on his wars with the bankers and speculators, he organized his own Liberty National Bank, and he also continued his program of stock sales to the multitudes through the Durant Corporation that had been the trigger of his misfortunes in 1920. Lastly, he himself sank deeper and deeper into the stock market. At age sixty-five Durant's persistent, sweeping, optimistic buying earned him the newspaper sobriquet of "King of the Bulls." Still dapper, soft-spoken, and persuasive, he preached the 1920s gospel of success through investment. He traded as many as 5 million shares a year through 15 or 20 brokers and earned enough to sustain a life-style that now allowed for occasional trips to Europe and lavish gifts for Catherine—but did not include any substantial sums to organized charity. Durant was not uncaring, but he simply did not think in philanthropic terms.

He became less of a production hero and more of an ephemeral figure of the Jazz Age, coupled in the financial news with now-forgotten speculators such as Jesse Livermore and Michael Meehan. His son Clifford, once a race car driver and Durant Motors executive, now plunged, like his father (and grandfather) into the world of stock speculation. His daughter Margery became a globetrotting, thrice-divorced socialite. And his last strong remaining tie to his old Flint life vanished in 1924 with the death of his mother.

Durant Motors struggled along in a market increasingly dominated by Ford, GM, and a new entry, the Chrysler Motor Corporation, founded in 1923. By 1928 these "Big Three" sold 70 percent of all new cars among them, leaving 40 other concerns, including Durant Motors, to fight for the rest. In the words of his longtime secretary and friend Winfred Murphy, Durant had "made some pretty good competition for himself."

The decline of Durant Motors was underway by the mid 1920s as the burden of indebtedness caused by too-rapid development was not relieved by sales revenues. The only remedy was to dismantle the new structure and dispose of its parts for ready cash. The costly factories in Elizabeth and Flint were sold to competitors. The Locomobile line fell by the wayside. A modest sales target of 94,000 units for the remaining divisions was set for 1927, but even that was not reached. In 1929, 75,000 Durant cars were sold, some 2 percent of the market. That left the net losses for the year at $980,000 and a total deficit of $12.8 million. Durant Motors was mortally wounded. The stock market crash and the onset of the Depression simply administered the coup de grace. The final expiration date was 1931.

Durant played only a small part in these losing battles. In 1926 he suffered severe head injuries in a railroad collision, and he used his temporary incapacitation as a reason to withdraw from active management of Durant Motors. He came back to its presidency in 1927, but the following year saw him once more turn executive responsibility over to others. This time it was a four-man team of hired experts, whose dismal performance he later blamed on insufficient zeal.

Meanwhile he toyed with projects of a kind that once would not have interested him, such as sponsoring an essay contest on how best to enforce Prohibition, or making public statements denouncing the belated attempts of the Federal Reserve Board to restrict brokers' credit and tame the surging bull market. Durant even secured an April 1929 audience with Herbert Hoover to press his point.

The great crash of October in that year completely devastated him. His paper fortune was eradicated by distress selling within a year of "Black Thursday." He continued to give cheerful interviews, declaring that the fault lay with conservative banking practices, and that an imminent return of confidence would improve conditions. But late in 1930 he told an old Chevrolet and GM colleague, John Thomas Smith (who had stayed successfully and profitably with GM as its general counsel) that he was "wiped out."

The remainder of the story is pathetic and brave. Amid a welter of lawsuits, Durant's remaining properties were liquidated. On February 8, 1936, he declared personal bankruptcy. His income that year was $5,420. In 1937 his son Clifford died of a heart attack. In 1938 Raymere and all its furnishings were sold at auction.

Yet Durant, in defeat, regained some of the amiability that had been lost in the 1920s and won admiration for uncomplaining acceptance of his lot. With the few dollars he had left he toyed with minor projects—a shopping center in an old Durant Motors showroom in Asbury Park; small real-estate operations around Deal; and in Flint, a spark plug company, and finally a bowling alley and lunchroom. He always remained neatly dressed, dignified and forward-looking in the interviews occasionally sought by editors looking for a "where-are-they-now?" story. "I never saw anybody like him," said Arch Campbell, a Flint partner in the spark plug venture. "Even when he should have been despondent and down in the mouth the average person who

Early Flint Road Cart Company wagon, 1886

had just met him wouldn't have known. He could take it."

His correspondence reveals forlorn hopes of still finding and marketing some invention that would end his exile from the mountaintop. But the big breaks would come no more, and age took its inexorable toll. In 1942 Durant suffered a stroke while visiting Flint. He declined steadily thereafter, passing time in correspondence with old friends and foes, making notes for an incomplete autobiography, and dreaming of might-have-beens. He was supported by a $10,000 annual retainer furnished by four onetime GM lieutenants–C. S. Mott, Alfred P. Sloan, Sam McLaughlin, and John Thomas Smith. On March 18, 1947, he died in his downtown New York apartment. It was a season of passing for the automobile pioneers. Henry Ford died almost in the same month. Walter Chrysler had gone in 1940, Ben Briscoe in 1945. Nash followed in 1948 and Olds in 1950, while America and GM rolled on toward what then appeared to be a limitless future. Durant's memory survives dimly if at all today, but despite that, it is safe to say that the nation would have been a very different place without him.

References:

Margery Durant, *My Father* (New York: Putnam's, 1929);

Lawrence R. Gustin, *Billy Durant: Creator of General Motors* (Grand Rapids, Mich.: Eerdmans, 1973);

Arthur Pound, *The Turning Wheel: The Story of General Motors through Twenty-Five Years, 1908-1933* (New York: Doubleday, Doran, 1933);

Richard P. Scharchburg, *W. C. Durant, 'The Boss'* (Flint, Mich.: GMI Press, 1973);

Bernard A. Weisberger, *The Dream Maker: William C. Durant, Founder of General Motors* (Boston: Little, Brown, 1979).

Archives:

Two important sources are in the General Motors Institute Alumni Foundation Collection of Industrial History. They are: Frank M. Rodolf, "An Industrial History of Flint," and Bellamy Partridge, "Chevrolet in Peace and War."

Durant left a miscellaneous and broken collection of personal and business correspondence, most of which is to be found in the General Motors Institute Alumni Foundation Collection of Industrial History in Flint. These are usefully supplemented by several ancillary collections of papers of associates Winfred W. Murphy, William S. Ballenger, George Willson, and Charles Stewart Mott, all in the same archive.

There is additional important material in the papers of Pierre S. du Pont and John J. Raskob in the Hagley Museum and Library, Wilmington, Delaware.

Duryea Motor Wagon Company

by George S. May

Eastern Michigan University

Charles Duryea once wrote an article entitled "It Doesn't Pay to Pioneer" in which he laid claim to having "designed and built the first gasoline automobile actually to run in America, sold the first car on this side, did the first automobile advertising and won the first two American races." The accuracy of these claims is highly debatable, but no one disputes Duryea's claim to having been a pioneer in the auto industry or that neither he nor his brother Frank received the kind of financial rewards one would expect from the fact that they were the first commercial producers of automobiles in America.

Charles Edgar Duryea was born in 1861 on a farm near Peoria, Illinois, the eldest of five children born to George Washington Duryea and Louisa Melvina Duryea. His brother James Frank Duryea (who as an adult did not use his first name), eight years younger than Charles, would be closely associated with him in his early work with automobiles. Charles was the more original of the two, the one with the ideas, while Frank was the more practical one, whose mechanical abilities were needed to make his brother's ideas work.

Charles Duryea claimed that even as a boy he was thinking about automobiles, at a time when virtually none existed. The principal of the school he attended confirmed that he could "remember distinctly his prediction and advocacy of horseless vehicles for the common roads, in those years." However, when Charles reached adulthood, he was swept up in the enthusiasm for the bicycle. He and Frank went to the East, where they became involved in the bicycle trade. Charles Duryea eventually manufactured a bicycle that included several features he had invented. But in the latter part of the 1880s, as he saw examples of the new internal combustion engines and read reports of the use Europeans were making of those engines to power road vehicles, his interest in horseless carriages was renewed.

Exactly when Charles Duryea began serious work on plans for such a vehicle is unclear, but he declared later that an announcement in 1890 by the sponsors of the World's Columbian Exposition to be held in Chicago in 1893 had a decisive effect. One exhibit called for "vehicles propelled by other than animal power," with rewards to be offered to the best examples. The announcement, Duryea said, encouraged him and others "who had been discouraged by ridicule and pity [to take] a fresh hitch at their trousers." By 1891 he had drafted plans for a motorized vehicle. He was living in Chicopee, Massachusetts, where the Ames Manufacturing Company was handling the production of his bicycle. Frank Duryea, by now a skilled mechanic, was employed by Ames as a toolmaker. Charles Duryea would later claim that with his brother's help, he built an engine, attached it to a carriage, and, on April 19, 1892, successfully tested the vehicle in a loft he had rented in Springfield, Massachusetts, where he had obtained financial support for his experimental work.

In actuality, however, in September 1892 Charles Duryea relocated his bicycle business back in Peoria, leaving his brother to carry on with the building of the automobile in Springfield. It is clear that at that time their vehicle was not operational and that Frank had to make numerous changes in his brother's plans before the vehicle could be made to work. It was not until September 20, 1893, that the first brief but successful test run was made on a Springfield street.

Other Americans were experimenting with horseless carriages powered by gasoline engines, and there is strong evidence that more than one successfully tested a vehicle prior to the date of the Springfield test. Nevertheless, the Duryea brothers are commonly credited with having built America's first successful gasoline car because they were able to proceed from the construction of one experimen-

*Producing cars in the confusion of the Duryea Motor Wagon factory, 1896
(courtesy of the Smithsonian Institution)*

tal vehicle to the production of multiple copies for sale to the public. There is no doubt that the Duryeas were the first to do that. Within two years the Duryea Motor Wagon Company had been founded, and by 1896 the first motor wagons had been sold.

How much each of the brothers contributed became a source of controversy that created lasting divisions in the family. In the fall of 1893 Frank Duryea came to Chicago, where he and his brother took in the exhibits in the closing days of the Exposition. It was too late to exhibit the vehicle there. It had made its first run only a few days before, and the brothers saw few other vehicles exhibited at the fair. They no doubt discussed the work that needed to be done with their automobile, but while Frank returned to Springfield, Charles went back to Peoria to run his bicycle business. He always maintained that even though he was in the West he continued to supervise the work, but that was disputed by Frank, who declared that his brother's involvement was minimal after he moved to Peoria.

By 1894 Frank had decided that he had gone as far as he could with the original Duryea vehicle, which never worked very well. He raised funds that enabled him to design a second vehicle, in which he replaced the 1-cylinder, 2-cycle engine with a 2-cylinder, 4-cycle engine he built. That was the type of engine virtually every gasoline car before long would be using. He also included in his second car advanced features such as pneumatic tires, clutch and gear transmission, three forward speeds, and reverse. The new motor wagon operated satisfactorily by April 1895, and by June, Frank could report to his brother, still in Peoria, that "actual orders" were being received. "An order received this A.M. says book me for two carriages to be delivered at earliest possible date."

In September 1895 Springfield backers organized the Duryea Motor Wagon Company with George Henry Hewitt as president. The two brothers were given equal shares in the company, but it was Frank who, as mechanical superintendent, was in charge of production. And it was Frank who drove a second version of his 2-cylinder motor wagon to victory in the Thanksgiving Day race in Chicago that year. The Thanksgiving Day race was not the first contest between horseless carriages held in the United States, but it was the first to attract widespread attention. Cashing in on the publicity, the winning Duryea entry was put into production, and 13 were sold in 1896, marking the beginning of the American automotive industry.

It was Charles Duryea who received sole credit as the inventor in the patent awarded on June 11, 1895, for the "new and useful improvements in Road Vehicles" even though there is little doubt that Frank was responsible for the improvements. It was also Charles Duryea who was pictured seated in a Duryea Motor Wagon in a leaflet the company distributed, which was not technically the first American automobile advertisement but was the first to advertise a production vehicle. And it was Charles Duryea who was elected president of the American Motor League, America's first automotive organization, formed in November 1895 in Chicago by those who were present for the Thanksgiving Day race won by Frank Duryea.

The first public indication of a developing fraternal rift came in February 1896, the month in which Frank Duryea made the first sale of a Duryea Motor Wagon. "In nearly all accounts of the Duryea motor wagon which have thus far appeared," an article in *Horseless Age* reported, "the name of Charles E. Duryea has been mentioned as the sole inventor, while the very important part performed by his younger brother, J. Frank Duryea, in the development of the machine has been lost sight of." The story went on to say that "the motor in its present form is the work of the younger brother," who, "with energy and persistence," had solved the problems with the original motor after his brother had left to go back to Peoria.

The article must have been written with Frank Duryea's assistance and quite probably at his suggestion. It had to help fuel the growing feud between the brothers, which has often been cited as the reason why the Duryea Motor Wagon Company went out of business in 1898. But that was not the only reason for the company's unexpected demise. Following up his triumph at Chicago, Frank Duryea drove a Duryea to victory in a Memorial Day race sponsored by John Brisben Walker, publisher of *Cosmopolitan* magazine, and later in 1896 the Duryeas took two of their motor wagons to England, where

they won the London-to-Brighton run held to celebrate the repeal of the Red Flag Act, which had been blamed for retarding the motor car's development in that country. In addition to those racing triumphs, a Duryea was also put on tour with the Barnum & Bailey Circus, displayed with the other marvels and oddities.

But if they had good ideas as to how to publicize the car, neither the Duryeas nor their Springfield backers had any experience in manufacturing such a complex product. A photograph taken of the interior of the Duryea factory in 1896 shows a hopeless tangle of machinery and workmen, which makes it easy to see why only 13 wagons were produced that year. Learning how to improve efficiency would take time and money. Annual sales of 13 cars hardly supplied that kind of cash, and in New England investment capital was already tied up in long-established industries. With one estimate placing production in 1897 at a mere three cars, it is remarkable that the company survived as long as it did.

In 1898 Frank Duryea departed. After several false starts he wound up designing a 2-cylinder, 2-seat car for the Stevens Arms and Tool Company of Chicopee Falls, Massachusetts, in 1901. In 1906 Stevens Arms was reorganized as the Stevens-Duryea Motor Car Company to produce expensive low-volume, high-performance cars. Frank Duryea became modestly well-to-do as a result, although a nervous breakdown in 1909 forced him to retire from the business. He made a brief return six years later.

Frank's affluence contributed further to the division between the brothers, since Charles, after the breakup of the original Duryea company, had a hard time making ends meet. He fronted a succession of companies in Reading and Wilkes-Barre, Pennsylvania, and Saginaw, Michigan, among other locations. His goal remained what had been set forth in the 1895 patent: to produce a car "not unduly heavy, simple and easy of control and comparatively inexpensive." The same approach made Henry Ford a billionaire, but there were few takers for outmoded Duryea models that for 20 years remained much like the 1896 motor wagon. Charles was also a frequent contributor of articles on automotive topics and on his claims to being the country's pioneer developer of the internal combustion automobile.

Charles Duryea died in 1938. His son, Merle Junius Duryea, continued the fight to gain the recognition he thought his father deserved. Frank Duryea was by no means silent in public airings of the family feud, but he was more inclined than his brother or nephew to use the pronoun "we" in discussing the development of the Duryea Motor Wagon. In 1946 he was an honored guest of the Golden Jubilee celebration the industry hosted in Detroit, although most of the attention was focused on the fact that Henry Ford and Ransom Olds tested their first cars 50 years earlier, not on the 1896 debut of the Duryeas' production car. Like a good many automotive pioneers, Frank Duryea lived to an unusually old age. He died in 1967, just short of his ninety-eighth birthday and some 74 years after that memorable test run in Springfield.

References:
Editors of *Automobile Quarterly, The American Car Since 1775* (New York: Dutton, 1971);
George S. May, *The Automobile in American Life* (forthcoming, 1990);
John B. Rae, *American Automobile Manufacturers: The First Forty Years* (Philadelphia: Chilton, 1959).

Archives:
The Charles B. King Papers in the National Automotive History Collection, Detroit Public Library, contains a good deal of primary material relating to the Duryeas. King was closely associated with the Duryeas in the mid 1890s, and in later years he made a hobby of collecting automotive materials not only on his own activities but on those of others from the early years.

Eaton Corporation

by George S. May

Eastern Michigan University

Eaton, the Cleveland-based automotive parts manufacturer, originated with the Torbensen Gear & Axle Company, founded in 1911. The present name of the company comes from a shop that Joseph Oriel Eaton opened in Bloomfield, New Jersey, in 1920 to produce heavy-duty truck axles. The business went into receivership and was purchased by Torbensen in May 1923, along with the Perfection Spring Company. The several businesses were consolidated in Cleveland that year as the Eaton Axle & Spring Company. In 1932 the name was changed to the Eaton Manufacturing Company.

Since that time there have been numerous other acquisitions as well as divestitures, the detailing of which takes up three and a quarter page-length columns in *Moody's Industrial Manual*. After World War II Eaton expanded into the European markets with acquisitions and joint arrangements that enabled it to supply axles and gears to Ford and General Motors (GM) operations in England and, through an Italian subsidiary, engine valves to Simca in France and Fiat in Italy.

Engine valves represented a move beyond the gears, axles, and springs that had been the company's mainstays. In 1958 Eaton added transmissions to its automotive product lines with the acquisition of the Fuller Manufacturing Company through an exchange of stock. The Fuller Company had its origins in 1902 when the Michigan Automobile Company was founded in Kalamazoo by Charles and Frank Fuller, whose family had prospered by making washboards. The new company produced a lightweight runabout, the Michigan, designed by Charles and Maurice Blood, but both the Fullers and the Bloods soon decided they would be better off manufacturing parts rather than complete cars. The Bloods left to form a company that manufactured a universal joint they had developed. This company eventually wound up as part of another giant parts corporation, Rockwell. The Fullers, meanwhile, transformed the Michigan Automobile Company into Fuller & Sons Manufacturing Company, which, after 1923, concentrated on transmissions for heavy-duty trucks. The company in 1928 was sold to the Unit Corporation of America, which went into receivership in 1932. The Kalamazoo transmission operation was salvaged and emerged as the Fuller Manufacturing Company. Some years after its acquisition by Eaton the Kalamazoo plant became simply the transmission division, but the Fuller trade name continued to be carried by the transmissions that it manufactured.

The acquisition of Fuller in 1958 was an early indication of the desire to add greater diversity to the company's products. Under John C. Verden, who was Eaton's president from 1958 to 1963 and then chairman until his retirement in 1969, the concept of diversification was extended beyond Eaton's traditional automotive interests to include a presence in the nonautomotive markets. The acquisition in 1963 of the Yale & Towne Manufacturing Company, the lock maker, marked the most important move in that direction. The merger, accomplished through an exchange of stock, was completed on December 31, 1965, with the resulting company being renamed Eaton Yale & Towne Inc.

Eaton Corporation, the firm's present name, was adopted on April 21, 1971. The dropping of Yale & Towne from the letterhead in no way signaled an end to the effort to lessen the corporation's dependence on the automotive market. Yale & Towne had added much-needed stability in the mid 1960s, when GM, a major customer, had reduced its purchases, and in the 1970s, when new conditions greatly affected the demand for American cars and parts. Eaton stepped up its diversification activities. Under E. Mandall de Windt, a career Eaton employee who became chairman in 1969, the expansion into world markets was emphasized along with a new focus on high technology. The most important acquisition in that area was that of the electronics company Cutler-Hammer, Inc. in 1978. The merger was carried through with Cutler-Hammer stockholders receiving either cash for their stock or subordinated installment notes from Eaton. James R. Stover, who succeeded de Windt as chairman in 1986, continued these expansionist policies, with the goal of making the new electrical and electronic controls segment contribute as much to Eaton's profits as its vehicle components segment. However, with the heaviest demand for Eaton parts coming from the industry's more stable truck producers, and with the strong revival of passenger car sales in the mid 1980s, vehicle component sales remained most important. In 1988, when Eaton sales were a record $3.5 billion, vehicle component sales exceeded $2 billion for the first time, with profits twice those of the electrical and electronic controls segment. A 70 percent stake in a joint venture with Nittan Valve Company, Japan's leading producer of engine valves, opened up the market for the sale of parts to Japanese car manufacturing subsidiaries in the United States, with shipment of valves to Honda's Ohio plant beginning in 1989.

References:

Thomas Derdak, ed., *International Directory of Company Histories*, volume 1 (Chicago & London: St. James, 1988);

George S. May, *A Most Unique Machine: The Michigan Origins of the American Automobile Industry* (Grand Rapids, Mich.: Eerdmans, 1975).

Electric Auto-Lite Company

by George S. May

Eastern Michigan University

Founded in 1911 in Toledo, Ohio, the history of the Electric Auto-Lite Company is characterized by mergers, acquisitions, and divestitures that have entirely altered its original product line and have resulted in various name changes. The business survives, still located in Toledo, as Prestolite Electric, Inc., a name that results from one of Electric Auto-Lite's most important acquisitions, the Prest-O-Lite battery operation.

A 6-volt generator developed by Sherman L. Kelly to power automobile lights led to the formation of Electric Auto-Lite by Kelly, Artemus Fisher, and Clement O. Miniger, a successful Toledo businessman. Studebaker and Packard were among the first customers for the company's generator. In 1914 the company was acquired by John North Willys, who converted it into the Auto-Lite Division of his Toledo-based Willys-Overland automotive company. Following World War I Willys's severe financial problems led to the Auto-Lite Division in 1922 being sold and reorganized again as the Electric Auto-Lite Company with Miniger, who had managed the Auto-Lite Division, as president. Miniger continued to be closely associated with Willys, and in 1929 he and his business associates purchased Willys's 800,000 shares in Willys-Overland. Miniger became a director of that company and was involved in the reorganization that resulted from the firm's Depression-era troubles.

At Electric Auto-Lite, Miniger aggressively pursued a policy of expansion by acquiring control of companies producing closely related automotive parts. Automotive wiring was picked up in 1923 with the purchase of the American Enameled Magnet Wire Company. In 1926 the starting, ignition, and lighting operations of the American Bosch Magneto Company and Gray & Davis, Inc., were acquired. In 1929 Electric Auto-Lite purchased the J. B. Brown Manufacturing Company, which made automobile lamps. In 1934 Electric Auto-Lite

merged with the Moto Meter Gauge & Equipment Company, whose president, Royce G. Martin, became Auto-Lite's president, succeeding Miniger, who became chairman, a post he held until his death in 1944.

In the late 1920s Miniger had moved his company into the production of batteries with the acquisition of USL Battery Corporation, Marko Storage Battery Corporation, and the storage-battery division of Westinghouse Electric. It was then, too, that Prest-O-Lite battery came under Electric Auto-Lite's control. The Prest-O-Lite Company, founded in 1904 in Indianapolis, had begun as a producer of automobile lighting that used acetylene gas, but it had then expanded into the production of batteries through the purchase of the Pumpelli Battery Company, a pioneer Indiana battery manufacturer. Prest-O-Lite's founders were Carl G. Fisher and James A. Allison, both of whom went on to bigger things. Together they founded the Indianapolis Speedway, where the famed 500-mile race was first staged in 1911. Allison continued in the racing field, establishing in 1915 the Allison Engineering Company to provide engines and other mechanical support for racing cars. It later expanded into the production of marine and aviation engines and, after Allison's death in 1928, was purchased by General Motors (GM), which used it to enter the growing aviation field. Fisher, in addition to being the principal founder of the Indianapolis 500, went on to be the successful developer of Miami Beach and of the Lincoln Highway, the country's first transcontinental thoroughfare.

In 1912 Fisher sold Prest-O-Lite to Union Carbide, the major producer of calcium carbide, used in acetylene lighting systems. In 1927 Union Carbide sold the battery division to Electric Auto-Lite but retained other Prest-O-Lite related products, including Prestone antifreeze.

By the 1930s Electric Auto-Lite was selling batteries under the Auto-Lite, Prest-O-Lite, and USL trade names, along with spark plugs, generators, lamps, ignition systems, and a variety of other automotive parts. It also produced such nonautomotive parts as marine and aircraft batteries and gauges, electric parts for tractors, and commercial aluminum and zinc die castings, the last following the acquisition in 1935 of the Alemite Die Casting Company.

In 1961 the Ford Motor Company purchased the Autolite spark plug operations and the rights to that trade name, which by then had become a single word. As a result of antitrust actions initiated by the federal government, the Supreme Court in 1973 forced Ford to sell its Autolite Division to the Bendix Corporation. Meanwhile, Electric Autolite in 1963 had merged with the Mergenthaler Linotype Company. The new company resulting from the merger became the Eltra Corporation, with its auto parts products being grouped under the Prestolite name, which by that time had also ceased to be hyphenated.

In 1979 the Allied Corporation acquired control of Eltra for $598 million. Three years later Allied acquired the Bendix Corporation in one of the most celebrated takeover battles of the 1980s. This brought the famous Autolite and Prestolite names together once again under one corporate umbrella, but not for long. Edward L. Hennessy, Jr., who had become chief executive of Allied in 1979, followed a policy of selling elements of Eltra and Bendix that did not fit in well with his plans to revitalize Allied, which had traditionally depended on products in the chemical field. Following the merger of Allied and the Signal companies in 1985, Hennessy, who emerged as the dominant executive in Allied-Signal, Inc., continued this policy. In April 1986 he sold the Prestolite Motor & Ignition subsidiary, which became a subsidiary of the PMI holding company. The automotive, aviation, appliance, and electronic wire production that had earlier been one of the Prestolite divisions in the old Eltra corporate setup is now a separate business, the Prestolite Wire Corporation, based in Farmington Hills, Michigan. Prestolite Motor & Ignition became Prestolite Electric, with some 5,000 employees in Toledo and at its branches in the United States, Great Britain, and Australia. It produces alternators, starting motors, voltage regulators, and other electrical products as original equipment and replacement parts for the automotive, aircraft, marine, farm, military, and industrial markets. Autolite survives as a division of Allied-Signal, producing spark plugs for automobiles, trucks, buses, tractors, recreational vehicles, and aircraft. Neither Prestolite nor Autolite produces batteries anymore.

References:

Automotive Industry of America (Southfield, Mich.: Prestige, 1979);

Thomas Derdak, ed., *International Directory of Company Histories*, volume 1 (Chicago & London: St. James, 1988).

Electric Automobiles

by Robert J. Kothe

Atlanta, Georgia

Since the beginnings of the automotive industry electric automobiles have been driven by motors drawing power from rechargeable storage batteries. Modern-day alternatives to that tried-and-true, if limited, power source include solar panels and nuclear reactors, but nothing has been able to supplant the original.

Early in automotive history both electricity and steam seemed as likely to propel cars as did the internal combustion engine. At the end of the 1890s production of both electrics and steamers exceeded that of gasoline-powered cars, and electrics were the overall leader. At the time storage battery technology was more advanced than gasoline, and electric motors were commonly used in a variety of industrial and business contexts.

A crude battery-powered vehicle built by Robert Davidson of Scotland is said to have appeared as early as 1839. The first American electric vehicles were built separately in 1888 by Phillip Pratt and William Morrison. Morrison, of Des Moines, Iowa, demonstrated his vehicle in Chicago in 1892 and exhibited it at the Columbian Exposition in that city in 1893. Production electric automobiles were sold in the United States by 1897 (they had gone on the market in Europe somewhat earlier). The best-known early manufacturers are Pope Manufacturing Company, which built about 500 electric cars in Hartford, Connecticut, in 1897 and 1898; Detroit Electric Company; Baker Motor Vehicle Company; and Rausch & Lang.

Early electrics enjoyed several advantages over gasoline and steam cars of the period. They were fairly simple to build, simpler than either steamers or gasoline cars. The power source was relatively safe. In gas cars of the time fuel was dispensed from cumbersome drums, which frequently spilled and caused fires. The gasoline was often contaminated and unreliable, and the engines required frequent maintenance. By the turn of the century most urban regions had reliable electric power, and it was not difficult to install a charging station in a home or commercial garage. The batteries needed topping off with water on a regular basis, but until they needed to be replaced that was about all one had to accomplish.

The primary advantage electrics had over steamers and gasoline cars was that they were easy to operate. The driver unplugged from the charging station and drove away. Steam cars were exceedingly complex and required a near-expert's technical knowledge, and cranking a gasoline car was physically demanding and potentially dangerous. In an electric usually a single pedal or lever controlled the speed and another pedal or lever controlled the brake, while early steam and gasoline cars often presented a confusing array of pedals and knobs. Ease of operation made electric cars the favorites of female drivers. The companies quickly picked up on the hint and began making their products resemble parlors on wheels, with overstuffed seats and luxury features.

Despite their seeming advantages over gasoline cars, however, the limited range of the batteries powering electric cars ultimately doomed them to near-extinction. In their heyday the typical range of electric cars was 40 to 50 miles. Range decreased when the batteries got old, when it was cold outside, and when the cars sustained high speeds. It took hours for the batteries to be recharged. Adding more batteries extended a car's range but at the cost of additional weight and the loss of passenger and payload space. The introduction of a nickel battery designed by the Edison company added some distance, but not enough to make any difference. Even modern batteries offer only slightly better performance.

Still, electric vehicles continue to enjoy some success, as fleet vehicles, delivery vans, and in other special services (such as in mines and other

Electric automobiles parked outside the Detroit Athletic Club, where members' wives were inspecting new facilities (courtesy of the Motor Vehicle Manufacturers Association)

cramped places where ventilation is a problem). Fleet vehicles utilize battery modules that can be replaced with fresh units. Electric power in urban delivery vehicles making frequent starts and stops makes sense because no power is consumed when the vehicles are stationary. Batteries are also widely used in golf carts and other recreational vehicles.

The introduction of a practical self-starter in the 1912 Cadillac meant the end of the electric as a serious contender for supremacy in the American automotive industry. The Detroit Electric Company, still in business as late as 1940, was one of the few firms able to continue. Interest in electrics was briefly revived during the period of World War II gas rationing, and before the advent of air conditioning utility companies occasionally tried to market electric cars as a way to boost demand for electricity during off-peak (evening) hours (when most of the cars would be recharging). Environmental concerns have recently boosted interest in electrics. The cars emit little pollution at the point of use, and some environmentalists argue that it would be easier to clean up a relatively small number of power plants (presumably burning coal) than it is to clean up the emissions of the tens of millions of gasoline automobiles presently on the road. But unless emission regulations become so strict that internal combustion engines are virtually banned, or there is a major breakthrough in battery technology, electrics seem unlikely to return to the marketplace as a major force. In 1989, though, a spokesman for Chrysler Corporation announced the company was testing an electric van. "The key is finding a battery with decent range," he said. "We can't ignore the electric powered vehicle."

Reference:

John B. Rae, *The American Automobile: The First Forty Years* (Philadelphia: Chilton, 1959).

Electric Vehicle Company

by John B. Rae

Harvey Mudd College

The Electric Vehicle Company was an early and unsuccessful attempt to establish a monopoly in the automobile industry. The company started in 1896 as the Electric Carriage and Wagon Company, founded by Henry C. Morris and Pedro G. Salom, and operated electric-powered cabs in New York City. A year later the company was bought by Isaac L. Rice, president of the Electric Storage Battery Company (Exide), and renamed the Electric Vehicle Company. Rice saw in electric cabs a potential outlet for his batteries. He expanded the original fleet of 13 cabs to about 100, and they attracted attention during a blizzard early in 1899, when all other street traffic in New York was stranded but the cabs were able to operate on the sidewalks.

The success of Rice's electric cabs attracted the attention of a syndicate of traction magnates headed by William C. Whitney and including P. A. B. Widener, Anthony N. Brady, and Thomas F. Ryan. It is unknown whether they saw the manufacture of electric cabs as a profitable adjunct to their traction interests, as a potential rival concern that they should control, or merely as a field for stock manipulation. At any rate, they bought out Rice and launched a grandiose scheme for operating electric cabs in all the principal cities of the United States. They contemplated building a fleet of 12,000 vehicles, a figure far beyond the immediate capacity of the American automobile industry, whose output in 1900 did not exceed 4,000 cars and trucks.

The first step in achieving that goal was to approach the Pope Manufacturing Company of Hartford, Connecticut, then the largest American producer of bicycles, which had begun in 1895 to build both electric- and gasoline-powered cars. The Whitney syndicate bought the Pope Motor Carriage Department and renamed it the Columbia Automobile Company, and Columbia Automobile and the Electric Vehicle Company became joint owners of the Columbia and Electric Vehicle Company, designed as the manufacturing agent of the new combine. The Electric Vehicle Company became the holding company for the subsidiaries that operated the cabs.

That complex corporate structure was ambitiously financed, at least on paper. The Pope-Electric Vehicle merger was capitalized at $3 million, and by 1902 the Electric Vehicle Company had issued $20 million in stock, some of it for the acquisition of smaller manufacturers of electric automobiles. If the syndicate's scheme for running electric cabs had worked out as planned, the aggregate capitalization would have been on the order of $200 million.

A genuine and fairly impressive production effort ensued. Columbia and Electric built some 2,000 electric cabs in the first large-scale production operation in the American automobile industry. The Electric Vehicle Company also made a few electric buses for the Fifth Avenue Coach Company, owned by the Whitney group, and some electric trucks for the U.S. Post Office Department and the United States Trucking Corporation, a merger of cartage companies in New York created with the assistance of Alfred E. Smith.

Unfortunately the promoters of the Electric Vehicle Company had backed the wrong horse, or more accurately the wrong horseless carriage. The electric automobile was not to be the wave of the future, and the electric cabs saw only brief service in New York, Boston, Chicago, Philadelphia, and Washington, D.C. The performance in the blizzard had been illusory. In normal service the cabs were clumsy, awkward vehicles, with 1,200-pound batteries that had to be replaced after every trip.

By 1900 the Electric Vehicle Company was in trouble. It was referred to in the press as the "Lead Cab Trust," and its reputation suffered from revelations of a $2 million loan from a New York bank controlled by the Whitney syndicate. Normal banking channels had been bypassed, and the loan was made on notes secured by Electric Vehicle stock and signed by a dummy director who proved to be Thomas F. Ryan's secretary. At the same time the operating subsidiaries, the companies that ran the cab fleets, were collapsing. By the middle of 1900 the Electric Vehicle Company had reverted to being a manufacturer of motor vehicles, liquidating the Columbia and Electric Vehicle Company. So it worked out that an organization dedicated to the electric automobile came to depend for survival on its possession of a patent claiming to be the basic patent on all road vehicles powered by the internal combustion engine.

The Electric Vehicle Company became a key element in the controversy over George B. Selden's patent for an internal combustion engine because when William C. Whitney was negotiating the purchase of the Pope Motor Carriage Department, he asked if there were any patents that might cause trouble. Herman F. Cuntz, an engineer who was in charge of patents for Pope, pointed out the Selden patent. Whitney was sufficiently impressed to consult Dugald Clerk, a British engineer who was considered the leading authority on the internal combustion engine. When Clerk gave a favorable opinion, an agreement was reached whereby Selden sold exclusive rights to his patent to the Electric Vehicle Company in return for $10,000 and a royalty of $15 on each vehicle sold under the patent, with a guaranteed minimum of $5,000 per year.

With its electric cab prospects deteriorating rapidly, the Electric Vehicle Company had a powerful incentive to make what it could from its patent rights. In 1900 it filed suit for infringement of the Selden patent against the Winton Motor Carriage Company of Cleveland, Ohio, at that time the largest American manufacturer of gasoline automobiles. Winton fought back for a while, but after an early court ruling seemed to favor the Electric Vehicle Company's claims, some 30 automobile firms, led by Henry B. Joy of Packard and Frederic L. Smith of the Olds Motor Works, reached a settlement with the Electric Vehicle Company in 1903.

By the terms of that agreement the participating members accepted the validity of the Selden patent and formed an organization, the Association of Licensed Automobile Manufacturers (ALAM) for the purpose of administering it. Authority to issue licenses under the patent was vested in an executive committee of five members, one of whom was always to be the Electric Vehicle Company. A royalty of 1.25 percent of the catalog price was imposed on every vehicle manufactured under license. Three-fifths of the proceeds would go to the Electric Vehicle Company and the rest to the association; one-third of the Electric Vehicle Company's share went to Selden.

The underlying reason for the formation of the ALAM was that both parties were negotiating from weakness. The automobile companies of that day were all small firms, none of them in a position to face prolonged litigation, and whatever they might think of the Selden patent, they had to face the prospect that the courts might uphold it. On the other side, the Electric Vehicle Company's precarious financial position made expensive litigation equally undesirable.

The ALAM's principal opponent was Henry Ford, who disapproved of both patents and business associations. After a protracted lawsuit the U.S. Circuit Court of Appeals upheld Ford in 1911, ruling that the Selden patent was "valid but not infringed." With that decision the ALAM collapsed. The Electric Vehicle Company had already done so. It went into receivership in the panic year of 1907 and was reconstituted as the Columbia Motor Car Company with a greatly reduced capitalization. Three years later Columbia became part of Benjamin Briscoe's United States Motor Company. When that organization collapsed in 1912, the Columbia Motor Car Company disappeared. Since the United States Motor Company was reorganized as the Maxwell Motor Car Company, which eventually became the Chrysler Corporation, it might be claimed that the Electric Vehicle Company was part of the Chrysler genealogy.

References:
William Greenleaf, *Monopoly On Wheels: Henry Ford and the Selden Automobile Patent* (Detroit: Wayne State University Press, 1961);

John B. Rae, "The Electric Vehicle Company: A Monopoly That Missed," *Business History Review*, 29 (December 1955): 298-311.

Elmore Manufacturing Company

by George S. May

Eastern Michigan University

The Elmore Company of Clyde, Ohio, was the outgrowth of the Elmore Bicycle Company. The Becker brothers, owners of the bicycle business, made a preliminary move into the automotive field in 1899, when they reportedly built ten cars. Three years later they reorganized as the Elmore Manufacturing Company and went into automobile production fulltime. During the next ten years the company produced a series of cars, moving up from the initial 1-cylinder models to 2-, 3-, and 4-cylinder cars. Production was halted permanently in 1912.

The only thing that distinguishes Elmore from the hundreds of other companies that likewise failed to survive the fierce competition of the early years of the automobile industry is that its cars used a 2-stroke, or 2-cycle, internal combustion engine in contrast with the 4-cycle engine that most companies used. The first practical gasoline internal combustion engines that had appeared in the 1860s had been of the 2-cycle variety, and this was the type used by Charles and Frank Duryea in their pioneering American gasoline car of 1893. It was also the type that George B. Selden used in the plans he drafted for a self-propelled vehicle in 1879 and on which he was granted a patent in 1895. Already by that year, however, the Duryeas and other automotive experimenters were abandoning 2-cycle engines in favor of the 4-cycle engines that had first been popularized by a German, Nicholas Otto, in 1876. The 2-cycle engine became a standard in the marine engine field, but it would be used very little in the automotive field after the early experimental period.

In 1903, when the Association of Licensed Automobile Manufacturers was formed by those companies that agreed to be licensed under the Selden Patent, the Elmore Company was one of the first companies admitted to membership. The ALAM leadership that rejected the Ford Motor Company's application at this same time perhaps accepted the small Ohio company because, although the patent

Advertisement for the only factory-made American automobile powered by a 2-cycle engine

was claimed to apply to all gasoline-propelled motor vehicles, they thought it would be wise to include a manufacturer that employed the kind of engine Selden had initially had in mind and that critics declared was the only type of propulsion the patent covered.

Six years later Elmore was one of the select group of companies acquired by the newly formed

General Motors (GM) Company. Why GM's creator, William C. Durant, would want to add to the ranks of such blue-blooded acquisitions as Cadillac, Buick, and Olds a company that produced what one writer called a "two-cycle monstrosity" may have puzzled some people, but it may have reflected his desire to cover all bases. Just as he picked up Cartercar on the chance that its friction-drive might win widespread acceptance, so, too, he took Elmore, with its 2-cycle engine. "That's the kind of thing they were using on motor boats," he later recalled; "maybe two-cycles was going to be the thing for automobiles. I was for getting every car in sight, playing safe all along the line."

However, even Durant, who was admittedly no expert on mechanical matters, ought to have seen that by 1909 the verdict was already in on the usefulness of 2-cycle engines in automobiles. It is possible that his real reason for acquiring Elmore was part of a stock-watering scheme that led him to pick up some other companies of even more dubi-

ous merit in order to inflate the value of General Motors securities artificially. In any event, in 1911 a federal court ruled that the Selden patent applied only to cars driven by 2-cycle engines. The patent's worthlessness was revealed by the fact that of the hundreds of cars on the market, the Elmore was apparently the only one the patent covered. In 1912, therefore, the bankers who had gained control of General Motors dumped the Elmore as part of their efforts to rid the company of such unprofitable curiosities.

References:

Nick Baldwin and others, *The World Guide to Automobile Manufacturers* (New York: Facts on File, 1987);

Beverly Rae Kimes and Henry Austin Clark, *Standard Catalog of American Cars, 1805-1942* (Iola, Wis.: Krause, 1985);

Bernard A. Weisberger, *The Dream Maker: William C. Durant, Founder of General Motors* (Boston: Little, Brown, 1979).

Everitt-Metzger-Flanders Company

by George S. May

Eastern Michigan University

Organized in 1908 at the same time William C. Durant was working to put together the consolidation that became General Motors (GM), the Everitt-Metzger-Flanders (E-M-F) Company provides another example of the trend toward automotive mergers and consolidations, which was already underway and which would eventually reduce hundreds of hopeful automakers to a handful. E-M-F, located in Detroit, represented the merger of two existing Detroit auto manufacturers, Northern and Wayne.

Northern, which had started out in 1902 as the Northern Manufacturing Company and had then been renamed the Northern Motor Car Company, was organized by William T. Barbour and G. B. Gunderson of the Detroit Stove Works to produce a 1-cylinder runabout developed by Jonathan D. Maxwell, an engineer at nearby Olds Motor Works. Maxwell, who had a hand in the development of the popular curved-dash Oldsmobile runabout, closely followed the design of that car in the

new model, which was introduced in October 1902. Because of its quietness it was advertised as the "Silent Northern." Charles B. King, another former Olds employee, soon joined Maxwell. He would claim that only after he corrected some of Maxwell's mistakes had the Northern runabout operated satisfactorily. The following year Maxwell left Northern, and under King's direction the company—while continuing the 1-cylinder runabout model for several years—followed the industry in moving to larger models: a 2-cylinder touring car in 1904 and a 4-cylinder model in 1906.

The Wayne Automobile Company was organized in 1903-1904 by Charles L. Palms and his uncle, Dr. James B. Book, who jointly possessed financial resources far exceeding those available to most other Detroit auto companies of the day, including Northern and the Ford Motor Company. But the cars the company began to offer in 1904 enjoyed only modest sales, possibly because chief engi-

Silent as an electric; amply efficient in its motive power; complete to the remotest detail in the refinement of its body; ready at any time to travel any-where, the Flanders "20" Coupé is the ideal vehicle to carry Milady on her expeditions into the shopping district or on her round of social duties.

Its comfort makes it a veritable drawing room on wheels.

This Coupé is luxuriously equipped, is finished in dark green enamel with nickeled trimmings, has English broad-cloth upholstering, and is fitted with interior and exterior electric lights.

The E-M-F Company
Automobile Manufacturers
Detroit, Mich.

Advertisement designed to attract electric-car devotees to the gasoline-powered automobiles of E-M-F Company, 1910

neer William Kelly, despite what the company claimed in its advertisements, was no match for Henry Ford or Charles King.

In the spring of 1908 Wayne underwent a major executive overhaul. Byron "Barney" Everitt, a veteran of the carriage industry who had become one of the largest producers of automobile bodies and trimmings, became company president. Joining him were several prominent former Ford executives, including E. LeRoy Pelletier, who had been Ford's advertising manager, and Walter E. Flanders, who in a year and a half at Ford had acquired a reputation as a production genius. It was soon apparent, how-ever, that those changes were but a prelude to big-ger developments. William E. Metzger, Detroit's pioneer auto dealer who had gone on to direct sales at Cadillac in that company's early years, acquired an interest in Northern, and a merger between Wayne and Northern was carried out. In the new company, which was formally announced on June 2, 1908, Barbour from Northern became vice-president, and Palms and Book from Wayne were

listed as the treasurer and a member of the board of directors respectively. The clear leaders were Everitt, who continued as president of the consoli-dated firm; Metzger, the sales manager; and Flan-ders, the general manager.

The new firm abandoned the old Wayne and Northern lines and announced it would begin pro-ducing a new car in touring and roadster versions in September 1908. Called the E-M-F, which joke-sters would declare stood for "Every Mechanical Fault," the cars were slow to appear. Early in 1909 Metzger explained the delay was "due to our deter-mination to have our cars right, and we closely scruti-nize each machine before it goes on the market." In April 1909 an agreement was announced whereby Studebaker—the South Bend, Indiana, carriage manu-facturer that had been seeking ways to increase its presence in the automobile field—contracted to sell the entire output of E-M-F for three years. The agree-ment, similar to one Reo had worked out with the veteran New York auto dealer Ray Owen in 1904, eliminated the need for Metzger to continue lining up dealers. It also quickly eliminated Everitt and Metzger, who left the company in May when their stock interests were purchased by Studebaker. That company's representatives replaced Everitt and Metzger on the board of directors. Walter Flanders remained, succeeding Everitt as president.

Metzger, Everitt, and William Kelly, E-M-F's chief engineer, went off to form the Metzger Motor Car Company, which began producing a car called the Everitt "30." Flanders took advantage of the infu-sion of Studebaker money to acquire the DeLuxe Motor Car Company, a Detroit luxury car manufac-turer since 1906 that had had little success. The De-Luxe factory was used to turn out the Flanders runabout as a less expensive companion to E-M-F models. The company also picked up other proper-ties and began to produce its own bodies, axles, crankshafts, and other parts. It also picked up a fac-tory in Windsor, Ontario, where it could produce E-M-F and Flanders cars for the Canadian market. By 1909 E-M-F was second only to Ford among De-troit auto producers, with an output of 8,000 cars. With 10,000 employees in its several plants it was, according to one account, Detroit's largest em-ployer by the end of 1909.

In December 1909 Flanders announced that he was canceling the contract with Studebaker, charging that the company had not fulfilled its part of the agreement. Studebaker went to court, seeking

E-M-F 30, circa 1911

to force E-M-F to honor the arrangement, while Flanders began to set up a separate network of dealers. It soon became evident, however, that both parties were simply maneuvering in a contest for control of the company. Studebaker, which controlled only 36 percent of E-M-F stock, upped its offer for the remaining shares after Flanders won the preliminary round in the fight over the sales agreement. On March 9, 1910, Studebaker, acting through its agent, J. P. Morgan and Company, purchased the remaining 64 percent for about $5 million. Book (who is reported to have received about $1.25 million for his shares), Palms, and Barbour retired from the auto business with a handsome profit. Flanders, who was paid $1 million for his stock, stayed on as president and general manager under a three-year contract. Pelletier also stayed on, as advertising manager. He reportedly handled the negotiations that brought about the sale to Studebaker and received $200,000 for his services.

In 1911 Studebaker consolidated its wholly owned companies under the name Studebaker Corporation. The E-M-F and Flanders names were retained on the cars coming out of the Detroit factory through the 1912 season, but after that the Studebaker name was adopted. Total production of the two cars from 1908 through 1912 was nearly 80,000. Studebaker continued to produce cars in Detroit until 1925, then it concentrated operations at its plants in South Bend. Walter Flanders remained with the Studebaker organization until early in 1912 when, by mutual agreement, he departed. He was soon reunited with Metzger and Everitt, combining the Metzger Motor Car Company with a truck company Flanders had established to form the Flanders Motor Company. That company went out of business by the end of the year. Everitt, Metzger, and Flanders, along with Pelletier, were reunited briefly in the early 1920s in still another ill-fated venture, Rickenbacker Motor Company.

References:

Nick Baldwin and others, *The World Guide to Automobile Manufacturers* (New York: Facts on File, 1987);

George S. May, *A Most Unique Machine: The Michigan Origins of the American Automobile Industry* (Grand Rapids, Mich.: Eerdmans, 1975);

John B. Rae, *American Automobile Manufacturers: The First Forty Years* (Philadelphia: Chilton, 1959).

Fageol Motors Company

by George S. May

Eastern Michigan University

Initially, when Frank H. Fageol, William B. Fageol, and Louis H. Bill organized the Fageol Motors Company in Oakland, California, in November 1916, their intent was to produce a 4-cylinder luxury car, using a Hall-Scott engine. However, the American entry into World War I a few months later caused Hall-Scott to concentrate on engine production for the armed forces, and fewer than 20 Fageol cars were assembled. Fageol also produced 4-wheel-drive orchard tractors, but they did not sell and were soon abandoned.

The Fageols had some experience with trucks, and the company decided to switch its emphasis, turning out 4-cylinder trucks of a conventional design except for the row of finned ventilators on top of the hood that would be the distinguishing characteristic of most Fageol vehicles. The trucks were built to deal with the steep grades encountered in California and other western states, and those same conditions led the Fageols in 1921 to branch out into bus production. The Fageol Safety Coach, as it came to be called, used a 4-cylinder Hall-Scott engine; a low, enclosed body carrying 22 passengers; and brakes designed for the rugged California terrain. A 6-cylinder, 29-passenger bus was soon added. The Safety Coach proved to be popular in the East as well as the West, and in 1924 the former Thomart Motor Company plant in Kent, Ohio, was obtained to serve as an assembly center for the eastern market. In 1924, 503 Safety Coaches were sold, twice the sales figure for 1923.

In 1925 Detroit's American Car & Foundry Company, a longtime producer of railroad cars and rolling stock, approached the Fageol company with a purchase offer as part of its effort to diversify into bus production. An agreement was reached to sell Fageol's Kent plant but not the Oakland factory, which remained a separate operation. The Fageol brothers became vice-presidents of American Car & Foundry, which moved the bus production

to Detroit in 1926. The Fageol name continued to appear on some of the buses that it produced, but the company's name appeared on other models after 1927. The Fageol brothers left the company at that time and returned to Kent, where they formed the Twin Coach Company. For a short time in the early 1950s the Fageol name was used on delivery vans that Twin Coach produced.

Meanwhile, the Oakland plant of the original Fageol company continued to produce limited numbers of buses and trucks in the latter part of the 1920s, but financial problems took the company into receivership and reorganization in 1932 as the Fageol Truck & Coach Company. Trucks now became virtually the only product of the company, with diesel-powered models introduced in 1932, and cab-over trucks introduced in 1937. However, Fageol's recurring money problems led to truck production being suspended on January 1, 1939, by the Sterling Motors Corporation of Milwaukee, a truck company that had acquired control of Fageol the previous November.

Later in 1939 Sterling sold the Oakland plant to T. A. Peterman, while retaining Fageol's sales outlets. Peterman formed the Peterbilt Motors Company, the name being derived from the custom of calling the Fageol trucks "Bill-Bilt," after the company's president. With the exception of the finned ventilators, the early Peterbilt trucks were much like the Fageol trucks. Peterman died in 1944; some employees bought the company and operated it until 1958 when it became a subsidiary of Pacific Car & Foundry, the giant truck manufacturer now known as PACCAR. In 1960 Peterbilt left the old Oakland factory for a newer, larger facility at Newark, California. Although originally designed for western driving conditions, Peterbilt developed a devoted national following among long-distance haulers, not only for its rugged qualities but also for the luxurious interiors available in the cab that have made it and Kenworth, another PACCAR subsidiary of western origins, favorites with owner-operators.

References:
Nick Baldwin and others, *The World Guide to Automo-*

bile Manufacturers (New York: Facts on File, 1987);
G. N. Georgano, ed., *The Complete Encyclopedia of Commercial Vehicles* (Osceola, Wis.: Motorbooks International, 1979).

Federal-Mogul Corporation

by George S. May

Eastern Michigan University

The Federal-Mogul Corporation, headquartered in the Detroit suburb of Southfield, has been a supplier of automotive parts almost from the start of the industry. The company had its beginnings in Detroit in 1899 when J. Howard Muzzy and Edward F. Lyon formed the Muzzy-Lyon Company, dealing in mill and factory supplies. Their major interest, however, was in developing new and better bearing alloys. An alloy of tin, antimony, and copper developed by Isaac Babbitt in the 1830s had served since then as the antifriction agent that kept rotating metallic shafts of locomotive engines from overheating and wearing out. Muzzy and Lyon reformulated the "babbitt metal" to meet the needs of the internal combustion engine. They formed a Muzzy-Lyon subsidiary, Mogul Metal Company, that became a leading supplier not only of babbitt metal but also of bearings produced by a new die casting method they had developed. An order from Buick in 1910 for 10,000 connecting rod bearings was an important breakthrough for the small company, although the desire to maintain the secrecy of the die casting process almost caused it to lose an order from Hudson that same year, because they would not allow Hudson engineers into the plant.

In 1923 a Kansas City parts distributor, Douglas-Dahlin, was threatened with bankruptcy. Muzzy-Lyon was concerned because Douglas-Dahlin owed the company a considerable amount of money. Also concerned was Federal Bearing and Bushing, another firm that would suffer a heavy loss if the Kansas City firm went under. Out of a discussion between the two came a decision to merge. Federal Bearing did not have sufficient facilities to produce babbitt metal, while Muzzy-Lyon lacked

bronze-foundry facilities. The two fit together perfectly. Federal-Mogul Corporation was incorporated on May 1, 1924. The new corporation in turn took over Douglas-Dahlin, thereby giving it a service outlet. Within two years Federal-Mogul sales tripled the combined sales of the two companies at the time of the merger.

Over the next three decades expansion through acquisition would greatly increase Federal-Mogul's production and service capabilities. Mergers with the Brown Roller Bearing Company in 1955 and the National Motor Bearing Corporation in 1956 put the company on the *Fortune* 500 list. The name was changed to Federal-Mogul-Brown Bearing Corporation in 1955 but was changed back to Federal-Mogul Corporation ten years later.

In the 1960s Federal-Mogul, which had acquired Canadian outlets in 1937, greatly expanded its presence in world markets by acquiring control of producers of bearings in Europe and Latin America. Acquisition in 1980 of the Huck Manufacturing Company, a producer of fastening systems for the aerospace, truck, trailer, and railroad industries, was part of diversification efforts designed to make Federal-Mogul less dependent on sales to the volatile auto industry, as were the acquisitions of a variety of toolmaking firms. Vehicle and machinery components remained the corporation's major focus, but even there greater emphasis was placed on tapping the replacement-parts market. A joint venture with the Japanese NTN Toyo Bearing Company and expansion into the production of oil seals, o-rings, fuel pumps, and electrical and lighting products were other indicators of the recognition of the need for greater diversity.

References:
Automotive Industry of America (Southfield, Mich.: Prestige, 1979);

Thomas Derdak, ed., *International Directory of Company Histories* (Chicago & London: St. James, 1988).

Fenders

by James Wren

Motor Vehicle Manufacturers Association

Mud guards, splash guards, and wings were a few of the terms used to designate automobile parts used to protect both vehicle and passenger from water and mud thrown up by the wheels. Such protective guards, whether made from metal, wood, or leather, were not new with the automobile, but had been used with bicycles and horse-drawn carriages. Sometime during the years 1905-1915 those guards became commonly known as fenders.

With the development of the automobile the importance of fenders also changed. At the beginning of the twentieth century, only 200 miles of paved road existed in the United States, all of it within cities. As cars became more reliable and began to venture outside incorporated areas, drivers were faced with more than 2 million miles of rutted, unim-

proved roads that were difficult to traverse in good weather and nearly impossible to negotiate in inclement weather. Some sort of protection was necessary if automobile travel were to be convenient and safe. The wood and leather appendages were soon modified into metal fenders, while the former became known as flexible or removable flaps.

In 1914 the fender became a part of the growing trend of more unified design when Pierce-Arrow mounted headlights on the fenders themselves. By the end of the 1910s metal platforms were mounted between the front and rear fenders, leading to the development of the running board. These changes in fender design and use were influential in the stylistic revolution that overtook the industry during the 1920s.

Ford Model T fender

Frederick Samuel Fish

(February 5, 1852-August 13, 1936)

by Donald T. Critchlow

University of Notre Dame

CAREER: City attorney, Newark, New Jersey (1880-1884); member, New Jersey General Assembly (1884-1885); member, New Jersey State Senate (1885-1887); attorney and chairman of the executive committee (1887-1911), president (1911-1915), chairman of the board, Studebaker Corporation (1915-1933).

In the nascent automobile industry, Frederick Fish cut a much different figure from industry leaders such as the mechanic, Henry Ford; the speculator and founder of General Motors (GM), William C. Durant; or even the production man, Alfred P. Sloan, Jr., who finally brought stability to GM. Fish represented the new managerial man, a corporate lawyer with close ties to Wall Street financial houses. He realized early that the automobile industry would be dominated by three or four major companies whose success would not come just in the field of product line or market domination but also on the financial front. Those companies that could mobilize financial forces would be the victors in this war of survival.

Frederick Samuel Fish was born in Newark, New Jersey, on February 5, 1852, the son of Henry Clay and Clara M. Jones Fish. Henry Fish was the pastor of the First Baptist Church of Newark and was the author of numerous religious books. Frederick received an A.B. degree from Rochester University in 1873 and was admitted to the New Jersey bar in 1876. He rose quickly in Republican politics, first being elected city attorney of Newark in 1880, and then to the New Jersey General Assembly in 1884. One year later Fish won a seat in the state senate, where he emerged as one of the party's young reformers. It was this reputation that enabled the thirty-five-year-old Fish to become the president of the New Jersey Senate in 1887.

In his inaugural speech as president of the senate Fish declared, in what must have been one of

Frederick Samuel Fish

the shortest speeches in the body's history (taking up only three lines in the senate journal), that the state would "... best succeed when the Senate meets every two years and not every year." Nonetheless, Fish emerged as an active force in the reform wing of the Republican party. In the mid 1880s the New Jersey Republicans had consciously set out to establish themselves as a party of progress sympathetic to the laboring classes. Fish, as a representative of Essex, a county that was rapidly industrializing with a growing population of immigrant workers that by 1900 would account for more than half the county's population, was ready to carry the banner of reform. Under Fish's leadership, the Republican-controlled senate passed legislation for the protection of industry and labor from prison factory production, the establishment of a state board of agriculture, a women's factory law, the opening of a state school for mutes, and the protection of the oyster and fishing industry. Fish also helped engineer a tax on railroad and canal corporations. Fish's political success was short-lived, however. In 1888 the Democrats made a comeback under their gubernatorial candidate, Robert Green. In the rout Fish lost his seat to his Democratic opponent. He returned to Newark where he once again took up the practice of law, quickly establishing himself as one of the state's most prominent corporate attorneys. In 1887 Fish had married Grace Studebaker, the daughter of John M. Studebaker, one of the founders of the Studebaker Brothers Manufacturing Company. When the couple left Newark four years later, the local press reported that Fish had firmly established himself as "a churchman, member of society, and citizen."

When Fish came to Studebaker, his reputation as a man with close ties to Wall Street and as a Republican concerned with the laboring classes fit the Studebaker brothers' perception of themselves as enlightened capitalists and progressive employers. Fish moved to South Bend, Indiana, as he later reported, only at "the repeated insistence of J. M. together with Clem and Peter." Fish joined Studebaker as the company's corporate counsel, assigned the primary task of assisting the Studebaker brothers on financial matters. Although he came with the understanding that he would be placed on an "equal footing" with the brothers, he was "loath" to leave New Jersey, where he was a well-established lawyer with hopes of renewing a career in politics.

The Studebaker Brothers Manufacturing Company had by the 1890s reached a scale of production and a volume of sales that necessitated new managerial organization. The company continued to operate as if it were a small partnership, even though it had incorporated in 1868. Organizational tasks, sales, production, purchasing, and finance were assigned to the various brothers, who conferred with one another on an infrequent and informal basis.

The Studebakers in 1891 called upon Fish to draft new organizational plans for the firm. Within a year he had totally reorganized the company along the lines of a modern corporation, including the establishment of a board of directors, an executive committee, and a divisional structure that clearly separated the finance, production, sales, and purchasing functions of the company. Each function now would be managed by a separate committee and would make detailed reports to the executive committee on a quarterly basis. Each committee was given the power to undertake day-to-day decisions, while long-term policy remained in the domain of the executive committee. Shortly after undertaking this major reorganization, the firm was confronted by the depression of 1893. Fish assisted in the recapitalization of the firm with the backing of J. P. Morgan, who acquired approximately one-sixth of the voting stock. In 1900 Fish employed the Chicago accounting firm of Haskell-Sells to install a new factory accounting system.

Fish's behind-the-scenes style fit the image of the new corporate man. As the son-in-law of John Studebaker, Fish understood the traditions of the company, its reputation for quality products, and its image as a progressive employer, but unlike the company's founders he rarely appeared before the press or in public relations promotions. Indeed, his 1936 his obituary received less space in the *New York Times* than his wife's did a decade later. For this reason Fish has been generally overlooked by historians, but insiders at the time understood his importance to the company. The accounting firm of Marwick Mitchell, assigned to investigate Studebaker as an investment opportunity in 1910, reported to J. P. Morgan that Fish was the "dominant force" on the board, the man responsible for making the basic decisions of the company and setting corporate strategy.

Studebaker's decision to enter the automobile industry marked a victory for Fish and his vision for the expansion of the corporation. Under his leadership the corporation moved steadily into the new industry, carefully responding to conditions that did not allow much room for caution. As the automobile industry left behind a trail of failed companies, product lines, and bankruptcies, Fish pushed Studebaker forward, first into electrics, then into high-priced gasoline cars with the Garford Company in Ohio, later into mass-produced, medium-priced automobiles with Everitt-Metzger-Flanders (E-M-F), and finally into its own multimodel line under its own name.

The choice to enter the newly created automobile industry was not simply one of going into automotive production or going under. In 1900 the wagon and carriage business continued to flourish, and even as late as 1919 the Studebaker wagon division, having a strong market in the South for its products, continued to make a profit. Furthermore, in their arguments with Fish the Studebakers were quick to point out that automobiles were expensive, often the toys of the very rich, and had by no means established a market for themselves. To convert a profitable company to a new line that had not yet proven itself, the brothers maintained, seemed rash and irresponsible. They pointed to the bankruptcies of those who had mistakenly left wagon manufacturing to enter the booming bicycle industry only to find that the fad soon ended. The Studebaker brothers warned that a successful business must be built on caution and careful business practices, not on current fad.

Fish's curiosity regarding the automobile had been heightened considerably in 1896 after a series of discussions with top officials in the Postmaster General's Office who told him that they had initiated experiments with a "horseless wagon" as a means for delivering the mail. Under these circumstances Fish felt compelled to urge the executive committee to explore the automobile industry by funding research and development of a prototype electric vehicle that could later be put into production. This proposal, however, set off a fight within the board between Fish and the Studebaker brothers.

As Fish picked his way along, the automobile industry mushroomed. In a single decade, 1900 to 1910, 270 new firms were formed, adding to the 30 firms that had been established prior to the turn of the century. In 1908 the Association of Licensed Automobile Manufacturers reported that of the more than 200 companies in the nation, 70 to 80 of these were considered important, although only 20 companies were making a profit. Later estimates showed that more than 600 firms had engaged in the automobile industry by 1908. In these unsettled conditions, Wall Street naturally shied away from investing in the industry. Indeed, most financial houses saw the automobile industry as an ominous sign of extravagance and waste that led men to liquidate and divert their investments away from more productive and solid companies.

Shortly before Clement Studebaker's death on November 27, 1901, a new board composed of Fish and his supporters, including Clement Studebaker, Jr., resolved to begin production of electric and gasoline automobiles. Production was limited to electrics, however, for the first two years.

The company entered the market for gasoline-powered automobiles in 1904 when Fish contracted with the Garford Manufacturing Company to supply Studebaker with chassis for a 2-cylinder machine. In spring 1906 Garford wanted to expand production to 1,000 vehicles per year. Studebaker provided the capital for the expansion. The following year Fish made a bid to acquire Garford, but much to his dismay the bid was turned down because, as Arthur Garford put it, the Studebaker Corporation did not "cut much of a figure in the auto business." Rejected but not defeated, Fish set out to acquire a controlling interest in Garford, whether welcomed or not. In November 1908 Fish informed Garford that the Elyria plant was to have a "Studebaker-Garford" sign installed over the main entrance. The Studebaker Corporation had acquired a controlling interest in Garford.

Within a decade after taking the company into the automobile industry, Fish realized that three or four firms would dominate the market. This entailed, as Fish accurately perceived, a high concentration of capital being placed within a single company, a degree of capital that in the case of the Studebaker Corporation went beyond family resources. At what point Fish realized that taking the company into the automobile business meant the loss of control of the corporation by the Studebaker family remains uncertain.

Even as Fish moved to acquire control of Garford, he pursued other avenues to expand Studebaker's stake in the automobile market. Aware that the company needed to enter into the medium-priced market, Fish opened negotiations with the newly formed Everitt-Metzger-Flanders Company to market their medium-priced E-M-F 30. Fish announced that a cooperative arrangement had been reached that obligated Studebaker to market 600 cars produced by E-M-F. The sale of these medium-priced cars would thereby supplement the sales of the higher-priced Studebaker-Garford autos.

Clem Studebaker, Jr., and Fish acquired one-third of E-M-F's stock in 1909. Within months after this stock acquisition, relations between

E-M-F and Studebaker began to sour. Byron F. "Barney" Everitt and William E. Metzger saw in the acquisition an attempt by Studebaker to take over the company. They resigned from E-M-F soon afterward in a dispute with Walter Flanders over how to fight Studebaker. Meanwhile, Flanders went so far as to accuse Studebaker of falling behind in its sales in order to drive E-M-F's stock down for easy purchase. In turn, Studebaker charged E-M-F with not delivering its production quota in an attempt to remove Studebaker representation from the E-M-F board. The final break came in 1909 when Flanders refused to deliver any further orders to Studebaker unless they were paid in advance. The matter went to the courts with each side arguing that the other had broken the marketing agreement.

After a bitter, public controversy, the courts ruled in favor of E-M-F. Then, in a surprise move, Flanders, who had secretly opened negotiations with Fish, accepted a Studebaker offer of $5 million to acquire E-M-F. In the process, Studebaker hired Flanders as production manager of the newly merged company.

To finance the purchase of E-M-F and to expand production, Studebaker had to recapitalize. Although the J. P. Morgan company, which financed the acquisition of E-M-F, initially had an option on the new stock, it told Fish that it would not be able to exercise its option. As a consequence, Fish was placed in a serious bind. Desperate to refinance the short-term notes used to buy out E-M-F, Fish finally turned to his old acquaintants the Goldmans, of Goldman, Sachs, who together with the Lehman Brothers financed the reorganization of the new Studebaker Corporation on February 14, 1911. As a consequence of this reorganization, J. M. Studebaker, now seventy-nine years old, was forced to relinquish active control of the corporation to Fish, who became president; J. M. moved to the position of chairman of the board. When J. M. retired from the corporation in 1915 and Fish became chairman of the board, Fish's prótegé, Albert Erskine, took over active control of the company. The new board agreed that the "name of the family be retained by the corporation for advertising value and for the preservation of good will, if for no other reason." J. M. Studebaker remained on the board of directors, as did his nephew George Studebaker, but the family's role in the company had been greatly diminished.

The merger of E-M-F and Studebaker occurred at an ideal time in the industry. Although the automobile market experienced a brief decline in 1910, the market quickly revived as consumers went on a spending spree. Studebaker soon expanded its line to include a Flanders 20, along with the E-M-F 30. Although relations between Studebaker management and the mercurial Flanders soon forced Flanders to resign in 1912, the new Studebaker Corporation soon emerged as a major competitor to Willys, Cadillac, and Buick. Henry Ford's Model T stood in a class by itself, but Studebaker had become a major manufacturer.

Fish, it appeared, had been proven right in his determination to enter the automobile industry. Fish's strategy in taking Studebaker into automobiles had been one of gradualism. This later led some historians to argue that Studebaker's management had been *too* conservative in moving into the new industry, given the intense competition and the emergence of large concerns such as GM and Ford. Yet under the circumstances, Fish's strategy of cautious exploration and gradual entrance into production proved successful. By maintaining the wagon division while experimenting with electrics, and then using Garford to produce the chassis for the first Studebaker gasoline cars, Fish had enabled his company to explore the market without a heavy output of resources or great capital investment. When it became clear that the automobile could provide huge profits, Fish moved swiftly, first acquiring controlling interest in Garford, then quickly entering the medium-priced field through his acquisition of E-M-F in 1910.

Fish continued as chairman of the board through the growth period of the 1920s. Then in his seventies, he was content to follow the lead of Erskine and the organization he had created. Fish stayed in that position until the company went into receivership in 1933. He died at age eighty-four in South Bend on August 13, 1936. He had proven to be one of the professionals capable of making tough choices in the new age of corporate capitalism.

References:

Albert Erskine, *History of the Studebaker Corporation* (Chicago: Poole, 1918);

Joseph F. Mahoney, "The Impact of Industrialization on the New Jersey Legislature 1870-1900: Some Preliminary Views," *New Jersey Since 1860: New Findings and Interpretation* (Trenton, 1972);

Lawrence H. Seltzer, *Financial History of the American Automobile Industry* (Boston: Houghton Mifflin, 1928);

William H. Shaw, *The History of Essex and Hudson Counties, New Jersey* (Philadelphia: Everts & Peck, 1884);

Shaw, *New Jersey Senate Journal* (Trenton, 1887).

Archives:

Material relating to Fish is located in the Henry Cave Papers, Detroit Public Library, Detroit, Michigan; the Arthur L. Garford Papers, Ohio Historical Society, Ohio State Museum, Columbus, Ohio; the Henry P. Joy Papers, Bentley Library, University of Michigan, Ann Arbor, Michigan; the Post Office Department, Record Group 28, National Archives, Washington, D.C.; and the Studebaker Corporation Papers, Studebaker National Museum, South Bend, Indiana.

Fisher Body Corporation

by Roger B. White

Smithsonian Institution

A leading manufacturer of bodies for passenger automobiles and delivery cars, Fisher Body Corporation built bodies for some General Motors (GM) companies beginning in 1910 and was a division of GM from 1926 to 1984. By 1919, when GM purchased a majority of its stock, Fisher Body was the world's largest manufacturer of automobile bodies. The six Fisher brothers who then managed the corporation were specialists in closed-body construction and staunch advocates of the wood-and-steel body; Fisher built more closed bodies than open by 1922, three years before closed-body production exceeded open-body in the automobile industry as a whole, and by 1926 the company controlled its supplies of glass and lumber. The firm's competence as a designer and producer of closed bodies was crucial to General Motors' emergence as the nation's leading automobile manufacturer in the late 1920s. Because of its large volume and its attention to quality and aesthetics, Fisher Body became a prominent contributor to the growing comfort, attractiveness, durability, and strength of low- and medium-priced automobiles.

The Fisher Body Company, principal forerunner of the Fisher Body Corporation, was organized in Detroit, Michigan, on July 22, 1908, by Albert Fisher and his nephews Frederic and Charles Fisher. The company was capitalized at $50,000, of which approximately $30,000 was supplied by Albert Fisher, an established manufacturer of carriages and wagons in Detroit and builder of automobile bodies for several leading firms. Frederic and Charles had been trained by their father, Lawrence Fisher, in his carriage-making shop in Norwalk, Ohio, and had worked at the C. R. Wilson Body Company in Detroit.

Fisher Body initially advertised both carriage and automobile bodies, but the rapidly growing automobile industry gradually became the firm's main concern. By 1911 the Fishers no longer advertised carriage bodies. Under the financial guidance of Louis Mendelssohn, a Detroit automobile manufacturer who purchased Albert Fisher's interest in the company soon after its founding, Fisher Body built open and closed bodies for many leading automobile manufacturers, including Ford, Cadillac, and Hudson. Frederic served as president and manager of the company, and Charles served as vice-president and superintendent.

The Fishers quickly moved to the forefront of automobile body design by learning to form and attach metal body panels. Bodies made of stamped-steel sheets instead of wooden panels were being adopted by several larger manufacturers, including Maxwell and Everitt-Metzger-Flanders, because steel could be shaped more rapidly than wood and was lighter and more durable. Within a few years high-grade manufacturers such as Pierce-Arrow were using cast-aluminum bodies. In 1909 Fisher Body advertised automobile bodies "of wood and metal," and two years later the company advertised bodies made of steel and aluminum. Fisher built Cadillac's first metal closed bodies in 1910, but Wilfred Leland, general manager of Cadillac Motor Car Company at the time, recalled that the bodies were unsatisfactory and that the Fishers had to cor-

The 1915 Buick Roadster with body by Fisher (photograph by Rick Lenz; courtesy of Automobile Quarterly)

rect them. By 1915 the composite body, consisting of sheet-steel panels attached to a wooden frame reinforced with steel braces, was gaining acceptance for automobiles of average quality, and by 1918 Fisher Body made extensive use of presses and woodworking machinery to make composite bodies for Ford, Hudson, Studebaker, Chandler, and other firms.

Many automobile manufacturers during the 1910s found it more economical to purchase bodies from specialists such as Fisher Body than to invest in the skilled labor and machinery needed to process sheet steel and wood. Buying an array of large dies and presses to stamp steel sheets required large amounts of capital and floor space. Woodworking machinery, painting facilities, and sheet storage also required space. Moreover, much skilled handwork was necessary: shaping dies, cutting wooden parts and sheet steel, screwing wooden parts together, and brushing and rubbing coat after coat of paint and varnish. Despite the slow, labor-intensive nature of its operations, Fisher Body expanded rapidly. Profits increased more than threefold between 1913 and 1916, and output rose from 105,000 bodies in 1914 to nearly 500,000 in 1917.

As late as 1918, however, Fisher Body's assembly methods still retained much of their shoplike character, in contrast with the specialized, integrated chassis-assembly lines at Ford. Although Fisher subassembled some frame sections by 1918, each frame was still fully assembled on a stationary jig, and steel panels were then screwed to the frame. Every order was unique; dies had to be changed, new patterns for wood and steel had to be drawn, and the flow of materials and partially finished bodies among the 16 Fisher plants had to be shifted. Not all bodies were fully assembled; the company built bodies for 1918 Ford Model T touring cars in sections that were paneled separately and shipped to Ford plants for final assembly. Virtually all other open bodies were taken by truck to other body companies to be upholstered and painted. Closed bodies alone were finished in Fisher Body shops.

Fisher Body's expertise in building closed bodies and its farsighted appraisal of their eventual popularity earned the company a huge share of the market for closed cars by 1920. Mendelssohn and the Fishers organized the Fisher Closed Body Company in December 1910. The vast majority of automobiles then in use were open touring cars and roadsters; closed bodies were available only on limited-production limousines, town cars, and coupes. A typical limousine sold for approximately $5,000. Though poorly suited to hot weather and unpaved rural roads, closed cars, including new family "sedans," enjoyed slowly growing sales as prices fell within reach of the middle class. By 1914 sedan tops that could be installed in winter and removed in summer were available as standard equipment on some makes and as aftermarket accessories. The Ford center-door sedan, introduced in 1915, was priced at less than $1,000, and by 1918 several sedans of substantial quality were priced at less than $2,600. By late 1916, after the August 22, 1916, consolidation of Fisher Body Company, Fisher Closed Body Company, and Fisher Body Company of Canada to form Fisher Body Corporation, the journal *Automobile* estimated that Fisher was building 60 percent of the industry's total output of closed bodies. In the year ending April 30, 1920, Fisher built about half as many closed bodies as the entire number produced in 1919, but most of its output still consisted of open bodies.

General Motors was one of the manufacturers that looked upon Fisher Body with growing respect and was the first to propose a partnership with the body firm. Beginning in 1915 Fisher built bodies for Buick and Cadillac. On November 9, 1917, at the urging of GM president William Durant, GM agreed to purchase "substantially all" of its bodies from Fisher for a period of ten years at cost plus 17.6 percent. But Fisher continued to build bodies for many of GM's competitors. The company built the popular 1919 Essex sedan body for Hudson, a leader in closed-car sales, and in 1920-1921 erected a large factory in Cleveland, Ohio, to build bodies for Cleveland and Chandler automobiles.

In planning GM's post-World War I expansion program, both Durant and chairman Pierre S. du Pont were convinced of the need for vertical integration to assure an adequate supply of parts and materials. They were particularly concerned that the most capable body manufacturer available, Fisher, might not meet their terms in future negotiations; worse yet, they learned that Fisher was discussing a partnership with an automobile manufacturer in Cleveland. In 1919 Durant, du Pont, and John J. Raskob negotiated the purchase of 300,000 shares (60 percent) of common stock in Fisher Body Corporation. The value of the shares was $27.6 million; a

cash payment of $5.8 million was made, and the balance was paid in five-year serial notes. The parties agreed on a new five-year contract paying Fisher the same rate as the 1917 contract. Frederic Fisher remained president and general manager of Fisher Body Corporation, and Louis Mendelssohn remained chairman. Five of Frederic's younger brothers—Charles, William, Lawrence, Edward, and Alfred—were actively involved in managing the firm and would assume more important roles during the subsequent two decades.

With an assured outlet and the expectation of steady growth, Fisher took steps to secure its own material needs. In 1920 the corporation paid approximately $7 million in cash for the Saginaw Plate Glass Company, the Columbia Plate Glass Company, and the Federal Plate Glass Company and merged them to form the National Plate Glass Company. In the same year the corporation acquired the Ternstedt Manufacturing Company of Detroit, which specialized in automobile-body hardware. Ternstedt developed a crank-type window regulator and other devices and fittings for Fisher but continued to sell products to automobile manufacturers outside of GM.

During the depression of 1920-1921 Fisher Body's output fell by more than half, but the affiliation with GM resulted in rapid growth when market conditions improved. Under the chairmanship of Pierre S. du Pont GM sought to upgrade the quality of its Oakland and Oldsmobile lines and increase its volume in the low-price field with Chevrolet models that were of better quality and priced slightly higher than the Ford Model T. Fisher was integrated into those plans in stages. In 1922 it began building Chevrolet bodies in Cleveland, and in that year Frederic Fisher was appointed to GM's Executive Committee to facilitate the coordination of body production and final assembly. In 1923 Fisher opened six new body-assembly plants, four of which were near Chevrolet chassis plants. By the following year Fisher built Oakland open and closed bodies and Oldsmobile bodies. Annual output rose from 158,224 in the year ending April 30, 1922, to 574,979 in the year ending April 30, 1924, and net operating income in the same period rose from $6,193,454 to $22,102,009. The number of non-GM Fisher customers decreased from seven to four.

Much of Fisher Body's renewed success resulted from the growing popularity of closed cars in the early 1920s. Sedans and coupes provided comfort and convenience in inclement weather, and they could be locked to prevent theft. The spread of paved roads made heavy closed bodies more practical, and falling prices generated further demand. A 1922 Ford Model T sedan could be purchased for as little as $645, and GM reduced the price of the least expensive Chevrolet sedan from $1,375 in 1921 to $875 in 1922. By 1924 closed cars accounted for 40 percent of GM's production. Some GM manufacturing divisions, including Chevrolet and Cadillac, built their own open bodies but ordered closed bodies from Fisher. In November 1924 GM increased its output of closed cars to 75 percent of total production, well above the industry average. In the 1925 model year Fisher built 40 types of closed bodies for GM, and Fisher assembly plants operated or were being constructed near chassis- and final-assembly plants for all GM makes.

By the mid 1920s Pierre du Pont greatly respected the Fishers as production managers and wanted them to become more deeply involved in GM management. He also wanted better coordination between Fisher Body and the automobile-manufacturing divisions. Du Pont apparently favored a merger of GM and Fisher Body to achieve those ends and to secure fully GM's supply of closed bodies. The Fisher brothers, who owned approximately 20 percent of Fisher Body Corporation's stock, resisted du Pont's suggestion because the corporation was highly profitable and because they did not wish to forfeit the family's identification with and partial control over the business.

When the 1919 body-purchase agreement between GM and Fisher expired in 1924, GM management offered the Fishers an informal means of further integrating the two firms, and the Fishers accepted the offer. Charles and Lawrence Fisher were appointed to GM's Executive Committee, and the three Fishers then on the committee concentrated on GM affairs while their brother William presided over the body firm. The Fishers' influence on the ten-member Executive Committee grew as du Pont and Raskob became less involved in its affairs, and the Fishers made a profound contribution to GM's marketing and product development during the next few years. In 1925 Lawrence Fisher was appointed president and general manager of the Cadillac Motor Car Company. During his nine-year tenure the division introduced the LaSalle line and the Cadillac V-16 and V-12 engines. Fisher also inaugurated an

expansion program at Cadillac, and soon Cadillac closely rivaled Packard as America's leading mass-produced luxury car. Frederic Fisher was appointed to GM's Finance Committee in 1924 and served on the study group that recommended the acquisition of Austin Motor Company, Ltd., in 1925 and Adam Opel A.G. in 1929. GM purchased the latter in 1931.

In 1926 du Pont and the Executive Committee formally proposed a merger of General Motors and Fisher Body. The younger Fishers at first declined to sell their interests, but after further discussion between du Pont and Frederic Fisher, GM accepted the latter's claim of "hidden values" not reflected in account books and offered the brothers an excellent exchange of stock. The Fishers then accepted the merger terms, and on June 30, 1926, GM traded 664,720 shares of its own common stock, having a market value of $136 million, for the remaining 40 percent of Fisher Body Corporation stock at the rate of one share of GM for one and one-half of Fisher. The latter firm became the Fisher Body Division of General Motors but remained under the managerial control of William Fisher. The new division included as subsidiaries the Ternstedt Manufacturing Company, the National Plate Glass Company, and other manufacturing, assembly, and supply units formerly owned by Fisher Body Corporation.

The merger of General Motors and Fisher Body resulted in great success, particularly in its bearing on marketing. A historic shift in the character of automotive demand was coming to fruition in the late 1920s. Most Americans buying cars for the first time or as replacements sought the comfort and convenience of all-weather, all-season closed bodies. Also, middle-class Americans were acquiring a taste for luxury and decoration in their cars, and many coveted low-priced automobiles with the cosmetic features of more-expensive makes: classic, artful lines; decorative color schemes and striping; fabric upholstery; and accessories such as interior lights, window shades, door pockets, and ashtrays. The price of a fully equipped sedan had fallen to as little as $695 for a 1927 Chevrolet two-door coach and $495 for a 1927 Ford Tudor sedan, but GM captured the emerging market by stressing quality and innovation along with low price.

Fisher Body's long-standing reputation for refined, well-built closed bodies, then a particularly valuable cachet, was touted in advertisements for all GM makes. A logo introduced in 1922 bearing an ornate Napoleonic-era coach and the phrase "Body by Fisher" was used more frequently in those advertisements. As early as 1922 Fisher hired professional body designers to work on custom bodies, and in 1926 an Oakland with body by Fisher had won first prize in its class in the annual French body competition. Fisher's Fleetwood Division, formed in 1925 through the purchase of Fleetwood Metal Body Company of Fleetwood, Pennsylvania, created special body lines, paint colors, hardware, upholstery, and decoration for limited-production Cadillacs and other luxury makes. The stylish Chevrolet two-door coach enjoyed rapidly growing sales after 1927, much as the utilitarian Ford Model T touring car had won motorists' approval and affection a decade earlier. In Pontiac, Oldsmobile, Buick, Oakland, and LaSalle GM offered a range of more-expensive models that Ford could not match. As part of an innovative marketing strategy conceived by GM management in 1921 and fully realized by 1927, each GM make represented a different level of price, luxury, and power to which prospective motorists could aspire. Although the quality of bodies and chassis varied from make to make, every GM automobile body bore a nameplate with the Fisher logo, another enticement to those who bought inexpensive models.

The value of the creative stylist came to the attention of GM management when Lawrence Fisher commissioned Harley Earl, a Los Angeles designer of custom automobile bodies, to style the 1927 LaSalle. Recognizing the stimulating effect that bold styling and annual styling changes could have on sales of all GM models, company president Alfred P. Sloan put Earl in charge of a newly created Art and Colour Section, which was placed under GM's central office on January 1, 1928. At first Earl met with resistance in translating his ideas into finished bodies for other GM models. Ten years later, however, the Art and Colour Section, renamed Styling, systematically met and compromised with each automobile manufacturing division's general manager and engineers. Earl and his large staff greatly influenced the appearance of Fisher bodies, but they were often forced to concede to Fisher and other division officials on practical requirements stemming from market research, chassis design, production volume, cost, and parts storage.

Although some automobile manufacturers changed to welded-steel bodies in the late 1920s,

the bodies styled by Earl in his first years with GM had wooden frames covered with sheet steel. Wood is both strong and resilient, and the Fishers maintained that such a frame was better able to withstand the stresses caused by rough roads, collisions, and upsets. That conclusion was confirmed by tests conducted by Fisher in which 9,000 pounds of pressure was applied diagonally across each body type. The wood-and-steel body deflected four inches with a minimum of distortion and cracked glass, but the welded-steel body deflected eleven inches and was crushed beyond repair. Fisher Body had established its own logging operations and sawmills by 1926, and as late as 1934 GM owned approximately 222,000 acres of hardwood timberland in Michigan and the South.

In contrast, some automobile and body manufacturers had become convinced that bodies with all-steel cowls, sides, and rear panels were superior to composite bodies. Hale and Kilburn, a Philadelphia metal-stamping firm, had built all-steel bodies for the 1912 Hupmobile touring car. The Edward G. Budd Manufacturing Company of Philadelphia, a specialist in steel automobile bodies, had built bodies for the 1913 Oakland and Garford touring cars and the 1915 Dodge touring car. Essex adopted steel bodies in 1926, and the 1926 Ford Model T's (except Fordor sedans) also had steel bodies. The Essex and Ford bodies, however, had wooden floors and wood-and-fabric roofs. In 1925 Chevrolet rejected an offer by Budd to build all-steel bodies. Six years later Fisher bodies still had hardwood frames but also had a steel or iron brace in place of wood at every joint; that type of construction continued in use for the next four years.

Fisher Body's metal-stamping abilities were more commensurate with those of Budd. By 1931 Fisher Body had installed large presses that stamped as one piece rear-quarter and back panels formerly stamped in several pieces and welded together. On some 1935 Chevrolets and other GM makes Fisher introduced the Turret-Top, its most important technical contribution to closed bodies. The first one-piece, stamped-steel roof in the automobile industry, the Turret-Top added strength and rigidity to bodies, enhanced safety and appearance, and facilitated streamlined styling. It was part of all GM closed cars for 1936. The 1936 Oldsmobile body frame was made of steel except for the body sills and window frames, and bodies for the 1937 Chevrolet and Oldsmobile were made entirely of steel. Inner and outer sheet-metal panels of these "Unisteel" bodies were welded together to form a rigid unit that was then welded to a steel framework.

In 1934 Frederic and Charles Fisher resigned their management positions at GM to concentrate on personal matters. By 1937 Lawrence, William, Edward, and Alfred Fisher reportedly wished to resign too, but they remained at GM through the strikes and violent incidents involving GM workers between 1937 and 1939 and the conversion to war production during World War II. Fisher Body built tanks, subassemblies for B-25 and B-29 bombers, aircraft instruments, anti-aircraft guns, experimental aircraft, and other war products. The four brothers resigned their management positions in 1944, before design and production of postwar automobiles could begin. Lawrence and Edward remained on GM's board of directors, however, the latter until 1969.

As part of a major restructuring of GM operating divisions, Fisher Body's primary manufacturing and assembly plants were transferred in 1984 to two new divisions, CPC (Chevrolet-Pontiac-GM of Canada) and BOC (Buick-Oldsmobile-Cadillac), or to other GM units. With that change, aimed at integrating production and marketing activities and reducing development time for new models, the Fisher Body Division ceased to exist. Eight Fisher Body parts-manufacturing plants, however, were combined with GM's Guide Division to form Fisher Guide, which manufactures hardware and lighting apparatuses for GM and other automakers.

References:

Alfred D. Chandler, Jr., *Giant Enterprise: Ford, General Motors, and the Automobile Industry* (New York: Harcourt, Brace & World, 1964);

Chandler, *Strategy and Structure: Chapters in the History of the Industrial Enterprise* (Cambridge, Mass.: MIT Press, 1962);

Chandler and Stephen Salsbury, *Pierre S. du Pont and the Making of the Modern Corporation* (New York: Harper & Row, 1971);

Arthur Pound, *The Turning Wheel: The Story of General Motors through Twenty-Five Years* (Garden City, N.Y.: Doubleday, Doran, 1934);

Alfred P. Sloan, Jr., *My Years with General Motors* (Garden City, N.Y.: Doubleday, 1964).

Henry Ford

(July 30, 1863-April 7, 1947)

by Richard B. Folsom

Henry Ford Estate—Fair Lane

CAREER: Engineer (1891-1893), chief engineer, Edison Illuminating Company (1893-1899); mechanical superintendent, Detroit Automobile Company (1899-1901); engineer, Henry Ford Company (1901-1902); partner, Ford & Malcomson Company (1902-1903); vice-president and general manager (1903-1906), president (1906-1919, 1943-1945), majority owner, Ford Motor Company (1919-1947).

Henry Ford, the most famous of all automobile manufacturers and perhaps the most important industrialist of the twentieth century, was born on July 30, 1863, in Springwells Township, Wayne County, Michigan. He was one of five children of William and Mary Litogot Ford who survived infancy and early childhood. William Ford, who was born in 1826, immigrated to the United States in 1847 from near Clonakilty, County Cork, Ireland. Mary Litogot was born to Mr. and Mrs. William Litogot of Wyandotte, Michigan, in 1839. She became an orphan in 1840 and was adopted by Patrick and Margaret O'Hern in 1842. William Ford and Mary Litogot were married in 1861 and proceeded to live with the O'Herns in a new house that William Ford had helped Patrick O'Hern build in the farming community of Springwells Township, located about ten miles west of Detroit. It was in this spacious new farmhouse that Henry Ford was born. In 1867 Patrick O'Hern sold his farm to William Ford with the stipulation that the O'Herns be allowed to continue living on the farm for the rest of their lives.

The Ford farm was both productive and profitable during the post-Civil War years. The 1876 *Wayne County, Michigan Atlas* even contained an il-

Henry Ford, 1904 (courtesy of the Ford Archives, Henry Ford Museum, Dearborn, Michigan)

lustration and description of the Ford farm—no doubt a source of pride to William Ford. For young Henry Ford life on his father's farm was typical of that of other children growing up in a Midwest farm setting—typical because of sunup to sundown backbreaking chores, combined with farming sans power machinery. As the eldest son of William Ford, Henry was expected to be a role model for the younger Ford children—especially his brothers. Stories of young Henry's lack of enthusiasm toward farm work abound. His sister Margaret reported that Henry would easily become distracted and walk away from an unpleasant farm chore. It was also said that he was sluggish on the way to a chore and light-footed on the way back. Henry had disdain for repetitious farm work and the excessive amount of time required to complete even the most basic tasks. "My earliest recollection," he later declared, "is that, considering the results, there is too much work on the place!"

The farm, with all its unpleasantness, offered Henry a unique opportunity to explore and develop his burgeoning interest in anything of a mechanical nature. Often he would travel from farm to farm throughout the Springwells Township countryside fixing his neighbors' broken farm tools and implements. He even built and repaired sleighs and wagons in his father's workshop. In 1876, when he was thirteen, his interest in farm machinery led to an additional enthusiasm for the intricacies of clocks, watches, and toys. He is said to have earned a reputation for being able to fix even the most complicated watches and clocks. Another positive aspect of growing up on the farm was that Henry Ford acquired a strong appreciation and love for nature. From childhood, he developed a love for bird-watching, which, as an adult, he pursued with enthusiasm.

During the winter months, when the amount of farm work decreased, Ford attended public school. He began school in January 1871, at the age of seven, and concluded his education in November 1879, at the age of sixteen. The first school that he attended was the Scotch Settlement School, located about a mile and a half from his home. Later he transferred to the Miller School. All during his formal education Henry worked hard to learn from his teachers, achieving various degrees of success. He excelled in mathematics. As was the case in many American schools during the 1870s, his reading and writing lessons were taught from William McGuffey readers. Although he did not learn to read or write with anything more than a small degree of proficiency, the moralistic stories of the McGuffey readers had a lasting impact on him. Many years later he enjoyed collecting and reprinting the books so that new generations of students could benefit from them. Also in later years he restored both the Scotch Settlement and Miller schools and moved them to his Greenfield Village outdoor museum in Dearborn, Michigan.

Ford's mechanical curiosity was not confined to the family farm. One day after school he instructed a group of boys in a project to build a dam and miniature mill on a creek that led past the Miller School. The mill was an engineering success, reportedly even strong enough to grind clay, potatoes, and small stones. Unfortunately, the boys did not dismantle the dam when they finished their experiment. During the night it caused the ditch to overflow, flooding a neighboring farmer's potato patch. The next morning the farmer expressed his anger toward the boys, ending the project. On another occasion, Henry is said to have supervised his friends in the construction and operation of a small coal-fired steam boiler, which blew up, injuring Henry and a couple of the other boys and causing a nearby fence to catch on fire. However, Ford's sister Margaret later declared that Henry Ford considerably embellished his recollections of boyhood. "It was neither as colorful and romantic as it has been painted," nor "was it as full of hardship."

In March 1876 thirty-seven-year-old Mary Litogot Ford died. Her death came 12 days after she gave birth to a stillborn baby. Her loss was especially tragic because the children she left behind were so young. Henry was twelve, and the youngest, Robert, was only three. Mary's death was a terrible shock to Henry. She was the parent who strongly encouraged his interest in mechanics. Years later Henry remembered that at the time of his mother's death he "felt a great wrong had been done to me. The house was like a watch without a mainspring."

Not long after the death of his mother Ford had an experience that profoundly affected him. In July 1876 he was riding on a farm wagon with his father when they came upon a self-propelled steam traction engine lumbering down the road ahead of them. Henry, who was not quite thirteen, had seen portable steam threshing engines drawn by horses and, of course, railroad locomotives, but he had never seen an engine that traveled under its own power on a country road. Without saying a word to his father, Ford jumped off the wagon and approached the iron monster. He was fascinated by the mechanical marvel hissing and clanking down the road ahead of him. Without hesitation he began walking quickly alongside the engine and shouting questions to the engineer about the machine's operation. The engineer was impressed with the young boy's inquisitiveness and answered each question put to him. Later that summer, and the next, Henry was allowed to help the engineer operate the same engine. The engine he encountered was the first of that kind he had ever seen in operation under its own power. The memory stayed with him the rest of his life.

On December 1, 1879, Henry decided he had had enough of farm life and walked to the city of Detroit in search of an opportunity to pursue his interest in mechanics. Detroit in 1879 was a city of approximately 116,000 people. It had the reputation of being one of the largest centers for iron stove manufacturing in the United States. There were also vast machine shops; iron, steel, and brass foundries; carriage and wagon works; engine manufactories; flour mills; breweries; pharmaceutical,

soap, and cigar plants; and railroad car assembly plants. It was to one of these plants of the Michigan Car Company works that Ford went looking for employment. He was hired immediately and started his new job with the title "Beginning Apprentice Engineer" at a very respectable wage of $1.10 per day. He lived with his aunt Rebecca Flaherty, who gave him free room and board. His feeling of good fortune quickly disappeared when he was fired from the Michigan Car Works after just six days. He later recalled that a large machine near his work station had broken down and that the experienced mechanics had spent most of the day trying to diagnose and fix the problem. After the men gave up and left, Henry walked over to the machine, intuitively identified the problem, and quietly fixed it. The shop foreman, considering the new employee too brazen and forward, promptly fired him. Reflecting on this incident, Henry vowed, "I learned then not to tell all you know."

Ford was not out of work very long. Upon hearing of his son's misfortune, William Ford came to Henry's rescue, taking him to the Flower Brothers Machine Shop, also in Detroit. The Flower brothers, James, George, and Thomas, were good friends of William. Henry thus began his second job at $2.50 per 60-hour work week. To be nearer his new job, Ford moved to the boardinghouse of Mrs. James Payton, who charged him $3.50 per week. To meet his expenses Ford found a part-time job repairing watches at the Robert Magill Jewelry Shop not far from the boardinghouse. Magill was impressed with Ford's ability to repair clocks and watches but insisted that he work in a room at the rear of the shop so that customers would not become alarmed from seeing a teenage boy working on their valued timepieces. Magill willingly paid Ford $3.00 per week for working six hours per evening, six days per week.

In August 1880, after assimilating all he thought he could learn at the Flower Brothers Machine Shop, Ford quit that job and moved on to the Detroit Drydock Company, the largest of Detroit's shipbuilding firms. To gain experience at a larger company Henry accepted a pay cut of 50 cents per week. Although he was working 96 hours per week during this period, he never considered his life difficult. "I was never tired," he said later. "I was always enjoying what I was doing and always had plenty of energy for it." During his apprenticeship at the Detroit Drydock Company from late fall

1880 to summer 1882, Ford was deeply influenced by Frank Kirby, the company's construction engineer. When Ford built his vast Dearborn Engineering Laboratory in the early 1920s, he ordered that the names of famous scientists and inventors be carved into the building's exterior walls. Among names such as Edison, Newton, and Galileo is Kirby, in honor of the Detroit Drydock Company engineer who gave young Henry valuable advice during his apprenticeship.

In August 1882 Ford completed his apprenticeship in Detroit and returned to his father's farm in Springwells Township. His grandfather, Patrick O'Hern, had just died, and William more than ever needed additional help on the farm. Not long after Henry returned, one of William's neighbors, John Gleason, hired Henry to operate a small portable steam engine he had just purchased but did not know how to operate. Henry operated the little engine for 83 days that summer, for $3.00 per day, cutting clover and corn, grinding feed, and sawing wood. News of Ford's ability operating Gleason's steam engine quickly spread. Late in the same summer of 1882 Henry was hired as a steam engine expert by John Cheny, district representative of the Westinghouse Engine Company of Schenectady, New York. His new job took him all over southern Michigan setting up and servicing Westinghouse steam traction engines. During his spare time he continued working for John Gleason and accepted odd jobs repairing machinery.

On December 1, 1884, Ford entered Detroit's Goldsmith, Bryant & Stratton Business University. There he studied mechanical drawing, bookkeeping, and business. Although he only attended school for a few months, he learned the basics of conducting business, and he would credit his understanding of the intricacies of business to his brief business school experience

On January 1, 1885, Henry attended a party sponsored by the Greenfield Dance Club at the Martindale House in Greenfield Township, about six miles north of the William Ford farm. There he met eighteen-year-old Clara Bryant, his future wife. Clara Jane Bryant was born on April 11, 1866, in Greenfield Township, Wayne County, Michigan. She was a graceful girl with chestnut-colored hair and a reputation for being clearheaded and practical. All these qualities attracted the twenty-one-year-old Henry. She was impressed by Ford as well. She told her parents that he was "quiet, pleasant, keen-

minded, and sensible." On April 19, 1886, Henry and Clara became engaged, and they were married on April 11, 1888.

William Ford presented his son with an offer he did not think Henry could refuse: if Henry would agree to turn 40 acres belonging to William Ford into a productive farm, the land would be legally turned over to him. Henry, however, did not begin farming as his father had hoped and expected. Instead, he cut down the timber on the property and sold it to neighbors and various factories and shipyards in Detroit. He also cut timber for his own use. He and Clara were planning to build a new, larger home on the property. This new home, known as the "square house," was completed in June 1889, and they lived in the house until September 1891.

Much to his father's consternation, Ford refused to farm the 40 acres. When he had finished cutting all of the timber, his main source of income stopped. He was then forced to think of a new way to make a living. In early September 1891 he went to Detroit and accepted a job as an engineer with the Edison Illuminating Company with the understanding that he would begin work as soon as possible. Clara was definitely not enthusiastic about leaving her comfortable new home, but she believed in her husband and wanted to see him have every opportunity. On September 25, 1891, Henry and Clara packed their limited possessions and traveled east to Detroit. Upon arriving, they moved into a small apartment on John R. Street.

Henry began his work as night engineer at the Edison Illuminating Company at a salary of $40 per month. Less than one month after Henry began his new job he was faced with a major problem when a critically important 100-horsepower steam engine broke down. Ford identified the problem and repaired it. The manager was so pleased that he raised Ford's salary to $45 per month in November and $50 per month in December. Ford also was allowed to use a small workshop at the rear of the Edison Plant. When he could not make parts for his mechanical projects in his workshop, he made them at the Detroit YMCA, where he taught an evening metalworking class from late 1892 to early 1893.

Not long after Henry received his raise at the Edison Illuminating Company, he and Clara packed up and moved to a new, more expensive apartment on Washington Avenue. This was but the first of eleven moves made between 1892 and 1915. Each time Ford received a pay raise, or when his financial situation improved, he and Clara moved to better and sometimes bigger quarters. On November 6, 1893, Henry and Clara became parents for the first and only time when their son, Edsel Bryant Ford, was born. Edsel was named after Edsel Ruddiman, one of Henry's closest boyhood friends and a schoolmate from back in Springwells Township. Three weeks after Edsel's birth, Henry was again promoted, this time to the position of chief engineer. His pay was raised to an impressive $100 per month. He would seem to have had an assured future in the electric power industry, but it was in this period that Ford's interests began turning toward automobiles.

Exactly when Ford moved into the activities for which he is best known is difficult to determine, because Ford's recollections of what happened are so unreliable. For decades he and the Ford Motor Company claimed that he had built and operated his first motor vehicle in 1893 and that he had driven it about 1,000 miles by 1896 before another gasoline-propelled vehicle appeared in Detroit. Finally, by the 1940s the claim was abandoned when it had become obvious that there was no supporting evidence that would substantiate it. In fact, it had always run counter to another claim Ford had made that he had not conducted his first tests of the engine used in the car until the last part of December 1893. Even that claim is suspect. There is no doubt that Ford had become knowledgeable about engines, and he may have, as he claimed, gained some experience with gasoline internal combustion engines as well as steam engines prior to the 1890s, but it is not until the end of 1895 that there is any corroborative evidence that indicates Ford was actually engaged in such experiments. Both Oliver E. Barthel and Charles B. King, acquaintances of Ford, recalled that it was the sight of an article on a gasoline engine in the *American Machinist* that was on King's desk that caused Ford to declare, "I want to build one of these." King's recollection of helping Ford test this engine in the Fords' kitchen corresponds closely to details contained in Ford's recollection of events, but it is obvious from King's account that the test occurred at the end of 1895 or the first part of 1896, not in 1893.

The advice and assistance Ford received from King, an experienced and talented engineer, was typical of Ford's entire life. Particularly in his early years Ford had an innate ability to get other men to help him with his experiments. Often, all he would have to do was pose a mechanical question, or suggest an intriguing experiment, and his friends or coworkers would spring into action. Early in 1896, when he had built a gasoline engine, Ford turned to the construction of the vehicle it would power. King provided aid and some materials, along with a small cadre of workers, including George Cato, James Bishop, and Edward "Spider" Huff. In 1896 Ford's workshop was a little shed behind his duplex at 58 Bagley Avenue. He even convinced his neighbor Felix Julian, who stored coal and wood in half of the shed, to allow him the use of the entire building so that there would be more room for construction of the automobile.

Ford was not the only person in Detroit working on an automobile in 1896. Charles King was completing his own horseless carriage at the same time, and when King tested his 1,300-pound vehicle in March 1896, a fascinated Ford followed him on a bicycle.

By June 1896 Ford was finishing the work on his first automobile. He decided to call the little vehicle a "Quadricycle" because he used the techniques of the bicycle maker in constructing the vehicle rather than taking an existing carriage or wagon, as King and most other American experimenters were doing. Ford completed the car at approximately 1:30 A.M. on June 4 and was so eager to test it that he refused to wait for sunrise. Of his associates, only Jim Bishop was present for the test-drive, which was delayed for an hour due to an unforeseen problem. In all their enthusiasm for getting the car ready, no one stopped to consider that the door on the shed was too narrow to allow the car to pass through. Ford immediately grabbed an ax and knocked out the door frame and enough bricks in the wall to allow the Quadricycle access to the outside world.

Ford pushed the car into the alley and tinkered with the engine for a moment. Then the little 500-pound vehicle, powered by a 2-cylinder engine, slowly came to life and moved down the alley toward Bagley Avenue.

From Bagley Avenue Ford proceeded slowly to Grand River Avenue, then to Washington Boulevard, where the Quadricycle suddenly stopped. Bishop and Ford pushed the car to the Edison plant, where they replaced a small nut and spring that had fallen off and caused the car to stop. As soon as the engine was started again, Ford returned it to the Bagley Avenue shed, obviously pleased with his success.

In July 1896 Ford, accompanied by Clara and Edsel and Charles King, drove the Quadricycle to the Ford farm to show his father what he had accomplished. Henry's sister Margaret remembered her father's reaction to the car. "He examined the machine, listened to Henry's explanation, but wouldn't get into the car. Father was a conservative farmer . . . he saw no reason why he should risk his life at that time for a brief thrill from being propelled over the road in a carriage without horses." William Ford later said to one of his neighbors, "John and William," Henry's brothers, "are all right but Henry worries me. He doesn't seem to settle down and I don't know what's going to become of him."

In August 1896 Ford attended a convention of the Association of Edison Illuminating Companies in New York. There he met Thomas Alva Edison for the first time. At a banquet, one of Ford's coworkers introduced him to Edison as "a young fellow who's made a gas car." After Ford responded to a dozen questions about how the car worked, Edison slammed his fist down on the table and said, "Young man, that's the thing. You have it. The self-contained unit carrying its own fuel with it! Keep at it!" Edison's encouragement was an inspiration to Ford. "That bang on the table was worth worlds to me," he later declared. "No man, up to then, had given me any encouragement."

Upon returning to Detroit, Ford began planning a new, more advanced automobile to replace his first. In November 1896 he sold the Quadricycle for $200. He had accomplished what he had set out to do with the little car; now he was anxious to leave it behind and build something better. Ford soon realized that the costs involved in building the second car were much greater than he had expected. He needed financial help. He got that help from William C. Maybury, a prominent Detroit attorney who was an old friend of the Ford family. Maybury, who became mayor of Detroit in April 1897, began to provide financial support for Ford's continuing experiments in January 1897. In a few months Maybury had brought together several other acquaintances who agreed to provide continuing support to Ford with the ultimate goal of forming a company to produce the automobile he developed.

Ford proved to be a perfectionist who never seemed to be satisfied with the vehicle he and his assistants were building. His backers became impatient at the resulting delays, pointing out that in this early stage of the automobile's development perfection was impossible to achieve. Finally, however, Ford's work had progressed enough so that other wealthy Detroit businessmen joined Maybury's group to organize the Detroit Automobile Company. Its articles of incorporation were filed on July 31, 1899, a factory was acquired, and Ford was hired as the mechanical superintendent in charge of production. On August 15 Ford resigned his position with the Edison company to accept the new job at a salary of $150 per month, the same wage he had earned at the power company.

Unfortunately, the Detroit Automobile Company did not prove to be a successful venture. Its failure can be traced to Ford's continuing dissatisfaction with what he had thus far accomplished and to his backers' unfamiliarity with how they should go about conducting the new business. Instead of producing Ford's automobile—the one that had convinced the stockholders to invest—the directors of the Detroit Automobile Company decided to produce a motorized delivery wagon that he had completed in spring 1899. It was favorably publicized by a *Detroit News-Tribune* reporter, who rode in the vehicle with Ford in early February 1900. The article's headline exclaimed, "Swifter Than a Race Horse It Flew Over the Icy Street. Thrilling Trip On the First Detroit-Made Automobile, When Mercury Hovered About Zero." The article described the vehicle's speed, quietness, reliability, and comfort. At one point, as the vehicle passed a team of horses attached to a big wagon, Ford turned to the reporter and said, "Those horses will be driven from the land. Their troubles soon will be over."

Ford was lucky that the delivery wagon didn't break down during his trip with the reporter. Each of the 12 motor wagons produced by the Detroit Automobile Company was very unreliable, and Ford, as mechanical superintendent, was unable to rectify the situation. The company's directors demanded production and profits while Ford insisted on quality and reliability. In addition, he had had no experience in directing a production operation, which caused further delays. The directors and stockholders expressed their dissatisfaction. Ford felt threatened and began spending less time in the plant. By January 1901 the company had been dissolved and

Ford (standing) and Barney Oldfield with the Ford-built racer, the 999 (courtesy of Ford Motor Company)

was out of business. Ford blamed the directors and stockholders for the company's failure. He called them "a group of men of speculative turn of mind whose aim was to exploit."

Not all of the investors of the failed Detroit Automobile Company had lost their confidence in Ford's ability. William Murphy, whose wealth came from lumber, still thought that Ford was on the right track and that given enough support he could design a satisfactory automobile. In February 1901 Murphy and four other men rented a small section of the defunct Detroit Automobile Plant and asked Henry to continue experimenting.

However, instead of designing a new automobile that could be put in production, Ford, by the summer, had turned his thoughts to a new national craze, automobile racing. With the financial help of Murphy and his associates, Ford hired a team of talented men to help him build a racing car. The car was completed by September 1901, and Ford began conducting speed trials. His first opportunity to test the car in competition came on October 10, when the first automobile races in Michigan were held at a dirt track in Grosse Pointe. In the featured race of the day Ford was pitted against Alexander Winton, the Cleveland automobile manufacturer

and America's leading racing driver, whose car was the only other entry in the race.

The race covered a distance of ten miles and took 13 minutes to complete. Winton held a commanding lead during the first six laps until Ford, gaining confidence in his ability to corner at high speeds, surged ahead on the seventh lap as Winton's machine developed mechanical problems. It began to smoke and fall behind. Ford increased his lead and won the race to the thunderous applause of the spectators. Clara Ford described the scene in a letter to her brother: "I wish you could have seen him. Also have heard the cheering when he passed Winton. The people went wild. One man threw his hat up and when it came down he stamped on it. He was so excited! Another man hit his wife on the head to keep her from going off the handle. She stood up in her seat and screamed, 'I'd bet fifty dollars on Ford if I had it.'"

On November 30, 1901, less than two months after Ford's victory, William Murphy and his four associates filed the articles of incorporation for the Henry Ford Company. Ford, they believed, had now proven his ability to design and build a "winning automobile." They decided the time was right to cash in on his success. Unfortunately for them, Ford was not ready to settle down and concentrate on building a production automobile. He had been bitten by the racing bug and could not stop thinking about building a larger and faster racing car. With his victory over Winton behind him, Ford became enthusiastic about the possibility of racing the world-famous Frenchman Henri Fournier. Ford was confident that he could capture the speed record from Fournier. In January 1902 Ford wrote to his brother-in-law, saying, "If I can bring Mr. Fournier in line there is a barrel of money in this business. I don't see why he won't fall in line. If he doesn't, I will challenge him until I am black in the face. My company will kick me about following racing but they will get the advertising. And I expect to make $ where I can't make ¢ at manufacturing."

Within two months of the incorporation of the Henry Ford Company, the investors discovered that Ford—against their specific orders—was spending all of his time and the company's money designing and building a new racing car. When he persisted in not working on a production car, the directors fired him in March 1902. They allowed Ford to keep the designs for his new racing car, and they gave him a $900 cash settlement. Later that year they turned for advice to Henry M. Leland, head of the Leland and Faulconer Machine Shop. Leland's staff came up with a 1-cylinder runabout they could put into production. The company was renamed the Cadillac Automobile Company, and by 1903 the Cadillac was becoming one of the best-selling cars in the country.

Meanwhile, far from being discouraged, Ford had moved his workshop into a small rented building on Park Place and continued design work on the new racing car. In May 1902 he joined forces with racing enthusiast Tom Cooper, who provided the money needed to build the car. Together they proceeded to build not one but two identical racing cars—the 999 and the Arrow. When completed in summer 1902, they were considered the largest and most powerful cars ever built in America. Ford and Cooper did not wish to race them themselves; they were intimidated by their creations. To drive the car Tom Cooper hired a fellow bicycle-racing enthusiast, Barney Oldfield. "Nothing's too fast for him . . . he'll try anything once," Cooper told Ford. Another race was to be held at Grosse Pointe on October 25, 1902, with Alexander Winton again participating. The 999 was entered, and on the day of the race it was towed to the track by horses. It

was too powerful and noisy to drive on city roads. Oldfield had never driven an automobile until he was hired to drive the 999, but his inexperience may have been an asset, because he had not had a chance to develop a fear of the machine he drove. When the starting flag was dropped, Oldfield put the accelerator to the floor and did not let it up (even on the curves) until he had won the race. Ford's reputation as a designer of "winning" automobiles was further enhanced.

In early summer 1902, when the 999 and the Arrow were nearing completion, Ford and his staff designed a small 2-cylinder automobile they believed could be sold at a reasonable price. Eager to build a prototype of the car, Ford approached an acquaintance, Alexander Y. Malcomson, seeking support. During his years as chief engineer of the Edison Illuminating Company, Ford had been responsible for purchasing coal for the company's furnaces, and he had often bought coal from a company owned by Malcomson, a Detroit coal merchant. After leaving Edison, Ford had continued to buy coal from Malcomson for home heating. Malcomson was well aware of Ford's racing success, and he was quickly convinced that the car Ford had designed had great sales potential, agreeing that the car's engine was its greatest asset.

On August 20, 1902, a partnership—Ford & Malcomson Limited—was formed. Under the terms of the agreement Malcomson provided enough financial support to build Ford's prototype. Once the car was completed, it was to be used to attract investors. When a sufficient amount of capital had been raised, production of the car was to begin. The partnership agreement was further enhanced in November 1902 when the two partners decided to form the Ford & Malcomson Company. Shares in the new company were established, and an effort was started to sign up investors. By spring 1903 an acceptable 2-cylinder runabout, which would be called the Model A, had been built, more through the efforts of C. Harold Wills, Ford's chief assistant, than Ford himself. Once they had a car in hand, Malcomson and Ford could make better progress attracting investors.

By June 1903 ten men (twelve, including Ford and Malcomson) had pledged their money, notes, equipment, and property to purchase the available 1,000 shares of stock. In addition to Ford and Malcomson the investors represented an interesting variety of professions. John S. Gray, Malcomson's uncle and a prominent Detroit banker, invested the most money, $10,500 in cash. John W. Anderson, one of Malcomson's lawyers, invested $5,000 in cash borrowed from his father. Horace H. Rackham, another lawyer who had also had dealings with Malcomson, invested $3,500 in cash and notes for $1,500 more. Charles H. Bennett, a manufacturer from nearby Plymouth, Michigan, invested $5,000 in notes. John F. and Horace E. Dodge, owners of a Detroit machine shop and builders of the mechanical components of the first Ford automobile, invested $7,000 in automobile parts and a note for $3,000. Vernon C. Fry, Malcomson's cousin, invested $3,000 in cash and gave a note for $2,000. James Couzens, Malcomson's office manager, invested $1,000 in cash and gave a note for $1,500. (Couzens also talked his sister Rosetta into loaning him $100 so that he could increase his original investment. When the company became a success, Couzens, instead of returning her $100, gave her one share of his stock. Ford purchased her interest in 1919 for $262,036 after she had collected a total of $95,000 in dividends.) Charles J. Woodall, a clerk in Malcomson's business, invested a note for $1,000. Albert Strelow, a building contractor and owner of the Mack Avenue Plant where the first Ford Motor Company automobiles were assembled, invested $5,000. Henry Ford and Alexander Malcomson were credited with investing their time, patents, machinery, and designs, worth a total of $51,000. Together they were given 51 percent controlling interest in the new company. Each man received 255 shares out of the 1,000 shares issued.

On June 13, 1903, during a meeting of the twelve stockholders, Malcomson proposed that the new company be named the Ford Motor Company. All agreed. On June 16, 1903, papers of incorporation were filed at the state capitol in Lansing, Michigan. Henry Ford's third automobile company in less than four years was now in business. John Gray was the company's first president. Ford was named vice-president and general manager in charge of production while Couzens was chosen to be secretary and was given direction of the business side of operations. His former employer, Malcomson, served as company treasurer.

The Ford Motor Company was one of hundreds of automobile companies organized in the early years of the industry. Most of the companies were located in the East or elsewhere in the Midwest besides Michigan, but in 1903 Oldsmobiles,

which were then produced in both Detroit and Lansing, had been for two years the country's most popular car, while Cadillacs, introduced at the start of 1903, were the most important of several other cars that were rapidly pushing Detroit and Michigan to the forefront of automobile production. None would do more, however, to solidify Detroit's lead than Ford's new company, but it got off to a shaky start as its bank balance in the first four weeks dropped from a comfortable $14,500 to a dangerously low $223.65. This situation was especially worrisome to the company's conscientious business manager, James Couzens, who watched the books like a hawk. Couzens was greatly relieved when an order for a Model A was received on July 15 from a Chicago dentist, Dr. E. Pfennig. The price of the car was $850. Other orders soon arrived, and the Mack Avenue mechanics worked as fast as they could to assemble 15 cars per day. On July 23, 1903, the first shipment was ready. But Ford, forever the perfectionist, came very close to endangering the new company before its first orders could be shipped. He held up delivery because he felt "they are not yet as good as I can make them!" Couzens was shocked by Ford's action. He even helped crate the cars and nail the doors closed on the freight cars. Ford, who came to admire Couzens's business sense, quietly allowed the cars to be shipped. An excellent working relationship soon developed between Ford and Couzens, and they became aligned on many company issues.

In October 1904 a second story was added to the Mack Avenue plant in order to increase production capacity. That same year three new models were introduced—Models B, C, and F. Sales and profits continued to rise. Henry was now, at last, a successful automobile manufacturer, but he was not completely in control of the company.

In 1904 Malcomson pressured a reluctant Ford into designing and placing into production a high-priced, 6-cylinder touring car—the Model K. Malcomson wanted to concentrate production on this one car instead of on the high-volume, low-profit Models C and F. Ford was strongly opposed, and a confrontation developed.

The Model K was a dismal failure, and the fact that it did not sell strengthened Ford's contention that the company's future lay in concentrating on the low-priced car market. At the same time the failure of the car he had backed weakened Malcomson's position in the company, a position

Ford at the wheel of the 999 on January 12, 1904, the day he set a world speed record of 91.3 mph at Lake St. Clair, Michigan (courtesy of the Ford Archives, Henry Ford Museum, Dearborn, Michigan)

that was even more damaged late in 1905 when he organized the Aerocar Company. The fact that he was heading up another automobile company while at the same time retaining his office as treasurer and director of Ford caused other directors and stockholders to ask for his resignation. Malcomson refused, but in the face of other actions engineered by Ford and Couzens that threatened to reduce the value of his Ford stock, Malcomson gave in and sold his stock to Ford in July 1906 for $180,000. Stockholders Bennett, Fry, Woodall, and Strelow, all Malcomson allies, also sold their stock. Henry Ford was now the majority stockholder in the three-year-old company and was free to direct it as he pleased.

In July 1906 Ford's authority was further enhanced when he became company president following the death of John S. Gray. The title did not change his easygoing personality. A Mack Avenue plant employee, Fred Seeman, described Ford during these years as an "agile, friendly man. A man that nobody need be afraid to approach at all." Ford broke the tension of stressful days at the plant by staging impromptu boxing matches among employees. He never lost his fondness for practical jokes. Occasionally, he nailed an employee's hat to a wall peg or electrified a doorknob so that an unsuspecting coworker would receive a slight shock.

In less than two years the strong demand for Ford automobiles had outgrown the limited production capacity of the Mack Avenue Plant. A new, larger plant was constructed on Piquette Avenue, where automobile production began in 1905. Orders for Ford cars began arriving from Canada and England as early as 1903. In 1905 Ford cars were being assembled in Windsor, Canada, under the direction of the newly formed Ford of Canada. In 1906 Percival Perry traveled from England to Detroit to meet Ford and begin negotiations to set up a Ford Motor Company franchise in London. Ford was so pleased with the prospect of Ford automobiles being produced in England that he insisted that the Perrys stay with the Ford family during their visit to Detroit. Perry remembered Ford as "a man to whom you would give your last penny."

Although the Ford Motor Company achieved impressive success within its first six months in business, a cloud soon shadowed the firm—a lawsuit. On October 23, 1903, the company became the target of a suit filed on behalf of George B. Selden, a Rochester, New York, patent attorney, and the Electric Vehicle Company. The celebrated Selden patent suit proved to be the first in a series of events that strongly influenced public attitudes toward Ford and the Ford Motor Company.

George B. Selden had filed a patent application in 1879 for a road vehicle he had designed but never actually built. For 16 years he delayed issuance of the patent by filing additions and changes. Finally, in November 1895, Selden obtained a patent for a "road-carriage," which, it was claimed, covered all gasoline-powered vehicles produced and sold in the United States. Any company wishing to produce such automobiles during the 17-year term of the patent would have to be licensed by Selden or else be guilty of violating his patent rights. In 1899 Selden assigned the patent to the Columbia & Electric Vehicle Company (reorganized as the Electric Vehicle Company in 1900) for $10,000 and a percentage of whatever royalties could be collected. Lawsuits were then filed against five automobile companies. Although most automobile men, including Ford, questioned the validity of the Selden patent claims, uncertainty as to how the courts might rule in these cases caused Detroit's Olds and Packard companies to take the lead in March 1903 in forming the Association of Licensed Automobile Manufacturers (ALAM). In return for acknowledging that the Selden patent applied to the cars they produced and agreeing to pay the patent holders a royalty of 1.25 percent of the price of every car they sold, the members of the association were given the authority to approve each new company that would be admitted to membership in the ALAM and would be granted a license under the Selden patent. By April 1903, 30 companies had joined the ALAM.

In February, and again in June 1903, Henry Ford and his associates approached the ALAM with a request to obtain a license for the Ford Motor Company. The ALAM turned down the request, stating that Ford did not qualify as a "creditable" member of the industry.

One of the objectives of the ALAM, its supporters contended, was to weed out the many fly-by-night companies that had sprung up and that threatened to undermine the public's confidence in the industry because of the shoddy products they put on the market. Ford's dismal record with the first two companies with which he had been associated certainly could have raised legitimate doubts about the chances of his success with his latest company. Others contend, however, that the real purpose of the ALAM was to gain a monopolistic control of the market for a small and select group of companies by denying licenses to others, regardless of how qualified they may have been.

No matter what may have motivated the ALAM's action, its rejection of the Ford company's application infuriated Ford, Couzens, and other company officials who decided to defy the Selden forces and proceed with production without a license. When advertisements appeared warning makers, sellers, and buyers of unlicensed cars that they would be liable to be sued for patent infringement, Ford placed rebuttal ads promising legal protection to its dealers and customers. Other unlicensed companies went about their business quietly, but the Ford company's open defiance of the ALAM and the Selden patent holders left them little choice but to answer the challenge by filing suit against Ford on October 22, 1903.

The ensuing battle proved to be a publicity bonanza for Ford and his company. Couzens later said, "The Selden suit was probably better advertising than anything we could put out." At a time when President Theodore Roosevelt was depicted as the "trust buster" for his efforts to restrain monopolistic practices, Ford was pictured as the little company fighting the powerful ALAM, which Ford ads referred to as "The Trust." The publicity helped make the Ford the best-known automobile in the United States.

The legal struggle dragged on for six years until a New York Federal District Court judge ruled that the Selden patent did indeed cover the cars produced by Ford and the other companies that had by then been added to the list of those being sued. Most of the companies accepted defeat and sought licenses on whatever terms were offered. Ford, however, decided not to give in. The lower court's ruling was appealed, and on January 9, 1911, the New York Federal Circuit Court of Appeals overturned the ruling, stating that, while Selden had a valid patent, the Ford Motor Company and nearly all other manufacturers were using an entirely different motor principle. The ALAM was disbanded, and Ford emerged victorious. He was lauded on all sides as a giant killer, as a symbol of revolt against the monopoly, and as a magnificent individualist, and was well on his way to becoming a folk hero of the twentieth century.

Publicity was also received through other means. In January 1904 Ford again put himself behind the wheel of a racing car to compete against time. He announced he intended to break the world's record for the mile in a car equipped with an engine practically identical to that of his new 4-cylinder touring car, the Model B. The test was to be made on the cinder-covered ice of Lake St. Clair, northeast of Detroit. After unofficially setting a new world's record on January 9, Ford repeated the run on January 12 with official timers on hand. He had indeed set a new world's record, covering the four-mile course in 39.4 seconds per mile (91.3 miles per hour). Ford raced again in 1905 in a new car based on the 6-cylinder Model K. The race took place at Cape May, New Jersey, but Ford could not make the car run faster than 41 seconds per mile. The Ford Motor Company continued to receive much favorable publicity from its racing successes between 1904 and 1907, and the company's cars were unbeaten in their class and frequently won contests with larger vehicles.

In spring 1906 production of the Ford Model N began. The car was designed to be compact, with a durable 4-cylinder engine. Its price was intended to represent the best value of any car on the market, although Ford's original intention to sell the car for $500 had to be altered when he discovered he could only make money if the car was priced at $600. Nevertheless, the Model N was a bargain at that price, and although Ford's able staff deserves much credit, it was Ford who was in charge and who authorized and ordered the actions that made the Model N a success. By September 1907 the Model N had set new sales records that made the company the country's leading car producer.

Ford instinctively knew he was on the right track. In early 1907 he set up a special workroom in the Piquette Avenue Plant and, along with a hand-picked team of workers, began designing a completely new car—the Model T. It was Ford's idea to incorporate in the new car all of the qualities he thought were important. The vehicle would be strong, durable, dependable, economical, and technically advanced, yet simple in design and priced within the reach of the largest number of potential buyers.

The Model T was introduced on October 1, 1908. It was an immediate success. By May 1, 1909, sales were so far ahead of production that the company stopped taking orders for nine weeks. Sales continued to climb during the next decade, some years showing more than a 100 percent increase over the year before. By 1914 the Model T was selling at the rate of 250,000 per year, and it had already attained a worldwide reputation enjoyed by no other car. The Model T was the practical embodiment of Henry Ford's vision. It was designed primarily for farm and family use. Utility, not stylish beauty, was its hallmark. Ford was pleased with the car's popularity among the "common folk." The Model T was reaching the people for whom it was intended, as evidenced in Henry Ford's statement, considerably embellished by his publicity staff, "I will build a motor car for the great multitude, constructed of the best materials, by the best men to be hired, after the simplest designs that modern engineering can devise . . . so low in price that no man making a good salary will be unable to own one—and enjoy with his family the blessing of hours of pleasure in God's great open spaces."

By far the most important element in merchandising the Model T was the price cut. Ford maintained that he gained 1,000 new customers for every dollar that the car was reduced in price. In 1908 the Model T touring car was priced at $850, a reasonable figure but still much higher than such previous Ford models as the Model N. Ford's attention now turned to finding ways of lowering the

Model T's price—and lower it he did. By 1910 the price had dropped to $690, and by 1915 it was down to an astounding $360. Total sales increased from 6,398 units in 1908 to 34,528 in 1910, and to 472,350 in 1915. These developments resulted from the full attainment of the achievement for which Ford is best known—the application of mass production to the manufacturing of automobiles. By 1908 production demands dictated the need for a larger factory. The Piquette Avenue Plant, birthplace of the Model T, was too small and congested to produce the increasing number of cars demanded by consumers. Construction began that year on the mammoth Highland Park Plant, located in Highland Park, Michigan, a community of 4,120 population surrounded by Detroit. Designed and built by America's greatest industrial architect, Albert Kahn, upon its completion in 1910 the plant was the world's largest automobile factory. The layout of the plant's interior, with the absence of the many supporting pillars that had characterized the old factories but which Kahn had reduced by his pioneering use of reinforced concrete construction, enabled the Ford staff to plan a smoother, less interrupted movement of the assembly operations throughout the plant. Walter E. Flanders, who had been the production chief from 1907 to 1908, had made important moves forward in assigning workers specific tasks to perform, rather than having them involved in assembling the entire car, as Ford and most other companies had initially done. When Flanders left in 1908, Charles E. Sorensen began the leading role in production that he would occupy over the next 35 years. But important as these staff members were, it was Ford who was in control and who had to give final approval to whatever was done.

Time-and-motion studies became popular in the Highland Park Plant soon after construction—cost-conscious James Couzens loved them. The studies proved that most of the workers were still performing too many individual functions during the assembly process. Also, too much time was being wasted with the workers bending, lifting, turning, and pulling. In summary, management decided that time was not being spent efficiently in the assembly process, and that machines were not being utilized to their maximum effectiveness.

In 1913, in a stroke of genius, Ford and his associates decided to reverse the techniques used in Chicago's animal slaughter/packing houses. That is, instead of disassembling a cow or pig on a sliding conveyor, Ford would begin with small parts on sub-assembly lines and feed them into a larger assembly line that would ultimately produce a completed automobile. Although Couzens resisted the initial costs involved in setting up the machines and conveyors involved in the line, Ford quickly convinced him of its ultimate benefit to the profitability of the company.

After months of trial and error and fine-tuning, the moving assembly line was running fairly smoothly by November 1913. Ford summarized the new system when he said, "The man who places a part does not fasten it. The man who puts in a bolt does not put on the nut; the man who puts on the nut does not tighten it. Every piece of work in the shops moves. It may move on hooks; on overhead chains; it may travel on a moving platform; or it may go by gravity, but the point is that there is no lifting or trucking. No workman has anything to do with moving or lifting anything. Save ten steps a day for each of 12,000 employees, and you will have saved fifty miles of wasted motion and mis-spent energy." The average time required to assemble a Model T fell from 12.5 man-hours per car to 93 minutes. Production increased dramatically to almost 250,000 cars in 1913-1914 compared to 168,000 cars produced in the 1912-1913 period.

In an effort to increase the efficiency of the assembly line, a decision was made to produce the new 1914 Model T in only one color—black. Thus the source of Henry Ford's most-quoted remark: "You can have any color you want, so long as it's black!" The reason was quite simple: black enamel paint dried faster than any other color, and therefore the speed of the assembly line could be increased. The Model T would not be offered in colors other than black until 1926, when the public was given the additional choice of blue, green, brown, or gray.

In 1913, $11.2 million in dividends and bonuses were distributed among Ford stockholders and executives. Henry Ford and James Couzens became colossally rich, and they paid executives higher salaries and bonuses. On October 1, 1913, every worker received a wage boost—the increase for all employees averaging 13 percent. The pay increase provided a minimum daily wage of $2.34, as good or better than any of Ford's competitors.

With the advent of the moving assembly line, a problem had developed that Ford had not anticipated. The employees in the Highland Park Plant found working on the assembly line to be monotonous and stressful. The turnover rate rose to unacceptable levels. Workers quit and accepted more-conventional jobs elsewhere in the industry. This situation, combined with the fact that the company's profits were growing to almost embarrassingly high levels, led Ford, Couzens, and others who were involved to make the momentous decision to institute a profit-sharing program in the form of providing employees with a minimum wage of $5 per day—double the previous rate.

When the $5-per-day plan was officially announced to the press on January 5, 1914, Ford became an immediate celebrity. Photos of Ford, along with newspaper and magazine articles describing the program, appeared across the United States and around the world. The day after the newspaper headlined the story, 10,000 men gathered at the Ford employment office looking for work. Riots broke out when the job hunters were told there were none available. City policemen turned fire hoses on them, despite the wintry conditions, before the crowd dispersed. The Ford residence was besieged by reporters, job seekers, and an admiring public trying to gain an audience with Ford. A security guard was hired to shield Ford at his home and as he traveled to and from the Highland Park Plant.

The Fords' life-style had changed dramatically as his company's rapidly increasing profits had brought him great wealth. After living in modest homes all of their lives, Henry and Clara now possessed the resources to build a dream house. In 1907 they had purchased a large lot in the fashionable Boston Edison residential development a few miles south of the future site of the Highland Park Plant. A substantial home was constructed of red brick with stone trim and a porch with large columns. Clara Ford hired an interior decorator to finish the house, which included a large living room, dining room (with butler's pantry), kitchen, three bedrooms, a study, a third-floor ballroom, and a maid's bedroom. A landscape architect was hired to plant a large variety of trees and shrubs. An impressive rose garden was designed and built under Clara's personal supervision. A butler and a maid were hired to maintain the home, allowing the Fords time to enjoy their luxurious surroundings. The total cost of the home by 1908, including landscaping, reached $283,253.

At the age of fifteen, Edsel Ford, who had been attending Detroit's public schools, was enrolled in the Detroit University School, a preparatory institution. In the late afternoons and evenings, Ford and his son often worked together at the Highland Park Plant, or in a small home workshop that was constructed for Edsel. In summer 1912 the Fords undertook their first European vacation. Ford visited his subsidiary organizations in England and France and discussed production and sales problems that were unique to each country. Visits were also made to Clara's mother's birthplace in Warwick, England, and to the famous cathedrals, castles, and gardens. During their first week in England the Fords stayed at the home of Percival Perry, manager of Ford operations in England. Perry was finally able to repay the Fords for the hospitality they had extended to him during his first trip to Detroit in 1906.

Now in 1914 the attention that was so difficult to evade at the Ford home in downtown Detroit led him to decide to move to the more-secluded confines of the 2,000 acres of farmland that he had acquired approximately two miles from his birthplace in what is now Dearborn. In 1909 he had built a bungalow on this property as a retreat from the city. Construction began in February 1914 on an Ohio marblehead limestone residence. The home and estate were named "Fair Lane" in honor of Ford's grandfather, Patrick O'Hern, who was born in County Cork, Ireland, on a road that led to the fairgrounds. The original architect was Marion Mahoney Griffin, who was employed by Von Holst & Fyfe, a Chicago firm. A disagreement with this firm concerning costs and architectural style led to the final design being executed by William Van Tine of Pittsburgh. Giving orders not to build lavishly, Mr. Ford set an initial budget of $250,000, but in order to complete the residence as quickly as possible, 500 to 800 men were employed in various trades, and final expenditures surpassed $2 million.

Jens Jensen, the internationally famous landscape architect, was hired to develop the estate until a disagreement occurred with Clara Ford. While Jensen felt that extensive formal gardens were contrary to American ideals, Clara, a devoted gardener, insisted on their inclusion. Eventually seven gardens, totaling 16 acres, were laid out, requiring 25 full-time gardeners during the growing season. The largest, a 3.5-acre rose garden, contained more than 10,000 bushes.

A love of nature was a central part of Ford's being, and he enjoyed walking along trails that crossed the unlandscaped portions of the estate. Ford imported more than 500 varieties of songbirds to be released on the estate, while a herd of deer and native small game filled the grounds with unspoiled wildlife. A combination powerhouse, garage, and laboratory was erected approximately 300 feet to the south of the residence and connected to it by a tunnel. In the powerhouse, two 55-kilowatt, water-powered generators and one emergency steam generator provided power for the estate. Additionally two coke-burning, 60-horsepower boilers provided heat for the residence. The cornerstone for this building was laid by Thomas Edison. Approximately ten other buildings completed the accommodations of Fair Lane.

Fair Lane was visited not only by Ford's close friends Thomas Edison, Harvey Firestone, and John Burroughs, but, as Ford's fame continued to grow, also by President Herbert Hoover, Charles A. Lindbergh, the Prince of Wales, Charlie Chaplin, George Washington Carver, and many other notables.

As soon as the $5-per-day plan took effect, the employee turnover rate declined sharply. Suddenly, Ford employees had a new incentive to continue working on the assembly line. The new pay scale, combined with a reduction in the workday from nine hours to eight hours, made working for Ford Motor Company a very attractive proposition. In addition to reaping the benefits of free publicity, a reduced turnover rate, and improved employee morale, the Ford Motor Company profited from the creation of the $5 day through the creation of a new market for the Model T. The very workers who were building the Model T were now better able to afford to buy one.

Ford's benevolence and concern for the welfare of his employees were not confined to the activities in the Highland Park Plant. In 1914 he felt it necessary to establish a department to oversee the private lives of Ford employees and make sure they were handling their increased income properly. Approximately 50 inspectors of the Ford sociological department visited the homes of employees and conducted detailed surveys regarding citizenship, marital status, religion, health, savings-account balances, cleanliness, hobbies, amounts of life insurance, whether alcohol and cigarettes were used, and what type of automobile, if any, was owned. In May 1914 the sociological department began teaching English-language classes to all foreign-born employees. Ford wanted to make sure that all of his

Twelve thousand Ford Motor Company employees outside the Highland Park, Michigan, plant in 1913 (courtesy of the Ford Archives, Henry Ford Musem, Dearborn, Michigan)

employees spoke English so that communication problems within the plant could be eliminated. Ford won the praise and admiration of many when he instituted a policy, carried through by the sociological department, to hire women, ex-convicts, and the disabled. The only people who were turned away from employment were those with contagious diseases.

Although the sociological department was created with good intentions and did indeed help thousands of people from 1914 to 1920, accusations from critics of paternalism and of company meddling in the lives of employees caused it to be closed. Some of the educational aspects of the sociological department continued when they were incorporated into the Henry Ford Trade School. Ford founded the school in 1916 to train indigent teenage boys who wished to acquire a trade.

One of Henry Ford's most important public service ventures began in 1914, when a campaign to construct a large, modern hospital in Detroit bogged down. Ford stepped in, reimbursed the original donors the $600,000 they had contributed, and proceeded to build a hospital, later named the Henry Ford Hospital. After its completion, Ford assumed total responsibility for administering the institution and worked out a type of hospital different from what had originally been planned. The institution allowed any doctor to bring his patients to the hospital, but, once inside, they could be treated only by Ford staff doctors. There were no class distinctions in the hospital. All charges were equal, the hospital's rooms were designed to be uniform in size, and all patients were given the same care. The Ford Hospital was one of the best-publicized medical institutions in America during the 1910s and 1920s, and it contributed considerably to Ford's reputation as a humanitarian.

When war broke out in Europe in August 1914, Ford did not hesitate to condemn it. A pacifist, Ford declared that he would rather burn his factory than let it produce cars that might be used for military purposes. He also said that he would "give everything I possess" to stop the war and the build-up of arms in America. A *Detroit Free Press* reporter working closely with Ford wrote numerous antipreparedness articles that appeared in newspapers all over the country over the industrialist's signature. Declaring that he would not let cars leave his plant if he thought they would be used in warfare, Ford announced that he would inaugurate a worldwide campaign, to be supported by a Ford-endowed $1 million fund, to show the benefits of peace and the horrors of war.

When an article expressing Ford's pacifist sentiments was scheduled to appear in the company's publication *Ford Times*, Couzens, who was a strong supporter of the Allied cause in the war and who was responsible for overseeing the magazine, refused to allow it to be printed. When Ford insisted that it appear, Couzens quit his job. A break had been coming for some time as the close relationship between the two men that had existed earlier became more strained when Ford was no longer willing to treat Couzens as an equal. As he departed,

Couzens declared that he was willing to work with Ford but not for him.

By August 1915 Ford's pacifist sentiments had attracted the attention of two peace advocates—Rosika Schwimmer, a Hungarian author and lecturer, and Louis P. Lochner, a former secretary of the International Federation of Students. In November 1915 the two presented Ford with a plan whereby President Woodrow Wilson might call for a peace conference where neutral nations would participate in "continuous mediation" for a peace acceptable to the warring nations. During a subsequent meeting at the White House, Wilson politely refused to endorse Ford's proposal. Undaunted, Ford traveled to New York and announced to the press that he was going to "get the boys out of the trenches by Christmas." He chartered an oceanliner, the *Oscar II*, to transport an American peace delegation to Europe, where it helped form a commission to mediate a peaceful solution to the war.

Although many prominent Americans were invited to sail on the *Oscar II* with Ford and his fellow peace advocates, few accepted. The ship departed on December 5, 1915, from Hoboken, New Jersey, amid much fanfare and enthusiasm. Thomas Edison and Clara Ford, both of whom declined to accompany Ford on the trip, stood at the pier along with an estimated 15,000 people as the ship began its voyage to Europe. Once the *Oscar II* was well out to sea, the 50 or so peace delegates began arguing among themselves about how best to achieve their goals and objectives. In the process, Ford, as the group's sponsor and its most notable personality, became the target of ridicule and criticism. He soon distanced himself from Schwimmer and the other delegates and spent the rest of the voyage in his cabin.

The press had a field day making fun of the mission, picturing Ford as a "Don Quixote at the wheel of a tiny Model T" or a "flivverboat" charging a huge war machine. When the ship docked in Oslo, Norway, on December 18, a discouraged and cold-ridden Ford disembarked but did not appear in public. Five days later he returned to New York. Although his departure grieved the delegates, Ford continued to finance the group until February 1917, when the hopelessness of attaining peace became apparent.

Ford became a "fighting pacifist" when America entered the war in 1917. In addition to his plants, he offered to contribute his time to the war effort and to "work harder than ever before." The Ford Motor Company made a substantial contribution to the American war effort. Six thousand ambulances and 33,000 cars and trucks were supplied to the American and Allied forces. Seven thousand tractors were sold to Britain at cost—$750 each. Ford also built the "Eagle" submarine patrol boats on an assembly-line basis. They were riveted together in an immense building on the site of the company's present River Rouge Plant. Sixty boats were built. The company also supplied steel helmets, caissons, submarine detectors for the British navy, lightweight armor plate for tanks, and 4,000 Liberty aircraft engines. Because of his war efforts Ford was frequently called "Germany's greatest individual enemy" and "the civilian who is more important to the conduct of the war than any other in the world." Perhaps nothing generated more publicity and goodwill for Ford and his company than his oft-repeated promise to return all war profits to the government. However, although the company's war profits totaled at least $8 million, there is no record of Ford returning any of the money to the government.

One case in which Ford was not praised for his actions during the war was his determined and successful effort to prevent his son Edsel from being drafted for military service. After he had graduated from the Detroit University School, Edsel, unlike most of his fellow students, had not gone on to college but had instead gone to work for his father's company. He perhaps would have liked to attend college, but he dutifully adhered to the wishes of his father, who felt he could get all the education he needed at the Ford Motor Company. Edsel was already familiar with many of the operations, and he soon demonstrated considerable managerial skills. When Couzens resigned in 1915, Edsel, only twenty-two years old, was named to replace him as secretary.

When the United States entered the war in April 1917 and shortly instituted the draft, Edsel, who was only twenty-three, indicated that he was willing to serve if drafted, as other young men he knew were doing. However, Ford insisted that Edsel should be exempted, on the grounds that his continued presence with the Ford company was required to ensure the successful completion of its war contracts. After prolonged negotiations, the local draft board finally agreed to place Edsel in an exempt status class, not so much because of its belief that his work at Ford was essential as because Edsel and his wife, Eleanor Clay Ford, whom he had married in 1916, had their first child, Henry Ford II, on September 4, 1917. This placed Edsel in the 2-A classification, along with many other young men with dependents, while as one deemed indispensable to a war industry he was classified 3-L. Although his exemption could be legitimately defended, Edsel had to live from then on knowing that many charged him with being a draft dodger, a charge that resulted from his inability to resist the wishes of his strong-willed father.

In 1916 and 1917 Ford became involved in a lawsuit with two of the company's stockholders, John and Horace Dodge. The statements Ford made in and out of court during the period did much to brighten his image as an American folk hero. The suit originated with Ford's plan to double the size of the Highland Park Plant, to construct a blast furnace and a foundry ten miles away on the Rouge River, and to suspend all but nominal dividends until the indefinite date of the expansion program's completion. Ford believed he had to increase productive capacity or risk falling behind his competition in the low-priced field. But the Dodges, who between them owned 10 percent of Ford company stock, were thoroughly alarmed by Ford's plans. From 1903 to 1914 they had produced most of the mechanical parts for the Ford cars but then in 1914 had decided to capitalize on the reputation they had gained by producing their own car. They had used several million dollars derived from their Ford stock dividends to launch their new company, and they were counting upon the continued flow of money from their Ford investment to expand production. Ford's decision had diverted $40 million of company profits into the expansion program. The Dodge brothers immediately filed suit against the Ford Motor Company, demanding resumption of dividend payments.

Characteristically, Ford at once took his case to the public, declaring in an interview that it was his desire to enable "a large number of people to buy and enjoy the use of a car" and to "give a larger number of men employment at good wages." He also stated, "I do not believe that we should make such an awful profit on our cars. A reasonable profit is right, but not too much."

On the witness stand Ford was asked by the attorney for the Dodges, "What is the purpose of the [Ford] company?" "To do as much as possible for everybody concerned," responded Ford, "to make money and use it, give employment, and send out the car where the people can use it . . . and incidentally to make money. . . . Business is a service not a bonanza." The last statement was obviously directed at the Dodge brothers and other stockholders.

In October 1917 the Ford Motor Company was ordered to give up its Rouge expansion plans and to declare a special dividend of $19,275,385. Ford appealed. In February 1919 the state supreme court held that Ford could proceed with the Rouge plans but had to pay the dividend ordered by the lower court. Ironically, as the majority stockholder Ford received the largest share of this dividend, but the decision made him determined to get rid of the minority stockholders, whom he had once equated with parasites. Even before his appeal was decided, he took a first step. On December 30, 1918, he resigned as president of the Ford Motor Company. Edsel Ford was elected to the presidency; his father retained his seat on the board of directors. Ford went to California and announced he planned to build a new and better car that would be less expensive than the Model T. The new vehicle would be built and marketed by a new company. He explained that the recent Dodge suit decision had been responsible for his astounding plan.

The public was shocked at Ford's announcement, and the stockholders were worried. Concerned that the value of their stock would decline sharply if Ford carried out his threat, they were prepared to sell when approached by agents acting secretly on Ford's behalf. The representatives were able to purchase the 8,300 outstanding shares for $12,500 per share (except in the case of Couzens, who insisted on $13,000). The transactions, completed in July 1919, cost Ford a total of $105,820,894.57. The approximately 41 percent of the company's stock that was obtained was placed in Edsel Ford's name. Ford abandoned his plans (assuming he ever really had any) for building a rival to the Model T. Edsel retained the title of president, but it was apparent that Henry Ford was in charge.

In order to finance the stock buyout, Ford was forced to borrow $60 million from a New York financial syndicate. Although he had freed himself of stockholders, he was now indebted to Wall Street. Payments on the loan continued until $25 mil-

Ford Model T, 1916: "the blessing of hours of pleasure in God's great open spaces"
(courtesy of Quadrant Picture Library, Sutton, Surrey)

lion was left to be repaid in spring 1921. Sharply declining sales resulting from the onset of a postwar depression in late summer 1920 threatened Ford's ability to meet his obligations. Wall Street became excited at the prospect that Ford would be seeking another loan. Instead, he first ordered a reduction in his production and office staff, leaving a small crew of managers and superintendents. Second, he ordered pressure put on his suppliers to reduce prices charged to the Ford Motor Company for parts. The third step was the most controversial. He ordered the Highland Park Plant and other Ford assembly plants around the country to begin producing cars from all available stock on hand. In February 1921, 30,000 unconsigned cars were shipped to dealers, who were forced to pay for them or risk losing their franchise. Many dealers protested, but in most instances they went to their local banks and took out loans for the amount required. Ford, instead of borrowing the money himself, had compelled his dealers to borrow for him. By April 1921 Ford had saved or procured $42.6 million—more than enough

to pay his debts in full. Ford, Clara, and Edsel were now the sole debt-free owners of the Ford Motor Company.

In the process of transforming the company into a family-owned business, however, Ford had sacrificed qualities that had provided much of the basis of the company's rise to greatness. Ford in his early years had been surrounded by strong-minded, able men who had not hesitated to speak their minds. There had been an exchange of ideas that Ford, although he had to make the final decision, had seemed to welcome. But then he had become more authoritarian and less willing to brook differences from others in the company. The departure of Couzens in 1915 had been an early sign of that change. The buyout in 1919 of the Dodges, who had contributed so much in earlier years both as stockholders and as producers of vital parts, and of the other minority stockholders removed another source of possible opposition to Ford's policies. Finally, the economic problems of the immediate postwar years gave him an excuse to get rid of such top executives as Norval Hawkins, who was responsible for much of the success the Ford sales department had enjoyed; Frank Klingen-Smith, the company's treasurer; John R. Lee, head of the sociological department; and William S. Knudsen, a production genius. All had contributed much, but their independent attitudes made them expendable to Ford's new way of thinking. Able executives such as Charles Sorensen remained, but they would survive only if they said or did nothing that ran counter to Ford's wishes.

Just as Ford was getting the stockholder situation under control, a trial began in a small Michigan town that again would bring the automobile magnate into the public eye—but in a rather different light than in the past. In this case Ford was the one bringing suit against another party. Ford's libel suit against the *Chicago Tribune* grew out of an editorial published in June 1916 entitled "Ford is an Anarchist." The *Tribune* had asked earlier whether large businesses would give financial aid to workers mobilized for National Guard duty along the Mexican border because of Pancho Villa's attack on Columbus, New Mexico. When the *Tribune* called the Ford Motor Company to see what its policy would be, Frank Klingen-Smith erroneously replied in the negative. The *Tribune* then suggested that Ford move his factories to Mexico. It added that, if Ford continued to deny aid to guardsmen, "he will reveal himself, not merely as an ignorant idealist, but as an anarchistic enemy of the nation." Ford demanded a retraction. The *Tribune* publisher, Col. Robert R. McCormick, rejected his request, and Ford filed suit.

Three years passed before the case came to trial in Mount Clemens, Michigan. Ford looked forward to expounding his views, as he had in the Dodge suit, before an appreciative audience. But in the Dodge suit the questioning centered around the Ford Motor Company, a subject familiar to Ford. In the *Tribune* case, however, the newspaper's attorneys attempted to prove that Ford was indeed an "ignorant idealist." They showed the manufacturer to be one of the least informed national figures in the country. Ford could not say when the United States was created, nor did he know when the American Revolution was fought—he guessed the year 1812. Asked to define the Monroe Doctrine, he replied that it was "a big brother act"; anarchy was "overthrowing the government and throwing bombs."

When asked who Benedict Arnold was, Ford replied, "a writer, I think."

Finally, on August 14 the case went to the jury, which ruled in favor of Ford. The *Tribune* was indeed guilty of libel, but Ford was awarded damages of only 6 cents, because the jury did not believe Ford had suffered financially from the *Tribune* editorial. The jury declared that it could not bring itself to admit that a man who had created an industrial empire could be ignorant. Ford declared victory because the verdict was in his favor. The *Tribune* claimed victory because the damages were insignificant.

The Ford Motor Company Rouge plant development began in 1918 when a gigantic building was hastily erected for the construction of Eagle boats. After the war the structure was converted into a body-making plant and during the next few years was rapidly surrounded by a complex that transformed raw materials into finished products within a matter of hours. Coke ovens went into operation in late 1919, a sawmill in early 1920, and Blast Furnace A in late 1920. In early 1921 tractor production began in the B Building, and in the same year a foundry and a power plant, both the largest in the world, came into operation. By 1924 the complex employed 42,000 workers and by 1928, more than 103,000. In 1926, still short of completion, the complex sprawled over 1,115 acres. Ninety-three separate structures stood on the site, 23 of which were classified as "main buildings." Railroad trackage covered 93 miles, and conveyors, 27 miles. By the mid 1920s, the Rouge was the company's primary manufacturing site and was the greatest industrial facility in the world.

In addition to beginning construction of the Rouge complex, fighting various court battles, and dealing with the normal production problems, Ford in 1918 decided to take the time to run for public office. In June, President Wilson, impressed with Ford's popularity and his support of Wilson's peace program, pleaded with Ford to enter the Michigan senatorial campaign. Ford reluctantly agreed to run, saying, "If they want to elect me let them do so, but I won't make a penny's investment." As an independent, Ford's name was entered in both the Democratic and Republican primaries, something that Michigan election laws then permitted. Most Democratic papers, identifying Ford with Wilson, were enthusiastic about his candidacy, and he had virtually no competition in the Democratic primary.

But in the Republican primary he was opposed by Truman H. Newberry, a former secretary of the navy, wartime lieutenant-commander, and a prominent stockholder in the Packard automobile company.

Ford easily won the Democratic nomination but lost the Republican nomination to Newberry, who spent lavishly in order to overcome his lack of name recognition in contrast to that which Ford possessed. In the general campaign Ford put forth little effort to win. He gave no speeches, gave out no statements beyond a declaration for woman suffrage, and did not spend a cent. Newberry, however, continued to spend heavy amounts of money, conducting a hard-hitting campaign on the theme of Americanism. The biggest issue became Edsel's draft deferment. Ford took full responsibility for retaining Edsel at Highland Park and remarked that, if Edsel did serve, he would be found "fighting, and not sticking his spurs into a mahogany desk in Washington," an obvious slap at Newberry's son, who served in Washington during the war.

Two days before the election the Republican Committee started a rumor that Ford was a "Hun-lover" and that he harbored German aliens and sympathizers in his Highland Park plant. Ford's reply arrived too late to counter the charge. Consequently, thousands of voters went to the polls aware of the accusations but not of Ford's defense. Ford lost the election by only 2,200 out of 440,000 votes. Within weeks he was accusing Newberry of exceeding the legal limits on campaign spending. Investigators were hired to gather evidence against Newberry. After four years of fighting the accusations in various courts, Newberry resigned from the U.S. Senate.

At the time Newberry resigned in 1922 a Ford-for-president movement had gotten underway, more or less spontaneously. When a Ford executive investigated and reported that many people believed Ford would make a better president than the incumbent, Warren Harding, Ford at first said he did not "want anything to do with it," but then later when some supporters planned to enter him in the Iowa primary Ford said to let them go ahead. "We might have some fun with these politicians." But with Harding's death in 1923 and the accession to the presidency of Calvin Coolidge, the Ford boom quickly died out. One report says that Clara Ford, who was well aware of her husband's limitations,

threatened to leave him if he did not end his quasi candidacy.

Beginning in 1918 Henry Ford's vacations and leisure life began to receive much publicity. Ford expended much time, energy, and money on extracurricular activities including camping trips, antique hunting, and dancing.

The camping trips enabled Ford to "get away from it all" for a few weeks and to enjoy nature with such "vagabond" friends as Thomas Edison, John Burroughs, Harvey Firestone, President Warren G. Harding, and others. The campers were chauffeured on their trips in a caravan of six specially equipped vehicles. A small army of reporters and photographers recorded their every word and activity. Ford commented in his autobiography that "The trips," which ended in 1924, "were good fun, except that they began to attract too much attention."

In 1919 Ford began to exhibit an interest in antiques and historic preservation that would last until his death in 1947. During the *Tribune* trial he had been humiliated when he could not accurately answer history questions, which he thought were unimportant. Because of this experience Ford decided to build a historical museum. Ford's collection of Americana began during his early camping trips when a few old farm implements were purchased. These items were soon augmented with a variety of antiques stored in the old Dearborn Tractor factory. Within a half-dozen years the building was filled.

Ford ordered his own birthplace restored, even having sections of earth near the home excavated so that pieces of dishes could be located, pieced together, and reproduced. After the home was restored, it was used to entertain special guests of the Fords. This project was followed by the purchase and restoration of the Wayside Inn of South Sudbury, Massachusetts, in 1923, and the Botsford Inn, northeast of Dearborn, in 1924. The latter was important to the Fords because they had attended dances there in the 1880s.

In 1927 Ford announced plans to build an "industrial museum" in Dearborn. The following year he revealed plans to supplement the museum with an early "American village" that would exhibit buildings representing several stages of American life or associated with important events and persons. The museum and village, although uncompleted, were dedicated by President Herbert Hoover on October

21, 1929, at a celebration of the 50th anniversary of Edison's invention of the electric light.

Ford's Henry Ford Museum and Greenfield Village grew steadily as the years passed. No expense was spared to acquire historically important buildings such as the Wright Brothers' bicycle shop, Noah Webster's home, a courthouse where Abraham Lincoln practiced law, and approximately 100 other buildings. Ford also moved to the village many buildings of personal importance, including the farmhouse in which he was born, the two schools he attended as a child, and the Bagley Avenue shed where he constructed his first automobile. Ford was especially proud of the private school system that he instituted within Greenfield Village. Three one-room schools were used to educate children in the elementary grades, while the remainder of the students were taught in a modern high school building near the museum. Reminiscent of the Henry Ford Trade School's vocational curriculum, the Greenfield Village Schools placed a heavy emphasis on learning-by-doing. The concept of Ford schools spread throughout the Ford empire. Although most of the schools were located in Michigan, others were established in Georgia, Massachusetts, and England.

During the restoration of the Wayside Inn in Massachusetts in the early 1920s, Henry and Clara Ford revived a long-dormant interest in old-fashioned dancing. In 1923 organized square dances became a regular activity at the Wayside Inn and were taught by dancing master Benjamin B. Lovett. In 1925 Ford announced a crusade to bring back old-fashioned dancing in the United States. Ford became so enthusiastic about such dances that he virtually forced about 300 friends and company executives into dance classes. To publicize his hobby, Ford arranged for his private orchestra to play old-fashioned dance music over nationwide radio networks during public showings of his new cars in January 1926 and January 1927. Ford also revived old-time fiddling, which went hand-in-hand with square dancing. The industrialist liked to fiddle and often played "Turkey In the Straw" and other tunes on a Stradivarius.

Ford's recreational activities and burgeoning interest in history did not overshadow the overriding importance of his position in the industry and his relentless quest to improve the efficiency of the Ford Motor Company. As David L. Lewis points out, "During the 1920s Ford developed America's first

vertically integrated, yet highly diversified industrial empire. His company mined coal, iron ore, and lead; owned timberlands, sawmills, dry kilns, a wood distillation plant, a rubber plantation, and a series of 'village' industries; operated a railroad, blast furnaces, coke ovens, foundries, steel mills, and lake and ocean fleets; produced glass, artificial leather, textiles, glass, gauges, paper, and cement; built airplanes; farmed 10,000 acres; and made Model T's, Lincolns, trucks, and the Fordson tractor. In addition, it prospected for oil, bought dolomite lands with the production of magnesium in mind; took steps to produce abrasives; processed soybeans; bought acreage in the Everglades and Brazil with the intent of planting rubber trees; and experimented with the development of power by burning coal. These multifarious activities received wide attention during the 1920s and contributed importantly to the view that Henry Ford had a daring and highly original mind, virtually unique technical skills, and a never-ceasing desire to serve mankind."

In addition to being the world's greatest producer of automobiles, Ford also became a leading tractor manufacturer. He began experimenting with tractors in 1907. By 1915 he was displaying a tractor at the Michigan State Fair. On July 27, 1917, he organized Henry Ford & Son Tractor Company, which, by the end of the year, had built 254 tractors. By the end of 1918, 34,000 tractors had been built. Ford had moved ahead of International Harvester to become the world's largest tractor manufacturer. Production rose to 57,000 in 1919 and 71,000 in 1920. International Harvester could not stave off the Ford challenge, and General Motors, which had launched its Samson tractor in 1918, closed out its entry in 1922 with a $33 million loss. Fordson tractors (as they were called) were sold without the company incurring any advertising or promotional expenses. Instead, Ford dealers were expected to foot the bill.

The tractor's success was especially gratifying to Ford because of the realization that he was making the farmer's life easier. Ford remembered vividly the backbreaking work required to manage a farm before the age of tractors. In 1928, after a decade of sales fluctuation and increased competition, Ford moved the tractor operation to a plant in Cork, Ireland. The advantages for the new location included lower labor costs and closer proximity to European markets.

Ford with Charles Lindbergh on August 11, 1927 (courtesy of the Ford Archives, Henry Ford Museum, Dearborn, Michigan)

In the early 1920s, with his reputation secure in the tractor business, Ford entered another commercial venture—luxury car manufacturing—by purchasing an existing manufacturer, the Lincoln Motor Company. Lincoln had been organized in 1917 by Henry M. Leland and his son Wilfred to produce Liberty aircraft engines during World War I. The company turned to automobile manufacturing after the war. Unfortunately, the car did not sell due to the depressed state of the market, and in late 1921 the Lincoln Company faced bankruptcy.

Ford purchased Lincoln in February 1922 for $8 million. Henry Leland, who had been brought back in 1902 to save the Henry Ford Company, and his son Wilfred turned in their resignations after working for Ford for only three months. Serious problems had developed between Ford and the Lelands concerning how the company should be run. Further problems developed after their resignations when Ford refused to compensate the Lincoln Motor Company's original 1,800 stockholders for their investments, although he did complete payment of $4 million to 900 creditors of the company. A lawsuit was filed by the Lelands, and in 1931 the case was ruled in favor of Henry Ford.

In 1922 Edsel Ford took over the direction of Lincoln, and under his able leadership the Lincoln automobile quickly gained a reputation as one of the most beautiful cars on the road. The Lincoln was not an outstanding sales success and would not be for a good many years, but with it Ford now had offerings at both ends of the market—the Model T was the lowest-priced car, and the Lincoln was one of the most expensive.

In addition to producing automobiles, trucks, and tractors, Ford also manufactured airplanes beginning in the late 1920s. His interest in aviation began in 1922 when he invested a small amount of money in the newly formed Stout Metal Airplane Company. Ford became interested in the pioneering ideas of William B. Stout, the company's founder. Stout convinced Ford of the commercial possibilities that aviation offered and asked for Ford's assistance in starting an airplane company. Ford agreed and promptly purchased Stout's company and incorporated it into the Ford Motor Company in 1925. On July 1, 1925, he began a Detroit-to-Cleveland air service, and in early 1926 the company was awarded government contracts to carry mail between Detroit and Cleveland and Detroit and Chicago. Ford also built the world's first airport hotel, the Dearborn Inn, completed in 1931. A tiny 40-horsepower "flivver plane" was constructed in 1926 with hopes of developing a mass market for low-priced aircraft. The idea was dismissed when the plane crashed, killing one of Ford's test pilots, Harry Brooks. More successful was the famous Ford Tri-Motor airplane, which the company began to produce in 1926, with a total of 198 units completed before the operation ended in 1932. The plane was 70 feet long and could carry eight passengers as well as freight. Henry Ford's venture into aviation ended when the depression of the 1930s sharply curtailed the market for commercial aircraft.

Between 1919 and 1927 Ford published a weekly magazine, the *Dearborn Independent*. Its circulation from 1925 to 1927 exceeded 500,000 copies per week. The publication was a sounding board for Ford's views on life and current events, but it is chiefly remembered for spreading Ford's anti-Semitic views. In a series of articles in which Ford appeared as the author, Jews were said to have caused most of the world's troubles. Ford maintained that Jews controlled the world's banks; Jews had started World War I and kept it going; and

Jews were plotting to destroy Christian civilization. The ultimate result was a suit brought by Aaron Sapiro that came to trial in Detroit in March 1927. The chief issue was the responsibility of Ford for the libelous material printed in the *Dearborn Independent*. The editor, William J. Cameron, Ford's longtime spokesman, testified that he had the sole responsibility for whatever the *Independent* had published, and that he had never discussed with Ford any article on Jews, had never sent Ford an advance copy, and had never seen Ford read a copy, even though he was supposedly the author. The defense took the position that Ford was unaware of what his editor had been printing and that he had simply been an innocent bystander.

Haunted by memories of the *Chicago Tribune* trial, Ford was naturally reluctant to testify. On the day before he was to appear, a coupe he was driving was sideswiped and forced off the road and struck a tree. The sixty-three-year-old Ford, badly shaken, bleeding, and dazed, staggered to the gatehouse of his estate. He then spent two days in the Ford Hospital. A legal technicality resulting from actions instigated by Ford's security chief Harry Bennett led to a mistrial being declared in April 1927. This gave Ford an opportunity to settle out of court, and on July 7 he published a personal apology to Sapiro and a formal retraction of all his attacks on the Jewish people. Although Ford worked hard to smooth over his troubles with the Jewish people, stories of his anti-Semitism continued ever after to shadow the automaker and his company. Rumors even circulated that Ford financially supported Hitler's rise to power in Germany. The fact that Henry Ford was the only American mentioned in Hitler's *Mein Kampf* did not help the automaker's image.

Despite such adverse publicity most of the attention Ford received in the 1920s was highly favorable. The public regard for him was rivaled by few contemporaries, but at the very time his popularity was at its peak, his company's position as the leading automaker was slipping. GM, which under its founder, William C. Durant, had never been able to rival Ford's sales despite its impressive lineup of cars, was placed under new management, headed by Alfred P. Sloan, Jr., at the start of the decade. Sloan installed a new administrative organization that became the model for all large corporations. New techniques promoted sales by emphasizing the changing look of each year's new models rather than less-visible mechanical improvements. And, most important of all to Ford, William S. Knudsen, the ex-Ford production executive, was hired to make Chevrolet competitive with the Model T in the low-priced market.

Ford's response to these challenges was to do nothing. He continued to believe he could run his company, guided only by his instincts, as he had in the past and was openly disdainful of the kind of formal administrative structure Sloan had established at GM. As for the evidence that the public by the 1920s wanted fancier and more stylish cars, such as those GM was putting out, Ford remained convinced that most people wanted a car that provided good, reliable transportation, such as the Model T, in spite of the efforts of some, including his son, to convince him otherwise. And with the Model T in the early 1920s accounting for more than half of all American car sales, it was difficult not to agree with Ford's reasoning.

By the mid 1920s, however, as GM profits for the first time topped Ford's and as Model T sales fell while Chevrolet's climbed, it was apparent that the era of the Model T was coming to an end. In 1926 the Model T received a face-lift, including larger fenders and nickel-plated radiators. It no longer was available only in black. Ford even reduced the price of the car, hoping it would spur sales. The improvements, however, did not stop the sales slide. Ford was finally convinced that his wonder car was outmoded, and on May 27, 1927, the car that had brought him fame and fortune became part of history when the 15-millionth Model T was driven off the assembly line by Edsel Ford, with his father as a passenger.

Between May and November 1927 the public waited anxiously for information about what Ford would come up with to replace the Model T. In the meantime Ford was grappling with the Herculean task of getting out a new vehicle. Sorensen directed the scrapping of 40,000 machines incapable of producing anything except the Model T and the rebuilding of the mechanism of the Ford plants to handle the production of a new car. The retooling of the Rouge complex, along with 34 domestic assembly plants, 12 overseas factories, and numerous suppliers' shops, constituted an unparalleled changeover.

On November 30, 1927, a press preview of the new Model A was held in Dearborn. Then on December 2 the car was shown to the public across the country. In just five days a total of 1.25 million

New Yorkers crowded into the Waldorf-Astoria Hotel to see the car. The 4-cylinder Model A was an overnight success, with 400,000 orders placed within a few days of its introduction. Between 1927 and 1931, 4.3 million Model As were built. The car's stylish looks plus Ford's reputation as a builder of quality automobiles assured its success, but it was not enough to enable Ford to regain for long the volume leadership it had lost to Chevrolet when Model T production had ended in 1927. The 1929 Chevrolet lineup included the 6-cylinder "cast-iron wonder" that Knudsen had rushed into production, and by 1931 Chevrolet was again on top and was rarely unseated in the years that followed.

On November 21, 1929, slightly less than one month after the great stock market crash, Henry Ford commented to the press on the worsening economic situation in the United States. "Nearly everything in the country is too high priced," he said. "The only thing that should be high priced is the man who works." Ford suggested that industry could defeat the Depression by increasing the general wage level. On December 1, 1929, Ford increased the minimum daily wage of his company to $7 per day. He also lowered the price of the Model A and announced a $25 million plant expansion program. The automaker believed that if other businessmen around the country followed his lead the economy would be stimulated enough to turn around the Depression. Ford continued with such off-the-cuff comments as the Depression worsened. In August 1930 he observed: "We are better off today than we have been for three or four years past. It was a mighty good thing for the nation that the condition which we misnamed 'prosperity' could not last." In October 1930 Ford announced "the depression is a good thing." In March 1931 he blithely maintained that "these are really good times, but only a few know it."

In 1931, as the Depression continued to worsen, sales of the Model A declined. Ford decided that a new and exciting car was needed to stimulate sales. For one last time Ford became personally involved in the design and engineering of the car. The result in 1932 was the Ford V-8. It was an outstanding car and enjoyed considerable popularity, especially with speed-loving criminals. John Dillinger wrote Ford, enthusiastically endorsing the V-8. "Hello Old Pal," Dillinger wrote, "You have a wonderful car. It's a treat to drive one. Your slogan should be Drive a Ford and Watch The Other Cars Fall Behind You. I can make any other car take a Ford's dust. Bye-bye." Clyde Barrow (of Bonnie and Clyde fame) wrote Ford an equally laudatory letter. However, good as the Ford V-8 was, it was not enough to prevent Ford, which had already fallen behind GM, from falling behind Chrysler into third place in 1933 in total sales, where Ford would remain nearly every year until 1952.

In 1933 the deepening financial problems of the Depression involved Ford in a banking crisis in Detroit. Ford's role became one of the more controversial of his business career. In January the Union Guardian Trust Company, part of a bank holding company of which Edsel Ford's brother-in-law Ernest Kanzler was chairman and Edsel was the largest stockholder, applied to the Reconstruction Finance Corporation for a $50 million loan to meet its creditors' demands. The government agency, which had loaned the parent holding company $15 million only two months before, agreed to loan $37 million if the major depositors, including Edsel Ford, put up the remaining $13 million. However, when James Couzens, now a United States senator, learned of the plan, he objected, saying that the Union Guardian Trust was "Mr. Ford's baby" and the Fords, not the taxpayers, should bail it out.

In the tangled series of events that followed, appeals were made to Ford to step in and save the bank. But Ford, who before this time had paid little or no attention to his son's banking activities, did nothing except to have company funds transferred to Edsel's account to cover his losses. Once that was done, Ford, who disliked Kanzler, a former Ford executive whom he had dismissed, refused to lift a hand, even though the trust company's collapse threatened the city's and the state's banking structure. If there was to be a crash, Ford said, so be it. Last-minute negotiations on the weekend before Lincoln's Birthday, a bank holiday, failed to move Ford, who instead threatened to withdraw all his company's funds from the banks when they reopened. Governor William A. Comstock, therefore, issued a proclamation extending the bank holiday for a week, after which he extended it again until President Franklin D. Roosevelt, when he was inaugurated in March, proclaimed a national bank holiday.

There is no better indication of the continuing high regard in which Ford was held in Detroit than in the fact that few people blamed him for the difficulties resulting from the bank closures, while Couzens, who raised legitimate questions concerning the use of government funds to help a bank out of problems that were largely of its own making, was denounced as a traitor to the community. On February 24 the Fords offered to take over most of Detroit's closed banks and form two new banks, to be backed by $8.25 million of their own money. The offer was turned down, but two new banks did emerge, the National Bank of Detroit, backed by GM, and the Manufacturers Bank, backed by Ford. Under stricter banking regulations, both prospered.

Hard on the heels of the banking crisis came another backlash from the disrupted Depression economy that again demonstrated the extent to which the aging Ford, always an independent person, stubbornly insisted on doing things only his own way. This new controversy grew out of enactment by the Roosevelt administration of the National Industrial Recovery Act (NIRA), signed into law in June 1933. The emergency measure provided that codes of fair competition dealing with wages, hours, working conditions, and the fixing of prices would be drafted for each of the nation's industries. All businesses were required to comply. A code was drawn up for the automobile industry, and although none of the companies was enthusiastic about the code, they agreed to comply with its provisions. But Ford would not. He believed that if he complied, he would be surrendering control of his business to the government. He also argued that his company already exceeded the code's requirements. The federal government tried to persuade Ford to change his mind and support the NIRA, but without any success. Although a boycott was declared against Ford vehicles by the federal government and several state governments, no other actions were taken to try to force Ford's compliance, a testimony to Ford's popularity, which the government no doubt feared would create a negative reaction among the public if they pushed Ford too hard. The nation's motorists applauded Ford's rugged individualism and his courage to stand up for what he believed.

Roosevelt was undoubtedly relieved, therefore, when the United States Supreme Court in 1935 declared the NIRA's industrial code provisions, which had never worked well anyway, to be unconstitutional. However, the court's ruling did not affect the act's provisions guaranteeing the rights of workers to collective bargaining. No issue would cause Ford and his company more trouble than his refus-

al in the next several years to permit his employees to exercise that right.

Ford was only one of many manufacturers opposed to organized labor. Other automakers, including GM and Chrysler, made extensive use of labor spies, private policemen, and various forms of coercion to keep workers from organizing. Depression-era labor problems for Henry Ford and his company had begun on March 7, 1932, when 3,000 men marched on the Rouge complex demanding that their grievances be heard. The men, who were mostly unemployed, hungry, and desperate for jobs, had many demands, including the right to form a union. They were met by Ford security forces as well as the Dearborn police. A confrontation led to four demonstrators being shot and killed and many others being injured. The "Hunger March," as it was called, set the stage for Ford's future relationship with his employees and with organized labor.

The United Auto Workers (UAW), which was formed to take advantage of the Roosevelt administration's sympathetic attitude toward unionization efforts, spent most of 1936 preparing to break the industry's opposition to unions. GM was struck in December 1936 and, after six weeks of turmoil, agreed to recognize the UAW. The union next turned to Chrysler, which gave in on April 6, 1937. It then turned its attention to Ford. By 1937 the labor practices at Ford plants were a far cry from the enlightened policies that had gained the company and Ford their enviable reputation before World War I. Ford no longer paid the highest wages in the industry, and its employees were subjected to harsh, often unfair treatment by the foremen. Ford labor policies were enforced by the service department, often described as the largest privately owned secret-service force in existence. The department was headed by Harry Bennett and consisted of ex-convicts and thugs. Henry Ford made no secret of his dislike for unions. In April 1937 Ford told Edsel and his executives that he would not allow any meetings with union officials. He decided that Bennett would be designated to "handle" the unions.

Bennett, an ex-sailor and boxer, joined Ford during World War I. He began his rise in 1919 when he was assigned various special tasks by Ford. Proud of these assignments, Bennett quickly gained a reputation as a man who could "get the job done." In 1921 he was put in charge of security at the Rouge complex. By the early 1930s he was probably the most powerful man in the company next to Henry Ford. Ford liked Bennett for several reasons. First, Bennett did anything Ford told him to do, quickly and without question. Second, Bennett had an open relationship with the Detroit underworld, which kept Ford and his family safe from criminals. Third, Ford believed that Bennett could protect the Rouge from sabotage and other disturbances. Finally, Ford found in Bennett many of the qualities and attitudes that he did not see in his son. Henry believed Edsel was not tough enough to run the company, although the industrialist had put a lot of effort into trying to change his son's character. Because of this, the relationship between father and son had greatly deteriorated, and Bennett had become something of a substitute son to Ford. The designation of Bennett to direct labor relations distressed Edsel, who argued that they should bargain with the union, since they could not in the long run avoid having to accept a collective bargaining agreement. Edsel and his father had heated debates over labor matters. On one occasion Edsel seriously considered resigning as president of the company. The labor issue had placed a wedge between father and son; they would never again be close.

The UAW launched its organizing drive at the Ford Rouge Plant on May 26, 1937. A group of union officials, including Richard Frankensteen and Walter Reuther, attempted to distribute pamphlets to Ford workers as they walked over and down a street overpass leading from the Rouge. The unionists were attacked by Ford security men in full view of reporters and photographers. Many organizers were severely mauled, including Frankensteen and Reuther. The reporters and photographers were also abused. Most had their notes and film confiscated. Some film escaped destruction, however, and the resulting photographs and reporters' stories appeared across the country, seriously damaging Ford's public image.

After the "Battle of the Overpass" the National Labor Relations Board (NLRB) accused the company of violating every unfair labor practice defined by the Wagner Act, passed in 1935 to substitute for the NIRA's earlier labor provisions. Ford's policy was to deny every charge. In addition, from 1937 to 1940 Ford Motor Company expended considerable effort to hide its views on labor from the public. The strategy worked, with many public opinion polls showing Ford was still regarded as a

friend to labor. For four years Bennett's tactics kept the UAW at bay, but by 1941 it began an all-out effort to organize Ford employees. On February 27 the UAW announced its intentions to call for a strike at all Detroit-area Ford plants unless the company agreed to 15 demands, including higher wages and improved working conditions. The threat was ignored. Ford, ever more out of touch with reality, announced that "unions are losing ground and haven't a leg to stand on."

On April 1, 1941, most of the Ford workers at the Rouge plant walked out, and the plant was picketed. Edsel Ford, who was in Florida when the strike started, returned immediately to Dearborn and demanded that the company negotiate with the UAW. During the strike a mediator was called in, and on April 7 the NLRB announced that elections would be held within 45 days to determine bargaining agents for the Rouge plants. On May 21 elections were held, and only 2.6 percent of the employees voted in favor of no union at all. According to one company executive, the vote was "perhaps the greatest disappointment Henry Ford had in his business experience." A weaker union, which Bennett had backed because he felt he could control it, received only limited support from the Ford workers, who voted overwhelmingly for the UAW as their agent.

When the agreed-upon contract was presented to Henry Ford on June 18, he announced that he would close the plant before he would sign a contract with the union. "Let the union take over," Ford snapped. The automaker was then told that, if he closed the plants, the government would reopen them under its own management. "Well," replied Ford, "if government steps in, it will be in the motorcar business and it won't be me." The next day, however, he shocked everyone by agreeing to sign the contract, with terms that were better than the union had gotten from the other automobile companies. The reason for Ford's capitulation is believed to have resulted from Clara Ford informing her husband that, if he did not sign with the union, he would have to choose between closing the plants and continuing their marriage. The couple had been married for 53 years. "What could I do?" Ford told an executive.

During the decade of the 1930s Ford's drive and attitude concerning the day-to-day activities of the Ford Motor Company changed appreciably. After taking a personal interest in building his "last

*Ford enjoying a McGuffey Reader in the restored William McGuffey home at Greenfield Village,
Ford's re-creation of the rural America of his youth (courtesy of the Ford Archives,
Henry Ford Museum, Dearborn, Michigan)*

mechanical triumph," the V-8, in late 1931 and early 1932, he began spending more of his time with his "hobbies"—Greenfield Village and the Henry Ford Museum, the "village industries," soybean experimentation, Ford schools, and tractor development. In 1933 Ford even stated that "the Rouge is no fun any more."

However, he did find enjoyment in his company's participation in the regional and world's fairs of the 1930s. During these years the company spent almost $12 million on exhibits that were visited by 56 million people. The building Ford constructed at the Chicago Exposition in 1934 was the largest structure built by any of the fair's exhibitors. The Rotunda, as it was called, was so impressive Ford ordered it disassembled after the fair and reassembled in Dearborn.

In 1936 Henry and Clara Ford decided to build a winter home on property they had accumulated near Savannah, Georgia. The area covered more than 120 square miles and included 530 par-

cels of property, villages, islands, marshes, dozens of plantations, timber, and schools. The Ford plantation, known as Richmond Hill, was built on the site of the former Richmond Plantation, which had been burned by Sherman on his march to the sea. The home cost a total of $362,000 and was built to resemble Savannah's famous "Hermitage." Ford also spent a considerable amount of money building 85 separate structures on his estate and in the local village.

During the 1930s Henry Ford became very interested in relating scientific technology to agriculture. This led to his extensive soybean experimentation and research into plastics and was keyed to his lifelong efforts to improve farming. Ford planted 300 varieties of soybeans on 8,000 acres of his farms in 1932 and 1933. By 1933 his experimentation, which cost $1.25 million, had been rewarded with the discovery of soybean oil, which made a superior enamel for painting cars, plus a soybean meal, which could be molded into such products as horn buttons, gearshift knobs, and accelerator pedals. Ford also produced an entire car made from soybean plastic. In addition to automotive applications, Ford developed hundreds of soybean-based foods, such as bread, milk, ice cream, and cookies. By 1941 Ford was even wearing soybean-based clothing.

In 1935 Henry and Edsel Ford became concerned when the Roosevelt administration instituted higher income and inheritance taxes. Estates valued at more than $4 million were liable to a 50 percent assessment, and from $50 million and up, the tax would rise to 70 percent. Father and son were concerned that, if either died, a large amount of family stock would have to be sold to pay estate taxes. A decision was made to convert all the company's existing stock into two classes: Class A took 95 percent of the stock, and Class B, 5 percent. None of the new shares would be available to the public. The Class B shares would be the only stock to possess voting rights. After the stock was reissued, Henry and Edsel set up the Ford Foundation on January 15, 1936, for the purpose of "receiving and administering funds for scientific, educational, and charitable purposes, and for the public welfare, and for no other purpose." Because charitable donations are tax-exempt, the Fords could now will their Class A stock to the foundation and avoid payment of tax on 95 percent of their wealth. In early February Henry and Edsel Ford signed wills to bequeath their Class A shares to the Ford Foundation.

Two days after the attack on Pearl Harbor, President Roosevelt declared that the fate of the United States and its allies would depend largely on America's industrial strength and capacity. From that moment on the spotlight was focused on the industrial scene, particularly on the biggest contractors. Of these, Ford Motor Company was the fourth largest. Between the outbreak of war in Europe in September 1939 and December 7, 1941, Henry Ford had been an outspoken opponent of America's entry into the war, supporting the isolationist America First Committee. When the United States in summer 1940 stepped up the production of military supplies, Ford turned down one contract because the supplies were destined to go to the British, but before the end of the year he had approved contracts for materiel to be used by American forces.

At the end of 1940 he agreed to look into a proposal that Ford build a bomber for the Air Corps.

The result was the most famous of all Ford's contributions to the war effort, the production of B-24 bombers at a gigantic plant designed by Albert Kahn and built at Willow Run, near Ypsilanti, Michigan. The plant impressed everyone by its size. The main building was 3,200 feet long, 1,280 feet wide, and had 2,547,000 square feet of floor space. In early 1942 the main building and flying field were completed. The interior of the plant, however, was in turmoil. Charles Sorensen, in charge of production, had set a goal of one bomber per hour, but little progress had been made toward reaching that goal. On September 18 President Roosevelt visited the facility as part of a tour of war plants. During their limousine tour Ford, never a Roosevelt admirer, sat between President and Mrs. Roosevelt but would not say more than a few words. When the president received a "deafening" welcome from the employees, Ford showed his resentment and was described as being gloomy and mean looking on the tour.

By the end of December Willow Run had made only 56 planes. Henry and Edsel Ford received national criticism when Willow Run was nicknamed "Will It Run?" In addition to production problems the factory could not seem to hire enough competent workers and keep them from quitting. With gas rationing, many workers found it difficult to commute from Detroit. For employees who did not commute, a severe housing shortage developed for those who tried to live near the plant. Nevertheless, the efforts of Sorensen and his hard-pressed staff finally resolved the problems, and by the end of 1943 the Willow Run plant was well on its way to meeting the production goal, and long before production was halted in 1945 had surpassed it. In addition to B-24 "Liberator" bombers, the Ford Motor Company also built aircraft engines, tanks, jeeps, trucks, amphibious jeeps, armored cars, universal carriers, gliders, and jet bomber engines.

Edsel Ford worked tirelessly during the first year-and-a-half of the war to solve the production problems at Willow Run. Tragically, he was not on hand to share in the plaudits for a job well done. Thwarted and opposed for years by his father and Harry Bennett, Edsel underwent an operation for stomach ulcers in January 1942. Although he was able to resume his duties after a short rest, he fell ill again—of stomach cancer—later in the year. To his wife, children, friends, and associates who suggested that he slow his pace, he merely shook his head and replied, "The war won't wait." Run-down and in almost constant pain, Edsel was further weakened by an attack of undulant fever. Only with a tremendous amount of determination was Edsel able to carry on his work until mid April 1943. He died on May 26, 1943, at the age of forty-nine. Almost to the end his father refused to believe him in danger: if Edsel would only change his diet and life-style to that which his father had found best, if he would stop worrying and listening to men of the wrong type, he would soon get well. But his son's death dealt Ford a blow from which he would never recover. One of Henry Ford's soy-bean chemists, Robert A. Smith, noted that "the day Edsel Ford died was the day the sparkle disappeared from Henry Ford's eyes."

A few days after Edsel's death Henry Ford, then almost eighty years of age, informed company executives and his family that he would resume the company's presidency, a post he had vacated in 1919. Ford had wanted to see Bennett become president, but Edsel Ford's wife, who blamed Bennett for much of her husband's troubles, was adamantly opposed to Bennett's selection. She preferred Ford for the position, even though it was apparent that the founder was mentally and physically unable to handle the job.

Henry Ford's physical condition was indeed deteriorating. In addition to suffering two mild strokes, one in 1938 and another in 1941, Ford was showing increasing signs of senility. During the winter of 1943-1944 his symptoms became more obvious. Often he was irritable, suspicious, confused, and disoriented. Ford's ability to run the company effectively was negligible.

After Edsel's death in May 1943 high government officials became concerned about the chaotic administration of the Ford Motor Company. Ford's grandson Henry Ford II was released from active service in the U.S. Navy by Secretary of the Navy Frank Knox in May 1943, in the hopes that he would be able to stabilize the management of the company and help it to realize its full war-production potential. Henry Ford II arrived at the Rouge complex on August 10, 1943.

As Ford's influence in company affairs declined, Bennett's increased. Bennett commanded the allegiance of many well-placed executives, as well as the strong-armed service department. Bennett had been jockeying for power and position for many years under the reign of Henry Ford. His

major rival had been Charles Sorensen, but by the end of 1943 Sorensen was on his way out. Henry Ford II realized that it would be difficult to unseat Bennett from his position of power and authority. However, he had the advantage of the Ford family behind him. It was only a matter of waiting for the right time to move against Bennett.

Behind the scenes Clara Ford, convinced that Henry II was capable of managing the company, pleaded for months with her husband to retire and transfer the presidency to his grandson. Henry refused. Finally, in September 1945 Mrs. Edsel Ford forced the issue. Confronting her father-in-law with an ultimatum not unlike the one he had given his minority partners a quarter-century earlier, she threatened to sell her family's stock holding (41.6 percent of the total) unless the old man yielded to her son. The founder yielded.

On September 21, 1945, the board of directors held one of the most important sessions in its history. Henry Ford's letter of resignation was read to the board by company secretary B. J. Craig. The eighty-two-year-old Henry Ford was now officially retired from the company he had founded 42 years earlier. Bennett was through with the Ford Motor Company shortly thereafter. At last Henry Ford II ruled the Ford empire.

During the last two years of his life Henry Ford resembled a blurred and faded photograph of his former self. Alert one moment, he was bewildered the next. Physically as well as mentally Henry Ford failed perceptibly during his final two years. He tired easily and often did not feel well. Sometimes he wore a shawl and increasingly appeared to be an enfeebled old man. Although Henry and Clara Ford attended numerous public events from 1945 to 1947, the press was usually kept at a distance. Clara and her chauffeur Robert Rankin watched over the patriarch of the Ford family as a mother would watch a child. Photographs of Henry Ford suggest he looked lost.

On March 31, 1947, on the way to Dearborn from Richmond Hill, Henry Ford made his last public appearance at the Martha Berry College, near Rome, Georgia. The Fords had been good friends of the school's founder, Martha Berry, since the mid 1920s and had contributed generously to its construction and operation. At the school Clara was granted an honorary doctorate; Henry participated in a tree-planting ceremony.

Henry Ford's funeral procession, April 10, 1947 (courtesy of the Ford Archives, Henry Ford Museum, Dearborn, Michigan)

Upon returning to the Fair Lane estate in Dearborn, Ford seemed to be in good physical condition. On April 7 his mind was clear, and he seemed interested in his surroundings. The Rouge River, which flowed behind the Ford mansion, was in flood, and, while the waters were not high enough to reach the castlelike structure, they did partly cover the estate's powerhouse a short distance downstream, knocking out heat, electricity, and telephone.

Ford spent the afternoon with his chauffeur inspecting damage caused by the flood and visiting familiar places in and around Dearborn. Their last stop before heading back to Fair Lane was the little Ford family cemetery on Joy Road. "Well," he told the chauffeur upon arrival, "this is where they're going to bury me when I die. In among the rest of my folks."

That evening, Henry and Clara retired at about 9 P.M., their bedroom illuminated by candles. At 11:15 Clara, realizing that her husband was seriously ill, summoned her maid Rosa Buhler and asked her to have the chauffeur summon her husband's physician, Dr. John G. Mateer.

"When I came into the bedroom, I saw that

Mr. Ford was dying," said the maid. "We propped him up and he put his head on Mrs. Ford's shoulder just like a tired child. She kept saying, 'Henry, please speak to me.' I said to her, 'I think Mr. Ford is leaving us.' She seemed paralyzed." The time was 11:40 P.M. Dr. Mateer, arriving at midnight, pronounced the cause of death a cerebral hemorrhage.

Ford's body lay in state on the first floor of Greenfield Village's Recreation Building. On April 9 more than 100,000 mourners waited patiently in a mile-long line to view Ford's body. The funeral service was held at St. Paul's Episcopal Cathedral in Detroit on April 10. After the service more than 30,000 people watched as Ford's $45,000 bronze casket was placed in a Packard hearse (a Lincoln or Ford hearse could not be located in time) and transported to the family cemetery. The coffin was lowered into the grave as heavy rain poured down on the 20,000 mourners.

Henry Ford, one of the world's great industrialists, had an extraordinary influence on the American scene. His Model T, mass-production methods, and wage/price theories revolutionized American industry and reverberated around the world. An indigenous folk hero, Ford appealed to millions of his countrymen because, in their view, he succeeded through his own creativeness and hard work and by supplying a product to meet the public's desires, rather than by manipulating money, natural resources, or people. He also was admired, despite his great wealth, for having retained the common touch. Regarded as an industrial superman and believed by many to typify American civilization and genius, he reminded people of an earlier, simpler society.

Controversial, paradoxical, colorful, Henry Ford was an enigma. An idealistic pioneer in some respects, he was a cynical reactionary in others. He had a selfish, mean, even cruel streak; yet often he was generous, kind, and compassionate. He was ignorant, narrow-minded, and stubborn; yet at times he displayed remarkable insight, vision, open-mindedness, and flexibility.

As Will Rogers once said of Ford, "It will take a hundred years to tell whether he helped us or hurt us, but he certainly didn't leave us where he found us."

Selected Publications:

The Case Against the Little White Slaver (Detroit, Mich.: H. Ford, c.1916);

Ford Ideals: Being a Selection From "Mr. Ford's Page" (Dearborn, Mich.: Dearborn, 1922);

The International Jew (Dearborn, Mich.: Dearborn Independent, 1922);

365 of Henry Ford's Sayings (New York: The League-for-a-Living, c.1923);

Today and Tomorrow (Garden City, N.Y.: Doubleday, Page, 1926);

My Philosophy of Industry (New York: Coward-McCann, 1929);

Edison as I Know Him (New York: Cosmopolitan, 1930);

Moving Forward (Garden City, N.Y.: Doubleday, Doran, 1930);

The Only Real Security: An Interview with Henry Ford (New York: The Chemical Foundation, c.1936);

Things I've Been Thinking About (New York: Revell, c.1936).

References:

Harry Barnard, *Independent Man–The Life of Senator James Couzens* (New York: Scribners, 1958);

Ford R. Bryan, *The Fords of Dearborn, An Illustrated History* (Detroit: Harlo Press, 1987);

Bryan, "Henry Ford's Experiment at Richmond Hill," *Dearborn Historian*, 24 (Autumn 1984): 103-116;

Bryan, " 'Sialia'–Henry Ford's Yacht," *Dearborn Historian*, 29 (Spring 1989): 46-55;

Roger Burlingame, *Henry Ford* (New York: Knopf, 1954);

Floyd Clymer, *Henry's Wonderful Model T 1908-1927* (New York: Bonanza, 1955);

Clymer, *Treasury of Early American Automobiles 1877-1925* (New York: McGraw-Hill, 1950);

Robert Conot, *American Odyssey* (Detroit: Wayne State University Press, 1986);

Jean M. Fox, *More Than A Tavern: 150 Years of Botsford Inn* (Farmington Hills, Mich.: Botsford Inn, 1986);

William Greenleaf, *From These Beginnings–The Early Philanthropies of Henry and Edsel Ford 1911-1936* (Detroit: Wayne State University Press, 1964);

Greenleaf, *Monopoly on Wheels: Henry Ford and the Selden Automobile Patent* (Detroit: Wayne State University Press, 1961);

Barbara S. Kraft, *The Peace Ship–Henry Ford's Pacifist Adventure in the First World War* (New York: Macmillan, 1978);

Robert Lacey, *Ford, The Men and the Machine* (Boston: Little, Brown, 1986);

Leo Levine, *Ford: The Dust and The Glory: A Racing History* (New York: Macmillan, 1968);

David L. Lewis, "Henry Ford's Other Car," *Chronicle, The Quarterly Magazine of the Historical Society of Michigan*, 19 (Summer 1983): 38-40;

Lewis, *The Public Image of Henry Ford* (Detroit: Wayne State University Press, 1976);

Dwight MacDonald, *The Ford Foundation–The Men and the Millions* (New York: Reynal, 1956);

Glen McCaskey, *The View From Sterling Bluff: From General Oglethorpe to Henry Ford to Today* (Atlanta: Longstreet, 1988);

Allan Nevins and Frank Ernest Hill, *Ford: The Times, the Man, the Company* (New York: Scribners, 1954);

Nevins and Frank Ernest Hill, *Ford: Decline and Rebirth 1933-1962* (New York: Scribners, 1962);

Nevins and Hill, *Ford: Expansion and Challenge 1915-1933* (New York: Scribners, 1957);

William Adams Simonds, *Henry Ford and Greenfield Village* (New York: Frederick A. Stokes, 1938);

Scott D. Trostel, *The Detroit, Toledo and Ironton Railroad* (Fletcher, Ohio: Cam-Tech, 1988);

Michael Williams, *Ford and Fordson Tractors* (Dorset, U.K.: Blanford, 1985).

Archives:

The Ford Archives at the Henry Ford Museum in Dearborn, Michigan, contains by far the most extensive collection of records pertaining to any automotive executive and company. In addition to Henry Ford's personal and business records, it includes transcripts of interviews with many of Ford's associates and others who had contact with him. The separate Ford Industrial Archives at the museum contains certain other records, which can only be used with company authorization.

Ford Motor Company

by George S. May

Eastern Michigan University

Among many things the Ford Motor Company is famous as the only American automaker of recent decades in which family members are still involved. In earlier years that kind of family involvement was true of many companies, often with a degree of control exceeding that exercised by Henry Ford in the Ford company, where for some time after the company's founding in 1903 his authority was not of the unlimited character it became by the 1920s.

Twice before—with the Detroit Automobile Company from 1899 to 1901 and the Henry Ford Company 1901 to 1902—Ford had failed to deliver the passenger car the investors were counting on. In spite of those failures, other Detroit investors were found who would support still a third venture to produce a Ford-designed car. As had been the case with the two earlier companies, Ford was not head of the Ford Motor Company when it was officially formed on June 16, 1903. Instead the office of president was held by John S. Gray, a Detroit businessman whose $10,500 investment topped that of all other investors. Ford was named vice-president and general manager in charge of production. In return for his services he was given 25.5 percent of the stock. An equal amount of stock, however, was given to Gray's nephew, Alexander Y. Malcomson, a Detroit coal dealer who more than anyone else was responsible for persuading most of the investors to commit themselves to the company.

Aside from Gray most of the stockholders were men of modest means who had scrambled to raise the few thousand dollars they invested or had given their notes, promising to pay for their shares at a later time. Thus, in July 1903 when Ford said he had found problems with the first assembled cars that would have to be corrected before they were shipped, he was quickly overruled by business manager James Couzens. With the company's bank balance nearly exhausted, Couzens knew the company had to raise cash immediately to survive.

Since it was unlikely that the stockholders could be persuaded to supply more money, the only way to raise money was by the sale of the cars. Accordingly, they were shipped out, and the money that came in put the company on solid financial ground.

The incident helped to establish Couzens's supremacy in directing the company's business affairs, and for a decade his authority in that area went generally unchallenged. Ford's control over product and production matters, on the other hand, did not go unchallenged. The Ford Model A, the first car the company produced, was a 2-cylinder runabout selling in the $800 to $900 range. The lightweight and relatively inexpensive runabouts had been popularized by the curved-dash Oldsmobile runabout, and Ford was following an industry-wide trend when he chose this type of car as the company's initial offering. Malcomson, however, was soon pushing for a heavier and more expensive car. By 1904 many in the industry were turning from the runabout to heavier touring cars, which were better suited to American road conditions than the fragile runabouts and were also more profitable. Ford was convinced that the future of the company lay in continuing to develop cars for the masses. Malcomson's influence in the company was great enough to force Ford to come up with bigger cars, including the 6-cylinder Model K selling for $2,800. The Model K was a failure, which served to weaken Malcomson's position with his fellow directors and stockholders. Whatever support he still had was lost when he formed a separate company late in 1905 to produce air-cooled touring cars at the same time he continued as treasurer and stockholder in the Ford Motor Company. Ford and Couzens joined forces to drive Malcomson out of the company, and in July 1906 Malcomson sold his stock interest to Ford. This transaction gave Ford a majority of the stock; when Gray died at this same time Ford was elected president.

BOSS OF THE ROAD
THE LATEST AND BEST

$850

The FORDMOBILE with detachable tonneau

THIS new light touring car fills the demand for an automobile between a runabout and a heavy touring car. It is positively the most perfect machine on the market, having overcome all drawbacks such as smell, noise, jolt, etc., common to all other makes of Auto Carriages. It is so simple that a boy of 15 can run it.

For beauty of finish it is unequaled, and we promise **IMMEDIATE DELIVERY.** We haven't space enough to enter into its mechanical detail, but if you are interested in the NEWEST and MOST ADVANCED AUTO manufactured to-day write us for particulars.

FORD MOTOR COMPANY
691 MACK AVENUE,   **DETROIT, MICH.**

Ford advertisement, 1903: no "smell, noise, jolt, etc."

Ford now moved ahead in his pursuit of the car he wanted the company to sell. The $600 4-cylinder Ford Model N, introduced in 1905, marked a major advance over the earlier low-priced models, but Ford and his staff continued the search for a car that would be sturdy and still inexpensive. With the development of the Model T, Ford felt that he had been successful. The Model T was introduced in fall 1908, and the same basic model was produced until May 1927. After spring 1909 it was the only model the company produced until 1921, when it acquired the Lincoln company and began to manufacture limited numbers of that luxury car. In order to reduce the price of the Model T to a point where it would be within reach of a wide group of consumers, Ford and his staff turned their attention to means of improving the production of the car, culminating in the development of the moving assembly line in 1913-1914.

The combination of the Model T and mass-production techniques, all achieved within a remarkably short span of time, made the Ford Motor Company far and away the largest automobile manufacturer in the world and Henry Ford the world's best-known manufacturer. Yet the course of developments might well have been far different if plans had gone ahead in 1908 and 1909 to include the Ford company in one of the efforts then being made to consolidate several companies into one large firm. In the early months of 1908 Ford was a participant in discussions that would have merged his company with Buick, Maxwell-Briscoe, and Reo. Those talks collapsed when both Ford and Ransom Olds of Reo demanded cash for control of their companies rather than the stock in the new company that William C. Durant of Buick, Benjamin Briscoe, and the Wall Street interests who were arranging the merger favored. In 1909 Durant agreed to Ford's asking price of $8 million to add Ford Motor Company to Durant's General Motors (GM) combination, and Briscoe also agreed to a similar price as he tried to create his own combination. But neither Durant nor Briscoe was able to obtain the necessary backing from the banks.

Ford's willingness to sell at a time when he was on the threshold of perhaps the most spectacular achievements of modern industrial history in part may have been due to his discouragement at

Advertisement in the Detroit Free Press,
July 28, 1903

the progress being made in dealing with another problem—the prolonged suit brought against the company by the Association of Licensed Automobile Manufacturers, which charged it with infringing upon the rights of the holders of the Selden patent. In 1909 the federal judge hearing the case, which had been filed in 1903, upheld the claim that the patent, awarded in 1895, covered all gasoline-propelled automobiles and that the Ford company, by producing such vehicles without a license from the patent holders, was guilty of infringement. It was while Ford and his attorneys were debating what to do next that the discussions were held with Durant and Briscoe. Ford decided to appeal the judge's decision, and early in 1911 an appeals court reversed the lower court's decision. That ended the case since, with the patent having only one more year to run, the Selden forces decided it was not worth the expense of carrying the appeal up to the Supreme Court.

Henry Ford's identification as the victor in the Selden case served to add further luster to the pub-

lic acclaim he had been receiving for his industrial achievements. That acclaim had resulted from the collaborative efforts of Ford and his able staff, but Ford was increasingly less willing to share honors with others or to tolerate contrary views. In 1915 Couzens resigned from the company because Ford was no longer willing to allow him to exercise control over business affairs to the extent he had enjoyed since 1903. About the same time Ford launched an ambitious project to develop a new production facility along the Rouge River in what is now the city of Dearborn, Michigan. He financed the development out of the profits of the company, drastically reducing dividends. Ford held a majority of the stock, but among the minority stockholders were John and Horace Dodge, who had been the major suppliers of parts for Ford until 1914, when they started their own automobile company, which they had planned to finance through their Ford stock dividends. They filed suit, arguing that Ford was violating their interests as stockholders by paying dividends at a rate far less than was justified. The Michigan Supreme Court ruled in their favor, ordering Ford in 1919 to pay $19 million in back dividends. Incensed by this opposition from the minority stockholders, whom Ford referred to as "leeches," he successfully maneuvered to buy them all out, transforming the company into an entirely family-owned business. However, with the removal of strong-minded individuals such as Couzens and the Dodges, who had not been afraid to stand up to Ford, the company now entered a period when only those who agreed with Ford could survive long. Within a few years it was evident that this would have tragic consequences for the company.

References:

Allan Nevins and Frank Ernest Hill, *Ford: Expansion and Challenge, 1915-1932* (New York: Scribners, 1957);

Nevins and Hill, *Ford: The Times, the Man, the Company* (New York: Scribners, 1954).

Archives:

The Ford Archives, established by the Ford company when Allan Nevins was engaged to write a history of the company, is the most complete archives of any automobile company. It is now located in the Henry Ford Museum in Dearborn, Michigan. In addition to company records it includes a vast collection of oral interviews with individuals associated with Henry Ford and his company and a large amount of other material.

Four Wheel Drive Auto Company

by Frederick I. Olson

University of Wisconsin–Milwaukee

Four Wheel Drive Corporation of Clintonville, Wisconsin, is the survivor of a series of corporate structures for making automobiles dating back to 1909 based on the notion that 4-wheel drive was a superior form of traction for passenger cars and trucks. Isolated in a small Waupaca County farm community remote from industrial supplies and skilled labor and chronically short of capital, the firm has survived for 80 years through periodic hard times punctuated by peaks of prosperity during two world wars.

In 1906 two Clintonville brothers-in-law, Otto Zachow and William Besserdich, blacksmiths by trade and operators of a threshing machine repair shop, took on an agency for Réo, the automobile company formed by Ransom Olds. Traction difficulties with the rudimentary mud roads of the time led Zachow to conceive of a 4-wheel-drive vehicle, for which he developed and forged a double-Y universal joint. For this he received a patent in 1908, unaware of the fact that sooner or later 70 or so other patents for 4-wheel drive would be entered, all without operational success. But Zachow and Besserdich successfully tested their device on a steam-driven vehicle in snow. In 1909, with financing from William H. Finney, a local physician, they incorporated as Badger Four Wheel Drive Auto Company and soon converted their vehicle to a 45-horsepower Continental gas engine with a total vehicle weight of 3,800 pounds. Difficulties persisted, however, and in 1910 the company was dissolved, soon to reemerge as Four Wheel Drive Auto Company under a new president, Walter A. Olen, the attorney who had assisted on the original patent, and without its two blacksmith founders. Of their initial effort, automobile historian John B. Rae writes: "In 1908 Otto Zachow and William Besserdich produced a four-wheel drive car in Clintonville, Wisconsin, the long-range precursor of the jeep."

Under Olen, though still undercapitalized, the company actually built ten production models incorporating many innovations. The U.S. Army in 1912 equipped one of these touring cars with a wagon body and successfully drove it a circuitous 1,509 miles from Fort Myer, Virginia, to Fort Benjamin Harrison near Indianapolis in seven weeks. This persuaded Olen of the 4-wheel drive advantage for trucks. He ordered the new factory superintendent and chief engineer P. J. F. Batenburg to produce for the Army a 3-ton model which was tested as a support vehicle on a 260-mile troop march from Dubuque, Iowa, to Sparta, Wisconsin, over nearly impassable dirt roads. But even this demonstration failed to produce the expected Army order for 4-wheel drive vehicles.

With the outbreak of World War I the company shipped two trucks to England, resulting in a British order for 50 trucks. By year's end the British had taken 288 vehicles, the Russians 88, and the order backlog was 200 per month. Up to then the company had made no profit, paid no dividends, and seemed ready for bankruptcy. But 1915 produced sudden and overwhelming financial success. In 1916 the U.S. Army ordered its trucks for the Mexican campaign, but this was only a prelude to the largest truck order ever placed, when the United States entered the war in 1917–3,750 trucks at the rate of 175 per month. Four Wheel Drive boomed. It built a boardinghouse to accommodate the workers recruited from nearby farms and cities, and it also licensed Mitchell Motor Car Company of Racine and Kissel Motor Car Company of Hartford, among others, to contribute to the production of 10,000 trucks in a year.

The sudden conclusion of the war halted the company's prosperity. Its Model B may have helped win the war, but the government, finding itself awash in new trucks, dumped half their stock in the private market and gave the rest to state and

A trainload of Four Wheel Drive ammunition trucks (made under license by the Kissel Motor Car Company) on their way to the war in Europe, 1918 (courtesy of the State Historical Society of Wisconsin)

city highway departments. Undaunted, Olen shifted his company's focus from production to parts manufacture and supply and to repair and service in the field. Thus the company survived for five postwar years while 70 other truck makers quit. The prosperity of the mid 1920s found Four Wheel Drive offering new, lighter, and better truck models geared to highway maintenance, fire fighting, and utility work. By 1929 the company finally seemed to be an established truck maker, with sales of $3.3 million, a profit of $213,000, and a work force of 768 in two shifts.

The depression that began in 1929, however, was as devastating as the postwar downturn. Sales declined sharply, inventories swelled, employment fell or became part-time at reduced wages, and the company resorted to scrip while coping with two local bank failures in 1933. Yet by 1935 production had recovered to 1929 levels, which were maintained until World War II. It was during the 1930s that Olen undertook to promote the company's 4-wheel drive principle by building a racing car, which qualified in each Indianapolis 500 from 1932 to 1937.

At the outbreak of World War II the U.S. government turned to Four Wheel Drive for help. The company produced 30,000 trucks in five years, mean-

while modernizing its factory, doubling its work force (at one time employing 3,000 in a community of about 4,000), and contracting with another truck maker for its domestic line while itself making troop carriers, earth borers, bridge builders, bomb disposal units, and specialized moving equipment.

By the end of the war more than half of America's truck makers used 4-wheel drive. The increased competition led to diversification and specialization at Four Wheel Drive. In 1963 it purchased the Seagrave Corporation of Columbus, Ohio, and moved that company's operations to Clintonville. Originally a maker of ladders for fruit harvesting, Seagrave converted its line from fire ladders to one featuring complete fire engines. It is now operated as a division of FWD Corporation. Local ownership, which had nurtured the company for so long, ended with the sale to out-of-state investors in 1958, and for 23 years the company floundered under a series of absentee owners. In 1981 Chapter 11 bankruptcy brought new on-site management, a sharp reduction in product lines, and adequate financing from state and federal governments and a regional bank. Approximately 450 production workers now focus their efforts on fire trucks, snowplows, and refuse trucks.

References:

"Auto That Put the Army on Wheels," *Milwaukee Journal*, December 17, 1967;

Clintonville Tribune Gazette, special edition, September 17, 1957;

"Government Helps in FWD Revival," *Milwaukee Sentinel*, October 13, 1988;

H. E. McClelland, "FWD: The Company That Put Clintonville on the Map," *Wisconsin Trails*, 12 (Autumn 1971): 4-9;

Howard William Troyer, *The Four Wheel Drive Story: A Chapter in Cooperative Enterprise* (New York: McGraw-Hill, 1954).

H. H. Franklin Manufacturing Company

by Beverly Rae Kimes

New York, New York

Decades after the last Franklin automobile was built, the factory of the H. H. Franklin Manufacturing Company in Syracuse, New York, was razed to make way for a new high school. Demolition experts wore out several steel balls trying to collapse the building. Ultimately a blasting specialist was called in with explosives. That finally did the job. And it also said a lot about Franklin, both the company and the car. They were solid—and obstinate.

The saga of the Franklin is among the most fascinating and bittersweet in American automobile history. The longest-lived and the most successful air-cooled automobile produced in this country, the Franklin enjoyed a devoted following and the rock-solid leadership of Herbert H. Franklin.

Unlike most early successful automobile manufacturers, Franklin did not enter the field for reasons of ardor. The newfangled horseless carriage did not even particularly interest him. A former newspaper publisher, Franklin was a prominent Syracuse industrialist at the turn of the century, making fine profits in the manufacture of die castings. Making no profit at all at this time was John Wilkinson, a recent engineering graduate from Cornell University, who had developed two air-cooled prototype cars for the New York Automobile Company but who had not been paid for his efforts. When the two men met, both their lives changed.

Given a ride in one of the Wilkinson prototypes in 1901, Franklin decided dispassionately that the car was a fine product worthy of the Franklin name. The New York Automobile Company, following a bit of litigation, was absorbed into Franklin's organization, and the Franklin automobile was born. The first production car was delivered in

June 1902. A dozen more Franklins were built and sold that year.

In addition to air cooling, other features set Franklins apart from the industry norm of that era. Cylinders numbered four, valves were overhead (and would be the only type used), steering was by wheel, and the carburetor was a float-feed type. The Franklin was a very progressive car.

And sales progressively increased, to more than 200 cars in 1903, 700 in 1904, and 1,000 in 1905. By 1910 the firm was at the 4,000 annual unit figure and steadily proceeding upward. When Franklin closed its doors in the mid 1930s, lifespan production totaled 152,000. A good many were still on the road. Among the facts with which Franklin had celebrated its 25th anniversary in 1927 was a very telling one: fully 75 percent of the automobiles the company had produced to date were still registered and in use.

That the Franklin was an excellent car is a commonplace. A Franklin's robust durability had been demonstrated early on—in 1904 when transcontinental driver L. L. Whitman drove one from New York City to San Francisco in just under 33 days, which cut the previous Winton and Packard records by almost half. And in the late 1920s the inimitable Erwin G. "Cannon Ball" Baker took to the wheel of a Series 11B for an extended array of endurance runs that saw the Franklin successfully challenge the continent, the Union Pacific Limited, and Pikes Peak. Said the "Cannon Ball" affectionately: "That old waffle iron was the greatest car I ever drove."

There was an appealing arrogance about the H. H. Franklin Manufacturing Company. Some as-

Drivers of two 1902 air-cooled Franklins allowing a nervous horse to pass (courtesy of the Albert Meacham Collection, Long Island Automotive Museum)

pects of its product never changed at all. The Franklin's full-elliptic suspension provides a good example. In addition to ensuring a superior ride, it made tire wear so minimal—a Franklin's tires were good for at least 20,000 miles over the lamentable roads of the period—that the firm did not offer detachable rims as standard equipment until 1922. Franklin persisted with its wood frame—for lightness—through 1928.

High quality with less weight was Wilkinson's guiding principle. The company's pacesetting use of aluminum pistons in 1915 was another result of this. Among the advanced features in earlier Franklins were shaft drive, 3-speed selective transmissions, and automatic spark advance. Only reluctantly had a fan been added since Wilkinson regarded one as superfluous. Absolutely anathema to him was a radiator. The forward end of a Franklin was a one-piece hood, hinged at the front and easily removable. Form following function was a Wilkinson commandment.

In 1923 Franklin dealers said that commandment should be broken. Wilkinson resigned in vigorous protest. H. H. Franklin had no choice but to agree with his dealers. For years the company had

prospered with its unusual look, but buyers of the early 1920s had begun to balk. When Franklin dealers said they stood ready to give up their franchises unless Franklin cars were designed with a conventional radiatorlike grille in front, H. H. Franklin made the obvious choice between new car or no car.

Although Wilkinson's exit resulted in a wholly different-looking Franklin, there was no immediate change in the way the company did things. Engineering development remained as high on the agenda as before. Indeed the company's engineering budget—carefully computed on a percentage of income basis—was among the highest in the industry. Just as carefully considered was the design of the new Franklin. Ideas were sought from the Walter M. Murphy Company in Pasadena, California, and from a brilliant New York City designer named J. Frank de Causse. De Causse was the victor; his concept became the new Series 11 Franklin, and he had a new job as head of the Franklin Custom Department.

Since 1913 Franklin had been the most enthusiastic champion of the sedan body style—so much so, in fact, that the marque had been sometimes lambasted as stodgy despite its excellent performance. Now de Causse added a long, low, and racy boat-tail speedster (Franklin was first to catalogue the body style that was a metaphor for the Roaring Twenties) and oversaw an expanding line of models with coach work by Holbrook, Brunn, Derham, Willoughby, Locke, and Merrimac. Following the death of de Causse in 1928, Raymond Dietrich became the Franklin designer. Arriving that year, too, was the Airman series, named for Charles Lindbergh, a devoted Franklin fan.

In 1929 the stock market crash signaled the beginning of the end for Franklin. From 14,000 cars that year, output plunged to 2,000 in 1932. By then a banking syndicate controlled the company, and H. H. Franklin could but accept the dictates of Edwin McEwan, the bankers' man. A V-12 was the new model; it eliminated the traditional Franklin full-elliptic suspension and tubular axles and was as heavy as a truck. The next Franklin was mostly Reo—the chassis and body from Lansing arriving in Syracuse where Franklin installed its Airman engine, a Franklin hood and Franklin emblems for the hubcaps, and the Reo dashboard where a water temperature gauge was installed.

In 1934 Franklin produced just 360 cars. Though his company was heavily in debt, H. H. Franklin insisted it was solvent. The banks decided otherwise. After nearly three decades, H. H. Franklin was out of a job. When he walked out the door of his Franklin factory, he left everything behind. He never looked back.

References:

Stan Grayson, "The Twelve at the End of the Road," *Automobile Quarterly*, 17 (Third Quarter 1979): 228-239;

Thomas H. Hubbard, "The Case for Franklin," *Automobile Quarterly*, 5 (Winter 1967): 228-243.

August Charles Fruehauf

(December 15, 1868-May 16, 1930)

by James Wren

Motor Vehicle Manufacturers Association

CAREER: Blacksmith's apprentice, Fent & Sons (1886-1890); independent horseshoer and blacksmith (1890-1893); founder and president, Fruehauf Company (1893-1918); president (1918-1929), chairman, Fruehauf Trailer Company (1929-1930).

August Charles Fruehauf is recognized as a leader in the American trailer-truck industry. Quality craftsmanship is part of his legacy. Fruehauf also pioneered products such as refrigerated trailers, platform trailers for lumbering purposes, drop-frame semitrailers for hauling gasoline, and carryalls for heavy machinery. Fruehauf was born on December 15, 1868, in Frazer, Michigan, one of eight sons and two daughters of Charles and Sophie Hoffmier Fruehauf, both natives of Saxony. Charles Fruehauf came to America as an experienced blacksmith and machinist. Fruehauf got his education at St. John's school in Frazer, where he gained the attention of teachers as an exceptionally bright student. He had to leave school at fourteen, however, to begin work at Moffat's Sawmill, where his father worked as an engineer. As the age of eighteen Fruehauf began a blacksmith's apprenticeship with the firm of Fent & Sons of Roseville, Michigan. While running errands for his new employer he met Louise Schuchard, whom he married on October 19, 1890, at St. Peter's Church in Detroit. The couple eventually had five children—four sons and a daughter.

After marrying, Fruehauf endured a period of business failure. A fire disaster, which also severely injured his wife, wiped out a blacksmith's shop he opened in Mt. Clemens, Michigan; his next shop was also destroyed by fire. Then in 1903 he opened another shop, called Fruehauf Company, this time in Detroit. Soon business was brisk, and within a decade he moved across the street to larger quarters. During that period he expanded into the manufacture of trucks and wagons to supplement his bread-and-butter business, shoeing horses. A Detroit neighbor recalled that Louise Fruehauf found time to help her husband despite their growing family.

Fruehauf Company trailer (courtesy of the Fruehauf Corporation)

One of her shop chores was painting Fruehauf wagons. "One might say," the neighbor continued, "she was also Fruehauf's first purchasing agent. His long hours didn't allow Fruehauf time, so she did the shopping."

The year 1914 was the turning point in Fruehauf's career. In the middle of that year Frederick Sibley, a Detroit lumberman, asked Fruehauf to "rig up a contraption to hook onto a Model T roadster to haul a boat for a 600-mile trip to a lake in Upper Michigan." The result was Fruehauf's first semitrailer, a sturdy 2-wheeler with a pole that acted as a brake. The trailer worked so well that Sibley ordered other trailers for heavier loads. Within nine months Fruehauf's business tripled.

By 1916 the Fruehauf Company was famous for its huge platform trailers, which it built for lumber companies. With sales reaching $150,000 annually, a local newspaper reported, "the blacksmith shop literally began bulging at its bay windows with workmen and trade." The company began to scout for land on which to expand production capability. In 1918 Fruehauf reorganized the company as Fruehauf Trailer Company. In 1920 the new factory, located on Hayes Avenue in Detroit, was completed, signaling the company's permanent commitment to trailer production. By 1929 sales reached $3.8 million, and Fruehauf, to use his own words, decided to become a "fifth wheel." He stayed on as chairman of the firm while son Harvey became president. All the Fruehauf boys went on to work in the firm their father founded.

Fruehauf died in his home at Grosse Pointe, Michigan, on May 16, 1930, approximately ten months after retiring. His blacksmith's shop had become a world leader in trailer production. In his last months he grew fond of explaining the secret of his success: "Do a good job . . . put everything into it of materials and workmanship . . . take pride in your work."

References:

Clarence M. Burton, *History of Wayne County and the City of Detroit* (Chicago: Clarke, 1930);

Fruehauf Corporation, *Fruehauf—The Front Runner* (Detroit: Fruehauf Corporation, 1987);

James Wren and Genevieve Wren, *Motor Trucks of America* (Ann Arbor: University of Michigan Press, 1979).

Arthur Lovett Garford

(August 4, 1858-January 23, 1933)

by Donald T. Critchlow

University of Notre Dame

CAREER: Bookkeeper, cashier, Savings Deposit Bank (1880-early 1890s); founder and president, Garford Manufacturing Company (1890s-1899); other financial and manufacturing interests (1897-1933); treasurer, American Bicycle Company (1899-1901); president, Automobile & Cycle Parts Manufacturing Company (1901-1905); president, Cleveland Automatic Machine (1902-1933); president, Garford Company (1905-1912).

Arthur Lovett Garford, inventor, industrialist, and politician, was born in Elyria, Ohio, on August 4, 1858. His parents, George and Hannah Lovett Garford, had acquired a farm in this small town in northern Ohio after emigrating from England in 1852. The senior Garford turned his experience as caretaker of an English estate into a successful landscaping business in his new homeland. Arthur's later interest in the lace industry can be traced to his maternal grandfather, who was a silk and lace manufacturer in England.

After graduating from high school in 1875, Garford went to work for Rice & Burnett, a large importing concern in Cleveland. In 1880 he returned to Elyria to work for the Savings Deposit Bank, where he rose from bookkeeper to cashier by the early 1890s. While at the bank he developed a new, more comfortable, leather bicycle saddle. The popularity of the seat led him to quit the bank. He went on to build his own factory, and the Garford Manufacturing Company was launched.

By 1895 he built a large home, the Hickories, in Elyria, where he resided with his wife, Mary Louise Garford, until his death in 1933, and where they raised two daughters. For many years he also maintained a winter home in Pasadena, California.

As a leading producer of bicycle seats Garford joined with the Pope Manufacturing Company in 1899 in the formation of the American Bicycle Company, for which he served as treasurer. Shortly be-

fore the demise of the so-called "Bicycle Trust" he left to form the Automobile & Cycle Parts Manufacturing Company in 1901, which later became the Federal Manufacturing Company. In 1904 Garford had contracted to build the chassis for gasoline-powered automobiles that were finished and sold by the Studebaker Brothers Manufacturing Company. Originally the chassis were equipped with 2-cylinder engines; Garford later supplied more powerful 4-cylinder engines. These automobiles were sold in the medium- to high-price range. Garford also supplied chassis and other parts to the Cleveland Motor Car Company and the Rainier Auto Company. In 1905 Garford left Federal, taking with him the automobile plants to establish the Garford Company.

In spring 1906 Garford's management proposed to expand production to 1,000 chassis a year through the construction of a new plant in Elyria. Studebaker financed the expansion and gained more control over the corporation. In 1907, with the construction of the new plant in Elyria under way, rumors began to circulate that machinists were planning to strike the Cleveland plants. Garford acted decisively by locking out the union men, thereby reducing the labor force from 500 men to less than 150 men. At the same time the transfer of machinery and production facilities from Cleveland to Elyria was sped up. Once in Elyria, Garford continued to confront labor difficulties. After the lockout few workers were willing to go to work for Garford. "Owing to the fact, " Garford management reported to Studebaker, "that it was generally known throughout the country's labor market that the Garford Company was out of sympathy with labor unions' demands and proposed to maintain an open shop, it was more difficult for us to acquire necessary help." Finally the company undertook a country-wide recruiting campaign, but

The 1910 Garford touring car

"the workers were poor and we did not keep but one third of them."

The following year Frederick Fish of Studebaker made a bid to acquire controlling interest in Garford, but much to his dismay the offer was turned down. Fish proceeded to purchase stock from other Ohio investors. In November 1908 Fish informed Garford that the Elyria plant was to have a "Studebaker-Garford" sign installed over the main entrance. The Studebaker Corporation had acquired a controlling interest in Garford. By 1912 the Studebakers and Garford sold their interests in the Garford Motor Car Company to John N. Willys of Willys-Overland Company. Garford left the automobile business, never to return.

Garford had other business interests to keep him busy. In 1902 he had developed an interest in a French-controlled company, Cleveland Machine Screw Company. That same year he acquired control of the company and became president of the renamed Cleveland Automatic Machine, which remained his chief business concern. In 1897 he helped to form, and became the secretary of, the Elyria Gas and Electric Company. Garford Manufacturing Company, formed in 1905, produced parts for telephone systems, rural electric light systems, automotive accessories, and phonographs. The Perry-Fay Screw Machine Company was formed in 1905. He was president of the American Lace Company, formed in 1907. In 1913 he was a founder and vice-president of the National Fire Insurance Company of Cleveland. He served as president of the Republican Printing Company, which published the Elyria *Evening-Telegram*. He had controlling interest in the Worthington Ball Company, a manufacturer of golf balls, and the Worthington Company, a producer of wheelchairs, bicycles, and children's cycles. He also became president of the Savings Deposit Bank & Trust Company and later was president of the Electric Alloys Company.

Garford participated in Republican politics, serving as the party's county and district chairman and as a party delegate to the national convention. He was a Theodore Roosevelt progressive Republican who hoped to reform the Republican party. An abiding interest in temperance led him to a favorable view of woman suffrage, which he felt would bolster the dry vote. He was also concerned about losing the black vote to the Democrats. While basically opposed to increasing tariffs, he opposed the lowering of the tariff under the Underwood Tariff Bill in 1916.

At the state Republican convention in 1912 Garford almost won the gubernatorial nomination as an anti-Taft Progressive. After the convention Garford, his business associate Walter F. Brown, and James R. Garfield defected from the Republican party to form the Ohio Progressive party. The party chose Garford as its nominee for governor. His platform called for labor reform, woman suffrage, and new regulation of business by government, but his bid was unsuccessful. In 1914 he ran for the U.S. Senate under the Progressive party banner. In 1916 Garford returned to the Republican party, but his interest in active politics had diminished.

Garford became interested in motion pictures around 1915 and entered into a business arrange-

ment to produce the Vanoscope, a flickerless motion picture projector. He also developed an interest in synthetic rubber. Over the years he invested in mining properties, and he devoted much to this enterprise in the 1920s and early 1930s. Garford died in Elyria on January 23, 1933.

References:
John B. Rae, *American Automobile Manufacturers: The First Forty Years* (Philadelphia: Chilton, 1959);
James H. Rodabaugh, "Arthur L. Garford," *Museum Echoes*, 28 (July 1955).

Archives:
Material on Garford is available in the Arthur Garford papers, Ohio Historical Society, Ohio State Museum, Columbus, Ohio; and in the Studebaker papers, Studebaker National Museum, South Bend, Indiana.

General Motors Corporation

by George S. May

Eastern Michigan University

The General Motors (GM) Corporation was incorporated under the laws of Delaware on October 13, 1916, but in actuality the biggest of the Big Three automakers was born on September 16, 1908, when the General Motors Company was chartered in New Jersey. The original GM was not a manufacturer, but was simply a holding company that controlled other firms that made motor vehicles and related items through its stock holdings. Unlike Ford, its principal rival over the years, GM was the result of the acquisition of existing companies and their eventual consolidation into one corporation rather than from the development and growth of a single automobile manufacturing firm. As such, GM is one of the most successful examples of the movement toward merger and consolidation that has so often characterized American industrial development over the past century.

GM's creator was William C. Durant, who had taken part in negotiations in the early months of 1908 to merge Buick, which he controlled, Maxwell-Briscoe, Ford, and Reo. When these negotiations collapsed in the summer, Durant went ahead

on his own to form the General Motors Company, organizing it under the laws of New Jersey rather than of Michigan, where Durant and his company were located, because New Jersey's corporation laws permitted one company to own stock in another company. Under Durant's direction, GM immediately acquired control of Buick and by the end of 1908 also controlled the Olds Motor Works. By the end of the next year GM was in control of Cadillac and the Oakland Motor Car Company—the future Pontiac Division—along with about a score of other automobile, truck, and parts manufacturers.

In most cases, these acquisitions involved the payment of little cash. Instead GM gained a controlling stock interest in a company through the exchange of the holding company's stock for the shares of the manufacturing company. Stockholders were persuaded that the value of the GM stock would ultimately far exceed the amount they could have received if they sold their stock to the holding company. Events would prove that this was indeed what happened, but in 1909 Henry M. Leland forced Durant to come up with $4.5 million in cash

Law Offices of
Ward, Hayden & Satterlee,
Equitable Building, 120 Broadway, New York
Telephone 3915 Cortlandt.

Cable Address,
Northward, New-York.

J. Langdon Ward
Henry W. Hayden
Herbert L. Satterlee
Curtis R. Hatheway
H. Kintzing Post
Thomas W. North

Sept. 10th, 1908.

W. C. Durant, Esq.,

    Hotel Manhattan,

        New York City.

Dear Mr. Durant:-

    Referring to our conversation during the past two days, we find it impracticable to use the "International Motor Company", incorporated by us recently under the laws of the State of New Jersey, for the purpose of taking over the stock of certain motor companies or to use that name in such connection, at present. It will be impossible to secure the underwriting by the parties with whom we have been in touch, until the inventories, appraisals and audits of all Companies have been finally completed. This would necessarily mean a delay of nearly two months, if not more, and would entirely preclude the plan of perfecting an organization and working out its details before the end of this year. We are convinced that not until after election can the new capital which we had in view be secured for the enterprise and it therefore seems best to incorporate another Company with similar powers, under another name, in New Jersey. We might use the "United Motors Company" were it not for the fact that there is already a "United Motor Car Company" in that State. We suggest the name, "General Motors Company", which we have ascertained can be used.

Letter from lawyer Curtis R. Hatheway recommending use of the name "General Motors Company" for William C. Durant's holding company, incorporated on September 16, 1908 (courtesy of Catherine L. Durant and Aristo Scrobogna) to acquire the Cadillac company. This expenditure, when combined with Durant's ambitious and costly programs to build up and expand such acquisitions as Olds and Oakland, left him dependent on the continued good sales of his top-selling cars, Buick and Cadillac, to provide the income needed to pay the bills.

In summer 1910 a brief economic slump led to a slowdown in car sales, and GM suddenly faced financial collapse as cash flow slowed. In desperation, Durant was forced to accept the offer of an eastern banking syndicate to provide funds to carry GM through the emergency. In return for the loan of $15 million the bankers insisted that the company be managed by a trust committee during the five-year term of the loan. Although Durant was a member of the five-man committee he was effectively removed from control of the company as the other members represented the bankers.

Under James J. Storrow, the leader of the bankers' group, GM was managed in a conservative manner. Some of the companies Durant had acquired that had proven to be liabilities were sold. The first tentative moves to establish some central controls over the operations of the companies of the holding company were also initiated. Manufacturing efficiency was improved through the efforts of Charles W. Nash, who, on Durant's recommendation, had been placed in charge of Buick in 1910 and who then was named president of GM in 1912, and Walter P. Chrysler, who was brought into the organization by Storrow and who succeeded Nash at Buick.

In the meantime, Durant had become involved in the organization of several new motor vehicle companies, the most important of which was the Chevrolet Motor Company, formed in 1911 to produce a car designed by Louis Chevrolet. Under Durant's direction, however, Chevrolet's plan to produce a relatively large, expensive car was replaced by 1913 with one featuring smaller, lower-priced models. Although Chevrolet production and sales did not approach those of Ford, which dominated the low-priced market, Durant was able to use Chevrolet to regain control of GM.

Durant had been purchasing shares of GM stock from investors who were dissatisfied at the slow progress made by the company under the bankers' management and especially by its failure to pay dividends. When the five-year period of the loan expired the bankers had expected to hold or influence enough stock to enable them to remain in control of GM. At a meeting in September 1915 to decide on a slate of directors to present at the annual stockholders' meeting in November, they discovered that Durant controlled a block of shares virtually equal to that which they held. The resulting deadlock was broken by an agreement that allowed each faction to name seven directors, with three others to be selected by Pierre S. du Pont, a GM investor since 1914 regarded by both factions as a neutral force. The slate of directors was accepted at the stockholders' meeting and du Pont was chosen to be chairman of the board. Nash continued to be president.

Determined to regain complete control of GM, Durant now reorganized Chevrolet under the incorporation laws of Delaware and offered to trade five shares of the new Chevrolet stock for one share of GM stock. There was a rush to accept this offer, with even du Pont taking advantage of the opportunity. By spring 1916 Durant controlled a clear majority of GM stock, and he moved quickly to oust the bankers. Nash was forced out as president, with Durant taking over that office. Nash and Storrow combined to acquire the Thomas B. Jeffery Company in Wisconsin, renaming it after Nash, but Durant foiled their effort to persuade Chrysler to go with them by offering Chrysler financial rewards totaling $500,000 a year to remain at Buick.

It was four and a half months after Durant took office as president on June 1, 1916, that the GM Corporation was incorporated. It was not until August 1, 1917, that the GM holding company was dissolved and its numerous wholly owned manufacturing companies were assimilated as operating divisions of the new corporation. As he had done during his first tenure at GM, Durant now added still more units to the corporation's already far-flung empire. In a very complicated transaction, spread over several years, Chevrolet, which, because of Durant's 5-for-1 stock offer, owned a majority of GM's common stock, was taken over and made into another of the corporation's operating divisions. Also acquired was United Motors Corporation, which Durant had created in summer 1916 by merging Hyatt Roller Bearing, Delco, Remy Electric, and two other parts manufacturers. A 60 percent stock interest was purchased in another parts manufacturer, Fisher Body, which, like the future AC Spark Plug Division, was not completely absorbed by GM until later in the 1920s. A non-automotive company, Guardian Frigerator, producer of the refrigerator later known as the Frigid-aire, was also acquired.

By 1919 virtually all the elements of the modern GM were in place. Durant, with the support of the du Pont interests that had now become the largest single stockholder in the corporation, launched a program to increase factory capacity in order to cash in on the anticipated post-World War I boom. However, Durant's failure to implement Alfred P. Sloan, Jr.'s, plans to provide tighter administrative controls over the loosely run maze of operating divisions left GM unprepared for the sudden drop in car sales that accompanied postwar depression in summer 1920. At the end of that year Durant was once more forced to relinquish control of the company, this time permanently. Instead, under the leadership of du Pont and Sloan, GM finally lived up to its potential and shortly supplanted Ford as the world's number one automaker.

References:

Ed Cray, *Chrome Colossus: General Motors and Its Times* (New York: McGraw-Hill, 1980);

James J. Flink, *The Automobile Age* (Cambridge, Mass.: MIT Press, 1988);

George S. May, *A Most Unique Machine: The Michigan Origins of the American Automobile Industry* (Grand Rapids, Mich.: Eerdmans, 1975);

Alfred P. Sloan, Jr., *My Years with General Motors* (Garden City, N.Y.: Doubleday, 1964);

Bernard Weisberger, *The Dream Maker: William C. Durant, Founder of General Motors* (Boston: Little, Brown, 1979).

Archives:

Material on GM and GM employees is located in the GMI Alumni Foundation Collection at GMI Engineering and Management Institute, Flint, Michigan.

Max Grabowsky

(1874-September 26, 1946)

by Genevieve Wren

Motor Vehicle Research Services

CAREER: Founder and president, Grabowsky Motor Vehicle Company (1900-1902); president, Rapid Motor Vehicle Company (1902-1908); founder and president, Grabowsky Power Wagon Company (1908-1912).

Max Grabowsky was a pioneer in the design and construction of gasoline trucks. As founder and president of Grabowsky Motor Vehicle Company, he built the forerunner of General Motors (GM) Company's first truck, introduced in 1908. In 1909 Grabowsky's company was purchased by GM and became General Motors Company (GMC) Trucks.

Grabowsky was a native Detroiter, born in 1874. He obtained an education in the Detroit public schools. Early on he displayed a talent for mechanics. While still in his teens he began experimenting with the construction of commercial vehicles. Later he obtained employment at Winder & Woodward, a locksmith, gunsmith, and bicycle repair concern. In 1900 he and his brother Morris succeeded in de-

signing a 1-cylinder commercial truck featuring a horizontal gasoline engine. The success of that prototype convinced Grabowsky and his brother to form the Grabowsky Motor Vehicle Company to manufacture and sell the design. "To my knowledge," Grabowsky reminisced in a 1946 interview, "that was the first gasoline-powered truck to be used on the streets of Detroit and one of the first in the country. We had to start from scratch. We used structural steel and tested it ourselves; then designed, forged, and machined every part of the vehicle in our own shop."

In 1902 the Grabowsky firm sold its first truck, a rear-drive chain model, to Detroit's American Garment Cleaning Company. Other models followed quickly, outfitted with improved double-opposed engines. Later that year the company reorganized as the Rapid Motor Vehicle Company, and in the next three years some 75 trucks, along with several passenger cars, were manufactured in the company's small factory. In 1904 Rapid Motor Vehicle incorporated with a capitalization of $13,000.

The company needed more space, so a new factory was constructed in Pontiac, Michigan, the first in the country to be built exclusively for the manufacture of gasoline trucks. Within two years the company was building 12 types of trucks, passenger buses, and a wide range of other vehicle styles. Trucks were even shipped to faraway Italy and Sweden. Their durability won Rapid Motor Vehicle widespread recognition. Grabowsky recalled, "Yes, trucks were built well in those days, but it took much longer to do it."

In 1909 General Motors purchased both the Rapid Motor Vehicle Company and the Reliance Motor Truck Company and consolidated them to form the General Motors Truck Company. The first trucks bearing the GMC name appeared on the market in 1911. But Grabowsky had not stayed to enjoy life under the GM banner. He left in 1908 to form the Grabowsky Power Wagon Company to continue to manufacture trucks under his own name. His new models featured a removable power plant, a convenient and widely imitated innovation. Beginning in 1909 the company built two different chassis and 12 different models, including one with a load capacity of two tons. By 1912 the company had introduced four types of light-delivery wagons and a new line of 4-cylinder trucks, including a 3-ton furniture truck and a 1-ton panel truck. In December of that year, however, the company went into bankruptcy. Grabowsky sold it to the Budd Manufacturing Company, also a truck manufacturer.

When World War I broke out, Grabowsky helped coordinate the manufacture of airplanes and automobile parts. Later he worked as a factory appraiser and participated in industrial associations. When World War II began, he offered his services to the Detroit Ordinance District and worked long hours overseeing war production in the city. He continued to serve the city faithfully until he died on September 26, 1946. Grabowsky was survived by his wife, Celia, and two daughters.

Reference:

James Wren and Genevieve Wren, *Motor Trucks of America* (Ann Arbor: University of Michigan Press, 1979).

John S. Gray

(October 5, 1841-July 6, 1906)

by George S. May

Eastern Michigan University

CAREER: Assistant, Pelgrim, Gray & Company (1861-1865); partner and chief executive, Gray & Toynton [later Gray, Toynton & Fox] (1865-1902); vice-president, National Candy Company (1902-1906); president, Ford Motor Company (1903-1906).

John Simon Gray, first president of the Ford Motor Company, was born on October 5, 1841, in Edinburgh, Scotland, the son of Philip C. and Amelia Tasker Gray. In 1849 Philip Gray, a crockery merchant, moved his family to the United States to take up farming in Wisconsin. When that did not work out, the Grays moved to Detroit, where Philip Gray purchased a toy store. John Gray attended school in Detroit and then taught in a country school near Algonac until he joined his father in the toy store business in 1859. Two years later Philip Gray disposed of the stock of toys and went into the candy making business, forming a partnership with another man under the name Pelgrim, Gray & Company. The elder Gray retired in 1865, and John Gray took over the business, which went through several name changes as new partners were added. In 1881 Gray purchased complete control of the business, and he continued to head it until 1902, when it was sold to the National Candy Company. He served as vice-president of that firm until his death in 1906. He also served as president of Detroit's German-American Bank, an influential office from which he obtained a position of community leadership and that made him an attractive source of automotive capital.

By 1902 Gray had had a long and satisfying career. He and his wife, Anna Hayward Gray, whom he had married in 1864, had three sons and one daughter. He indulged his love of travel in visits to Europe and the Orient. He served on the library commission of the Detroit Public Library and was an active member of the Christian church. Those who

John S. Gray

knew him agreed he was "a man of high probity and attractive personality." In business he was known for his "prudent conservatism, setting much store by economy and solidity."

Gray's nephew, Alexander Y. Malcomson, had developed the largest coal business in Detroit, and in the winter of 1902-1903 he had been able to get his uncle to approve a loan to expand operations. At the same time, Malcomson was engaged in organizing a company to produce the car Henry Ford was developing. By April 1903 he had lined up several investors, and the Ford Motor Company was incorporated later that year. John and Horace Dodge, operators of a machine shop in Detroit, had contracted to produce most of the mechanical parts for the car, and their initial payment totaling $10,000 was due from Ford by April 15. Ford and Malcomson did not have that kind of money, and Malcomson, who had not wanted to tell his uncle of the venture into automobiles when he was already heavily in debt from his expansion of the coal business, was forced to approach Gray for help. Gray was initially horrified when Malcomson

told him what he had done, but when he was shown Ford's work, he agreed to provide the $10,000 needed to satisfy the Dodges, plus $500 more, in return for which Gray received 105 Ford shares and the assurance that he would be named president of the firm. True to his conservative nature, Gray also exacted the promise that if after a year he was not satisfied with the company's progress, Malcomson would refund what Gray had contributed.

When the 12 original stockholders of the Ford Motor Company assembled on June 18 they elected Gray president without difficulty. The stockholders, including the Dodges, were not wealthy men, and they were no doubt impressed by Gray's standing in the business community. Malcomson, who had to abandon his initial hope of becoming president to get his uncle's money, hoped to take over as business manager while Ford handled production. But Gray insisted that Malcomson devote his time to running the coal business to repay the bank loan. Malcomson protested that his bookkeeper, James Couzens, was capable of running the coal business, prompting Gray to reply, "If Couzens is so good, then you can send him to the automobile business. He can watch that for you." Couzens became Ford's business manager while Malcomson was given the far less time-consuming job of treasurer.

If Gray had done nothing more as president of the Ford Motor Company than to secure Couzens's appointment as business manager, he would have made his mark, because Couzens proved to be a brilliant executive, perhaps more important to the company's early success than Ford himself. Malcomson subsequently sought to remove Couzens as business manager, and when that failed he tried to influence company policy in other ways. Gray, although he personally liked his nephew, consistently threw his support to Ford and Couzens.

Gray did not attempt to make the Ford presidency a full-time responsibility. He was content to allow Ford and Couzens to run things. On one occasion, when Percival L. D. Perry, who was serving with several others as a Ford dealer in England, came to Detroit to try to persuade the company to establish a British branch, he found Gray in his shirtsleeves in his modest office at the German-American Bank. When Perry explained his mission, Gray, whom Perry described as "a dear old man," told him, "Well, I guess you'll have to see Henry," and he sent Perry off to the Ford factory.

*Ford Motor Company's Mack Avenue plant, Detroit, 1903, during Gray's first year as company president
(courtesy of the Ford Archives, Henry Ford Museum, Dearborn, Michigan)*

Still, Gray was by no means an inactive president. In 1905 he went with Ford and Couzens on trips to Boston, Buffalo, Chicago, Kansas City, and Cleveland to set up branch stores. Couzens had no difficulty persuading the economy-minded Gray that branches would save the company money by circumventing the price discounts awarded to franchised dealers in those cities. Gray also strongly backed Ford and Couzens in their determination to fight the suit brought against the company by the holders of the Selden patent.

Soon after its incorporation the company had approached the Association of Licensed Automobile Manufacturers (ALAM), which licensed automobile manufacturers under the Selden patent. After an initially unfavorable response, Gray insisted on further negotiations. At a luncheon meeting with Frederick Smith of the Olds Motor Works, president of the ALAM, Gray, according to Smith, "put [the Ford company's] case so fairly and simply that I had a guilty feeling of 'sassing' my elders and betters when I, in turn, tried to state the A.L.A.M. policy and purposes." The meeting ended in discord, with Ford and Couzens expressing defiance at the threat of a suit if they went ahead with production. Gray had been through patent fights before, having fought "a memorable legal battle in defense of his rights to certain glucose patents." He decided to retain an attorney, Ralzemond A. Parker, to fight the Selden group. Parker assured Ford stockholders

that they could win the suit—and after eight years the victory was achieved.

Gray did not live to see the Selden victory. He died on July 6, 1906. Henry Ford was elected to succeed him as Ford president, and not until 1960 would someone other than a member of the Ford family hold that job again. David Gray succeeded his father on the board of directors. One of his father's Ford shares was placed in his name, and the other 104 shares were held by the Gray estate. As the Ford company developed into the largest car producer in the world, the estate received millions of dollars in dividends from the stock John Gray purchased in 1903. In 1919, when Henry Ford bought out all outside stockholders and converted the company into a family-owned business, the estate received a payoff of $26,250,000. Gray's heirs had no reason to fault his business judgment.

References:

George S. May, *A Most Unique Machine: The Michigan Origins of the American Automobile Industry* (Grand Rapids, Mich.: Eerdmans, 1975);

Allan Nevins and Frank Ernest Hill, *Ford: The Times, The Man, The Company* (New York: Scribners, 1954).

Archives:

Material relating to John S. Gray's activities as president of the Ford Motor Company is in the Ford Archives at the Henry Ford Museum, Dearborn, Michigan.

A. B. C. Hardy

(November 19, 1869-November 22, 1946)

by Richard P. Scharchburg

GMI Engineering & Management Institute

CAREER: Secretary, superintendent, Wolverine Carriage Company (1892-1895); vice-president and general manager, Diamond Buggy Company (1896-1898); vice-president (1898-1900), president, Durant-Dort Carriage Company (1900-1902); president, Flint Automobile Company (1902-1904); secretary and general manager, Waterloo Carriage Company (1904-1909); general manager, Welch-Detroit Motor Company (1909-1910); general manager, Marquette Motor Company (1910-1911); vice-president and general manager, Little Motor Car Company (1911-1914); vice-president, Mason Motor Company (1911-1914); vice-president and general manager, Chevrolet Motor Company (1914-1916); assistant to the president (1916-1920), member of Operations Committee (1921-1925), president and general manager, Olds Motor Works (1921-1925); director (1922-1925), vice-president, General Motors Corporation (1922-1925).

Like so many of the early pioneers of the automobile industry, Alexander Brownell Cullen Hardy was a product of Michigan. He was born November 19, 1869, in Ypsilanti. Hardy was educated in the Ypsilanti public schools, and after graduating from high school he attended the University of Michigan for two years. He did not complete his degree, leaving in 1889 to help support a younger sister. That was the extent of his formal education. Because his marks had been exceptionally high, he was able to induce James B. Angell, president of the university, to recommend him for a teaching position in the public schools. He taught school for two and a half years at Grosse Isle, Michigan. He left the teaching profession in 1892 and joined the Wolverine Carriage Company in Davison, Michigan, as secretary of the firm. He advanced to superintendent but left the firm in 1895.

In January 1896 he took over management of the Diamond Buggy Company in Flint, Michigan, becoming vice-president and general manager. This company was backed financially by William C. Durant and the Durant-Dort Carriage Company, also of Flint. In 1898 Hardy accepted the position of vice-president of the Durant-Dort Carriage Company, advancing to the presidency in 1900. That same year he left for Europe for a much-needed and deserved rest. He spent three months traveling and after returning briefly to Flint sold all his stock in Durant-Dort; he was formulating plans of his own for an entirely new manufacturing venture. He returned to Europe and spent practically all of 1901 studying European automobile manufacturers, especially those in France, Germany, and Italy.

In 1902 he returned to Flint and organized the Flint Automobile Company, the first automobile company ever started there. By spring 1903 the fledgling company had built and sold 52 "Flint Roadsters," all painted vivid red and priced from $750 to $850. Accused of violating the Selden patent, which related to motor vehicles powered by internal combustion engines and which was held by the Association of Licensed Automobile Manufacturers, Hardy refused to acknowledge the patent rights and felt he had no choice but to go out of business or face endless and costly litigation. Sales did not meet expectations, and the company's financial condition quickly degenerated. Hardy was, no doubt, relieved to close up shop.

From the knowledge and experience gained in his automobile venture, Hardy believed that the carriage business would remain strong for about ten years. In 1904 he returned to the carriage business and for four years was secretary and general manager of the Waterloo Carriage Company in Waterloo, Iowa. In July 1909 he was recalled to Michigan by Durant, who had formed the General Motors (GM) Company in 1908. Hardy was placed

*A. B. C. Hardy (center), with General Motors president
William C. Durant and Durant's wife Catherine, 1919*

in charge of the Welch-Detroit Motor Company, a GM subsidiary, in Detroit.

When Durant lost control of GM in fall 1910 and a group of bankers headed by James J. Storrow took charge, Hardy was asked to make a confidential report on GM's Rainier Motor Company in Saginaw. His detailed report impressed the GM board of directors to such an extent that he was called upon to discuss his findings at a board meeting. He had condemned management and working conditions at the factory, and the board believed that anyone able to prepare such a critical report was also the man to set things right. Hardy was ordered to move tools and machinery from the Welch plants in Detroit and Pontiac to Saginaw and combine them with Rainier to form a single unit for the production of a line of cars called the Marquette, to be sold by the Buick organization.

Hardy agreed to undertake the task upon assurance that when the operation was completed he would be allowed to design and produce a new line of low-priced cars at the Marquette factory.

Hardy's recommendations were made at a time when Chevrolet was still a high-priced experiment in Detroit and Ford had not yet achieved his enormous output. Hardy thought the tremendous organizational task before him would be worthwhile if he could achieve his goal of building a small car at a price within the means of thousands of people.

When the GM board later withdrew its promise to produce Hardy's car, he resigned and was immediately invited back to Flint to take charge of Durant's latest promotion. While Hardy was engaged in GM affairs in Saginaw, Durant had been busy in 1911 establishing another automobile empire independent of GM, the Little Motor Car Company in Flint. Hardy was made vice-president and general manager of Little and also vice-president of the Mason Motor Company in Flint, yet another Durant creation.

In 1913 Durant decided to move his newly created Chevrolet Motor Company from Detroit to Flint and combine all his Flint automobile plants under the Chevrolet banner. In 1914 Hardy was

sand dollars, was convicted, and served a short prison term. He never tried to hide his past, admitting, "I put $3,000 of the money into the oil business and, besides, I was always a pretty good liver." He later used himself as an example of how anyone could triumph over adversity if he had the will to do so.

Hawkins, who was a CPA, launched the Hawkins-Gies accounting firm in 1898. On May 2, 1904, it did its first audit of the fledgling Ford Motor Company. Hawkins's firm continued advising Ford on various financial matters until fall 1907 when James Couzens hired him to be a full-time commercial manager in full charge of sales.

Although Henry Ford did not believe in meticulous cost accounting, Hawkins did, and from the beginning he worked to improve the company's methods of bookkeeping, purchasing, stockpiling, and distribution. But Hawkins's chief contribution to the company was in marketing. When Ford asked him in 1907, "Where do you expect to start selling cars?" Hawkins pointed to a grocery store on the opposite corner and said, "I think we should start there, and then weave the web around until we reach a point where the freight rates change, which means Chicago or Buffalo."

According to Hawkins, it was the settling of the Selden Patent Case in 1911 that allowed the Ford Motor Company to develop its vast national and international network of dealers. Before the case was thrown out by the courts, dealers were afraid that they too could be held accountable for any settlement that might be rendered against Ford.

Before 1911 existing dealers had been granted exclusive agencies for entire counties and, in some cases, entire states. To Hawkins this meant that many potential buyers were never reached, and he restricted a dealer's territory to a township or to a territory of similar size. He reasoned that the smaller the territory, the more intensive the required selling process would have to be. He also divided the United States into thirty branch agencies. Each had its manager who maintained direct contact with Detroit while supervising the dealers in his region; however, Hawkins continued to determine the specific territory a dealer might have. He also established nine such agencies in Canada, three in Europe, and one each in Australia and South America.

Before Hawkins was through, Ford averaged three dealers for every county in the United States, and its sales network extended to the far corners of the earth. In a 1913 speech in which he compared the growth of the Ford Motor Company to the miraculous creations that sprang from Aladdin's lamp, Hawkins said, "We are as well represented in Bangkok, Siam, as we are in any city here of similar size."

Hawkins picked his field personnel with considerable care. He sent out "road men" to keep track of dealer finances, the state of their buildings, and their standing in the community. Hawkins himself often went into the field to maintain direct contact with his sales force, and he clearly enjoyed the opportunity for "hands-on" selling:

> Dealers were required to keep a list of prospects. . . . It was the work of these road men, when they went into a man's place, to ask for his prospect list. I have done this myself many a time. I have said to a dealer, 'Let us look at your prospect list,' and he would take out a bunch of maybe a hundred cards. . . , and I would say to him, 'Pick out five real buyers out of that list of a hundred cards,' and he would shuffle the cards for some little time, and finally decide he had picked out five. Then I would say, 'Let us, you and I, get in a car and see if we can't sell these five cars today or tomorrow and bring in some money for the fall season.'

One of Hawkins's most ingenious schemes was the offering of rebates to buyers at the end of that particular selling year if a certain total of cars were sold. This turned customers into salesmen as they aggressively encouraged neighbors, friends, and family to purchase a Ford.

Hawkins was also involved in the day-to-day operation of the factory. Until 1913 production schedules depended largely on anticipated future sales, and it was Hawkins who made these estimates. As such he was responsible for the pace of production as well as improving industrial efficiency. Hawkins was always proud of the fact that not a single Model T was manufactured without already being spoken for by a buyer. Ford sold 76,000 cars in 1912, and by the close of the year it had 20,000 unfilled orders. Hawkins assured Ford that he could sell all the cars the company could manufacture in 1913, and production jumped to 180,000 cars with annual sales of $100 million.

Hawkins also involved himself in shipping. He once spent six weeks loading and reloading freight cars to find the best way of transporting cars to the dealers. Previously, only completed cars had been sent, but under Hawkins's supervision the cars were broken down into their interchangeable pieces and assembled at various locations around the United States.

On April 15, 1908, Hawkins started the *Ford Times*, an in-house illustrated monthly (later bimonthly). It was usually 16 to 40 pages in length and featured cartoons and jokes, verbal nuggets, countless pictures of Model Ts doing miraculous things, as well as items about car design and production, the work of the branch managers and dealers, testimonials of buyers, and selling hints. Hawkins himself wrote many of the articles, including a regular listing of suggestions under such titles as "Profit Chokers," "Profit Makers," "Old Saws Re-Set," "Dont's [sic] for Salesmen," and "Thoughts for Salesmen."

A tall, lean man with sharp, gray eyes and a machine-gun delivery so rapid that stenographers had trouble keeping up, Hawkins annually invited his dealers and managers to Detroit for his sales seminars. He informed one such 1913 gathering that "the only reason the twentieth century is so full of civilization is because its transportation is so far ahead of the means our ancestors had of getting around." He urged the assembled dealers to forget "social affairs, amusements and the theatre" in exchange for hard daily pursuit of prospects to whom they could sell Ford cars. He also urged them to avoid negative image-making; hence, they should not erect glass partitions between their showrooms and their repair shops lest potential customers be reminded of all the things that could go wrong with their Model Ts. He also ruled against advertising antiskid chains because drivers might think of accidents, and he strongly suggested that dealers tow disabled Fords only under the cover of darkness.

He pitted dealer against dealer and threatened to reduce their territory if they did not sell sufficient numbers of automobiles. But such tactics did not deter those wanting Ford franchises. According to Ford biographer Allan Nevins, "Mayors, Congressmen, and ex-Governors were among the applicants" waiting in line for the lucrative dealerships.

In spite of the company's continued growth and tremendous financial success, by World War I Henry Ford had become increasingly disenchanted with Hawkins. He thought his sales manager had become too independent in his decision making, a trait Ford did not admire. Nor was Ford comfortable with Hawkins's unrelenting penchant for effi-

ciency. Once, when Ford himself was asked to sign for a part, he ordered the offending clerk to bring him every similar form he could find and proceeded to burn them. Ford was also upset when Hawkins took a leave of absence to assist the War Department in its production of military vehicles. After Hawkins's return from wartime service, Ford demoted him to special sales manager for Europe and South America. In April 1919 Hawkins resigned and, like so many former Ford executives, took his talents elsewhere at considerable cost to the Ford Motor Company.

In 1921 Hawkins went to work for GM at an annual salary of $150,000 as general consultant to the executive committee in relation to advertising, selling, and servicing GM products. More specifically, he helped Alfred P. Sloan, Jr., and Pierre S. du Pont with the reshaping of the corporation. He urged an end to intracompany competition and the return of Chevrolet to being the low-priced volume car in the GM line. And, as he had done so well for Ford, he continued his cost-saving methods and improved shipping efficiency.

He resigned his GM position in December 1923 to set up the Sturgis Steel Gocart Company of Sturgis, Michigan, a $3 million concern which manufactured baby perambulators. He also served as chairman of the board of the Detroit Lubricator Company, and his Detroit-based accounting firm opened offices in New York, Chicago, and Toledo. He taught classes in salesmanship, advertising, and business efficiency, was a popular and effective speaker, and wrote *The Selling Process* (1918) and *Certain Success* (1920), both of which laid out his selling principles and sold over 80,000 copies.

Hawkins was a gifted fund-raiser. He organized the Boys Club of Detroit and, as its treasurer, raised thousands of dollars to keep it going. Once, while a patient in a hospital, he complained about the sorry conditions he found there. When informed that there was no money to correct matters, he raised $55,000 for the needed improvements.

He served as a member of the State Board of Accountancy from 1907 to 1910 under Governor Fred M. Warner and again from 1932 to 1935 under Governors Wilber M. Brucker and William A. Comstock. He was active on the Detroit Board of Commerce and served as a trustee of the Detroit Bureau of Governmental Research. But in November 1933 he filed for bankruptcy, declaring he was unemployed and with liabilities of $350,377.46 (he was precise to the end), while claiming assets of only $293.45. His entire personal fortune, including $1 million in stocks, had been carried away by the collapse of the Detroit banking structure in 1933. "Every one of the obligations I owed the Detroit banks, " he testified, "was secured by collateral consisting of shares of stock in the Detroit banks and trust companies. When the crash came, it wiped me out." Three years later, on August 18, 1936, Norval Hawkins died of a heart attack in his home at 470 Merrick Avenue in Detroit. He was sixty-nine years old.

In spite of his achievements in selling and management, Norval Hawkins is today a virtual unknown. The fame and lasting recognition went to such giants in the automobile industry as Henry Ford, Ransom Olds, Henry Leland, William Durant, and Alfred Sloan. But Hawkins's contributions to America's automotive industry—indeed, to the nation in the early twentieth century—are also of giant proportion. A prominent Detroit attorney

rated him "perhaps the greatest salesman the world has ever known . . . original in ideas, forcible in presenting them, a perfect dynamo for work, and a man who got the quickest execution of any man I ever knew." Certainly Hawkins did as much as any other man to convince a generation of Americans that, as he himself once told his regional managers, "The Ford car is part of human life, the necessity of every civilized man and woman."

Publications:
The Selling Process (Detroit, 1918);
Certain Success (Detroit, 1920).

Reference:
Allan Nevins and Frank Ernest Hill, *Ford: The Times, the Man, and the Company* (New York: Scribners, 1954).

Archives:
The Ford Archives at the Henry Ford Museum in Dearborn, Michigan, contains the complete record of Hawkins's years with the Ford Motor Company.

Elwood Haynes

(October 14, 1857-April 13, 1925)

by Ralph D. Gray

Indiana University

CAREER: Professor, Eastern Indiana Normal School (1885-1886); superintendent, Portland (Indiana) Natural Gas & Oil Company (1886-1890); field superintendent, Columbus Construction Company (1890-1892); manager, Indiana Natural Gas & Oil Company (1892-1901); partner (1898-1901), president, Haynes-Apperson Company (1901-1905); president, Haynes Automobile Company (1905-1925); president, Haynes Stellite Company (1912-1920).

Elwood Haynes was an automobile inventor and manufacturer as well as a metallurgical genius who discovered both Stellite and stainless steel. An intuitive experimentalist and instinctive businessman, he manufactured Haynes (originally Haynes-Apperson) automobiles for 30 years and Stellite and other alloys he had developed for eight. Still, he considered himself primarily a scientist, a chemist, or, specifically, a metallurgist, and he aban-

doned the business office in favor of the scientific laboratory whenever possible. Despite a late start in higher education, he managed to convert a good scientific education (at Worcester Polytechnic Institute and Johns Hopkins University) into a series of useful inventions and discoveries that helped transform and modernize the world in which he lived.

Haynes was born in the small agricultural village of Portland, Indiana, on October 14, 1857. He was the son of Judge Jacob M. and Hilinda Haines Haynes, pioneers who had come, separately, to Jay County (organized in 1836) in its earliest years from Massachusetts and Ohio, respectively. They married in 1846 and became the parents of ten children, eight of whom lived to maturity and became prominent citizens. By the time of Haynes's birth in 1857—he was the sixth child—his father was already one of the most distinguished men of the county. As a circuit judge, however, he traveled extensively (usually by horse and buggy), thereby leaving most

Elwood Haynes

of the responsibilities of child rearing in the capable hands of Mrs. Haynes. The results were auspicious. Among the children were a teacher, a banker, a lawyer, a miller, a farmer, a merchant—and Elwood. This sometimes dreamy lad caused no little concern among the family as to his ability to earn a living, but he himself had no such doubts. His early drive was for an education, which he eventually managed to acquire.

This involved not only much independent study and the conduct of some crude, often dangerous experiments, but also, when a high school was finally established in Portland in 1876, his return to school when he was nearly nineteen years old. His two years there qualified him for admission to the Worcester County (Massachusetts) Free Institute of Industrial Science (now Worcester Polytechnic Institute), where he was able to continue his technical education at minimum expense to his family. The school, as its original name indicated, was free to residents of Worcester County, so Haynes moved there in 1878. He completed the three-year program on schedule, although the course of study proved to be quite rigorous (especially that "wicked algebra").

Moreover, despite being the oldest student in the class and a full three years above the average age, Haynes was popular with his classmates, served as class president his junior year, and laid the foundation for his eventual career in metallurgy. For his senior thesis he analyzed the effect of tungsten upon iron and steel, a topic to which he returned 20 years later. It was the addition of tungsten to his binary (two-part) alloys of either cobalt and chromium or nickel and chromium that transformed them into the incredibly hard tool metals (named Stellite by Haynes) that revolutionized the machine tool industry in the 1910s.

Upon graduation from Worcester in 1881, Haynes returned to Portland and embarked upon a teaching career, an activity in which he showed great talent and enjoyed considerable success. He worked his way up from the proverbial one-room schoolhouse, teaching in district schools in Jay County, to the still new Portland High School, serving also as principal, and finally, after additional graduate work at the newly established Johns Hopkins University in Baltimore during 1884 and 1885, he spent one year as professor of science at the Eastern Indiana Normal School in Portland. "I like teaching first rate," he confided to his friend Bertha Lanterman, then living in Alabama, "and the more I teach the better I like it."

This pleasant and comparatively tranquil position was given up, however, upon the discovery of natural gas in Portland in 1886. Haynes had given valuable assistance to the company drilling Jay County's first well in March and April, and subsequently he was persuaded to enter the business full-time. The work proved congenial to Haynes, who supervised the drilling of wells, the piping of the city, and the office operations of the Portland Natural Gas & Oil Company for four years. His talents for invention were utilized in this job, for he designed and installed gas meters suitable for various-sized pipes and variable pressures, an "automatic gas regulator" or thermostat, and a specially made alarm system placed in his home to notify him of any sudden changes in the gas pressure in the lines. His new employment also enabled him, at age thirty, to marry Bertha Lanterman.

Haynes's outstanding management of the Portland gas company brought him to the attention of a Chicago firm, the misnamed Indiana Natural Gas & Oil Company, which was seeking to monopolize the supply of gas to the city of Chicago. Masterminded by Charles T. Yerkes, an urban corruption-ist whose scandalous career supplied novelist Theodore Dreiser with the basis for his central "Frank Cowperwood" character in his trilogy about urban society (*The Financier, The Titan, The Stoic*), the plan called for constructing a pipeline from the heart of the Indiana gas field west of Portland to the Indiana-Illinois border near Lake Michigan. As this project was an unprecedented undertaking, company officials carefully searched for a man to direct the field operations. They decided upon Elwood Haynes, whose name had come up repeatedly as the most knowledgeable natural gas man in the state. Ostensibly working for the Columbus Construction Company, and perhaps unaware of the company's secret ownership by the Yerkes group in Chicago, Haynes accepted the new challenge, moved to Greentown, Indiana, and supervised the construction of two 120-mile-long, 8-inch pipelines across northwest Indiana.

This job, too, required innovation, including Haynes's solution—since used universally—of dehydrating the gas prior to its being pumped through the lines. It was also necessary to erect a pumping station at Greentown, the "largest plant of its kind" in 1901, to install feeder pipes from the many wells surrounding Greentown to the company's reservoir, and to travel extensively along the main line from Greentown to Hammond during the construction period. It was this travel that rekindled Haynes's desire for a mechanical vehicle, one that would relieve his horses of their drudgery and long hours in harness. During a lull in construction activity in 1891 caused by a lawsuit contesting the company's right to ship Indiana gas to points outside the state, Haynes used his free time to make preliminary drawings for a self-propelled vehicle, but he put them aside when construction resumed.

Perhaps Haynes had a chance, following completion of the pipeline, to join the INGO staff in Chicago, but he chose instead to become manager of its Kokomo plant, moving there in December 1892. There his first surviving child—a daughter, Bernice—was born shortly afterward, soon to be followed by a son, March. Haynes lived in Kokomo the rest of his life. His gas company duties afforded him time for other activities, and he soon made important advances in the two careers—as an automobile inventor and manufacturer and as a metallurgical inventor and producer—to which he devoted himself subsequently while employed at the gas company. In-deed, some of his earliest alloys were produced in his gas company office—at night—using tiny crucibles the size of teacups and small gas-fired furnaces to melt the ingredients, and the frame of his first automobile was built from sections of small-diameter gas pipes.

As early as 1890 Haynes wrote to the editors of *Scientific American* to inquire about the most suitable power sources for self-propelled road vehicles: electricity, steam, or gasoline. The editors recommended steam, saying the other types were unproven, but Haynes was not convinced. He made other investigations and drew up preliminary sketches for a vehicle, but he was unable to devote much time to the project until the pipeline to Chicago had been completed and he had moved to Kokomo to open the gas company office there. Soon the city was piped and the plant established, and in 1893 Haynes began serious work toward building his first car. A breakthrough came in fall 1893 when he attended the Chicago World's Fair and visited the exhibit of the Sintz Gas Engine Company of Grand Rapids, Michigan. Believing the Sintz engine, manufactured in different sizes for various marine or boating purposes, could also serve his purposes, Haynes ordered a small, 1-cylinder, 1-horsepower model upon his return home. Delivered in November 1893, Haynes immediately and with near-disastrous results tested it in his home. Shaken loose from its mounting by vibration, the engine careened across the kitchen floor until the battery wires came loose. The reactions of Mrs. Haynes are not known, but soon thereafter Haynes arranged to have further testing of the engine, and a vehicle designed to accommodate it, conducted in a local machine shop, Elmer Apperson's Riverside Machine Works. Apperson agreed to do the job during slack time at a rate of 40 cents an hour for himself and his men, including his younger brother, Edgar, and Jonathan D. Maxwell.

After several months of intermittent labor and some modifications to Haynes's original plans, the vehicle was ready for its initial test run on July 4, 1894. Because of the crowd in town for the national holiday, Haynes and Apperson decided to have the machine towed by horses to the outskirts before attempting to operate it. To the delight of the builders, the engine caught at once (having no crank initially, it was push started), and the car moved off under its own power, reaching a speed of 7 to 8 mph. After traveling a mile and a half eastward, Haynes permitted the car to coast to a stop (it also had no brakes), whereupon it was turned around and driven all the way back to the shop. Unknown to Haynes and his associates, J. Frank Duryea had road-tested his first vehicle the previous fall (in September 1893), but its initial run was far less successful than the "Pioneer's."

As Haynes later described his first car, the framework for the motor "consisted of a double hollow square of steel tubing, joined at the rear corners by steel castings, and by malleable castings in front. The hind axle constituted the rear member of the frame and the front axle was swiveled at its center to the front end of the 'hollow square' in which the motor and countershaft were placed." There were only two forward speeds and no reverse, with the low speed barely "strong enough to move the machine up a 4 per cent. incline. . . . On the other hand, it moved right off on the level road. . . ." Despite the promising beginning, there were still problems to be solved. The engine was too small, and a second, 2-cylinder model obtained from the Sintz company was also unsatisfactory. Subsequent Haynes and Apperson cars featured their own "double opposed" 2-cylinder engines. The steering mechanism on the Pioneer was also unreliable, "positively dangerous," in fact, according to Haynes, and this, too, was modified in subsequent vehicles.

In 1895 Haynes and Apperson, now in partnership, built a second car to enter a race held in Chicago on November 28, 1895. This race, the first in America for automobiles, had but a few entrants, including European cars and electric cars. Only the Duryea brothers, who won the race, and Haynes-Apperson were on hand with gasoline-powered vehicles built in America. Unfortunately, the Haynes-Apperson car damaged a wheel en route to the starting line on race day and was unable to compete. The company won a prize, however, for its "double opposed" engine, and the interest the car attracted in Chicago induced Haynes and Apperson to continue their partnership and begin producing automobiles on order. In 1898 they organized the Haynes-Apperson Company to begin relatively large-scale production (50 cars a year were targeted), and the company enjoyed reasonable success for nearly 30 years.

At the outset Haynes and Apperson made several notable improvements in their automobile. Some of their ideas were patented, but others were merely incorporated into their cars without protec-

tion. Of particular pride to Haynes were the metallurgical innovations. He was the first manufacturer to use aluminum in an engine and a nickel-steel alloy elsewhere in the car. Another distinction of the company was an early long-distance travel record. In 1899 Haynes and Edgar Apperson fulfilled the terms of a buyer's agreement by driving one of their automobiles to New York, perhaps the first 1,000-mile trip by automobile in the nation.

Apperson withdrew in 1901 to start, with his brother, his own automobile company, at which time Haynes left the gas company to devote himself, briefly, full-time to the automobile business. Haynes personally managed the company only in times of crisis—following Apperson's departure, after a 1911 fire, and during the financial problems of 1923 and 1924. In 1905 Haynes changed the corporate name to Haynes Automobile Company. In the years that followed, both Haynes and Apperson, now competitors, stressed the longevity of their careers and vied with each other for recognition as the builder of "America's First Car" (the Haynes Automobile Company slogan), a contest in which Haynes prevailed.

Indeed, as early as 1908 Haynes was generally recognized in the United States as the inventor of the American automobile. He enjoyed this reputation throughout his lifetime, although critics from time to time sought to strip it from him. Charles Duryea was particularly upset at the neglect of the Duryea claim to priority, but he damaged his cause by claiming an 1892, not the proper 1893, date for the first Duryea and by claiming personal credit for things his brother had done. Henry Ford and others were similarly vague and misleading, if not intentionally dishonest, in dating their first vehicles. As a result of the confusion created, Haynes's claims to priority were not challenged successfully until after his death. It must have been especially gratifying for Haynes when he led the "historical section" of a 2,000-car parade down New York City's Broadway in April 1908. The celebration, designed to commemorate the first decade of the automobile in New York, featured an evening parade headed by Haynes driving the Pioneer, followed by ten other Haynes automobiles, one for each year of the decade. What may have pleased the inventor even more was the performance of his first car, then 15 years old and once termed by Haynes as "never much account." While testing it shortly after its arrival by train on the afternoon of the parade,

Haynes in his first car, tested (contrary to the sign) on July 4, 1894 (courtesy of the Motor Vehicle Manufacturers Association)

Haynes was arrested by a New York City policeman for speeding. Two years later, the Haynes Pioneer was donated to the Smithsonian Institution, where it is on permanent display.

In 1919, when asked to comment on a biographical sketch of himself being prepared for publication, Haynes gave his own view of his role in developing the automobile. He took exception to a statement "which gives me credit for originating the automobile. I have never claimed this distinction, and I do not believe that it belongs to me. It is generally conceded, however, that the little machine which I constructed in 1893-1894 was the first complete gasoline automobile built in the United States. Some attempts were being made in Europe at the time, but I was not aware of them."

Neither was automobile manufacturing his sole, or even his primary, activity. He gave personal direction to the automobile company from 1901 to 1905, when a reorganization took place and he was able to return to some metallurgical experiments that had reached a promising point just before their abandonment in 1901. Only slight growth occurred

in the automobile company, however, during the next few years. Production had averaged just under 250 cars per year early in the new century, and annual output rose to approximately 350 cars by 1910. At first Haynes not only wrote the advertising copy for the automobile company, as is clear from the heavy doses of technical information included, but he also published accounts in trade journals, especially *Horseless Age*, which analyzed, for example, the merits of the hydrocarbon (gasoline) engine over rival sources of power. In 1902 and 1903 he wrote a series of advertisements featuring such "good points" of the Haynes-Apperson car as its "famous double cylinder balanced motor," its 3-speed transmission (far superior to the "French gear"), its "new carburetors" (one for each cylinder), and its improved steering and suspension systems. From the beginning, Haynes also emphasized the antiquity of his company—"*Notice When We Commenced—1893*"—and the remarkable performances of Haynes-Apperson vehicles in all the early speed and endurance contests they had entered.

The first cars were simply identified by year and type—surreys, standards, or runabouts—but in 1902 letters began to be used. The surrey became Model A; the standard, Model B; the runabout, Model C. In 1903 these models were, respectively, G, H, and I. In 1904 only two models (F and J) were produced, but the next year the company introduced its first 4-cylinder cars (Model K). Subsequently the company concentrated on either 30- or 50-horsepower touring cars, the latter being similar to the racing models entered in the first two Vanderbilt Cup races in 1904 and 1905 (won by Frenchmen). Rather than racing, however, Haynes preferred the endurance or reliability runs of the type sponsored by Charles J. Glidden, and Haynes frequently participated in them personally. He also was the star attraction on a transcontinental tour undertaken by some 22 Indiana-made cars and trucks in 1913.

By that time the Haynes Automobile Company had become the largest manufacturing concern in Kokomo. As early as 1908 the Haynes plant, occupying three large factory buildings, employed approximately 500 workers, and its production capacity exceeded 350 cars a year. Small in comparison with the automotive leaders in Detroit, Haynes nevertheless was one of the largest 20 or 25 companies in the United States by the time Henry Ford introduced his Model T, and it continued to produce a sizable number of good, reliable, medium- to high-priced automobiles for a decade. Sales averaged more than 4,000 cars a year from 1910 to 1923 but tailed off precipitously after that.

Haynes had been called back into active service with the automobile company in 1911 after a disastrous fire, and he oversaw the rebuilding of a modernized manufacturing plant. This, coupled with another management reorganization, kicked off the most prosperous period in Haynes Automobile Company history. The 1913 Haynes cars featured electric lights, a self-starter, and a new 6-cylinder engine. These "Light Six" models were popular, and during 1915 and 1916 the Haynes plant operated day and night to keep up with demand. This led to additional plant expansion and modernization in 1916. A. G. Seiberling, who returned from the Apperson company to become general manager at Haynes in 1912, is usually given credit for the company's rapid development, which saw sales reach peak levels of more than $10 million on a volume of 7,100 units in 1916.

The succeeding war years, however, were difficult ones, and Seiberling's postwar plans for a small car were scuttled. In the meantime, his overly eager purchase of high-priced raw materials to replenish plant inventories plunged the company into debt, from which it never recovered. A successful $1 million bond drive in Kokomo in 1923 kept the company going for another year, but it failed in 1924. The final cars, assembled from stock on hand, rolled off the line in February 1925.

There had been an unfortunate advertising war in 1920 with the Apperson company, initiated by the advertising departments of the rival Kokomo firms, over who deserved major credit for building what both misnamed "America's First Car." This might be seen as a rather desperate attempt by both companies to retain an adequate share of the automobile market for cars in their price range, which, while dropping, could not compete with the far-greater production economies being realized in Detroit. Nothing could save them: Ford controlled 55 percent of the market in the early 1920s, and soon, by the mid 1920s, such industry pioneers as Winton and Maxwell, as well as Haynes and Apperson, disappeared from the scene.

Long before that happened, Haynes had made his mark in the world as a metallurgist. He had experimented with metals throughout his life—as a boy in Portland, for his senior thesis at Worcester, in his spare time in Portland, in Greentown, and in Kokomo, while engaged primarily in the natural gas and automobile industries. Eventually two companies based upon his metallurgical discoveries—Haynes Stellite and American Stainless Steel—were established. The initial development work for both was done in a small laboratory the gas company permitted Haynes to establish in the room above his office. A subsequent series of metallurgical experiments, conducted between 1904 and 1912, was carried out in a converted barn located at the back of Haynes's residential property.

As early as 1887, while still in Portland, Haynes began a series of experiments in search of an alloy that "would resist the oxidizing influences of the atmosphere, and . . . take a good cutting edge." In other words Haynes was searching for a nontarnishable metal suitable for table cutlery. At first he tested various copper alloys but considered them unsuitable; he next worked with minor success with some of the rarer metals. His first satisfactory alloy, a pure nickel-chromium combination, was produced in 1898, and the following year he made a pure alloy of cobalt and chromium. The two binary combinations were the first ones Haynes patented, claiming the general properties of durable luster, resistance to atmospheric oxidization, and hardness. He suggested that the cobalt-based product, which he subsequently named Stellite (for its starlike brilliance), could be "substituted for mild tempered steel in the manufacture of edge tools, as table and pocket cutlery, physicians' and dentists' instruments, or standards of weight [and] measures." These alloys were announced to the scientific and industrial world in 1910 at the San Francisco conference of the American Chemical Society, where Haynes presented a paper.

The paper aroused considerable interest in the alloys. Not only did Haynes receive several orders (which he was unable to fill) but he also came in contact with Thomas Southworth, an official of the Deloro Smelting & Refining Company in Canada. The Deloro firm, located near Cobalt, Ontario, was seeking an outlet for its vast supplies of cobalt, then considered a nearly worthless by-product in the production of silver. Its primary use prior to the development of Stellite was as a coloring agent in the manufacture of ceramics. Haynes arranged to obtain a supply of cobalt from Southworth, who in turn obtained a license to produce Stellite in Canada and certain other countries. Southworth also provided assistance through various Sheffield, England, firms in fabricating Stellite tableware. The cutlers there soon learned, as did American firms Haynes engaged to produce pocketknives, that Stellite's hardness made it very difficult to manipulate for those purposes.

Consequently, Haynes investigated other possible uses for his alloys. A major step forward came when Haynes added tungsten and molybdenum to the cobalt and chromium. This made an alloy of remarkable hardness, and machine tools made from it proved far superior to the "high speed steel" tools being used. Haynes applied for patents on three tool-metal alloys in July 1912, which were promptly granted, and he began the manufacture of Stellite in fall 1912.

He erected a small factory, barely 50 feet by 50 feet, near the site of his automobile plant; the initial work force consisted of only four people. As explained by a secretary years later, Haynes had an office where he worked with and then weighed the different materials before taking them into the fur-

nace room. He experimented "almost every day," and after being in the furnace room with its "terrific heat and noise" would come "hurrying in and write the results in a notebook." During this time, indeed, Haynes was more interested in doing experimental work and developing new and unusual uses for Stellite than in producing large quantities of the metal. He also was lax in establishing quality-control methods. The business grossed only $7,000 in 1913, its first full year of operation, $11,000 in 1914, and $48,000 in 1915 (the year of incorporation). Three grades of tool metal were then being produced, using a battery of 16 tiny gas furnaces. The crucibles held 15-pound charges, which melted in approximately 90 minutes. Later Haynes converted to electric arc furnaces, which took charges up to 500 pounds. In 1918, the banner year for the Haynes Stellite Company for more than two decades (because of the demands of wartime production), all of the Stellite produced in the United States came from three Snyder electric furnaces housed in a small concrete block building in south Kokomo. Their combined capacity exceeded four tons per 11-hour day, with total sales for the year exceeding $3.5 million.

By this time Union Carbide & Carbon Corporation was taking an increased interest in the Indiana firm, and purchase negotiations began in 1919. An excess profits tax then in effect required that 80 percent of the purchase price above the capitalization figure (still at $50,000) go to the federal government, or more than $2.5 million, so the sale fell through. A year later, however, a transfer was effected by means of a stock exchange, and Union Carbide operated a Stellite division for 50 years. Sold in 1970 to Cabot Corporation, greatly expanded and diversified Stellite plants in Kokomo and elsewhere continue to produce a variety of high-performance alloys, precision castings, and powdered ceramics for an international market.

During the last years of his life, Haynes was intimately connected with a second metals company, the American Stainless Steel Company, but it remains moot whether or not Haynes should be credited with the discovery of stainless steel. Metallurgist Carl A. Zapffe, a careful student of the history of high-chromium iron and the gradual development of stainless steel, considers the discovery a European advance, made from 1903 to 1908, and he credits Haynes and an Englishman, Harry Brearley, with its commercial development. These statements are based upon a thorough knowledge of the metallurgy involved and a broad study of the printed records, but he did not examine Haynes's work in detail. Zapffe stated, moreover, that the work of some of the men involved was perhaps conducted "without foreknowledge of the investigations" in Europe. The case is not unlike that involving the automobile—many people in Europe and America were at work on both developments simultaneously, both resulted from a cumulative process, and in both instances Europeans were in the forefront. It seems clear, however, that Haynes—working alone and without knowledge of events abroad—both produced an early American automobile and learned that stainlessness could be imparted to steel by the addition of sufficient quantities of chromium. Haynes made the latter discovery in a series of experiments carried out between November 1911 and April 1912.

When inquiries made by Haynes among the steel trade revealed that "a non-rusting or non-tarnishing" alloy could not be purchased because "no such alloy existed," he was encouraged to seek a patent for his new discovery. Chrome-iron alloys, of course, were not new, as Haynes recognized, but his discovery was not the alloy but the fact that chromium above a certain percentage imparted immunity to atmospheric influences. The patent office, however, rejected Haynes's application in May 1912, and it was not until March 1915 that he reapplied. This was prompted by reports from England of a similar discovery, but Haynes's application antedated by nearly a year that of Harry Brearley for the "rustless iron" he had developed. Even Haynes's reapplication, after a second rejection, came two weeks before the Brearley petition. Haynes was again denied, but Brearley received a patent in September 1916. Haynes filed for an interference, which he eventually obtained, and was granted a patent on stainless steel in April 1919. By that time, however, Haynes and Brearley had merged their interests in the American Stainless Steel Company, a licensing company that was successful in having its two stainless steel patents upheld in court. Virtually all of the stainless steel producers in America during the 17-year life of Haynes's patent paid a small royalty to the American Stainless Steel Company.

It may be said of Haynes that he enjoyed success in numerous undertakings. He was an effective teacher, but he gave up that career to become the builder of a fine municipal gas system and an unpre-cedentedly long pipeline to Chicago. Later he invented one of the first automobiles in America, and he subsequently manufactured automobiles until 1925. His greatest work, however, was in the development of new alloys, both ferrous and nonferrous, that helped pave the way for the great technological strides of the twentieth century.

Good fortune, happy circumstance, and timing played a role in his success, but Haynes had an uncanny ability to be at the forefront of most of the exciting new industrial and technological breakthroughs in his state during his lifetime. The first can be ascribed primarily to preparation and circumstance—Indiana's first commercial gas well was drilled in Portland—but Haynes placed himself in the right place at the right time to initiate the automobile industry in Indiana, to account for the development of Stellite, and to participate in the commercial development of stainless steel. Neither exceptionally bright nor a fast learner, Haynes had the capacity to absorb completely that which he had learned, and he exhibited rare tenacity and perseverance in pursuing his goals and fighting for his just rights of invention and discovery. He was quick to turn away from the daily routine of business, however, in favor of furthering his research endeavors and promoting various "causes," of which there were many. His most cherished reform was Prohibition, something for which he had worked since the 1870s, but he also strongly advocated United States adoption of the metric system and entry into the League of Nations, and he warmly supported many religious and charitable organizations. His final struggles were to save the Haynes Automobile Company, which failed in late 1924, and the validity of his Stellite and stainless steel patents. Success in the latter two efforts came shortly after his death in April 1925.

Selected Publications:

"Natural Gas," in *Biographical and Historical Record of Jay and Blackford Counties, Indiana* (Chicago: Lewis, 1887), pp. 217-226;

"The Hydrocarbon Engine as a Source of Energy," *Horseless Age* (January 17, 1900): 14-15;

"The Characteristics of the Gasoline Motor," *Horseless Age* (December 18, 1901): 822;

"Alloys of Nickel and Cobalt with Chromium," *Journal of Industrial and Engineering Chemistry*, 2 (1910): 397-401;

" 'Stellite': A New Alloy," *Scientific American* (November 19, 1910): 398;

The Complete Motorist (Chicago, 1914);

"The Uses of Stellite in the Machine Shop," *Iron Age*, 93 (January 8, 1914): 148-149;

"How I Built the First Car," *Haynes Pioneer* (July 1918): 5-7, 11;

"Stellite and Stainless Steel," *Proceedings of the Engineering Society of Western Pennsylvania*, 35 (1920): 467-482.

References:

Jacob Piatt Dunn, "Elwood Haynes," in *Indiana and Indianans: A History of Aboriginal and Territorial Indiana*, 5 volumes (Chicago: American Historical Society, 1919);

M. J. Duryea, "America's First Automobile Controversy," *Antique Automobile*, 1 (December 1953): 125-147;

O. D. Foster, "How Elwood Haynes Came to Build First 'Horseless Carriage,' " *Forbes*, 15 (March 1, 1925): 679-682;

Ralph D. Gray, *Alloys and Automobiles: The Life of Elwood Haynes* (Indianapolis: Indiana Historical Society, 1979);

Gray, *Stellite: A History of the Haynes Stellite Company, 1912-1972* (Kokomo, Ind., 1974);

Mary Ellen Harshbowser, "Elwood Haynes: Scientist with a Social Conscience," dissertation, Ball State University, 1964;

Clifton J. Phillips, *Indiana In Transition: The Emergence of an Industrial Commonwealth, 1880-1920* (Indianapolis: Indiana Historical Society, 1968);

Joseph S. Powell, "History of Elwood Haynes and the Automobile Industry," thesis, Indiana University, 1948;

Carl A. Zapffe, "Who Discovered Stainless Steel?," *Iron Age*, 162 (October 1948): 120-129.

Archives:

The major collection of Elwood Haynes's papers is located in the Elwood Haynes Museum in Kokomo, Indiana; it includes family and business correspondence for the years between 1878 and 1925, but is reasonably complete only for the period after 1913. The business records of Haynes's three companies—the Haynes Automobile, the Haynes Stellite, and the American Stainless Steel companies—have not survived, but other materials relating to Haynes are scattered in contemporary newspapers and journals, scientific and technical publications, and various special collections in libraries in Detroit, Indianapolis, and Kokomo.

Headlamps

by James Wren

Motor Vehicle Manufacturing Association

During horse-and-carriage days the lighting of vehicles for night travel consisted of lanterns used as markers or signals to alert oncoming pedestrians or other carriages. Candles were the initial light source, used until coal-oil or kerosene lanterns were adequately developed for motor vehicles.

Headlamps were not included by the pioneer manufacturers on early automobiles. Consequently, at that time automobile travel was usually restricted to the daylight hours. If desired, however, lights could be added through a carriage-equipment supplier.

The increased speed and power of automobiles after the turn of the century necessitated the use of additional lights mounted in front of the vehicle so the driver could see the road or obstacles ahead. Reflectors were eventually placed behind the carriage-type lamps in an attempt to project the light further, but the light was initially inadequate for good visibility.

By 1902 the carbide lamp was made available as an accessory item by some automobile firms. The carbide light source was derived from acetylene gas, which was generated when sodium carbide was placed in contact with water. The result of burning the acetylene gas was a flickering light that later was amplified by parabolic reflectors.

The use of carbide lamps continued until about 1908, but the system proved too hazardous and was a maintenance nuisance. Removal, disassembly, and cleaning of the burner lights, reflectors, and diffusers were major chores. Despite the use of divergent lenses to alter the annoying glare from the lamps, and despite improvements in the gas generator by 1908, the gas lighting system was giving way to electric lighting systems such as the Apple system, which used small belt-driven dynamos in conjunction with a storage battery.

In 1910 the Peerless Company offered the Gray Davis positive drive dynamo as standard equipment for lighting. But the dramatic breakthrough occurred in 1911 when Delco introduced the battery-generator electrical system, which provided high voltage for starting and lower voltage for lighting and ignition. A workable system had been devised, but focusing the light beam continued to be a problem.

Manufacturers experimented with ways to lower the headlamp beam for several years. Finally, in 1915 Cadillac offered tilt-beam headlights that provided adequate illumination but could also be adjusted so as not to disturb oncoming motorists.

Magnus Hendrickson

(1864-1944)

by Genevieve Wren

Motor Vehicle Research Services

CAREER: Logger and laborer, Wisconsin and Michigan (1888-1896); bicycle shop owner, Chicago (1896), White Cloud, Michigan (1896-1900); co-owner, Hendrickson-Danielson Machine Shop (1900-1902); owner and partner, automotive firms (1903-1907); chief engineer, Lauth-Juergens Motor Company (1907-1913); founder, Hendrickson Motor Truck Company (1913).

In 1906 Magnus Hendrickson invented the hollow-spoke wheel, which is still used in trucks today. He is also famous as the designer of the tandem-axle suspension system, introduced in 1926. Born in Sweden in the rural community of Mangskog in 1864, Hendrickson began to display an interest in engineering early in his life. As a youngster he spent hours in his uncle's machine shop, intrigued with the mechanics of construction and repair. He ceased formal education at the grammar school level, but he continued to study informally for the rest of his life. As an adult he spoke fluently on almost any subject, from religion to politics to the fine points of mechanical engineering.

After a year with the Swedish Army Corps of Engineers Hendrickson sailed from his native country to America in 1887. He went to Chicago and fell in love with the booming young city, "flexing its muscles for the coming of the twentieth century." He loved the "clattering and clanging of raw materials that flowed in by barge, engine, and rail" to be fashioned by men and machines. He settled in the city and married Edla Nyman there in 1888. The couple would have five children: Esther, Bob, George, Agnes, and Carl. Hendrickson's three sons displayed his talent for mechanics and eventually succeeded their father in the family trucking business.

After marrying, Hendrickson and his wife lived in rural Wisconsin and Michigan, where Hendrickson found work machine jobbing and logging. In 1896 the couple moved back to Chicago, and Hendrickson started a bicycle shop. Then with a partner he began manufacturing the Gladstone bicycle in White Cloud, Michigan. At the same time he began experimenting with various types of gasoline engines, starting with a 4-cylinder version that lay flat in a configuration now popular in city buses. He never completed it. Still, one of his sons remembered, "he couldn't shake ideas about building trucks." In 1900 he returned to Chicago to found the Hendrickson-Danielson Machine Shop with his brother-in-law with the idea of furthering his engine experiments.

In the new shop Hendrickson built one of his first trucks, equipped with regular wagon-type wooden-spoke wheels with steel bands for tires. He also began working on passenger-car designs and sold a passenger car, a 1-cylinder model built entirely with his own hands, to a local doctor in 1902. The following year he designed a clutch that is still in use and built several more cars and trucks. Also in 1903 he reorganized the Hendrickson-Danielson company in partnership with J. Lauth to custom-build cars and trucks. That company continued until 1907, when it became the Lauth-Juergens Motor Company, located in Fremont, Ohio.

Meanwhile, motivated by growing industry dissatisfaction with the reinforced wagon-type wooden-spoke wheels used in the vast majority of cars and trucks of the day, Hendrickson invented the hollow-spoke steel wheel in 1906. The design, a major breakthrough, resulted in lighter yet stronger wheels and in the trucking industry opened the door to bigger vehicles and greater payloads.

Hendrickson served as chief engineer at Lauth-Juergens from 1907 to 1913. During that time he helped pioneer the manufacture of tilt-cabs, three-speed truck transmissions capable of moving loads at 60 mph, a two-speed bevel-gear transmission for chain-drive cars, and improvements in truck axles and transmissions.

In 1913 Hendrickson moved back to Chicago to begin the Hendrickson Motor Truck Company with sons George, Bob, and Carl. The firm began to supply trucks to meat, cheese, and candy wholesalers, coal dealers, stone haulers, refuse collectors, and building contractors. The firm prospered, branching out to manufacture custom-built trucks and its own patented truck hoists. In 1926 it introduced the Hendrickson 6-wheeler, featuring a tandem suspension unit using an equalizing beam to distribute the load evenly and at the same time reduce the effects of bumps in the road by 50 percent. The success of the design ensured good business and full employment for the firm even through the Depression.

In 1933 the Hendrickson company signed a 20-year contract to produce heavy-duty tandem suspensions for International Harvester. The company's product line further expanded that year with the introduction of diesel engines. In the late 1930s Hendrickson started installing Cummins diesel engines in International Harvester trucks. New methods, new machinery, new materials, and new products led to continual expansion. The war emergency of the 1940s meant even greater production rates, now for the Allies. Another boom followed the peace. Two out of every three trucks manufactured in America today are equipped with Hendrickson tandem suspensions. Hendrickson's sons continued their father's sound management of the company after he retired. Hendrickson died in 1944.

References:

Hendrickson Manufacturing Company, *The Second Fifty* (Avon, Ill., 1964);

James Wren and Genevieve Wren, *Motor Trucks of America* (Ann Arbor: University of Michigan Press, 1979).

George M. Holley

(April 14, 1878-June 27, 1963)

by George S. May

Eastern Michigan University

CAREER: General manager, Holley Motor Company (1899-1905); president, Holley Brothers Company (1905-1917); president (1918-1930), chairman, Holley Carburetor Company (1930-1963).

George Malvin Holley, whose name has been on auto carburetors since the start of the twentieth century, was born in Port Jervis, New York, on April 14, 1878, the son of Ada E. and Franklin Pierce Holley, a businessman and hotel owner. Young Holley attended a military school, Clinton Liberal Institute, in Fort Plains, New York, and Stevens Preparatory School in Hoboken, New Jersey. While still in school in Hoboken he worked in a shipyard, and in 1896, after leaving school, he gained experience as a machinist.

Like so many mechanically minded young people of his generation, Holley was swept up in the enthusiasm for motorized vehicles. In the mid 1890s he built a 3-wheeled automobile, but then he and his younger brother Earl became interested in motorcycles. They built and sold a few motorcycle engines before forming the Holley Motor Company in 1899 to produce a motorcycle of their design. George Holley served as general manager of the Bradford, Pennsylvania-based firm, and over the next three years between 200 and 300 of the 2-wheelers were produced. George Holley claimed that the Holley was the first practical motorcycle. Its 2.25-horsepower motor was attached at the crank handle, the lowest and strongest part of the vehicle's frame, providing an improved distribution of weight that eliminated much of the vibration common to earlier motorcycles. The low attachment point also enabled the motor to perform more efficiently, so that the cycle could ascend a 20-percent in-

George M. Holley

cline "without the aid of pedals."

To demonstrate the superiority of the Holley cycle, George Holley raced it, setting several speed records in 1901. In 1902 he received a medal from the Metropole Cycling Club of New York for riding one of the bikes from Boston to New York in the country's first motorcycle endurance event. That year also saw the appearance of the Holley Motorette, a small 1-cylinder car. Perhaps 100 were sold, with one version in 1903 including kerosene lamps and a steering wheel that could be tilted and locked in place.

Had they continued with vehicle production, like nearly all early auto companies tried to do, the Holleys would probably not have survived for long. Fortunately for them, they also got into the manufacture of carburetors. They had become the American sales agents for the French Longuemare carburetor, which they used in the original Holley motorcycle, but George Holley worked on developing an improved carburetor, and the company began to manufacture it. Although a few were sold to such eastern automakers as E. R. Thomas and George N. Pierce, the orders the Holleys got from Detroit convinced them to abandon the effort to produce entire vehi-

cles and instead specialize in the production of one part.

Sometime in 1903 or 1904 George Holley came to Detroit and obtained an order from the Olds Motor Works to supply carburetors for a 2-cylinder Oldsmobile the company was preparing to produce. Back in Bradford, a telegram from Henry Ford assured the success of the operation. Ford had seen an article on the Holley carburetor in a trade journal. Although he had received a patent on a carburetor in 1898, neither the one he had designed nor others he had tried had proved entirely satisfactory, so he asked George Holley to come to Detroit, and Holley went back for a meeting. Holley recalled some 40 years later that he found Ford and C. Harold Wills, Ford's principal engineering associate, "sitting in the pattern shop on a bench. . . . They told me they would like to have me design a carburetor for their new car." The encouragement Holley received from that contact, combined with the earlier order from Olds, convinced him and his brother in 1905 to sell the Holley Motor Company and move to Detroit. They formed the Holley Brothers Company with George Holley as president and began manufacturing their carburetor in space rented from the Michigan Lubricating Company.

Although the Holley carburetor would be used by many companies, the Ford Motor Company was by far the most important customer. Henry Ford had few if any close friends, but he took a liking to George Holley. He sometimes brought the younger man into the experimental room where Ford and his staff worked on plans for new models. Ford had his playful moods, and one worker recalled that Ford and Holley would be having a discussion, "and the first thing you knew, they'd both be on the floor wrestling." Holley was present at some of the planning sessions for the Model T, and when the prototype of that car was completed, Ford had Holley take him on a test run through downtown Detroit. Ford, exulting in the car's performance, had Holley drive past the office of Alexander Malcomson, the cofounder of the Ford Motor Company who had left in 1906 in part because he did not agree with Ford that the company should be producing a low-cost car.

George Holley had a special interest in the Model T, for it included a new carburetor he and his brother had designed. They first built a brass carburetor but then turned to a lighter, lower-cost iron version that was used in all of the more than 15 million Model T's produced from 1908 to 1927. The unprecedented volume of Model T production soon absorbed the entire output of the Holley Company. In 1917 the brothers sold it to Ford.

The following year the Holley brothers formed the Holley Kerosene Carburetor Company, with George Holley again serving as president. The company soon expanded beyond the kerosene carburetor the brothers designed for the new Ford tractor and was renamed the Holley Carburetor Company. The brothers continued their close relationship with Ford, and the new company supplied half of the carburetors used in the Ford Model A (which replaced the Model T late in 1927). Holley also expanded into the production of accelerator foot pedals, cooling fans, distributors, and heat regulators. In 1927 it entered the aviation field with a carburetor for a Curtiss-Wright plane, and in 1935 it made a variable Venturi carburetor for the Douglas DC-3 that eliminated most of the problems with icing. During World War II Holley carburetors were used in many American and British planes as well as in PT boats and jeeps. Turbine controls, afterburner controls, and miscellaneous valves and actuators were also produced for Westinghouse and Pratt & Whitney gas turbine and turboprop engines.

In May 1946 the automobile industry celebrated the 50th anniversary of auto production in the United States at a banquet in Detroit, and George Holley was seated at the head table with such other surviving industry pioneers as Ransom E. Olds, J. Frank Duryea, and Henry Ford. "Here we are," Ford said to Holley. "Two old buddies growing old, and drinking milk together." Ford, 15 years older than Holley, had indeed grown old and feeble. He was no longer head of the Ford company, and within a year he would be dead. Holley, however, was still very active. He was a member of professional and social organizations and clubs in Detroit, Grosse Pointe, Michigan, and Palm Springs, California, and he enjoyed horseback riding, square dancing, and raising purebred cattle at a ranch in Lake Placid, New York. He was also still

very much involved in the Holley Carburetor Company. Since 1930 he had been chairman of the board, and in the postwar boom period he would oversee the expansion of Holley operations. All Ford, Lincoln, and Mercury cars and trucks used carburetors, distributors, and heat regulators built by Holley or produced under Holley's authorization. Holley fuel and ignition parts were used in Mack, GMC, White, and International trucks, and Holley's aircraft division produced parts for military planes.

George Holley married Margery Corliss in 1909, and they had three children. Following Holley's death on June 27, 1963, the oldest child, George M. Holley, Jr., who had joined the company in 1938, moved up to chairman of the board. In April 1968, 50 years after it had been founded, the Holley Carburetor Company was acquired by Colt Industries. One of the early conglomerates, in 1964 Colt had acquired its corporate name from the firearms maker that had been one of its early acquisitions. The Holley takeover marked the beginning of Colt's automotive business, one of the strongest elements in the often-troubled conglomerate, which went private in 1988 through a leveraged buyout. From their headquarters in Warren, Michigan, the Holley Automotive and Holley Replacement Parts divisions of Colt continue to supply carburetors, fuel injection systems, and other parts to the Big Three, to other transportation equipment manufacturers, and to the parts and replacement market.

References:
Robert Lacey, *Ford: The Men and the Machine* (Boston: Little, Brown, 1986);

Eugene W. Lewis, *Motor Memories: A Saga of Whirling Gears* (Detroit: Alved, 1947);

Allan Nevins and Frank Ernest Hill, *Ford: The Times, the Man, the Company* (New York: Scribners, 1954).

Archives:
Material on George M. Holley can be found in the Ford Archives, Henry Ford Museum, Dearborn, Michigan.

Horns

by James Wren

Motor Vehicle Manufacturers Association

Since the beginning of recorded history man has used audible signals and devices to announce his arrival, departure, or location. With the advent of steam locomotion the use of steam whistles developed. The introduction of the bicycle marked the first use of a driver-actuated sound device for individualized transportation. A bell or an air-bulb horn was attached to the handlebars of the bicycle within easy reach of the rider.

With the arrival of the horseless carriage, whistles, air-bulb horns, and bells were quickly adapted as audible signals. The foot-operated bell was a particular favorite on electric vehicles, the pull-string steam whistle continued to find favor with steam-vehicle users, and the hand-operated rubber air bulb was used on gas-operated motor cars. The air bulb dominated the field. It was not only inexpensive but could be mounted in various locations. The basic air bulb was attached to a short brass horn. However, lengthy, curving brass horns—often in the shape of a serpent—became a fad, especially for the roadsters or sportier touring cars. The operation of a bulb horn merely required squeezing the rubber air bulb, and the sound was produced by a vibrating reed.

In 1908, when the Lowell-McConnell Manufacturing Company purchased the patent rights to a horn, its founder F. W. Lowell coined the term *Klaxon* for his product. The company then contrived a most ambitious advertising scheme by locating signs throughout the United States on major highways, especially on curved roads, advising motorists to "Sound Your Klaxon." The success of their endeavor resulted in the Klaxon almost becoming the generic expression for an automobile horn.

By 1915 a diaphragm-type, electrically operated motor horn became standard equipment on many cars. The diaphragm was of thin vanadium steel and was vibrated about 3,000 times a minute by a rotor or toothed wheel. Dry cells or a storage battery provided the electricity for operation of the horn. The sizes of motor horns and their prices diminished over the years until the 1940s, when the technology stabilized.

Air-bulb horn on a Ford Model T, circa 1909

Hudson Motor Car Company

by George S. May

Eastern Michigan University

With the formation of Hudson Motor Car Company in 1909 several former employees of the Olds Motor Works finally achieved control of their own firm. Early in 1906 Roy Dikeman Chapin, former sales manager at Olds, persuaded the Buffalo automaker E. R. Thomas to back a new company, E. R. Thomas-Detroit, with Chapin, Howard E. Coffin (Olds' former chief engineer), and two other Olds alums, Frederick O. Bezner and James J. Brady, as stockholders and officers with Thomas. E. R. Thomas-Buffalo handled sales of the Detroit car, which was designed by Coffin. In 1908 Thomas decided not to continue actively in the business and sold out to Hugh Chalmers, formerly of the National Cash Register Company, and Thomas-Detroit was renamed Chalmers-Detroit.

In February 1909 Chalmers, Chapin, Coffin, Bezner, Brady, and Roscoe B. Jackson (a new recruit from Olds who was married to Hudson's niece) formed the Hudson Motor Car Company, named after principal investor Joseph L. Hudson, owner of Detroit's largest department store. Initially, the firm was a kind of subsidiary of Chalmers-Detroit, producing a lower-priced car. But by the end of the year a complete break between the two was arranged. Chalmers sold his 1,334 shares of Hudson stock to Chapin, Coffin, and Bezner for $80,040, and they sold their 7,880 shares of Chalmers stock to Chalmers for $788,000. They also bought Brady's Hudson stock for $54,150. In the ensuing reshuffling of Hudson personnel Chapin became president of the company, Coffin vice-president and chief engineer, Bezner secretary, and Jackson treasurer and general manager. Joseph Hudson served as chairman, but aside from asserting himself on some financial matters he left the management of the company to Chapin and the others. At the time of Hudson's death in 1912 Chapin, Coffin, and Bezner each owned 20,772 shares in the company; Jackson had 11,007; Hudson's nephew,

R. H. Webber, had 7,200; and the executor of Hudson's estate controlled another 7,200. The only other person owning Hudson stock was W. J. McAneeny, a Hudson executive recruited from Pope-Hartford.

Under the direction of Chapin, Coffin, Bezner, and Jackson, Hudson quickly established itself as one of the industry's strongest and most innovative companies. One thousand small 4-cylinder cars were produced in the first year of operations, and in 1910 the company moved into new and larger Detroit facilities, and production rose to 4,500. With Coffin in charge of design and Jackson directing production, in 1912 Hudson introduced a 6-cylinder model with a Delco self-starter that had been introduced earlier that year on the Cadillac. In 1915, when total sales were nearly 13,000, Hudson was the largest producer of 6-cylinder cars in the world. The company's reputation was further enhanced in 1916 when it introduced the first dynamically balanced crankshaft, which eliminated the vibration and rattle so characteristic of early cars.

Despite that record Hudson's profits were disappointing. For a time in 1916 Chapin and his associates were apparently ready to surrender their independence and make Hudson part of a new combination also to include Chalmers, Willys-Overland, and Electric Auto-Lite (all controlled by John North Willys), and the United Motor Company, a new combination of five parts manufacturers that William C. Durant had put together. The new company was to be called American Motors. For some reason, probably because New York banker and close Durant ally Louis H. Kaufman could not arrange the financing, the deal fell through.

Chapin and his associates were probably not unhappy to see the merger plans misfire. They then concentrated on improving Hudson's profitability. They cut costs by producing more parts in-house, and, more important, they expanded the company's

The 1910 Hudson Model 20

product lines. Little came of Chapin's suggestion that Hudson move into the production of trucks and tractors, but the partners agreed on the need to provide dealers with a lower-priced car to go along with the medium-priced Hudson. In September 1917 they formed the Essex Motor Car Company, a separate concern controlled entirely by Hudson stockholders, to make the new car. World War I prevented them from immediately producing the new 4-cylinder model, but toward the end of 1918 a few were turned out in a factory where Hudson made shells during the war. By the early part of 1919 the Essex, priced about $800 less than the Hudson, was being assembled at a rate of 15 to 20 per day, and by the end of 1919 about 20,000 had been produced, equaling the number of Hudsons produced that year. With the completion of new assembly facilities, Essex was soon the volume leader of the two companies.

In 1925 Hudson production rose to 110,000 and Essex production to 160,000, with the majority of those cars being closed models. Therein lay the greatest contribution of Roy Chapin and his company to automotive design. In 1919 some 90 percent of all cars had open bodies, and closed bodies were found on only the most expensive models. Production of Hudson, and especially Essex, closed sedan models at prices that were only slightly greater than those for open cars revolutionized car-buying habits, forcing other companies to follow suit. By 1925 closed car production exceeded that of open cars for the first time. Automobiles could now be used in all seasons, and sales boomed.

The success of the Essex led to the merger of Hudson and Essex (under the Hudson name) in 1923. At the same time Hudson went public, and shares in the company were quickly snapped up. The company's founders retained a controlling financial interest but no longer involved themselves in day-to-day operations. Bezner had gone to Europe in 1913 to supervise Hudson's export business, which boomed in the 1920s, and he continued to live there. Coffin would not officially retire until 1930, but from the time of World War I his function was largely a consultative one. Chapin turned over the Hudson presidency to Jackson in 1923. Chapin became chairman, a position that may not have been entirely honorary but which allowed him ample time to become the most recognized spokesman for "good roads" in the industry.

In 1929 Hudson production topped 300,000, but that year also saw the untimely death of Jack-

Herbert Hoover and his 1917 Hudson during Hoover's term as U.S. Food Administrator in Europe after World War I (courtesy of Chrysler Corporation)

son and the beginning of the Great Depression. Hudson sales collapsed to a mere 40,000 in 1933, and heavy losses threatened the company with bankruptcy. W. J. McAneeny, who had been president of Essex when that company was formed in 1917, was named to succeed Jackson as president, but he was unable to halt the slide in sales. So in 1933 Chapin, who served as U.S. secretary of commerce in the last months of the Hoover administration, resumed his earlier role as Hudson's president. By 1934 he had gotten the company out of the red, and by 1935 sales were up more than 100,000. But the strain of the effort, combined with the long hours he spent on behalf of the industry, probably caused his death in 1936.

A. E. Barit, who had started at Hudson as a stenographer in 1910, succeeded Chapin as president. Production fell during the recession of 1937-1938 but rebounded to 88,000 by 1940. By that time all the vehicles were Hudsons. The Essex had been re-

named the Essex Terraplane in 1932, and before long they were known simply as Terraplanes.

Hudson produced guns, marine engines, and aircraft components during World War II. Like all the surviving independents, the company enjoyed big sales following the war. Sales rose to nearly 150,000 per year by the end of the 1940s. The distinctive Step-Down body design of the 1948 Hudson was one of the more famous of the postwar models and was reminiscent of the innovations for which Hudson had been renowned before the war. But once the Big Three got fully into gear the independents were unable to hold the market they had gained. By 1953 Hudson sales had fallen to 76,000, and the company suffered heavy financial losses. The 6-cylinder Hornet and the compact Jet, introduced in 1951 and 1953 respectively, flew in the face of buying trends favoring big, 8-cylinder cars.

George Mason, head of Nash-Kelvinator, had foreseen the problems smaller car producers would face. Not long after the war he discussed with Barit the possibility of a merger of their companies. At the time Barit had not been interested, but by June 16, 1953, when the two men met again, Barit had little choice but to accept an offer. The Nash and Hudson directors approved the merger on January 14, 1954. Hudson stockholders, with only a few dissenters, went along with the decision, which created the American Motors Corporation (AMC) on May 1, 1954. Nash-Kelvinator was much the stronger of the two companies: Nash stockholders received one share of American Motors stock for each of their Nash shares, while Hudson stockholders had to exchange three shares of Hudson stock to obtain two AMC shares. Mason became head of the new company, while Barit served only as a director and a consultant. Production of Hudsons was moved to Kenosha, Wisconsin, home of the Nash, but the cars carrying the Hudson name were such close duplicates of the Nash models that observers suggested the company's cars should be called "Hash." Both the Nash and Hudson names were discontin-

ued in 1958 in favor of the American Motors designation. The Rambler models that replaced them were models Nash had developed. Roy Dikeman Chapin, Jr., the original partner's son who had risen through the ranks of the Hudson company, served as head of American Motors from the late 1960s to the late 1970s. Unlike his father, he lived to see the demise of the company when it was acquired by Chrysler Corporation in 1987.

References:

Richard M. Langworth, *Hudson: The Postwar Years* (Osceola, Wis.: Motorbooks International, 1977);

John D. Long, *Roy D. Chapin* (N.p.: Privately published, 1945);

"Overland, Hudson, Chalmers, Auto-Lite and United Motors in Monster Merger," *Automobile*, 34 (June 8, 1916): 1049.

Archives:

The papers of Roy D. Chapin are in the Michigan Historical Collections, Bentley Historical Library, University of Michigan, Ann Arbor.

Robert Craig Hupp

(June 2, 1877-December 7, 1931)

by Charles K. Hyde

Wayne State University

CAREER: Vice-president and general manager, Hupp Motor Car Company (1908-1911); president, Hupp-Yeats Electric Car Company (1910-1912); president, Hupp Corporation and R.C.H. Corporation (1911-1913); president, Monarch Motor Car Company (1922-1924); assistant general manager, Four Wheel Hydraulic Brake Company (1922-1924).

Robert Craig Hupp, automobile manufacturer, was born on June 2, 1877, to Charles J. and Anna Klinger Hupp of Grand Rapids, Michigan. Charles J. Hupp moved to Detroit in 1884 and held the position of assistant general freight agent of the Michigan Central Railroad from 1884 until 1907, when he became general freight agent. Robert C. Hupp attended Detroit schools, including Central High School. Among other interests, he served as quarterback for the Detroit Athletic Club football team in 1896. He began his first full-time job with

the Olds Motor Works in Detroit in 1902. There, he started as an unskilled laborer but quickly advanced to more skilled jobs. He assembled engines, then had the responsibility of testing engines, and finally became an inspector and tester for the entire automobile. Hupp left Michigan and the automobile industry in fall 1905 and had a job for nine months with a Chicago firm that made soda fountains. He then returned to Detroit and worked for the Ford Motor Company from summer 1906 until January 1908, holding a variety of positions in the sales, service, and shipping departments.

Hupp served a brief stint as a clerk in his father's office at the Michigan Central Railroad in the early part of 1908 but spent much of his energy trying to build a medium-priced, high-quality automobile. With the help of E. A. Nelson, an engineer at the Packard Motor Car Company, and several investors who sank $11,000 into the venture, Hupp established the Hupp Motor Car Company on

Advertisement for the 1912 Hupp 25-horsepower automobile (courtesy of the National Automotive History Collection, Detroit Public Library)

November 8, 1908, with a capital stock of $25,000. By that time he had finished a prototype car, which was exhibited in February 1909 at the Detroit Automobile Show, where it earned rave reviews. In later years Henry Ford noted, "I recall looking at Bobby Hupp's roadster at the first show where it was exhibited and wondering whether we could ever build as good a small car for as little money." The 4-cylinder Hupmobile was a popular automobile right from the start, with sales that jumped from 1,618 units in 1909 to 6,079 units in 1911.

Robert Hupp is naturally associated with the Hupmobile, which enjoyed great popularity over its lifetime from 1908 through 1941. But in 1911 Hupp left the firm that bore his name and launched a series of additional automobile companies and related businesses. He introduced a luxury car called the "RCH" (1911-1914), the Hupp-Yeats Electric car (1911-1919), and the Monarch (1914-1916), a lightweight, 6-cylinder model. He also founded the Rotary Valve Motor Company in 1910 to manufacture 6-cylinder engines, as well as a series of other firms, including a foundry, forge, machine shop, pattern shop, and a construction company. After

leaving the Hupp Motor Car Company, he consolidated his businesses into the Hupp Corporation, established in May 1911 and capitalized at $700,000, but was forced to change the firm's name to the R.C.H. Corporation in February 1912, following a successful lawsuit by his former partners, who wanted to monopolize the Hupp nameplate. Robert Hupp left the Hupp-Yeats firm in 1912, the RCH was a dismal failure, and the Monarch fared no better.

Robert Hupp left Detroit in 1916 and moved to Forest Hills, New York, where he remained until 1921. He volunteered for military service and was about to receive a commission as captain in motor transport when World War I ended. He remained in New York state, worked as an automotive consulting engineer, and helped launch the ill-fated Emerson car, made in Kingston, New York.

Hupp returned to the Detroit area in 1921 and worked as an automotive engineering consultant until his death in 1931. He was a major figure in the development of 4-wheel hydraulic brake systems for use in passenger automobiles. In 1922 Hupp road tested a Model A Duesenberg with 4-wheel brakes, and at the end of the year, he joined the Four Wheel Hydraulic Brake Company as assistant general manager. The firm owned patents awarded to Malcolm Loughead and by early 1923 was producing the Lockhead Hydraulic Brake system. This system was introduced on the Chalmers models in 1923, and most American automobile manufacturers adopted this improved braking system in 1924 and 1925.

Hupp married the former Elsie Eugenia Winn, daughter of Henry R. Winn, a prominent Detroit printer, and the marriage produced two sons, Robert C. Hupp, Jr., and Craig Anthony Hupp, and a daughter, Marion Hupp. The automotive pioneer died on December 7, 1931, at age fifty-five, from a massive cerebral hemorrhage, at the Detroit Athletic Club following a squash match. Robert Craig Hupp was one of dozens of entrepreneurs who emerged during the early decades of the automobile industry, had great short-term success and made great fortunes, but often lost much of his wealth on later ventures.

References:
"The Automobile Industry in Michigan," *Michigan History Magazine,* 8 (1924): 247-251;
Clarence M. Burton, *The City of Detroit, Michigan, 1701-1922* (Detroit: Clarke, 1922);

Jeffrey I. Godshall, "Hupmobile: Always a Good Car," *Automobile Quarterly*, 16 (1978): 62-97;

Albert N. Marquis, ed., *The Book of Detroiters* (Chicago: Marquis, 1908);

Allan Nevins, *Ford: The Times, The Man, The Company* (New York: Scribners, 1954);

Arthur Pound, *The Turning Wheel: The Story of General Motors Through Twenty-Five Years, 1908-1933* (Garden City, N.Y.: Doubleday, 1934);

"The Rapid Rise of Robert C. Hupp," *Detroit Free Press,* August 14, 1910, section 1, p. 20;

"Robert C. Hupp, Automobile Pioneer," *Detroit Saturday Night*, September 16, 1911.

Archives:

The Burton Historical Collections, Detroit Public Library, has a Hupp Family vertical file, with miscellaneous newspaper clippings, including obituary notices in a half-dozen newspapers, December 8 and December 9, 1931. The National Automotive History Collection, Detroit Public Library, has records of the Monarch Motor Car Company and photographs of Robert C. Hupp.

Hupp Motor Car Company

by Charles K. Hyde

Wayne State University

In summer 1908, Robert C. Hupp, who had previously worked at the Olds Motor Works in Detroit and for the Ford Motor Company, prepared to build a car of his own, with the aid of E. A. Nelson, a designer with the Packard Motor Car Company. Hupp convinced several Detroit investors to advance him $11,000 to build a prototype. Once he finished the work, they established the Hupp Motor Car Company on November 8, 1908, with a capital stock of only $25,000. J. Walter Drake was president of the new firm, Hupp served as vice-president, while E. A. Nelson was chief engineer. Charles D. Hastings, formerly Olds's sales manager, advanced an additional $8,500 to enable Hupp to exhibit the new model at the Detroit Auto Show in February 1909.

The original Hupmobile, a two-seat runabout with a 4-cylinder, 2.8-litre side-valve engine, sold for about $750 and was an immediate success. The firm struggled to produce 1,618 cars in 1909 but manufactured 5,340 in 1910, 6,079 the following year, and 7,640 in 1912. The company received an enormous amount of favorable publicity as the result of an around-the-world tour that ran from November 1910 through January 1912, when a Hupmobile traveled 40,000 miles through 23 nations.

Robert Hupp sold his stock in the firm in 1911 and founded the Hupp Corporation in May 1911, but the major stockholders of the Hupp Motor Car Company pursued a lawsuit to prohibit Hupp from using the Hupp name on any new firm or automobile. Hupp lost the case in February 1912 and changed his firm's name to the R.C.H. Corporation. The original Hupp firm reincorporated in November 1915 as the Hupp Motor Car Corporation, with capital stock of $6.5 million. Production climbed steadily for the rest of the decade and reached a peak of 19,225 units in 1920. By the late 1910s the firm had a labor force of about 1,700 men at its new factory on Detroit's northern outskirts.

Charles D. Hastings replaced J. Walter Drake as the firm's president in early 1920, and Hastings held the post through 1925. DuBois Young, who joined the automaker after working for a Jackson, Michigan, gear manufacturer acquired by Hupp in November 1915, became president and general manager in 1926. The company enjoyed considerable success in the 1920s. Sales jumped from 13,626 cars in 1921 to more than 34,000 in 1922 and then, in 1928, reached a peak of nearly 66,000. By the mid 1920s, the firm employed about 5,000 workers. In 1925 Hupp introduced a medium-priced straight-eight in January, followed by a 6-cylinder car in October, replacing the firm's popular but outdated 4-cylinder model. Hupp also moved in step with the other major producers in adopting the closed-body style. In 1922 only one-fifth of Hupp's production had closed bodies but in 1926 nearly nine-tenths did.

The Depression years devastated smaller automobile companies such as Hupp. Sales dropped from about 50,000 cars in 1929 to 17,450 in 1931,

The 1911 Hupmobile

then plummeted to about 9,500 cars in both 1934 and 1935. Sales stood at $53 million in 1929 but fell to a low of $6 million in 1935. Hupp also suffered through a series of internal struggles, including lawsuits in the years between 1933 and 1936 over control of the firm. Hupp suspended production for much of 1936, resumed briefly in 1937, but made only 1,752 cars. A court-appointed receiver took over the firm in June 1938, and Hupp was able to resume production the following year only after the city of Detroit wrote off more than half of the firm's tax liability. In a final, desperate move in 1939 and 1940, the firm produced about 1,500 Skylarks, luxury cars with Cord bodies on Hupmobile chassis. The company declared bankruptcy in November 1940, was reorganized, and began war production.

At the end of World War II, the board of directors decided not to resume automobile production and changed the firm's name to the Hupp Corporation. William S. Knudsen from General Motors be-

came the chairman of the board at Hupp in 1946. Hupp sold its Detroit manufacturing complex to Midland Steel Products Company in 1950, moved its headquarters to Cleveland, and diversified into the manufacture of home appliances and electronics. It became a subsidiary in 1967 of White Consolidated Industries.

References:

"The Automobile Industry in Michigan," *Michigan History Magazine*, 8 (1924): 247-251;

Clarence M. Burton, *The City of Detroit, Michigan, 1701-1922.* (Detroit: Clarke, 1922);

Jeffrey I. Godshall, "Hupmobile: Always A Good Car," *Automobile Quarterly*, 16 (1978): 62-97;

Allan Nevins, *Ford: The Times, The Man, The Company* (New York: Scribners, 1954).

Archives:

Material on Hupp Motor Car Company is located in the National Automotive History Collection at the Detroit Public Library.

John Wesley Hyatt

(November 28, 1837-May 10, 1920)

by Genevieve Wren

Motor Vehicle Research Services

CAREER: Apprentice printer, Illinois (1853-1863); journeyman printer, Albany, New York (1863-1869); partner, Embossing Company of Albany, Albany, New York (1869-1872); inventor and manufacturer, celluloid plastic, Newark, New Jersey (1872-1881); partner, Hyatt Pure Water Company, Newark, New Jersey (1881-1891); founder and president, Hyatt Roller Bearing Company, Harrison, New Jersey (1891-1917).

John Wesley Hyatt was an inventive genius who secured more than 250 patents covering several industries. Today automobiles use Hyatt roller bearings, axles, transmissions, and valve rocker-arms. The Hyatt name is also prominent in the agricultural-industrial field, where Hyatt shaft wheels contribute to long life for farm machinery. Hyatt bearings are used in oil wells, textile and steel mills, railroad-related machinery, and in other industrial equipment. In addition, Hyatt invented celluloid pyroxylin plastic in 1869, a filter-pump system for water filtration in 1881-1882, and precision gauges and other tools especially helpful in optical measuring.

Hyatt was born on November 28, 1837, in Starkey, New York, the son of John Wesley and Ann Gleason Hyatt. He received a common-school education and then attended Eddytown Seminary for a year, especially excelling in mathematics. When he was sixteen he moved to Illinois, where he was employed as a printer for ten years. He obtained his first patent in 1861, for a solid emery wheel used to sharpen knives. In 1863 he moved to Albany, New York, to work as a journeyman printer. In Albany he also worked on developing an "artificial ivory" for use in billiard balls, in response to a public offer of $10,000 by Phelan & Collander of New York. He developed several plastic compositions, all of which proved unsuitable, but used some of the technology in partnership

John Wesley Hyatt (courtesy of the Smithsonian Institution)

with his two brothers, forming the Embossing Company of Albany to manufacture checkers and dominoes out of pressed wood. Hyatt finally succeeded in developing a billiard ball substitute in 1869, using a combination of paper flock, shellac, and collodion (a nitrocellulose solution) that achieved wide use in the industry. He continued experimenting with nitrocellulose, discovering that a mixture of that substance with camphor and a small amount of alcohol becomes viscous when heated but hardens at room temperature. With the help of his brother Isaiah Smith Hyatt he moved to Newark, New Jersey, in the winter of 1872-1873 to set up a factory to manufacture this celluloid plastic. He continued to refine complicated techniques and designed machinery for the manufacture and manipulation of the material. Along with several others, notably Alexander Parkes and Daniel Spill, Hyatt is credited with beginning the plastics revolution in industrial history. He went on to obtain many patents on machinery to manufacture commercial articles and novelties from celluloid.

In 1881 Hyatt and his brother Isaiah started the Hyatt Pure Water Company to market their patented process to clean water with coagulants without the need for extended-period settling. Paper and woolen mills and public water systems adopted the Hyatt system in the United States and Europe.

In 1888, while working to develop an improved mill for crushing sugar cane, Hyatt became frustrated over the inadequacy of existing bearings. After extensive research, he developed a roller bearing wound from flat strips of steel in a coil or helix. The bearing greatly increased the load-carrying ability of machinery, required a minimum of lubrication, and increased the efficiency of power transmission. In 1891 he started the Hyatt Roller Bearing Company in Harrison, New Jersey, to manufacture the bearings. Then he went on to finish the sugar mill system. Hyatt bearings had already proven themselves by the time the automobile came along, and car designers were quick to adopt them when suitable versions appeared in 1896. The first production Oldsmobiles and Fords used Hyatt automobile bearings. More than 20 car companies used them by 1908. In 1917 the Hyatt Roller Bearing Company became part of General Motors Company.

Hyatt was married on July 21, 1869, to Anna E. Taft. The couple had two sons, Ralph and Charles, the latter of whom became an electrical engineer. Hyatt died in Newark on May 10, 1920, after a long retirement.

References:

Cycle and Automobile Trade Journal (December 1, 1924);

Arthur Pound, *The Turning Wheel* (Garden City, N.Y.: Doubleday, Doran, 1934).

Jackson Automobile Company

by George S. May

Eastern Michigan University

Although Detroit is the Michigan city always associated with the auto industry, automobile companies sprang up throughout southern Michigan at the start of the twentieth century. One, the Jackson Automobile Company, organized on July 23, 1902, seemed to have as much of a chance of success as most. Its three founders were men of stature in Jackson, which was an important center of industrial activity in south-central Michigan. George A. Matthews owned the Fuller Buggy Company, the largest of the city's carriage manufacturers, and Charles Lewis owned the Lewis Spring & Axle Company, which supplied parts to the carriage industry and became a supplier to auto companies. Byron J. Carter had the least impressive business credentials as the operator of a bicycle shop and a print shop, but he was responsible for the car the Jackson company produced.

Carter had experimented with both gasoline- and steam-propelled cars, and when the Jackson company got into production at the end of 1902 it followed the rather unusual practice of turning out both a 3-cylinder steam runabout and a 1-cylinder gasoline runabout. The steamer was publicized when news of the company's organization appeared, but when the two runabouts, called "Jaxons," were exhibited at the Chicago auto show in February 1903, Carter noted that the gasoline version "seemed to be preferred." As a result the steam models were dropped after 1903, and the Jackson company followed the rest of the Michigan automotive firms, which concentrated almost solely on gasoline cars. The company also began calling its cars "Jacksons," using a picture of Andrew Jackson as an advertising symbol and describing them as being "Sturdy as Old Hickory."

*Jackson advertisement for its 1910 model line,
marketed safe from the threat
of Selden patent litigation*

Jackson automobiles continued in production until 1923. The Jaxons had been priced less than $1,000, but as the company followed the trend away from the lightweight 1-cylinder runabouts and introduced 2-cylinder Jacksons in 1904 and 4-cylinder models in 1905, prices went up. In 1907 the 2-cylinder touring car sold for $1,250 and the 4-cylinder for $2,500. By 1910 only 4-cylinder Jacksons were being produced. A 6-cylinder model appeared in 1913, but in 1916 both 4-cylinder and 6-cylinder Jacksons were replaced by V-8 models. Six-cylinder Jacksons were reintroduced after World War I, and they were the last to be offered when production ended in 1923.

The fact that the Jackson company disappeared while other Michigan companies are still operating is attributable not so much to the inferiority of Jackson products as to the management of the company, which lacked the skill and imagination that enabled the others to prosper. Among the three founders of the company, Carter and Lewis were the most active in the initial stages of operations, but neither stayed active for very long. Lewis

soon devoted his full attention to the spring and axle business, and Carter left the company in May 1904 after developing a light car using friction drive. Since the Jackson company had already made one shift in its product line when it dropped the steam cars, Carter's colleagues may not have wanted to follow that up so soon with friction-drive models. Carter got the support he needed in Detroit, where he produced the friction-drive Cartercar before his untimely death in 1908. Carter was no Henry Ford or Ransom Olds, but his departure from the Jackson company nevertheless removed the one person who had provided the same kind of leadership and inspiration that Ford and Olds provided to their companies. Although the Jackson advertising slogan, "No Sand Too Deep—No Hill Too Steep," is widely remembered, the leadership of the company missed opportunities that would have made the Jackson stand out. The great race driver Bob Burman persuaded the company to allow him to drive one of its cars in a 50-mile race in Detroit in 1906. He won and followed it up with another win over well-known cars and drivers in a 24-hour endurance race at St. Louis. But the company let Burman get away, and he became one of a team of crack drivers William C. Durant used with spectacular success to promote the Buick. In the same period, when R. Samuel McLaughlin, whose family owned Canada's largest carriage-manufacturing company, came to Jackson looking for a car the McLaughlins could manufacture in Canada, he became interested in the Jackson and bought two of the cars. But again the company let an asset get away, and in 1908 McLaughlin accepted Durant's offer to manufacture Buicks in Canada.

That same year saw the organization by Durant of General Motors (GM) holding company, and Buick was the first company to come under that banner. Had Durant gone after the Jackson company it might have survived, but although Durant was thoroughly familiar with the city of Jackson, where he had the Buick assembled for several years, he does not seem to have actively sought to gain control of Jackson. With the departure of Carter and Lewis the company was headed by George Matthews until his death in 1914. Matthews's sons continued to run the company until the early 1920s. In 1922 the company did become part of a consolidation, Associated Motor Industries, but the attempt failed, and Jackson cars were gone by the end of 1923.

References:

Nick Baldwin and others, *The World Guide to Automobile Manufacturers* (New York: Facts on File, 1987);

W. O. MacIlvain, "Jackson Automobile Co., Jackson, Michigan," *Bulb Horn*, 13 (October 1952): 14-15, 25;

George S. May, *A Most Unique Machine: The Michigan Origins of the American Automobile Industry* (Grand Rapids, Mich.: Eerdmans, 1975).

Thomas B. Jeffery Company

by Beverly Rae Kimes

New York, New York

The first Jeffery-built car carried no name at all. A plaque had either been forgotten or there had not been time to affix one. Displayed at the first automobile shows held in America–in Chicago in September 1900, followed by one in New York that November–the vehicle created a good deal of attention among journalists, who alternately referred to it as the G & J or the Rambler. G & J was the name of the tire company that was owned by R. Phillip Gormully and Thomas B. Jeffery (and would ultimately become part of United States Rubber). Rambler was the name of the bicycle Gormully and Jeffery manufactured; their bicycle factory in Chicago was the second largest in the United States.

Although Gormully had remained steadfastly unenthusiastic about the horseless age, Jeffery's enthusiasm had grown steadily since the 1895 *Chicago Times-Herald* contest where he and his son Charles saw their first automobile and decided they could do better. The sudden death of Gormully a few years later sealed that resolve. By now Col. Albert Pope was creating his bicycle empire, and Jeffery had no desire to compete against a conglomerate. Instead he sold out to Pope for what was described as "a princely sum," which provided him the cash necessary to purchase a gigantic building in Kenosha, Wisconsin, in 1900. There he and his son Charles pursued their automotive plans. The building's price was $65,000–a bargain possible because the plant was abandoned. Ironically, it had been home to the Sterling bicycle, which, like many of the companies Pope bought for his empire, had already gone under.

In Kenosha, Thomas B. Jeffery & Company flourished. In negotiating with Pope, Jeffery had insisted upon retaining rights to the Rambler name, and now it graced his 1-cylinder automobile. Production in the firm's maiden year of 1902 was 1,500 cars, a figure exceeded only by Ransom Olds with his curved-runabout. Unlike Olds, Jeffery did not long remain content with a 1-cylinder. By 1904, when production reached 2,342 units, Ramblers were available as 2-cylinder touring cars as well. By 1905 the factory focused on only these larger automobiles, and sales increased to 3,807 cars. A 4-cylinder model followed in 1906.

By now, Thomas B. Jeffery & Company was an industry leader. Its Rambler was among the nation's most respected medium-range cars. Its advertising–courtesy of Ned Jordan, who both worked for the company and married one of the Jeffery girls–was pleasantly progressive. Its publicity department never missed a good photo opportunity–be it the presidents Roosevelt or Taft parading in a Rambler, Mark Twain or Buffalo Bill riding with friends in the same. The Kenosha factory was not only the largest in the United States but was reputed to be the best equipped as well. Nonetheless, mass production did not interest the Jefferys. They were making a fortune with an annual output of 3,000 cars in any case. They could enjoy the good life.

On April 2, 1910, having returned to the Grand Hotel after visiting the ruins at Pompeii, Thomas Jeffery died of a heart attack at the age of sixty-five. The news from Italy stunned Kenosha. Jeffery's estate was valued at $3.3 million, and the terms of his will stipulated that his firm be incorporated (for $3 million) as the Thomas B. Jeffery Company, with ownership remaining entirely in the hands of the Jeffery family. Son Charles assumed the helm, as he and his father had been virtual partners from the beginning. Except for raising annual production by about 500 cars a year, Charles Jeffery did not much alter procedures in the Rambler factory. The big change came in 1914, when

A 1914 Jeffery Quad truck negotiating difficult terrain (courtesy of the Chrysler Corporation)

the new model was introduced as the Jeffery, as Charles said, "to the end that his name may remain in the memories of men." Discarding the name of one of America's most respected automobiles in favor of one honoring his father was a decision motivated by sentiment. But it worked. The new Jeffery quickly earned a reputation as meritorious as the old Rambler. Gone as well was the old Rambler limited-production policy; Charles would build Jefferys to market demand. He also entered the commercial field with a truck called the Quad. Production in 1914 totaled 10,417 Jeffery cars and 3,096 Jeffery trucks. For 1915 priorities were reversed; with war raging in Europe and the likelihood that America would be drawn into it, the focus was on truck manufacture, with the 7,600 Quads produced being twice the number of Jeffery cars built.

Then fate intervened. In May 1915 Charles Jeffery set sail for Europe on what ostensibly was just another of his routine business trips to the Continent. His ship was the *Lusitania*. Jeffery survived the torpedo attack, but "the lasting memory of its horror"—he was in the icy Atlantic for four hours before being rescued by a trawler—haunted him thereafter in Kenosha. Probably his father's sudden death also made him aware of his fragile mortality. At the age of forty, Charles Jeffery decided to retire. In 1916 he sold the Thomas B. Jeffery Company to Charles Nash.

Reference:

Beverly Rae Kimes, "A Family in Kenosha: The Story of the Rambler and the Jeffery," *Automobile Quarterly*, 16 (Second Quarter 1978): 128-145.

Jordan Motor Car Company

by George S. May

Eastern Michigan University

The automotive historian Beverly Rae Kimes presents some strong arguments in support of her contention that the 65,000 or so Jordans produced between 1916 and 1931 were cars of considerable distinction. She admits, however—like everyone who writes about the Jordan Motor Car Company—that the car is best remembered for the way in which it was advertised.

Edward S. "Ned" Jordan was born in 1882 in Merrill, Wisconsin, and after working his way through the University of Wisconsin as a reporter for the *Wisconsin State Journal,* he went on to take a job in the sales department of the National Cash Register Company. Jordan moved to the Thomas B. Jeffery Company in 1906, where he became the advertising manager. Marrying one of Jeffery's daughters may have helped him get the job, but he soon began to employ to good advantage his copywriting skills in promoting the company's Rambler automobiles. Some years later he left Jeffery, and after a brief stint writing copy for the great Chicago Lord & Thomas ad agency, he formed the Jordan Motor Car Company in Cleveland, Ohio, with $300,000 supplied by bankers in that city and Chicago.

With the exception of the bodies, which Jordan made, the cars that appeared in late summer 1916 were assembled from parts obtained from outside suppliers. Even the bodies of many of the later Jordans were also produced elsewhere. The term "assembled car" had come to have negative connotations: in the views of critics a car that contained nothing that was original with the manufacturer whose name was on the vehicle. Ned Jordan blunted such criticism by putting together distinctively designed vehicles that had the look of custom cars. A roadster that Florenz Ziegfeld had had custom-built for his wife, Billie Burke, was the model used for Jordan's most famous car, the Jordan Playboy, introduced in 1919.

The sporty roadster, whose name was supposedly inspired by John Millington Synge's drama *The Playboy of the Western World,* originated one night, Jordan related, when a girl with whom he was dancing urged him to build a car "for the girl who loved to swim and paddle and shout . . . and for the boy who loves the roar of the cut-out." If this was actually how he got the idea for the Playboy, he should have also credited the girl with suggesting how he should promote the car. The ads that he wrote said little about the car but much about the pleasures that were to be experienced by the happy occupants of a Playboy, driving along with "the blue sky overhead, the green turf flying by and a thousand miles of open road."

The ad for which Jordan is most famous was inspired when, during a train trip in 1923, he glanced out the window and saw a beautiful girl riding a beautiful horse across the plains. "Where are we?" he asked a companion. "Oh," came the reply, "somewhere west of Laramie." Thus was born the title of the ad that appeared in the *Saturday Evening Post* of June 23, 1923. The ad showed a cowboy astride a horse, and a girl at the wheel of a Playboy racing through the open country. The girl was described as "a bronco-busting, steer-roping girl," "the lass whose face is brown with the sun when the day is done of revel and romp and race," a girl who "loves the cross of the wild and the tame." "The truth is," Jordan declared, as he warmed up to his topic, "the Playboy was built for her." So, too, it was built for all who, "when the hour grows dull with things gone dead and stale," wanted to drive off "for the land of real living with the spirit of the lass who rides, lean and rangy, into the red horizon of a Wyoming twilight."

"Somewhere West of Laramie" makes nearly everyone's list of the greatest advertisements of all time. It was not the first of its kind. Others before had broken away from the nuts-and-bolts approach used in the first automobile ads, but none could equal the wildly evocative appeal of Jordan's copy. But the copywriter's "word magic" was not enough to enable the Jordan to survive the increasingly brutal competitive forces that favored the big companies over the smaller producers. By 1926, 8-cylinder cars had replaced the earlier 6-cylinder models, and Jordan sales hit a peak of more than 11,000 cars. But in 1927 the company suffered its first loss for a year, with sales of barely 6,000 cars. The Little Custom, a small, 6-cylinder luxury car introduced that year, failed to attract enough buyers among those who preferred big luxury cars. Jordan tried to recoup by bringing in veteran automobile executives, first Edward Ver Linden, formerly with General Motors (GM) and Peerless, and then John McArdle from Chrysler. But it was to no avail. The onset of the Great Depression at the end of 1929 caught Jordan with a lineup of 8-cylinder makes, one of which, the Model 2 Speedway Ace, sold for $5,500. Within a year and a half the company was in receivership, and it was out of business by 1932, joining the depressingly long list of Cleveland automobile companies that failed. Jordan, who continued in various advertising and public relations jobs, died in 1958.

References:

Nick Baldwin and others, *The World Guide to Automobile Manufacturers* (New York: Facts on File, 1987);

Beverly Rae Kimes and Henry Austin Clark, *Standard Catalog of American Cars, 1805-1942* (Iola, Wis.: Krause, 1985);

George S. May, *The Automobile in American Life* (forthcoming, 1990).

Henry Bourne Joy

(November 23, 1864-November 6, 1936)

by Charles K. Hyde

Wayne State University

CAREER: Clerk, paymaster, and assistant treasurer, Peninsular Car Company (1886-1887); assistant treasurer and director, Fort Street Union Depot Company (1891-1896); president and director, Detroit Union Railroad Depot and Station Company (1896-1912); treasurer and director, Peninsular Sugar Refining Company (1899-1906); receiver, Chicago & Grand Trunk Railway (1900-1903); general manager (1902-1909), director (1903-1917), president, Packard Motor Car Company (1909-1916); director, Michigan Sugar Company (1906-1908); president, Joy Realty Company (1910-1936); director, Federal Reserve Bank of Chicago (1913-1914); president, Lincoln Highway Association (1913-1917); director, Wabash Railroad (1916-1917).

Henry Bourne Joy, automobile manufacturer, was born on November 23, 1864, in Detroit, Michigan, the son of James Frederic and Mary Bourne Joy. He was one of James F. Joy's six children from two marriages. The elder Joy was a major nineteenth-century Michigan business leader who promoted the canal and locks at Sault Ste. Marie in the mid 1850s, launched railroad and banking ventures throughout the Midwest, and served as president of the Michigan Central Railroad.

Joy attended public elementary schools in Detroit, the Michigan Military Academy, and Phillips Academy in Andover, Massachusetts, graduating in 1883. He attended the Sheffield Scientific School at Yale University until 1886, his junior year, when he returned to Detroit to work for the Peninsular Car Company, a large manufacturer of railroad cars. He started as an office boy, earning $15 per month, but within two years quickly advanced to the positions of clerk, paymaster, and assistant treasurer. Joy left Detroit in 1887 because of failing health and spent nearly two years in the silver mining industry in Utah.

When Joy returned to Detroit in 1890 he served as secretary for the Fort Street Union Depot Company, a firm that his father had founded. He became assistant treasurer and director of the firm in 1891. Shortly thereafter, at the age of twenty-seven, he married Helen Hall Newberry, a member of one of Detroit's oldest and wealthiest families, on October 11, 1892. With the death of James F. Joy in 1896, the younger Joy became president of the re-

Henry Bourne Joy (courtesy of the Motor Vehicle Manufacturers Association)

named Detroit Union Railroad Depot and Station Company, a post he held until 1912.

Joy was one of the founders of the Michigan State Naval Brigade, established on February 22, 1894. He served in this naval reserve unit for nine years, including his last three as navigation officer for the U.S.S. *Yantic*. During the Spanish-American War, Joy served as chief boatswain's mate on the U.S.S. *Yosemite*, manned by the Michigan Naval Brigade. This vessel performed blockade duty off San Juan, Puerto Rico, where it sank a Spanish armed transport, the *Antonio Lopez*, on June 28, 1898. All crew members received a double bonus for this action, with Joy's share amounting to $206.05. The *Yosemite*'s tour of duty was not entirely glorious, however. On June 16, 1898, the vessel had failed to pursue and capture a Spanish prize ship, the *Purisima Concepcion*, and a subsequent navy report blamed the failure on the officer on watch, Lt. Gilbert Wilkes. Henry Joy was the last surviving member of the *Yosemite*'s crew, and, following his death, his widow, Helen Newberry Joy, published a defense of Wilkes that Joy had written earlier. Joy claimed that the errors were made by Capt. Wil-

liam H. Emory, who covered up the facts in his official report and shifted the blame to Wilkes. Joy's strong desire to clear Wilkes nearly 40 years later is evidence of his strong sense of personal loyalty and justice.

Joy returned to Michigan at the end of the Spanish-American War and helped establish the Peninsular Sugar Refining Company, one of the first beet sugar processors in Michigan. He was company treasurer until 1906, when the Michigan Sugar Company acquired Peninsular, and continued as a director of the new firm until 1908. Joy also served as a receiver for the bankrupt Chicago & Grand Trunk Railway in the years 1900 through 1903. However, it was his interest in the nascent automobile industry, beginning in the mid 1890s, that led Joy to his long association with the Packard Motor Car Company.

Joy was a business associate and friend of Charles B. King, a Detroit inventor who manufactured pneumatic drills and marine engines in the 1890s. King built the first gasoline-powered car in Detroit in 1896, was an early promoter of improved roads through the American Motor League, and enlisted Joy's support to help promote the automobile. Joy's mechanical interests, initially limited to marine engines, broadened to include automobiles. Joy tried to buy a Duryea car in 1895 and one of Henry Ford's experimental vehicles a few years later, but the inventors would not part with them.

Joy and his wealthy brother-in-law, Truman H. Newberry, visited the New York Automobile Show in November 1901 in search of automobile manufacturers as potential investments. The two were observing a steam-powered vehicle in operation, when the sight glass for the boiler exploded in Newberry's face. Shortly thereafter, while the two men were admiring a pair of automobiles parked in front of the Adams and McMurtry Packard Agency on West 59th Street, two men ran out to the cars, intending to chase fire trucks to a fire. Both cars started easily, and Joy was so impressed that he decided to buy one. The automobiles were Packards, manufactured in Warren, Ohio, by the Ohio Automobile Company and named after James Ward Packard, the engineer who had designed them.

Joy was impressed with the design of the Packard and concluded that the firm that made it might be a good investment opportunity. In late 1901 and in January 1902 he acquired 250 shares of Ohio Automobile Company stock for $25,000. Joy began to correspond with James W. Packard, visited his manufacturing plant in July 1902, and discovered that the Ohio firm wanted to expand but was short of capital. He returned to Detroit and convinced several of his millionaire friends to invest a total of $250,000 in the firm, with an additional $125,000 promised if Packard would move his manufacturing operations to Detroit. Russell A. Alger, Jr., invested $75,000, while Joy, Newberry, and Philip H. McMillan put $50,000 apiece into the venture.

The Ohio Automobile Company reorganized as the Packard Motor Car Company in October 1902, with Packard serving as president and Joy as general manager. The Detroit investors held a majority of the stock and gave Joy the authority to run the firm. The major Ohio stockholders quickly resigned their management posts in Packard in November 1902 and January 1903. Joy exerted his influence by offering J. W. Packard detailed advice on personnel and design matters. In the early months of 1903 Joy insisted that J. W. Packard name Charles Schmidt company engineer, and Packard did so. After Newberry had sent Packard a nasty letter on July 1903, criticizing his design of the Model K Packard car, Packard decided to resign from the firm that bore his name. Joy asked Russell Alger, Jr., to visit Packard in Warren, Ohio, and persuade Packard to remain with the firm. Alger was successful, and Packard remained the titular head of the Packard Motor Car Company until 1909.

When the firm moved to Detroit in October 1903, Packard remained in Ohio to manage his electrical goods manufacturing business. Joy was the only Detroit investor to show much interest in the day-to-day operations of Packard, and the other Detroit capitalists saw Joy as the guardian of their majority interests. By the end of 1903, at the age of thirty-nine, Joy had assumed control of the firm, and his elevation to the presidency in 1909 simply confirmed his power. He remained as president until June 1916, when Alvan Macauley, Packard's general manager, assumed the post. Joy remained on the board of directors until July 1917, when he entered the U.S. Army.

Joy made the Packard Motor Car Company the distinctive automobile company that it remained for its entire corporate history—a producer of high-quality luxury cars with the greatest prestige of any American nameplate. He was the driv-

ing force within the firm from 1902 until 1917. Joy planned the company's move to Detroit, the introduction of new models, the maintenance of the highest quality production in the industry, and the development of the Packard's image as the premier American luxury car. In May 1903 Joy purchased the tract of 66.4 acres in Detroit that became the site of Packard's main manufacturing complex. He decided in January 1903 to employ Albert Kahn to design Packard's Detroit factory, and so provided Kahn his first automobile industry project. The first nine buildings Kahn executed for Packard were standard mill buildings, but Building Number Ten (1905) was the first reinforced concrete factory building in Detroit. In 1911 Kahn also completed the massive Packard Forge Shop, a radical design in steel and glass.

When he took control of Packard, Joy decided that the firm's major goal was to produce automobiles that would sell for $3,000 to $5,000 but yield a profit of $1,000 per vehicle. He had accomplished that goal by 1906. Joy recognized from the start that even a producer of luxury cars had to be efficient in order to earn profits. He insisted on rigid, standardized accounting practices and in 1909 brought Frederick W. Taylor to Detroit to study Packard's manufacturing efficiency. He also established a research-and-development department, known as the Experimental Branch, and hired Milton Tibbetts to supervise industrial research at Packard. Joy increasingly delegated the responsibility for day-to-day operations at Packard to Alvan Macauley, whom he hired as general manager in 1910.

Throughout his tenure at Packard, Joy insisted that the firm maintain the highest possible standards of quality. He personally tested every new model, often subjecting them to severe speed and durability runs. As late as June 1915 Joy drove Packard's new Twin Six model from Detroit to San Francisco. He routinely climbed under the vehicle to inspect the undercarriage during that trip. Joy realized that the Packard's reputation was vital to the firm's success. He was active in Packard's operations until 1916, when he gave up the presidency. Joy remained on the Packard board of directors, but his efforts to enlarge the firm through mergers with other automobile producers gained no support from his fellow directors. When Joy resigned as a director in July 1917 he sold his stock in the firm.

Joy not only managed the Packard Motor Car Company but was extensively involved in the American automobile industry in other ways. He was one of the founders of the Association of Licensed Automobile Manufacturers (ALAM), established in 1903 to lease and control the patents of George B. Selden. After the Selden patent was declared irrelevant by the courts in 1911, the ALAM became the Automobile Manufacturers Association.

Joy was also one of the key participants in the Automobile Manufacturers' Tariff Committee, which lobbied successfully to keep duties on imported automobiles at 45 percent ad valorem when the Payne-Aldrich tariff was written in 1909. He delivered speeches before the National Association of Manufacturers and gave testimony before Congress on the issue. Joy and other automobile producers later fought unsuccessfully against a reduction of duties from 45 percent to 30 percent that was incorporated in the Underwood tariff passed in 1913. He testified before the Senate Finance Committee in March 1912 that European automakers were low-wage competitors who would drive American automobile manufacturers from the field, but to no avail.

Joy clashed with the Progressives on the issue of retail price setting by manufacturers. The courts were increasingly interpreting the Sherman Anti-Trust Act as prohibiting the practice of retail price maintenance. Joy did not propose repeal of the Sherman Act and remained strongly opposed to monopoly, but he believed that the Sherman Act should not apply to retail price maintenance agreements. He argued that it was "the natural right of business" that manufacturers have the "sole right to vend" (set their own retail prices). According to Joy, price-cutting was unfair competition for retailers and consumers alike.

Joy became a major figure in the debate, wrote several articles in national magazines on the issue, addressed a meeting of the Association of National Advertising Managers in May 1913, and served as a spokesman for the National Association of Manufacturers before the House Committee on Interstate and Foreign Commerce in 1914. Joy also served as a director of the Federal Reserve Bank of Chicago in 1913 and 1914, appointed to one of three positions reserved for members of the business community who were not bankers.

Joy was also active in the movement to promote improved roads in the United States. He first de-

veloped a serious interest in western highways after he tried to drive from Omaha to San Francisco in 1912 and discovered that there were simply no roads at all through much of the West. At the same time, Carl G. Fisher of Indianapolis proposed the construction of a highway, named after President Abraham Lincoln, linking New York City with San Francisco. Fisher and Joy founded the Lincoln Highway Association, which held its initial meeting in Detroit in June 1913. Joy was elected president and held the post until he entered military service in 1917. He devoted much time and energy from 1913 to 1915 working out the route that the Lincoln Highway would follow, often personally surveying stretches in Utah and Nevada. Much of the western portion was completed by 1916, but the Lincoln Highway did not extend coast-to-coast until 1923.

Joy also became embroiled in one of many disputes between the city of Detroit and the private street railway system, the Detroit United Railway. In 1920 Mayor James Couzens had ignored his own Railway Commission's proposal that the streetcar lines operate on a strict "rides-at-cost" basis, with no subsidies of any kind. Joy discredited Couzens's argument that this would violate the city charter, and went on to accuse the mayor of misrepresenting the situation in order to build public support for a municipal takeover of the streetcar system.

Joy did not limit his public advocacy to domestic issues. During World War I he viewed American neutrality as immoral and unrealistic, and in 1915 he became a major advocate of "preparedness," believing that United States entry into the war was inevitable. He launched a blistering attack on Henry Ford's pacifism in April 1915 and subtitled one of his pamphlets "A Reply to the Peace-at-any-Price Propaganda of Henry Ford." In September 1915 he produced a series of articles in *Leslie's Illustrated Weekly Magazine* on the dangers of military and naval unpreparedness. Joy consistently argued for universal military training, even in peacetime. His public campaign continued until the United States entered the war in April 1917. To be sure, the Packard Motor Car Company earned profits from the production of war goods, as did the other automakers, including Ford. But Joy's stance on the war seemed to flow from genuine patriotic fervor, not simply from a lust for profits.

Joy dressed for the road in a Packard Model 24 (courtesy of the National Automotive History Collection, Detroit Public Library)

Packard's first connection to the war in Europe came in the form of truck sales to the Allies, with roughly 1,500 trucks sold in both 1915 and 1916. The firm also filled several orders for trucks for the Mexican campaign against Pancho Villa beginning in March 1916. Joy generated favorable publicity by accompanying the Expeditionary Force to observe firsthand his trucks' performance. The reliability of Packard trucks and Joy's willingness to satisfy the army's requirements won Packard substantial orders in 1916 and 1917.

Joy was particularly interested in military aviation and advocated the deployment of a fleet of lighter-than-air ships to aid in coastal defense. He purchased a 640-acre tract northeast of Detroit, on Lake St. Clair, in 1915 and developed Joy Aviation Field there. At Joy's urging, the National Advisory Committee for Aeronautics visited the facility in November 1916 and recommended that the Federal government lease it from Joy. The army leased the property, renamed it Selfridge Field, and established a pilot training base there. Joy eventually sold the property to the government in 1921 for $190,000, the price he had paid for it in 1915.

Joy's most important contribution to the Allied war effort was a gasoline engine for military aircraft. The Packard Twin Six motor, introduced in September 1915, was modified into an aircraft engine, the Packard 299 (the displacement, in cubic inches) in early 1916. The design for a second motor, the Packard 905, also with 12 cylinders but with three times the displacement of its predecessor, was completed in December 1916. Between April 1917 and July 1917 engineers from Packard and several aircraft manufacturers substantially modified the design of the original Packard 905 to produce the Liberty motor. The government then ordered 22,000 of them from six manufacturers. By the end of the war, Packard had produced 6,000 Liberty motors, but several other automobile companies shared the contracts, including the Lincoln Motor Car Company, initially launched for that purpose. Packard, Lincoln, Ford, and Cadillac made 90 percent of the total. The Liberty motor contributed greatly to the Allied air forces' success against German aviators in the closing year of the war.

Joy demonstrated his patriotism in a variety of other ways as well. He was active in the Liberty Loan drives and in January 1916 was elected vice-president of the National Society for the Advancement of Patriotic Education. He enlisted in the U.S. Army (Signal Corps) in July 1917 with the rank of captain. Joy helped organize four motorized regiments that served in France and was promoted to the rank of lieutenant colonel before his discharge in July 1918.

He continued to speak on international issues after the end of the war. Joy opposed American support for the League of Nations, in part because the league could not prevent war but primarily because membership would reduce America's freedom to pursue its own interests internationally. He attacked President Wilson for linking approval of the League of Nations to the peace treaty and then trying to force both down the throat of the U.S. Senate. Joy did not favor leniency toward Germany, especially in the matter of reparations. He argued at length in 1923 that the United States should support France in its efforts to extract reparations from its defeated enemy, citing German treatment of France at the end of the Franco-Prussian War as justification.

However, in the late 1920s he joined the American Association Favoring Reconsideration of the War Debts, a group that advocated the drastic reduction of war debts owed to the United States by its allies. In an open letter to the American business community in 1928, Joy pointed out that most of the Allied war debts were incurred after the United States had entered the fight. During the long period when America contributed little to the war effort, France and Great Britain committed vast resources, including millions of men, to the struggle. The American government could produce an equitable adjustment of the war debts by simply eliminating all debts incurred after the United States entered the war.

Joy's most notable venture into the public policy arena was his lengthy campaign to repeal the Eighteenth Amendment. He favored temperance, but argued that national Prohibition was the work of fanatical Protestant churchmen and represented a serious erosion of individual rights. The power to regulate alcohol should be returned to state and local governments, which better reflected opinion in those jurisdictions. In his mind, Prohibition created more evil than it eliminated. In a February 1926 issue of *Manufacturers Record*, Joy called Henry Leland and other supporters of Prohibition "fanatics" and advocated breaking the law as a statement of personal liberty. Leland wrote an eight-page re-

sponse, delineating the "evils of drink" in ghastly detail.

In the late 1920s Joy helped launch two anti-Prohibition organizations, the Crusaders and the Association for the Repeal of the Eighteenth Amendment. In 1930 he testified against Prohibition before the House Judiciary Committee in February, delivered a series of public addresses, and published letters and other documents opposing the Eighteenth Amendment. He resigned from the Detroit Republican Club the same year, citing his own stance on Prohibition and protesting the hypocrisy of the Republicans. Joy's attacks on the advocates of Prohibition became increasingly strident after 1930. He argued that the Anti-Saloon League was the creation of a small group of Protestant prelates whose ultimate goal was the subversion of American liberties.

Joy spent his last few years attacking liberal Protestant churchmen. He wrote a series of pamphlets in 1935 and 1936 with titles such as "The Enemy Within Our Gates" and "Our Pro-Socialist Churches," in which he accused the Federal Council of Churches of Christ in America of serving as a propaganda machine promoting Prohibition, pacifism, and communism. He published a collection of documents in 1936 outlining conspiratorial connections between the Federal Council of Churches, the Protestant Episcopal Church, the Church League For Industrial Democracy, the American Civil Liberties Union, the Communist Party of America, and various labor unions. Joy argued that those groups were a serious threat to American liberty.

Joy had many interests in addition to business and public policy. His marriage to Helen Hall Newberry resulted in four children: Helen Bourne, Marian Handy, James Frederic, and Henry Bourne. The family enjoyed the trappings of wealth, including three homes and several yachts. In 1908 Joy commissioned Albert Kahn, who had designed most of the Packard Motor Car Company factory complex, to plan a residence on the Detroit River in Grosse Pointe. The resulting house, completed in 1910 and dubbed "Fair Acres," was a relatively simple Georgian design featuring extensive windows. The Joy family also owned a summer home at Watch Hill, Rhode Island.

The style of living that Joy preferred was best reflected in a simple wooden house he built on the Joy Ranch near Mt. Clemens and Lake St. Clair, northeast of Detroit. This was an informal house reflecting the kind of ranch living Joy enjoyed so much during his brief time in the Rockies. The enormous wooden mantle over the living room fireplace bore the motto, "Industry is Fortune's Right Hand." After retiring from Packard, Joy spent most of his time at his "ranch," enjoying his house and nature. Each year around St. Patrick's Day a flock of geese stopped at one of the ponds at the Joy Ranch, and he dubbed these visitors his "Irish Geese."

Joy had two major hobbies—skeet shooting and amateur radio broadcasting. His father had been a world-class skeet shooter, and Henry Joy held several world records in the sport, including shooting a run of 157 without a miss. He invented an electric, automatic target-release device, made several experimental models in 1932 and 1933, and then introduced the "1934 Joy Ranch Single Lever Control Skeet Timer," which he patented and sold commercially.

Joy's interest in radio had its roots in his youth, when he was attracted to telegraphy and had mastered the Morse Code. Shortly after his marriage he built a telegraph system linking his office with his home, enabling him to stay in constant touch with his wife. He was an early member of the Radio Relay League, an organization of radio amateurs. In the early 1920s, when voice transmission became practical, both he and Helen Newberry Joy became avid radio operators. He built elaborate radio transmission facilities at "Fair Acres," the Joy Ranch, his summer home in Rhode Island, and aboard his yacht *Spray III*.

Joy was actively involved in numerous Detroit area social and charitable organizations. He and Frederick K. Stearns, a Detroit pharmaceutical manufacturer, revitalized the Detroit Athletic Club in 1912. He was a major donor to the YMCA, the Red Cross, and the Salvation Army. Joy converted part of his Mt. Clemens estate into a bird sanctuary. He even purchased one of George Washington's diaries and donated it to the Detroit Public Library, where it remains to this day. Joy died in Detroit on November 6, 1936, after suffering from heart disease for many years. Helen Newberry Joy remained an energetic supporter of dozens of Detroit cultural and charitable organizations until her death in 1956.

Selected Publications:

Price Maintenance, Discussion Before Members of the Association of National Advertising Managers, May 14, 1913 (Detroit: Packard Motor Car Company, 1913);

Millions For Tribute, Not One Cent for Defense: A Reply To Henry Ford (Detroit, 1915);

Germany vs. America, France, England, Italy, Belgium, et al (Detroit, 1923);

War Debts: An Argument For Fair Re-Adjustment, Made To American Business Men (Ashburnham, Mass.: American Association Favoring Reconsideration of the War Debts, 1928);

Appeal to President Coolidge's "Court of Last Resort" in Defense of the Constitution of the United States and the Bill of Rights Against the XVIIIth Amendment (Detroit: Henry B. Joy, 1930);

Reference Material Printed For Preservation by Henry B. Joy, With Reference To Federal Council of Churches of Christ In America and Subsidiary Coordinated Councils and American Civil Liberties Union and National Religion and Labor Foundation and Communist-Socialist-Pacifist Activities (Detroit: Henry B. Joy, 1936);

The USS Yosemite, Purisima Conception Incident, June 16, 1898, Also A Brief History of the USS Yosemite (Detroit: Helen Newberry Joy, 1937).

References:

Clarence M. Burton, *The City of Detroit, Michigan, 1701-1922* (Detroit: Clarke, 1922);

Robert Campbell, "Henry B. Joy—He Never Does A Thing Halfway," *Detroit Sunday Times*, December 3, 1922;

Stephen I. Gilchrist, "A Four-Station Radio Amateur," *Detroit Saturday Night*, March 10, 1928, p. 10;

Gilchrist, "Henry Bourne Joy," *Detroit Saturday Night*, November 14, 1936, p. 6;

Grant Hildebrand, *Designing For Industry: The Architecture of Albert Kahn* (Cambridge, Mass.: MIT Press, 1974);

"Henry B. Joy," *National Cyclopedia of American Biography*, 27 (New York: White, 1939);

Beverly Rae Kimes, ed., *Packard: The History of the Motor Car and the Company* (New York: Dutton, 1978);

Albert N. Marquis, ed., *The Book of Detroiters* (Chicago: Marquis, 1914);

Joe McCarthy, "The Lincoln Highway," *American Heritage*, 25 (June 1974): 32-37, 89;

Alan Nevins, *Ford: The Times, The Man, The Company* (New York: Scribners, 1954).

Archives:

Joy's papers are found primarily in a massive manuscript collection at the Bentley Historical Library at the University of Michigan. The Burton Historical Collection of the Detroit Public Library has a small collection of his papers, as well as Joy's publications, extensive clippings files, and photographs. Finally, the National Automotive History Collection at the Detroit Public Library has additional photographs of Joy and miscellaneous materials on the Packard Motor Car Company.

Albert Kahn

(March 21, 1869-December 8, 1942)

by Charles K. Hyde

Wayne State University

CAREER: Office boy, John Scott & Company (1883-1884); office boy, draftsman, and architect (1884-1890), chief designer, Mason and Rice (1892-1895); partner, Nettleton, Kahn and Trowbridge (1896-1897); partner, Nettleton and Kahn (1897-1900); partner, Mason and Kahn (1900-1902); principal architect, Albert Kahn, Architect, Ernest Wilby, Associate (1902-1918); principal architect, Albert Kahn Associates, Architects and Engineers (1918-1942).

Albert Kahn, the most important influence on the design of automobile factories, was born on March 21, 1869, in Rhaunen, Westphalia, Germany, the first of eight children of Joseph and Rosalie Cohn Kahn. Because Joseph Kahn worked as an itinerant rabbi and teacher, the family lived a nomadic life. When Albert was six, they settled in Echternach, Luxembourg, where he spent the rest of his childhood. He attended school there and became an accomplished piano player at age seven. The Kahns immigrated to the United States in 1880 and came directly to Detroit. Albert was only eleven at the time but never resumed his formal education. Because Joseph Kahn was not a particularly good provider, Albert was forced to seek work to help with the family's finances. Like many other architects of the time, he learned his craft as an apprentice to an established architect.

Albert Kahn began working as an office boy for the architectural firm of John Scott & Company in 1883, performing errands and menial work for no pay. While he was working for Scott, the sculptor Julius Melchers allowed him to attend Melchers's drawing classes at no cost. In March 1884 Kahn worked as an office boy at the architectural firm of Mason and Rice. George D. Mason, who was only twenty-six years old, encouraged Kahn to develop his skills as an architect and soon paid him $3.50 a week to help prepare details of

Albert Kahn

working drawings. Mason gave Kahn greater responsibilities over time, and in 1888 Kahn supervised the design and construction of a large residence in Detroit, the Gilbert W. Lee House.

In late 1890 Kahn won the $500 Travelling Scholarship awarded by the *American Architect and Building News*. Starting in December 1890, he spent a year traveling in Europe, visiting England, France, Italy, Germany, Belgium, and Luxembourg. During four months of the trip, Kahn traveled with Henry Bacon, later the architect of the Lincoln Memorial, and from him learned much about aesthetic values in architecture.

After Kahn returned to Detroit in early 1892, Mason and Rice appointed him chief designer for the firm. He designed a variety of residences and in January 1896 established an independent practice with two other Mason and Rice architects, George Nettleton and Alexander B. Trowbridge. Kahn then married Ernestine Krolik of Detroit, daughter of a dry goods merchant, in September 1896. The marriage produced four children: Lydia, Edgar Adolph, Ruth, and Rosalie. After Alexander Trowbridge left the firm in 1897, it continued as Nettleton and Kahn through 1900. Nettleton died in 1900, and Kahn reunited with Mason to form Mason and Kahn, which survived until 1902.

Kahn designed public buildings, private residences, and industrial buildings between 1892 and 1902. His first factory project was a small building of standard mill design, which he completed for the Boyer Machine Company of Detroit in 1901. Joseph Boyer subsequently commissioned Kahn to design the Burroughs Adding Machine Company's Detroit manufacturing plant, built between 1905 and 1919. More important, Boyer was a major stockholder in the Packard Motor Car Company and introduced Kahn to Henry B. Joy, the Packard general manager. When Packard began building a new manufacturing complex in Detroit in 1903, Joy chose Kahn to serve as the firm's architect. The Packard plant became Kahn's first reinforced concrete factory building design, the first of his major contributions to industrial architecture.

Kahn first used reinforced concrete for the floors of the Palms Apartment Building in Detroit, a six-story structure with load-bearing limestone walls designed by Mason and Kahn and built in 1901-1902. Kahn brought his brother Julius, who held an engineering degree from the University of Michigan, into the architectural firm as chief engineer. The two shared an interest in reinforced concrete, which they used as the frame for the University of Michigan Engineering Building, completed in 1903. Julius also established the Trussed Concrete Steel Company in Detroit to manufacture his own reinforcing bars, and the two brothers worked together for more than a decade.

Starting in 1903, Kahn designed a series of buildings for Packard using standard mill construction, with load-bearing masonry walls and the extensive use of interior timber or cast-iron columns to support the wood floors. When he designed Building Number Ten in 1905, he adopted reinforced concrete throughout, producing the first reinforced concrete factory building in Detroit. His work on the Packard complex, which had grown to 1.6 million square feet by 1911, established Kahn as the premier factory architect for the automobile industry. In the course of his career, he completed a dozen major projects for the University of Michigan; several notable commercial buildings, including the vast General Motors Building (1922) and the Fisher Building (1928), both in Detroit; theaters and other public buildings; and more than a dozen residences, mainly for his industrial clients. Still, his most significant work was his industrial architecture, primarily for the automobile industry.

Kahn's success was in part a result of his willingness to specialize in industrial architecture while situated in Detroit on the eve of the explosive growth of the automobile industry. He was one of the earliest proponents of reinforced concrete in factory design, which proved particularly suitable for automobile manufacturers. Compared to standard mill designs of the nineteenth century and before, reinforced concrete buildings were much stronger, particularly in resisting vibration, as well as virtually fireproof. They typically featured 30-foot clearances between columns, whereas standard mill construction rarely exceeded 20-foot clearances.

Reinforced concrete buildings were relatively low-cost as well, because they were built with unskilled labor and cheap materials. Finally, the design could be built quickly, a great advantage in a rapidly expanding industry. At the end of April 1910 John Dodge gave Kahn preliminary plans for a new factory, and Dodge approved the final plans on June 3. Construction was virtually completed by mid October, and Dodge Brothers Company began production in their new plant at the end of November.

Most of Kahn's factory designs executed between 1905 and the early 1920s used reinforced concrete framing for the major multistory buildings and steel-framed designs for the remaining one-story structures. Starting with the Ford Highland Park plant, begun in 1909, he used steel-sash windows exclusively. After his major work for Packard, Kahn designed most of the new plants in the automobile industry: the enormous George N. Pierce plant in Buffalo, New York (1906); the Grabowsky Power Wagon factory in Detroit (1907); the Chalmers Motor Car Company complex in Detroit (1907); the first portion of the

Dodge Brothers Company plant in Hamtramck, Michigan (1910-1914); the Ford Motor Car Company plant in Highland Park, Michigan (1910-1918); the Hudson Motor Car Company plant in Detroit (1910); the Continental Motors Corporation factory in Detroit (1912); and a series of Fisher Body Company plants in Detroit (1919-1922) and in Cleveland (1921).

Albert Kahn's firm expanded as the volume of work grew. In 1902 Ernest Wilby joined the firm as chief designer, and from 1902 until 1918 all work was completed under the imprint, "Albert Kahn, Architect, Ernest Wilby, Associate." In 1910 Albert Kahn brought his brother Louis into the firm as a manager, and Louis quickly became second in command. The office staff, which included architects and engineers, stood at 40 in 1910 and then grew to 80 by 1918, when the firm began to operate under the title, "Albert Kahn Associates, Architects and Engineers," followed by a list of his associates. Ernest Wilby, who left the firm in 1922, apparently worked primarily on the firm's residential and commercial projects, as well as on decorative detailing for the factories.

Despite his growing wealth and fame, Kahn remained a quiet, unassuming, and intensely private man throughout his life. He built an unostentatious house in Detroit in 1907 and lived there until his death. Even the summer home he built at Walnut Lake, Michigan, in 1917 was a modest residence for a person of his wealth. He took his wife Ernestine on an extended European tour in 1911-1912, but that was one of the few luxuries he allowed himself. Well into the 1920s he drew a salary of only $40 a week and lived modestly. Habits he had developed during an austere and difficult youth remained for the rest of his life.

Most of Kahn's industrial work between 1905 and 1915 was executed in reinforced concrete, but he again revolutionized factory design beginning in the 1920s with his sprawling single-story buildings utilizing steel frames encased in glass. Kahn had executed steel-and-glass designs as early as 1904, when he built a large single-story building with sawtooth roofs for the Burroughs Adding Machine Company. The machine shop (1910) at the Ford Highland Park plant used a similar configuration. His design for the Packard Motor Car Company forge shop (1911) foreshadowed his later work. This large steel-framed building, encased in glass, had a column-free floor 72 feet in width.

Kahn executed his first major factory designs in steel and glass at the Ford Motor Company River Rouge complex in Dearborn, Michigan. The Ford Eagle Plant (1917), built for the manufacture of submarine chasers, was 1,702 feet in length and was divided into five aisles 51 feet wide. This enormous building, featuring glass walls and butterfly roof monitors with clerestories to admit light and provide ventilation, was the first major expression of the new industrial architecture. Kahn went on to design a glass plant (1922), foundry (1923), open hearth building (1925), pressed steel building (1925), motor assembly building (1925), and a half-dozen additional structures at the Ford Rouge Plant in the 1920s. His other major automobile factory projects of this era, including the Buick Motor Car Company plant (1919) in Flint and the Chrysler Corporation Lynch Road Assembly Plant in Detroit (1928), utilized the same design principles.

Although he did considerable work for a large number of clients, Kahn's factory designs for Henry Ford were by far the most significant. Both pioneers were unpretentious, self-made men equally suspicious of book learning. Kahn once remarked that "architecture was 90 percent business and 10 percent art," sentiments that Ford certainly shared. They developed a long-term working relationship in which Kahn produced innovative factory designs to match the automaker's innovative manufacturing concepts. Ford's respect for Kahn, a Jew, overruled the automaker's often-virulent anti-Semitism.

During the 1920s Kahn was easily the most important industrial architect in the world, in terms of the design innovations he introduced and in terms of the sheer volume of work his firm completed. He designed 50 major factory complexes, primarily for automobile manufacturers, in addition to numerous public and commercial buildings. His brother Moritz, who had previously worked with Julius Kahn, joined Albert in 1923. The firm had a staff of 400 by 1929, but its founder continued to leave his imprint on every project. Kahn's international reputation was confirmed when the government of the Soviet Union approached him in April 1929 with a commission to design much of the country's expanding factory space. He accepted the proposal and established a branch office in Moscow to manage the work. When the Soviets terminated the relationship in March 1932, Kahn's staff had designed 521 plants, including an enormous tractor plant at Cheliabinsk.

The Depression brought an abrupt decline in the construction of new manufacturing plants until the late 1930s. Kahn's major work from then until his death in 1942 was almost entirely industrial. He completed major projects for the Burroughs Adding Machine Company, Republic Steel, the Glenn L. Martin Company, Kelvinator Corporation, and others, but his work remained heavily focused on the automobile industry. Some of his most striking and beautiful designs appeared in the last phase of his career, including the DeSoto Press Shop (1936) in Detroit and the Chrysler Corporation Dodge Half-Ton Truck plant (1938) in Warren, Michigan. Other notable automotive projects included the Ford Motor Company Tire Plant (1936) at the Rouge complex, the General Motors Diesel Engine Plant (1937) in Detroit, and the Ford Motor Company Press Shop (1939), also at the River Rouge complex.

Kahn's energies focused on defense work during the last three years of his life. His firm received more than $200 million in defense contracts between December 1939 and December 1941. As defense work expanded dramatically, Kahn increased his staff to more than 600 by 1941. His last major projects included the Chrysler Corporation Tank Arsenal (1941) in Warren, Michigan; the Willow Run Bomber Plant (1943) near Ypsilanti, Michigan; and the Chrysler Corporation Dodge Chicago plant (1943). Over the course of his career, Albert Kahn designed factories worth more than $2 billion.

Kahn suffered his first heart attack in 1939, while visiting a prospective client in Cleveland. His third heart attack, in mid November 1942, left him weakened and bed-ridden. He died in Detroit on December 8, 1942, of a bronchial ailment.

Albert Kahn's contributions to industrial architecture were widely recognized at home and abroad. In 1937 he was made a chevalier of the Legion of Honor in France and received a gold medal at the International Exposition of Arts and Sciences in Paris. The American Institute of Architects gave him a special award in 1942 for his work in concrete-and-steel factory design. Shortly after his death, the Franklin Institute awarded Kahn the Frank P. Brown Medal for his achievements in industrial architecture. He was the most important industrial architect of the twentieth century, primarily because of the large, innovative manufacturing plants he designed for the automobile industry.

Selected Publication:

"Industrial Architecture," *Michigan Engineer*, 57 (January 1939): 8-18.

References:

"Albert Kahn," *Architectural Forum*, 69 (August 1938): 87-142;

Albert Kahn, Inc., *Architectural Catalogue, October 1921* (New York: Architectural Catalogue Company, 1921);

Albert Kahn, Inc., *Industrial and Commercial Buildings* (Detroit: Albert Kahn, Inc., 1925);

Albert Kahn, Inc., *Industrial and Commercial Buildings* (Detroit: Albert Kahn, Inc., 1936);

W. Hawkins Ferry, *The Legacy of Albert Kahn* (Detroit: Detroit Institute of Arts, 1970);

Grant Hildebrand, *Designing For Industry: The Architecture of Albert Kahn* (Cambridge, Mass.: MIT Press, 1974);

Edgar Kahn, "Albert Kahn: His Son Remembers," *Michigan History*, 69 (July/August 1985): 24-31;

Sol King, *Creative, Responsive, Pragmatic: 75 Years of Professional Practice, Albert Kahn Associates, Architects-Engineers* (New York: Newcomen Society, 1970);

David Lewis, "Ford and Kahn," *Michigan History*, 64 (September/October 1980): 17-28;

Michigan Society of Architects, *Weekly Bulletin, Albert Kahn Memorial Issue, Featuring Some Recent Works of Albert Kahn Associates, Architects-Engineers, Inc.*, 17 (March 30, 1943);

George Nelson, *Industrial Architecture of Albert Kahn* (New York: Architectural Book Publishing, 1939);

Lydia Robinson, "Albert Kahn," *Architectural Review*, 152 (June 1975): 349-357.

Archives:

The largest collection of materials on Kahn's work can be found in the archives of Albert Kahn Associates, Architects and Engineers, Detroit, which includes the original drawings for virtually all of his work, plus an extensive collection of photographs. Few of the business records have survived, and family members hold most of the remaining private papers. The Bentley Historical Library, University of Michigan, has miscellaneous Kahn materials as well.

Kelsey-Hayes

by George S. May

Eastern Michigan University

Long one of the best-known names in the auto-parts industry, the firm of Kelsey-Hayes resulted from a 1927 merger of the Kelsey Wheel Company and the Hayes Wheel Company. The Kelsey company was organized in Detroit by John Kelsey and several others in 1909. Kelsey, whose businesses are not to be confused with the two short-lived automobile ventures organized in the East a few years later by Cadwallader W. Kelsey, had developed a spring automobile wheel. It proved to be impractical, however, and at Henry Ford's suggestion Kelsey turned to the production of standard wooden wheels. Ford sales got the Kelsey company off to a good start; almost $185,000 of its first-year sales of $229,000 came from sales of wheels for the Model T. Fearful of being too dependent on Ford, Kelsey then sought to limit sales to Ford to no more than one-fourth of his annual output. By 1915 Kelsey had acquired from 15 to 20 percent of the market for wheels, with annual sales more than $3.5 million. Ford accounted for some $695,000 of that figure, with the rest accounted for by purchases from Cadillac, Chalmers, Hupmobile, Hudson, Paige, Saxon, and Studebaker, among others. In addition to wheels, Kelsey also produced wooden auto bodies, supplying as much as 20 percent of Ford's needs. However, when Ford, following the industry trend, turned to steel bodies in the 1920s, Kelsey chose not to make the necessary adjustments and shortly ceased body production.

The Hayes Wheel Company was founded in 1908 by Clarence B. Hayes, not to be confused with H. Jay Hayes, whose Hayes Manufacturing Company of Detroit was during this period one of the largest manufacturers of automobile bodies. Clarence Hayes was an experienced manufacturer of carriage wheels, having managed the Standard Wheel Company of Kalamazoo in the 1890s. In 1899 he became president and general manager of the Imperial Wheel Company, a subsidiary of the giant Durant-

Dort carriage combine. With the growth of the automobile industry, which drew William C. Durant and J. Dallas Dort into auto manufacturing, Imperial, under Hayes's direction, soon produced wheels for motor vehicles as well as for buggies.

In 1908 Hayes left Imperial and took over the National Wheel Company in Jackson, renaming it the Hayes Wheel Company. It quickly emerged as the largest of the automobile wheel manufacturers, eventually turning out more than 50 million wheels at plants in Jackson, Flint, St. Johns, and Albion, Michigan; Anderson, Indiana; and Nashville, Tennessee. By 1921 it was supplying as much as 60 percent of the industry's needs and was selling $1 million worth of wheels each month to Ford alone, one-third of the combined annual sales of Durant-Dort carriage operations in 1900. Like Kelsey, Hayes produced wood wheels, and by the 1920s a move to wire wheels was gaining momentum. The threat that presented was the primary motive behind the 1927 merger.

In 1935 Clarence Hayes, while remaining a director of Kelsey-Hayes, formed Hayes Industries in Jackson (later Hayes-Albion), which built auto parts and airplane wheels. That gave Clarence Hayes the distinction of having "spanned the three phases of modern vehicular wheel making" during his career.

In the 1920s Kelsey began producing a wire wheel of its own design, but the threat of a costly patent fight (over claims that the wheel infringed on the wire wheel patent of Edward P. Cowles) led Kelsey-Hayes to purchase the Wire Wheel Corporation of Buffalo in 1929. That company licensed wheel production under the Cowles patent. It turned out, however, that the Cowles patent was not owned by Wire Wheel but by the Packard Motor Car Company. Kelsey-Hayes later bought the patent from Packard for $500,000, and by licensing other wheel manufacturers, such as the Budd

Company, was able to recover the money, after which it lifted further restrictions on the patent's use.

Acquisition of Wire Wheel was part of an expansion following the merger of the two wheel companies. In 1929 the purchase of the General Motors (GM) subsidiary Jaxon Steel Products Company of Jackson gave Kelsey-Hayes greater access to GM's automotive divisions, since Jaxon had been supplying much of those divisions' wheels. In 1928 Kelsey-Hayes began producing brakes for the new Ford Model A, inaugurating a product that would continue to be a major element in the corporation's increasingly diversified lines. In later years Kelsey-Hayes moved into the production of wheels, rims, and brakes for trucks and tractors; electric brakes and axle assemblies for mobile homes; recreational vehicles; light commercial trailers; and transmissions, gearbox assemblies, actuators, and other parts for the aviation industry. In 1956, in recognition of those changes, the company became simply the Kelsey-Hayes Corporation. Nevertheless, wheels remained its mainstay, and in 1955 it introduced the industry's first aluminum wheels for passenger cars.

In 1973 Kelsey-Hayes became a wholly owned subsidiary of the Fruehauf Corporation. Under the new arrangement Kelsey-Hayes continued to be the largest independent supplier of automobile wheels, disc brakes, and skid control systems in the country. In 1989, in a complicated series of moves that resulted in the divestiture of Fruehauf's trailer operations, Kelsey-Hayes became the corporation's primary remaining operation. In recognition the corporation's name was changed from Fruehauf to that of the K-H Corporation.

References:

Automotive Industry of America (Southfield, Mich.: Prestige, 1979);

George S. May, *A Most Unique Machine: the Michigan Origins of the American Automobile Industry* (Grand Rapids, Mich.: Eerdmans, 1975);

Allan Nevins and Frank Ernest Hill, *Ford: The Times, the Man, the Company* (New York: Scribners, 1954).

Charles Brady King

(February 2, 1868-June 23, 1957)

by George S. May

Eastern Michigan University

CAREER: Draftsman, Michigan Car Company (1889-1892); representative, World's Columbian Exposition, Russell Wheel & Foundry Company (1893); owner, Charles B. King Company (1893-1901); engineer, Olds Motor Works (1900-1901); engineer, Michigan Yacht & Power Company (1901-1902); chief engineer, Northern Motor Car Company (1902-1907); chief engineer, King Motor Car Company (1910-1912); aeronautical mechanical engineer, U.S. Army Signal Corps (1916-1919).

Few of the pioneers of the American automobile industry had as varied and as interesting a career as Charles Brady King, although he is mostly remembered for having built and driven the first gasoline automobile in Detroit. He was born on February 2, 1868, at Camp Reynolds on Angel Island in San Francisco Bay, the son of Col. John Haskell King and Matilda Davenport King. King's father had been in the army since 1837, serving in the Indian campaigns in Florida, the Mexican War, and coming out of the Civil War brevetted major general (an honorary rank). Until Colonel King retired in 1882, his son's boyhood was punctuated by continual moves from one army post to another, an experience, Charles King would say, that led him to develop "an early interest in transportation."

When John King retired from the army, he moved his family to Detroit, the hometown of his wife. Charles King was sent to an Episcopal private school in Port Hope, Ontario, which he attended for two years before being enrolled in 1886 in the Cascadilla school at Ithaca, New York, a preparatory school for Cornell University. In 1887 King entered Cornell's Sibley School of Mechanical Engineering, where he not only began gaining the engineering knowledge that would be so important in his business career but also practiced music and

Charles Brady King (courtesy of the Motor Vehicle Manufacturers Association)

graphic arts, both of which were notable features of his later years.

The death of his father in 1888 forced King to withdraw from Cornell and return to Detroit, where he got a job as a draftsman with the Michigan Car Company, the largest of several firms that made Detroit a center for the manufacture of railroad cars and equipment. A handsome, confident, and talented young man, King was soon given more responsible positions in the company before moving on to take a job with another Detroit manufacturer of railroad equipment, the Russell Wheel & Foundry Company, which in 1893 named King as its representative at the World's Columbian Exposition in Chicago.

King's experiences in Chicago from the time the fair opened in May until it closed in October marked the turning point in his life. The Russell company that he represented won an award for its logging cars, but King also received the exposition's highest award, a bronze medal and a diploma, for a pneumatic hammer he had designed in 1890, which he described as the first practical tool of this type developed in the country. A steel brake beam

that he would later patent was also displayed on several refrigerator cars exhibited at the fair. King's sale of the patent rights to the brake beam to the American Brake Beam Company in 1894 was the first of the benefits he reaped from the 64 patents he obtained during his lifetime that eventually made him independently wealthy. The most important result of his Chicago experience, however, was the stimulus that it provided to an interest he had already begun to develop in the newly emerging automotive field.

Not far from the Russell exhibit in the transportation building was an exhibit of the Daimler Motor Company. A gasoline-propelled car was part of this exhibit, but in later years King could not remember having seen it. This is perhaps because he was more interested in the Daimler engines that he saw there and that William Steinway, the piano manufacturer, who was Daimler's authorized American agent, was primarily interested in promoting at that time. Steinway's representative at the Chicago fair, a Mr. Weinman, proposed to King that the Russell company could manufacture the engines under a license from Steinway. King did not pursue the idea, in part because he saw some difficulties involved with manufacturing the engine and in part because the royalties that Russell would have to pay would not have made the deal a very profitable one. But for this, King noted, the Russell Wheel and Foundry Company could have become Detroit's first automobile parts manufacturer.

Although King examined and rode in the electric vehicle that a Chicago battery company exhibited at the fair and was undoubtedly familiar with the experimental steamers that had been around for many years, he apparently was convinced from the outset that the gasoline internal combustion engine was the most efficient means of powering horseless carriages. He was attracted, however, not by the possibilities offered by the Daimler engine but those of a 1-cylinder, 2-cycle engine produced by the Sintz Gas Engine Company of Grand Rapids, Michigan. It was designed to be used as a marine engine, but King, when he saw the Sintz exhibit, felt he could adapt it to power a land vehicle, and in July 1893 he ordered a Sintz engine to be delivered to him in Detroit that fall.

When he returned to Detroit, King decided to go into business for himself, although whether the Charles B. King Company was established at this time or somewhat later is not clear. The money he received from the sale of his patented brake beam provided the financial foundation for the business, which initially centered on the production of King's pneumatic hammer. Through an arrangement worked out with John Lauer, this tool was produced in Lauer's Detroit machine shop at a moderate charge to King, who rented office space on the second floor of the shop. Lauer, whom King considered at least as capable a machinist as Henry M. Leland, Detroit's most famous machine shop operator, even allowed King to supervise the production of the pneumatic hammer. In 1894 King hired a young assistant, Oliver E. Barthel, whose fluency in German enabled him to communicate King's instructions to Lauer's predominantly German-speaking work force.

Brake beams and pneumatic hammers were both an indication of King's wide-ranging mechanical interests and a source of income for him. But his main concern at this time was to construct a horseless carriage. Late in 1893 he had drafted plans for both 3-wheeled and 4-wheeled carriages, the latter including a left-hand, wheel-steering arrangement that was in contrast to most systems employed by other American experimenters of that period, which placed the driver on the right-hand side, steering with a lever. The carriage was designed to be powered by the Sintz engine, to be attached beneath the body of the carriage, but as King began working with that engine he soon concluded, as did Elwood Haynes, the Apperson brothers, and Frank Duryea, who also experimented with this engine, that the 2-cycle engine provided insufficient power. He then set to work to build an engine of his own design. Exactly when he completed this engine and used it to power a car has been a subject of some controversy. The claim that he conducted tests of a vehicle late in 1894 was widely circulated for many years, particularly after the King Motor Car Company included it in advertisements for its cars, which began to appear in 1910. However, when the *Chicago Times-Herald* in summer 1895 announced it would sponsor America's first automobile race that November, King sent in his entry, only to withdraw it a few weeks later, explaining that he could not finish building his car by the date of the race. This caused the historian Milo M. Quaife to ask King in 1940 that if he had driven his car in 1894 "wouldn't you have been able and ready to go to the race at Chicago a year later?" Obviously taken aback by the question, the

seventy-two-year-old King replied, "That is a thought."

The first public demonstration of a King-built, self-propelled vehicle actually did not take place until March 6, 1896. Private tests may have preceded the public debut, but certainly not by more than a few days. Predating the successful launching of an automotive pioneer's work, as the King company did in its ads, was not unusual. For 40 years Ford Motor Company insisted that Henry Ford's first car was driven three years before he actually drove it. Since King in later years seems to have been genuinely uncertain as to the year in which his first car became operational, it is possible that he and the King company were unaware that the 1894 date was incorrect.

Barthel later claimed that much of the work on the horseless carriage had been completed when he came to work for King late in 1894. King's limited financial resources seem to have been the major cause of the delay in completing the vehicle, which made the $5,000 in prize money to be awarded to the winners of the *Times-Herald* race a special inducement in 1895. He described his entry as a light vehicle weighing 675 pounds, driven by a 4-horsepower 100-pound engine. Indicating that he intended to manufacture the car, he estimated that it would "probably be sold for about $600." Although he never got the car into production, King's plans in 1895 foreshadowed the later approaches of Ransom Olds and Henry Ford to concentrate on low-priced, lightweight cars. It was soon apparent, however, that King was not as far along on the vehicle as Barthel later claimed, and by the latter part of September King had advised race officials to withdraw his name. He would claim that problems in getting pneumatic tires forced his withdrawal, but in 1940 he told Quaife, "I didn't have money enough to get it through."

As it turned out, King was a participant in the race after all. Of the more than 80 entries received, only six vehicles made it to the starting line on Thanksgiving Day. Each was assigned an umpire to see that the driver abided by the rules of the contest, and King was the umpire assigned to an imported Benz driven by Oscar Mueller of Decatur, Illinois, who was, with his father, the owner of the car. Mechanical problems prevented Mueller's Benz from getting underway until 10 A.M., an hour after the other cars, but it and the winning Duryea Motor Wagon, driven by Frank Duryea, were the only entries to finish the 53-mile, snow-covered course. Driving conditions and more mechanical troubles hindered Mueller's efforts to make up the lost time, and late in the day fatigue, a lack of much food since morning, and the cold weather caused Mueller to collapse. King was able to stop the car, and since the rules specified that the driver at the start of the race must still be in the car at the finish, he shoved the unconscious Mueller into the passenger's seat while he took over the driving. Holding Mueller with one hand and steering with the other, King drove the rest of the way, finishing the race at 8:53 P.M., more than an hour and a half after Duryea.

Aside from the thrill of having taken part in the race, King benefited greatly from his contacts with those who shared his automotive interests, and who had been attracted to Chicago by this event. During the preceding year King had subscribed to a French newspaper and to a New York clipping service as part of his effort to learn more about automotive developments in Europe and elsewhere in the United States. Now, recognizing the opportunity that would be offered by the assembling of like-minded individuals in Chicago, King, in a letter dated October 8, 1895, which was published in the *Times-Herald* and other publications, called for the formation of an organization of those "interested in the coming revolution, the motor vehicle . . . in order to pave the way for the early success of this vehicle of the future." The response was favorable, and in November the American Motor League (AML), the name King had suggested, was organized in Chicago, with the members on the day after the Thanksgiving Day race electing officers that included Charles Duryea as president and King as treasurer.

The AML was soon to be replaced by more effective organizations that represented automotive interests, but as the first such group in the country the league signaled the emergence of a new era. King's role in organizing the league grew out of his realization that the manufacturing of motor vehicles was, as he told a correspondent, becoming "a reality." The first issue of *Horseless Age*, in November 1895, included an advertisement for "King's Patent Gas Engine for Vehicles, Launches, etc." Within two months, he told a correspondent, he hoped to have on the market a 2-cylinder engine "designed exclusively for vehicle use." But then he received a letter from one of the Duryea brothers, whose Duryea

Motor Wagon Company was capitalizing on its victory in the *Times-Herald* race by pushing ahead with the production of its motor wagon at its plant in Springfield, Massachusetts. King was asked whether he would be interested in manufacturing the Duryea engine. He responded in the affirmative, and on January 18, 1896, he signed an agreement with the Duryea company to manufacture in Detroit the engine developed by Frank Duryea, which would, however, be called the Duryea-King Gas Engine, with the Duryea company receiving a ten percent royalty on all the engines King sold. The engines were for other users of gas engines, but King was willing to supply the Duryeas with engines "at a very low figure" if the demand for their motor wagons outstripped their ability to meet their own engine needs.

Frank Duryea later declared that the agreement was of great importance to his company because it constituted "our first recognition by one who really knew engines." But for King the agreement proved of little value. Despite his best efforts to drum up business, including contacts with the Packard brothers of Warren, Ohio, future developers of the Packard automobile, he made only one sale. One engine, produced for King in John Lauer's shop, was purchased by the Emerson & Fisher Company of Cincinnati, carriage builders who had been commissioned to build a horseless carriage that would be used by the Robinson & Franklin Brothers Circus as one of its attractions. In April 1896 King spent a week in Cincinnati supervising the installation of the engine. He warned the head of the circus, John Robinson, that it would not be able to make it up steep hills under its own power, and Robinson assured him that in such cases he would have his biggest elephant walking behind, ready to push the carriage the rest of the way.

King's view that the Duryea-King engine, like the earlier Sintz engine, did not provide sufficient power led him to turn back to the engines of his own design. Early in 1896 he took the 4-cylinder engine out of the still-uncompleted motor car he had been working on since 1894 and installed it in an iron-tired wagon that H. D. Emerson, a Cincinnati carriage builder, let him have to conduct his experiments. It was this self-propelled wagon, with a left-hand drive and a tiller, rather than the steering wheel that had also been part of King's original plans of 1893, that King, at 11 P.M. on the evening

King (right) and his assistant Oliver E. Barthel in King's first car, publicly demonstrated on March 6, 1896

of March 6, 1896, drove out of the shop and over to Detroit's main business thoroughfare, Woodward Avenue. The local papers reported the appearance of what one newsman described somewhat redundantly as "a most unique machine." King, however, assured the reporter that such vehicles were already becoming more commonplace elsewhere in the United States and in Europe and that he was "convinced they will in time supersede the horse."

King announced that he intended to have a motor carriage on the market before long. Although the Duryeas, who touched off the commercial phase of the automobile's development in America, had sold their first motor wagon only a few days before King's test drive on the streets of Detroit, a good many individuals hoped to be producing horseless carriages in a short time. Among these were Henry Ford, who tested his quadricycle in Detroit on the night of June 4, 1896, and Ransom Olds, who had built and driven two steam-powered carriages some years earlier and who tested his first gasoline-powered carriage in Lansing on August 11. King had only secondhand information concerning

Olds, but he had a hand in the work that led up to Ford's test of the quadricycle. King had become acquainted with Ford because of the latter's frequent visits to John Lauer's machine shop in connection with the work Ford did for the Edison Illuminating Company. In winter 1895-1896 King and his assistant Barthel had called Ford's attention to an article in a technical magazine that described a gasoline internal combustion engine. This inspired Ford to build what King and Barthel declared was the first such engine he had constructed. King provided advice and some material and worked with Ford until 3 A.M. one night to get the engine working in Ford's kitchen. This was the engine that Ford used to power the vehicle he tested the following June. Later that summer King rode with Ford when he drove the horseless carriage out to his father's farm in Dearborn. King declared that the father "was ashamed of a grown-up man like Henry fussing over a little thing like a quadricycle. We'd gone and humiliated him in front of his friends." Finally, a heartbroken Ford said to King, "Come on, Charlie, let's you and me get out of here."

It was to be several years before either Ford or Olds would have many of their cars available for the public to buy, but for King it would be much longer. And his position in the company that finally began producing cars bearing his name was much different from that held by Ford and Olds in their companies. Following his test run in March 1896, King sold the 4-cylinder engine he had used at that time, together with its blueprints and patterns, to Charles Annesley, a Detroiter who later bought Ford's quadricycle before moving to Buffalo, where he became involved in the manufacture of the engine King had designed. King then designed a 2-cylinder engine that he used in a second experimental vehicle that he was testing in summer 1896. He succeeded in selling a few of the engines, and by early 1897 he also had for sale several other automotive parts. But money remained a problem, as King explained to John Brisben Walker when he urged Walker to increase the prize money Walker was offering in a race sponsored by his *Cosmopolitan* magazine on Memorial Day, 1896. "This art is at present in a crude state," King said, "and is mainly in the hands of the inventor, who has not as yet been encouraged by capital." In 1897 three of King's wealthy Detroit friends, Henry B. Joy and Truman and John Newberry, who a few years later would be principal backers of the Packard Motor Car Company, provided King with some financial help for the production of marine engines. Of necessity, marine engines now became the main focus of the work of King's company, although he continued to advertise the availability of automotive engines and other parts.

At the outbreak of the Spanish-American War in spring 1898, King, who was a member of the Michigan Naval Reserve, was called into active service, along with Joy, the Newberrys, and many other Detroit socialites who were part of this organization and who served in the war on the *U.S.S. Yosemite*. While King, who was a chief petty officer, was off to war, Barthel looked after King's business. Later in the year, after the end of the war and the return of the sailors to Detroit, Joy and the Newberrys pulled out of King's company, leaving him to his own resources. He continued to try to promote automotive sales, but aside from selling the carriage he had been working on from 1894 to 1895 to Byron J. Carter, future developer of the friction-drive Cartercar, in June 1899, he had little success. His efforts on the marine side of the business did lit-

tle better. In January 1900 he wrote to Mrs. J. A. Vanderpoel of Boston begging that he be paid the remainder of his bill for the $10,000 yacht he had designed and built for her and her husband: "I am badly in need of funds and have stood off my creditors regarding the yacht as long as possible."

Shortly thereafter King sold his marine engine business to the Olds Motor Works, which had been established in Detroit the previous year to produce the automobile Ransom Olds had developed. The company also produced gasoline engines, and King went to work for the company as an engineer involved with the production of the marine engines. Later, after a fire destroyed much of the Olds plant in March 1901, Olds sold the marine engine division to Detroit's Michigan Yacht and Power Company, with King going along to handle engine design and production for that company. In May 1901 King sold his pneumatic tool business, which he had left in the hands of Barthel when he went to work for Olds. Thus ended the independent business operations that King had started with such high hopes after his return from the Chicago World's Fair.

In 1902 King left the Michigan Yacht & Power Company to become chief engineer for the Northern Manufacturing Company, shortly renamed the Northern Motor Car Company. Northern was a new Detroit company that had been formed by William T. Barbour and G. B. Gunderson of the Detroit Stove Works to produce a lightweight car originally designed by Jonathan D. Maxwell, a former colleague of King's at the Olds Motor Works. Although King is said to have recommended Maxwell to Olds, he developed a low opinion of Maxwell's engineering abilities, claiming that the Northern runabout did not work properly until he joined the company and corrected Maxwell's errors. In 1903 Maxwell left Northern, taking with him King's chief draftsman, who, King declared, did most of the work on the car that the new Maxwell-Briscoe company began to produce in 1904.

King remained with Northern for five years. Despite a promising start the company failed to become one of the leaders in the industry, and in 1908 it was merged with the Wayne Automobile Company to form the more successful Everitt-Metzger-Flanders (E-M-F) company. While King was in charge of its design, the Northern included advanced features on which he received five patents in

1907 and 1908. But before all of those patents had been awarded to him, King had left the company. In summer 1907 the company announced that in August he was going to Europe for three months to study foreign automobile construction, presumably to gain ideas for the next Northern models. A short time later King resigned as the company's chief engineer.

The reasons behind King's resignation are not known, but it may have had something to do with his desire to travel in Europe for longer than three months. He was away for two years, and during much of that time he was concerned not only with automobiles but also with the opportunity he had to develop his artistic talents, which were of a high order. He painted in oils and watercolors, but he became best known for black-and-white etchings, which were exhibited at the annual Paris Salons. One of these, "A Rainy Day—Fifth Avenue," appeared for many years in the annual handbook of the New York Public Library. Apparently King's once-limited financial resources had now been increased sufficiently so that he could support himself in Europe, although it is possible that he may have received some support through his wife, Grace Fletcher, whom he had married in 1901 and who was the daughter of George Nichols Fletcher, a wealthy Michigan lumberman.

Toward the end of 1909 King returned to Detroit and became involved in the formation of a new company that produced a car designed by him and carrying his name. However, aside from claiming that the car he designed introduced the cantilever spring, the central-control gearshift, and improved placement of the front lamps (it also included left-hand steering, which King claimed to have been the first to employ in his 1907 Northern), King in later years made few references to the King company. The early Kings were 4-cylinder cars that were replaced by 8-cylinder models beginning in 1914, when the King was the first American car to follow Cadillac's lead in using a V-8 engine. The King was a reasonably good car that was produced in limited numbers until 1924, when production ceased at the plant in Buffalo, where operations had been shifted the previous year. Charles King left the company in 1912 and had nothing to do with it or its cars thereafter.

At the time he left the King Motor Car Company he regained control of his patents. The sale of the rights to some of these patents to companies such as GM, Reo, and the Splitdorf Electrical Company, producer of ignition systems, plus the royalties he received from those patents that he retained, provided King with the freedom to be entirely on his own. Although he could have had his choice of high-ranking executive positions in numerous automotive companies, he was never again so employed during the remaining 45 years of his life. Increasingly his experimental work turned to the aviation field, and in 1916 he was appointed aeronautical mechanical engineer in charge of the division of engine design in the U.S. Army Signal Corps, which was at that time in charge of army aviation. During World War I King directed the development of three aircraft engines, including guns mounted to fire through the propeller shaft. In the case of the 450-horsepower, 15-cylinder King-Bugatti engine, 2,000 of which were produced, he also mounted a Browning gun that was synchronized to be fired between the rotating propeller blades. In addition he provided assistance from his office in Washington to the automotive engineers in Detroit who designed the famous Liberty aircraft engine, a name suggested by King.

King, a veteran of two wars, "had no wish to continue on the governmental payroll in time of peace," and thus in 1919 he resigned his position in the Signal Corps, never again to be on anyone's payroll. He did not return to Detroit. "The spadework was over in Detroit," he told Brendan Gill of the New Yorker in 1946. "The fun was going out of it." He and his wife moved to Larchmont, New York, where King had bought an old brick carriage house and stable that overlooked Long Island Sound. "I had so many . . . things to try," King said: "architecture, music, painting, travel! I knew there wouldn't be time enough for them all!" For three or four years in the 1920s King used his latent architectural talents to rebuild and enlarge his new home, creating a massive residence that Gill described as "a combination of styles in which Norman and modern predominate," with "walls as thick as those of a fortress and great windows of plate glass. It also has the look of having been lovingly and rashly assembled from a hundred sources," which, King told him, was "precisely what had happened." At the time King was working on the house, the W. K. Vanderbilt mansion in New York was being torn down, and King brought out 35 truckloads of Vanderbilt material that he installed in his house: "dormer windows, beams, pillars, marble handrails, fireplaces, even a spiral staircase."

Here, in the quadrangular-shaped home that he named after the dolphins and the court in the center, but which he spelled "Dolfincour," "just to be different," King spent most of the rest of his life. He enjoyed his artwork, which was displayed throughout the house, the several different musical instruments that he could play with considerable skill, and the 50 model engines that filled one of the rooms in the home. He continued to experiment with new products. During World War II he did some work for the government on a new torpedo, and he still enjoyed working on automotive products. He told Gill in 1946 that acquaintances said he should manufacture an unusual new automobile reflecting device that he had designed and installed on his Lincoln Zephyr, "but I don't want to put anything into production. Just want to go on making things."

King's wife died in 1941, and increasingly in the years that followed King devoted much of his time to his collection of manuscripts and books relating to his own work and the work of other automotive pioneers that he had been assembling for decades and that he donated to the Detroit Public Library in 1952. In the same period he gave his collection of engines and automobile models, valued at $500,000, to the Henry Ford Museum in Dearborn, whose founder King in his later years had helped to find some of the material used in that museum and the adjacent Greenfield Village. In 1946 King, Ford, Frank Duryea, and Olds were among the honored guests at the automobile industry's Golden Jubilees celebration of the momentous events that had occurred in 1896. In the 1950s, "after some 'trivial' driving accidents," King's insurance company canceled his car insurance, and when other companies were unwilling to insure him, the New York Motor Vehicle Bureau ruled he could no longer have a driver's license. Late in 1954 fire caused considerable damage to King's mansion, and he moved to a new residence that he purchased in Rye, New York, where he died on June 23, 1957, at the age of eighty-nine. Four days later he was buried in Elmwood Cemetery in Detroit, which, although he had spent little time there for more than four decades, he had wanted to be his final resting place. There, George W. Stark of the *Detroit News* noted, "He rests with the lumber barons, the ship captains, the iron mongers, the stove makers and all that brave company of dreamers and doers who loved Detroit and years ago dedicated it to great things."

Publications:
Psychic Reminiscences (N.p., 1935);
A Golden Anniversary, 1895-1945: Personal Side Lights of America's First Automobile Race (New York: Super-Power, 1945).

References:
Nick Baldwin and others, *The World Guide to Automobile Manufacturers* (New York: Facts On File, 1987);
Brendan Gill, "To Spare the Obedient Beast," *New Yorker*, 22 (May 18, 1946): 30-39;
Eugene W. Lewis, *Motor Memories, A Saga of Whirling Gears* (Detroit: Alved, 1947);
George S. May, *A Most Unique Machine: The Michigan Origins of the American Automobile Industry* (Grand Rapids, Mich.: Eerdmans, 1975).

Archives:
The Charles B. King collection in the National Automobile History Collection of the Detroit Public Library is one of the more important collections of primary sources on the early history of the industry in the United States, containing not only King's own papers but also material he obtained from others, such as Frank Duryea and the automotive journalist David Beecroft.

Kissel Motor Car Company

by Frederick I. Olson

University of Wisconsin–Milwaukee

The Kissel Motor Car Company was a family concern that contributed for a quarter of a century to the industrial growth of Hartford, Wisconsin, produced custom-crafted passenger cars of advanced design, and expired early in the Depression that began in 1929.

Louis Kissel, a German immigrant farmer in Washington County since 1857, moved to the nearby city of Hartford, 35 miles northwest of Milwaukee, in 1883 to enter business. He opened a hardware store, bought into a local farm equipment manufacturer, and soon became the community's most aggressive developer and its mayor. He and his four sons were in real estate, home building, building supplies, banking, and electrical generation. Their recruitment and employment of workers, their platting of subdivisions, and their promotion of local industrial growth changed Hartford from a farm center to a manufacturing city in 40 years, though it never became a company town. Its 1900 population of 1,632 grew to 4,575 by 1920.

In 1905 Kissel and two sons built an experimental motor car and soon were making gasoline engines. President William Kissel and secretary-treasurer George Kissel incorporated the Kissel Motor Car Company in 1906 as a family business to produce touring cars, runabouts, and trucks "on a large scale." They established a network of distributors across the country and by July 1907 had orders for 425 of their 1908 models. Employment at the factory passed 400 in 1908, and a Kissel truck was produced in 1910. The capitalization of the firm was increased to $1 million in 1912 to fund their expansion. World War I brought more rapid growth in sales and the manufacture of diverse automotive products. In 1920 a nearly integrated factory complex for automobile production on one large site in Hartford was completed. From a styling standpoint Kissel passenger cars became famous in the 1920s, but production actually peaked in 1920. At one time Kissel employed 1,400 workers, but it began a slow decline through the decade. Efforts were once again made to enter new markets, for example, through a contract in 1929 to make 500 Yellow taxicabs for Bradfield Motors. The firm tried in vain to obtain financing from federal government sources such as the Reconstruction Finance Corporation to keep the factory open after the onset of the Depression. The company declared bankruptcy and entered receivership in September 1930, suspending automobile production. The company's properties were liquidated by their sale to another Kissel enterprise, Kissel Industries, in July 1932, and the Kissels soon utilized the plant in starting a successful firm supplying outboard motors to Sears Roebuck. The factory site and the business still survive after several changes of ownership.

Two German immigrants contributed to the mechanical and style characteristics that made Kissel passenger cars famous. Herman Palmer, trained at the University of Cologne, joined the company in 1906 and became chassis designer and chief engineer for Kissel. Even more influential was J. Frederick Werner of Munich, whose family had designed carriages for European royalty. He came to the United States in 1908 from Germany's Opel Motor Works. Werner designed bodies with unusual attention to detail. The traditions of these two men account for Kissels being essentially handmade cars. The factory made a high percentage of the cars' components during the first decade and a half; after 1924 more items were purchased for assembly. The cars were sold by dealers, though distribution was very limited in some parts of the nation, and also directly at the factory. A buyer was entitled to select a wide array of options and even to order custom changes. The assembly or production line was very slow, and inspection was unusually

The 1909 Kissel Kar Model L-D9

careful. Total production was thus limited during Kissel's 25 years in the business.

From the very beginning Kissel introduced mechanical and stylistic innovations. Among the former were the double-drop frame, balloon tires, 4-wheel hydraulic brakes, straight-8 high compression engines, lightweight aluminum pistons and connecting rods, dual-jet carburetors, small-diameter wheels, and rubber spring, engine, and body mounts. In 1915 Kissel pioneered a convertible as an all-year car, with a removable top bolted to the body. In the mid 1920s it built both coupes and sedans with folding tops. In an age of drab exterior colors it offered several brilliant ones. Its interiors included leather; the best mohair; mahogany and walnut woods; and padding. It was known from the beginning as an easy-riding car, possibly because of its use of wire wheels. In the 1920s it mounted two spare wire wheels, one on each side.

In the 1920s Kissel was recognized as an American style leader. The most famous Kissel Kar was the Gold Bug speedster of 1922 (first produced in 1919), a long, low-slung 2-passenger roadster of bright chrome yellow, with bullet-shaped headlamps, curved body lines, and arched radiator. Its

6-cylinder engine could reach 75 to 80 miles per hour, while its low center of gravity, generous padding, deep upholstery and cushioning, and adjustable driver's seat provided the ultimate ride of the Roaring 'Twenties. Throughout the decade Kissel continued to make quality 6- and 8-cylinder cars at a reasonable price, generally ahead of competitors in beauty, ride, and handling, and remarkably free from squeaks, rumbles, and rattles. Its 1929 White Eagle De Lux Straight 8-126 was powered by a Lycoming engine capable of 95 to 100 miles per hour and was most admired in the 4-passenger Sport Tourster.

Kissel also produced general utility and "freighter" trucks, notably during World War I, as well as hoppers and other road building equipment, and provided engineering services to road contractors. It also made on order funeral cars, hearses, and ambulances in the 1920s.

The sudden demise of Kissel Motor Car Company early in the Depression, after a decade of seeming passenger car success, may be attributed to three factors: its relatively weak distribution and dealer setup, which was undercut by factory sales and optional designs; its continued use of custom craftsmanship, when the industry trend was toward efficient assembly and mass production; and its undercapitalization as a small-town family business.

References:

Carl Quickert, ed., *History of Washington County, Past*

and Present (Chicago: Clarke, 1912);

John N. Vogel, "Louis Kissel and Sons Thematic Resources of Hartford," *National Register of Historic Places Inventory–Nomination Form* (Wisconsin), June 8, 1988.

Henry Martyn Leland

(February 15, 1843-March 26, 1932)

by John B. Rae

Harvey Mudd College

CAREER: Apprentice machinist, Crompton and Knowles Loom Works, Worcester, Mass. (1859-1862); machinist, United States Armory, Springfield, Mass. (1862-1865); machinist, Colt Armory, Hartford, Conn. (1865-1870); machinist, Brown and Sharpe Manufacturing, Providence, R.I. (1872-1898); general manager, Leland, Norton and Faulconer, Detroit, Mich., (1890-1893); general manager, Leland and Faulconer Manufacturing Company (1893-1904); general manager, Cadillac Motor Car Company (1904-1917); president, Lincoln Motor Company (1917-1922).

Henry Martyn Leland, engineer and automobile executive, was born in Danville, Vermont, on February 15, 1843, and died in Detroit on March 26, 1932. He was the eighth child of Leander Barton and Zilpha Tifft Leland. His father was a farmer who supplemented his income by driving freight wagons between Boston and Montreal. The farm failed and the family moved to the vicinity of Worcester, Massachusetts, where Henry received a common-school education. At the age of sixteen he became an apprentice machinist at the Crompton and Knowles Loom Works in Worcester, makers of textile machinery. When he completed his apprenticeship in 1862, Leland went to work at the U.S. Armory in Springfield, Mass., motivated at least in part by a desire to be of service in the Civil War.

When the war ended the armory's operations were reduced, and Leland found another post at the Colt Armory in Hartford, Conn., where he stayed for five years. He therefore had a thorough training in two of the most important contributors to the creation of the "American System" of machine manufacture of standardized and interchange-

Henry Martyn Leland (courtesy of the National Automotive History Collection, Detroit Public Library)

able parts, which would in due course lead to mass production. However, Leland was not happy at Colt. He was engaged to a Worcester girl named Ellen Hull, and so he returned there in 1867. The marriage took place on September 28. They had three children, Gertrude, Wilfred, and Miriam. For some time afterward, Leland worked at a variety of jobs in the Worcester area, and then in 1872 he began his career in earnest by going to work for the Brown and Sharpe Manufacturing Company of Providence, Rhode Island, one of the country's leading tool manufacturers.

Soon after he went to Brown and Sharpe, Leland was placed in charge of the screw machine division of the sewing machine department; Brown and Sharpe made the Wilcox and Gibbs sewing machine under contract. He improved the accuracy of the screw machines and also recommended that screws and other small parts be kept in stock rather than turned out for every job. In addition, he recommended that the company manufacture hair clippers. After some hesitation his advice was accepted, and the hair clippers became a very profitable line. His reputation was such that in 1878 he was made head of the sewing machine department. He accepted the appointment on three conditions: that he could abolish the inside contracting system in the department, establish a piecework payment system, and determine the wages of all members of his department. A cost analysis of the sewing machine department completed a year later found a 47 percent reduction in labor cost, due to the end of the contract system and the adoption of piece work. There was also an improvement in the quality of the work, so much so that detailed inspection sheets demanded by the Wilcox and Gibbs Sewing Machine Company could be eliminated because they were no longer necessary.

Beyond this, Leland introduced significant improvements in production techniques. One was to grind to gauge sewing machine parts after they had been hardened, since the hardening process tended to warp or distort them. In formulating the technique, Leland induced Brown and Sharpe to develop a universal grinding machine and a grinder for straight work. He also instituted a system whereby all operations on specific parts were enumerated on sheets along with the necessary tools, jigs, and gauges. With those records foremen could follow work more accurately, and materials could be moved more smoothly in the proper sequence. The steps were not only valuable contributions to production at Brown and Sharpe, they were also part of Henry Leland's education in production technology.

Leland's years at Brown and Sharpe were professionally rewarding but not particularly remunerative. He strengthened his reputation as a stickler for precision and accuracy and was by nature a hard worker. Overwork and a bout of typhoid fever in

1883 led him to seek a less-demanding position in Columbus, Ohio, but the factory was destroyed by fire a year later, and he returned to Brown and Sharpe, where he became a traveling representative for the company. However, by that time he was determined to go into business for himself, and the opportunity finally came in 1890. Charles Strelinger, a Detroit businessman who sold tools, introduced Leland to a successful Michigan lumberman, Robert C. Faulconer, who was looking for investment opportunities; Faulconer agreed to finance a machine shop.

The company was organized as Leland, Norton and Faulconer, the second partner being Charles F. Norton, another Brown and Sharpe alumnus and the inventor of the automatic grinding machine. Faulconer became president and Leland became vice-president and general manager. Faulconer contributed $40,000 of the initial $50,000 capital. Leland put in $1,600 of his own money and $2,000 loaned by Lucien Sharpe through the influence of Richmond Viall, who had been Leland's immediate superior at Brown and Sharpe. The rest of the shares were divided between Norton and Strelinger. Wilfred Leland joined the company after a brief apprenticeship at Brown and Sharpe to begin a career as his father's principal assistant. Norton left in 1893 to concentrate on developing his grinding machine, and the firm became the Leland and Faulconer Manufacturing Company. It appears that one of Norton's reasons for leaving Detroit was that his wife left him for Faulconer. What the deeply religious and straitlaced Leland thought of that is unknown. Presumably he regarded it as outside the scope of business relations.

Leland and Faulconer emphasized the precision and accuracy in its products that Henry Leland had come to personify. When it established a foundry in 1896 for making high-grade iron castings, the company advertised that it would not attempt to compete with the average foundry in price. It appealed for business only to those who wanted the best. Leland's supervision was so rigorous that for some time half the castings were rejected, much to Faulconer's distress. Leland simply said that there always was and always would be conflict between Good and Good Enough, and he made it abundantly clear where he stood.

In addition to the castings and a wide variety of machine-shop products, Leland and Faulconer also manufactured typewriters. Inevitably, at this stage of industrial history and in Detroit, Henry Leland became interested in gasoline engines, and in 1899 Leland and Faulconer began to make them in some quantity for marine use, specifically in motor boats on the Great Lakes. Possibly that activity directed Leland's interest to the automobile industry, but it is hardly likely that a man of his technical skill and interests could have remained untouched for long by Detroit's growing preoccupation with the motor vehicle.

As it happened, Leland's introduction to the automobile did not come through his engines. The Olds Motor Works had moved from Lansing to Detroit in 1899, and Leland was called in to find a remedy for noisy transmissions. He did, and for a time Leland and Faulconer made transmissions for the Oldsmobiles. Then in March 1901 the Olds factory burned down. All that was saved was the prototype of the 1-cylinder buggy that became the famous "Merry Oldsmobile." To continue production Olds placed large orders for engines with Leland and Faulconer and for transmissions with another Detroit machine shop owned by the brothers John and Horace Dodge. There was nothing revolutionary about the arrangement. All early automobiles were assembled from parts manufactured by independent supplier firms. What was different was the scale of the transactions. The first order from Olds to Leland and Faulconer was for 2,000 motors, considerably more than any single engine builder had made in any previous year. After all, the total output of American motor vehicles in 1900 had been only 4,000 units.

To fill the order Leland and Faulconer designed a 1-cylinder motor delivering 3.7 horsepower. Oddly, there was difficulty in getting information or specifications from Olds at the start. Finally, Leland solved the problem by buying an Oldsmobile, his first car, and having the engine removed, taken apart, and reassembled.

In August 1902 Leland was visited by two Detroit businessmen, William Murphy and Lemuel Bowen, both former associates of Henry Ford. Murphy and others had formed the Detroit Automobile Company in 1899, with Ford as superintendent, to make cars of Ford's design. That enterprise lasted just more than a year. Ford, still with Murphy's support, turned to building race cars and driving them competitively. He gained enough publicity so that the backers of the Detroit Automobile Company returned to finance the Henry Ford Company, again

with Ford as superintendent. That venture was no more successful; evidence indicates that Henry Ford was still so obsessed with racing that he neglected commercial production. He left the company in March 1902, and the discouraged backers decided to liquidate the business. That was the reason for calling on Leland; they wanted him to appraise the property.

Leland's response was hardly what the partners anticipated. After he inspected their plant at 1363 Cass Avenue in Detroit, Leland told Murphy and his associates that it would be a great mistake for them to go out of business. He argued that the automobile had a bright future and then showed a new motor that he had designed and was prepared to offer them. From the same cubic capacity as the one his company was selling to Olds, it produced 10.25 horsepower.

Murphy and his friends were sold, provided Leland would join them and assist in reorganizing the company. He agreed and was made a director of the new Cadillac Automobile Company, named for the founder of Detroit, Antoine de la Mothe Cadillac. Leland and Faulconer received the contracts for making Cadillac motors, transmissions, and steering mechanisms.

The new car, a buggy selling for $750, was quite well received, but the company suffered from the lack of a management structure clearly designating who was in charge. After a 1904 fire destroyed most of the plant, Murphy and Bowen appealed to Leland and Faulconer to take charge of production. It soon became clear that Leland could not manage both companies, and by now his interest was predominantly in the automobile business. A new Cadillac Motor Car Company was organized in 1904 to consolidate the Cadillac Automobile Company and the Leland and Faulconer Manufacturing Company. Henry Leland became general manager and Wilfred assistant treasurer. Faulconer was in poor health and chose that opportunity to retire.

The first Cadillacs came on the market as low-priced cars, but given Henry Leland's emphasis on quality over price, it was inevitable that the Cadillac would eventually rise to be a luxury vehicle. The change can be dated to 1909, when a 4-cylinder engine was introduced after sales of the 1-cylinder models had begun to sag, but it was fully predictable in terms of the dictum that Leland laid down to the young Alfred P. Sloan, Jr., when the latter, as head of the Hyatt Roller Bearing Company, went to Detroit to investigate complaints about bearings sold to Cadillac by Hyatt. Leland greeted Sloan with, "Young man, Cadillacs are made to run, not just to sell." It was unfortunate for the American automobile industry that half a century later its management seemed to have reversed that principle to something like: "Our cars are built to sell; whether they run or not is immaterial."

Leland's insistence on precision was dramatically demonstrated in 1908, when Cadillac's British agent, Frederick S. Bennett, entered a standardization test announced by the British Royal Automobile Club (RAC). As it turned out, the Cadillacs were the only entrants. Three of the 1-cylinder engine models were taken apart at the RAC's test track at Brooklands, just south of London, dismantled under the eyes of officials of the RAC, and the parts put in a single pile and scrambled. The RAC officials next removed 90 parts from the pile, selected at random, and those were replaced from the stocks of Bennett's agency, the Anglo-American Motor Car Company (Cadillac). Then mechanics from the agency went to work on the pile of parts, under the rules of the test using only wrenches, screwdrivers, and hammers, and in due course reassembled the Cadillacs, which completed the final requirement of the test by being driven 500 miles around the Brooklands track. All finished with perfect scores.

The British were much impressed by the demonstration. It was freely conceded that the British motor industry could not match that level of standardization and interchangeability. For the achievement, the Cadillac Motor Car Company received the Sir Thomas Dewar Trophy, awarded annually by the RAC for the most meritorious performance of the year.

Four years later Cadillac again received the Dewar Trophy, this time for the introduction of the electric starter. In those days automobile engines were started with a crank handle, an operation that required considerable muscular power and was both difficult and hazardous. It was necessary to adjust the spark and throttle properly in order to avoid the risk of having the crank handle kick back when the engine started, and that could happen even if the spark and throttle were adjusted. The operator could be injured if he failed to get out of the way in time. ("He" is intentional; cranking a car was almost impossible for a woman.) Broken wrists and arms were a commonplace result of cranking.

There had been efforts to solve the problem, using compressed air, clockwork, and even electric systems, but until 1912 none of them had worked.

The role of Cadillac in the development of the electric starter was complicated and somewhat controversial, because it was worked out in collaboration with Charles F. Kettering, who has traditionally been given credit for the invention and who certainly took it. Leland's interest in the electric starter is alleged to have been triggered by an accident to a friend, who had stopped to assist a woman driver whose car had stalled on a bridge in Detroit's Belle Isle Park. Unfortunately, she had not retarded the spark, so that when Leland's friend turned the crank handle it lashed back and broke his arm and his jaw. A few weeks later he died of pneumonia. Leland was very upset and called a special meeting of the Cadillac engineering staff to instruct them to give priority to a self-starter.

However important the incident may have been, it seems certain that Leland and his engineers had already given thought to the starting problem and done some preliminary work. They had adopted for Cadillac cars a wet-battery ignition system devised by Kettering to replace the less satisfactory dry-battery systems then in use, and from that they could conclude that a wet battery could provide the power needed to turn the engine over. The main problem then was to find a starting motor that could turn the engine over and still be small enough to fit under the hood of a normal-sized car. One Cadillac official, who had previously worked for the National Cash Register Company, recalled that Kettering, then with Dayton Engineering Laboratories Company, had successfully designed a small motor for electric cash registers when he had worked for National Cash Register. The principle was that the motor did not have to carry a constant load; it just had to deliver an occasional surge of power. Kettering was able to solve the problem of the starting motor, based on his cash register experience. On February 27, 1911, with both the Lelands and Kettering present, an engineer turned the starting switch on a Cadillac car, the motor caught, and the electric self-starter was practical technology. It was a cooperative achievement, but the initiative came from Henry Leland and the Cadillac Motor Car Company.

While Leland and Cadillac were registering those technological triumphs, the company was undergoing a significant change of status. In 1908 Wil-

*Leland and the first closed-body Cadillac, a 1-cylinder model constructed in 1905
(courtesy of Donald Macaulay)*

liam C. Durant incorporated the General Motors (GM) Company in New Jersey. His objective was to create a vast structure of motor vehicle and parts manufacturers to provide insurance against the fluctuations in market demand and consumer preferences that could be disastrous for a one-model producer. Presumably, bringing vehicle and supplier firms into the same organization could also eliminate the vexing problem of erratic deliveries of parts and components. The concept was sound enough, but the execution left something to be desired. That story is told elsewhere. What matters for Henry Leland is that GM bought the Cadillac Motor Car Company for $4.4 million. It was a cash sale, an important factor in the history of GM. Durant's other acquisitions were paid for in GM stock, and while the Cadillac purchase was certainly one of his soundest moves, it drained him of most of his available cash. Leland was somewhat reluctant to see Cadillac lose its independence, but his stockholders had no such hesitation. They had been the backers of the Detroit Automobile Company and the Henry Ford Company. The Cadillac ex-

perience had been an improvement, but Cadillac sales had slumped, along with all others, in the recession of 1907. Consequently, they saw the GM offer as a welcome opportunity to recover their investment and get out of what to them had become a precarious enterprise. However, Leland was able to stipulate that he remain in full charge of the Cadillac Motor Car Company. Durant said that was exactly what he wanted, which was good news for Leland but not necessarily for GM. It was an early indication that Durant preferred not to be bothered with details of management.

The combination Durant put together was a hodgepodge of vehicle and parts companies with no unifying organizational structure. Buick, with which Durant had started, and Cadillac were the only profitable automobile manufacturers in the collection, and Buick's financial resources had been severely depleted in order to finance the other acquisitions.

The Leland-Durant relationship has been described as "cordial though never close." Durant left Cadillac to Leland management while he pressed his plans for the expansion of GM. Henry and Wilfred Leland were uneasy about Durant's lavish spending but accepted his assurance that he could raise the money he needed from any of the principal banks of the country. There seemed so little cause for concern that in summer 1910 Henry Leland went on a trip to visit European industries with the American Society of Mechanical Engineers. He had scarcely arrived when word came that GM was in serious trouble. Durant had miscalculated the willingness of the banking community to support him.

Durant embarked on a frantic search for money, frequently taking Wilfred Leland with him to give the bankers information on Cadillac affairs, which were the one bright spot in the GM picture. Invariably, the result was to bring a response that if Cadillac stood alone, the bank would be happy to help, but Cadillac was now part of GM, and GM was a poor risk. There was reason for that attitude. Buick was a popular car, but the Buick company owed $3 million in short-term loans and $5 million for materials and supplies. The Oldsmobile had declined in popularity, and the Oakland was an untested newcomer whose management confessed that they did not know how much their company owed. None of the other car companies that Durant had so freely collected could be considered an asset.

The crisis came to a head with a bankers' conference in September 1910. GM was on the verge of receivership, and the initial attitude of the bankers was that perhaps Buick could be salvaged and the rest of the organization dissolved. Cadillac was evidently seen as a separate case. It had no bank indebtedness, and it was late in the day before Wilfred Leland was asked to describe the condition of the Cadillac company. His presentation led to an evening meeting at which he spoke eloquently of the future of the automobile and urged that GM be saved. The result was an agreement to lend GM $15 million and to put its affairs for five years in the hands of a bankers' trust headed by James J. Storrow of Lee, Higginson and Company of Boston. Durant remained a director but had to step down from his leadership role in the company.

The terms of this agreement have frequently been criticized as unduly harsh, but it must be borne in mind that the banking syndicate was taking a substantial risk. In 1910 the automobile industry was regarded as speculative and volatile (as indeed it was), and there was a strong belief in some quarters that the automobile was a fad whose popularity was bound to collapse just as the bicycle boom had ten years before. There was no assurance for the bankers that the organizational and financial tangle of GM could be straightened out. That they decided to try was a tribute to the prestige and credit of Henry and Wilfred Leland and the Cadillac Motor Car Company.

As a reward the Lelands had their salaries cut in half by the trust committee as part of a move to reduce GM's expenses. The members of the trust had not been present at the sessions in New York when the decision was taken to try to resuscitate GM, so it is quite possible that they were unaware of the crucial part the Lelands had played. Henry Leland was naturally indignant and contemplated resigning, but then he decided that he must honor the commitment his son had made to the bankers, that the Lelands would use their experience and skill to help rebuild the firm.

What Henry Leland had to contribute was, of course, technical expertise. During the period of the trust he spent much of his time visiting other GM plants and inculcating his own exacting standards of precision and accuracy. He trained all of the machinists in the use of Johansson blocks, which had been introduced at Cadillac in 1908, possibly a year earlier. His relations with Storrow and Charles W. Nash, who became president of GM in 1912, were good. Storrow, like Durant, was content to leave the management of Cadillac to the Lelands. He had enough on his hands in trying to straighten out the financial and organizational affairs of GM as a whole.

Consequently, it made little difference to Henry Leland that in 1915 William C. Durant recovered control of GM with a combination of support from the du Pont family and the profits of his most recent venture, the Chevrolet Motor Car Company. Durant professed great gratitude for the role the Lelands had played in rescuing GM from its difficulties and promised them a block of stock to reimburse them for the reduction in salary. Unfortunately, he then plunged into another period of aggressive expansion and forgot his promise.

During the trust period the Cadillac car underwent important changes, quite apart from the electric starter. In 1912 the standard Cadillac touring car had a 4-cylinder engine and sold for $1,975, that price including the top, the windshield, demountable rims, electric lighting, and a self-starter.

A year later a 6-cylinder engine was introduced, but it had problems with periodic vibrations in the crankshaft. While work was being done to try to remedy that difficulty, Wilfred Leland, brooding on it during a train trip to New York, came up with the idea that if two of the successful 4-cylinder motors, with smaller and lighter blocks and pistons, were to be combined at a V-angle, they might give the desired smooth operation without the troublesome long crankshaft of the in-line sixes and eights.

It was not a completely novel idea. Engines of that type had already been built in Europe, and the Cadillac engineers studied a DeDion-Bouton V-8. They found it below Cadillac standards of quality but were able to get some ideas from it. When the decision was made to design a Cadillac V-8 motor, the company felt that the project should be kept secret until a V-8 car was ready for the market. The manufacture of parts was spread out among half a dozen firms in New England that Henry Leland knew from his past experience, in such a way that those firms could not know that the parts were for a V-8 engine. The parts were delivered to a dummy company called the Ideal Manufacturing Company, with a building some distance from the main Cadillac plant. The new car, with its V-8 engine, was put on the market in 1914 to the accompaniment of a good deal of skepticism and criticism from within the automotive industry, generally to the effect that such a complicated engine would create problems for motorists. However, the engine proved entirely satisfactory and was standard for all Cadillac cars until 1927.

When Durant resumed the presidency of GM, his relationship with Leland temporarily resumed its previous pattern. Cadillac was doing well, and Leland was left to manage it as he saw fit. However, there was an important difference that would shortly disrupt the relationship. In 1916 war was raging in Europe. Leland had forecast the outbreak of war as a result of his visits to Europe with engineering groups. He believed that the war would threaten the existence of Western civilization, and he was convinced that the United States must sooner or later become involved. Consequently, when the United States did enter the war, he urged Durant to agree to the conversion of Cadillac facilities to the manufacture of aircraft engines, specifically the Liberty motor. Durant refused, whereupon Leland flew into a rage and resigned as president of Cadillac. Differences over Leland's management of Cadillac also contributed to the break and, according to Charles S. Mott, a GM director, led to Leland being dismissed as president, not to his resignation.

Leland's son, Wilfred, left with him and together they founded the Lincoln Motor Company for the purpose of building Liberty engines. Leland refused to give the company his own name; it was named in honor of the man he admired most and for whom he had cast his first vote in 1864 as a young man of twenty-one. The company was capitalized at $1.5 million and raised $2 million in loans. Much of the stock was purchased by Leland's former associates in the founding of Cadillac, including William Murphy. At the end of August 1917 the Lincoln Motor Company was awarded a contract for 6,000 Liberty Motors, the first such contract to be given. The company still had no manufacturing facilities. It had begun to build a factory in Detroit as soon as it was organized, designed to produced twenty 8-cylinder or fourteen 12-cylinder Liberties a day. Then the Army asked for expanded production, and a new and larger plant had to be constructed. Both factories were built under conditions of high cost and shortages of materials and labor. They were completed and in production by February 1918, a feat that would have been impossible without the goodwill that Henry Leland had accumulated in American industry over many years.

Henry Leland was spending much time in Washington consulting on the development of the Liberty motor. He had previously been in Britain to study and advise on British aircraft engine production, so he had some firsthand knowledge of the problem. The Liberty was designed late in May 1917 by Jesse G. Vincent of Packard and E.J. Hall of the Hall-Scott Motor Company of San Francisco, working under instructions to use only known and tried technology and design an engine that could be produced rapidly and in quantity by existing automobile engine plants. Two designs were considered, eight and twelve cylinders in line, but the eight was discarded on advice from France that twelve cylinders developing 400-horsepower were required. Leland's role was to aid in the elaborate testing that was required, a process that generated intense public and congressional impatience, since it had been lightly assumed that the automobile industry could immediately start to turn out airplanes and en-

Leland (center) overseeing a dynamometer test on a Packard 905 V-8 engine, 1917 (courtesy of the National Automotive History Collection, Detroit Public Library)

gines by the thousands. The same illusion still existed during World War II.

Once the plant was ready and the Liberty motor had been worked into acceptable condition, production moved rapidly. Besides the Lincoln Motor Company, Liberties were made by Packard, Nordyke and Marmon, Ford, Buick, and Cadillac (Durant changed his mind too late to keep the Lelands in GM). In July 1918 Lincoln received a new fixed-price contract for 9,000 engines, with a further 8,000 available if the government wanted them at $4,000 each. The change was made because part of the criticism of delay in war production focused on alleged abuses of cost-plus contracts.

The Lincoln record was impressive. When the war ended, the company had built the greatest number of Liberty engines in a single day, the greatest in a single month, and the greatest number by any manufacturer (6,500). Financially, the situation was less bright. The expansion required to meet the government's demands had put the company heavily in

debt, most of it in government loans. If the total of 9,000 engines had been made and sold, all would have been well, but when the war ended the government requested abrogation of the contract, and Leland acceded. Production of Liberty motors stopped in January 1919.

At that point Henry M. Leland was seventy-six years old. He might well have chosen to conclude a long and successful career, but he did not. He returned to the automobile industry. The Lincoln Motor Company was reconstituted, without change of name, as a Delaware corporation, transferring assets valued at $5.5 million, and the plants were refurbished for the manufacture of another fine car. The car was to be called Lincoln; Leland still refused to give it his own name. The retooling of the factories was done in the period of high inflation that immediately followed the war and amid a good deal of confusion and unrest. Congress and the Wilson administration had made no better preparation for peace than they had for war.

The result was that although Leland had hoped to have the Lincoln car in production by spring 1920, it did not appear on the market until September, just in time for the economic slump of 1920-1921. Sales were low, and by the beginning of 1921 the company's affairs were in crisis, and sharp policy disputes had developed between the Lelands and their largest stockholders. It was unfortunate for the Lelands that the aging William Murphy had turned the management of his affairs over to his nephew, Dr. Fred Murphy, because Wilfred Leland was sure that the doctor was trying to take over the company. The squabbling did nothing to raise money for the financially strapped Lincoln Motor Company. Then, on November 7, 1921, while the two Lelands and other directors were in New York to negotiate with banks, the U.S. Treasury Department presented a claim of $4.5 million in income taxes on earnings from wartime operations, asserting that some of the depreciation taken by the Lincoln Motor Company was not allowable. That was the second such tax claim. The first had eventually been successfully contested and withdrawn. The same would eventually happen to the second, but in the meantime no bank would risk lending money to a company with such a tax lien hanging over it. The Lincoln directors reluctantly agreed that receivership was the only course open to them.

Then, with the company in receivership, the Lincoln story became complicated, controversial, and insoluble. Leland was a respected, well-liked citizen of Detroit who had given much time and effort to community affairs. There was a powerful sentiment in Detroit that someone with the necessary resources should come forward to rescue him and his company. In 1922 that someone could only be Henry Ford, still the dominant figure in the automobile industry. One of the unanswered questions in the Lincoln situation is whether Ford or Leland made the first approach. Ford is known to have rejected several proposals that he should step in and save the Lincoln company, but he finally agreed to a meeting late in November 1921. There is some suggestion that Mrs. Ford urged it on him out of sympathy for the Lelands, and it is known that Ford's son Edsel was eager to acquire Lincoln. At any rate, a meeting was arranged between Wilfred Leland and Henry and Edsel Ford at which Henry Ford expressed his desire to acquire Lincoln. Other meetings followed, attended by other Ford executives,

and an agreement was reached for the Ford Motor Company to buy the Lincoln Motor Company and pay off its creditors. This much is certain; what else was agreed became the subject of bitter controversy. When the negotiations were completed, Wilfred Leland had an agreement ready for signature, but Henry Ford said that there was no need for a formal agreement; they understood each other thoroughly. Wilfred Leland said later that the agreement included assurances that he and his father would continue to run the Lincoln plant and that the Lincoln stockholders would be reimbursed as well as the creditors. Edsel Ford, who can be considered an honest witness, denied that any provision was made for the stockholders, and it became obvious later that Ford and the Lelands had quite different interpretations of what the authority to run the plant meant. That acquiescence in an unwritten agreement was to prove disastrous for the Lelands.

Henry Ford's motives for acquiring Lincoln remain obscure. At the time there was much publicity to the effect that he had intervened to help an old friend who had got into difficulties, and Ford unhesitatingly accepted that role. Yet he and Leland had never been more than acquaintances at best, certainly not friends, and Ford's subsequent treatment of Leland displayed neither friendship nor generosity. At the receiver's sale Ford offered $5 million for the Lincoln Motor Company but was compelled by the court to add another $3 million in order to satisfy the Lincoln creditors. An alternative explanation, equally plausible, is that Henry Ford had resented Henry Leland's replacing him at the Henry Ford Company 20 years before and was finally paying off that old score. Actually, Ford had left the Henry Ford Company several months before Leland was asked to take charge of it, but Henry Ford always had a conveniently flexible memory. It is quite definite that Mrs. Ford sympathized with Leland and that Edsel wanted to buy Lincoln, and it is likely that Henry Ford was finally attracted to the idea of having a high-prestige car in the Ford line to accompany the indisputably plebian Model T.

Troubles started immediately. As soon as the sale of the Lincoln Motor Company was completed, Ford executives, conspicuously the top production men, P. T. Martin and Charles E. Sorensen, looked over the Lincoln plant. When Leland protested, he was told that they were there to inspect and make recommendations for improving production. Here again there are conflicting and irreconcilable accounts of what happened. Leland objected that the Ford people were not just inspecting but also issuing orders without regard for the fact that he was still in charge. It may have been that he could not adjust to the fact that he was now an employee of the Ford Motor Company. True, he had previously been an employee of GM, but there Durant had never interfered with his management of Cadillac. Henry Ford's style was different. The Lincoln situation called for goodwill and tact on both sides, but for that Ford could have picked no worse emissaries. Neither Martin nor Sorensen understood the meaning of those words.

It took just five months to generate an explosion. Leland at one point offered to raise money to repurchase the Lincoln company, but that must be regarded as a desperation appeal, and he was ignored. In June 1922 he and his son were ordered out of the Lincoln plant, and Leland's distinguished career in American industry came to an end.

Leland did not give up easily. There was no possibility of recovering his position at the Lincoln Motor Company, but during his remaining years he and his son kept trying to persuade or compel Henry Ford to fulfill what they believed to be his obligations to the Lincoln stockholders. Finally, in 1927 they took Ford to court. Unfortunately, their case was that Ford had agreed to recompense the bona fide stockholders but not the speculators who had come in when Lincoln was in difficulties. Eventually, the Supreme Court of Michigan ruled that if Henry Ford had made such an agreement it was illegal and hence unenforceable, because there could be no discrimination among stockholders. Efforts to remedy that defect in the case proved futile, and shortly before his death Leland had to inform Lincoln stockholders that nothing more could be done.

The Lincoln failure was an unfortunate end to a distinguished career in American industry. To some extent Henry Leland was responsible. His insistence on high-quality precision tooling for the Lincoln plant was in accordance with his lifelong standards, but it had to be done in a period of high costs, with the result that the company was left with insufficient liquid capital to meet an unexpected emergency. There were also deficiencies in the early Lincolns, particularly in body design, that Leland may have been slow to acknowledge. However, there was another adverse element in the overall automotive situation over which Leland had no control and of which he and the other leaders of the automobile industry were basically unaware.

That was, very simply, that the introduction of the moving assembly line had doomed the small-scale, one-model automobile manufacturer to extinction, even at the luxury-car level, which was the least susceptible to assembly line techniques. The process was slow and unrecognized but inexorable. Several such companies entered the market at the same time as Lincoln, notably Duesenberg, Rickenbacker, and Wills St. Clair. All failed, although Duesenberg lasted into the 1930s as part of a merger arranged by E. L. Cord. With the passage of time it became increasingly evident that the large companies could dominate the luxury car market as well as the low-priced market. GM could build Cadillacs, and Ford could build Lincolns, with the overhead costs spread over a broader base than any small company could match and with marketing facilities well beyond the capacity of smaller firms.

Leland's reputation rests primarily on his career in the automotive industry and especially on his insistence on exacting standards of precision. But he had other interests and characteristics. Perhaps the most conspicuous of these was his intense religious faith. During his Detroit years he was an active member of the Westminster Presbyterian Church. He had previously been a Baptist, a Congregationalist, an Adventist, and a Quaker. He gave generously to religiously oriented causes, including the YMCA and the Anti-Saloon League, and he was an ardent prohibitionist. Occasionally he preached sermons himself.

His religious commitment undoubtedly also gave Leland his strong sense of community service. He was a founder and for many years (1911-1925) president of the Detroit Citizens' League, which was organized to work for civic improvement in Detroit. Its initial objective was to eradicate corruption in the government of the city. It was not an easy task, and Leland had to devote much time and effort to it, but encouraging progress had been made by the time he gave up office. He founded the Miriam Hospital as part of the Grace Hospital in Detroit in 1908, in memory of his youngest daughter, who had died in 1894. It is understandable that in his later years he was known as the "Grand Old Man of Detroit."

Leland's patriarchal appearance showed a benevolent rather than a forbidding character. He was much interested in helping young people.

While he was president of Cadillac, he established the Cadillac School of Applied Mechanics for training young men in the skills needed to advance in the automobile industry. The students had to have some skill in arithmetic, had to be of good moral character, and were forbidden to use tobacco and alcohol. They were given two years of instruction in machine-shop work and earned money in the Cadillac plant as well. They were not obligated to remain at Cadillac, but those who agreed to stay for two years received additional instruction. To his staff and work force Leland was known as "Uncle Henry" or "H. M."

In politics as in religion Leland was conservative. He was a lifelong Republican. He publicly defended the right of labor to organize as a necessary protection against unscrupulous employers, but he also insisted that workmen's organizations be balanced by employer organizations. He was active in the Detroit Employers' Association, a major force in keeping Detroit an open-shop city.

Leland also was deeply involved in professional activities. He was president of the Society of Automobile Engineers from 1909 to 1914, and he was a founder of the National Metal Trades Association and the National Founders Association. In addition, he was active in the American Society of Mechanical Engineers and the National Association of Manufacturers.

All this would constitute an impressive record for any man. It is all the more impressive when we realize that most of these achievements came after Leland had already passed the age when most men retire.

References:

Mrs. Wilfred C. Leland, with Minnie Dibbs Milbrook, *Master of Precision: Henry M. Leland* (Detroit: Wayne State University Press, 1966);

George S. May, *A Most Unique Machine: The Michigan Origins of the American Automobile Industry* (Grand Rapids, Mich.: Eerdmans, 1975);

Allan Nevins and Frank E. Hill, *Ford: Expansion and Challenge, 1915-1932* (New York: Scribners, 1957);

Arthur Pound, *The Turning Wheel* (New York: Doubleday, 1934);

John B. Rae, *American Automobile Manufacturers: The First Forty Years* (Philadelphia: Chilton, 1959).

Locomobile Company of America

by James M. Laux

University of Cincinnati

The steam-powered automobiles made by Locomobile at the beginning of the twentieth century were the first motor cars produced in large numbers in the United States. Small and lightweight, the Locomobile steamers illuminated the possibilities for quantity production and sales of small cars and may well have influenced entrepreneurs in Detroit—Ransom Olds, Henry Ford, and Henry Leland (Cadillac)—and elsewhere in the Midwest to manufacture small cars in large numbers.

The Stanley brothers (Francis E. and Freelan O., who were twins) designed the car that became the Locomobile. Operating a photographic dry-plate business in the Boston suburb of Watertown, the Stanleys, prototypical Yankee tinkerers, constructed several steam cars in 1897-1898. The two smaller models resembled a small steamer built by George Eli Whitney in Boston in 1896. They obtained many of the components—the 2-cylinder, 3.5-horsepower steam engine, and wheels, for example—from shops in the region. One of their machines, weighing under 600 pounds loaded, won considerable interest and praise for its performance at a Boston fair in October 1898. Immediately the Stanleys began manufacturing a batch of perhaps 100 of them in Watertown. That the brothers late in 1898 undertook producing this many cars was almost unprecedented in the United States. There were only a few other automobile makers at this point. In the Midwest Alexander Winton was the biggest with an output of 22 cars in 1898, but only the Pope company of Hartford, Connecticut, made more than a few dozen (electric) cars in this year. The Stanleys' decision to make small and inexpensive cars initiated an important pattern.

Yet in May 1899 they sold their infant enterprise to two New York City capitalists for $250,000, more than ten times their original invest-

Advertisement for the "noiseless, odorless" Locomobile, 1899

ment. John Brisben Walker, owner and editor of *Cosmopolitan* Magazine, and Amzi Lorenzo Barber, the dominant figure in asphalt street paving in the United States, each used the Stanley design to make his own automobiles: Walker in a new factory in Tarrytown, New York, where he produced some 600 Mobile cars from 1900 to 1903, and Barber first in the Stanley works in Watertown under the name Locomobile. The Stanley brothers had stayed on to manage the Watertown operation but left after a few months. In 1901 they returned to steam car production, selling a few hundred under their own name every year until their firm folded in 1924.

Barber expanded Locomobile with parts-making operations in a former bicycle factory in Westborough, Massachusetts, and in another machine works in Worcester. Barber had brought his son-in-law Samuel T. Davis, Jr., who held an engineering degree from Rensselaer Polytechnic Institute, into Locomobile from the beginning. They decided to move its operations closer to New York

City and chose Bridgeport, Connecticut, as a new location. In March 1900 they sold the Watertown facilities back to the Stanley brothers for just $20,000 and moved the assembly operations to a disused bicycle factory in Bridgeport. Then in June 1901 Locomobile production was centralized in a large new factory in this city. L-shaped with two long, narrow wings of four floors each, this building resembled the traditional textile mill of New England, not the extensive one- or two-floor layout that would later characterize auto factories. Originally, power to operate the machines was supplied by steam engines that drove shafts and belts. Soon large electric motors powered those shafts in each section of the factory, and the company generated its own electricity. Except for engine castings, wooden bodies, and wheels, the company made all its own parts.

There is no evidence of the use of continuous-flow assembly, nor was it needed. Output of 15 cars per day was quite exceptional, and on most days it fell far short of this figure. Production of the little steam cars was large for the period, an estimated 600 in 1899, 1,600 in 1900, and 1,400 in 1901. This total was much larger than any other American producer in these years, and probably exceeded that of De Dion-Bouton of Paris, the largest European maker at the turn of the century. Locomobiles were suitable for city driving but risky on the poor roads in the countryside.

Its Model 2, introduced late in 1899, weighed 640 pounds empty and cost $750. Its water tank held 21 gallons, enough for about a 20-mile journey. Despite the large sales, Locomobile steamers had problems. Starting them was a complex and time-consuming 30-minute task. Boilers frequently burned out, and the gasoline burners that heated the boilers sometimes backfired and set a car on fire, but the boilers did not explode. Water consumption was high because the Locomobile did not condense and reuse the exhaust steam.

When sales in 1901 declined from those of 1900, Barber and Davis decided to investigate the possibility of adding a gasoline car to the Locomobile line. In 1902 they hired Andrew L. Riker to develop this. Riker had been working with automobiles for several years and had experience with both electric and gasoline types. By the time Riker's 2- and 4-cylinder gasoline cars were offered to the public in November 1902, Locomobile's sales of steam cars had declined further, to about

1,100 for the year 1902. The gasoline machines appealed to well-to-do persons who could afford the price, which rose to $5,000. They marked a shift in the company's strategy from aiming at the low-priced mass market to elegance for the elite. Production of gasoline types gradually rose, and 1904 saw the last of Locomobile's steamers.

Thereafter Locomobile concentrated on the high-price segment of the market, with a switch to trucks during World War I. In the 1920s Locomobile struggled in the overcrowded luxury car market, for a time as one part of a group of companies controlled by Emlen S. Hare, and later as part of a conglomerate put together by W. C. Durant. It finally died in 1929. Its significance in the automobile industry was to demonstrate in the years 1899 to 1903 that there was a market for small, low-priced cars. It supplied some 5,200 steamers to this

market. From 1903 on, midwestern producers of gasoline automobiles would exploit Locomobile's vision.

References:

Thomas S. Derr, *The Modern Steam Car and its Background* (Los Angeles: Clymer, 1942);

L. J. Andrew Villalon, "The Birth of an Early Automobile Company," *Bulb Horn* (April-June 1981): 11-21;

Villalon, "The Locomobile Company of America, 1899-1905," *Bulb Horn* (July-September 1986): 16-28;

Villalon and James M. Laux, "Steaming through New England with Locomobile," *Journal of Transport History*, new series 5 (1979): 65-82.

Archives:

The Locomobile Collection and A. L. Riker Papers are located in the Bridgeport Public Library, Bridgeport, Connecticut.

Mack Trucks, Inc.

by George S. May

Eastern Michigan University

"Built like a Mack truck," a familiar phrase used to describe something or someone of a particularly sturdy, durable build, appears to have originated during World War I as a result of the performance of heavy-duty Mack AC trucks that were used to haul military equipment. A British officer, faced with the job of moving an artillery piece that was bogged down in mud, is said to have shouted to the driver of a Mack truck, "Bring that bulldog over here." The term stuck, and eventually a determined-looking bulldog came to symbolize the ruggedness of the Mack company's product.

The founders of the company were Augustus F., William, and John M. Mack, sons of a German immigrant farmer in Lackawanna County, Pennsylvania. In the 1890s they acquired a small Brooklyn, New York, carriage and wagon manufacturing company that they renamed the Mack Brothers Wagon Company. Experiments with methods of making a self-propelled vehicle finally resulted in their introduction in 1900 of what is often referred to as America's first successful bus, a 4-cylinder, 20-passenger sight-seeing vehicle. It was operated as a bus until

1908, when it was converted into a truck and was driven for another nine years, becoming Mack's first "million-miler." By 1905, 15 of these buses, trade named Manhattans, had been built and were in use in Boston, New Orleans, Havana, and New York.

In 1905 the three brothers moved their company, now incorporated as the Mack Brothers Company, to Allentown, Pennsylvania, where they were joined by a fourth brother, Joseph S. Mack, who owned a successful textile company in Allentown. There the Macks, in addition to continuing to produce buses, by the end of 1905 had brought out their first trucks. At a time when the market for trucks was still quite limited, the Macks came out with a full range of models with capacities from 1- to 7.5 tons. Like the buses, they were sold under the Manhattan name until 1910, when all the company vehicles took the Mack name. The Macks pioneered the forward-control, what later became known as the "cab-over," truck design and provided parallel lines of conventional or normal-control models.

By 1911 the Mack company, which earlier had been averaging fewer than 100 vehicles a year, had increased annual production to 600 trucks, buses, and fire engines. This expansion created financial problems that led to Mack and the newly organized Saurer Motor Company of Plainfield, New Jersey, in October 1911 being taken over by the J. P. Morgan-backed holding company International Motor. It also acquired control the following March of the Hewitt Motor Company of New York, a truck manufacturer founded in 1905. For several years production of the three makes continued separately, although sales were combined under one management. After 1916, however, Macks were the sole surviving products. In 1937 the International Motor name was dropped, and the company became Mack Manufacturing Corporation until 1956, when it became simply Mack Trucks, Inc.

The company's headquarters remained in Allentown, but the Mack brothers had little to do with it after the changes of 1911 and 1912. In 1912 Joseph and Augustus Mack left for California, where they acquired extensive land-holdings in the San Diego area. John Mack also left in 1912 to form a new truck company, Mac-Carr, later Maccar Truck, which produced trucks in Allentown and, until 1935, in Scranton, Pennsylvania. In its later years in Allentown, Maccar was linked with two other truck producers, Hahn and Selden. The fourth brother, William, remained with International Motor until retiring in the 1920s, but in 1916 and 1917 he also had his own company, Metropolitan Motor, in Bronx, New York, which turned out a handful of light trucks he called Mackbilt.

Despite the departure of the Macks, the great days of the vehicles carrying their name lay ahead. In 1914 the medium-sized, 4-cylinder Mack AB appeared, replacing the earlier light Mack trucks that had been known as Mack Juniors. The AB truck continued to be produced until 1936, with production totaling 51,613 by that time. In addition, more than 3,800 AB-based buses were produced between 1921 and 1934.

In 1916 came the Mack AC, the heavy-duty truck that took the place of the earlier Mack Seniors in the 3.5-ton to 7.5-ton range. This was the truck that saw service in the war that earned it its reputation as one of the most durable trucks of all time. By 1938, when AC production ended, 40,299 of these trucks had appeared, and many remained in service for 30 to 40 years after they were built.

By 1927 Mack production was more than 7,000 units a year with sales having increased from $22 million in 1919 to $55 million. A 6-cylinder Mack bus introduced in 1926 marked a break with the 4-cylinder vehicles the company had always produced and also helped to keep Mack up with the increased demand for buses, which were replacing streetcars as the heart of urban mass transportation. Six-cylinder Mack trucks, introduced in 1927, filled the need to provide trucks capable of operating at higher speeds than had been available with the 4-cylinder models. Diesels gained support during the Depression because of their lower operating costs, and in 1938 Mack, which had used Cummins and Buda engines in its first diesel trucks, became the first truck manufacturer to produce its own diesels.

By the start of the 1940s, Mack was firmly established as the country's largest producer of heavy trucks, with annual production of more than 10,000 units. Following the war, which saw Mack build trucks, power trains, and other equipment for the armed forces, the company struggled through financial difficulties that have been a chronic problem since that time. In spite of the introduction of several new bus models, Mack's buses, although admired for their durability, had a reputation of being too expensive to operate, and declining sales finally led to their abandonment in 1960. Truck production, on the other hand, was greatly aided by the popular new "B" series models that appeared in 1952, which rang up sales of more than 127,000 trucks before they were discontinued in 1966.

But despite these good truck sales, earnings in the 1950s and 1960s declined sharply as a result of chronic labor unrest and a management that was dominated by executives with little or no experience in or understanding of the production side of the business—those whom the critics called "bean counters." A promising proposal in the mid 1960s to merge Mack with Chrysler was vetoed by the Justice Department's antitrust division. Finally, in 1967 the company's desperate need for cash led it to agree to an affiliation with Signal Oil & Gas Company that allowed Mack to continue to operate autonomously. However, with profits going to Signal, Mack was still ill-prepared to deal with the severe problems that beset the industry in the 1970s and that by the end of the decade left most of the major independent truck producers on the verge of collapse.

Mack 5-ton beer truck, 1911

Help for Mack began to appear in 1979, when the French auto company Renault, anxious to strengthen its weak presence in the American market, acquired a 41.9 percent interest in Mack. By 1988 this had been increased to 44 percent. In addition to much-needed new capital, Renault aided Mack by providing its dealers with Renault-built buses and medium trucks to sell while at the same time providing new outlets for the sale of Mack's light trucks. Additional cash became available in 1983 when the company for the first time in its history went public following Signal's divestiture of its control of the company. The price of the new Mack stock showed little movement on the over-the-counter market, but by the end of the decade there were definite indications that the rigid cost-cutting measures instituted in the 1980s by the company's new chief executive, J. B. Curcio, had put the company back on the road to prosperity. Its break-even point had been reduced from 1979's 37,000 vehicles to about 23,000 in 1988. The number of truck lines had been cut from sixteen to eight, but its Class 8 diesels remained the workhorses in the country's heavy-duty truck fleets. In 1986 a new computerized plant in Winnsboro, South Carolina, replaced the sixty-year-old Allentown assembly plant as Mack's main production facility. The highly touted savings that would be generated by the new facility at first were not forthcoming, as com-

puters that did not work properly, workers who were unfamiliar with their jobs, and parts that did not arrive led to a pileup of 2,000 unfinished trucks, a fall in Mack's share of the market for heavy-duty trucks at a time when demand was booming, and heavy losses on the company books. However, Curcio turned things around in 1988 by lowering the production quotas at Winnsboro, so the problems with the new plant could be more easily resolved while increasing output at other Mack plants. Prospects for the nearly ninety-year-old company brightened. With annual sales of $1.8 billion, Mack showed a profit again in 1988, and as for the future, "the company has a terrific reputation," as a *Forbes* analyst noted. "People still say: 'It's built like a Mack.' "

References:

Automobile Quarterly, The American Car Since 1775 (New York: Dutton, 1971);

Thomas Derdak, ed., *International Directory of Company Histories*, volume 1 (Chicago & London: St. James, 1988);

G. N. Georgano, ed., *The Complete Encyclopedia of Commercial Vehicles* (Osceola, Wis.: Motorbooks International, 1979);

Kerry Hannon, "On the road again," *Forbes*, 141 (May 16, 1988): 37-38;

Zenon C. R. Hansen, *The Legend of the Bulldog* (New York: Newcomen Society, 1974).

Alexander Young Malcomson

(June 7, 1865-August 1, 1923)

by George S. May

Eastern Michigan University

CAREER: Owner, several coal companies and mines in Detroit; Harlan, Kentucky; and elsewhere (1890s-1923); partner, Ford & Malcomson (1902-1903); treasurer and director, Ford Motor Company (1903-1906); president, Aerocar Company (1905-1907); vice-president, treasurer and director, United Fuel & Supply Company (1914-1923).

Alexander Young Malcomson, who more than anyone else was responsible for organizing the Ford Motor Company, was born in Dairy, Ayrshire, Scotland, on June 7, 1865, the son of William George and Bridget Rogers Malcomson. After attending schools in Scotland, Malcomson immigrated to the United States when he was fifteen and settled in Detroit. He worked for a time as a grocery clerk, but, unlike the stereotypical Scotsman, Malcomson, his son Allan later declared, was "the plunger type, a man who did not hesitate to take chances." He shortly struck out on his own, establishing his own grocery store.

In the early 1890s Malcomson turned to the coal business, starting with one small yard and a horse and wagon for deliveries. He aggressively pursued new business, and before long his wagons, carrying the slogan "Hotter Than Sunshine," were seen all over town. He gained new customers by dealing with people in a fair manner and not taking advantage of the opportunity to raise prices during periodic coal shortages. During one coal strike, when his supply of coal and that of other dealers was exhausted, Malcomson held his customers and gained new ones by getting coal from the gas company, which had more than it needed. By 1902 Malcomson had thousands of commercial and residential customers and was probably Detroit's largest coal dealer, with several yards in the city, an interest in a Toledo fuel company, and 1,000 acres of West Virginia coal land. At the same time that he continued to expand his coal interests, borrow-ing heavily to do so, Malcomson's instincts led him to take a gamble in a new area, the automobile industry.

Like many in the younger generation of that day, Malcomson had become an automobile enthusiast. He bought a Winton, one of the best-known cars of the day, and enjoyed driving this new means of transportation at the same time that his coal business still relied on horse-drawn vehicles. Malcomson had also followed the developments in Detroit that were promising to make it an important center of car production. Among those who were engaged in these activities, Henry Ford was a familiar figure to Malcomson: he had known Ford since the mid 1890s when he sold coal to the Edison Illuminating Company, where Ford served as the chief engineer. When Ford left the Edison company in 1899 to join the first of the automobile companies with which he would be connected, he had continued to buy coal from Malcomson for use in his home. Whether from contacts with Ford or through reading the local newspapers, Malcomson was certainly well aware of Ford's up-and-down career in the new industry, first with the Detroit Automobile Company, which had been dissolved early in 1901 because of Ford's failure to produce a passenger car. Ford's fortunes had then been revived by his victory in a car that he and others had built in a race with Alexander Winton in October 1901. This race had led to the formation of the Henry Ford Company, but when Ford spent his time developing a bigger racing car and not a passenger car for the public, his backers in the new company dismissed him in March 1902.

During the next several months, while Ford was engaged in well-publicized efforts to build the most powerful racing vehicle the world had yet seen, his plans to develop a passenger car drew him to Malcomson. It is not clear who made the first overture but Ford needed money to proceed with the

Alexander Young Malcomson (second from left) in the office of his coal company. Standing to his left are James Couzens and an unidentified man. The man seated to Malcomson's right is possibly John S. Gray (courtesy of Ford Motor Company)

building of his prototype model and Malcomson saw an opportunity to do what others had failed to do in the past–capitalize on the reputation Ford had begun to acquire as the builder of winning racing cars. On August 16, 1902, the two men sat down in the offices of Horace H. Rackham and John W. Anderson, two attorneys who had done work for Malcomson in the past. An arrangement was worked out which was formalized in a partnership agreement signed four days later, whereby Malcomson agreed to furnish the money Ford needed to build his pilot car. In return, among other things, Ford agreed that the two would control an equal share of a majority stock interest in the firm.

To keep his financial involvement in this venture secret from the bankers who had loaned him money to expand his coal business, Malcomson established a separate account to handle the funds Ford would be using and placed the account in the name of the coal company's office manager, James

Couzens. Although Ford had indicated to Malcomson that $3,000 would be all the money he would need, Couzens soon had to report that Ford was exceeding this estimate by a considerable amount. Nevertheless, by November in 1902, encouraged by the progress that had been made and by the victory of the Ford-designed "999" over a car driven by Alexander Winton in a race held in October, Malcomson went ahead to have the partnership with Ford converted to a corporation, sometimes referred to as Ford & Malcomson and sometimes as Malcomson & Ford. The corporation was to issue 15,000 shares of stock at $10 each. According to Allan Nevins, Ford and Malcomson were to receive 6,900 shares "in return for their patent rights, designs, and the time, money, and effort they were spending. They would also pay $3,500 in cash for 350 additional shares. This would leave 7,750 shares to be sold." The division, if reported correctly, is somewhat strange, since it left Malcomson and Ford controlling less than the majority of the stock. But in any event, subsequent developments rendered moot the questions raised by the stock split of November 1902, since the two men did indeed end up with a majority of the stock in the Ford Motor Company when it was incorporated in June 1903.

In winter 1902-1903 and the following spring, while Ford, together with his small crew of workers, proceeded from the first prototype model to the construction of a second model, Malcomson assumed the principal responsibility for promoting interest in the new company and its car. By the early part of 1903 he was placing advertisements in trade papers for the "Fordmobile," produced by the "Fordmobile Co., Ltd.," Detroit. The runabout model was to sell for $750 and the tonneau for $850. Production of either model was nowhere in sight at the time, but a few orders did come in, which were of some help to Malcomson in drumming up interest among potential investors. By March contracts were being signed with parts suppliers, and by April the assembling factory that had been leased was being put in readiness.

At that point, Malcomson faced a financial crisis that threatened to abort the entire operation. John and Horace Dodge, operators of a Detroit machine shop who had taken on the contract to build the engines and chassis for the car, insisted upon being paid the $10,000 that had been promised to them by April 15. Ford & Malcomson did not have the money. The investors that Malcomson had been able to recruit were, for the most part, not affluent and in a number of cases had provided only promissory notes. Malcomson's uncle, John S. Gray, was the president of the German-American Bank, one of Detroit's smaller banks, which had provided the money Malcomson had had to borrow during the winter to expand his fuel business further. Although he had not wanted to do it, Malcomson was forced to go to his uncle and ask for his help in getting the money the automobile venture needed to survive. Gray is reported to have blanched when he learned that his nephew, already deeply in debt as a result of one business, had become involved with such a risky business venture. However, he agreed to bail out Malcomson after he had been shown the solid work that had already been done on the car and the production plans. He provided the $10,000 plus an additional $500 in return for 105 shares of stock in the new company and a promise that he would be named company president and

that if after a year he was not satisfied with his investment Malcomson would buy him out.

Gray's money, the largest single cash investment in the company, saved the day, and within two months the Ford Motor Company was organized. The dozen stockholders, nearly all of whom had been brought in through Malcomson's efforts, held their first meeting on June 18, 1903, to elect officers. Altogether, $100,000 in stock had been distributed, but only $28,000 in cash had been received. Malcomson and Ford each held 255 shares, giving the two former partners a bare majority of the voting stock. Neither had paid anything for the stock, which was awarded to them for the time and effort they had put forth to make the company possible. Ford was elected vice-president in charge of production. There was apparently no thought of choosing him as president. In accordance with the promise that had been made earlier, Gray was elected president. Malcomson, who had certainly expected to get that job until he had been forced to give it up in order to secure his uncle's contribution, wanted to become the Ford Motor Company's business manager, handling that side of operations while Ford dealt with production. Although he had not paid for the stock he had received, he had spent thousands of dollars to keep the developmental work going and had devoted many hours to lining up investors and obtaining the space where the company workers would assemble the car. As an experienced businessman, Malcomson had good reason for feeling he deserved to be business manager. But it was not to be. Gray liked his nephew but was insistent that he should remain full-time at the coal business in order to make sure that the fuel company's bank loans were paid off. Malcomson objected, declaring that Couzens was a very able man who could look after the coal business, leaving Malcomson free to handle the auto company's affairs. Couzens had been able to scrape together enough cash to buy 25 shares in the company, and so Gray declared that if Couzens was as capable as Malcomson said he was, "then you can send him to the automobile business. He can watch that for you." As a result, the stockholders elected Couzens to be the secretary and business manager, while Malcomson had to be satisfied with the less important post of treasurer.

It must have been a bitter disappointment to Malcomson to have been denied the position he felt he so richly deserved. To be sure, in addition to being the treasurer he was also, along with Gray,

Ford, John Anderson, and John F. Dodge (who, along with his brother, had 100 shares of stock), one of the five directors chosen at the June 18 meeting, but it was soon evident that Malcomson was in the minority in the company and that any ideas he might have as to how the company should be run were not likely to receive a favorable reception. Gray sided with Ford and Couzens because he felt that no matter how much he liked his nephew his keen sense of business told him that the policies advocated by Ford and Couzens were better for the company than those proposed by Malcomson. John Dodge could usually be counted on to throw his support to Ford and Couzens because he did not like Malcomson. When Malcomson realized that Couzens was not going to follow his former employer's dictates but was going to act in accordance with what he felt was good for the Ford Motor Company, Malcomson sought to have Couzens removed as business manager and to have the job turned over to him. But only John Anderson, among the other directors, supported Malcomson. Then, despite the success of the small Ford models that were first introduced, Malcomson pressed for the introduction of bigger models. In this case, Malcomson could cite support in the industry as a whole, where, by 1905, there was a noticeable shift away from the light, low-priced runabouts to sturdier, bigger cars that were also much higher priced and more profitable. Malcomson gained enough support to force Ford, who continued to favor a policy which concentrated on the lower-priced models, to come out with bigger cars, including the 6-cylinder Model K, selling for $2,800, three times the price of the 2-cylinder Ford Model A, which had been the company's initial entry in the marketplace in 1903.

The Model K was a commercial disaster, and its failure further weakened Malcomson's position in the company. However, although he was in a minority on the board of directors, he still might have been able to round up enough support among the stockholders to gain majority control had he not announced the formation late in 1905 of a new company, Aerocar, to produce air-cooled touring cars. For one person to hold an interest in more than one automobile company was not unheard of, and it could be argued that the Aerocar would not be competing with the type of cars Ford was putting out, but the other directors, and at least some of the other stockholders, did not see it that way.

They saw a Ford executive who was also the majority stockholder and president of another automobile company whose sales, it was felt, were bound to have an impact on Ford sales. The directors adopted a resolution, which was seconded by Henry Ford, asking Malcomson to resign as treasurer and director within five days.

Malcomson refused to resign, declaring he saw no conflict of interest. He reminded the directors that he was, with Ford, the largest stockholder in the Ford Motor Company, and it was obviously in his best interest to take no action that would reduce the value of that stock. On the other hand, Ford and Couzens, with support from several other stockholders, had formed the Ford Manufacturing Company to produce parts for the best-selling new Ford Model N. Malcomson had not been invited to be a stockholder in this new company for the simple reason that Ford and Couzens were using it as a means of siphoning off some of the Ford Motor Company's profits and thereby forcing Malcomson out. In this aim they were successful. On July 12, 1906, six days after John Gray died, Malcomson sold his 255 shares of Ford stock to Henry Ford for $175,000 (at the time of the company's incorporation, the stockholders had agreed to sell their stock only to each other, not to outsiders). This gave Ford the majority stock control that increasingly led him to do what he wanted to do, regardless of others' views. Malcomson could have retained his stock, but without support within the company he was simply delaying the inevitable day when Ford would have his way in most, if not all, matters.

Had Malcomson held on to his stock until 1919, when Ford bought out all the other stockholders, he would have received in dividends since 1906 and in the price Ford paid for the stock in 1919 about $100 million. Had his Aerocar Company been a success, Malcomson might have felt vindicated, but that company, like the great majority of manufacturers, went bankrupt, its assets being picked up in 1907 by Alfred O. Dunk, a legendary Detroiter who made a tidy living for many years by buying and selling the assets of automobile companies that had gone under. Malcomson continued in the coal business, merging his Detroit coal interests in 1914 with the C. H. Little Company to form the United Fuel & Supply Company. He was director, vice-president, and treasurer of the company, in which he had the largest individual holding, and at the same time retained coal interests in Harlan, Kentucky, and other commercial interests in and around Detroit.

Malcomson was married twice, first to Sarah Jane Mickleborough of Toronto in 1889 and then, after Sarah's death in 1901, to Alice Schofield of Detroit in 1903. He had seven children, five by his first wife and two by his second. He was active in many community activities, a communicant of the Church of Christ, and a well-liked, kindly man. But his success in the coal business meant little in a city that came to associate success with the automobile industry. In the 1940s, some two decades or so after Malcomson's death on August 1, 1923, John Gunther, when he was doing research for *Inside U.S.A.*, published in 1947, ran across Malcomson's name in the list of the original Ford stockholders. After some inquiries, he said that it appeared "that he was a coal dealer, and Couzens was a clerk in

his office. Ford must, of course, have bought him out many years ago. . . . I was unable to find anybody in Detroit who knew further about Mr. Malcomson."

References:

John Gunther, *Inside U.S.A.* (New York: Harper's, 1947);

David L. Lewis, *The Public Image of Henry Ford: An American Folk Hero and His Company* (Detroit: Wayne State University Press, 1976);

George S. May, *A Most Unique Machine: The Michigan Origins of the American Automobile Industry* (Grand Rapids, Mich.: Eerdmans, 1975);

Allan Nevins and Frank Ernest Hill, *Ford: The Times, The Man, The Company* (New York: Scribners, 1954).

Archives:

Much material relating to Malcomson's activities in the Ford Motor Company can be found in the Ford Archives, Henry Ford Museum, Dearborn, Michigan.

Marketing

by George S. May

Eastern Michigan University

In the years after the first American cars were produced in the 1890s, the industry enjoyed the marketing advantage of offering the public a product their customers had never owned before. It was, in short, a seller's market, and these conditions continued to govern the market for cars until the 1920s, when, for the first time, the majority of cars sold were purchased as replacements for cars the buyers had purchased in a previous year.

In theory, the seller's market during the industry's first three decades seemed to mean that until the great pool of first-time buyers had been significantly drained, little effort was needed to sell a car. Instead, a company's major concern should be directed toward expanding production to meet an insatiable demand. Although important adjustments and new emphases did indeed have to take place in marketing practices in the 1920s because of the buyer's market that emerged, the job of promoting and selling their product was not something that automakers prior to the 1920s could afford to neglect.

Although it was true that the demand greatly exceeded the supply and that any car that ran—or even appeared to be able to run—was almost certainly going to be bought, the buyer still had to be made aware of the car's existence. In an era when there were hundreds of companies producing motor vehicles, the task of making the consumer aware of all the differing makes was not as simple as it became in later years when only a handful of companies, all with familiar names, were still in business. To promote a greater awareness of these novel vehicles and of particular companies and their cars, the industry from the very outset staged annual shows where a wide selection of new cars could be viewed in one place. Influenced by the earlier practices of the bicycle industry, individual companies sought to draw attention to themselves and their vehicles by entering them in races, hill-climbing events, and endurance runs that, if the entries won, demonstrated the superiority of the company's product. Both newspapers and mass circulation magazines gave considerable coverage to these events. In addition, new magazines were already beginning to appear in the mid 1890s that were devoted entirely to matters of interest to the automobile industry and its customers.

Although Henry Ford and his company were the recipients of so much free publicity that he did not for some years have to spend any money on advertising in order to maintain a healthy growth rate in sales of his Model T, most companies felt the need to keep their name before the public through paid advertising on billboards and particularly in newspapers and magazines. Much of this early advertising emphasized a nuts-and-bolts approach, as the public was still unfamiliar with the automobile's mechanical features. Although the message of these ads differed from the more sophisticated appeals of later years, the volume of car ads in the early twentieth century was already making this new industry one of the major sources of income for the nation's ad agencies.

Promotions and advertising were a means of acquainting potential customers with the product, but a direct contact had to be made to bring about a sale. Initially, this contact was with the company itself as many cars were bought directly from the factory, a practice that remained fairly common for many years. Aside from small-scale operations, such as those of custom car builders who counted on making the major share of their sales at the annual salon shows, the direct-sales approach was not practical for manufacturers producing a significant volume of cars that they hoped to sell across the country. Thus, by the 1920s only 4 percent of General Motors (GM) sales were handled in this fashion. The other 96 percent resulted from contacts the buyers made not with the factory but with an agent in or near their hometown who was authorized to sell the products of GM's car divisions.

A variety of methods were tried in establishing networks of outlets for a company's products. The most common approach in the early period was to contract with a distributor who acted as a wholesaler or middleman who subcontracted with local agents or dealers in the area that the company had assigned to him. This might be part of a state, an entire state, or several states. In a few instances a company awarded the exclusive rights to handle sales of its cars nationwide to one company or individual. Thus, in 1909 Studebaker contracted to sell the entire output of the new E-M-F company. In a more famous case, Ray M. Owen, who had been

the Oldsmobile distributor for Ohio and the New York area, in 1904 became the national distributor for Ransom E. Olds's new Reo. The advantages to the manufacturer of such a system, whether the distributors handled sales in a region or in the entire country, was that it allowed him to devote most, if not all, of his attention to production matters. The disadvantage was that the manufacturer gave up his ability to control sales of his cars at the local level, depending on the distributor to handle these for him. Disputes between E-M-F and Studebaker over the latter's performance resulted in Studebaker taking over control of E-M-F in 1910. In the case of Reo, after ten years the dissatisfaction of its management with Ray Owen's performance led to cancellation of the contract with him in 1914 and the company's taking over the distribution of its cars to the local dealers. By the 1920s most companies had eliminated the distributors and were handling the wholesaling of their products through their own sales departments.

A variation on the system of regional distributors was that employed by Ford, Packard, and other companies, which involved setting up company branches in various parts of the country. Unlike the regional sales offices that the industry would ultimately adopt as the method of handling distribution, these branches sold cars to individuals as well as saw that the dealers were supplied with the cars and parts they needed. On the whole, this system did not work especially well and was eventually abandoned. Salesmen at the branches were salaried company employees who were not inclined to be as aggressive as dealers' salesmen who worked on commissions. Branch managers sometimes gave their customers repair services too generously, charging the costs to the company. Also, the building housing the branch was often an elaborate showplace, in keeping with the reputation of such companies as Packard. The system worked best for Ford since the low-priced Model T had no real competition, making it unnecessary for its "stores," as Ford called its branches, to resort to the tactics used by other companies' branches to keep pace with the competition.

No matter what method of distribution was used, however, the strength of any company's ability to sell its cars ultimately rested with its local dealers. Finding good people to fill these positions was difficult, which is one reason why companies in the early years were inclined to pass the job along to regional distributors who might be more familiar with the talent available in their area. Demonstrated ability as a salesman was an obvious criterion. William E. Metzger, who opened Detroit's first retail automobile business in 1898, had previously sold bicycles and cash registers. Within a short time he had a large establishment in which he acted as the local agent for Oldsmobiles, Waverly Electrics, the Mobile steamer, as well as Olds and Lozier engines, bicycles, and furniture. His ability as a salesman soon led him to be hired by Cadillac as its first sales manager, and later to his association with other automotive companies.

Dealers who sold more than one company's cars were common in this early period, but before long the larger companies increasingly insisted that a dealer be their agent exclusively. Particularly as the regional distributors were phased out and companies established direct contacts with their dealers, the special conditions of this relationship became clear. A dealership was not the same kind of business as a grocery store, whose owner stocked his shelves with a variety of competing products that he obtained through wholesalers. In the automobile industry the manufacturer became the wholesaler, who awarded the dealer a franchise authorizing him to sell that company's product. The dealer had certain rights under that franchise agreement, but the company also had rights, including the preeminent right to cancel the agreement if the dealer failed to live up to the conditions spelled out in the agreement. The threat of cancellation only added to the risks the car dealer faced in a business that was inherently risky because of the fact that so many car manufacturers went bankrupt, leaving their dealers high and dry. Nevertheless, for those who were fortunate enough to obtain a franchise from one of the major successes, such as Ford, Buick, Cadillac, or Packard, a dealership could be a highly lucrative business well worth the risks.

That business could not have survived, however, if the method by which the product had been sold in the pre-1920 era had remained in effect in later years and credit not been made available to car buyers. Selling a product on the installment plan in America went back at least as far as 1856 when the Singer sewing machine company allowed customers to buy one of its machines by putting $5 down and paying off the remainder of the cost at $3 to $5 a month. Some other merchandisers adopted the same financing approach, including

shops selling bicycles in the 1890s. Although an automotive trade publication in 1899 reported "one of our large capitalists" predicting that within less than a year similar credit arrangements would be made available to some car buyers, the business was carried on during its first two decades almost entirely on a cash basis. The industry could not have survived on any other basis. The automobile companies typically started their operations with limited funds from their investors, just enough, if they were lucky, to get the parts they needed to build their first cars. With little hope of financial assistance from bankers, who had to be convinced that the automobile was more than a passing fad, these pioneer companies insisted that their dealers pay cash upon the receipt of a shipment of cars in order for the company to be able to get more parts to build more cars. The dealers, in turn, demanded full payment from their customers when they received delivery of their car. The banks were just as unwilling to assist dealers and their customers in financing a car purchase as they were in providing assistance to the manufacturer, and few dealers were in a position to bear the expense of such a credit arrangement on their own. Besides, with cars in such short supply there was no inducement to offer credit terms. If a sale was lost because the buyer could not pay the full price of the car, someone else would soon come in who could meet the dealer's demand for cash on delivery.

By 1910 questions were being raised as to whether the industry's growth could be sustained on a cash-only basis. Reports, probably greatly exaggerated, that many people had mortgaged their homes in order to buy a car sparked much discussion in the press, with most comments, including those from the industry, deploring the practice. Nevertheless, it underlined the need for some means of relaxing the existing purchase arrangements.

Although Studebaker in 1911 began providing help to its dealers who sold cars on the installment plan, the biggest impetus to the emergence of the new approach came in 1915 when John North Willys formed the Guaranty Securities Company to support credit purchases of the cars of Willys-Overland. For one-third down, a buyer could begin driving an Overland touring car by agreeing to pay off the remainder of the $750 price of the car in eight monthly installments of $50 to $75. A few months later Guaranty Securities was reorganized as Guaranty Securities Corporation of New York, and it began financing installment sale purchases of other cars besides those produced by Willys-Overland. The idea of relieving the dealer of the burden of financing time payments by taking over the loans he negotiated, paying him the money he was owed, and collecting the monthly installments, with interest, from the car buyer caught on quickly. By the early 1920s several hundred such loan companies had been established, GM had established its own credit agency, General Motors Acceptance Corporation, and the ground had been broken for the

boom in automobile sales during the course of that decade, the bulk of it financed by credit, not cash.

References:

James J. Flink, *The Automobile Age* (Cambridge, Mass.: MIT Press, 1988);

George S. May, *The Automobile in American Life* (forthcoming, 1990);

Allan Nevins, *Ford: The Times, The Man, The Company* (New York: Scribners, 1954);

Alfred P. Sloan, Jr., *My Years With General Motors* (Garden City, N.Y.: Doubleday, 1964).

Walter L. Marr

(August 14, 1865-December 11, 1941)

by Richard P. Scharchburg

GMI Engineering & Management Institute

CAREER: Apprentice, J. Walker & Sons (1882-1887); machinist, Wickes Brothers (1887-1898); bicycle manufacturer (1898-?); chief engineer, consulting engineer, Buick Motor Company [later Buick Motor Division, General Motors Corporation] (1903-1920s).

Outstanding among pioneer automobile engineers, Walter Lorenzo Marr is best known for his part in the development of the Buick "valve-in-head" engine. He brought remarkably broad mechanical knowledge, skill, and experience to the early motor industry. Marr was born in Lexington, Michigan, on August 14, 1865. He began his mechanical career in 1882 as an apprentice with J. Walker & Sons, a machinists' firm located in East Tawas, where his family had moved in the late 1860s. In 1887 he took a job with Wickes Brothers, sawmill and steamboat engineers in Saginaw.

While in Saginaw, Marr worked on his first automobile. Steam automobiles were receiving a lot of attention at the time, and the Wickes superintendent was interested. He built a steam car, but Saginaw authorities would not allow him to run it on the streets. Marr became the protégé of the superintendent and was allowed to borrow and study his prized collection of German magazines dealing with topics of a mechanical nature. Unable to understand the German text but able to understand the pictures, Marr secured a fair knowledge of mechanics,

giving him an advantage over most would-be engine designers. He began to develop gasoline engine designs, eventually producing a workable valve-in-head motor.

After leaving Wickes Brothers in 1898, Marr started a bicycle manufacturing plant in Detroit. After several reorganizations the firm became known as the Marr Cycle Company. He continued his experiments with motorized transport, producing a "motor tricycle" and a "motor wagon" in 1899. About that time he met David Buick, a former plumbing supply manufacturer who was getting into the automobile business as well. Buick convinced Marr to leave the bicycle business to devote full time to automotive design. Marr and Buick could not get along, however, and soon Marr struck out on his own, in the first of several stops and starts in their relationship. By 1903 he had produced a vehicle he called the Marr Auto-Car, which he exhibited in the Chicago auto show that spring. The car never got into production.

In the fall of that same year David Buick's Buick Motor Company was purchased by Flint Wagon Works interests and moved to Flint, Michigan. Buick and Marr apparently agreed to forget past differences and to continue work on developing an automobile, to which the Wagon Works management reluctantly agreed. By May 27, 1904, a 2-cylinder valve-in-head engine of Marr's design had been perfected. On July 9, 1904, Marr and

Walter L. Marr (left) and Tom Buick, son of Buick Motor Company director David Buick, in Flint, Michigan, after driving to Detroit and back in the first Flint-made Buick, July 9-12, 1904

Buick's son Tom drove a Buick from Flint to Detroit in record-breaking time. The company soon started producing cars in a new plant built south of the Wagon Works on West Kearsley Street. Thirty-seven cars were made that year.

In the early years of the twentieth century the standard way for budding automobile manufacturers to impress prospective automobile buyers with their product was to enter races and contests. Marr convinced William C. Durant, who had taken over management of Buick, to enter a Buick car in the 1905 Eagle Rock (New York) Hill Climbing Contest. The Buick won handily, defeating entries including a White Steamer and other gasoline powered cars–a Napier, a Pope-Toledo, a Pierce Arrow, and several imported models. Marr entered other contests with similar results. By the end of 1905 he later stated, "the buying public of our Nation had been convinced of Buick's superior qualities. . . . The Buick valve-in-head engine was looked upon as the greatest car built. It became more famous each

month and year as it went on lowering records and winning new victories over all competitors."

In 1907 Durant formally authorized the organization of a Buick racing team including drivers Louis and Arthur Chevrolet, "Bob" Burman, and Louis Strang, and Marr as chief engineer. The team accumulated 500 trophies and many speed records in two seasons.

In 1910 Marr and the Buick team, now part of the General Motors (GM) combine, startled the racing world by introducing two almost identical race cars, quickly nicknamed "Bugs" because their profiles resembled a June bug, at the new Indianapolis Speedway. They painted a goat's head on the hood of each racer, which according to Marr "indicated that Buick was butting into the racing game." The Bugs, driven by Bob Burman and Louis Chevrolet, lapped off the miles so fast that the car driven by Burman was clocked at an astonishing 105.8 miles per hour. Chevrolet's Bug developed trouble and never got to the starting lineup for the inaugural race at the speedway. Burman entered the race but finished behind the winner. Later the Buick Bugs shattered records all over the United States. Financial troubles at Buick and at GM brought a halt to the racing program.

In 1914, when cycle cars were in vogue, Marr developed a model for his personal use. According to an article in the October 22, 1914, issue of *Automobile Industries*, the Marr Cyclecar "was not built with the specific idea of manufacturing it for the public." Unless manufactured in quantity its selling cost would have been prohibitive. The car had a 36-inch tread, a 100-inch wheelbase, and weighed a mere 600 pounds. Its motor was of the 4-cylinder water-cooled type. Its body was arranged for tandem seating. The radiator shell was plated with German silver, and the car's interior was finished in buff with brown leather upholstering. Deep "Turkish cushions" were fitted, and the driver's compartment was roomy and comfortable. A special feature was "the adjustable steering wheel which may be raised or lowered on its spindle to meet the requirements of the driver."

Those early years in the motor industry were hard on the men vital to its development. Some of the pioneers wore out quickly. Marr's health was often poor, and he took long vacations. As early as 1909, when he took a vacation in Colorado because of an attack of tuberculosis, he did a little flying and soon became interested in airplane engines. Experiments led to his patenting a new type of rear rudder control, which in 1910 was adopted on the first plane built in Flint—the "Flint Flyer." The Flyer never flew more than a few feet and eventually cracked up on a rail fence. Marr retired to the Signal Mountain area near Chattanooga, Tennessee,

in 1912 but kept an airplane to use on trips. An airport in Chattanooga, for which he donated the land, was named "Marr Field." In 1920 he predicted that "flying is the coming mode of travel."

After his retirement Marr still continued as consulting engineer for Buick until the mid 1920s. He kept a suite of offices near his home, where he worked when he saw fit. Reportedly all new motor developments at Buick were submitted to him at Signal Mountain for approval. Sometimes he commuted to Flint in his private plane.

By all accounts Marr was a colorful figure. He wore a Van Dyke beard throughout his life. Designing engines and cars for the successful Buick racing team was the key activity of his professional career. He was often seen at racetracks and hill-climbing events. Marr enjoyed many years in "retirement" at Signal Mountain. He died on December 11, 1941, after a long illness.

References:

Terry B. Dunham and Lawrence R. Gustin, *The Buick: A Complete History* (Princeton: Princeton Publishing Co., 1985);

Arthur Pound, *The Turning Wheel* (New York: Doubleday, 1934);

Frank Rodolf, *An Industrial History of Flint* (Flint: Flint Journal, 1949);

Richard P. Scharchburg, *W.C. Durant: the Boss* (Flint: GMI, 1973);

Bernard A. Weisberger, *The Dream Maker: William C. Durant, Founder of General Motors* (Boston: Little, Brown, 1979).

Archives:

The Wilkerson Collection in the GMI Alumni Foundation Collection of Industrial History contains material on Walter Marr. Several of the cars he designed are housed at the Sloan Museum in Flint, Michigan.

Mass Production

by James J. Flink

University of California, Irvine

The term "mass production" dates from an article by that title actually written by William J. Cameron, but attributed to Henry Ford, in the thirteenth edition (1926) of the *Encyclopaedia Britannica*. It is described there as "the focusing upon a manufacturing project of the principles of power, accuracy, economy, system, continuity, speed, and repetition." Prior to this, the system of continuous flow production techniques implemented at the Ford Highland Park plant in 1913-1914 to produce the Model T in ever greater numbers at an ever lower price was popularly known as "Fordism." Despite the earlier origin and use of the constituent elements of the Ford production system, their integration and refinement at Highland Park was unique. As David A. Hounshell concludes in his definitive history of the rise of mass production, "it is only with the rise of the Ford Motor Company and its Model T that there clearly appears an approach to manufacture capable of handling an output of multicomponent consumer durables ranging into the millions each year."

Up to the innovations at Highland Park, "artisanal" methods prevailed in the production of automobiles. Skilled machinists, capable of operating efficiently many general-purpose machine tools, predominated in the work force and directed production in the workplace. They were aided by unskilled helpers, who performed the menial labor, such as carting and hauling material, at about half the pay of the skilled machinists. Increasingly, semiskilled specialists who could operate one or more specialized machines were also employed, especially in the United States. The skilled machinists had wide latitude in determining the pace of work, in setting the standards of production, and in hiring and firing their unskilled and semiskilled helpers. Consequently, there were few purely supervisory personnel, such as foremen, in the shops and small factories where components were made or assem-

Assembling magnetos at Ford Motor Company's Highland Park factory, 1913 or 1914 (courtesy of Ford Motor Company)

bled into completed automobiles.

General purpose machine tools predominated over more specialized machines; there was a relative absence of specialized jigs and fixtures to position the work; and tool benches equipped with the machinists' personal hand tools were placed in close proximity to machine tools. Machine tools of the same or similar type were grouped together, and material was conveyed by hand from one group of machines to another to be processed. Final fitting and finishing to acceptable tolerances generally involved hand filing or grinding. The principal component remained stationary on the shop floor until assembly was completed, while other components were brought to it and affixed. Thus chassis stood in rows as assembly crews moved from one to another affixing bodies and wheels.

The initial capital as well as the managerial and technical expertise needed to enter automobile manufacturing was most commonly diverted from other closely related business activities, particularly from the manufacture of machine tools, bicycles, and carriages and wagons. The requirements for fixed and working capital were also met by shifting the burden to parts makers. The automobile was a unique combination of components already standardized and being produced for other uses—for example, stationary and marine gasoline engines, carriage bodies, and wheels. Consequently, the manufacture of components was jobbed out to scores of independent suppliers, minimizing the capital requirements for wages, materials, expensive machinery, and a large factory. So once the basic design of his car was established, the early automobile manufacturer became merely an assembler of major components and a supplier of finished cars to his distributors and dealers. The modest assembly plant needed could be rented as easily as purchased, and the process of assembling was shorter than the 30- to 90-day credit period that the parts makers allowed. Operating on this basis, for example, the Ford Motor Company was able to start in business in 1903 with paid-in capital of only $28,000, a dozen workmen, and an assembly plant just 250 feet by 50 feet. The chassis components (engines, transmissions, and axles) of the first Ford car were supplied by the Detroit machine shop of John F. and Horace E. Dodge, who became minority stockholders.

So long as and wherever such "artisanal production" persisted, labor productivity was extremely low. At Renault, the largest French producer, some 3,900 workers produced only 4,704 cars in 1913. British labor productivity was even lower. At Austin in 1913, 2,300 workers produced a mere 1,500 cars. Morris Motors, entirely an assembly operation, was the only British maker in 1913 with an annual production of more than one car per worker. Labor productivity was equally low among the makers of luxury cars in the United States. Even after Frederick Winslow Taylor's principles of scientific management of labor had been adopted to rationalize production, at Packard in De-

troit in 1913 it still took 4,525 workers to produce only 2,984 cars, an annual production rate of about 1 car for every 1.5 workers.

The major reason for this extremely low labor productivity (and correspondingly high prices for cars) was excessive reliance upon skilled workers, especially in Europe. For example, at Daimler's Stuttgart plant, the most integrated in the industry, the breakdown of its 1,700 production workers in 1909 was 69 percent skilled, 11 percent semiskilled, and 20 percent unskilled. In 1920 at the Peugeot plant at Souchaux 65 percent of the workers were skilled, 25 percent semiskilled, and 10 percent unskilled laborers.

Data for the Ford Motor Company are in sharp contrast. On the eve of innovation of the moving assembly line in 1913, the labor force of 13,304 workers at Ford already was classified as only 2 percent "mechanics and subforemen," versus 26 percent "skilled operators," 51 percent "operators," and 21 percent "unskilled workers." Even in its first year of operation, 1903-1904, the Ford Motor Company produced about 12 cars annually for every worker it employed. A comparable production rate was not achieved by Morris Motors, the largest and most efficient British producer, until a generation later, in 1934, when Morris turned out 11.6 cars per worker. Average output at that date for the British automobile industry was only about 6 cars per worker. Similarly, by 1927, when the Model T was finally withdrawn from the market, the manufacture of an automobile took 300 mandays of labor in the United Kingdom compared with 70 in the United States.

The volume production of standardized commodities had early become a pervasive feature of American industrial history. It had been encouraged by the absence of tariff barriers among the states, a high per capita income, more equitable income distribution than in European countries, and a chronic shortage of skilled labor that necessitated the mechanization of industrial processes. Firearms, sewing machines, typewriters, watches, and bicycles were among the consumer-goods items standardized and produced in volume prior to the automobile.

The most significant single contribution to the volume production of standardized commodities was the development of truly interchangeable parts—an essential element of mass production—by John H. Hall at the United States Harper's Ferry Armory in the 1850s. Henry M. Leland, a precision toolmaker prior to entering automobile manufacturing, pioneered parts interchangeability in the automobile industry in his 1904 Model B Cadillac, which was awarded the 1908 Dewar Trophy of the Royal Automobile Club of England for the achievement of previously unparalleled interchangeability of parts.

Ransom E. Olds became the first volume producer of American-made gasoline-powered cars. Some 425 units of his $650, 1-cylinder curved-dash Olds were produced in 1901, 2,500 in 1902, and 4,000 in 1903, giving Olds about a third of the market in the United States. However, Olds attempted volume production at too early a stage in the rapidly developing automotive technological art. The 3-horsepower curved-dash was a primitive motorized horse buggy, obsolete even at its introduction compared with the 35-horsepower, pressed-steel-frame 1901 Mercedes, called by Lynwood Bryant "the first modern motorcar in all essentials." The problem was to produce in volume a car of comparable quality at a moderate price.

Ford succeeded where Olds and others had failed because his Model N and Model T were truly advanced automotive designs for their day. The 4-cylinder, 15-horsepower, $600 Model N was one of the better-designed and better-built cars available at any price in 1906. *Cycle and Automobile Trade Journal* reported that "the Model N supplies the very first instance of a low-cost motorcar driven by a gas engine having cylinders enough to give the shaft a turning impulse in each shaft turn which is well built and offered in large numbers." Deluged with orders, the Ford Motor Company installed improved production equipment and after July 15, 1906, was able to make daily deliveries of 100 cars. Henry Ford boasted to reporters: "I believe that I have solved the problem of cheap as well as simple automobile construction" and that the Model N was "destined to revolutionize automobile construction."

Encouraged by the success of the Model N, Ford was determined to build an even better low-priced car. At $825 for the runabout and $850 for the touring car, the 4-cylinder, 20-horsepower Model T was first offered to dealers on October 1, 1908. Extensive use of new heat-treated vanadium steels made the Model T a lighter and tougher car, and new methods of casting parts (especially block casting of the engine) kept the price still within the reach of the middle-class purchaser. Ford's advertising boast was essentially correct: "No car under $2,000 offers more, and no car over $2,000 offers more except for trimmings."

Committed to large-volume production of the Model T as a single, static model at an ever-decreasing unit price, Ford innovated modern mass production techniques at its Highland Park plant that permitted prices to be reduced by August 1, 1916, to only $345 for the runabout and $360 for the touring car. Production of the Model T in 1916 was 738,811 units, giving Ford about half the market for new cars in the United States. Antedating the introduction of the moving assembly line, in 1912 the initial price of the Model T first dropped below the average annual wage in the United States at $575 for the runabout. By withdrawal of the Model T from production in 1927, more than 15 million units had been sold, and its price had been reduced to a low $290 for the coupe.

Charles E. Sorensen, who was in charge of production at Ford, was keenly aware that the contribution of the Ford Motor Company to mass production lay primarily in its refinement of the integration and coordination of the process of final assembly. Sorensen recalled in his 1956 autobiography: "Overhead conveyors were used in many industries including our own. So was substitution of machine work for hand labor. Nor was orderly progress of the work anything new; but it was new to us at Ford until Walter Flanders showed us how to arrange our machine tools at the Mack Avenue and Piquette plants." The significant contribution that Sorensen claimed for the Ford Motor Company was "the practice of moving the work from one worker to another until it became a complete unit, then arranging the flow of these units at the right time and the right place to a moving final assembly line from which came a finished product. Regardless of earlier uses of some of these principles, the direct line of succession of mass production and its intensification into automation stems directly from what we worked out at Ford Motor Company between 1908 and 1913."

Prior to the innovation of the moving assembly line at the Ford Motor Company, continuous flow production had been innovated in a grain mill designed by Oliver Evans in the late eighteenth century, and in Admiral Isaac Coffin's 1810 oven for baking ships' biscuits in England. By the late nineteenth century in the United States it was common in flour milling, oil refining, breweries, canneries, and the disassembly of animal carcasses in the meat packing industry.

Furthermore, recognition that the Ford Motor Company led the industry in developing the mass-produced and, as a consequence, low-priced car should not obscure the fact that Ford's effort to increase output greatly after 1908 was far from unique in the American automobile industry. With the appearance of the first reliable, moderately priced runabouts in the Ford Model N and Model T and the Buick Model 10, many of Ford's competitors also began to attempt to cut manufacturing costs and capitalize on the insatiable demand for motorcars by working out similar solutions to their common production problems. For example, innovations to reduce the time and cost of final assembly similar to those worked out at Ford were independently conceived by Walter P. Chrysler after he replaced Charles W. Nash as head of Buick in 1912. Buick production was more than quadrupled from 45 to 200 cars a day by changing outmoded procedures for finishing the body and chassis, which had amounted to "treating metal as if it were wood," and by installing a moving assembly line that consisted of "a pair of tracks made of two by fours" along which a chassis was moved from worker to worker by hand while being assembled. Chrysler recalled that "Henry Ford, after we developed our [assembly] line, went to work and figured out a chain conveyor; his was the first. Thereafter we all used them. Instead of pushing the cars along the line by hand they rode on an endless-chain conveyor operated by a motor."

The moving assembly line was first tried one Sunday morning in July 1908 at the Ford Piquette Avenue plant during the last months of Model N production. The parts needed for assembling a car were laid out in sequence on the floor; a frame was next put on skids and pulled along by a towrope until the axles and wheels were put on, and then rolled along in notches until assembled. However, this first experiment to assemble a car on a moving line did not materialize into moving assembly lines being installed at Ford until 1913 because the extensive changes in plant layout and procedures, in Sorensen's words, "would have indefinitely delayed Model T production and the realization of Mr. Ford's long cherished ambition which he had maintained against all opposition."

There was general agreement in the automobile industry that the 62-acre Highland Park plant de-

Conveyor system for wheels, fenders, and running boards at Highland Park, 1914 (courtesy of Ford Motor Company)

signed by Albert Kahn that opened on January 1, 1910, possessed an unparalleled factory arrangement for the volume production of motorcars. Its well-lighted and well-ventilated buildings were a model of advanced industrial construction. However, it is clear from the fact that much of the plant was several stories high that it was not designed with using moving assembly lines in mind.

In a plant that employed fewer than 13,000 workers, by 1914 about 15,000 specialized machine tools had been installed at Highland Park at a cost of $2.8 million. "The policy of the company," relate Allan Nevins and Frank E. Hill, "was to scrap old machines ruthlessly in favor of better types—even if 'old' meant a month's use." After 1912 the 59 draftsmen and 472 skilled toolmakers in the tool department were constantly devising new specialized machine tools that would increase production. By 1915 they had turned out more than 140 specialized machine tools and several thousand specialized dies, jigs, and fixtures. Jigs and fixtures to set up and/or position the work were called "farmers' tools" because with them green hands could turn out work as good as or better than skilled machinists. Machine tools became larger, more powerful, more specialized, and semi-automatic or automatic. A prime example was a special drilling machine supplied by the Foote-Burt Company. This machine drilled 45 holes simultaneously in four sides of a Model T cylinder block and was equipped with an automatic stop and reverse. The cylinder block was positioned by a special jig, so all the operator had to do was to pull the starting lever and remove the finished block.

Elementary time and motion studies begun at the Piquette Avenue plant were continued at Highland Park and in 1912 led to the installation of continuous conveyor belts to bring materials to the assembly lines. And with the move to Highland Park, manufacturing and assembling operations began to be arranged sequentially, so that components traveled to completion over the shortest route possible with no unnecessary handling. This entailed the abandonment of grouping machine tools together by type in plant layout.

Magnetos, motors, and transmissions were assembled on moving lines by summer 1913. After production from these subassembly lines threatened to flood the final assembly line, a moving chassis-assembly line was installed. It reduced the time of chassis assembly from twelve and a half hours in October to two hours and forty minutes by December 30, 1913. Moving lines were quickly established for assembling the dash, the front axle, and the body. The moving lines were at first pulled by rope and windlass, but on January 14, 1914, an endless chain was installed. That was in turn replaced on February 27 by a new line built on rails set at a convenient working height and timed at six feet a minute. By the summer of 1914 productivity in assembling magnetos had more than doubled, and chassis assembly took under two hours, about one-sixth the time required with artisanal production methods. "Every piece of work in the shop moves," boasted Henry Ford in 1922. "It may move on hooks or overhead chains going to assembly in the exact order in which the parts are required; it may travel on a moving platform, or it may go by gravity, but the point is that there is no lifting or trucking of anything other than materials."

At the industrial colossus that Ford began building on the River Rouge in 1916, Fordism was intensified. Nevins and Hill write that by the mid 1920s "in conveyors alone it was a wonderland of devices. Gravity, belt, buckle, spiral, pendulum gravity roller, overhead monorail, 'scenic railway' and 'merry-go-round,' elevating flight—the list was long both in range and in adaptation to special purpose." They recount that "at the entrance of the machining department, the various castings were routed mechanically to 32 different groups of machine tools, each unit then passing through a series of machine-tool operations—43 in the case of the Ford [Model T] cylinder block—before the finished shining element emerged, ready to be routed to assembly." By 1924 the River Rouge foundry cast over 10,000 Model T cylinder blocks a day, and by 1926 the 115-acre plant boasted some 43,000 machine tools and employed 8,000 tool and die makers. At the changeover to Model A production in 1927 the Ford Motor Company was estimated to have about 45,000 machine tools worth $45 million.

The mass-production techniques innovated at Highland Park were widely publicized and described in detail, most notably by Horace L. Arnold and Fay L. Faurote in their 1915 *The Ford Methods and the Ford Shops*. Within a few years moving assembly lines had been installed by all major American automobile manufacturers. Production reached peak efficiency at Hudson, where by 1926 assembling an automobile took only 90 minutes, and cars rolled off its four final assembly lines every 30 seconds.

Because cars could be shipped cheaper by rail in knocked-down form, Ford branch assembly plants were built beginning in 1909 at Kansas City, Missouri. Under the supervision of William S. Knudsen, by the end of 1912 other branch assembly plants had been opened in St. Louis, Long Island City, Los Angeles, San Francisco, Portland (Oregon), Seattle, and outside the United States in Canada and at Trafford Park, Manchester, England.

The industry leaders early had turned to integrated manufacturing operations to improve the quality and ensure the supply of components. In 1911 Ford purchased the John R. Keim Mills of Buffalo, New York, a leading manufacturer of pressed and drawn steel components. The plant's modern machinery and technical experts were moved to Highland Park, giving Ford the capacity to make its own crankcases, axles, housings, and bodies. With the inauguration of mass production at Highland Park in 1913 came complete independence from the Dodge brothers for the supply of engines and complete chassis.

Body assembly at Willys-Overland Company, 1920 (courtesy of the Budd Technical Library)

The era of artisanal production and freewheeling competition ended as, led by the Ford Motor Company, automobile manufacturing became capital intensive and economies of scale became essential for success. Capital investment in plant in relation to revenue at Ford increased from 11 percent in 1913 to 33 percent in 1926, even as Ford inventories shrank and the time to fabricate a Model T from scratch fell from fourteen days to four. The number of active producers in the American automobile industry concomitantly shrank from 253 in 1908 to 44 in 1929, with Ford, General Motors, and Chrysler responsible for about 75 percent of the output.

References:

Horace L. Arnold and Fay L. Faurote, *The Ford Methods and the Ford Shops* (New York: Engineering Magazine, 1915);

Jean-Pierre Bardoux and others, *The Automobile Revolution: The Impact of an Industry* (Chapel Hill: University of North Carolina Press, 1982);

Gerald R. Bloomfield, *The World Automotive Industry* (Newton Abbott, London & North Pomfret, Vt.: David & Charles, 1978);

James R. Bright, "The Development of Automation," in *Technology in Western Civilization*, volume 2, edited by Melvin Kranzberg and Carroll W. Pursell, Jr. (New York: Oxford University Press, 1967), pp. 635-655;

Lynwood Bryant, "The Beginnings of the Internal Combustion Engine," in *Technology in Western Civilization*, volume 1, edited by Kranzberg and Pursell (New York: Oxford University Press, 1967), pp. 648-663;

Walter P. Chrysler, in collaboration with Boyden Sparkes, *Life of an American Workman* (New York: Dodd, Mead, 1937);

Hugh Dolnar, "The Ford 4-Cylinder Runabout," *Cycle and Automobile Trade Journal*, 11 (August 1, 1906): 108;

James J. Flink, *The Automobile Age* (Cambridge, Mass.: MIT Press, 1988);

Henry Ford, in collaboration with Samuel Crowther, *My Life and Work* (Garden City, N.Y.: Doubleday, Page, 1922);

David A. Hounshell, *From the American System to Mass Production: The Development of Manufacturing Technology in the United States, 1800-1932* (Baltimore: Johns Hopkins University Press, 1984);

George S. May, *R. E. Olds: Auto Industry Pioneer* (Grand Rapids, Mich.: Eerdmans, 1977);

Stephen Meyer III, *The Five Dollar Day: Labor Management and Social Control in the Ford Motor Company, 1908-1921* (Albany: State University of New York Press, 1981);

Allan Nevins and Frank E. Hill, *Ford: The Times, the Man, the Company, 1865-1915; Ford: Expansion and Challenge, 1915-1933;* and *Ford: Decline and Rebirth, 1933-1962* (New York: Scribners, 1954, 1957, 1963);

Emma Rothschild, *Paradise Lost: The Decline of the Auto-Industrial Age* (New York: Knopf, 1973);

Charles E. Sorensen, with Samuel T. Williamson, *My Forty Years with Ford* (New York: Norton, 1956).

Hiram Percy Maxim

(September 2, 1869-February 17, 1936)

by John B. Rae

Harvey Mudd College

CAREER: Superintendent, American Projectile Company (1892-1895); chief engineer, Motor Carriage Department, Pope Manufacturing Company (1895-1899); chief engineer, Electric Vehicle Company (1899-1901, 1903-1907); engineer, Westinghouse (1901-1903); partner, Maxim-Goodridge Company (1906-1909); president, Maxim Silent Firearms Company (1909-1936).

Hiram Percy Maxim, engineer and inventor, was born in Brooklyn, New York, on September 2, 1869, and died in La Junta, Colorado, on February 17, 1936. He was one of three children, the only boy, of Sir Hiram S. Maxim, the inventor of the Maxim gun, and Jane Bidden Maxim. Hudson Maxim, also a famous inventor, was his uncle. Percy Maxim, as he was usually known, graduated from the Massachusetts Institute of Technology in 1886, the youngest member of his class. He worked for the Sun Electric Company of Woburn, Massachusetts, and the Jenny Electric Company in Fort Wayne, Indiana, before becoming superintendent of the American Projectile Company in Lynn, Massachusetts, in 1892. This company was a subsidiary of the Thompson-Houston Electric Company, which later became part of General Electric.

According to his own account, Maxim first conceived of a motor vehicle while he was bicycling from Salem to Lynn late one night in 1892 after visiting a young lady in Salem. It occurred to him that a small motor on the bicycle would make his journey much easier. He relates that, although he was a graduate of M.I.T. and knew the theory of the internal combustion engine, he had never actually seen one until he went to observe a 4-cycle stationary Otto gas engine after he began his own experiments. He knew nothing of the work of Benz and Daimler in Germany or the active commercial development of the automobile in France. He did not even know if gasoline could be used as a fuel, and he made some tests in a corner of the American Projectile Company property with a half-pint of gasoline and some empty shell cases. Fortunately he managed to avoid injury and satisfy himself that a gasoline explosion in a cylinder could be controlled.

The vehicle he used for his experiments was a second-hand Columbia tricycle (made by the Pope Manufacturing Company) that he bought for $30, all that he could afford at the time. It took him until 1895 to design an operational motor. His trial run was only a qualified success, because he had overlooked the need for a clutch, so that he had to start the machine by rolling down a steep hill, and when he tried to stop he had to run into a plowed field. Nevertheless, when he visited the Pope Manufacturing Company in Hartford shortly afterward, his work interested Hayden Eames, the manager of the Pope Tube Department, whom Maxim had known when Eames was a naval inspector at the American Projectile Company. Negotiations followed with Henry Souther, head of research for Pope and also an M.I.T. graduate, and then with George H. Day, vice-president and general manager of the Pope Manufacturing Company. The result was that Maxim was offered and accepted the post of chief engineer of a newly formed Motor Carriage Department headed by Eames. Maxim moved to Hartford in July 1895 and for the next several years worked in designing motor vehicles. He was somewhat handicapped because neither Albert A. Pope nor George Day saw any future for the gasoline car and preferred to concentrate on electrics. Pope said to Maxim at one time, "You can't get people to sit over an explosion." Nevertheless Maxim was able to do a fair amount of experimenting. He built some cars using an electric transmission designed by Justus B. Entz. It worked well, but it was too com-

Maxim in his first automobile, designed for Pope Manufacturing Company in 1895

plicated and expensive for ordinary use. He also designed a gasoline-powered tricycle for use in making package deliveries.

By 1899 the Motor Carriage Department had produced approximately 500 electric and 40 gasoline cars, making Pope by far the largest American manufacturer. Then, as is recounted elsewhere, Pope sold its Motor Carriage Department to the Electric Vehicle Company. The ensuing corporate manipulations did not directly affect Maxim's position, although he disapproved of the transaction, observing astutely that it appeared to be a scheme to unload stock on the public.

Trouble developed in 1901 when the Electric Vehicle Company bought the Riker Motor Vehicle Company of Elizabethport, New Jersey, its principal competitor in the manufacture of electric road vehicles. Andrew L. Riker became superintendent of the Electric Vehicle Company, and, when George H. Day became ill, Riker took charge with a heavy hand. Friction developed immediately. Riker transferred much of the Electric Vehicle operation, including the main office, to Elizabethport, and Maxim and Eames resigned. Maxim went to the Westinghouse Company in Pittsburgh, where he spent two

years designing a complete line of electric motor controllers. When Day recovered and resumed the management of the Electric Vehicle Company, he reversed Riker's actions and moved the head office back to Hartford. Day was able to persuade Maxim to return to the Electric Vehicle Company, where he remained until the company went into receivership in 1907. Eames never went back, and his talent for organizing production must have been missed. Maxim's inventive mind would never have let him settle down to routine work, and during this second session with the Electric Vehicle Company he continued to experiment with gasoline engines and produced another model with electric transmission, which again was not a commercial success.

By the time the Electric Vehicle Company failed he was ready to leave the automobile industry in order to develop the invention for which he is best known, the Maxim Silencer for firearms. In 1907 he formed a partnership with T. Goodridge, a former Studebaker executive, as the Maxim-Goodridge Company. This was an interim arrangement for engineering consultation and experimentation. In 1909 Maxim was ready to form the

Maxim Silent Firearms Company, which he headed for the rest of his life.

The Maxim Silencer offers a striking example of transferring technology from one area to another. At the beginning of his career Maxim's familiarity with projectiles and explosives led him to gasoline as the fuel for a self-propelled road carriage. Then his experience with gasoline engines gave him the idea for the silencer, which was based on the automobile muffler. The basic principle for silencing an explosion in a cylinder was the same.

Maxim's fields of interest outside his business affairs were also primarily technical. He founded and was president of the Amateur Cinema League of America, and he was also president of the International Amateur Radio Union, which fostered the de-

velopment of shortwave radio. He was a lieutenant commander in the United States Naval Reserve. In 1898 he married Josephine Hamilton, the daughter of a former governor of Maryland. They had two children, a son and a daughter.

Publications:
Gun Report Noise (Washington, 1917);
Life's Place in the Cosmos (New York: Appleton, 1933);
A Genius In the Family (New York: Harper & Brothers, 1936);
Horseless Carriage Days (New York: Harper & Brothers, 1937).

Reference:
John B. Rae, *The American Automobile* (Chicago: University of Chicago Press, 1965).

Maxwell-Briscoe Motor Company

by George S. May

Eastern Michigan University

Although to many in the later years of the twentieth century the Maxwell is remembered only for its use by the comedian Jack Benny as a butt of humor on his popular radio and television programs, the Maxwell was for 20 years at the start of the century one of the better-known and, for a time, one of the more popular American cars. It got its name from its designer, Jonathan Dixon Maxwell, who was born near Russiaville, Indiana, on September 3, 1864. At the age of fourteen he went to work for the Star machine shop in Kokomo, Indiana, and during the next dozen years or so learned the machinist's trade there and at shops in Peru and Huntington, Indiana; Chicago; and Brainerd, Minnesota. In 1891 he returned to Kokomo and worked in the Riverside Machine Shop, operated by Elmer and Edgar Apperson. In 1893 Maxwell became the supervisor at the Star works where he had apprenticed.

In 1894 Maxwell worked on the construction of the automobile developed by Elwood Haynes and the Apperson brothers, which received its test run on July 4 of that year. Over the next five years he continued working with Haynes and the

Appersons as they progressed to limited production of an improved car by 1898. The following year Maxwell went to Montreal, Canada, where he was hired to build an experimental gas-propelled plow, although the resulting machine, designed like a traction engine, was not of a practical nature.

In 1900 Maxwell took a job with Detroit's Olds Motor Works. There he was involved in the development of the famed curved-dash Oldsmobile runabout. In later years it was claimed that Maxwell was primarily responsible for the runabout's design, but Horace Loomis, the engineer to whom Ransom Olds gave his preliminary plans for the car in fall 1900, said that Maxwell's role was limited to work on the transmission. Later, in 1901, Maxwell and Roy D. Chapin publicized the little cars by driving them in one of the first races held in Michigan, with Maxwell coming in third behind Chapin, who finished second.

Next to the Olds factory in Detroit was the Detroit Stove Works. Maxwell became acquainted with the head of the company, William A. Barbour, and took him on test runs of the Oldsmobile. This gave Maxwell a chance to tell Barbour of plans he

The 1915 Maxwell 25

had in mind for a better runabout. As a result, Barbour and his business colleague, G. B. Gunderson, formed the Northern Manufacturing Company, which produced Maxwell's car. By the latter part of 1902 the new runabout, called the "Silent Northern" because it operated so quietly, was on the market. Maxwell was credited as the designer, although Charles B. King, who had built the first gasoline car to be driven in Detroit and had been a colleague of Maxwell's at Olds, declared that the car did not work properly until he joined the Northern as its chief engineer and made the necessary corrections in Maxwell's design.

Maxwell did not remain with Northern for long. Wishing to put out a car that bore his own name, he approached Benjamin Briscoe, with whom he had become acquainted because of the radiators and other auto parts produced by Briscoe's Detroit sheet metal company. Briscoe and his brother Frank had begun to think that they might like to get into producing the entire car, not just some parts, when they had provided financial backing to David D. Buick, but by 1903 they had despaired of Buick

being able to develop and manage a successful operation and in September had disposed of their controlling interest in the Buick company to a group of Flint businessmen. Benjamin Briscoe was no doubt happy to be rid of Buick, because Maxwell, with greater experience in automotive development, seemed to be a much better prospect. Therefore, on July 4, 1903, Briscoe and another Detroit businessman, C. W. Althouse, agreed to put up $3,000 to enable Maxwell to build a prototype of the car he had in mind. Ill health forced Althouse to withdraw, but on Christmas day Briscoe witnessed the successful test of Maxwell's new car, a light car that, like the earlier Northern, owed much to the popular Oldsmobile runabout. King, who did not have a high regard for Maxwell's ability as an engineer, declared that it was King's chief draftsman, whom Maxwell took with him when he left Northern, who should have been credited with the Maxwell's design.

Early in 1904 the Maxwell-Briscoe Motor Company was organized, and Jonathan Maxwell had the satisfaction of seeing himself appear first in the company name and in seeing his name on the car that company would produce. No matter what King may have thought of Maxwell or what Briscoe's feelings may have been (and he later admitted that he and Maxwell had serious disagreements), company ads would quote Briscoe as declaring that Maxwell was "the foremost automobile designer of the world." But Briscoe did not make the mistake Alexander Malcomson had made in giving Henry Ford an equal voice in the Ford Motor Company that Malcomson had helped organize. There was never any doubt that while Maxwell might supervise production, Briscoe controlled the company.

Briscoe's attempts to secure financial support for his new company in Detroit met with little success. Although Detroit bankers became famous for their generous treatment of the automobile industry, the reluctance Briscoe encountered in the winter of 1903-1904 may have resulted from the banks' fears that the rate at which new companies had been emerging posed a threat to the local economy's stability. But Briscoe was fortunate in not being dependent on local financing. Some years before he had obtained financial help for the sheet metal company from New York's J. P. Morgan, and he now returned to Wall Street and got a quarter of a million dollars from a sale of bonds handled by the Morgan company plus $100,000 from the banking house of Richard Irwin & Company. As part of these arrangements, Briscoe agreed to lease the Tarrytown, New York, factory where the Mobile steamer had been built until 1903 when that company went out of business.

By June 1904 Maxwell-Briscoe had begun operations in its new quarters, and, after a slow start that saw only ten cars produced that year, production of more than 2,000 units by 1906 made it the leader among the automobile companies in the East and one that seemed ready to challenge the supremacy of the Michigan companies in the production race. The first lightweight Maxwells were followed by heavier models and also a light truck, and to keep up with the goal of expanding production Briscoe had added plants in Pawtucket, Rhode Island, and Newcastle, Indiana, in addition to the Tarrytown plant, which the company bought in 1906.

A brief but sharp drop in sales that accompanied the financial panic of 1907 led Briscoe to follow the suggestion of his Wall Street advisers that he should strengthen his operations by merging the company with other manufacturers. According to Briscoe, the Morgan interests were earning a healthy 20 percent on their investment in Maxwell-Briscoe, but they had always sought to create more economic stability by promoting mergers of several competing companies into one large, dominating corporation. Thus, late in 1907 Briscoe broached the subject of merger with William C. Durant, who had, ironically, made a huge success of the Buick operation that Briscoe had given up on in 1903. Out of this discussion came a series of meetings in 1908 between Briscoe, Durant, Henry Ford, Ransom Olds, and a representative of J. P. Morgan with the object of arranging a merger of Maxwell-Briscoe, Buick, Ford, and Reo, the four leading car producers. The negotiations broke off when Ford and Olds insisted that they must receive $3 million or $4 million each to bring in their companies, whereas Briscoe and Durant and the Morgan company were thinking in terms of an exchange of stock of the companies for stock in the new corporation, with little cash involved. By August 1908 efforts to merge only Buick and Maxwell-Briscoe had also collapsed, apparently because the Morgan company, which was to have handled the financing of the merger, was no longer interested in going ahead with the deal.

Durant then went on by himself in September to form the General Motors (GM) holding company, which by the following summer had acquired control not only of Buick but also of the companies that made the Oldsmobile, the Oakland, and the Cadillac, along with several lesser lights. Briscoe had also tried to go it alone, but his inability to raise the money needed to purchase the 60 percent interest in Cadillac that he said he was offered in November 1908 did not speak well for his chances of success. Later in summer 1909 he and Durant worked out a plan that would have brought Maxwell-Briscoe, as well as Frank Briscoe's Brush Runabout company and the Briscoe brothers' sheet metal company into the GM fold for $5 million in GM stock. Briscoe pointed out in 1921 that that stock by then would have been worth about $100 million, but the exchange never took place because of the Morgan company's insistence that GM also pay $2 million in cash, besides the stock.

Finally, early in 1910, Briscoe, with backing from the Morgan interests and Anthony Brady, another Wall Street promoter, formed the United States (US) Motor Company, with Maxwell-Briscoe as its first acquisition and Benjamin Briscoe as its president. Jonathan Maxwell, who became a vice-president of US Motor, is said to have opposed the merger, and, as it turned out, with good reason. Although US Motor eventually controlled about 130 companies, most of these were small businesses making parts. With production by 1910 of around 10,000, the Maxwell remained one of the best-selling cars in the lower end of the medium-price range, but none of the other companies that became part of US Motor was of comparable worth, and the company was forced into bankruptcy in 1912. Various causes have been advanced for US Motor's failure, but the most commonly cited is that the profits of Maxwell-Briscoe were not enough to overcome the losses sustained by many of the other subsidiaries.

Maxwell was salvaged from the US Motor wreckage and was reorganized as the Maxwell Motor Car Company. Briscoe's name was dropped as he went his separate way with two new automotive ventures before going on to a variety of other business activities before he died in 1945. Jonathan Maxwell stayed on for a short time before leaving. For a while he had plans for a new car he had designed and had purchased a factory in Indianapolis where it would be assembled, but he abandoned the project following the American entry into World War I in 1917. Although he served as president of a company that dealt in automobile accessories, Maxwell's career as an automobile manufacturer had been over for a good many years when he died on March 8, 1928.

The Maxwell name continued to appear on cars until three years before his death. Direction of the post-1912 Maxwell company had been given by the bankers who carried through it reorganization to Walter E. Flanders, a veteran of service with several companies, most notably Ford, Everett-Metzger-Flanders, and Studebaker. Flanders, who received $1 million plus $2.75 million in stock for taking over Maxwell, produced a 4-cylinder Maxwell in the Dayton, Ohio, plant formerly used by Stoddard-Dayton, a US Motor company that did not survive the 1912 bankruptcy. In the Detroit plant that had been used by Flanders's own Flanders Company, which the banks purchased in order to acquire his services, he produced what had been the Flanders Six but which now became the 6-cylinder Maxwell. In 1914 the 4-cylinder Maxwell 25, priced at $750, was introduced, and it boosted company sales to

more than 17,000 in 1914 and by 1917 to 75,000—plus 25,000 Maxwell trucks that used the same 4-cylinder engine.

In 1917 Flanders became president of Detroit's Chalmers company as well as continuing as president of Maxwell. Chalmers, under its founder Hugh Chalmers, had overexpanded, building new factories whose production capacities greatly exceeded Chalmers's needs. Thus, a semimerger was arranged, enabling Maxwell, which needed more production space, to transfer production to Chalmers's underutilized facilities. Following the war, Flanders, like all automakers, moved to take full advantage of the anticipated postwar boom, but the unexpected depression that struck in summer 1920 caught the company completely off guard. Instead of the announced 1920 goal of 100,000 cars, only 34,168 were produced and the company was heavily in debt. Adding to these woes was the murky corporate relationship with Chalmers, which was in worse shape, and consumers' complaints about recent Maxwell models that had greatly damaged its once excellent reputation, making it all the more difficult to dispose of a huge inventory of unsold cars.

In an involved and often confusing corporate reorganization, Maxwell's principal creditors dumped Walter Flanders and brought in Walter P. Chrysler to run another salvage operation. Chrysler, who had become famous for his work in revitalizing Buick production, had been paid $1 million in 1920 to try to "straighten out Willys-Overland," but he now agreed to only $100,000, plus stock options, to become the chairman of the Maxwell reorganization and management committee because he saw an opportunity to own his own company.

Chrysler managed to put Chalmers and Maxwell through what was termed a "friendly receivership," after which he bought the assets of the two troubled companies, which were combined as the Maxwell Motor Corporation. In 1921 he cut the price on the existing Maxwell models which he advertised as the "Good Maxwell," to distinguish them in the public's mind from the old Maxwells that had caused their owners so much grief. Then under his direction a redesigned 4-cylinder Maxwell was brought out in 1922 which was not only the "Good Maxwell," but the "New Series Maxwell." Sales rebounded, and 67,000 Maxwells were built in 1922 to meet a demand that was in sharp contrast with the sales of 16,000 in 1921.

Meanwhile, plans were going ahead for an entirely new 6-cylinder car that would carry Chrysler's own name. The car appeared in 1924, replacing the Chalmers. The new Chrysler outsold the Maxwell, and the result was that in 1925 Walter Chrysler reorganized the business once more, changing its name to the Chrysler Corporation. The Maxwell was dropped, but the 4-cylinder Chrysler 58 that was introduced for the 1926 model year had the same engine that had been used in the earlier 4-cylinder Maxwell. That same engine, plus some other parts of Maxwell origins, was used in 1928 in the new Chrysler-Plymouth, later simply the Plymouth. Thus both Jonathan Maxwell and Benjamin Briscoe lived to see their old company, in

a very real sense, live on in the Chrysler Corporation, the last of the country's Big Three automakers to appear.

References:

Nick Baldwin and others, *The World Guide to Automobile Manufacturers* (New York: Facts on File, 1987);

Tad Burness, *Cars of the Early Twenties* (New York: Galahad, 1968);

Walter P. Chrysler, *Life of An American Workman* (New York: Dodd, Mead, 1950);

George S. May, *A Most Unique Machine: The Michigan Origins of the American Automobile Industry* (Grand Rapids, Mich.: Eerdmans, 1975);

Alfred Reeves, "Benjamin Briscoe, 1867-1945," *Old-Timers News* (July 1945): 31-33.

Mercer Automobile Company

by George S. May

Eastern Michigan University

During the 16 years between 1909 and 1925 that it was in business, the Mercer Automobile Company produced about 25,000 cars, a fair number for a firm that never intended to be a high-volume manufacturer. But Mercer is one of America's most celebrated automotive names because of only 500 of those cars, the Mercer Type 35 Raceabout.

The Mercer took its name from Mercer County, New Jersey, where Trenton, the city in which the cars were built, is located. Members of the Roebling engineering family, famous as the builders of the Brooklyn Bridge, had been involved in the production of a very expensive car designed by Etienne Planche, called the Roebling-Planche. In 1909 the company and the car it produced adopted the Mercer name, the company first being called the Mercer Autocar Company and then in 1910 the Mercer Automobile Company. Several models appeared before the legendary Type 35 Raceabout was introduced in 1911. It was designed by Finlay Richardson Porter, the company's new chief engineer, and what Porter came up with was the ultimate sports car, a term not yet in vogue. Speed and acceleration were goals of other automotive engineers of that period, but they usually combined these with a desire to provide space for several occu-

pants to ride in some comfort. Not so in Porter's case. His Raceabout contained nothing but the bare essentials: a 4-cylinder, 55-horsepower T-head engine, four wheels, two seats, a gas tank, and two spare tires. The car's appeal, Ralph Stein declares, is that "it wasn't stylized," the term used to describe cars that emphasized a pleasing physical appearance. On the other hand, the Mercer Raceabout was not like Henry Ford's earlier barebones "999," described by its driver, Barney Oldfield, as "a bed frame with wheels . . . ugly as sin." The Raceabout's brass-bound radiator, the hood, with its strap, the slanted mahogany board that faced the driver, with its brass-cased instruments and the brass tube carrying the steering wheel, and the sketchy mudguards were features that combined to give the car a classic, timeless look, which, aside from a bit of striping in the paintwork and the gleaming brass, contained nothing that could be termed a concession to those who felt a car had to be dressed up to make it attractive. The Mercer Raceabout did not need that. "Its appearance," Stein contends, "is but the happy result of its parts being so disposed for efficiency that their very placement makes the whole good to look upon." All of this for a car that cost about $2,200.

The 1913 Mercer Type 35 Raceabout

The Type 35 Raceabout was designed for the enthusiast whose interest in the car was not as a means of transportation but as a machine to be driven at top speed, under his complete control. Mercer advertised the Raceabout as "The Champion Light Car," implying that the success that drivers such as Oldfield, Ralph de Palma, and Eddie Pullen had with it in actual racing events had been with stock Raceabouts, whereas the cars they drove were especially prepared racing versions of the Mercer. However, few owners could have been disappointed by the performance of the Raceabouts they drove out of the dealers' showrooms. Stein, who drove one that had been restored years later, declared that its steering was better than that of modern sports cars and was comparable to the great Bugattis and Alfa Romeos of the 1930s. In first gear the engine, even at 75 mph, turned over at only 2,000 rpm. "But drop down into second or third at 2,000 rpm," he reported, "and the Raceabout turns into the wildcat it was designed to be." The car's drawback was "its miserable braking," which could create problems when the car was being driven in first gear and the driver, lulled into thinking "he was just loafing along," encountered a situation that required a quick stopping of the vehicle.

In 1915 the Type 35 Raceabout was replaced by the L-head 22/70 Raceabout. It was designed by Erik H. Delling, who had replaced Finlay Porter, who had left Mercer to go off on his own. The new Raceabout had a more powerful engine, which was guaranteed to propel the car from 0 to 60 mph in 48 seconds, 3 seconds faster than the Type 35's guarantee, but for the car buff it was not the same as Porter's Raceabout. A windshield, electric starting, a more conventional body including doors, and left-hand rather than right-hand drive were concessions that made the model, even though it sold well, much less acceptable to the sports car devotee.

In the postwar period the Roeblings were no longer involved with Mercer. The company from 1920 to 1922 was, with Locomobile and Crane-Simplex, part of a combine of luxury cars that Emlen Hare of New York tried to put together. After the end of Hare's Motor Group, Mercer continued for three more years. New designers put out new Raceabouts, still further removed from Porter's original. Touring or sedan models, which had been available during much of Mercer's history, dominated from 1923 to 1925, when only 6-cylinder cars were available. Production ended in the latter year, and efforts to bring the name back with an 8-cylinder Mercer in 1931 died before any cars were produced.

References:

Nick Baldwin and others, *The World Guide to Automobile Manufacturers* (New York: Facts on File, 1987); Ralph Stein, *The Treasury of the Automobile* (New York: Ridge, 1961).

Metz Company

by Beverly Rae Kimes

New York, New York

In its obituary of the Metz Company in 1925, *Motor* magazine noted that the Waltham, Massachusetts, firm was one of the few in the automobile industry to fail for reasons of "conservatism rather than enthusiasm." But the company's status as a footnote to automobile history was deserved for more than that negative factor.

During summer 1909 Charles Herman Metz incorporated the Metz Company as successor to the Waltham Manufacturing Company. He had been in charge at Waltham twice. Founding that firm in 1893 for the production of Orient bicycles, Metz had moved Waltham into automobile production in 1898 and then moved out in 1901 following a dispute with his board of directors regarding the direction of the firm. The direction subsequently taken was obviously lamentable because when Metz got his company back during summer 1908, it was debt ridden and saddled with a gigantic inventory of car parts. Lacking the capital to proceed into serious manufacture immediately, Metz came up with a clever scheme to turn his inventory into quick profit. "$350 Buys This $600 Car," the ads said. The only catch—and an insignificant one, Metz insisted—was that the owner had to put the car together himself. It arrived in packages priced at $25 each, 14 of which made up the whole (the starting handle was appropriately in the last package).

The "Metz Plan" car was aimed at those people who could not afford or were disinclined to invest substantially in an object that was still widely regarded as an invention and not a wholly viable necessity. The installment payment program had no deadline for each package purchase; thus the purchaser was guided only by his pocketbook or the time he required to get package A put together before proceeding to package B. "Remember, the motor, transmission, shafts, wheels, magneto, carburetter [*sic*] and all parts are assembled as units at the factory," Metz said. "You simply put them

Advertisement for the 1914 friction-drive Metz 22. Metz switched from its outmoded friction transmission to a conventional geared arrangement in 1919, too late to save the company.

in place in the same manner you would as a wheel on your buggy or handle bar on your bicycle. There are no holes to drill, no filing or fitting." Doubtless it was not quite that simple.

But the idea paid off. By the time Metz renamed Waltham for himself, the company was out of debt. That December the per-package price of a Metz was raised to $27, and the factory was assembling the car for purchase as well (price tag: $600). Admittedly, it was not a very good automobile. The brake, for example, resembled an enlarged version of that used for a bicycle.

The Metz Plan car survived into 1912, when declining installment sales indicated the wisdom of proceeding with factory-manufactured vehicles only. Production capacity was 5,000 cars annually. The Waltham facility was grand: 40 acres of the former Gore estate, with the Governor Gore mansion serving as the Metz executive offices. From the 2-cylinder, 12 horsepower "Plan" car, Metz automobiles had grown to 4 cylinders and 22 horsepower by 1912. Retained, however, were the chain drive and friction transmission that had been featured from the beginning and which by now were decidedly derriere-garde. But when a three-car Metz team finished the 1913 Glidden Tour with a perfect score (the only team to do so), no one at the Metz Company saw a compelling need to change. The year 1915 was Metz's best year ever, with sales of 7,200 cars.

Truck production was launched in 1917, just about the time car sales began to take a nose dive. Production was suspended altogether in 1918, and

the trade press reported that Metz was contemplating selling part of its facilities to liquidate debts. Instead Metz returned in 1919 with a brand-new car: the Master Six with geared transmission and shaft drive. "A New England Product Honest Through and Through" was the homey slogan. But it was too late. The Metz name by now was indelibly associated with an out-of-date car. Late in 1921 the firm was reorganized as Waltham Motor Manufacturers. But selling a Metz as a Waltham did not work either. In August 1922 the company was petitioned into bankruptcy by three creditors, one of them the Johns-Manville Company. In October 1925 the Metz property in Waltham was sold at auction to satisfy creditor claims. The winning bid was $196,000.

Reference:

Beverly Rae Kimes and Henry Austin Clark, Jr., *The Standard Catalog of American Cars, 1805-1942* (Iola, Wis.: Krause, 1985).

Monroe Auto Equipment

by David J. Andrea

University of Michigan

The Monroe Auto Equipment Company was founded in 1917 from the corporate remains of the Brisk Blast Manufacturing Company. Throughout its history Monroe has targeted the automotive service and repair market. Monroe's original product offering, the automotive hand tire pump, was bought by motorists through gas stations, dealerships, and mail order catalogs as an important maintenance tool, because early roads, usually made of packed dirt, brick, or wooden boards, contributed to frequent flat tires. Headquartered in Monroe, Michigan, Monroe enjoyed additional success as Detroit's vehicle manufacturers began to equip cars with tire pumps as standard or optional equipment. However, as spare tires became standard vehicle equipment, Monroe's air-pump market evaporated.

Adapting its steel-cylinder production equipment and expertise, and, to some extent, the hand pump's general operating principles, the company

turned its attention to the shock absorber. Monroe produced its first shock absorber in 1926 and has to this day concentrated its efforts in this market. Monroe began producing shock absorbers for many markets under a variety of trade names, some of which still exist today: Monroematic, Load-Levelers, E-Z Ride, and Monroe standard. This market coverage built a level of customer awareness and loyalty known to few companies.

Monroe expanded to Europe in 1960 by opening a sales and engineering office. The company's first European manufacturing operation began soon after in Belgium. Based on Monroe's strong brand awareness, high-quality reputation, and strong sales, Tenneco, Incorporated, purchased the company in 1987. Monroe continues as a cornerstone of Tenneco's automotive parts operation along with Walker Manufacturing (producing mufflers and exhaust pipes) and Speedy Muffler Shops (providing automotive service).

Throughout its history Monroe has reduced its dependence upon the repair and service aftermarket. Monroe supplies directly to Ford Motor Company and Chrysler Motors Corporation and has entered into joint-research efforts with an automotive electronics supplier to develop and produce sophisticated electronically controlled suspension systems. Monroe also produces specialty shock absorbers for nonvehicle applications.

Moon Motor Car Company

by George S. May

Eastern Michigan University

The longest lasting of the several cars that were produced in St. Louis, the Moon was an outgrowth of the carriage industry. Its origins go back to the Moon Brothers Carriage Company, established in 1873, and the later Joseph W. Moon Buggy Company, founded in the 1890s. In 1905 Joseph Moon, while continuing to build buggies, started a separate Moon Motor Car Company to build a 4-cylinder car designed by Louis P. Mooers, formerly with Cleveland's Peerless company. Priced in the medium to upper medium price range, the Moon was a well-made car that enjoyed modest sales growth, with production by 1915 being only around 1,000 cars for the year. From 1914 to 1917 a 4-cylinder truck was also produced.

Following the death of Joseph Moon in 1919, his son-in-law and successor, Stewart McDonald, directed a growth in sales that was sparked by the postwar Victory Six model that included a radiator with lines that closely resembled those of the Rolls-Royce. A car in the $2,000 price range that looked like a Rolls was a bargain, and sales rose to 3,195 in 1921 and, despite depressed conditions that affected industry sales in the early 1920s, hit 7,500 in 1922. Borrowing a design from another automaker was typical of an approach that made Moon by the 1920s one of the best known of what was termed an "assembled car." In its early years Moon produced its own engines and, because of its links with the carriage industry, its own bodies. But after 1914 it bought its engines from Continental and shortly was also getting most, if not all, of its bodies from outside suppliers. By the postwar period little if anything that went into the Moon was not manufactured somewhere else, a fact that the company freely admitted. Calling the Moon "A Car of Specialists," its advertisements listed the car's "proven units": Continental Red Seal motor, Delco starter and ignition, Timken axle, Spicer universal joints, Brown-Lipe transmission, Borg & Beck clutch, Rayfield carburetor, Exide battery, Fedders radiator, Gemmer steering gear. In response to critics who used the term "assembled car" to denigrate one containing nothing for which the company assembling it had been responsible the company declared: "Practically every car in America today is using units made by specialists—whether few or many." All Moon had done was to carry "the advantages of specialism out to their logical and complete conclusion," thereby freeing its staff to concentrate on designing the complete car, rather than its components.

Sales rose to nearly 13,000 by 1925, at which time McDonald added to the wide variety of body styles in which the Moon was available a new marque, the Diana, an 8-cylinder car with a radiator design lifted from that of the prestigious Belgian luxury car, the Minerva. The Diana was designed to appeal to women, and the company claimed that nearly four times as many women as men bought the new car. But overall sales declined sharply, falling to 5,276 in 1927. A low-priced Moon, introduced in 1927, failed to turn things around, and in 1928 the Diana was dropped, to be replaced by a new straight-8 model, the Aerotype, with styling by Howard "Dutch" Darrin, a designer later famous for his work on the Kaiser-Fraser models, who was paid $3,000 for three days' work.

Early in 1929 still another new 8-cylinder car, the Windsor White Prince, was introduced, and in

The 1911 Moon 30/35 roadster

April the remaining Moon model was also given the Windsor name, ending the use of the founder's name on the company's product. The company went so far as to use the coat of arms of the Prince of Wales on the Windsor White Prince, after whom that car had been named, but protests from the British Royal Family led to the end of that practice. With total production in 1929 of 1,333 cars, the end of the company was also in sight.

In April 1930 Archie M. Andrews acquired control of Moon, despite the opposition of Carl W. Burst, who had succeeded McDonald as president in 1928. Andrews needed a factory in which to produce the Ruxton, a low, 8-cylinder sedan designed by William J. Muller of the Edward G. Budd Company, the body producer of which Andrews was a director. Together with Muller, C. Harold Wills of the recently defunct Wills Sainte Claire company, Frederick W. Gardner, the Cleveland automobile executive, and William V. C. Ruxton, Andrews had formed the New Era Motor Company in 1929 to produce Muller's car. He then went in search of facili-

ties where the Ruxton could be assembled. Within two months after the acquisition of the Moon company production of the Ruxton had begun at the St. Louis plant, but the Depression was no time to start up a new business venture. When the Kissel Motor Car Company, which was supplying transmissions for the Ruxton, filed for bankruptcy in September, Ruxton production came to a halt, and two months later Moon also declared bankruptcy. The plant was sold for $86,000 in 1935, but it was another three decades before legal obstacles were overcome that permitted the company's creditors to receive payments of about seven cents for every dollar of the outstanding claims against the company.

References:
Nick Baldwin and others, *The World Guide to Automobile Manufacturers* (New York: Facts on File, 1987);

Tad Burness, *Cars of the Early Twenties* (New York: Galahad, 1968);

Beverly Rae Kimes and Henry Austin Clark, *Standard Catalog of American Cars, 1805-1942* (Iola, Wis.: Krause, 1985).

Charles Stewart Mott

(June 2, 1875-February 18, 1973)

by Richard P. Scharchburg

GMI Engineering & Management Institute

CAREER: Director (1896-1913), secretary and superintendent, Weston-Mott Axle Company (1899-1913); director (1913-1973), vice-president, General Motors Company [later General Motors Corporation] (1916-1937); founder and president, Charles Stewart Mott Foundation (1926-1973).

Born on June 2, 1875, in Newark, New Jersey, Charles Stewart Mott served in a diversified range of occupations during his career: automotive engineer, public servant, soldier and sailor, corporation executive, banker, philanthropist, educational innovator, and community leader. Although Mott's parents were living in New Jersey when he was born, his father's base of business was the Boukville, New York, farm of S. R. Mott, Charles Stewart Mott's grandfather. Mott's father, John Coon Mott, was living in New Jersey to be convenient to volume markets for the cider and vinegar produced on the Boukville farm. Like most farm families of the period, the Motts were closely knit and hardworking, and of necessity every family member was expected to perform daily chores around the home. Even though the family prospered from the cider and vinegar business, they practiced the kind of thrift that was to become a Mott "trademark" later in his life. "Mother used to make my clothes from material from Father's [old] suits. Short pants and so tight that the boys used to ask if I was poured into them."

Mott's chief memories of his early years were of vacations on his grandfather's farm at Boukville, where he once fell in the Erie Canal and where he liked to go hickory-nutting in the hills nearby. The family moved from Newark to New York City in 1880, and Mott got his early education in five New York public schools. After another move in 1888 to East Orange, New Jersey, Mott entered Stevens High School, which prepared students to enter Stevens Institute of Technology in Hoboken, New Jersey. He graduated in 1892 and entered Stevens Institute planning to earn a degree in mechanical engineering. His father would have much preferred him to study the chemistry of fermentation, which was directly related to the family cider and vinegar business. Two years later his father did in fact persuade Mott to take time from his engineering studies to study zymotechnology—the science of fermentation—in Copenhagen and Munich. While studying in Europe, Mott rode a bicycle through the countryside whenever time permitted. With all the enthusiasm and energy of youth he went to concerts and art galleries and participated in the life of the places he visited. He developed an appreciation of the wide variety of people he met on his travels. He eventually collected dozens of paintings by great masters—Sir Thomas Lawrence and Sir Joshua Reynolds, Goya, Peter Rubens, Winslow Homer, William Tryon, and Frederic Remington. His favorites, however, were the nineteenth-century Dutch painters. Anton Mauve and the brothers Marals were of particular interest, and over the years he acquired a splendid collection of that pastoral school.

After returning to the United States, Mott reenrolled at Stevens Institute and completed a degree in mechanical engineering in 1897. With his formal education in place he was well prepared to make the transition from the old rural, agrarian economy to the new urban, industrial enterprise of the twentieth century. It was obvious that his interests and talents lay in engineering, and his father was determined to keep him in a family business.

In 1896, while Mott was finishing his studies at Stevens Institute, his father and his uncle Frederick bought the I. A. Weston & Company of Jamesville, New York, which had manufactured bicycle hubs and wheels since 1884. The company was reorganized as the Weston-Mott Company with Frederick Mott as president and manager and

Charles Stewart Mott

Charles Stewart Mott as a director, and it continued the same line of products as before.

The day after Congress declared war on Spain in 1898, Mott volunteered for active duty in the navy. He served as a gunner's mate on the USS *Yankee*, and his letters home during the period reveal the enjoyment of adventure, the enthusiasm, the pride of accomplishment, the acceptance of discipline, and the sense of personal responsibility notable throughout Mott's life.

While Mott was serving in the navy, the Weston-Mott Company moved to a new factory in Utica, New York. In the late 1890s the bicycle craze was beginning to wind down and the demand for wheels declined sharply, so the company began a search for new products and markets, striking out in several directions at once. One venture involved a new type of light carriage with drop-forged axles and wire wheels with cushion rubber tires. The company started making those axles and wheels as well as "fifth wheels" for the undercarriage mechanism. It also made wire wheels for pushcarts, implements, wheelchairs, and jinrikishas, and it soon added wheels for automobiles. Mott and his father, agents for the company's products, would sell wire wheels to such early automobile makers as Canda Quadricycle, Grout, Autocar, Oldsmobile, Packard, Cadillac, Elmore, Blomstrom, Whiting, Ford, and Buick.

On June 2, 1899, Mott's twenty-fourth birthday, his father died. His interests now settled firmly on manufacturing, and a few months later he went to Utica to take over purchasing and engineering as secretary and superintendent of the Weston-Mott Company.

Mott's uncle, president of the company, was in the process of withdrawing from active management, and in addition to bringing his nephew from New York, he interested a Utica man, William G. Doolittle, in joining the company as part owner and treasurer. The company was still struggling to adapt to the changes in vehicle manufacturing, but it was soon apparent that the future of Weston-Mott lay with the rising automobile industry.

Most early automobiles were equipped with wire wheels, and when the Olds Motor Works began the automobile industry's first quantity production operation in 1900, Weston-Mott was asked to quote prices on 1,000-wheel lots. The company was momentarily unprepared for such a volume of business. However, over the next two years Weston-Mott furnished some 3,000 sets of wheels to Oldsmobile. When Packard and Cadillac became customers, the capacity of the company reached its peak. On June 14, 1900, while he was struggling with the Olds deal, Mott married Ethel Culbert Harding, a daughter of one of his mother's girlhood friends. The couple would have three children: Aimee, Elsa Beatrice, and Charles Stewart Harding.

Suddenly in 1902 the Olds company canceled all orders for wire wheels, and when other automobile companies did the same, the Weston-Mott company, barely recovered from the loss of the bicycle market, faced another business crisis. Mott had to travel to the factories of automobile manufacturers to try to sell them the now-favored wooden-spoked artillery wheels with which his company had neither experience nor production capabilities. Under those conditions sales were difficult. Mott also discovered that a change in manufacturing techniques in automobile plants called for sets of front wheels and rear wheels with chain-drive axles. To attract sales he had to design rear axles with wheels included, make the drawings and blueprints, and at the same time solicit business for a line of goods with which the company had no experience. Subsequently the factory had to be retooled to manufacture the new product. Mott recalled: "Those were not the days of the 40-hour week. Our factory started at 7:00 A.M. and ran until 6:00 P.M.—one hour for lunch—10 hours per day, 60 hours per week. I used to get to the factory at 6:00 A.M., taking my lunch with me, and work till 7:00 P.M. trying to construct axles which would do the job, and it was several months before it was accomplished." With the new product Weston-Mott soon recovered its financial position, and profits over the next few years steadily rose until the company's earnings in 1905 were $601,572 and its operating surplus had accumulated to $191,073.

When William C. Durant, founder of General Motors, took over the Buick Motor Company in Flint, Michigan, in 1905, he recognized the necessity of having parts suppliers close at hand. So on June 4 he wrote to Mott inviting him to move Weston-Mott to Flint to produce axles for Buick. Not having received a favorable reply, Durant and his partner in the carriage business, J. Dallas Dort, visited the Weston-Mott factory in Utica on the Fri-

day before Labor Day. The Flint men toured the factory and invited Mott and Doolittle to visit Flint, hoping that once they saw the city they could be persuaded to move to Michigan.

Arriving in Flint the next day, Mott, Doolittle, and their wives were entertained by one of the city's most prominent banking families, the Arthur G. Bishops. Flint's business and industrial leaders were most persuasive, and after being given property on which to erect a new plant next to the Buick complex on Industrial Avenue, Mott and Doolittle agreed to form the Weston-Mott Company of Michigan to take over the business of the Weston-Mott Company of Utica, providing Durant and Dort would guarantee $100,000 for additional capital to build the new axle plant. Mott and Doolittle returned to Utica. Many Utica employees made the move to Flint when the plant was completed, and on August 8, 1906, the power was turned on for the first time in the new Weston-Mott factory, which was soon steadily turning out axles and wheels.

The Weston-Mott plant became the largest axle manufacturer in the world, and when Durant organized General Motors (GM) Company in 1908, he acquired 49 percent of the stock of Weston-Mott in exchange for GM stock. Since William Doolittle's death in 1908 Mott had become sole owner of Weston-Mott's non-GM stock, and in 1913 he exchanged his remaining 51 percent of Weston-Mott stock for GM stock, making Weston-Mott a totally owned subsidiary of GM. Mott still remained active in the management of the company. In the same year he also became a director of General Motors, a position he retained until his death 60 years later.

It had taken bold planning and tremendous effort to bring the comparatively small Weston-Mott Axle Company to its dominant position in the automotive world. But in spite of the demands Mott imposed on himself to develop his business, he found time for his family, his friends, his church, and for community affairs.

In 1910 Durant lost control of General Motors, and a considerable reorganization of GM operations ensued. Many talented men followed Durant into a new venture—Chevrolet. Mott, however, remained loyal to GM and was in Flint to welcome Charles W. Nash as Durant's successor at Buick. Nash eventually hired Walter P. Chrysler to manage

Buick operations when he was elected president of General Motors in 1912.

Partly as a result of the fears engendered by the threat to the existence of General Motors a year earlier, Flint elected a Socialist mayor in 1911. Mott was persuaded by his friends to run for the office in 1912. He did so and was elected. Running again in 1913, he was reelected, but he was defeated in 1914.

After the 1914 election Mott toured Europe. When he returned, a banquet was given in his honor. Such friends as W. H. Little, Charles Nash, and Dallas Dort presented tributes. The highlight of the evening was the presentation of a cup on which was engraved: "Presented by His Friends and Fellow Townsmen to Hon. Charles S. Mott, Twice elected on a non-partisan ballot Mayor of Flint, 1912-1913–In grateful recognition of his unselfish devotion to the public welfare and his insistence upon the application of business principles in municipal government." Other close friends during this period were Harry H. Basset and Walter P. Chrysler, both of Buick, and Albert Champion, founder of AC Spark Plug Company.

These were challenging years of growth for Flint, caused mainly by the rapid influx of people seeking jobs in the booming automobile factories. The north side of Flint had been farm country a few years earlier, lacking such amenities as sewers and sidewalks. Workers were living in tents and tar-paper shacks, and beds in rooming houses were rented in three shifts conforming to working hours in the plants. During his administration Mayor Mott worked to improve living conditions for the residents of the industrial area. Buick's employment was high, as was his own Weston-Mott Company, and when Chevrolet announced late in 1912 that it would be moving from Detroit to Flint, the strain on the city's utilities and housing mounted. It was fortunate that Mott skillfully planned for expansion of city services.

Although Mott was spending a lot of time in Detroit, his life was still centered on his home in Flint. In 1918 he bought 26 acres from Dallas Dort and 38 adjacent acres from Charles Nash, creating a farm almost in the middle of Flint at 1400 E. Kearsley Street. He built a fine house, and because he was proud of his farm background, he named his estate "Applewood." Again his Flint friends urged him to run for mayor. He was elected for one term and was also appointed a major in the

U.S. Army and chief of the automotive branch of the Quartermaster Corps. In 1920 Mott sought nomination as the Republican candidate for governor of Michigan, but he was not well known in those days beyond the Flint area and was not successful. That was Mott's final effort to attain high political office.

When the postwar depression shook General Motors loose from Durant's control for the last time in 1920, Pierre S. du Pont assumed the presidency of the corporation. There was serious need for a stabilizing influence at GM because of the magnitude of the changes and problems confronting it. In April 1921, to provide that influence, Mott was appointed chief of the corporation's advisory staff, with headquarters in Detroit. Mott served on most of GM's most powerful standing committees and was often called upon to perform special assignments whenever his talents could be used. He was respected for his analytical and perceptive investigations and his careful attention to detail. He retired as a vice-president of GM in 1937 but remained a director until his death. Years later Pierre S. du Pont referred to Mott as having been a "tower of strength" during the difficult period of readjustment following Durant's final departure from GM.

In the days when Mott was getting started in the axle business, he had become the good friend of Alfred P. Sloan, Jr., manager of the Hyatt Roller Bearing Company. In 1916, with the purchase of Hyatt, Durant brought Sloan into General Motors. Thus, when Sloan became president of the corporation in 1923, he and his friend Mott were occupying key GM positions. Their relationship was congenial, and they liked to work together.

Among Mott's many accomplishments as chief of staff was the hiring of William S. Knudsen. In 1920 Knudsen left a $50,000-a-year job as production manager for Henry Ford over a disagreement on the hiring and firing of personnel. Mott contacted him and, after conferring with Sloan, offered Knudsen the post of manufacturing manager of Chevrolet. In 1922 Knudsen was promoted to general manager of Chevrolet and then was elected an executive vice-president of GM and put in charge of all car, truck, and body manufacturing operations. In 1937 he was elected president of General Motors and served until 1940, when he left at President Franklin Roosevelt's request to head the Office of War Production.

Mott (second from left) with past and future General Motors executives Alfred P. Sloan, Jr., Charles W. Nash, and H. H. Bassett (courtesy of the General Motors Institute Alumni Foundation Collection of Industrial History)

Mott became group executive for GM car divisions, in which capacity he promoted the use of ethyl gasoline, which had been developed under the direction of his friend Charles F. "Boss" Kettering. Mott also is credited with encouraging the development of the Pontiac automobile and the use of Duco paint, and for advocating the use of common bodies for GM cars, an idea that was never adopted. Mott also was intimately involved in an advisory capacity during the developmental stage of GM's copper-cooled engine, introduced in experimental form in the early 1920s. When an air-cooled engine developed by Kettering failed in performance tests, Mott was among those who recommended that the whole project be scrapped along with the 1923 Chevrolet cars, which were recalled shortly after their release to dealers.

Mott next took a philanthropic step that was to have effect throughout the country and abroad, when he incorporated the Charles Stewart Mott Foundation in 1926. In its early years the foundation contributed to many charitable and community endeavors in Flint, as well as churches, universities, and a camp for underprivileged boys. However, it was not until 1935 that the Mott Foundation found the pattern for which it has since become known in many parts of the world. On June 21, 1935, Mott heard Frank J. Manley speak at a Rotary Club meeting about the youth problems of Flint. Later that summer they got together on a plan by which Mott would supply funds to open a few Flint schools after regular hours to provide supervised recreation for young people. That was the genesis of the Mott Program of the Flint Board of Education and what was to become known as the "community school." The original concept kept broadening and intensifying, until the whole community, not just the school or some after-hours recreation, became involved. The adults of the community became involved because they set patterns for the young. While the chief areas of foundation operation remained in the fields of health, recreation, and education, the concept of working with all the elements that shape a young person's life eventually carried foundation activities into a whole complex of programs. During Mott's third term as Flint mayor he instituted and contributed to a pioneer program to correct the dental defects of children. In 1937 a foundation plan, the Mott Health Achievement Program, was instituted. This "whole-child" approach led to the development of the Mott Children's Health Center in Flint, Michigan, with its vast medical and dental assistance programs.

Mott's wife, Ethel, met a tragic death in 1924, when she fell from a second-story window at the couple's home on Kearsley Street in Flint. During the next 10 years Mott married twice. His second wife died suddenly following a short illness, and his third marriage ended in divorce. Mott had no children from either of those unfortunate marriages. While vacationing in the West and visiting relatives in Texas, Mott met a distant cousin, Ruth Mott Rawlings, and on October 13, 1934, they were married. Ruth Mott shared her husband's philanthropic interests. Three children were born to the couple: Susan Elizabeth, Stewart Rawlings, and Maryanne Turnbull.

Meanwhile, the development of adult education opportunities through Mott Foundation support had been extended to college level classes for credit, and the University of Michigan published a brief study of the foundation's activities under the title "An Experiment in Community Improvement." During World War II Mott carried out a special responsibility assigned to him by the National Office of Production Management, helping to locate people with the experience and ability to assist national defense production. He was also instrumental in organizing the Genesee County War Board and served faithfully and effectively on Flint's Civilian Defense Council. Thus, his efforts aided his country in three wars.

More than 5,000 persons attended a community party given for Mott on his seventy-fifth birthday in 1950 at the Industrial Mutual Association Auditorium. After expressing his thanks to Frank Manley, his staff, and the Flint Board of Education for developing the Mott Program, he pledged to give $1 million for development of "a four-year community college or branch of the University of Michigan" if the public would vote a millage issue on behalf of needed facilities. The millage was approved by a 4-to-1 vote, and the first impetus was given to opening a branch of the University of Michigan in Flint.

When a tornado devastated a suburb of Flint in June 1953, Mott was among the thousands who volunteered for the "Operation Tornado" rebuilding project—and he even brought his own hammer. That was not merely a dramatic gesture but was a simple act of good citizenship to help where help was needed. In the same spirit his son Harding and grandson Harding, Jr., also worked on the project.

It was with particular pleasure that Mott contributed $188,810 in 1954 for construction of a swimming pool, because the pool was to be named in honor of his longtime friend Frank Manley. That same year he himself received a high tribute. Harlow H. Curtice, then president of General Motors, announced a corporation gift of $3 million to the Flint College and Cultural Center, of which the Flint Community Junior College was a component. In announcing the GM gift, Curtice said: "The Junior College Science and Arts Building, now nearing completion on this campus, will be dedicated to Charles Stewart Mott. This very campus we owe to his generosity. The Mott Foundation has a nationwide reputation for accomplishments."

Honors came to Charles Stewart Mott from around the nation. President Dwight D. Eisenhower conferred the International Big Brother of the Year Award on him for his "outstanding work with the Flint Youth Bureau for broad Humanitarian endeavor." He received an honorary life membership in the American Federation of Labor. A resolution adopted by both houses of the Michigan Legislature commended him for "contributions made throughout the years." Among the developments most gratifying to him was passage by the legislature in 1955 of a bill establishing a branch of the University of Michigan in Flint. After the dedication of the Science and Arts Building, Mott moved across the campus to break ground for the University of Michigan Building—all this on land that a few years before had been part of the Mott farm. In 1956 Mott received the American Legion's Distinguished Service Medal, and the next year the Michigan Society of Professional Engineers named him Michigan Engineer of the Year.

The Flint College of the University of Michigan opened in 1956, and the enlarged Flint Community Junior College enrolled the largest numbers of students in its history. Following Mott's death on February 18, 1973, its Board of Trustees renamed the community college the Charles Stewart Mott Community College.

References:

Walter P. Chrysler, *Life of An American Workman* (New York: Dodd, Mead, 1937);

B. C. Forbes and O. D. Foster, *Automotive Giants of America* (New York: Forbes, 1926);

Arthur Pound, *The Turning Wheel* (Garden City, N.Y.: Doubleday, Doran, 1934);

John B. Rae, *American Automobile Manufacturers* (Philadelphia: Chilton, 1959);

Lawrence H. Seltzer, *A Financial History of the American Automobile* (Boston: Houghton Mifflin, 1928);

Alfred P. Sloan, Jr., *My Years With General Motors* (Garden City, N.Y.: Doubleday, 1964);

Clarence Young and William A. Quinn, *Foundation for Living* (New York: McGraw-Hill, 1963).

Archives:

The Charles Stewart Mott Papers are in the GMI Alumni Foundation Collection of Industrial History at GMI Engineering & Management Institute, Flint, Michigan.

Mufflers

by James Wren

Motor Vehicle Manufacturers Association

Two of the greatest objections to early motor vehicles were the raucous noise emitted from the rapid explosions in the engine cylinders and the exhaust smoke. Early automobile builders were well aware of the noisy nuisance, which not only created havoc among the horses pulling carriages and wagons but irritated the community as well. The Duryea automobile of 1895 was equipped with a muffler that served to silence the exhaust. However, the Duryea was an exception. Mufflers, or silencers or exhaust boxes, as they were originally called, were not essential to the efficiency of the motor. In fact, if not properly designed, a muffler would create a back pressure on the engine, which could result in a power reduction. But power loss was not as important as silencing the noise and occasional loud explosive backfire, which was frightening to the pedestrians as well as the horses.

Silencing the exhaust requires passing the exhaust from the exhaust manifold, through an exhaust pipe, into the muffler of a larger diameter, and then through the tailpipe. The muffler also serves to cool the exhaust gases. Some early designers developed "expanding" mufflers, which allowed the hot gases to expand and cool before expulsion, but most manufacturers used "separating" mufflers that broke up the gases by directing them through numerous passages and baffles, which helped to silence the engine but created back pressure and diminished power.

It was also common practice for early motorists to use a cutout in exhaust systems so that the exhaust would bypass the muffler. That system also allowed the mechanic to hear the detonations more clearly for the reason of determining the running condition of the engine. The cutout was placed before centering the muffler so that the exhaust could go directly into the atmosphere before the muffler. Many cities prohibited the use of cutouts, especially because of the "scorchers" or fast drivers who delighted in the increased power and noise of an unmuffled engine.

One of the major problems of the muffler was that the oxidation caused by the high temperature of the exhaust gases and the water produced from combustion of gasoline and mixing with acids quickly rusted the interior of the muffler. The location underneath the vehicle also made the muffler vulnerable to the elements of nature and poor terrain. Because of these faults, the muffler quickly became one of the most frequently replaced parts of the automobile.

There were numerous attempts to alleviate the problems. Some mufflers contained holes for draining the water. Several parts manufacturers even riveted asbestos paper against the inner walls of the muffler. Some used sound-absorbent glass fiber blankets while others attacked the problem by using various materials for the muffler such as aluminized-steel mufflers and ceramic-lined designs. The idea of using dual mufflers and exhaust pipes for separat-

ing the exhaust to improve the silencing problem
and reducing back pressure appeared early in 1905
when the Northern automobile used dual mufflers.
The Lexington automobile in 1917 also used a dual

exhaust system. With the widespread use of the
V-type engine, the dual exhaust system became standard.

Charles W. Nash

(January 28, 1864-June 6, 1948)

by Richard P. Scharchburg

GMI Engineering & Management Institute

CAREER: Laborer, trimming department foreman,
trimming department superintendent (1891-1904),
vice-president and general manager, Durant-Dort
Carriage Company [Flint Road Cart Company to
1895] (1904-1910); president and general manager,
Buick Motor Company (1910-1912); president,
General Motors Company (1912-1916); president
(1916-1932), chairman, Nash Motors Company
(1932-1937); president, LaFayette Motor Company
(1919-1923).

Charles Williams Nash, president of Buick
and later General Motors (GM) in the early years
of those companies and later head of his own firm,
was born in DeKalb County, Illinois, on January
28, 1864, the first of two children of Charles William and Anna Caldwell Nash. Accounts of what
happened to his parents vary: they either were separated, divorced, or died. Six-year-old Nash was
made a ward of the court, and a judge "bound"
him out to a farm couple near Flushing, Michigan.
He ran away at age twelve and got a paying job on
a farm near Grand Blanc, south of Flint. He picked
up carpentry skills, worked during the off-season
on the farm, and managed to save some money. He
invested his scanty savings in a few sheep, put the animals out with another farmer's "to double," and
they doubled so well that by the time he was eighteen Nash had 80 sheep in his flock; with wool selling at good prices in Genesee County his investment provided good returns.

In 1884 Nash found a job as a foreman on a
nearby farm. With increased responsibilities (and
pay) there were also increased "fringe benefits": to
serve for his living quarters, a house was furnished
as part of the bargain. The salary was $300 per
year, and he soon had need for the cottage. He mar-

*Charles W. Nash (courtesy of the General Motors
Institute Alumni Foundation Collection of
Industrial History)*

ried Jessie Halleck of Flint shortly after moving in.
The couple had three daughters: Mae, Lena, and
Ruth. Following the common practice, Nash continued to look around for work during the offseasons. His search took him into Flint, where he
worked in several odd jobs. One day in 1890, carriage manufacturer William C. Durant noticed how
hard Nash was working at his job in a local hardware store. Writing to Nash in 1942, Durant recalled, "I remember so well meeting you in the
hardware store, at which time I was very much inter-

ested in you. I suggested that you come over to the factory and you promptly accepted."

Nash started at the Flint Road Cart Company, (known as the Durant-Dort Carriage Company beginning in 1895) as a laborer in 1891. He worked in various departments—blacksmithing, upholstery, trimming, and shipping—at a starting pay of a dollar a day. Nash was always making suggestions to his employer. When working in the blacksmith shop Nash convinced Durant's partner J. Dallas Dort that the purchase of a $35 power hammer would double the output of the blacksmiths. His employers were pleased with Nash's initiative, but fellow workers often complained that the hardworking Nash made them look bad. When Nash moved over to operate a hand drill-press, Dort noticed that he rigged the press so it could be operated by foot, leaving both hands free to again double the output. Dort, the production expert of the Durant-Dort team, realized he had a budding management candidate on his hands. He advanced Nash to foreman of the trimming department, and within a year Nash became department superintendent, eventually earning $1,200 annually—the top Durant-Dort salary.

Durant left active management of Durant-Dort in 1904 to oversee operations at Buick Motor Company, and Nash became general manager of the carriage firm. Two years later sales peaked at 56,000. But the days of profitable carriage manufacturing were numbered. The company began to move into the production of automobile bodies. Meanwhile Durant founded General Motors Company in 1908 to oversee his growing automotive interests. In 1910, when financial difficulties forced Durant to reorganize, Nash became president and general manager at Buick. Buick was only a few blocks northeast of the carriage factory, so he simply transferred his base of activities from carriages to automobiles.

Hardly was he inside the plant gates before Durant was gone, ejected from GM along with William H. Little and several other key people at Buick. Nash quickly took charge. Firmly backed by the banker management then in control of GM, he pushed the development of a new 6-cylinder Buick and reduced inventories and discontinued production of unprofitable models. He generally commanded the situation so well that he is credited with pointing Buick toward its brilliant future. In 1912, on the recommendation of James J. Storrow,

president of GM and spokesman for the bankers, Nash brought a thirty-six-year-old former railroad mechanic, Walter P. Chrysler, into the Buick organization as works manager. Nash was preparing to move on. In the same year, 1912, the onetime bound-out farm boy assumed the presidency of General Motors.

As GM president Nash served as an appointee of the bankers' trust just as he had at Buick. He was charged with the imposing task of not only producing Buick, Cadillac, Oldsmobile, and Oakland cars in enlarged quantities but also with continuing to reduce the $15 million debt (funded by a five-year note issue of 1910) that had been underwritten by eastern bankers. Conservatively inclined and well aware that time was fleeting, he whittled faithfully at the debt. By 1915 he was entirely on top of the debt problem and could recommend a sizable dividend to the patient holders of GM common stock. But the dividend payment did not come soon enough to satisfy the stockholders. As president of Chevrolet, Durant had recouped his losses from the earlier GM venture, and GM stockholders responded positively to his offer to exchange Chevrolet for GM stock in 1916. Nash was not inclined to return to his former status as second or third in command, and so he left GM, and Durant resumed the company's presidency.

Nash looked around for a suitable opportunity elsewhere in the automotive business. He was now inclined toward ownership. He had prospered, and in addition to personal resources he enjoyed the continued backing of the investment group headed by Storrow. With backing from Storrow, he bought the Thomas B. Jeffery Company of Kenosha, Wisconsin, makers of the original Rambler, for $5 million and renamed it Nash Motors Company. Nash took the job of president of the new firm.

He immediately set his engineers to the task of developing a new 6-cylinder engine and began an expansion program to provide for a larger volume of business. At the time Nash took over, the company was manufacturing lackluster 6-cylinder cars and 1-ton, 2-ton, and quad trucks. The expansion of the passenger car business had to be delayed because of World War I. Although the company had the first Nash car on the market in 1917, full conversion to automobile production was not achieved until 1919.

In 1918 Nash decided that the company would continue to produce trucks. Truck produc-

The 1918 Nash touring car

tion represented something of a departure from standard practice among passenger-car builders. Though Nash's move was not without precedent, the company entered the field so forcibly as to become the industry's largest producer of trucks for a short period. Nash challenged such established names as Mack, International Harvester, White, Reo, and Autocar—all veterans in the truck-building business.

Entering the automobile market in one of the most competitive price classes, that of medium-priced vehicles, Nash quickly became one of the most successful of American automobile manufacturers. Producing 12,179 vehicles in 1917, 21,019 in 1918, and 29,841 in 1919, the company showed a net profit of $5,089,036 in 1919 (net profits for the first two years exceeded $3.4 million). The profit figure for 1919 represented about the same amount Nash, Storrow, and associates had paid for the Kenosha facilities. In October of that year, in order to assure quantity production of automobile bodies, Charles Nash recommended the acquisition of a 50 percent interest in the Seaman Body Corporation of Milwaukee (the company purchased the remaining 50 percent in 1936). Nash next directed his attention to expanding the Nash car line by opening a second assembly plant in Milwaukee. The new plant initially produced a 4-cylinder and later the new 6-cylinder Nash.

The Nash company also became involved in an effort to expand into the luxury end of the automobile market after the war. Nash acquired the LaFayette Motor Company of Indianapolis in 1919 to manufacture and sell a V-8 automobile designed by D. McCall White, who designed Cadillac's first V-8 car in 1914. The sale of LaFayette's capital stock was underwritten by Lee, Higginson & Company, who agreed to participate only if Nash would take over the LaFayette presidency. Soon after LaFayette began production in Mars Hill, Indiana, a suburb of Indianapolis, it encountered financial difficulties, and large loans were obtained from Nash Motors. Only about 1,000 cars were built. In 1922 Nash recommended that the LaFayette Motor Company be reorganized and refinanced by Nash Motors. The Nash Motors directors, headed by Storrow, underwrote an entire issue of new stock to the extent of $2.2 million.

In early 1923 LaFayette operations were moved from Indianapolis to the Nash plant at Milwaukee. But in spite of all Nash's efforts, the firm continued to lose heavily. In August a letter to LaFayette stockholders bearing the signatures of Storrow and Nash announced that "the company has not been able to overcome the difficulty of unprofitable operation" and advised that they agree to the sale of LaFayette to Ajax Motors Company for $225,000.

Ajax was formed by Nash and friends to manufacture a light, 6-cylinder automobile. The plant of the former Mitchell Motors at Racine was purchased at a receiver's sale and equipped with the machinery from the LaFayette plant, which Nash sold to Ajax at a $1,775,000 loss. Ajax began production in 1925 under the supervision of David Averill, a former associate of Nash at Durant-Dort who had also been associated with Chevrolet in its early days and had most recently been general manager of the Dort Motor Car Company in Flint. The company continued as a separate corporation (wholly owned by Nash Motors) until December 1, 1926, when it was merged with Nash. In the whole LaFayette/Ajax affair it appears that Nash and Storrow were playing some of the same cat-and-mouse games for which they had condemned Durant when they forced him out of GM in 1910.

Following the death in 1926 of Nash board chairman James J. Storrow, that office remained vacant until 1932, when Nash stepped aside as president in favor of E. H. McCarty to assume the chairmanship. In no sense of the word did he retire. He retained a firm hand on the business through thick and thin. He and his associates had earned almost $100 million for the company, but they and all the nation's businessmen were to encounter a period of high competition and, at the same time, national depression. However, as he had demonstrated in the past, Nash was equal to the task, though he and the new Nash president had to face a drop in production down to 17,600 cars in 1932. Nash and his idea-men fought against the Depression with an entirely new low-priced Nash LaFayette model, produced from 1934 to 1940.

In 1936 Nash negotiated with George W. Mason of Kelvinator Corporation in Detroit to achieve a merger that was finalized in January 1937. The new company was called the Nash-Kelvinator Corporation. At the time of the merger with Nash, Kelvinator was making 250,000 refrigerators per year. Its merger with the automotive company brought Mason the presidency, and Nash prepared to retire to California. One of the last transactions in which Nash participated was a far-reaching arrangement with Edward G. Budd of Philadelphia to provide unitized bodies for a new car designed to compete in the high-volume market. The "new car" became the Nash 600, the forerunner of the Rambler. Sales of the 600 moved Nash sales to 80,000 units by 1941.

In retirement Nash seldom left his mountainside home in Beverly Hills, California. On June 6, 1948, at age eighty-four, he died. At the time of his death his estate was valued in excess of $40 million.

The Nash company was merged with Hudson in 1954 to form the American Motors Corporation, which remained in business until 1987, when it was acquired by the Chrysler Corporation. Thus, after 70 years Nash and Chrysler were symbolically in business together, as Storrow and Nash had originally planned in 1916. Nash's impact on the automobile industry continues by a line of direct succession.

References:

Frank Donovan, *Wheels for a Nation* (New York: Crowell, 1965);

John B. Rae, *The American Automobile: A Brief History* (Chicago & London: University of Chicago Press, 1965);

Bernard A. Weisberger, *The Dream Maker: William C. Durant, Founder of General Motors* (Boston: Little, Brown, 1979).

National Association of Automobile Manufacturers

by James Wren

Motor Vehicle Manufacturers Association

The first automotive manufacturers' trade association was the National Association of Automobile Manufacturers (NAAM). During the first New York auto show in October 1900 a group of eight automobile and three automotive supplier companies met at the Hoffman House in response to a call from the publishers of the *Motor Vehicle Review*. The purpose of the meeting was to consider a permanent organization of motor vehicle and parts manufacturers. Charles Duryea served as temporary chairman, and a committee was appointed to arrange a second meeting at the close of the show on November 10, 1900. At the second meeting plans were made for a permanent organization. The group appointed a committee of manufacturers, drafted a constitution and bylaws, elected officers for the coming year, and secured a certificate of incorporation.

The permanent organizational meeting of the NAAM convened on December 1, 1900, with 24 motor vehicle manufacturers and 14 parts suppliers in attendance. The supplier companies were designated associate members. The primary purposes of the new association were to "advance and protect the interests of the trade, to procure an adjustment of freight rates, to promote good roads, to procure proper legislation and modify rulings of the United States Treasury Department, to take needed action regarding future shows and exhibitions, and for such other matters as may properly come before the meeting." Samuel J. Davis, Jr., of Locomobile Automobile Company was elected as the association's first president. The NAAM also arranged to manage the receipts and operation of auto shows in conjunction with the Automobile Club of New York and the Chicago Automobile Club. By 1902, when Milton Budlong was elected the second NAAM president, membership had grown to 129. That same year Samuel A. Miles became general manager and conducted the Chicago Auto Show.

The NAAM employed several strategies to promote the automotive industry and its products. It sponsored endurance contests and tours to demonstrate the practicability of motor transportation. It began a successful program of parts standardization, although it had no capacity to enforce its own recommendations. All customers of member companies received a 60-day guarantee on their purchases courtesy of the association. The NAAM also instituted a lobbying program, petitioning Congress for nationwide licensing fees and for funds to construct a transcontinental highway.

In 1905 parts and accessories companies withdrew from the NAAM to form a Motor and Accessory Manufacturers group, but they continued to participate in the NAAM shows. The NAAM continued to promote street and highway improvements, oppose anti-automobile legislation, and popularize automobile use. Membership was almost exactly that of the rival Association of Licensed Automobile Manufacturers (ALAM). With the conclusion of the Selden patent case in 1911 and the dissolution of the ALAM later that year, the Automobile Board of Trade was formed to protect the legal rights of its members and to promote the industry and their products. In 1913 the Automobile Board of Trade and the NAAM merged to form the Automobile Chamber of Commerce. That organization became the Automobile Manufacturers Association in 1935, and then the Motor Vehicle Manufacturers Association in 1972.

Archives:

Material pertaining to the National Association of Automobile Manufacturers is at the Patent Library of the Motor Vehicle Manufacturers Association, Detroit, Michigan.

National Automobile Chamber of Commerce

by James Wren

Motor Vehicle Manufacturers Association

The National Automobile Chamber of Commerce (NACC) was organized as the successor to the National Association of Automobile Manufacturers (NAAM) and the Automobile Board of Trade (ABT). The NAAM was formed in 1900 and was the first automotive trade association. The ABT was formed after the 1911 dissolution of the Association of Licensed Automobile Manufacturers (ALAM), which followed that association's loss in a suit filed by Ford Motor Company contesting the validity of the Selden internal combustion engine patent. Since the concerns of the NAAM and the ABT overlapped, in 1913 the two groups voted to combine.

The new NACC continued to promote the objectives of its predecessors: the advancement of the automotive field through technical exchange, parts, standardization, publicity and advertising, lobbying in favor of the industry, good-roads promotion, and record keeping and other monitoring. Charles Clifton, former president of the ALAM and its successor, the ABT, was chosen NACC president and served for 23 years. Three vice-presidents were appointed, to handle passenger vehicles, commercial vehicles, and electric vehicles. NACC directors met monthly, and the chamber held meetings three times a year. Automobile companies designated an officer or stockholder to represent them in chamber matters. Requirements for admission included the recommendations of two members.

Departments dealing with such areas as traffic, patents, shows and promotions, roads, trucking, and political action required staffs. In addition, a wide range of special assignments—responses to industry changes and crises—were handled as events dictated.

As legislation relating to the automotive industry was proposed in Congress and in the states, the NACC worked to educate lawmakers in favor of its positions. The chamber consistently opposed such suggestions as horsepower taxes, gasoline taxes, and nonresident state driver's license requirements. Under the auspices of the Show Committee, NACC auto shows were held annually in New York and Chicago and were major attractions in those cities.

The most significant NACC accomplishment advancing the industry was the Patent Cross-License Agreement of 1915, by which automotive companies (NACC members) agreed to exchange patent rights without payment of royalties or threat of penalty for ten years. Each member contributed patents it controlled to the pool and received licenses from other members in return. Many of the gigantic strides the industry took in the period from 1915 to 1930 occurred as a result of the agreement, which was extended several times for periods ranging from five to ten years. The agreement helped avoid costly litigation and also created an atmosphere in which other cooperative activities flourished. In a monograph prepared for the Temporary National Economic Committee in 1941, Professor Walter Hamilton of Yale University Law School commented, "It is hard to think of a form of cooperation between competitors which has brought as much benefit to the public as the Cross-Licensing Agreement in respect to the automobile."

NACC membership reached a peak of 131 member companies in 1922. Membership slowly declined to 31 companies. In 1934 the NACC moved its headquarters to Detroit, Michigan, when it also changed its name to the Automobile Manufacturers Association.

References:

Automobile Trade Journal (December 1, 1924);
National Automobile Chamber of Commerce, *The Organization: What It Does and What It Has Done* (New York, 1915).

Navistar International Corporation

by George S. May

Eastern Michigan University

Although other farm equipment manufacturers, including J. I. Case and John Deere, expanded into motor vehicle production in the early years of the auto industry, none rivaled the giant in the farm equipment business, International Harvester, whose motor vehicle production continues today under the Navistar International banner. Navistar can lay claim to being one of America's oldest manufacturing firms, for its origins can be traced back to the 1830s, when Cyrus H. McCormick invented and began to produce and sell his revolutionary mechanical reaper. In 1902 the McCormick Harvesting Machine Company was consolidated with four other farm machinery manufacturers to form the International Harvester Company (IHC), one of the largest mergers that took place in American industry in that period. The merger aroused cries from anti-monopolists and presaged similar developments in the auto industry, most notably the formation of General Motors in 1908. Cyrus H. McCormick, the eldest son of the first McCormick and the first president of International Harvester, defended the merger on the grounds that it provided the new firm with the resources to do things that would have been beyond the capability of the five companies had they remained independent.

Late in 1906 International Harvester brought out its Auto Buggy, one of the first of the high-wheeler vehicles designed to negotiate the heavily rutted dirt roads of rural America. The Auto Buggy was designed by E. A. Johnston, who had begun experimenting with horseless carriages at the McCormick company in 1898. The buggies were powered by IHC engines, which were also used to power International's farm tractors, also introduced in 1906. The buggies were first produced in Chicago, the headquarters of International Harvester's activities, but were moved in 1908 to a plant in Akron, Ohio, where load-carrying high-wheel Auto Wagons were

introduced in 1909 to join the passenger-carrying Auto Buggies.

High-wheelers proved to be a fad. Farmers adopted the Ford Model T in ever-increasing numbers after that sturdy car was introduced late in 1908. International Harvester abandoned its Auto Buggy in 1912 after somewhat more than 6,000 of the 4-cylinder cars had been manufactured. Although the company went out of the passenger car business, the 4,100 Auto Wagons that had been turned out since 1909 marked the debut of the International name in the truck field. High-wheeler motor trucks were produced until 1916, a year after conventional trucks had been introduced. In the post-World War I period trucks became an ever more important part of International's product line, as road improvements promoted the increasing use of what had been until then a greatly underutilized means of hauling freight. By 1921 IHC truck production was 7,000, and the company emerged as the largest manufacturer of heavy trucks in the country.

By the end of the 1940s the company's annual sales had passed the $1 billion mark. By that time trucks had become the company's most important product. In addition, an 18-ton crawler tractor for the construction industry had been introduced, and in late 1960 the company reentered the passenger car trade to a degree, with the debut of the Scout, modeled after the immensely popular Jeep. Actually, IHC had produced station wagons intermittently since 1936. Trucks, however, remained by far the company's most important products, comprising nearly half of all sales by 1964 and accounting for 31 percent of the heavy truck market, the largest share held by any truck producer.

After World War II International Harvester came under heavy criticism for what was described as its conservative, antiquated style of management. Over the years the company had shown a willingness to develop new products and expand into new areas, but the expansion had been carried out in a haphazard manner that demonstrated little awareness of the need for the kind of balance between centralized and decentralized authority, which Alfred P. Sloan, Jr., had employed so effectively at General Motors. Division managers did not have the authority to arrive at even minor decisions before clearing them through the central office. And new blood was not brought into the executive ranks, as the company followed a policy of in-house promotions that only strengthened the traditional, conservative managerial approach. That conservatism in part stemmed from the fact that the company had become so dominant in some areas that innovative approaches, which might have expanded its market share, raised concern that the company might become a subject of antitrust attacks. But it also resulted from a stand-pat management that was content with the status quo. "For too many years," a director later recalled, "as long as there was cash to cover the dividends, few executives really cared about how much the company made." Little effort was made to upgrade old plants or to drop losing lines. One truck with poor sales was kept in production for years for no other reason than that it had always been part of a plant's output.

By the 1960s International Harvester, despite its size, was losing its leadership position to more efficient competitors. Brooks McCormick, grandnephew of Cyrus H. McCormick, took over in 1968 and made some changes, closing old plants (including the great McCormick Works in Chicago), cutting the fat from the ranks of International's bloated dealer ranks, and bringing in new people. But the profit picture only worsened, with sales of more than $3 billion in 1971 resulting in only $45 million in profits. The oil crisis of 1973-1974 and the resulting recession had a crippling effect on the company, as it did on the industry as a whole. Archie R. McCardell was brought in from Xerox in 1977 to head the company. Although his drastic cost-cutting moves boosted profits from $203.7 million in 1977 to $370 million in 1978, the moves also triggered a bitter strike in 1979-1980, which, when combined with the onset of another recession, plunged the company into the red. By the time McCardell resigned in 1982, his austerity program had cut the company's work force by half. With debts in the billions, bankruptcy appeared to be a certainty.

Bankruptcy was avoided, however, by a massive overhaul of IHC. Its construction division was sold to Dresser Industries for $100 million and its axle division to Rockwell. The biggest change came in 1985, with the sale of the farm equipment holdings to Tenneco for $485 million. International Harvester also agreed to give up that famous name within five years. A great deal of time and money was spent on finding a new corporate name, Navistar International. Company chairman Donald D. Lennox admitted that Navistar was not a real word, but he said it had a "determined" and "futuristic" sound that was just the image the company wanted to project.

The new name was adopted at the start of 1986, signaling a new corporation whose eight plants, comprising 7.5 million square feet, contrasted with the 47 plants and 38 million square feet that International Harvester controlled as recently as 1980. The reduction to a great extent resulted from the fact that trucks were now virtually all the company produced. Other motor vehicles such as the Scout and the station wagons had been dropped in the earlier austerity programs. Instead of the gasoline-powered trucks for which the company had been long famous, the trucks, still carrying the International name, were now all diesel powered. Navistar manufactured its own diesels for its medium trucks but bought diesels from manufacturers such as Cummins for its heavy trucks. In the latter category International trucks still held about a quarter of the market.

At the end of 1986 the company posted a yearly profit for the first time since 1979. It was a minuscule $2 million on sales of $3.4 billion, but it was nevertheless a sign that the company had turned the corner. By the end of the decade a firm that had seemed doomed only a few years earlier was given a favorable rating by industry analysts.

References:

Nick Baldwin and others, *The World Guide to Automobile Manufacturers* (New York: Facts on File, 1987);

"The Name Game," *Newsweek*, 107 (January 20, 1986): 46;

Barry Stavro, "A surfeit of equity," *Forbes*, 138 (December 29, 1986): 62-64.

Archives:

The McCormick Collection in the State Historical Society of Wisconsin, Madison, Wisconsin, has papers of the McCormick family that relate to the origins of International Harvester. That corporation, in addition, was a pioneer in developing a corporate archives available to scholars.

Oakland Motor Car Company

by George S. May

Eastern Michigan University

The Oakland Motor Car Company of Pontiac, Michigan, was one of the lesser acquisitions made by William C. Durant when he was putting together General Motors (GM). The Oakland Company, formed in August 1907 by Edward M. Murphy, remains, under a different name, as one of GM's most important divisions. Murphy's Pontiac Buggy Company, incorporated in 1891, had helped make Pontiac a major center of the carriage industry, but by the early twentieth century Murphy, like a number of other carriage manufacturers, saw future sales threatened by the burgeoning popularity of automobiles. As a hedge against such a development, Murphy decided to expand into the production of automobiles.

Murphy liked the Brush Runabout that Alanson P. Brush had designed and which Frank Briscoe had begun to produce in Detroit in 1907. He asked Brush if he could provide a car that Murphy might put on the market. Brush had been Cadillac's chief engineer until 1905, and, as part of an agreement whereby Cadillac paid him $40,000 for the use of his patents and designs for two years, he had agreed not to engage in any activity that would compete with Cadillac during that period. With the expiration of the two years Brush welcomed the chance to return to automobile manufacturing, and he joined Murphy, becoming, in effect, the co-founder of the Oakland company, whose name was that of the county in which Pontiac is located.

As Oakland's chief engineer, Brush brought with him the design for a 2-cylinder car that he had prepared while at Cadillac but which that company had not used. It now became the first Oakland model to be produced. Brush followed it in 1908 with a more powerful 4-cylinder Model K that attracted considerable attention by its success in hill-climbing competitions. But this would be the last of the Brush-designed Oaklands, as the company early in 1909 came under the control of William C.

Durant and his GM holding company.

It is not immediately apparent why Durant should have been interested in Oakland. Because of his own experience in the carriage industry he was well acquainted with Edward Murphy and respected his ability, but there was little reason to be impressed with Murphy's new company, which, at the end of 1908, had thus far turned out only 278 cars. However, Oakland showed promise, and, most important, Durant needed to acquire control of more companies to increase investors' interest in GM, which then controlled only Buick and Olds.

According to Durant's unpublished autobiography written many years later, all of Oakland's stockholders except Murphy agreed to exchange their stock for shares of GM stock, but without Murphy's holdings Durant did not have control of the company. Durant used his legendary persuasive powers to break down Murphy's resistance and, according to Durant, got his stock just days before Murphy's death. Brush's widow held that Brush, who, she said, held the largest block of Oakland shares, was the one who opposed the GM takeover but that he was out-voted by the other stockholders and had no choice but to go along with the transfer of control.

Brush did not stay on at Oakland under the new regime. Instead, Durant persuaded him to move to Buick to fill in for the ailing Walter Marr as chief engineer. Meanwhile, Durant, in his characteristically impetuous way, sought to build up Oakland and make something of his new acquisition. He came to Pontiac and visited the Oakland plant. Lee Dunlap, the general manager, thought Durant intended to stay for several days so they could have a chance to go over plans carefully for the company's development. But after a short time Durant said, "Well, we're off to Flint." When Dunlap said they needed more time to go over possible expansion of the facilities, Durant took a quick

The 1912 Oakland Model 23 (courtesy of Rick Lenz)

look at the factory, agreed that it needed to be expanded, and told Dunlap to bring some plans with him to Durant's office in Flint on the following day.

No plans had been drafted, so that night Dunlap and his staff hastily drew up an outline of the grounds and made up some cut-out objects to represent different factory units. The next day, Dunlap, with some hesitation, presented this improvised layout to Durant, who, however, was "pleased pink" with it. "We placed those new buildings first here, then there, debating the situation," Dunlap recalled. "When we agreed as to where they should go, he said, 'Glue them down and call W. E. Wood [a contractor].' Mr. Wood came in after a few minutes and received an order for their construction. Wood had men, materials, and machines moving toward Pontiac within 24 hours and we were installing machinery in part of the structure within three weeks."

The money Durant spent on expanding Oakland and some of GM's other acquisitions placed a strain on the company's resources. A crisis arose in 1910, and Durant was forced to step aside in order to get the financial help needed to save GM from collapse. However, the efforts to upgrade Oakland continued with a series of 4-cylinder and then 6-cylinder and 8-cylinder models selling in the medium-price range. By 1917 Oakland's annual sales were near the 35,000 level. In that year Oakland, which had remained a separate company whose stock was held by GM, was transformed into an operating division of the GM Corporation, which succeeded the earlier holding company and took over its assets. Among these, Oakland seemed to be increasing in value as its output in the post-World War I boom year of 1919 soared to 52,000. When that boom collapsed in the last half of 1920, Oakland's production and sales, like those of the industry as a whole, dropped off, but Oakland's decline to only 11,852 units in 1921 was sharper than many other makes, such as Buick and Chevrolet, GM's top volume producers.

One source of Oakland's problem was the quality of the product. In 1921 one GM executive, John Lee Pratt, reported that Oakland's management had been working to improve its quality but with only limited success. "Some days they produce ten cars and some days they produce 50 cars. . . . they turn out a lot of cars that are not what they should be and then they have to fix them up." Oakland's 6-cylinder power plant was the major source of trouble. The division's general manager George H. Hannum and his staff were therefore more receptive than their counterparts at Chevrolet to the use of Charles Kettering's controversial air-cooled or "copper-cooled" engine—until tests on an Oakland late in 1921 revealed the defects that would eventually lead GM to abandon the engine's development.

By 1923 a new water-cooled, 6-cylinder engine had been introduced in the Oakland models for that year. These were also the first automobiles to use the disc wheels that Kettering's research department had developed; they were also the first to use the fast-drying Duco paints that Kettering and du Pont had produced. Blue was the only color then available, hence the "True Blue" label was attached to the 1923 Oaklands. These changes revived consumer interest in Oakland, bringing production levels by 1926 back to those achieved in 1919, but which by that time placed Oakland well down on the list of producers.

The corporate reforms pushed through by Alfred P. Sloan, Jr., successor to Durant as GM's executive leader, had slotted Oakland in the price range between the less-expensive Oldsmobile and the more-expensive Buick, eliminating the chaotic conditions that had earlier seen Oldsmobiles and Oaklands competing in the same price range. As it turned out, however, the future of the Oakland division lay in the area between Chevrolet, GM's lowest-priced car, and Oldsmobile. Sloan's strategy was to promote sales by enticing buyers to move up from one price range to the next, but the difference between the prices of Chevrolets and Oldsmobiles was so great that the decision was made to develop a new car that would bridge the gap. George Hannum, in October, 1924, proposed that Oakland be given the job of developing and producing the car, which was already being called the Pontiac. To save costs, Sloan had much of the engineering handled by Chevrolet, which also supplied many of the parts for the car, but responsibility for the final development, production, and sales of the Pontiac was assigned to Oakland.

The Pontiac Six was introduced in the 1926 model year and was an instant success. The Pontiac coach was priced at $825, roughly halfway between the Chevrolet coach's $645 price tag and the Oldsmobile's $950. The price of the Pontiac, which came only in closed body models, also undercut the price of Hudson's Essex, which had been the lowest-priced closed-body car on the market. Although the Pontiac came in as Oakland's lower-priced companion car, Oakland's importance was diminished greatly by the Pontiac's popularity. The tripling of the division's output in 1926 was due almost entirely to the demand for Pontiacs, and by the end of the decade the division was selling six Pontiacs for every Oakland. By 1932 the Oakland was dropped and the unit was renamed the Pontiac Motor Division.

In the 1930s Pontiac generally ranked fifth among all cars in sales, with production in 1941 of 282,087 placing it only 34,000 units behind Buick's figures. After the war Pontiac continued to hold the fifth position, rising to a production of more than 467,000 in 1950. However, Pontiacs did not seem to fit in with the trends in the industry toward flashier, more-powerful cars that appealed to younger drivers. Pontiacs had a reputation as good, dependable family cars which, like the Chevrolets, were referred to as "old ladies cars." In the middle of the decade, as GM was moving toward offering a greater variety of models in each division and away from the price compartmentalization of the earlier period, questions were raised as to whether there was a need to keep Pontiac.

In 1955 Semon E. Knudsen, son of William B. Knudsen, the man who had revitalized Chevrolet in the 1920s, was named Pontiac's general manager, with orders essentially either to make something of the division or to oversee its dismantlement. Working with Elliot "Pete" Estes and John Z. DeLorean, Pontiac's engineers, Knudsen moved quickly to change Pontiac's staid image. The traditional Indian-head logo was scrapped. Powerful new engines were developed that enabled Pontiacs in the late 1950s to pile up an impressive record of victories on the stock-car racing circuit. The sporty image was further enhanced by the adoption of longer, lower, wider bodies. Knudsen was successful in creating a new image that made Pontiac a favorite with the younger set. Sales at times in the 1960s pushed Pontiac into third place among all cars, ranking only behind Chevrolet and Ford. It was not possible always to hold on to that position in later years, but Pontiac models bearing such names as "Firebird," "Grand Prix," and "Grand Am" testified to the continued emphasis that the division was now the one where, as the ads claimed, "We build excitement."

References:

Ed Cray, *Chrome Colossus: General Motors and Its Times* (New York: McGraw-Hill, 1980);

Lawrence P. Gustin, *Billy Durant: Creator of General Motors* (Grand Rapids, Mich.: Eerdmans, 1973);

George S. May, *The Automobile in American Life* (forthcoming, 1990);

Alfred P. Sloan, Jr., *My Years With General Motors* (Garden City, N.Y.: Doubleday, 1964).

J. Patrick Wright, *On a Clear Day You Can See General Motors* (Grosse Point, Mich.: Wright Enterprises, 1979).

Ransom E. Olds

(June 3, 1864-August 26, 1950)

by George S. May

Eastern Michigan University

CAREER: Part-time employee (1880-1883), machinist and bookkeeper (1883-1885), partner (1885-1890), secretary-treasurer, P. F. Olds & Son (1890-1897); president, Olds Gasoline Engine Works (1897-1903); general manager and treasurer, Olds Motor Vehicle Company (1897-1899); general manager (1899-1904), vice-president (1899-1900, 1901-1904), president, Olds Motor Works (1900-1901); president (1904-1923, 1934), general manager (1904-1915), director (1904-1936), chairman, Reo Motor Car Company (1923-1936).

Although Ransom Eli Olds was technically an active figure in the automobile industry for some four decades, it was only during the first ten years of that period that he exerted a major influence. However, what he did during that brief period went far to determine the course of subsequent developments, making Olds one of the industry's most important founders.

Olds was born in northeastern Ohio in the town of Geneva on June 3, 1864. He was the youngest of five children born to Pliny Fisk and Sarah Whipple Olds. The Olds family's roots in America go back to about 1670 when Robert Ould, as the name was then spelled, came to Connecticut from England. In the early nineteenth century Ould's great-great-grandson, Jason Olds, went to Ohio, where his son, Pliny, was born in 1828. Pliny Olds married Sarah Whipple twenty years later, and the couple shortly settled in Geneva, where Pliny Olds opened a blacksmith shop. In 1870 he traded the business for a house and lot in Cleveland where he had been named superintendent of the Variety Iron

Ransom E. Olds (courtesy of the Clarence P. Hornung Collection)

Works. Four years later he gave up this job to take up farming at Parma, nine miles south of Cleveland. The economic conditions of that period did not make this an opportune time to go into farming, and after struggling to make a living for four years, Olds took a job in 1878 as a pattern maker in Cleveland. Unable to sell the farm, he had to take a room in the city while his family continued living in Parma. Finally, in 1880, although the details of what happened are not clear, an opportunity arose for Pliny Olds to go into business for himself, and he traded his Ohio property for property in Lansing, Michigan, where he opened a machine shop under the name of P. F. Olds & Son.

For the remaining seventy years of his life, Lansing was home for Ransom Olds, except for one brief period when he lived in Detroit. During the years when he was growing up in Ohio, he had begun acquiring a knowledge of machines from his father, visiting him at the ironworks in Cleveland and then later on the farm helping his father in the little blacksmith shop he built to repair farm tools. When the family moved to Lansing, Olds was only sixteen. The son in P. F. Olds & Son was an older brother, Wallace, but Ransom Olds worked in the shop after school, on Saturdays, and during vacations, getting paid 50 cents a day at first and then after a year or two getting a raise to $2 a day. Olds dropped out of school before graduating, as both he and his father felt that it was more important for him to work full time in the shop. However, in addition to the training Olds had received from his father in the machinist's trade, he did take some courses at the Lansing Business College in 1882-1883 that both father and son agreed would be of practical help as Ransom became more involved in the affairs of the family business.

In 1885, when he turned twenty-one, Ransom Olds bought out his brother's share of the business, although he had to borrow some money from his father to do so. Wallace Olds continued to work in the shop, but his younger brother had now assumed the role of partner. Up to this time, P. F. Olds & Son had been engaged mostly in repair work. It had built a few wood- and coal-burning steam engines, but these do not seem to have been a very important part of a business that was not doing very well. Despite the great difference in age between Ransom Olds and his father, the young son seems to have quickly asserted himself as the dominant force in the company, assuming the role, with or without the title, of general manager. Pliny Olds accepted the leadership role his son had assumed, eventually telling him that he recognized that the son had the ability that he lacked to move the company ahead. Officially Pliny Olds retained

the title of president, but by the 1890s he was taking less and less of a role in the business, and by the latter part of the decade he had retired and moved with his wife to southern California.

Shortly after he had assumed the partnership in the firm, Ransom Olds took the initiative in developing a small steam engine, which, by using a gasoline burner, achieved the desired steam pressure more quickly than one using coal or wood. Olds guessed that there was a market for such an engine among businesses, such as print shops, that only needed power for their operations on an intermittent basis. He guessed right. Between 1887 and 1892 some 2,000 of the engines were sold, with sales in the last year totaling over $20,000, a four-fold increase in the company's annual income since 1885. In spite of the depression that began in 1893, sales continued to rise, reaching $29,000 by 1896. The small plant the shop had originally occupied was twice expanded, the number of employees increased from 12 in 1887 to 23 in 1893, and in 1890 the company was incorporated. The business was capitalized at $30,000 with 3,000 stock shares issued. Originally Pliny and Ransom Olds each held 1,450 shares and Wallace Olds 100, but by 1897 the father's holdings had been reduced to only 50, Wallace, who had acquired additional shares as the father began disposing of his holdings, owned 200 shares, and Ransom Olds held 2,600 shares. Madison F. Bates, a company employee, owned the remaining 150 shares, the first shares not held by the family.

Under Ransom Olds, P. F. Olds & Son, although it still did repair work and sold other products, achieved widespread recognition for its engines, which were advertised in publications such as *Scientific American* by the early 1890s. Although he may have started out with the idea that the engines would be used for industrial purposes, he soon was exploring other possible uses. He installed one in a launch which he operated on the Grand River in Lansing in the latter part of the 1880s, beginning a love of powerboating that stayed with him for the rest of his life. He also sought to use his steam engine (which, because of the use of a gasoline burner to heat the water, was inaccurately advertised as a "gasoline engine") to power a road vehicle.

No contemporary evidence has survived that indicates exactly when Olds began his steam carriage experiments. Although claims were later made that he tested it in 1886 or even earlier, the best indications are that these tests took place in summer 1887, although he may well have been working on the vehicle for a year or more. If Olds had much information concerning the steam carriages that others elsewhere had built in earlier years, he did not seem to have learned much from them. His first steamer was crude compared to those that the American steam pioneer Sylvester H. Roper had built in Massachusetts as early as the 1860s, some of which had been exhibited and demonstrated in the Midwest. The Olds carriage was a box mounted on three wheels—one in front and two in the rear—steered by a tiller. A little 1-horsepower Olds steam engine was at the rear of the vehicle and was supposed to propel the carriage at speeds of 5 to 10 miles an hour. However, when Olds took the carriage out for its first run he found that the engine did not have enough power to keep the vehicle moving when any bump or incline was encountered. He made the test in the predawn hours so no one would see him if the machine failed, but the engine made such a racket that the entire neighborhood was awakened, and the embarrassed Olds had plenty of witnesses to the difficulties he had in getting his steamer back to the shop.

Pliny Olds is said to have told an acquaintance: "Ranse thinks he can put an engine in a buggy and make the contraption carry him over the roads. If he doesn't get killed at his fool undertaking, I will be satisfied." In light of the public's familiarity with the use of steam engines to power railroad locomotives and ships, as well as self-propelled steam-powered farm equipment that had been seen in rural areas of the Midwest for many years, Olds may have been exaggerating in his later years when he told of how much ridicule he received for his early experiments. However, the ultimate result of those experiments was to convince Olds that a steam engine was not the best source of power for passenger road vehicles. He boosted the power by substituting a 2-horsepower engine for the 1-horsepower unit he had first used. He found that it still did not provide sufficient power. Finally, around 1890, as he continued his experiments in his spare time, he dismantled the first steamer and built a second 4-wheeled steamer. A photograph that survives shows Olds and a passenger seated high off the ground on a seat built up over the out-sized front wheels. Looming up behind them, mounted on a low platform, were two

2-horsepower engines, linked together to form one unit that was directly connected to the driving wheels, eliminating the transmission and gears that had been among the problems in the earlier steamer. Over it all was a fringed canopy that added a touch of elegance to the strange-looking machine.

This second Olds steamer worked sufficiently well to attract the attention of a reporter for *Scientific American* who wrote a laudatory story about the steamer which Olds had demonstrated for the writer. The 1,200-pound vehicle could travel at a rate of 15 miles an hour, and its "great advantage," Olds declared, was "that it never kicks or bites, never tires out on long runs, and during the hot weather [the driver] can ride fast enough to make a breeze without sweating the horse. It does not require care in the stable, and only eats while it is on the road, which is no more than at the rate of 1 cent per mile." However, Olds apparently did not tell the reporter that the water in the boilers had to be replaced every ten or fifteen miles, the vehicle could not be put into reverse, and, although it had more power than the first steamer, Olds still, as he later admitted, "dreaded the sight of a hill." There were questions about the steamer's ability to make it up the hill, but if Olds had to stop on an incline the brakes were of such a doubtful nature that it was always the job of Olds's wife, Metta Ursula Woodward, whom he had married on June 5, 1889, to get out and place blocks of wood behind the wheels.

The story about the Olds steamer appeared in the May 21, 1892, issue of *Scientific American* and was reprinted in the July 1892 issue of *The Hub*, a leading trade paper for the carriage industry that would begin to pay attention to the growing phenomenon of horseless carriages. It may well have been the first national publicity that had appeared about any such activity occurring in the state that would soon be the center of the horseless carriage industry. The publicity attracted the attention of the Francis Times Company of London, England, a patent medicine firm, which contacted Olds and in 1893 bought the steamer for $400 and had it shipped to the company's branch office in Bombay, India. A good many writers have incorrectly called this the first sale of an American-made motor vehicle, which it was not, but it may well have been the first such sale to a foreign buyer. What happened to the vehicle is not known, but it is clear that Olds was glad to be rid of it. Nevertheless, although Olds did not return to further experiments with steam-powered horseless carriages, the knowledge he gained was of great value to him later. At the start of the automotive industry none of the other major pioneers had been working with motor vehicles as long as Olds.

The decision Olds made not to continue with steamers quite likely had its origins with his visit to the Chicago World's Fair in June 1893. There he had a brief ride in a European-made gasoline-powered automobile that was on exhibit, but the large number of gasoline internal combustion engines on display seems to have convinced him that these, not steam engines, represented the wave of the future. Upon his return to Lansing, Olds shortly began to work on designing a gasoline engine that P. F. Olds & Son could manufacture. On August 24, 1895, Olds and Madison F. Bates of his staff applied for a patent on a "gas or vapor engine." The patent, which was awarded to them a year later, one of 34 patents credited to Olds during his lifetime, was for an engine that emphasized the same elements of simplicity, efficiency, and safety of operations that had been featured in the earlier Olds steam engines and which later were featured in his automobiles. By spring 1896 the new Olds engine had been put into production. Although steam engines continued to be produced, they soon took second place to the gasoline engines that boosted company sales to $42,208 in 1897, necessitating a 10,000-square-foot addition to the factory.

Once the new engine was developed and put into production, Olds returned to his work on horseless carriages, realizing, he said, "that I ought to make a move at once in this direction, or all my former experience would be fruitless." The interest that had been shown in the *Chicago Times-Herald*'s automobile race, held in November 1895, had provided the first indication of the large number of Americans who were working on the development of horseless carriages. Few of them, as it turned out, had much success, but Olds, not having any way of knowing that, was stimulated to build a new vehicle, using the Olds gasoline engine as the source of power. By June 1896 the vehicle was completed, and on August 11, with a reporter for a local paper as his passenger, Olds gave it its first public demonstration. The vehicle consisted of a carriage supplied by a local carriage manufacturer, Clark & Son, with two seats, the rear seat being ad-

justable so that it could be placed facing backwards, the *dos-a-dos* seating arrangement. Attached beneath the carriage was a 1-cylinder, 5-horsepower engine. Ball bearings were used throughout, and the wheels were fitted with cushion tires, although a later version of this vehicle, which survives in the Smithsonian Institution, has solid rubber tires.

Cranking up the motor, Olds climbed into the driver's seat, which, as in virtually all of these early horseless carriages, was on the right side. With his right hand Olds shifted via a lever from low to high gear or into reverse, while using a tiller with his left hand to steer the vehicle. The 1,000-pound carriage had a maximum speed variously estimated at from 18 to 25 miles per hour, and its 3-gallon tank provided enough fuel for 25 to 50 miles of travel, depending on road conditions. The vehicle was put through a series of tests, including runs up the dreaded hills, at the end of which Olds exclaimed "Eureka," as an expression of his satisfaction with the performance. The reporter, who was obviously impressed, told the newspaper's readers the next day: "There is no doubt that the much mooted question of the horseless carriage has been successfully solved by Messrs. Olds & Clark."

Although Frank G. Clark, an Olds acquaintance who had supplied the carriage for the project, was for a time involved in the efforts to put this horseless carriage into production, there was never any doubt that Olds was the dominant figure in the endeavor. In September a Detroit patent law firm filed with the patent office an application on behalf of Olds on his claim to having invented certain new features in what the Detroit firm described as an "auto-mobile carriage," a very early use of the French term in the United States where "horseless carriage" for several years continued to be the common name for these new machines. In the application Olds declared that "the object of my invention is to produce a road vehicle that will meet most of the requirements for the ordinary uses on the road without complicated gear or requiring engine of great power and to avoid all unnecessary weight." What Olds was proposing was precisely the kind of car that would provide enough power to meet the average driver's normal needs that would come to be the mainstay of the Michigan-based automobile industry, enabling it within less than a decade to seize hold of the leadership of an industry in which much of the effort elsewhere was placed on the production of bigger, high-powered, and expensive cars for a much more limited clientele. But it was five years from the time of that August 1896 test run before any significant quantity of Olds-made cars reached the market.

Initially Olds thought production models of his car, which would be priced at around $1,000, could be put together in the shops of P. F. Olds & Sons, using engines manufactured there together with bodies provided by Frank Clark's company and wheels and other parts obtained from other suppliers. Several orders were received before the end of 1896, but by the following summer it is doubtful if any of these orders had been filled. The demand for the Olds gasoline engine was so great that Olds apparently did not feel that he could afford to divert any of the energies of his work force to the production of the Olds automobiles. Until this time the growth of the Olds business had been financed by the profits made from the sales of its products. Now for the first time Olds decided that he must seek outside investment if he was to establish motor vehicle production that would be separate and independent from the engine manufacturing business.

Olds got the help from Edward W. Sparrow, a Lansing businessman who had acquired a considerable fortune through real estate investments in that city and especially from large holdings of mineral sites and timberlands in northern Michigan. He had become familiar with Olds's latest invention by seeing it driven on the streets of the city. Whether he approached Olds or Olds broached the subject of an investment to him is not clear, but in any event a meeting was held in Sparrow's office on August 21, 1897, at which time the Olds Motor Vehicle Company was formed for the purpose of "manufacturing and selling motor vehicles." The company had a capitalization of $50,000, of which $10,000 in cash was actually paid in by Sparrow and several other businessmen with close connections to Sparrow. Sparrow was chosen to be the president of the new company while Olds, who was awarded half the stock in the company, was named general manager and treasurer.

The founding of the Olds Motor Vehicle Company is the basis for Oldsmobile's claim that this General Motors (GM) operation dates from 1897. But if it was born at that time it came perilously close to dying in infancy. For the investors the $10,000 they had put up was an interesting gam-

ble. "I am sure I did not see any great future for the invention," Eugene F. Cooley, who became vice-president of the company, later declared, "and I do not think others did, but we felt that, if developed, the power vehicle would have some sale and that a business possibly could be developed which would show a profit. I am free to say that I had not the faintest vision of what has eventuated in the automobile business." In 1897 Cooley and his colleagues may have seen their investment mainly as a means of acquiring some influence over the thriving Olds engine business, and, indeed, that fall P. F. Olds & Son was reorganized and recapitalized as the Olds Gasoline Engine Works. Ransom Olds now assumed the presidency that his father had previously held in what had been a family-owned business but which now for the first time received significant outside investments from Cooley, who became vice-president of the engine works, and others. To get the help he felt he needed, Olds had been forced to relinquish the freedom he had enjoyed in P. F. Olds & Son. Although he controlled half the stock in the motor vehicle company and a majority of the stock in the engine works, the wishes of men like Sparrow and Cooley could not be dealt with in the same fashion as Olds may have treated the ideas of his father or his brother.

Therein lay part of the problem the new company faced. Pliny, Ransom, and Wallace Olds had shared a common knowledge and understanding of their company's products. This was not the case with the investors in the Olds Motor Vehicle Company. At the company's first board meeting, Sparrow said, "Olds, we want you to make one perfect horseless carriage." Olds may have boasted to reporters earlier about how perfectly his vehicle operated, but now in private he told Sparrow that what he was asking was impossible, that at the present state of automobile development Sparrow "shouldn't even expect" him to be able to construct a "perfect" horseless carriage. Olds was able to prevail at this time, and in the minutes of the meeting the secretary drew a line through the word "perfect" to make the motion read that Olds was directed to build a carriage "in as nearly perfect a manner as possible." Olds was to discover, however, that differences he may have with stockholders could not always be so easily resolved in his favor.

Although $10,000 may have been all that Sparrow and his colleagues were willing to provide, Olds was greatly mistaken if he allowed himself

Olds driving the gasoline-powered car of his design he first tested on August 11, 1896

and them to believe that would be enough money to launch the production of the car. Such an investment was insufficient to finance the setting up of a separate manufacturing operation, and, with the assembling of the Olds automobile still dependent on the ability to fit this work into the tight work schedule and the facilities of the engine works, little progress was made. By the end of 1898 no more than a half dozen motor vehicles had been produced and sold—and there is some doubt that the number was even that great. The engine business continued to prosper, but the future of the motor vehicle business was most unpromising.

By summer 1898 Olds was looking for more money. He made some contacts in Detroit and Chicago that may have been genuine sources of investment or which he may have used only as a means of pressuring the Lansing investors to put more money into the business to keep it from being moved elsewhere. Late in 1898, however, Olds went to New York, where Lansing bankers are said to have aroused interest among some New York financiers in backing the establishment of the Olds Au-

tomobile Company at an eastern location. Olds is even said to have selected a factory site in Newark, only to find the necessary funding not forthcoming from the New Yorkers. Details regarding these negotiations are sketchy at best, but it does lead to some interesting speculations as to what might have happened to the industry had the Olds car production been located in the East and not in Michigan.

Upon his return to Michigan, Olds finally received the funding he needed and that assured the continued presence of his business in that state. The help came from Samuel L. Smith, who was living at this time in semiretirement in Detroit but who in earlier years had made a fortune in Michigan's copper-mining district in the Upper Peninsula and then subsequently through land investments which he made in association with Edward Sparrow. It was no doubt because of Sparrow that Smith had been one of the investors in the Olds Motor Vehicle Company in 1897. Now, as a result of his talks with Olds, he agreed to put up $200,000, but he was too shrewd a businessman to put up that much cash to support an untested product such as the

Olds automobile. Instead, he insisted that the ailing motor vehicle company be consolidated with the highly profitable Olds Gasoline Engine Works, thereby virtually guaranteeing Smith that even if the automobile side of the business failed, sales of the Olds engines would keep him from suffering a loss on his investment.

Details of the merger were worked out in spring 1899, and on May 8, 1899, the Olds Motor Works, which survives as GM's present Oldsmobile operation, was formed. It was capitalized at $500,000, but only 35,000 shares of stock at $10 a share were first issued. In return for his investment, Samuel Smith received all of the initial distribution of $200,000 in stock except for 10 shares each which went to Olds, Sparrow, Smith's son Frederic, and Smith's brother-in-law, James H. Seager. Smith soon recouped some of his investment by selling some of his stock to wealthy Detroit acquaintances, while the number of shares held by Olds was greatly increased as a result of the stock that he and the other shareholders in the engine company and the motor vehicle company received for permitting these companies to be absorbed by the Olds Motor Works. (Officially, the engine works continued to exist, with Olds as its president until 1903, when the parent company divested itself of the subsidiary.) Thus the first annual report of the new company reveals that Olds controlled the second largest holding of stock in the business, 7,500 shares. (Pliny Olds was listed as owning 125 shares.) But Smith still had by far the largest number of shares, 12,085, and these, when added to those held by Frederic Smith and another of Smith's sons, Angus, various Smith relatives, and such close business associates as Sparrow and the new Detroit investors, provided Smith with an overwhelming controlling interest.

At the outset Smith was named president of the Olds Motor Works while Olds was vice-president and general manager. By the beginning of 1900, however, the two had switched offices, with Smith becoming vice-president and Olds, who remained general manager, assuming the office of president. Whatever the reason for the change, it was probably based on the majority stockholders' recognizing that Olds was the one who knew the products and that he should be given the authority needed to handle the manufacturing side of the business. He must have been aware, however, that these same stockholders had the power to strip him of that authority if they wished to do so.

With the infusion of the money that he had long sought, Olds moved quickly. At the time of the formation of the Olds Motor Works a search for a permanent location for the company was launched. Hopes in Lansing that the Olds business would remain there were short-lived. The engine plant remained in operation in Lansing, but a new plant opened on a site obtained on the Detroit River in Detroit. That site was also the location of the company's main offices. The fact that the Smiths and other leading investors lived in Detroit may have had something to do with the decision to move the bulk of the Olds activities to that city, but Detroit's transportation facilities, its large pool of skilled workers, and problems that Olds had had with the machinists' union in Lansing, which had led him to fire his brother Wallace who was supporting the union's demands, were no doubt also contributing factors.

By the end of 1899 Olds, his wife, and their two daughters had left Lansing and moved to Detroit where Olds took charge of the operations in the new factory which was nearing completion. By March 1900 more than 100 men were at work in the Detroit plant, and the automotive journal *Motor Age* was predicting that before long "a goodly number" of cars would be coming into the market every week. But month after month passed, and most of the manufacturing that took place in the plant was not that of automobiles but of engines. The delay stemmed from an uncertainty on the part of Olds as to what kind of a car to produce. He and his staff worked on about a dozen different models, including "a handsome electric stanhope" that was the only car the company exhibited in September 1900 at one of the country's first automobile shows in Chicago. This gave Olds the distinction of being one of the very few automotive pioneers who built cars using all three sources of power that were then available. However, as he had indicated in 1897 in a talk that he gave to a group of engineers, he regarded the gasoline engine as the most suitable energy unit for a horseless carriage, and any interest he showed later in electrics only resulted from his recognition that this type of car would enjoy some short-term popularity until road conditions and gasoline cars were improved, making it possible to use the latter type for long trips that were impossible in an electric because of the limits imposed by its batteries.

Very few Olds electrics were actually produced, and the same was true of Olds gasoline cars, some of which were much larger and more expensive than the type Olds in 1896 had indicated he was interested in producing. After more than a year the automotive side of the business still had little to show except losses, which had risen to some $80,000. Gasoline engine sales continued to boom, accounting for most of the income of $186,000 in 1900, up from $120,000 the previous year. But now that he had the funding, the factory, and the staff that the earlier motor vehicle company had lacked, Olds felt under increasing pressure to do something to justify the continued existence of the automobile section.

Sometime in late summer or early fall 1900, Olds, "after a long sleepless night," came into the office and gave one of his engineers, Horace Loomis, a rough sketch of a vehicle which marked a return to the lightweight, inexpensive, simple car he had outlined in his 1896 patent application. He told Loomis that "what we want to build is a small, low-down runabout that will have a shop cost around $300 and will sell for $650." That would be half the price of the cheapest of the existing Olds models, one of which was priced as much as $2,750. Loomis, together with other engineers, including Jonathan D. Maxwell, who would later go on to build a car that bore his own name, fleshed out Olds's ideas and by October had built the car and were putting it through its tests. By the end of the year the first advertisements appeared, offering the car for a price of $600, although that had to be raised to $650 a year later. That remained the price of the car until 1907 when production ceased.

The car that Olds and his staff designed—the curved-dash Oldsmobile runabout—became one of the most famous in automotive annals. A runabout was a standard carriage model developed in the 1880s. It was a popular model because it was lightweight and could be pulled by only one horse. At a time when the American automobile was actually a horseless carriage, the runabout had been chosen by some automakers as early as 1899 as the body for the lightweight, low-priced car that would be their equivalent of the little *voiturette* that the French company, DeDion-Bouton, had marketed with such success within Europe. The Oldsmobile runabout was basically the same as the other run-

about models that had already been introduced. It was an open vehicle (a fabric top would be offered later as an option) with room for two people, the driver sitting on the right and operating the vehicle in the same way that Olds had operated his first gasoline car in 1896. The 1-cylinder Olds engine was mounted beneath the body, at the rear. The one distinguishing feature was the dash in front. The standard runabout had a straight dash, and most automakers retained this when they adopted a runabout as a body for their car. The Oldsmobile's dash, however, curved out, up, and then in, which Olds claimed deflected air currents down over the car's radiator, located in the footboard, "thereby greatly assisting in the dispersion of the heat." Whether this was true or not, it gave the little 600- to 700-pound car an unmistakable profile that Olds sought to protect from imitators by applying for and receiving a patent on the design.

Although the Oldsmobile has often been referred to as the cheapest car on the market when it was introduced, that is not true. There were numerous cars that were available at the same price or at a considerably lower figure. Nevertheless the car attracted a degree of attention that none of the company's earlier offerings had enjoyed, and by early March 1901 more than 300 orders had been received. Confident that they had finally found what they had been looking for, Olds gave his production superintendent directions to gear up to turn out 1,000 of the runabouts by year's end.

On March 9, 1901, Olds and his family returned to Detroit from California, where they had spent several weeks visiting Olds's parents in San Diego. As they were riding the streetcar from the railroad station to their home, Olds happened to glance at a newspaper and saw to his horror that the Olds factory in Detroit had been burned to the ground earlier that afternoon. He hurried to the site where he and Fred Smith, the company secretary who was already there, began to assess the damage. Olds told reporters that there could not have been a "more inopportune time for such a calamity" since the buying season would soon start, and they had had at least a score of vehicles under construction in the plant getting ready for the market. However, he declared that "in two or three weeks time we shall be running as though nothing had happened." It took a little longer than that, but by sometime in April the first curved-dash runabout had been produced, and before the year was up about

425 more had followed, not the 1,000 that Olds had aimed for but very large figures for a company at this stage of the industry's development when total American car production was only a few thousand units a year. By 1902 Oldsmobile production was in the neighborhood of 2,500, although accurate figures are hard to find in this period, and by 1904 output had doubled.

By the end of 1902 there is little doubt that the Olds Motor Works was producing more cars than any other American maker and probably more than any company in Europe, where commercial production had started ten years earlier than in the United States. One of the most persistent legends in the industry attributes the Olds' success to the March fire. According to this story, all that survived the fire was one curved-dash runabout that an employee managed to push out of the burning plant. All the other models that the workers had been working on, together with the plans and drawings for the models, were destroyed. Olds, who had vacillated as to which models to produce, was now left with no other choice than the runabout, which was all he had left to work with. Luckily for him, the car proved to be a popular one. In order to get back into production as soon as possible, Olds was forced to contract out the production of the various parts which made up the runabout, thereby inaugurating a practice of buying many of parts from outside suppliers that would be common throughout the industry.

This story is nonsense, even though Olds, who seemed to enjoy making it appear that his accomplishments were due to chance rather than to his own abilities, loved to tell it in later years. Well before the fire Olds had already determined to concentrate on the production of the runabout. As for the other models, the plans for them had not been destroyed but, as Olds told a reporter at the time, had survived undamaged in the vault where they were kept. The fire may have caused Olds to abandon completely these models sooner than he would have done otherwise, but that was certain to happen in any event in order to focus all of the attention on getting out the one car that the public was interested in. As for the decision to contract out parts production, that was something that Olds and all other manufacturers were doing to lessen the financial risk of automotive business. Long before March 1901, Olds had contracted with Weston-Mott in Utica, New York, to make his wheels, a Cleveland com-

Olds after he founded the Reo Motor Car Company in 1905 (courtesy of the Motor Vehicle Manufacturers Association)

pany to supply batteries, and, among others, the C. R. Wilson Body Company of Detroit to supply bodies, and the Dodge Brothers machine shop of the same city to make engines, a product that one might think the Olds company could have handled itself but which Olds decided to contract out, leaving the engine division free to fill its backlog of orders from other customers. After the fire, as the demand for the runabout grew, Olds turned to other companies to supply more parts, but it was not a practice that had been forced on him by the fire.

The fire did, however, force decisions to be made regarding the permanent location of Oldsmobile operations. Temporary quarters were used where the parts that were delivered could be assembled, and the decision was made to rebuild at the site of the destroyed plant. But news of the fire led officials in Lansing to come up with an attractive offer of land in southwestern Lansing where a new

Olds plant could be built. The Olds company was quick to accept the offer. A compelling reason in favor of the move was that the amount of land offered was much greater and the price far less than anything that could have been obtained adjacent to the Detroit factory. The latter was rebuilt, and, with the completion of the new Lansing plant, Oldsmobiles were being produced at two sites by the beginning of 1902. Ultimately by 1905, however, the decision was made to concentrate Oldsmobile production in Lansing where it continues to the present day.

Olds had nothing to do with that decision, for he was no longer associated with the Olds Motor Works in 1905. His departure, however, probably had its origins in the decision to build a second plant in Lansing. Olds had had little to do with that decision, for the stress resulting from his efforts to get production going after the March fire had caused him to be hospitalized in April and to continue to suffer from ill health for some time thereafter. The negotiations that wrapped up the acquisition of the Lansing property were handled largely by Fred Smith, an aggressive man, several years younger than Olds, who began to take a greater interest in the running of the company than his duties as secretary would normally suggest. When the Lansing plant was completed, it was decided that Olds, while continuing as general manager in charge of all operations, would move back to Lansing to look after the day-to-day activities at the plant there while Fred Smith would keep an eye on the Detroit plant. Early in 1901 Olds and Samuel Smith again shifted offices, Smith resuming the presidency, while Olds took on the title of vice-president. This may have been an early sign of the Smiths' dissatisfaction with Olds's leadership, but Olds, who was no administrator, may have suggested the change in order to allow him more time to handle production.

For a time there did not seem much cause for disagreement within the organization. Under the direction of Olds, production of the runabout grew at an unparalleled rate for that day. To keep up with the demand Olds instituted some changes in production techniques, assigning workers a certain limited number of tasks to perform, rather than having them involved in assembling the entire car, and having them carry out those jobs along a primitive sort of production line. These changes enabled annual production to increase from a few hundred to a few thousand cars and foreshadowed the far greater production changes that would be forthcoming a few years later at the Ford Motor Company. It was also apparently Ransom Olds who was responsible for having Roy D. Chapin drive one of the runabouts from Detroit to New York City in time for it to be displayed by the company at the annual automobile show in Madison Square Garden in November 1901, and which the company made effective use of in its advertisements. Olds, who had publicized his first gasoline car by demonstrating it at county fairs in southern Michigan, also helped to promote the company by driving a specially built Olds racer on the packed sands of the Ormond-Daytona Beach area of Florida in April 1902.

But by summer 1902 a rift between Olds and Fred Smith was clearly developing. Smith had assumed responsibility for sales, and Olds expressed some disagreement with the policies pursued by Smith and Roy Chapin, whom Smith had taken under his wing and who later became the company's sales manager. However, it was when Smith interfered in the production side the business, which Olds considered to be his exclusive domain, that the trouble really began. Smith was concerned at the number of complaints that were received from runabout owners about the problem they had with the car, and he began to demand that Olds take action to correct these problems. Although the curved-dash Olds was probably as well made as most of that period's cars, Olds seems to have had a rather casual attitude toward quality control, and Smith no doubt was correct in believing that more attention should be given to locating defects in a car before it left the factory rather than waiting for these to be pointed out by customers, which seemed to be Olds's approach.

The runabout was a fragile little car which Roy Chapin was able to drive to New York only by taking along a large stock of spare parts that he used to make the numerous repairs needed as a result of the pounding the car took on the wretched roads. Although Fred Smith recognized that the Oldsmobile would continue to be popular with most users, few of whom at this time would be thinking of taking it on cross-country trips, he felt that Olds should also design a touring car, a bigger, more powerful car that would be better suited to those who did want to take long trips. This has often been regarded as the major cause of the split between Smith and Olds that led to Olds being forced out of his company, but this exaggerates the importance of this issue. Olds did not see the urgency of this matter and did not push ahead with the development of the new car with any great speed, but it cannot be said that he opposed building the bigger car. He disagreed on the timing of the change, but by 1903 there is little doubt that Olds agreed that the market demanded a bigger car, in addition to the small runabout, which he and Smith agreed should continue to be produced. But what Olds did object to was Smith's intrusion into an area that Olds regarded as his own responsibility.

The final break between the two men came in spring 1903 when Smith, who had often expressed his dissatisfaction at Olds's failure to do more to improve the company's products, established an experimental engineering shop in the Detroit plant under Smith's supervision. Three months later Smith applied for a patent on improved springs to replace those that Olds had developed that worked satisfactorily, Smith said, only in lightweight vehicles. When Olds heard, "by a round about way," that Smith had set up this experimental operation without consulting him or obtaining his authorization, Olds, who usually gave the impression of being good natured and mild mannered, exploded. "Now if this is your policy to do business underhanded and unbeknown to me, as you have several other things," he informed Smith in a letter on May 1, "I do not care to be associated with you. I am Vice-President and Manager of this company and such things should not be taken up without my consent or the consent of the board. I have had all I want of this treatment."

From this time on, although Olds and Smith seem to have tried to carry on their relationship in a correct, professional manner, there could have been little doubt that Olds was on his way out. Olds had already realized that his ability to maintain control over production decisions was being undermined as Fred Smith gained increasing confidence in his own ability to run the company. As early as 1902 Olds had begun selling some of his stock, and by the end of 1903 he had sold more than 3,000 shares, about 40 percent of his holdings. Such actions would seem incompatible with a desire on his part to fight to retain his authority. In December 1903 Olds himself moved at the directors' meeting that he should be reassigned to work on engineering and experimental activities, while Charles B. Wilson would be given the job of supervis-

ing production in the Lansing and Detroit plants. At the annual stockholders' meeting on January 11 Olds was reelected to the board of directors, along with Samuel, Fred, and Angus Smith, James Seager, Henry Russel, a prominent Detroit attorney who held the job of president of the Olds Motor Works after Samuel Smith had surrendered the post in 1902, and Eugene Cooley, the only Lansingite besides Olds on the board. At the board meeting later that day, Seager moved, with Cooley's support, to turn over to Fred Smith the jobs of vice-president and general manager previously held by Olds. Although Olds would later claim that he had opposed the motion but had been voted down, the board minutes indicate that the motion passed unanimously.

Olds was still a director and could no doubt have continued with that title, but such a role would have been a meaningless one and would, he said, have amounted to admitting that the board had made the right decision in turning over his managerial job to Smith. He was soon trying to dispose of the remainder of his company stock and, in fact, had apparently made an agreement with Fred Smith to step down as general manager without a fight in return for Smith's help in selling his stock. The bitterness between the two men grew even greater when Olds charged that rather than helping him Smith had hurt him by advising brokers that $10 a share was a good price to pay for the stock, whereas Olds claimed he had gotten $30 a share for the stock he sold in 1902 and 1903. However, Smith's price quote in 1904 was quite reasonable, since Olds seems to have forgotten the 4-for-1 stock split that had been approved in 1903.

By summer 1904 Olds had sold all of his stock and had resigned from the board of the Olds Motor Works, severing his last ties with the company that had developed from the Olds's family business established 24 years earlier. But Olds, who was only forty years old, had no intention of retiring. He invested some of his money in real estate, which ultimately became his major business interest, but in 1904 he was still too close to the automobile business to give it up entirely. In February 1904, when he and his wife and daughters made their annual trip to California to visit Pliny and Sarah Olds, he stopped off in Los Angeles to meet with Reuben Shettler, a former Lansing businessman and acquaintance who had become an Oldsmobile distributor in California. The two men came to an understanding that as soon as Olds sold the rest of his Olds stock they would organize a new automobile company, with Shettler handling the financing of the business. When Olds returned to Lansing he hired Horace Thomas, a former Olds Motor Works engineer, to begin work on the design of the car the new company would produce. Shettler, meanwhile, was arranging to dispose of his Oldsmobile agency, after which he came to Lansing in June to begin lining up financial support. He seems to have had little difficulty in finding individuals in Lansing who jumped at the chance to have a piece of a company headed by Olds, who, despite his departure from the Olds Motor Works, remained probably the best-known name in the industry. On August 16, 1904, therefore, the R. E. Olds Company was incorporated. "Lucky Lansing," the Detroit *Free Press* declared, to have a resident whose "connection with the new enterprise will give it immense prestige."

Typically, Olds claimed to have been totally surprised by the development. He had been vacationing in northern Michigan, he said, when he received a message from Shettler asking him to return to Lansing. When he got off the train in the state capital, he later recalled, "I was met by an old friend who handed me a very interesting looking paper. Reading it I found that a group of my friends had organized a half-million dollar company of which I was to be the head, and within three hours had raised the money to finance it. Of this I was to have a controlling interest, or $260,000. To say that I was astounded would be putting it mildly." He might say that, but the truth was that he had carefully planned it that way. He would be president and general manager of the company, but, to avoid the problems he had encountered at the Olds Motor Works, he would also control 52 percent of the voting stock, which he was awarded in return for the use of his name, rights to certain patents, and certain other considerations, but no cash. This time around Olds was going to be in complete control.

With the formation of the new company, developments moved ahead at an amazing pace. Only one serious obstacle had to be cleared away. When the Olds Motor Works learned of the name of the new firm, it immediately objected. Fred Smith insisted that Olds had sold the rights to the use of his name to the Olds Motor Works and that its use in the name of the new company and on its cars would be an infringement of the rights of Olds's for-

mer company. Olds denied that he had sold the rights to the use of his name, but when attorneys whom he consulted declared that the Olds Motor Works stood a good chance of winning a suit if the matter were brought to court, Olds and his fellow stockholders on September 27, 1904, changed the name to the Reo Car Company, later amended to the Reo Motor Car Company. Whether they realized that *reo* is the Greek verb meaning "to run" is not known, but it is certain that they felt that Olds's initials, plus his appearance in Reo ads, would link him with the new cars just as much as if his name had appeared on the cars.

While these legal matters were being settled, work was beginning on the construction of a factory on land in south Lansing, not far from the Oldsmobile operations. Temporary facilities were obtained where Olds, Horace Thomas, and other staff members worked on the development of the cars that would be put into production. In recruiting his staff, Olds turned to those with whom he had worked in the past. In addition to Thomas, who was named chief engineer, Richard H. Scott, whom Olds had hired in 1898 to be plant manager of the gasoline engine works, now became the factory superintendent at Reo and in a few years became the dominant figure in the company. Ray M. Owen, whom Olds had persuaded in 1901 to become the Oldsmobile distributor in the New York City area and to agree to contract to sell 1,000 cars the first year, an astonishing figure at that stage of the industry's development, now contracted to sell the entire Reo output. This was a somewhat unusual arrangement, but by contracting out to a private company the selling of the company's product, Olds and his staff were free to devote their full attention to the production side of the business.

By October the first Reo cars were being tested, by November the first ads were appearing, and by the time of the automobile shows in January 1905, the Reos were on display and were soon being sold. There was a Reo runabout, as was to be expected, as one ad declared, from "the inventor of the first practical gasoline Runabout." It was priced at $650, the same as the curved-dash Oldsmobile, but it did not have a traditional runabout profile. Instead, there was a hood in front, although it housed the gas tank, radiator, and batteries, the engine was still was attached beneath the body. But the Reo runabout played second fiddle to the 5-passenger, 1,500 pound, 2-cylinder, 16-horsepower Reo touring car, which carried a $1,250 price tag. This was the kind of car that Fred Smith had been pushing Olds to come out with at the Olds Motor Works and which Olds, with an understandable affection for the money-making little Oldsmobile runabout, had been reluctant to develop with any great haste. But the fact that this was the model that received most of the attention in Reo promotions is a clear sign that Olds, like Smith, recognized that the runabout fad was on the way out as the public desired a car that was better able to withstand the abuse it received when driven extensively on the roads of that era. By going to the touring car, however, Olds was abandoning the low price that had been one of the main attractions of the runabout. His Reo touring car was an indication that he felt that sacrifice had to be made in order to provide the stronger car the times demanded. He thereby ceased to be the champion of the low-priced car, a role that would soon be taken on by Henry Ford, who proved with the Model T that it was possible to build a tough, durable car and still sell it at a price comparable to the earlier price of the runabout.

Despite the unfamiliar association of the Olds name with a higher-priced car, the Reos did very well, with production for the first fiscal year, which ended August 31, 1905, totaling 864 cars, a respectable figure when it is considered that most of this occurred after January 1. The next year production rose to 2,458, and records continued to be broken with production for the period September 1908 to August 1909 reaching 6,592. Olds's new company was an outstanding success. Its sales ranked it among the top four or five companies in the country, and its profits, as measured by the dividends it paid, were cited by an early automotive historian, James Rood Doolittle, as an example of the kind of money that well-run automobile companies could make in these early years.

By 1909, however, Olds had lost interest in being involved with his company on a day-to-day basis. Part of his motivation in organizing the company undoubtedly had been to prove to his former colleagues in the Olds Motor Works that he could get along without them. Under Fred Smith's direction, the Olds company, although it kept the curved-dash runabout in production until 1907, moved too hastily into the production of much bigger cars, and sales suffered so that within a couple of years the upstart Reo company had moved ahead of Olds-

mobiles in sales, and the gap between the two widened further in Reo's favor by 1908. By 1906, therefore, Ransom Olds, having proved his point to the Smiths, and also probably recognizing that he had no real taste for the less exciting job of running an established company, began to give greater responsibility to Richard Scott and to spend more and more time away from the office. Winter vacations in Florida became a yearly routine after his parents moved there from San Diego. In the summer it was trips to northern Michigan or, before long, to other parts of the country or abroad. Boating became an increasing interest which Olds could now afford to indulge with larger and larger yachts in Florida and on the Great Lakes.

Olds, of course, did not spend all of his time in leisure activities. Shortly after Reo was formed, he had taken the lead in organizing several companies in Lansing that supplied parts for the Reo and other automobiles, and he also became involved in banking activities in Lansing. Florida real estate developments, hotels, a brief fling in the aviation field, the development and manufacturing of one of the first gasoline-powered lawn mowers, diesel engines—these were among numerous interests that occupied his attention in his later years. But in the field with which he was most associated, automobiles, he was trying to get out by 1908. That year he was involved in negotiations that sought to merge Reo, Ford, Buick, and Maxwell-Briscoe into one big corporation. These failed because of the insistence of Olds and Henry Ford that they be paid cash for control of their companies, not the stock in the new corporation that William C. Durant of Buick and Benjamin Briscoe favored. When other attempts to sell Reo also failed, Olds in 1910 fought an attempt by Reuben Shettler to turn over control of the company to Ray Owen. Olds kept his control, but he assigned the actual administrative authority to Richard Scott. In 1915 he officially relinquished the title of general manager to Scott and in 1923 turned over the presidency to Scott as well, taking on the new and largely honorary title of chairman of the board. Problems created by Scott's unwise moves to expand the Reo output of cars in the late 1920s, compounded by the onset of the Depression, forced Olds to assume a stronger role in Reo's management. A bitter proxy fight, which Olds won in 1934, led to Scott's resignation from the company and Olds's return to an active management role. Briefly his reawakened creative juices led him to propose drastic actions to revitalize the company but his fellow directors rejected his suggestions. By the end of 1934 he had given up his management role, and two years later he resigned as a director of Reo, his last remaining office with the company. Reo stopped producing cars in 1936, concentrating on trucks, the production of which Olds had launched in 1911 and which continued until 1975.

Olds died at his Lansing home on August 26, 1950. His wife, who had been ill for several years, fell and broke her hip at the funeral. She contracted pneumonia and died on September 2. The couple were survived by their daughters, Gladys Olds Anderson and Bernice Olds Roe, and several grandchildren and great grandchildren. The last years of their lives had been relatively peaceful ones. Each year Olds's birthday was the occasion for civic celebrations and newspaper articles recalling his long and notable career. Olds, however, came to feel, naturally enough perhaps, that outside of Lansing his importance as an automotive pioneer had not received the attention it deserved. He was privately resentful of the praise heaped on his old friend Henry Ford, but he need not have been. His contributions, which had been substantial, could not be forgotten. He had been responsible for two motor vehicle operations that were still going at the time of his death, but of greater importance was the role he had played in stimulating and encouraging others to enter the field. Roy Chapin and several other Olds employees had used the experience they had gained there to form the Hudson company, long one of the more important independent automakers. Jonathan Maxwell joined with Benjamin Briscoe, who had made sheet metal parts for Olds, to form a company that later became part of what is now the Chrysler Corporation. Henry Leland, who made engines for the Oldsmobile, was primarily responsible for developing the Cadillac, which started out imitating the runabout that Olds had popularized. The Dodges went on to produce parts for Ford before striking out to build their own car. Finally, Henry Ford, after two earlier failures, owed much of the support he gained for his third and successful venture to the fact that Olds had demonstrated that there was money to be made in producing a low-priced car. Ford pursued that idea to an extent far beyond what Olds had attempted, but it was Olds who had blazed the way. He was the pathfinder.

Publications:

"The Horseless Carriage," in *Michigan Engineers' Annual, Containing the Proceedings of the Michigan Engineering Society for 1898* (Battle Creek: Michigan Engineering Society, 1898);

"Revolution of the World for Good," *Bankers Home Magazine,* (March 1921).

References:

George S. May, *A Most Unique Machine: The Michigan Origins of the American Automobile Industry* (Grand Rapids, Mich.: Eerdmans, 1975);

May, *R. E. Olds: Auto Industry Pioneer* (Grand Rapids, Mich.: Eerdmans, 1977);

Glenn E. Niemeyer, *The Automotive Career of Ransom E. Olds* (East Lansing: Michigan State University, 1963);

Duane Yarnell, *Auto Pioneering: A Remarkable Story of Ransom E. Olds, Father of Oldsmobile and Reo* (Lansing, Mich.: Privately published, 1949).

Archives:

The papers of Ransom E. Olds are in the Historical Collections of Michigan State University, East Lansing, Michigan. Almost nothing survives relating to the period before 1900, but the records for the years after 1900 are extensive, including correspondence and a complete run of Olds's pocket diaries. The same collection has the business records of the Reo Motor Car Company from its beginnings in 1904 to the demise of its successor company in 1975.

Olds Motor Works

by George S. May

Eastern Michigan University

The Olds Motor Works, now the Oldsmobile Division of General Motors (GM), was formed on May 8, 1899. It represented the merger of two Lansing, Michigan, businesses: the Olds Motor Vehicle Company and the Olds Gasoline Engine Works. Although the new company was soon famous for the production of an automobile developed by Ransom E. Olds, it was the successful gasoline engine that Olds had developed and marketed that undoubtedly persuaded the Detroit capitalist Samuel L. Smith to invest $200,000 in the venture. The company's headquarters were moved to Detroit, where a new factory was built for the production of automobiles, but it was the engines that were produced in the plant in Lansing, and also, for a time, in the Detroit plant, that were the company's only money-making products during its first two years in operation.

Although Samuel Smith for a time served as the president of the new company and together with his sons Frederic, who became the company's secretary, and Angus held by far the largest block of stock, they and the other investors from Detroit and Lansing relied upon Ransom Olds as the person who would be in charge of production. Olds, who had developed a gasoline automobile in 1896, had been unable to produce the car in any quantity because of the inadequate financial backing of the earlier Olds Motor Vehicle Company. Now that he had that support and a new factory that was completed by the end of 1899, he still failed to achieve any significant production for many months because of his inability to decide on the type of car that would have the most commercial appeal. Finally, after coming up with several models that failed to arouse much interest and caused the automobile side of the company's operations to sustain heavy losses, Olds settled upon a runabout. By October 1900 the Olds staff had built the prototype of this model, and by the end of the year preliminary an-

nouncements were made that this car, the first one to carry the Oldsmobile name, would soon be available. With its distinctive curved-dash front end, the 1-cylinder car, weighing around 600 pounds, sold for $600, half as much as the next-cheapest car that the company had been offering. Although this did not make the Oldsmobile runabout the cheapest automobile on the market and the price was shortly raised to $650, the price certainly helped stimulate sales that by 1902 made the Olds Motor Works the country's largest volume producer of cars.

Runabout production had barely begun when a fire on March 9, 1901, destroyed the Detroit factory where the cars were assembled. The strength of the company was quickly demonstrated by the fact that within little more than a month production of the runabout had been resumed. Ransom Olds had already, before the fire, contracted with various companies to build the parts used in the curved-dash Oldsmobile, and these parts were assembled by Olds employees in temporary facilities later that spring. By the end of the year about 425 Oldsmobiles had been produced, far short of the 1,000 cars that Olds had set as the goal for the year but still enough to put the company ahead of all but two or three other American companies. The Detroit plant was rebuilt and a second constructed in Lansing. By the end of 1902 production was over 2,500 for the year, and it was twice that by 1904 (although exact production figures are not available in these early years).

Although Ransom Olds deserves to be given the major responsibility for this success, his position in the company deteriorated to the point that by 1904 he had severed the ties with the firm that bore his family's name. This development had its beginnings with the decision in 1901 to maintain assembly operations in both Detroit and Lansing. Olds, who had moved to Detroit following the for-

The 1902 Oldsmobile curved-dash runabout

mation of the Olds Motor Works in 1899, moved back to Lansing where he took over the supervision of the new plant there, while also retaining his position of overall management of the company's entire operations. Frederic Smith, the company secretary, took on the day-to-day management of the Detroit plant. By 1902 Smith was beginning to question some of the ways in which Olds was managing production. He expressed concern that Olds was not acting quickly enough to respond to the complaints that were received about the runabout's quality. He also seems to have felt that Olds was not moving fast enough in the development of a bigger car to go along with the little runabout. Both men agreed upon the need for such a car, but Olds, who naturally felt a special attachment to the curved-dash runabout, does not seem to have felt the need was as immediate as did Smith and some others in the company. Finally a blowup between the two men occurred in spring 1903 when Smith went ahead with an action which Olds declared only he, as general manager, could authorize. The following January

Olds was replaced as general manager by Smith, and in August 1904, having sold his stock in the Olds Motor Works, he resigned as a director of the company and devoted all of his attention to his new automobile company whose name was an acronym formed from his initials, Reo.

Under Smith's management, the Olds company continued to prosper for a time. Production reached about 6,500 cars in 1905, which kept the company at the top of the list. Production that year was concentrated entirely in Lansing, which from then on remained the center of Oldsmobile production. Shutting down the Detroit operations was a cost-saving measure, although it was also claimed that the company feared that the sharp increase in the number of automobile companies in Detroit would make it more and more difficult to secure enough labor for the Detroit plant. Smith continued the curved-dash runabout in production until 1907, but well before then he had turned his attention to the introduction of bigger, more expensive 4-cylinder and 6-cylinder models. The shift from a

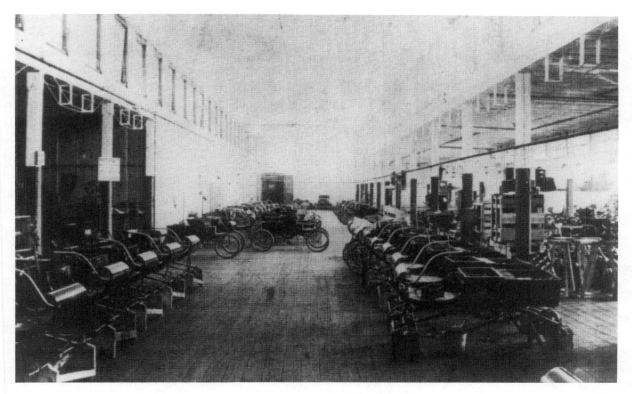

Assembly room at Olds Motor Works, 1903

company that had been known for its low-priced cars to ones with price tags four times that of the runabout was apparently made too suddenly, and by 1908 sales were down to only 1,000 cars for the year and Smith's father had to advance the company more than $1 million to keep it going.

The Olds Motor Works may have been saved from going under by the fact that William C. Durant, head of the Buick company, had become involved in negotiations to merge Buick with several other automobile firms. When these talks collapsed, Durant went ahead in September 1908 to form the General Motors (GM) Company, a holding company that would acquire control of other companies by obtaining control of the stock in those firms. Buick was the first company that GM came to control in this way, but one company was scarcely enough to create the kind of interest in GM's stock that Durant was hoping to stimulate. Durant therefore approached the Olds Motor Works, which he had already learned from discussions with the Smiths was ripe for the taking. After some negotiations, a deal was completed on November 12, 1908, whereby Olds became the second company to come into the GM fold. GM agreed to reimburse Samuel Smith for the money he had loaned the company, but otherwise little money changed hands. In exchange for Olds stock having a par value of $2 million but a market value only half that amount, Olds stockholders received about $3 million in GM stock plus only $17,279 in cash.

Under the holding company arrangement, the Olds Motor Works continued to exist as a separate company, the only difference being that virtually all of its stock was now held by GM (six individuals, owning from 10 to 50 shares of Olds stock, had still not taken advantage of the opportunity to exchange those shares for GM stock by summer 1909). Fred Smith retained his managerial position in the company, in keeping with Durant's announced intention of retaining the existing management in the firms that GM took over. But Durant recognized that the Olds company was not the company it had been a few years before. As he told an associate, what he got was mainly a lot of Oldsmobile roadside signs. But it was the very fact that the Oldsmobile name was still so visible and well known that he was counting on to enable him to reverse the downward trend in its sales figures. By

September 1909 the Smiths were out, and new managers, more attuned to Durant's ideas, took over.

For a decade or more only limited progress was made in restoring the Olds Motor Works to the prominence that it had in the period from 1901 to 1905. At that time it had been the leading producer of cars in the low-priced field, but when GM acquired control that field had been preempted by Ford. Durant, therefore, tried to find a niche for the Oldsmobile in the higher-priced brackets, with big, powerful models selling for as much as $7,000. When slight interest was shown in such luxury-level Oldsmobiles, the emphasis was shifted to the medium-priced range. With production rising to over 22,000 by 1917, the evidence indicated that the move had been a wise one.

On August 1, 1917, the Olds Motor Works ceased to be a separate company and became an operating division of the new GM Corporation which had succeeded the earlier holding company. Ultimately, on January 1, 1942, the division's name was changed to that of the car it produced. That name was Oldsmobile, of course, although the division briefly in 1929-1930 produced a higher-priced car that was called the Viking. In the 1920s, as part of Alfred P. Sloan, Jr.'s, move to place each of GM's cars in a distinct price range, Oldsmobile was assigned a position that would, by the 1930s, rank it in terms of its price between Cadillac and Buick at the upper end and Pontiac and Chevrolet at the lower end of the scale.

Oldsmobile's status was enhanced by its emergence as an innovator. In 1937 a semiautomatic transmission was offered on 8-cylinder Oldsmobiles, and two years later the model for 1940 included the option of the first true automatic transmission. By 1941 half of the Oldsmobiles sold that year included this system, known as the Hydramatic transmission, foreshadowing the adoption of automatic transmissions on the vast majority of American cars in later years. After the war the Futuramic Olds models, introduced in 1948, included the high-compression Rocket V-8 engine that ushered in the high-performance era of the 1950s. In 1966 the division was again a pioneer with its front-wheel drive Toronado. In a little more than a decade front-wheel drive was adopted throughout the industry as part of its response to the need to build more fuel efficient cars in the face of skyrocketing gas prices. These prices were a factor in Oldsmobile's move in the late 1970s into diesel-powered cars, another of its firsts at GM. In this case, however, Oldsmobile was not a trendsetter as rising diesel prices and the lack of availability of the fuel at many stations caused most buyers to opt for the more familiar gasoline-powered cars. Nevertheless, in spite of the failure of its diesel cars, Oldsmobiles were generally the third-best-selling American cars in these later years.

References:

Nick Baldwin and others, *The World Guide to Automobile Manufacturers* (New York: Facts on File, 1987);

Beverly Rae Kimes and Richard M. Langworth, *Oldsmobile: The First Seventy-Years* (New York: Automobile Quarterly, 1972);

George S. May, *A Most Unique Machine: The Michigan Origins of the American Automobile Industry* (Grand Rapids, Mich.: Eerdmans, 1975);

May, *R. E. Olds: Auto Industry Pioneer* (Grand Rapids, Mich.: Eerdmans, 1977).

Packard Motor Car Company

by Charles K. Hyde

Wayne State University

The brothers who founded Packard Motor Car Company, James Ward Packard and William Doud Packard, were natives of Warren, Ohio, where they established the Packard Electric Company in 1890 to manufacture electric lamps. J. W. Packard, who graduated from Lehigh University in 1884 as a mechanical engineer, developed an interest in gasoline-powered automobiles in the mid 1890s but did not become involved in the fledgling industry until 1898. In that year he bought an automobile from the Winton Company of Cleveland, but the Winton machine ran so poorly that Packard decided to build his own. Using the shops of the New York & Ohio Company, a Packard Electric Company subsidiary, he completed his first car in November 1899 and drove it on the streets of Warren. In order to keep the automobile venture separate from the electric lamp business, Packard and George Weiss established a partnership on December 30, 1899.

Packard and Weiss established the Ohio Automobile Company on September 10, 1900, with a capital stock of $500,000, but with $100,000 subscribed and only $10,000 actually paid-in. The Packard brothers and George Weiss owned 98 of the 100 shares issued. Production in 1900 amounted to five 1-cylinder vehicles. The firm received valuable publicity, which boosted sales during its infancy. At the first national automobile show in New York City in November 1900 the Ohio Company sold two cars to William D. Rockefeller, while at the same time *Horseless Age* reproduced the firm's first advertising brochure verbatim, citing it as a model of business literature. Five Packards entered the New York to Buffalo endurance race in September 1901, which ended at Rochester because of President McKinley's death. All five Packards finished the race, with two among the top ten (second and fifth place) of the 89 entrants.

One Ohio Automobile Company employee achieved national notoriety in 1901 when he was ar-

Packard board chairman James Ward Packard (right) with company general manager Alvan Macauley in 1915 (courtesy of the National Automotive History Collection, Detroit Public Library)

rested after he drove a Model C Packard through the streets of Warren at 40 miles per hour. The firm also first used its trademark slogan in an advertisement in *Automobile Topics* on November 23, 1901. J. W. Packard allegedly coined the phrase more than a year earlier, when a customer asked him for literature on the Packard car. Because the firm had not yet produced any promotional materials, he could only respond, "Ask the man who owns one." The Ohio Automobile Company manufactured 160 cars in 1901 but could barely keep up with demand.

Henry Bourne Joy, a Detroit capitalist with an enormous interest in the early automobile industry, quickly became involved in the firm's affairs in late 1901. Joy and his wealthy brother-in-law, Detroiter Truman H. Newberry, attended the New York Automobile Show in November 1901 looking for investment opportunities in the fledgling industry. They had been admiring two Packard automobiles parked in front of the Adams & McMurtry Packard Agency in New York, when two men ran out to the cars, started them with ease, and drove off in pursuit of a fire engine. Joy was so impressed by this performance that he bought a Packard and decided to invest in the firm that made it. He bought 250 shares of stock for $25,000 in December 1901 and in January 1902 began to correspond with J. W. Packard, and he finally visited Packard at the Ohio plant in July 1902. Joy learned that the firm was strapped for capital and offered to raise at least $250,000 in new investments, and possibly more if Packard would relocate his factory in Detroit. J. W. Packard agreed, and Joy returned to Detroit to launch a new chapter in the firm's history.

On October 2, 1902, the directors of the Ohio Automobile Company incorporated as the Packard Motor Car Company in the state of West Virginia and agreed to move manufacturing operations to Detroit. By the end of October Henry B. Joy had sold $250,000 in Packard stock to fellow Detroit capitalists, giving them a majority of the $400,000 in outstanding shares. Russell and Fred Alger invested a total of $75,000, Henry Joy and his brother Richard took another $50,000 in stock, Truman and John Newberry took a similar amount, Phillip Macmillan also invested $50,000, and three others took the rest.

J. W. Packard became president of the new firm and Joy the general manager in October 1902, but Joy quickly dominated the company's affairs, simply because the Detroit stockholders authorized him to represent their majority interests. Most of the major stockholders from the Ohio Automobile Company, including George Weiss and William A. Hatcher, withdrew from the new firm by January 1903. By that time Joy was already offering strongly worded, detailed suggestions to J. W. Pack-

ard regarding personnel, product design, and promotional strategies. Joy insisted that Packard name as company engineer Charles Schmidt, who had designed automobiles in France for eight years, and grant Sidney D. Waldon broad authority over advertising and dealerships.

J. W. Packard's relationship with the Detroit investors deteriorated and reached a crisis in July 1903, after Truman Newberry had sent Packard an ill-tempered letter criticizing the design of the Model K Packard automobile. Packard decided to withdraw from the firm that bore his name but changed his mind after Joy sent Russell Alger, Jr., to Warren to pacify him. Alger succeeded and J. W. Packard remained the titular head of the Packard Motor Car Company until 1909.

Joy almost single-handedly planned the erection of a new plant in Detroit and the relocation of the Ohio operations to Michigan. In May 1903 Joy directed the purchase of 66 acres of land in Detroit, at a cost of about $20,000, for a new plant site. He selected the Detroit architect Albert Kahn to design Packard's manufacturing complex and thus provided Kahn with his first automobile factory project. Once Joy approved the plans for the buildings in July, construction took only three months but cost $117,000, an enormous investment at that time. When the firm moved its machinery and workers from Warren to Detroit in October 1903, J. W. Packard remained in his hometown to manage his electrical goods factory.

The move to Detroit left Joy firmly in control of Packard. One of his first goals was to produce 1,000 cars at a profit of $1,000 per car. During the initial fiscal year in Detroit (1903-1904), Packard produced only 192 cars with a labor force of about 250 men and had losses of $200,000, but the next year production of 481 cars yielded profits of $216,000. Packard first achieved Joy's goals in fiscal year 1906-1907, when the firm manufactured 1,188 cars carrying price tags ranging from $4,000 to $5,325 and earning profits of $1,386,000.

Automobile production climbed steadily to 3,106 units in calendar year 1909, then fluctuated between roughly 2,500 and 3,000 units from 1910 to 1915. In parallel fashion the Detroit manufacturing plant grew from its initial size of about 100,000 square feet to 600,000 square feet by June 1907. Joy informed his board of directors in August 1911 that Packard employed 7,575 men in a factory complex of 1.6 million square feet. The labor force

Packard in his custom-built 1902 Packard Model F (courtesy of Terry Martin)

then climbed to around 13,000 by 1916 and remained at about that level until 1929.

Joy was not only an excellent manager of finance and production but was also a gifted promoter of the Packard automobile. With Joy's full support a Model F Packard began a cross-country trip from San Francisco to New York City on June 20, 1903. The Packard, dubbed "Old Pacific," arrived in New York City on August 21, 1903, and was the first automobile to achieve that feat, travelling 5,600 miles in two months. One of Packard's employees drove "Old Pacific," but Marius Krarup, editor of the *Automobile,* accompanied him and wrote daily reports for his magazine and for several newspapers. Packard received substantial free publicity as a result. Joy also agreed to build a Packard race car, the "Grey Wolfe," in July 1903, and it created outstanding publicity for the firm by breaking several world speed records in 1903 and 1904. Joy was also willing and able to exploit his own social position to promote Packard. He arranged for a photograph of himself with Charles M. Schwab, president of United States Steel, in Schwab's Packard.

The Packard Motor Car Company enjoyed more than two decades of nearly uninterrupted growth and prosperity, beginning with the move to

Detroit in October 1903. By the end of 1903 the paid-in capital stock was increased from $400,000 to $650,000 to pay for expansion, and by January 1907 it stood at $1 million. The Packard Motor Car Company was reorganized on August 31, 1909, as a Michigan corporation, with capital stock of $10 million. Joy was elected president at that time, and J. W. Packard became chairman of the board of directors. The firm's capitalization increased to $16 million in 1913, to $20 million in 1916, and in 1929 stood at $50 million.

Packard's early automobiles were all 1-cylinder designs, but Charles Schmidt's first product, the Model K, had a 4-cylinder engine located in front of the passenger compartment under a hood, one of the first American automobiles to use that design. Two 4-cylinder models, the "24" and the "30," named after their horsepower ratings, were Packard's mainstay between 1905 and late 1911, when the firm introduced the "48," a 6-cylinder machine. The 48, available in more than a dozen body styles, was Packard's most popular car through 1915.

Packard introduced the Twin Six model in 1915. It featured the revolutionary V-12 engine designed by Jesse Vincent, who had moved from the

Burroughs Adding Machine Company to Packard with Alvan Macauley. The firm offered the Twin Six Packard in 22 separate body styles, and it was Packard's chief product for six years. In 1916, the first full year of production, Packard manufactured 10,645 Twin Sixes, quadrupling the output level of 1915. The Twin Six was adapted to racing and on August 24, 1918, established a new speed record of 117.11 miles per hour at Sheepshead Bay, Long Island. By the end of Joy's tenure at Packard the firm's product philosophy was well established. Packard changed its products reluctantly and gradually, usually producing its models for five or six years, with only minor alterations. The Packard automobile could be purchased in a wide variety of body styles, using the same chassis, but over time Packards grew larger, had more powerful engines, and became more expensive.

The Twin Six motor, after a series of design mutations, became the Liberty motor, the power plant for thousands of Allied military aircraft in World War I. Under Joy's direction Packard engineers modified the original Twin Six motor in early 1916 to serve as an aircraft engine. The resulting Packard 299 (the displacement, in cubic inches) was not powerful enough, so by the end of 1916 the firm designed a new V-12 engine, the Packard 905. Between April and July 1917 engineers from Packard, several aircraft manufacturers, and the U.S. government greatly modified the Packard 905 to produce a hybrid engine, the Liberty motor. Six firms agreed to produce 22,000 Liberty engines, and Packard eventually manufactured 6,000. The four largest producers, Packard, Lincoln, Ford, and Cadillac, accounted for 90 percent of the total.

The Packard Motor Car Company was also a significant truck manufacturer from 1908 until 1923. The firm produced 50 light delivery trucks in 1904-1905, but these were really automobile chassis with a truck body. Packard introduced an entirely new vehicle in 1908, with a 144-inch wheelbase and a 3-ton capacity and manufactured 548 of them from 1908 to 1910. The firm followed with a 1.5-ton truck in 1911 and a 5-ton model in 1912, with combined sales in 1911-1912 of nearly 2,000 vehicles. In 1915, when Packard offered a variety of models ranging in capacity from 1 to 6 tons, truck output reached 4,000 units, compared to 2,645 passenger cars.

The U.S. War Department ordered trucks from Packard for the campaign against Pancho Villa in March 1917, and the solid performance of Packard trucks brought substantial orders from Allied and American governments alike. Packard was easily the largest single producer of trucks for the Allied war effort. Packard truck production reached 7,116 in 1917 and fluctuated between 6,000 and 7,000 from 1918 to 1920. Even during the peak years Packard never accounted for more than 6 percent of American truck production. Packard's output fell to only 1,331 trucks in 1921, the worst year of the postwar depression, and recovered to 2,145 vehicles in 1922. The firm decided to give up truck manufacturing in 1923, in part because of growing competition from specialized companies such as Mack, White, and International.

Joy resigned from the Packard board of directors in 1917 and sold his stock in the firm, reportedly as a result of disagreements with other board members over the issue of potential mergers with other firms, which Joy favored. He had officially served as president from 1909 through 1916 but in fact had run the firm since 1903. Joy hired James Alvan Macauley as general manager in 1910, and Macauley became the president of the firm in 1916. Macauley had studied engineering at Lehigh and law at George Washington University, began working as a patent attorney, but entered the field of industrial management when he took a position with the National Cash Register Company. He joined the American Arithmometer Company in St. Louis in 1899 and remained with the firm when it became the Burroughs Adding Machine Company and moved to Detroit in 1904. Joseph Boyer, president of Burroughs and a Packard stockholder, introduced Macauley to Joy.

Macauley left his imprint on the middle stage of Packard's corporate life, much as Joy had done for the early years. Macauley served as president from 1916 until 1939 but remained as chairman of the board of directors through 1948. Packard's production methods changed considerably under Macauley. Through the end of World War I Packard manufactured virtually all the parts and components used in its vehicles and assembled its products individually, by hand. In 1919-1920 the firm adopted the typical assembly line methods used in the rest of the industry. Packard continued to cast its own engines but increasingly bought parts, including frames, bodies, bearings, and wheels, from other manufacturers. Macauley recognized that increased reliance on outside suppliers

The 1915 Packard Model 3-38 (courtesy of the National Automotive History Collection, Detroit Public Library)

might impair quality, so he established a quality engineering department in 1923 to institute rigid quality control. The Packard Proving Grounds, opened in June 1928 near Utica, Michigan, was another of Macauley's efforts.

Packard enjoyed great success in the 1920s in terms of production, popularity, and profits. Automobile output in 1920 was about 6,200 units but increased to over 15,000 in 1922, 32,000 in 1925, and then climbed to about 50,000 cars in both 1928 and 1929. The firm introduced its first 8-cylinder car in 1923, replacing the Twin Six, and for the rest of the 1920s Packard produced a 6-cylinder automobile along with the 8-cylinder but introduced no new models. Early in the decade Packard enjoyed profits ranging from $6.4 to $11.1 million but then earned almost $22 million in 1928 and $26 million in 1929.

The positive public perception of Packard and its products probably peaked in this prosperous period. In a statement Macauley prepared for Packard employees around 1925, he observed, "There is an iron tyranny which compels men who do good work to go on doing good work. The name of that beneficent tyranny is reputation." On the eve of the Great Depression Macauley discussed the importance of stability for the Packard Motor Car Company. He argued that the firm's success had been the result of stability of its workers, management, and dealers, as well as the stable appearance of the Packard automobile.

Packard suffered through the early years of the Great Depression along with the other car manufacturers. Production dropped sharply to about 13,000 cars in 1931, then skidded even further to 6,000 units in 1934. The firm suffered multi-million-dollar losses in 1931, 1932, and 1934 but enjoyed a small profit of about $500,000 in 1933. At the urging of Packard's production manager, George T. Christopher, the firm decided in 1934 to enter the medium-priced car market, largely because of the loss of much of the luxury market to Cadillac.

Packard introduced a 6-cylinder model in 1936 and enjoyed a substantial revival from 1935 until the start of World War II. Production climbed to 81,000 cars in 1936, reached nearly 110,000 the next year, and after a sharp decline in 1938 rebounded to about 77,000 units in both 1939 and 1940. Christopher drastically reorganized production and achieved large cost savings as a result. Packard's labor force, about 4,500 in June 1934, jumped to 16,600 in June 1937, but output grew much more rapidly in the interim. To the surprise of company management, a majority of Packard workers joined the United Automobile Workers union in 1937.

World War II brought new management as well as new products to Packard. Max Gilman replaced Macauley as president in 1939, and he served until April 1942, when he resigned for reasons of health. George Christopher, whom Gilman had hired out of retirement from General Motors (GM) in 1934, became president and held the post until 1949. In the late 1930s, under Christopher's direction, Packard became a mass producer of medium-priced cars.

Well before American entry into the war Packard was heavily committed to war work. In October 1940 the firm agreed to manufacture 9,000 Merlin aircraft engines, designed by Rolls-Royce, with two-thirds destined for Great Britain and the rest for the U.S. government. A year later Packard committed more than 1 million square feet of space and about 10,000 production workers to this work. By the end of the war Packard manufactured nearly 56,000 Merlin engines as well as military marine engines used in PT boats and other applications. Production of more than 12,000 marine engines, together with aircraft engines, comprised virtually all of Packard's war work. Automobile production, drastically curtailed in late 1941, ceased altogether in February 1942.

Packard had greater difficulties than many other car manufacturers in reconverting to civilian production. In 1941 Packard agreed to stop making bodies and to buy them exclusively from the Briggs Manufacturing Company. In late 1945 and early 1946 strikes and other problems at Briggs resulted in costly shutdowns at Packard. The postwar steel shortages hit smaller firms much harder than the Big Three. Packard managed to produce only 2,722 cars in 1945, but then a respectable 42,000 the next year. The company was not able to regain production levels of 100,000 units until 1948 and 1949. Packard's innovative Clipper models of 1942, after a four-year hiatus, were the firm's only offerings until 1948.

The Packard Motor Car Company continued to introduce innovations in its automobiles in the early 1950s, following a tradition from the firm's early years. Packard cars were the first to have a steering wheel instead of a tiller and the first to use the H-gear shift configuration that became standard in the industry. Other Packard innovations included forced-feed lubrication (1913), the straight-8 engine (1923), air conditioning (1939), power windows and seats (1947), and the use of tubeless tires as a standard feature (1954). But in the postwar years, styling seemed more important to consumers than design or even comfort.

Packard never regained the position it had held in the automobile industry through the 1930s. By the early 1950s, when the postwar "seller's market" had finally disappeared, the remaining "independents" in the industry were severely handicapped by their relatively low volume of production and high costs. Ford and GM engaged in a brief price war in 1954 and 1955, further eroding Packard's market position. The combined sales of all of Packard's 1954 models was a disastrous 32,000 units. After Chrysler purchased Briggs in late 1953, the new owner informed Packard that it would no longer supply them with bodies. James J. Nance, Packard's president from 1952 until July 1956, compounded these problems by making several crucial blunders from 1954 on.

In April 1954 several New York City investment bankers suggested a merger of Packard and the Studebaker Corporation. At Nance's urging, Packard purchased Studebaker on October 1, 1954, and formed the Studebaker-Packard Corporation, a failing enterprise almost from the start. Once the merger was consummated, Packard's experts concluded that the break-even point for Studebaker was nearly double its 1954 output. The Studebaker plant in South Bend, Indiana, was grotesquely inefficient, with labor costs that were twice the industry average. In addition, Studebaker-Packard lost virtually all of its defense contracts in 1954, in part because of new policies initiated by Charles Wilson, the secretary of defense and a former GM executive.

The new firm suffered huge losses and faced severe cash-flow problems in 1955 and 1956. A 36-day strike at the South Bend Plant in early 1955 added to the troubles. The firm lost nearly $30 million in 1955 but in 1956 suffered losses of $103 million on sales of only $303 million. Sales in 1956

Packard Motor Car Company's first automobile, the 1899 Model A (courtesy of the National Automotive History Collection, Detroit Public Library)

amounted to 82,000 units, only a third of the estimated break-even sales level. Nance decided to
solve Packard's body supply problems by leasing an
old Briggs plant in Detroit and building an entirely
new assembly line there, a costly decision that only
worsened the firm's cash-flow crisis in early 1956.
The end for Packard came in June 1956, when
Nance suspended manufacturing operations in Detroit in favor of the South Bend plant. Although the
firm produced a few automobiles bearing the Packard nameplate in the South Bend plant until 1958,
the closing of the Detroit plant marked the demise
of this proud, distinguished manufacturer of luxury
automobiles.

References:

Michael Aiken, Louis A. Ferman, and Harold L.
   Sheppard, *Economic Failure, Alienation, and Extrem-
   ism* (Ann Arbor: University of Michigan Press,
   1968);

Eugene Ballou, *Facts About the "Silent Knight" Motor*
   (Toledo, Ohio: Toledo Legal News, 1913);

Nathaniel T. Dawes, *The Packard: 1942-1962* (South
   Brunswick, N.J.: Barnes, 1975);

Phillip S. Dickey III, *The Liberty Engine, 1918-1942*
   (Washington, D.C.: Smithsonian Institution, 1968);

Arthur N. Einstein, "The Advertising of the Packard
   Motor Car Company, 1899-1956," Thesis, Michigan
   State University, 1959;

Gwilyn G. Griffiths, *Packard: Advertising Highlights,
   1900-1956* (Timonium, Md., 1973);

Morton Jaffe, *Alvan Macauley: Auto Industry Leader
   and Pioneer* (Detroit: Privately printed, 1957);

Beverly Rae Kimes, ed., *Packard: The History of the
   Motor Car and the Company* (New York: Dutton,
   1978);

Richard M. Langworth, *Studebaker: The Postwar Years*
   (Osceola, Wis.: Motorbooks International, 1979);

Alvan Macauley, *Reputation* (Detroit: Packard Motor
   Car Company, n.d.);

Macauley, *Stability: An Informal Statement From the President of the Packard Motor Car Company* (Detroit:
   Packard Motor Car Company, n.d.);

"Packard: Golden Anniversary, 1899-1949," *Detroit
   Times*, November 6, 1949;

John Parker, "A History of the Packard Motor Car Company from 1899 to 1929," Thesis, Wayne State University, 1948;

Otto A. Schroeder, *Packard: Ask the Man Who Owns
   One* (Arcadia, Cal.: Post-Era, 1974);

Michael G. H. Scott, *Packard: The Complete Story* (Blue
   Ridge Summit, Pa.: Tab, 1985);

Robert E. Turnquist, *The Packard Story: The Car and the
   Company* (New York: Barnes, 1965).

Archives:

The major source is the massive Packard Motor Car
Company Papers at the Studebaker Archives, Studebaker
National Museum in South Bend, Indiana. In addition,
the Burton Historical Collections and the National Automotive History Collections, both located at the Detroit
Public Library, have miscellaneous materials, including annual reports, advertising literature, and photographs of
Packard automobiles and the Detroit factory. The archives of Albert Kahn Associates, Architects and Engineers, also has materials on the Packard manufacturing
plant.

Patent Cross-License Agreement

by James Wren

Motor Vehicle Manufacturers Association

The Patent Cross-License Agreement among members of the National Automobile Chamber of Commerce (NACC) was finalized on January 1, 1915. By that single act the automotive industry became stable in regard to patent lawsuits and could devote its time and energy solely to making and selling vehicles.

The Selden internal combustion engine patent had been held "valid but not infringed" by the U.S. Court of Appeals in 1911, but the specter of patent litigation remained. When patents were contested, the lengthy process of settlement by negotiation slowed planning and production. Through the auspices of the NACC Patents Committee, Howard E. Coffin, vice-president of Hudson Motor Car Company, and C. C. Hanch of Marmon (chairman of the committee) conceived of the idea of exchanging patents so that every chamber member had access to the ideas of the others. By that means manufacturers would be able to proceed without legal concerns. The overwhelming majority of NACC members approved the plan. Even the smallest company admitted to NACC membership had free access to the hundreds of patents under the NACC banner.

Many business historians cite the Cross-License Agreement as a main reason for the rapid expansion of the automotive industry after 1915. In turn, automotive expansion stimulated steel making, road construction, and the rubber and petroleum industries.

The initial patent agreement covered a period of ten years. In 1925 it was extended for a period of five years, with respect only to patents that were in the original agreement. New patents were excluded in a ten-year extension in 1930 and in a subsequent extension, approved in 1940. Patents of subsidiaries of the member companies were excluded from the Cross-License Agreement. It was also agreed that design patents would not be included in the original pool. Later, patents on trucks and special vehicles such as ambulances and taxis were also excluded. In 1956 auto manufacturers decided to drop the Cross-License Agreement, stating that it had outlived its usefulness. The agreement was quietly discontinued in 1957.

References:

George E. Folk, *Patents and Industrial Progress* (New York: Harper, 1944);

William Greenleaf, *Monopoly on Wheels: Henry Ford and the Selden Automobile Patent* (Detroit: Wayne State University Press, 1961).

Peerless Motor Car Company

by Beverly Rae Kimes

New York, New York

"All That the Name Implies" was the inspired slogan for the Peerless, but scarcely peerless at times was the management of this respected automobile company in Cleveland, Ohio. Had the quality of the product been matched in the front office, the marque may have survived longer than three decades.

The Peerless Company was founded in Cincinnati in 1869 for the manufacture of clothes wringers. The move to Cleveland followed in the mid 1880s, by which time the product was exported worldwide. With profits accrued, the company launched into cycle manufacture in 1891. That venture was profitable as well—until the turn of the century when the bicycle boom went bust.

Like many former cycle builders, Peerless elected to try the automobile next. Lacking technical expertise, the firm negotiated a license with the pioneering French firm of DeDion-Bouton to manufacture its Motorette in the United States and then advertised for an engineer to adapt the car for American roads. Answering the ad was Louis P. Mooers of Watertown, Massachusetts, who had already built an automobile but had been unable to secure the financing for manufacture.

Mooers and Peerless were made for each other. Arriving in Cleveland in 1900, the engineer began Americanizing the DeDion but quickly concluded that the design left no room for development, and that the American market would be best served by a car built specifically for American conditions. (European roads were vastly superior to those in the United States at the time.) By the spring of 1901 Mooers was designing a brand-new car. By 1902 the Peerless Motorette was being phased out of production and the Mooers Peerless phased in. Ninety cars were built that year, and the firm name was changed to Peerless Motor Car Company.

The product was exemplary and innovative. It featured a front-mounted engine, shaft drive, and a bevel-geared full-floating live rear axle. The 4-cylinder Peerless introduced in January 1904 had a pressed-steel channel frame, a forward-tilting steering wheel, and side-entrance tonneau and limousine models. Pace setting, too, was the Peerless assault in European motor sport. Few American companies crossed the Atlantic to race in those days, and after Mooers crashed his Peerless in the 1903 Gordon Bennett Cup in Ireland, the Cleveland firm decided to follow the decision of the majority.

Racing continued at home, however, and aggressively. Mooers designed a gargantuan racer called the Green Dragon, which the already legendary Barney Oldfield was hired to drive. The result was a splurge of speed records and headlines from coast to coast. Oldfield made the Peerless name famous, but his off-track carousing embarrassed Peerless management. Already the company was becoming renowned as one of the "Three P's"—and neither of the other two (Packard or Pierce-Arrow) indulged in raucous motor sport. Luxury cars and the Oldfield image were incompatible, so Barney was sent packing. Following him out of Peerless was Mooers, who joined the Moon Company in St. Louis. Taking Mooers's place in 1905 was Charles B. Schmidt, who was hired away from Packard. Taking the Peerless presidency was Lewis H. Kittredge, an 11-year veteran of the firm who had worked his way up through management ranks. That year Peerless built 1,176 cars, approximately 500 fewer than Pierce-Arrow or Packard.

Kittredge, who would also serve as president of the National Association of Automobile Manufacturers in 1910, was widely respected throughout the industry. But he did not have an easy time of it at Peerless. The company was early to market with a 6-cylinder car in 1907 and quickly followed Cadillac with a V-8 for the 1916 model year. Advanced en-

Barney Oldfield in the Peerless Green Dragon race car, 1903 or 1904 (courtesy of General Motors Corporation)

gineering features were the norm at Peerless. But so were upheavals within the company. In 1913, its capital stock at $4.2 million, Peerless came under the control of the National Electric Company. In 1915 New York financier Harrison Williams led another consortium into Peerless control. General Electric (GE) was purportedly behind that takeover, which involved a capitalization of $20 million. Three years later GE eased itself out, however, and the Cleveland old guard—led by B. G. Tremaine and F. S. Terry—bought back control. Employment stood at 4,000. Net income of $670,628 in 1919 rose to $1.1 million in 1920. The company surplus was $5.6 million and assets nearly $14 million. Six thousand cars were produced that year.

During the depression year of 1921, however, production fell to 3,500 units, and Tremaine and associates decided to ease themselves out of the rigors of the car business. Easing himself in that October was R. H. Collins. Kittredge, who had survived the previous Peerless upheavals, did not survive this one. Neither did William R. Strickland, who had become chief engineer shortly after the French-born Schmidt returned to his native land during World

War I and who now joined Cadillac. Meanwhile, former Cadillac people moved into Peerless, among them a quartet of engineers led by Benjamin H. Anibal and known in Cleveland as the "Four Horsemen." ("They rode in over the top of us," a Peerless engineer of the period would recall.) Collins had formerly been president and general manager of Cadillac, and as Peerless majordomo he brought some of his old Cadillac marketing and sales colleagues with him. A good many Peerless people in Cleveland found themselves without jobs.

Peerless production rose from 4,240 cars in 1922 to 5,700 in 1923. By the end of the latter year the Collins team had left, however. Part of Cleveland's attraction to the former Cadillac president's overtures had been his promise to develop a medium-priced 6-cylinder car for Peerless. Indeed, Collins and his Four Horsemen had independently developed a prototype during the short period between the Cadillac and Peerless regimes. Aware that both Packard and Pierce-Arrow were in development on less pricey models, Cleveland regarded the 6-cylinder as vital to future profits. But the Collins and company 6-cylinder never made it to production.

Taking over the Peerless helm was Edward Ver Linden, former Oldsmobile president; Fred Slack, a Peerless veteran of 15 years, was the new chief engineer. The new Peerless 6-cylinder (which borrowed liberally from the Collins prototype) was introduced in 1925. It sold in the $1,500 range, considerably lower than the prestigious V-8's $4,000 price tag. Advertisements claimed, "Now There's a Peerless for Everyone."

But the Peerless revolving management door revolved once again in 1928. Ver Linden left for Jordan, vice-president Leon R. German took over, and numerous other top-level executive chairs were occupied by new bodies. About the same time the announcement came that control of Peerless had been acquired in a transaction involving some $3.5 million in stock by a Detroit group led by Alfred A. Wallace. That announcement was followed within months by another: German was out; James A. Bohannon was in.

Formerly the vice-president of Marmon, Bohannon seemed the answer to Peerless's prayers. Both dreamer and pragmatist, he inaugurated a five-year prosperity program in 1929. Old inventory was cleared, mortgage and bank loans were paid off, overhead was reduced by $1 million, and plants were modernized. For the 1930 model year the Peerless line was straight-8 across the board—and, if technically lackluster, the new cars were a styling tour de force, courtesy of Count Alexis de Sakhnoffsky, the brilliant Russian-born émigré hired for the job. Then the stock market crashed.

Unaware of the repercussions to follow (as were most), Bohannon announced further expansion in May 1930 via a 100 percent increase in common stock, which put $1 million immediately at Bohannon's disposal. Eastern capitalists and the wealthy Van Schweringen family of Cleveland were demonstrably behind the president. Peerless sales

from 1926 through 1930 were 10,164; 9,872; 7,748; 8,318; and 4,021. The decreasing figures indicated the turmoil within Peerless during the middle 1920s; the slight increase in 1929 coincided with the Bohannon arrival; 1930 was bad, but the entire industry suffered that year, and Peerless did not fare as badly as most.

In the wings was the grandest Peerless of all, a car Bohannon was sure would put the company at the top of the luxury car ladder. It boasted 16 cylinders, 464 cubic inches, 173 horsepower, styling by the Walter M. Murphy Company, and aluminum virtually throughout the construction (Peerless had collaborated with the Cleveland-based Alcoa aluminum firm).

On June 30, 1931, the last Peerless to be delivered to a customer left the Cleveland assembly line. The next year the fabulous V-16 Peerless was tested at more than 100 mph at Muroc Dry Lake. But it would never be marketed. Bohannon's dream gave way to pragmatism. With the Depression deepening, the introduction of a no-compromise luxury car made no sense. Neither did continuing automobile manufacture at all. Only the automotive giants could survive the bad times, Bohannon reluctantly concluded; the independents had no chance. Now the question was what to do with the vast Cleveland plant.

On June 30, 1934, the Peerless Motor Car Company was succeeded by Peerless Corporation, brewers of Carlings ale. "It was a long jump from motors to malt and from hub caps to hops," Bohannon later reminisced. But the leap made sense with the repeal of Prohibition—and its wisdom has since been proven by history.

References:

Maurice D. Hendry, " 'All That the Name Implies': The Peerless Story," *Automobile Quarterly*, 9 (First Quarter 1973): 78-101;

Richard Wager, *Golden Wheels* (Cleveland, Ohio: Western Reserve Historical Society, 1975).

Edward Joel Pennington

(1858-March 5, 1911)

by Genevieve Wren

Motor Vehicle Research Services

CAREER: Apprentice pattern maker, J. A. Fay Company (1871-1879); treasurer, Industrial Factory & Company (1880-1883); founder, Standard Machine Works (1885); founder, Standard Manufacturing Company (1887); president, Pennington Pulley Works (1887-1888); vice-president, Pennington Machine Works (1887-1888); founder, Mt. Carmel Machine and Pulley Works (1890); founder, Mt. Carmel Aerial Navigation Company (1890); founder, Aerial Mail Express and Construction Company (1893); partner, Kane-Pennington Company (1895-1900); partner, Anglo-American Automobile Syndicate (1899); partner, Pennington and Baines, Ltd. (1902).

Edward Joel Pennington was a flamboyant, colorful hustler and confidence man with grandiose but shady plans for building huge manufacturing complexes during the formative years of the automobile industry. He promoted gargantuan schemes for the imaginary production of monorails, airships, fire engines, military vehicles, freight elevators, machine-powered pulleys, and other inventions—none of which was sufficiently perfected to materialize. Yet he operated in dozens of states and even in Great Britain, seizing millions of dollars in funds from gullible investors. Pennington's style was to breeze into a town radiating a display of pseudo-wealth before bankers' and businessmen's clubs. An impressive (but for the most part financially useless) array of patents—each an officially certified parchment document complete with wax seal and ribbons—bolstered his expertise in the eyes of those about to be taken. A name-dropping session—Rockefeller, Carnegie, Morgan, du Pont—usually finished the job. Plus, Pennington placed great emphasis on fine clothes and flashy jewelry, fine appointments and hotels, and all the other accoutrements of wealth.

Tracing Pennington's history is far from easy. He avoided close scrutiny and traveled constantly. The chronology of the companies he started and lost—many with six-figure capitalizations—and the patents he acquired from 1880 to the 1910s has yet to be established. Patents were easier to obtain at the turn of the century than they are today. Paradoxically, much of Pennington's work exhibits evidence of genius. Had he truly desired to live an honest life, he probably would have been more successful.

Pennington was born in the village of Milan in Ripley County, Indiana, in 1858, the fourth of five children of Joel and Catherine Dorsch Pennington. His father was a blacksmith, sawmill proprietor, and itinerant Baptist preacher. Pennington attended the village school in his hometown and spent his spare hours getting into trouble, to the despair of parents and teachers. At thirteen he was packed off to school to prepare for the ministry. Soon he changed his mind and turned in his books. He bummed his way to Cincinnati and found work as an apprentice pattern maker with the J. A. Fay Company, makers of woodworking machinery. He stayed eight years at Fay, favorably impressing his employer, who predicted "a brilliant future in the technical field" for him.

In 1880 Pennington applied for a patent (granted July 12, 1881) for a reciprocating cylinder head for planing machines. The invention helped lessen the tendency of the planing blades to nick, improving the quality of machined boards. Later in the year he married Mary Butler. Little is known of his activities in the following few years after he left the Fay company. He certainly continued his developmental work. It is suspected that he engaged in con artistry at least part of the time, for he next turned up in Fort Wayne, Indiana, in 1887, supposedly loaded with $3 million and looking for a factory site on choice land. City officials and bankers were impressed by his patent credits and willing to wait

A Pennington tandem motorcycle featuring the inventor's supposedly unpuncturable balloon tires, for which he received a patent in 1894 (courtesy of the Montague Motor Museum, Beaulieu, England)

for Pennington's cash. They even advanced him $20,000 to tide him over until his money came from New York, money they never saw again. He was making other deals at the time. The state of Indiana chartered several Pennington corporations that same year, including Pennington Machine Works and Pennington Pulley Works, capitalized at $50,000 apiece. The two businesses existed for one year only and disappeared as mysteriously as they appeared. The Elevator Machine Company, capitalized at $100,000, sprouted in Fort Wayne, and two million-dollar companies also made appearances: one making freight elevators in Oswego, Kansas, the other making wooden pulleys in Cincinnati.

In 1889 Pennington jumped to Edinburg, Indiana, where he fleeced the townspeople to the tune of $50,000 in another pulley-factory scheme. From 1890 to 1892 he headquartered in Mount Carmel, Illinois, where he set up the Mt. Carmel Aerial Navigation Company, capitalization $250,000, and the old standbys the machine and pulley works, this time combined in the Mt. Carmel Machine and Pulley

Works and capitalized at $100,000. In 1890 he hinted to the newspapers that he was readying an airship to fly from Mount Carmel to New York City; in January 1891 he exhibited the airship at the Old Exposition Building in Chicago. The display model turned out to be a varnished-silk tube, about 30 feet long and 6 feet in diameter, filled with hydrogen. An electric-motor-driven propeller lifted the ship about 40 feet, but the batteries for the motor remained on the ground, connected by cable. Skeptics were getting wise: *Engineering News* headlined the event "The Latest Aerial Humbug." The unsophisticated public was entranced.

In 1893 Pennington promoted another grandiose plan, but this one never got off the ground. Under the name Chicago and Central Indiana Electric Railway he proposed to construct a 150-mile monorail track equipped with cars outfitted like hotel rooms. Meanwhile he was becoming involved in the automotive industry. In March 1893 he applied for the first of his many automotive patents, for two versions of a motor-powered bicycle, which

Pennington 3-wheeled "Torpedo," 1896

he planned to manufacture under the auspices of the Motor Cycle Company of Cleveland—another scam.

In the summer of 1894 Pennington talked C. B. Hitchcock, president of a leading New York producer of wagons, buggies, and bicycles, into forming a partnership to produce a line of Pennington-designed motorcycles and four-wheel vehicles. The prototype was unable to run for more than a block without overheating. Pennington left town, and Hitchcock went into receivership. In the fall of that same year Pennington applied for a patent for oversized pneumatic balloon tires, which he called "unpuncturable," designed for two-wheeled vehicles. The tires were far from unpuncturable, but the patent is often cited as evidence that Pennington was the first to invent a balloon tire. Pneumatic tires would end up providing one of the most crucial links in the modern automotive chain.

Finally in 1894, when industrialist Thomas Kane offered Pennington development money, Pennington moved to Wisconsin to organize the Racine Motor Vehicle Company. Kane had profitably manufactured gasoline engines and even school and church furniture, and he was anxious to break into the new business. Pennington was provided with engineering and manufacturing facilities on a scale he had previously only imagined. But old habits died hard. In 1895 he produced an "igniter for explosive engines" based on his "long-mingling spark ignition

system," which supposedly did away with the need for a carburetor and even for highly refined gasoline. He liked to show a model of the device that ran on mere bits of candlewax. A few of the engines were placed in Pennington cars, but none ran very far, and they all overheated. A patent for the invention issued in 1897 was taken out in Kane's name.

Pennington promised faithfully to build four entries for the *Chicago Times-Herald* automobile race to be held in July 1895. Even though the race was delayed until nearly winter, he could not field a car. He was in England when the race was finally run. There he met Harry J. Lawson and convinced him to put up about $500,000 for another abortive automobile venture. He continued in the same pattern just as he had in America. By 1900 he faced several British suits. He declared bankruptcy and in 1901 went into receivership. In 1903 his and his second wife's clothing was put up for sale to pay hotel debts. Pennington drops out of the historical record at this point. He died on March 5, 1911, in a Springfield, Massachusetts, hospital.

Reference:

Robert F. Scott, "The Elusive Mr. Pennington: A Study of Inventive Genius and Gyp Artistry," *Automobile Quarterly*, 5 (Spring 1967): 362-373.

Pierce-Arrow Motor Car Company

by Beverly Rae Kimes

New York, New York

"Birdcages to Bankruptcy" was the headline *Time* magazine used in 1938 to announce the death of the Pierce-Arrow Motor Car Company. Alliterative and accurate, yes; witty, perhaps—but that trio of words deftly ignored what Pierce-Arrow had represented in the automobile industry for more than three decades. It was among the proudest and most prestigious marques in America.

Humble beginnings have not been unusual in American automotive history. Arch-rival Peerless commenced business in Cleveland, Ohio, with the manufacture of clothes wringers in 1869, just about the same time the firm of Heintz, Pierce and Munschauer began producing household products, including bird cages, in Buffalo, New York. In 1872 the middle partner bought out his associates' interests and reorganized as the George N. Pierce Company.

By the mid 1890s bicycles had joined bird cages in the product lines, and Charles Clifton joined the company as treasurer. Clifton began investigating the possibility of Pierce entering the automobile field. The first experimental car—a steamer completed during the summer of 1900—was a dismal failure. Then Clifton traveled to Europe to check out the state of the automotive art there and returned to Buffalo recommending utilization of the French DeDion gasoline engine.

Parallels to the early Peerless experience were striking, but while the Cleveland manufacturer elected to build the DeDion-Bouton Motorette under license, Pierce chose to purchase the engine and design a Motorette-like car in Buffalo. This was partly because of the entrance of David Fergusson onto the scene. English-born, Fergusson had enjoyed extensive experience in locomotive and stationary engine design prior to his arrival in America in 1899. Edward Joel Pennington had been responsible for Fergusson's emigration, though, thankfully for the engineer, Fergusson did not re-

Commemorative Pierce-Arrow advertisement, 1912

main with the promoter long, joining the E. C. Stearns Company in Syracuse instead. There he was dismayed by Stearns's reluctance to disavow its steam car for the gasoline version he had designed. Learning of Pierce's dismay with steam power altogether, Fergusson made a trip to Buffalo, drawings in hand—and Pierce had its chief engineer for the next two decades.

By the spring of 1901 the first two Fergusson-designed, DeDion-engined Pierce Motorettes were on the road. Testing the cars and introducing them to Pierce bicycle agents throughout the country followed. Manufacture began late that year; by the end of 1902 sales totaled 150 cars. Pierce would remain with its Motorette a bit longer than Peerless. Chiefly that was because the car's success in reliability trials of the period—including the Automobile Club of America's New York-Boston-New York run of 1903—was doing a fine job of introducing Pierce to the automobile-buying public. Sales remained commendable.

Meanwhile Fergusson was designing new models different from the primitive Motorette. One such 2-cylinder model was designated the Arrow. Its success prompted development of a model with twice the cylinders and a price tag more than twice as high. Fifty of those $4,000 Great Arrows found buyers in 1904—and Pierce found the market niche in which it would spend the rest of its life.

In 1905 a Great Arrow driven by Percy Pierce (son of George) won the inaugural running of the Glidden Tour, the famous reliability trial sponsored by Charles Jasper Glidden. The next four events were also won by Great Arrows—an astounding feat. The Buffalo firm celebrated in 1909 by changing its corporate marque names to Pierce-Arrow. "Great" was dropped as redundant.

In 1910 George Pierce died, and because his son Percy had decided he preferred bicycles to cars two years earlier, Pierce-Arrow's future rested in the hands of Clifton. By now all Pierce-Arrow models had 6 cylinders, and advertising was both lavish and grand. More than any other automobile manufacturer in America, Pierce-Arrow was responsible for adding aesthetics to the matter of selling automobiles. Graphics had been strictly an afterthought. With the help of pioneer adman Earnest Elmo Calkins, Pierce-Arrow changed that, hiring many of the nation's top illustrators (N. C. Wyeth, J. C. Leyendecker, Edward Penfield, Gil Spear, Edward Borein, and Adolph Treidler among them) to render the Pierce-Arrow into advertisements that were literally works of art.

That aesthetic approach, backed by a superlative product, paid big dividends. By January 1915 Pierce-Arrow built its 12,000th car and was preeminent in the highest echelon of the luxury market. Only Packard built more luxury cars. But, though an estimable marque as well, Packard did not produce a 6-cylinder as supreme as Pierce's, which, at 824.8 cubic inches, shared honors with a Peerless as America's biggest-ever production engine.

World War I saw Pierce-Arrow profitably engaged in building trucks for the Allies. One month before the Armistice the company introduced its postwar model: the Dual Valve Six. Continuing with a 6 when other top-echelon manufacturers had moved on to 8 and 12 cylinders was a decision of dubious merit. The Pierce-Arrow engine retained its reputation for producing power in blessed silence (and would be favored by rumrunners for their boats for that reason), but progress seemed to be shuffling past the Buffalo company.

Still, marching to its own drummer had long been the Pierce-Arrow way. Although the company would pioneer in the extensive use of aluminum and in power braking, it preferred right-hand drive until 1920 (when switching the steering wheel to the other side of the car was demanded by dealers) and retained its idiosyncratic headlamps until virtually the end (introduced and patented in 1913, the fender-mounted lamps were a Pierce-Arrow signature).

Even before the first roar of the 1920s a change was obviously necessary. Sales of between 1,200 and 2,000 cars annually were dismal, particularly in view of the lavish plant facilities and the company work force. Nearly 2,000 on the payroll produced less than one car per year per employee. But the only change immediately forthcoming was in management. The Pierce-Arrow old guard retired, and the firm's fortunes were placed in the hands of New York bankers (the Seligman Company) who offered Pierce-Arrow stock on the market and engaged George Goethals's consulting engineering firm to take care of things in Buffalo. Among the ideas for turning Pierce-Arrow around was development of a sleeve-valve engine. Fergusson was furious and abruptly resigned. His successor was Barney Roos, who resigned almost as abruptly. Succeeding Roos was Charles L. Sheppy. Clifton moved up to the chairmanship of the board in 1921, and Pierce's presidential chair was taken by treasurer Myron Forbes.

The 1920s were boom years for most established American manufacturers, but not for Pierce-Arrow. Styling clung tenaciously to the traditional; cylinders remained 6. In 1928 the respected Clifton died at the age of seventy-five. He had been president of the National Automobile Chamber of Commerce from its inception in 1913 until his retirement in 1927, and his death was mourned throughout the industry. Shortly thereafter, believing death was imminent for independent automobile manufacturers as well, Myron Forbes engineered a merger with Albert R. Erskine of Studebaker in South Bend, Indiana. The honeymoon was fine. A line of straight-8 Pierce-Arrows—designed earlier in Buffalo—was rushed to market, and Pierce sales doubled to 10,000 units. But the marriage was ultimately a disaster. Forbes resigned in 1929, and Erskine added the Pierce presidency to the one he already had in South Bend.

The stock market crash that October did not dissuade Pierce-Arrow from beginning development the following year of a new 12-cylinder car. Pierce virtually had no choice but to do so, since other luxury manufacturers were moving to 12s and 16s. The Pierce V-12 was designed by new chief engineer Karl Wise. Its introduction in November 1931 was followed in 1932 by wonderful news stories of Ab Jenkins's 24-hour record-breaking run on the salt flats of Bonneville, Utah. Jenkins both averaged more than 125 mph during the last hour and shaved so that he could be photographed without stubble as he alighted from the car.

Meanwhile events were taking a tragic turn in Buffalo. By 1933 Studebaker was in receivership, and Albert Erskine committed suicide. Pierce-Arrow had functioned as an independent operating entity since the merger, and now a group of Buffalo bankers got together and bought the company. Retained as president was Arthur J. Chanter, a former Studebaker man who had assumed that post during the final few desperate months of Erskine's life.

But now the question was whether new life could be breathed into Pierce-Arrow. Certainly the effort was formidable. The introduction of hydraulic tappets in 1933 had been an industry first, and even more sensational was the brand-new car. Startlingly streamlined and a smash hit at all the automobile shows, the Silver Arrow was a pacesetter in automotive design. But the pace in Buffalo continued to slow. Sales totaled 2,152 units in 1933, 500 less than the year before and nearly 1,000 less than the break-even point; 1934 was no better. In 1935 Arthur Chanter noted with some pride that, alone among America's automakers, Pierce-Arrow was committed to luxury car manufacture exclusively. But not for long. Just 875 luxury Pierces found buyers in 1935. In 1936 sales totaled 787; in 1937, only 167. On Friday the 13th of May 1938 the Pierce-Arrow company went to the auction block. In the vast but silent factory in Buffalo, several prototypes of the 1939 Pierce-Arrow were parked in a corner.

References:

Brooks T. Brierley, *There Is No Mistaking a Pierce-Arrow* (Coconut Grove, Fla.: Garrett & Stringer, 1985);

Maurice D. Hendry, "Pierce-Arrow: An American Aristocrat," *Automobile Quarterly*, 6 (Winter 1968): 240-265;

Hendry, *Pierce-Arrow: First Among America's Finest* (New York: Ballantine, 1971);

Beverly Rae Kimes, "The Artists Who Painted for Pierce-Arrow: Automobile Advertising's Grandest Era," *Automobile Quarterly*, 14 (Third Quarter 1976): 228-235;

Marc Ralston, *Pierce-Arrow* (New York: Barnes, 1980);

Bernard J. Weis, *The Pierce-Arrow Motor Car* (Atlanta: Pierce-Arrow Society, 1981).

Pistons

by David J. Andrea

University of Michigan

A piston is an engine component that seals the combustion chamber, the cylinder, from the engine block and crankcase. Every reciprocating engine uses a piston variation. In gasoline and diesel internal combustion engines the piston is a round bucket-shaped part. Made typically from cast iron or aluminum, pistons are a precision machined part.

During 4-cycle engine operation, the piston takes the initial impact of the exploding air and fuel mixture. This explosion occurs at the height of compression against the piston head, or crown. The piston, attached by a movable pin, transfers this energy to the connecting rod. Operating in a harsh environment, piston design must endure intense temperatures, resulting expansion and contraction of piston material, and corrosive exhaust gases. Thin metallic rings called piston rings encircle the piston just below its top to ensure a tight, flexible seal between the piston and cylinder wall.

Although the function and shape of the piston has remained the same since N. A. Otto patented the first gasoline internal combustion engine in 1877, piston design and materials have changed. Packard introduced the aluminum piston in the 1915 V-12. The drive to reduce weight and increase fuel economy has led many manufacturers to use aluminum on inexpensive subcompact vehicles as well as high-performance and luxury cars. As operating temperatures increase in engines, some pistons need ceramic coatings to control material heat expansion and increase durability.

References:

C. Lyle Cummins, Jr., "Early IC and Automotive Engines," Society of Automotive Engineers West Coast Meeting, San Francisco, August 9-12, 1976;

Cummins, Jr., *Internal Fire* (Portland, Oreg.: Carnot, 1976);

K. Newton, W. Steeds, and T. K. Garret, *The Motor Vehicle* (Kent, U.K.: Butterworth, 1985).

Albert Augustus Pope

(May 20, 1843-August 10, 1909)

by John B. Rae

Harvey Mudd College

CAREER: Union army officer (1862-1865); merchant (1865-1877); president, Pope Manufacturing Company (1877-1899, 1902-1907); president, American Bicycle Company (1899-1902).

Albert Augustus Pope, bicycle and automobile manufacturer, was born in Boston on May 20, 1843, and died in Cohasset, Massachusetts, on August 10, 1909. He was the son of Charles and Elizabeth Borgman Pope. He was educated in the public schools of Brookline, Massachusetts, but had to leave school at age sixteen because of financial reverses in the family. In 1862 he was commissioned second lieutenant in the 35th Massachusetts infantry and served with distinction throughout the Civil War, rising to the rank of lieutenant colonel. When the war ended, he returned to Boston and went into business as a merchant. In 1871 he married Abbie Linden; they had four sons and one daughter.

In 1877 Pope founded the Pope Manufacturing Company for the purpose of making small patented articles. A year later he turned to bicycles, which had not previously been built in the United States. Pope had become interested when he saw British-made bicycles at the Philadelphia Centennial Exposition in 1876. He became an importer of these machines, with results good enough to satisfy him that there was a promising American market for bicycles. He arranged to have the actual manufacturing done by the Weed Sewing Machine Company of Hartford, Connecticut, a company which was one of the leaders in the application of the "American Systems" of machine production of standardized and interchangeable parts. This was undoubtedly Pope's reason for selecting Weed, since he had decided that his bicycles, unlike British practice, should be built with machine-made interchangeable parts. The bicycles were sold by the Pope

Albert Augustus Pope (courtesy of the Motor Vehicle Manufacturers Association)

Manufacturing Company under the trade name "Columbia."

The early Columbias were the high-wheeled "ordinaries" of the period, for which the market was limited because only men of some muscular strength and agility could ride them. The introduction in Britain of the geared, low-wheel "safety" bicycle in 1885 made a dramatic change, because this machine could be ridden by practically anyone, women and children as well as men. A bicycle boom developed, of which Pope took full advantage, with production of Columbias rising to 60,000 per year in the 1890s. In 1890 he bought the Weed factory and devoted it entirely to bicycle manufacturing. He maintained and indeed improved upon the high production standards of the Weed Sewing Machine Company. By 1894 his company had its own tire factory in Hartford and what was then the most up-to-date mill in the country for making cold-drawn steel tubing, managed by an ex-naval officer, Hayden Eames. There was also a research department for testing metals and improving bicycle design, headed by Henry Souther, a graduate of the Massachusetts Institute of Technology. The vice-president and general manager of the Pope Manufacturing Company was George H. Day, who had a similar position in the Weed Sewing Machine Company.

Three aspects of Pope's management had some significance for his later career in automobile manufacturing. One, when he found that patents were causing problems, he made a point of acquiring control of every patent dealing with bicycles that he could. Two, he built a second bicycle factory in Hartford, not officially part of the Pope Manufacturing Company, to turn out a lower-priced bicycle called the Hartford. The minimum price of a Columbia was $120, but while Pope realized that there was a demand for lower-priced machines, he was unwilling to allow the Columbia name to be used for them. Three, he did not create a marketing organization. Columbias were sold in general stores or through dealers who handled several makes of bicycles. Since the Pope organization was the country's leading bicycle producer and was collecting royalties from most if its competitors, a marketing organization probably seemed unnecessary, certainly while the bicycle boom lasted.

Pope also worked actively to encourage bicycling. He was one of the principal sponsors of the League of American Wheelmen, established in 1880 to promote the interests of bicyclists. He founded the magazine *Wheelman* in 1882, with S. S. McClure as its editor, and two years later merged it with *Outing*. He was also an enthusiastic supporter of the Good Roads Movement of the 1880s and 1890s, which achieved the formation of the Office of Road Inquiry in the United States Department of Agriculture. This agency eventually became the Bureau of Public Roads, later the Federal Highway Administration. In addition, Pope financed instruction in highway engineering at the Massachusetts Institute of Technology and Harvard's Lawrence Scientific School.

In the 1890s Pope, like other bicycle manufacturers, became interested in motor vehicles, which were just then appearing on the American scene. At Souther's suggestion, Hiram Percy Maxim, the builder of one of the earliest American gasoline automobiles, was brought into the tube department as a motor carriage expert in July 1895, and shortly afterward Pope organized a motor carriage department headed by Eames and with Maxim as chief engineer. Maxim was an enthusiast for the gasoline automobile, but both Pope and Day favored electric propulsion, and so the motor carriage department emphasized electric cars. Pope is said to have told Maxim that people would never sit over an explosion, an understandable enough attitude at a time when gasoline engines were noisy and odoriferous and American gasoline cars were still built as buggies with the engine usually under the driver's seat.

The motor carriage department's products first appeared on the market in 1897, still under the name Columbia, and in the next two years it built 500 electric and 40 gasoline cars. The latter included gasoline-powered tricycles for use in package delivery, and since merchants were frequently hesitant to rely on these new fangled contraptions, the Pope Manufacturing Company organized its own delivery service.

At this point in his career Pope appeared to be in a thoroughly enviable position. He dominated the bicycle industry, and he now had a substantial foothold in the nascent automobile industry, with the largest output of any American motor vehicle manufacturer. The preference for electric automobiles proved to be a mistake, but it was an understandable mistake in the late 1890s, and it could have been corrected. Instead, in just three years Pope had lost both his bicycle and his motor vehicle business and was in effect having to start over again.

In July 1899 Pope sold the motor carriage department to the Electric Vehicle Company and turned his attention to the formation of the American Bicycle Company. The great bicycle boom of the 1880s and 1890s was fading, and the Pope organization felt some financial pressure as a result. At any rate Pope and his principal executives, Day and Eames, were all very pleased at the prospect of a million dollars coming in from the Electric Vehicle Com-

Two Pope cars struggling on a Virginia road, 1904 (courtesy of the Smithsonian Institution)

pany. None of them seem to have considered the possibility that the products of the motor carriage department might soon have more than made up for their lost bicycle sales.

At first the motor carriage department became the Columbia Automobile Company, owned jointly by the Pope Manufacturing Company and the Electric Vehicle Company, but in a series of corporate manipulations it became completely an Electric Vehicle property by 1902. One result was that Day, Eames, and Maxim all left the Pope organization. Pope himself displayed no interest in keeping his foothold in the automobile industry. He was busy organizing a "bicycle trust," the American Bicycle Company, which was an effort to rescue an industry that had overbuilt during the boom and was now desperately trying to adjust to rapidly declining sales.

The American Bicycle Company was planned on an ambitious scale. It was capitalized at $40 million and included 45 firms operating 57 plants. It took over all the property of the Pope Manufacturing Company except the tube plant in Hartford, and when that was sold to the National Tube Company a year later, the Pope Manufacturing Com-

pany went out of existence. It was an impressive show, but that was all it was. Within three years the American Bicycle Company was bankrupt and vanished from existence. It never approached being a "bicycle trust." Pope's principal competitor, Thomas L. Jeffery, who made the Rambler bicycle (and later the Rambler car) in Kenosha, Wisconsin, would have nothing to do with the American Bicycle Company and even disregarded many of Pope's patent claims.

Pope made two major mistakes, the first being to dispose of a promising start in the automobile industry and the second being the effort to control a declining bicycle industry. He may have been one of the many people of that era who believed the automobile was a fad for the wealthy that would sooner or later pass away, and if he did accept that idea, he might well have assumed that the bicycle would come back. In the late 1890s that would have been a reasonable enough position to take. The future of the motor vehicle was still uncertain. There was a strong body of opinion holding that its future was limited.

When the American Bicycle Company disintegrated Pope realized his mistake, and whatever else he may have lacked, it was not entrepreneurship. Even before the final collapse, he was moving toward reentry into automobile manufacturing. Two of the "bicycle trust's" properties were already making motor vehicles. One was the Waverley Company of Indianapolis, which had been making electric automobiles since 1896. The other was the Toledo, Ohio, plant of H. A. Lozier & Company, which began to make steam trucks, based on British models, in 1899. These were combined as the International Motor Car Company in 1901, and under Pope's management the steam trucks were phased out and replaced by gasoline cars. Then, since the Hartford bicycle plant was not being used to capacity, Pope converted part of it to automobile production—this time gasoline cars. The electric automobile was no longer the Pope favorite.

When the American Bicycle Company passed out of existence, its remaining assets were taken over by a new Pope Manufacturing Company, with a capital of $22.5 million and this time directed at motor vehicle manufacturing. The new company absorbed the International Motor Car Company and the Hartford plant. To these it added a factory in Hagerstown, Maryland, and another in Westfield, Massachusetts, which was still making bicycles. Since the Columbia name had gone to the Electric Vehicle Company, the new line of cars carried the Pope name, in a way that gives Pope some credit for pioneering the idea of offering models at various price ranges. The top of the line was the Pope-Toledo, built as the name indicates in the Toledo plant. It was a luxury car, compared in its day with the Packard, and it was the best known of the Pope products. Then came the Pope-Hartford, a medium-priced car made in Hartford, and finally the Pope-Tribune, a low-priced car made in Hagerstown. There was also the electric car, the Pope-Waverley, but electric automobiles were a minor factor in the market by this time. In this second Pope Manufacturing Company, Pope's cousin George Pope played an important role in management. He had also been involved in the first company, notably as manager of the factory that made the Hartford bicycle.

Pope can hardly be credited with more than a glimmering of the idea that led William C. Durant to the creation of General Motors and that Alfred P. Sloan subsequently implemented as "a car for every purse and every purpose." There is nothing in his career to show that Pope ever looked toward a mass market. Earlier when he decided to produce a low-priced bicycle, it was not allowed to be called Columbia or even to be built in the same factory. Now his lowest priced car was made in Hagerstown, an unlikely site to pick if production on a large scale for a mass market was contemplated, and the Pope-Hartford was introduced initially to utilize excess capacity in the Hartford bicycle factory. The aristocrat of the line was made in Toledo, which would have been an excellent site for large-scale production. The concentration of motor vehicle manufacturing in the general region about Detroit was not yet established when the second Pope Manufacturing Company was formed, but it became clearly visible in the next two to three years, and Pope could have adjusted his operations accordingly.

Pope may simply have lacked the resources to adapt to changing conditions in the automobile industry. His company was after all an assortment of bits and pieces salvaged from the wreckage of the bankrupt American Bicycle Company. It lacked financial strength, and in contrast to the situation of the motor carriage department in the 1890s, it was operating in a highly competitive industry where a number of powerful rivals had come or were coming into existence. There was not enough reserve strength to carry the company through the recession year of 1907. It had to go into receivership, and this marked the end of Pope's active business life.

His son Albert L. Pope and his cousin George took charge of a reorganized Pope Manufacturing Company with its capital scaled down to $6.5 million and its properties limited to the Hartford and Westfield factories. The other plants were sold, the one in Toledo going to John N. Willys, who made it the headquarters of Willys-Overland. A syndicate formed by Herbert L. Rice, who had been Pope's advertising manager and would later be president of Cadillac, bought the Waverley factory in Indianapolis and continued to make electric automobiles there until 1915. The reorganization failed to remedy the Pope Manufacturing Company's lack of working capital, and in 1915 it finally went out of business. George Pope took charge of liquidating the assets and, with the assistance of the industrial boom that World War I brought, did well enough to enable the creditors to receive 92 cents on the dollar.

Pope's career offers an intriguing comparison of success and failure. He founded the American bicycle industry and, in both the United States and Europe bicycle manufacturing, was an important, indeed essential, precursor to automobile manufacturing. In the fabrication of bicycles, a number of techniques were evolved that contributed significantly to the fabrication of motor vehicles. These techniques did not by any means come exclusively from the Pope Manufacturing Company, but Pope was a fairly large part of the overall process. Moreover, the widespread use of the bicycle revived the popularity of travel by road, which had been almost extinct since the phenomenal growth of the railroad in the nineteenth century. Pope contributed heavily to this change through his energetic support of the League of American Wheelmen and the Good Roads Movement.

From bicycles Pope moved to a promising start in motor vehicle manufacturing. His motor carriage department entitled the city of Hartford to claim to have been the "cradle of the American automobile industry." What would have happened if Pope had continued on the same path is impossible to determine, but a cradle seldom becomes a permanent home, and it is more than likely that the industry would have gravitated eventually to the magnetic attraction of the Midwest.

At this juncture Pope made some major mistakes. The first, the emphasis on electric cars, was remediable. The motor carriage department also made gasoline cars, and it would not have been difficult to change the emphasis. However, the other errors sent his career irreversibly downhill. One was the premature withdrawal from automobile manufacturing through the sale of the motor carriage department to the Electric Vehicle Company. The other was his futile effort to revive the bicycle business through the American Bicycle Company. When he returned to automobile manufacturing, it was too late. He was no longer a pioneer. New and formidable competitors were now in the field.

Although his business operations centered in Hartford, he remained a resident of Boston. He established the Pope Dispensary at the New England Hospital in Boston, in honor of two of his sisters who became physicians, and he gave 74 acres of land and $100,000 to establish a park in Hartford.

Publications:

Highway improvement. An address by Albert A. Pope before the Carriage Builders' National Association, at Syracuse, N.Y., October 17, 1889 (Boston?, 1889?);

The movement for better roads: An address before the Board of Trade, at Hartford, Mass., February 11, 1890 (Boston? 1890);

The relation of good streets to the prosperity of a city. An address by Albert A. Pope (Boston?, 1890?);

A catalogue of books, pamphlets, and articles on the construction and maintenance of roads/Presented by Col. Albert A. Pope (Boston, 1892);

Errors in school books (Boston: A. A. Pope, 1892);

A memorial to Congress on the subject of a comprehensive exhibit of roads, their construction and maintenance, at the World's Columbian Exposition (Boston, 1892);

The movement for better roads. An address by Albert A. Pope before the Board of Trade at Hartford, Conn., February 11, 1890. An open letter to the people of the United States. Relating to a department of road construction and maintenance at the World's Columbia Exposition. Width of tires. Extracts from recent special consular reports on streets and highways in foreign countries (Boston: Pope Manufacturing, 1892);

Wagon roads as feeders to railways (Boston: Albert A. Pope, 1892).

References:

Henry Cave, "Hartford—The Incubator of the American Automobile Industry," *Old Time's News*, 2 (April 1944);

David A. Hounshell, *From The American System to Mass Production* (Baltimore: Johns Hopkins University Press, 1984);

John B. Rae, *American Automobile Manufacturers: The First Forty Years* (Philadelphia: Chilton, 1959).

Pope Manufacturing Company

by John B. Rae

Harvey Mudd College

The Pope Manufacturing Company was founded in 1877 to build bicycles. Its founder, Col. Albert A. Pope, was attracted by British-made bicycles on display at the Centennial Exposition in Philadelphia in 1876. He arranged to have the construction done in the factory of the Weed Sewing Machine Company in Hartford, Connecticut, which was one of the leaders in applying standardization and interchangeability to the manufacture of sewing machines. Until the late 1880s the product was the high-wheeled bicycle, but when the Starley safety bicycle was introduced in Britain, Pope promptly turned to it. By 1890 the bicycle business had become so large that the Pope company bought the Weed factory and terminated the manufacture of sewing machines in it. By this time the Pope Manufacturing Company was the largest maker of bicycles in the United States, with an output of more than 60,000 annually, sold under the trade name Columbia.

It became a highly integrated, technologically innovative organization, introducing improved methods for the manufacture and assembly of bicycle parts. It had its own tire factory in Hartford, the most up-to-date mill in the country for making cold-drawn steel tubing, and a research department for improving design and for testing metals.

In 1895 the company established a motor carriage department under Hayden Eames, a former naval officer, with Hiram Percy Maxim, builder of one of the first American gasoline automobiles, as chief engineer. It emphasized electric automobiles, much to Maxim's disapproval, because both Pope and his general manager, George H. Day, were convinced that the noisy and smelly gasoline car would never sell. In four years this department built some 500 electric and 40 gasoline cars, still using the name Columbia. Then in 1899 the motor carriage department was sold to the Electric Vehicle Company.

The rest of the Pope Manufacturing Company was taken over by the American Bicycle Company, an unsuccessful attempt at a "Bicycle Trust" promoted by Pope. It was an effort to deal with declining bicycle sales; the bicycle boom of the late 1880s and 1890s was over. The American Bicycle Company was dissolved in 1902, but it left Pope with two plants that were making automobiles: the former Lozier bicycle plant in Toledo, Ohio, and the Waverley Company of Indianapolis, which had been building electric automobiles since 1896. These were combined as the International Motor Car Company. Then, since the bicycle plant in Hartford had excess capacity, Pope resumed the production of motor vehicles. A new Pope Manufacturing Company was formed that took over the remaining assets of the American Bicycle Company and the International Motor Car Company.

One consequence was that the Pope Manufacturing Company and the Electric Vehicle Company were now building automobiles competitively in adjacent factories in Hartford, but the new Pope organization went beyond that. It was making cars in Indianapolis, Toledo, and Hagerstown, Maryland, as well. Since the Electric Vehicle Company had acquired the name "Columbia," the new Pope products were called Pope-Toledo, Pope-Hartford, Pope-Tribune (made in Hagerstown), and Pope-Waverley.

These categories represented the first attempt by an American automobile manufacturer to offer cars at various price levels. The Pope-Toledo was the high-priced and best-known model. In its brief appearance on the market it was considered to be in the same category as the Packard. The Pope-Hartford was the medium-priced entry, and the Pope-Tribune, built in Hagerstown, was aimed at the low-price market. There is no indication that Pope management had any strong interest in the mass market. The Toledo factory was the largest;

The 1907 Pope-Waverley electric

the Hagerstown plant was not equipped for large-scale production.

This arrangement might have been changed in time, but time was running out for the Pope Manufacturing Company. Declining bicycle sales were hurting it in the late 1890s and may have been an incentive for the sale of the motor carriage department to the Electric Vehicle Company. The failure of the American Bicycle Company weakened the Pope organization further so that, like the Electric Vehicle Company, it could not survive the panic of 1907. There was a receivership, from which the Pope Manufacturing Company emerged with sharply reduced capitalization and only two factories, the Hartford automobile plant and a bicycle plant in Westfield, Massachusetts. The Toledo factory was bought by John N. Willys and became the home of the Willys-Overland Company. The Hagerstown plant was also sold. A separate organization bought Waverley Electric and kept it in production until 1916. This reorganization did nothing to strengthen the Pope Manufacturing Company's fi-

nances. Another receivership in 1913 resulted in liquidation.

The Pope enterprise made a promising start in the automobile industry, enough to give Hartford a plausible claim to be "the cradle of the American automobile industry." The company had a solid foothold in motor vehicle production, and then foolishly gave it up. It may be that the Midwest was bound to become the center of American automobile manufacturing, but it is interesting to speculate on what might have been if the Pope Manufacturing Company had kept its motor carriage department, shifted its emphasis from bicycles to automobiles, and turned earlier from electric to gasoline cars.

References:
The Pope Manufacturing Company. An Industrial Achievement (Hartford, Conn.: Pope Manufacturing Company, 1909);

John B. Rae, *American Automobile Manufacturers: The First Forty Years* (Philadelphia: Chilton, 1959).

Races and Tours

by George S. May

Eastern Michigan University

The initial promotional efforts of those engaged in manufacturing automobiles were centered on efforts to convince the public that these vehicles actually worked. That was accomplished through public demonstrations of the car's capabilities. Hill climbs were popular events for some years, with Pike's Peak, which John Brisben Walker successfully ascended in 1900 in one of his steamers, being the most enduring challenge of a car's ability to negotiate even moderate inclines. However, long-distance runs and races proved to be the most popular means of testing the performance levels of the horseless carriages.

The state of Wisconsin in 1878 offered a $10,000 prize to the winner of a 200-mile race that was designed to promote the development of a "cheap and practical substitute for the use of horses and other animals on the highway and farm." However, since the only entrants were two steam "road locomotives," weighing from 5 tons to 7 tons, the winner received only $5,000 because it was judged not to have fulfilled the requirement of being a cheap and practical alternative to the horse. Thus, a 53-mile run from Chicago to Evanston and back, sponsored by the *Chicago Times-Herald* on Thanksgiving Day, 1895, is usually regarded as the first true test of self-propelled road vehicles designed for conveying passengers. The sponsor sought to promote an interest in this new mode of transportation by presenting awards to those entrants that operated most economically, that could be controlled most easily, and that had the best design. But it was the $2,000 that was awarded to the Duryea Motor Wagon that Frank Duryea brought home ahead of the other entrants that attracted the most attention. From then on, the emphasis in these events was on the fastest car and not on the other categories, to which the *Times-Herald* had sought to devote equal space.

The fact that the Duryea Motor Wagon remained in production for only a short time proved that it took more than mechanical excellence to assure the success of an automobile manufacturer, even though the car achieved victory in the *Times-Herald* race, a Memorial Day race sponsored by John Brisben Walker's *Cosmopolitan* magazine in May 1896, and the London-to-Brighton run later that year celebrating the repeal of the British Parliament's Red Flag Act. But that did not deter others from trying to use this technique to boost their sales. Alexander Winton pioneered the long-distance trip as a publicity gimmick when he drove one of the cars of his new Cleveland company to New York City in 1897 in ten days time. Two years later, Winton repeated that trip, and the resulting publicity led to sales of Wintons to the general public, while earlier sales had been mainly to engineers.

Winton's Cleveland-to-New York trips inspired a host of imitators, most notably Elwood Haynes and Edgar Apperson, who drove one of their Haynes-Apperson cars from Kokomo, Indiana, to Brooklyn, New York, in summer 1899, and who repeated that feat in summer 1901. That fall, Roy D. Chapin drove a curved-dash Oldsmobile runabout from Detroit to New York, a trip that attracted little attention at the time and which fell more than 200 miles short of the distance Haynes and Apperson had driven. But the trip's subsequent unfounded acclaim as having been the record-setting American long-distance automobile trip testified to the ability of a successful manufacturer to convince the media of its superiority over less well known and less-enduring competitors.

Once Winton and Haynes had demonstrated that cars of that day could be driven several hundred miles, the attention then shifted to the possibilities of a much longer trip, from coast to coast. The first to make such a trip were Dr. Horatio Nelson Jackson and Sewall K. Crocker, who drove a

Buick head William C. Durant at the wheel of the 1907 Glidden Tour winner

2-cylinder, 20-horsepower Winton from San Francisco to New York in 64 days in summer 1903. Within a few weeks, a Packard and an Oldsmobile had been used to duplicate Jackson and Crocker's feat. The manufacturers of these two cars sponsored the trips, and both made extensive use of them in publicizing their products. Jackson financed his own trip and refused offers of assistance from the Winton's manufacturer, but nevertheless the Cleveland company, like the Packard and Oldsmobile companies, took full advantage of Jackson's achievement to draw attention to the merits of its car.

Two years later, Charles J. Glidden, a retired telephone company executive, inaugurated an annual long-distance automobile tour which quickly became the preeminent motoring event of its type. Glidden intended his tours to be a means of promoting interest in motoring and not of promoting a particular car. To achieve that end, Glidden limited entries to owner-driven cars, but since the owners who participated included such figures as Ransom Olds, Benjamin Briscoe, Albert Pope, Walter White, and Percy Pierce driving one of their own compa-

nies' cars, the attention of the public was naturally focused on these manufacturers. By routing the tour into different areas of the country each year and by emphasizing that reliability, not speed, was the objective the entrants were to demonstrate, Glidden succeeded in introducing motoring to many people who had had little opportunity to witness this new means of travel. The fact that nearly all participants in these tours completed the course with relatively few mishaps "proved," as a participant in the 1905 tour declared, "that the automobile is now almost foolproof" and that "American cars are durable and efficient." But it was the entrant who won the Charles Glidden Trophy who received the most publicity. The fact that a Great Arrow, manufactured by the George N. Pierce Company of Buffalo—the car that was shortly renamed the Pierce-Arrow—was awarded the trophy at the end of each of the first five tours led to a sharp drop-off in the interest of other manufacturers, some of whom suggested that the judging may have been rigged. The tours were abandoned after 1913, although they were revived many years later as a popular annual event for owners of antique automobiles.

Long-distance endurance runs have continued to be employed to demonstrate a particular car's ruggedness, fuel efficiency, and overall performance capabilities. But increasingly, the competitive nature of these events, which made them more races than tests of the automobile's reliability, caused more and more manufacturers to turn to racing events in which speed alone determined the winner. The Duryeas, Alexander Winton, and Henry Ford provided early proof of the publicity that resulted from victories in races, and none went about exploiting this source of public attention more than Buick, which in the period from 1906 to 1909 hired a team of top drivers, spent $100,000 a year, and obtained free publicity on the nation's sports pages by entering every available competition. In 1909 Buick claimed it finished first in 90 percent of these events. "Tests Tell," Buick ads proclaimed, "Could you ask for more convincing evidence?"

In 1909 the Indianapolis promoter and automotive parts manufacturer Carl G. Fisher began staging annual races that evolved in 1911 into the annual Memorial Day 500-mile race that became the most popular of all American automobile competitions. The Indianapolis 500 was run on a closed track, the format that would be adopted by nearly all racing events in the United States. The Vanderbilt Cup races, held on Long Island, New York, from 1904 to 1910, followed the prevalent European practice of staging competitions on public highways, but in the United States road racing fell out of favor because of the outcry over the dangers these races presented not only to the drivers but to spectators. Closed-track races did not necessarily prove to present less of a threat to human life, but the format conformed more closely to that of traditional races, further removing these contests from the kinds of general tests of a car's reliability and durability that had earlier been favored as means of promoting a manufacturer's products.

Some companies continued to participate in races such as the Indianapolis 500, with Marmon, Mercer, and Stutz making effective use of their successes in these races to boost sales of their passenger cars. The fact that their successful racing vehicles bore little or no relationship to the vehicles they sold to the public led to criticism that the companies were guilty of false advertising when they implied that their passenger cars were capable of the same kind of performance as their racers. The design of the Indianapolis-type racing machines soon made it impossible to continue that kind of charade, although the emergence of stock car racing in later years saw the return to racing of cars whose outer look and name were familiar to the spectators. Even though it was well known that these cars were souped-up versions of the cars available in the showrooms, Pontiac changed its entire image with victories in stock car races in the late 1950s. These victories came at a time, however, when the industry as a whole had come to frown upon such corporate involvement in racing because of concern over its image. Nevertheless, the ability of a car to be driven at fast speeds has remained one of the most constant themes of automobile advertising and promotions, especially among those cars whose appeal is directed at younger drivers.

References:

Joel W. Eastman, *Styling vs. Safety: The American Automobile Industry and the Development of Automotive Safety, 1900-1966* (Lanham, Md.: University Press of America, 1984);

George S. May, *The Automobile in American Life* (forthcoming, 1990);

Julian Pettifer and Nigel Turner, *Automania: Man and the Motor Car* (Boston: Little, Brown, 1984);

Stephen W. Sears, *The Automobile in America* (New York: American Heritage, 1977).

Reo Motor Car Company

by George S. May

Eastern Michigan University

Reo, for 70 years a well-known name among motor vehicles, had its origins shortly after Ransom E. Olds was not reelected as general manager of the Olds Motor Works, an office he had held since the company's formation in 1899. Although the public was told that Olds wanted to be relieved of these duties in order to devote more time to other interests, Olds, who was not yet forty, was not ready to retire from an industry to which he had been such a major contributor. Within less than a month, plans for his comeback were underway.

Early in February 1904, when Olds was in California visiting his parents, he met with Reuben Shettler, a former Lansing businessman who was the Oldsmobile distributor in southern California. Shettler had played a key role in the opening of Oldsmobile production in Lansing in 1901, and he was the major force in establishing a new automobile company, Reo, in Michigan's state capital. It is not known whether Olds or Shettler first proposed the idea, but, despite his later claims to have been taken by surprise when he was offered the control of the company, Olds was involved with Reo's development from the outset. While Shettler laid the groundwork for the firm's financing, Olds disposed of his remaining shares of stock in the Olds Motor Works and began planning the cars the new company would produce. By midsummer the organizational work had been completed, and the R. E. Olds Company was incorporated on August 16, 1904.

The investors, who included Shettler and several prominent Lansing businessmen, placed their hopes for success on the presence of Olds, as the name chosen for the company indicated. Olds's name was probably the best known in the industry, a fact that immediately caused the Olds Motor Works to object that its use infringed upon the rights that Olds's former company had to his name. Faced with the threat of legal action which their at-

torney advised them they would probably not win, the stockholders on September 27, 1904, changed the name to the Reo Car Company, shortly amended to the Reo Motor Car Company. Adopting the acronym would not seriously damage the public's ability to connect Olds with the firm since, it was claimed, his initials were almost as well known as his full name. In any event, *reo*, which also is the Greek verb meaning "to run," must rank with Fiat and Saab as among the most successful examples of an acronym used as the name of a motor vehicle.

In return for his reputation and experience, Olds, who put no money into the business, was awarded a 52 percent interest and was named company president and general manager. He quickly swung into action. Within three days after the company's incorporation, draftsmen were working on the drawings for the patterns of the cars, the design of which Olds and Horace T. Thomas, an automotive engineer whom Olds had put on his payroll the previous spring, had developed in the preceding months. Thomas, who was now appointed Reo's chief engineer, had served with Olds at the Olds Motor Works, and he was soon joined by numerous other former employees of that company. The most important of these was Richard H. Scott, who before long assumed the actual direction of Reo operations. Ray M. Owen, the most important of the Oldsmobile distributors, was awarded the exclusive rights to sell the new company's cars, a somewhat unusual arrangement which enabled the Reo staff to concentrate entirely on the production side of the business.

By the first weeks of 1905 the first Reos were coming out of the southside Lausing factory, not far from the Oldsmobile factory. Although Reo offered its version of the runabouts that Olds had popularized with his curved-dash Oldsmobile, it was the larger, more powerful, and more expensive Reo touring car that was most heavily promoted, as Olds fol-

Ransom E. Olds driving President Theodore Roosevelt and others in a Reo automobile, May 31, 1907
(courtesy of Michigan History Division)

lowed the industry-wide trend away from the frail little runabouts to sturdier models. The cars were a marked success with production of 864 in the first year of operations that ended on August 31, 1905. Production figures soon rose into the thousands, reaching 6,592 units by 1909, and placing Reo among the top half-dozen producers in the industry. James R. Doolittle, the pioneer automotive historian, singled out Reo's dividend record during this period as evidence of the astounding profits that successful companies were able to earn in those early years. However, already by 1909 Reo's share of the market, which had stood at more than 9 percent in 1907, had shrunk to only about 5 percent, and the promise that Reo would remain one of the big automakers faded.

The reasons for that decline are not hard to find. Ransom Olds, the man most identified with the company, seems by 1906 to have lost interest in remaining in close contact with Reo's day-to-day operations. Once Reo's sales surpassed those of the Olds Motor Works the challenge that may have moti-

vated Olds to prove that he could outperform the company from which he had been forced to step down was gone, and Olds was content to leave most management matters in the hands of Richard Scott, the factory superintendant. Scott was a capable manager in many ways, but his assumption of Olds's responsibilities, plus the time that Scott devoted to the Anti-Saloon League, aroused opposition from Reuben Shettler and some other stockholders. In 1910 Shettler, the vice-president, tried to remove Scott from power and replace him with Ray Owen, but the plans went awry, and it turned out to be Shettler who was out while Scott remained firmly in control. Shettler's plan had also called for Olds to sell most of his Reo stock and to turn over to Owen most of his administrative responsibilities and to continue as president in name only. Olds at first at least had been willing to go along with this since it fit in with his desire to get out of the business. In 1908 he had been willing to sell control of Reo to the combination that William C. Durant and Benjamin Briscoe were trying to put together if their backers had agreed to the price he asked. Such agreement was not forthcoming, and the reception to subsequent offers made by Olds over the next several years was similarly unfavorable.

Olds's price was judged to be excessive for a company whose sales declined after 1909 and which in 1911 omitted dividend payments for the first time. A celebrated advertising campaign mounted by the great advertising copywriter Claude C. Hopkins that sought to picture the 1912 Reos as striking new models in sharp contrast to the prevailing view of earlier models as basically unchanged since 1904, had only a limited and temporary impact in reversing the downward trend. The one bright ray was the decision, for which Olds probably deserves the major credit, to branch out into the production of trucks. These began to appear in 1911 and shortly began to bear the Speed Wagon name that would become one of the most famous in the trucking industry. By 1919 Reo truck sales surpassed those of the company's passenger cars, and during the following years the truck division usually maintained this lead.

In December 1915 Olds turned over to Richard Scott the title of general manager, a job that Scott had been unofficially holding for some time. In the 1920s Olds finally found a buyer for his Reo stock, selling back to the company a huge block in 1923 and disposing of smaller amounts at other times until by 1928 he and his family retained only token amounts of Reo holdings. In confirmation of this withdrawal from Reo's affairs, Olds on December 20, 1923, relinquished the title of president to Scott and assumed the newly created and essentially honorary post of chairman of the board. With the added prestige that his title had given him, Scott, who had been managing the company in a safe and conservative manner, launched a program of expansion. The vacant Duplex Truck factory in Lansing was purchased in 1923 to permit an increase in truck production, but Scott's major effort was to expand the company's car offerings and to break out of Reo's traditional spot in the medium-price range. Early in 1927 the Reo Flying Cloud was introduced to critical acclaim. The prices of the car, available in four body styles, were higher than those of the 1926 Reos. Later that year came the Wolverine, priced below the figure to which Reo customers had been accustomed. The same year also saw the ap-

pearance of a low-priced truck, the Reo Speed Wagon Junior.

Scott's diverse offerings briefly boosted sales. Passenger car production in 1927 exceeded Reo's truck production for the first year since 1918, and the following year Reo came out with new Flying Cloud models, priced between the original Flying Clouds and the lower-priced Wolverine. But 1928 also saw Reo trucks again move ahead of Reo passenger cars. The Wolverine, which had not done well, was dropped, and although sales at the start of 1929 were the best in the company's history these soon dropped off. With the depressing effect of the stock market crash in October, Reo by the end of 1929 was clearly in trouble.

Ransom Olds, who believed that Scott had been unwise in trying so radically to expand the company's offerings in early 1930, persuaded a majority of the board of directors to replace Scott as general manager with William Robert Wilson, an experienced automotive executive. Scott retained the title of president. Wilson, however, went ahead with the plans that were already underway to introduce still more models, including an entry in the luxury car field, the Reo Royale. Introduced in October 1930, the Royale, designed by the stylist, Amos Northup, is one of the most celebrated products of the golden age of American car design, but it proved to be a financial disaster for Reo which is reported to have lost more than $6 million on the car. This aggravated other losses that Reo, like all other companies, suffered in the depths of the Depression in the early 1930s. A bitter struggle ensued for control of the company. Wilson's contract as general manager was terminated in September 1931, and Scott resumed that position. The collapse of two Lansing banks in 1933 added to Reo's financial woes and exacerbated the division between Olds and Scott.

In December 1933 Olds announced he was resigning from the board of directors because he could not agree with the policies of Scott's management. The directors persuaded him to reconsider and to head a special executive committee that would control the management of the company until the stockholders' meeting the following April. Scott was again removed as general manager, and he allied himself with dissidents seeking to overthrow the control of the pro-Olds forces at that April meeting. When Scott realized that the dissidents could not win the proxy fight, and that they

REO LIGHT TOURING CAR
With Cape Top and Full Lamp
Equipment. $1,325 f.o.b. Factory
Searchlight extra

16 horse-power. 1,600 pounds. 90-
inch wheel base. Five passengers.
Side-door stationary or detachable
tonneau. Two speeds and reverse. Speed 35 miles per
hour. With cape top,
front and rear oil lamps
and 2 gas lamps as
shown in cut.

Reo advertisement, 1906 (courtesy of the Free Library of Philadelphia)

did not have the company's interests in mind, he threw his support to the Olds group. At the same time he withdrew from the company and was succeeded as president by Olds who was full of ideas for rejuvenating the company. When these were rejected by the directors as too risky to undertake, Olds resigned as president at the end of 1934. Two years later he resigned from the board, a few weeks after the decision had been made to abandon passenger car production and to concentrate solely on trucks.

The decision, which was long overdue, kept Lansing's Reo factory operating for another 39 years. The company changed its name to Reo Motors, Inc., in 1940, and it enjoyed a modest return to prosperity as a producer of commercial vehicles, including buses and trucks for civilian and military use. In 1957 Reo was acquired by the larger Cleveland truck manufacturer White Motors. White also acquired Chicago's Diamond T Motor Truck Company, moved it to Lansing where it was combined with Reo to produce Diamond-Reo trucks beginning in 1967. Four years later White sold the Lansing truck operations, which now became Diamond-Reo Trucks, Inc. Despite sales of over 9,000 of the big Diamond-Reo rigs in 1974 finan-

cial difficulties forced the company into bankruptcy on May 30, 1975. Rights to the Diamond-Reo name were purchased by Consolidated International of Columbus, Ohio, which also supplied parts to owners of the 200,000 Reos, Diamond Ts, and Diamond-Reos still in service. The Osterlund Company of Harrisburg, Pennsylvania, was licensed by Consolidated to manufacture trucks under the Diamond-Reo name, keeping alive to that extent the Reo name. But the company founded in 1904 had come to an end, and the ancient red-brick Lansing factory was auctioned in October 1975 and eventually torn down.

References:

Nick Baldwin and others, *The World Guide to Automobile Manufacturers* (New York: Facts on File, 1987);

Beverly Rae Kimes, "Reo Remembered: A History," *Automobile Quarterly*, 14 (First Quarter 1976): 4-35;

George S. May, *R. E. Olds, Auto Industry Pioneer* (Grand Rapids, Mich.: Eerdmans, 1977);

Glenn E. Niemeyer, *The Automotive Career of Ransom E. Olds* (East Lansing: Michigan State University Press, 1963).

Archives:

An extensive collection of Reo company records from its beginnings to the 1970s, along with papers of Ransom E. Olds, is in the Historical Collections of the Michigan State University Library, East Lansing, Michigan.

Andrew Lawrence Riker

(October 22, 1868-June 1, 1930)

by Genevieve Wren

Motor Vehicle Research Services

CAREER: Founder and president, Riker Electric Motor Company (1888-1899), Riker Electric Vehicle Company (1899-1902); vice-president and chief engineer, Locomobile Company of America (1902-1921); vice-president, Investing and Manufacturing Company (1924-1928); vice-president, Ventilouve Company (1929).

Andrew Lawrence Riker, automobile designer, electrical and mechanical engineer, and inventor, was one of the few automotive pioneers to work in all three propulsion mediums: electric, steam, and gasoline. He was born in New York City on October 22, 1868, the son of William James and Charlotte Lawrence Stryker Riker. His interest in motorized transport began early; he built his first vehicle, an electric tricycle, when he was sixteen. Each rear wheel of the tricycle was powered by a separate motor and battery. He later wrote of it, "Not too practical, although it ran." About a year later he left for Columbia University, but he spent only a year there. He began to devote all of his time to engineering.

Riker founded the Riker Electric Motor Company in 1888 to manufacture and sell his motor designs, one of which featured a slotted armature core that greatly improved the conventional surface-wound configuration. In 1894 he developed a gasoline-propelled tricycle and a very fast electric racing car. In 1895 he built his first 4-wheel vehicle by joining two bicycles with cross tubes and outfitting them with a common rear axle and two heavy electric motors. Soon after he began manufacturing 4-wheel vehicles commercially. In 1899 he reorganized to form the Riker Electric Vehicle Company, built a factory in Elizabethport, New Jersey, and marketed a line of passenger and commercial vehicles. A year later he introduced trucks capable of carrying five tons.

Andrew Lawrence Riker

Before 1899 Riker had been particularly successful in the construction of electric racing cars, and he had even raced some himself. In 1899 he won a three-heat affair at the Rhode Island State Fair in an electric racer of his own design. Later in 1899, on Long Island, he established a speed record of one mile in 63 seconds in the first race ever held on a closed track.

His company did not do so well. By 1902 Riker realized that the electric field was limited and began developing a gasoline car. The design impressed officials of the Locomobile Company of America, steam-car makers based in Bridgeport,

Connecticut, and they invited him to join the company to produce the car. It featured a steel frame, a sliding gear transmission, and a gear-driven electric generator. Riker became vice-president and chief engineer at Locomobile and quickly won recognition for the superior design and workmanship of Locomobile cars, which continued to set standards of style and performance through the 1910s. He also continued to design racers, including a 1904 model with 90 horsepower. In 1908 Riker's Locomobile No. 16 broke all existing records at the Vanderbilt Cup race, attaining an average speed of 64.5 mph.

Riker continued at Locomobile until 1921, taking a break in 1915 to serve on the U.S. Naval Consulting Board as an expert on internal combustion engines. He went on to serve as vice-president of the Investing and Manufacturing Company and then the Ventilouve Company, both of Bridgeport. He died at his home in Fairfield, Connecticut, on June 1, 1930.

Reference:

Motor Vehicle Manufacturers Association, *Motor Vehicles of America* (Detroit: Wayne State University Press, 1974).

Pedro G. Salom

(April 12, 1856-December 31, 1945)

by Genevieve Wren

Motor Vehicle Research Services

CAREER: Assistant assayer, U.S. Mint, Philadelphia (1876-1879); assistant chemist, Pennsylvania Railroad Company (1879-?); chemist and superintendent, Chester Rolling Mills (?); president, Standard Steel Casting Company (?-1886); cofounder and director, Electric Carriage Wagon Company (1896-1899).

Pedro G. Salom gained fame for mounting a fleet of splendid Hansom Electrocabs in New York and Philadelphia in 1896 and 1897–the first electric cabs to operate in large numbers in those cities. The cabs were a sensation, not only because of their excellent design, but also because they seemed incredibly elegant and clean when compared to horses. Salom was born on April 12, 1856, in Philadelphia and received an education in Philadelphia public schools. In 1876 he graduated from the University of Pennsylvania with a degree in chemical engineering.

Salom won early acclaim as a chemical and metallurgical engineer. After graduation he took a job as assistant assayer at the U.S. Mint in Philadelphia, where he worked for three and a half years, until he assumed the position of assistant chemist for the Pennsylvania Railroad Company, based in Altoona. He then served as chemist and superintendent of Chester Rolling Mills, leaving that job to

Morris and Salom Electrobat cab, which won a gold medal for design excellence at the Chicago Times-Herald *race in 1895 (courtesy of the Free Library of Philadelphia)*

assume the presidency of Standard Steel Casting Company. Salom married Julia Ward in 1885. They had four children, two boys and two girls.

Salom and Henry Morris in their "Skeleton Bat" experimental electric, 1895

Also in 1885 Salom teamed up with inventor Henry Morris, who had introduced a variety of mechanical devices and served as a director of several companies, to work on electrical storage batteries. Salom left the business world for nine years beginning in 1886 to devote himself exclusively to the development of an improved chemical battery for transportation purposes. Salom and Morris also worked to develop electric vehicles. The duo reached a point of triumph in 1895, when an electric vehicle of their design—the Electrobat 2—won a gold medal for excellence in design and craftsmanship at the *Chicago Times-Herald* Thanksgiving Day race. The race was run, however, on a bitterly cold, slushy day, which made it impossible for the Morris-Salom entry and the other electric entries to finish.

In 1896 Salom and Morris founded the Electric Carriage and Wagon Company to manufacture the pioneering Electrocab fleet and several other electric lines. The Electrocab was unique in design; it featured an extended hansom capable of carrying the necessary bulky batteries (with a 50- to 100-mile range), front-wheel drive, rear-wheel steering, and a pedal-controlled disc brake arrangement on each axle. The speed-control lever was located at the driver's left side, and a steering lever was mounted on the right. The company introduced cab service on New York's Fifth Avenue and shortly after in Philadelphia.

Salom and Morris's cabs could not sustain their initial favorable reception. The public enjoyed the comfort, silence, and ease of operation of electrics, but improvements in gasoline engine technology drew attention to the electrics' excessive weight and limited range. Sales declined rapidly, and the firm was purchased by the rival Electric Vehicle Company in 1899.

Salom went on to continue his engineering career in nonautomotive fields and then enjoyed a long retirement. He died in Philadelphia, aged eighty-nine, on December 31, 1945.

Reference:

James Wren and Genevieve Wren, *Motor Trucks of America* (Ann Arbor: University of Michigan Press, 1979).

Archives:

Material on Pedro G. Salom can be found at the University of Pennsylvania Library and Alumni Records Office.

Seaman Body Corporation

by Frederick I. Olson

University of Wisconsin, Milwaukee

Seaman Body Corporation evolved from a pioneer furniture manufacturer and retailer into an independent maker of passenger car bodies, and finally into a division of Nash Motors Company and American Motors Corporation.

Alonzo D. Seaman opened a fine-furniture shop in 1847 in Milwaukee, Wisconsin. By his death in 1868 the business employed 200 workers, with annual sales of $120,000 and a St. Louis outlet. His sons William and Harry carried on as the Milwaukee Parlor Frame Company on the city's south side. In 1881 William created the W. S. Seaman Company and contracted to produce for Western Electric Company a soundproof telephone booth to ensure privacy in public places; Seaman also made switchboards and other telephone equipment until World War I. In 1906, after his factory burned, William rebuilt on the north side of the city a larger plant than he needed for his current products. One of his tenants, Petrel Motor Car Company, made a friction-drive automobile, for which Seaman supplied wood bodies beginning in 1909. For nearly a decade thereafter Seaman produced passenger car bodies for automobile makers such as Moline, Rambler, Marmon, Chicago Electric, Velie, Dorris, Columbia Taxicab, Kissel, and FAL, as well as winter tops for Ford and Cadillac. In 1910 Seaman became the first automobile body builder to reinforce wood with steel. During World War I Seaman built thousands of sidecars for Harley-Davidson Motorcycles of Milwaukee, ordered for combat use by the United States Army, as well as ammunition boxes, gun mounts, and other war materiel under subcontract for the Velie Motor Car Company of Moline, Illinois.

By fall 1917 it became evident that Seaman was overextended. It therefore terminated its telephone equipment contracts and restricted its body production to Nash Motors Company of Kenosha, Wisconsin. The Thomas B. Jeffery Company, which had produced Ramblers in Kenosha since 1902, had been sold to Charles W. Nash, formerly president of General Motors, in 1916. Nash's production of 11,000 trucks in 1918, said to be more than any other maker in a single year, contributed to its decision to purchase a half interest in Seaman in 1919, accompanied by a name change to Seaman Body Corporation. Seventeen years later Nash bought out the rest of the Seaman family interest. As the Seaman Body Division of Nash-Kelvinator Corporation and American Motors, it continued to produce auto bodies until AMC was purchased by the Chrysler Corporation in 1987. The Milwaukee plant was then closed by Chrysler.

Reference:

William George Bruce, *History of Milwaukee City and County,* volume 3 (Chicago-Milwaukee, 1922), p. 489.

Seats

by David J. Andrea

University of Michigan

Automotive seats provide many functions: sitting structure and comfort, occupant protection, style and fashion, and storage (map pockets and under-seat compartments). As a combination of horse carriages and mobile power sources, early motor vehicles derived their seating directly from horse wagons and carriages. Pioneering vehicles such as the 1886 Daimler were hand built and expensive. With cost no object, leather was used for durability and appearance. Open vehicles of the day made durability important, as the interior was completely exposed to the elements; occupant comfort took a lower priority. In the early 1900s seats typically placed two abreast and consisted of a padded bench with metal or wood side rails for armrests and narrow, unpadded backrests. More luxurious vehicles such as the 1906 Mercedes featured full backrests and elaborate, buttoned leather upholstery.

As vehicle bodies became enclosed and production increased during the 1920s, woven fabrics replaced leather as the primary automotive upholstery. Used also in carriages and wagons, these fabrics were coarse but durable. A fabric named Leatherette (also marketed under the Rexine trade name) became widely used. A reasonably inexpensive fabric, it consisted of a cloth backing with a flexible, "leather-like" coating on the reverse side.

Other cost reductions occurred as the petrochemical industry grew and plastics became less expensive. Plastic webbing and foam rubber replaced horsehair and rubber air bladders as the primary method of cushion construction. Development of the well-known zigzag steel-wire seat springs completely eliminated animal hair cushions.

Up to the late 1930s most seats incorporated a fixed seat back. In 1936 G. H. Robinson invented a cam-system that allowed the back to recline. This system, initially applied to European vehicles, incorporates the design universally applied today. The recliner mechanism remained the same until 1951, when a German firm applied a spring mechanism allowing full reclining and adjusting capabilities.

Today seats are mass-produced by a variety of methods. A popular method, foam-in-place, injects foam rubber directly into fabric laid in a cushion mold. This allows further production cost and time reductions. "Cut and sew" shops produce seats in the more traditional manner: fashioning fabric seat covers to slip over foam rubber cushion forms.

Automotive seats now come with a wide spectrum of options. Low-priced seats in small, inexpensive vehicles are not significantly different from seats of ten years ago. Seats in expensive vehicles may cost $2,000 to $3,000 a pair and contain electric motors to control placement, inflatable air bladder back support, headrest audio speakers, and electronic memory chips to adjust seat position for different drivers automatically. The bench seat—more comfortable but similar to the seats of the early 1900s—is still the most popular seat for large and luxury vehicles. However, the bucket seat, once used only in small vehicles with manual transmissions, is growing in popularity as American consumers demand greater seat comfort and support.

Reference:

John Day and C. Eng, *The Bosch Book of the Motor Car— Its Evolution and Engineering Development* (New York: St. Martin's, 1975).

Selden Patent Case

by James Wren

Motor Vehicle Manufacturers Association

The Selden patent case was one of the most spectacular events not only in automotive history but also in American legal history in general. It was spectacular not for courtroom dramatics or revolutionary legal tenets, but for its cast of characters, which featured some of the nation's leading industrialists, including Henry Ford. At stake was the validity of U.S. patent number 549,160, issued on November 5, 1895, to lawyer and inventor George B. Selden of Rochester, New York, for an "improved road-engine" that Selden claimed represented an original and fundamental combination of features employing internal combustion engine technology. The patent covered "the combination with a road locomotive, provided with suitable running gear including a propelling wheel and steering mechanism, of a liquid hydrocarbon gas-engine of the compression type, comprising one or more power cylinders, a suitable liquid-fuel receptacle, a power shaft connected with and arranged to run faster than the propelling wheel, an intermediate clutch or disconnecting device and a suitable carriage body adapted to the conveyance of person or goods." The outcome of the case was vital to the financial and commercial interests of the fledgling automotive industry.

By 1903 a group of automakers recognized the validity of the patent in return for an exclusive license to manufacture cars under its stipulations. They formed the Association of Licensed Automobile Manufacturers (ALAM) for the purpose of enforcing their license, agreeing to pay royalties to Selden on each car manufactured under the patent. Later in 1903 Henry Ford and other officials of Detroit's Ford Motor Company applied to the ALAM for a license, but they were denied on the grounds that Ford was merely an "assemblage plant." Doubtlessly the ALAM also viewed Ford's two previous failures in the automotive business as grounds for denial. The ALAM held that the function of the association was to prevent disreputable

manufacturers from entering the business. Others, including the Ford company officials, viewed the ALAM as an impediment, intent on establishing a monopoly of American car manufacturers.

After the ALAM denied Ford the right to build cars under the Selden patent, it issued threatening advertisements aimed at frightening prospective automotive consumers away from purchasing cars from unlicensed makers. Ford countered with its own advertising, in which the company vowed to protect Ford owners from prosecution. Ford further challenged the ALAM by declaring that he would donate $1,000 to the association if it publicized the Ford Motor Company by filing an infringement suit.

The ALAM reply was not long in coming. On October 22, 1903, the association filed suit on behalf of Selden and the Electric Vehicle Company (the original patent licensee) in the U.S. District Court for the Southern District of New York against Ford and the C. A. Duerr Company, Ford's New York agent, for infringement. Soon after, the ALAM filed suit against the O. J. Gude Company for purchasing a Ford automobile in violation of the patent. In December the association filed suit against unlicensed foreign manufacturer Panhard et Levassor and its New York branch manager, Andre Massenat. Late in 1904 the association filed against Henry and Albert Neubauer as unlicensed importers of Panhard and Renault automobiles. The ALAM had engaged a domestic manufacturer, Ford; a sales agent, Duerr; a purchaser, Gude; a foreign manufacturer, Panhard et Levassor; and importers, the Neubauers. Eventually the five cases were consolidated into two test cases, the Ford and Panhard suits, and then into a single case.

As battle lines were drawn, distinguished patent attorneys prepared their cases. The ALAM and the Electric Vehicle Company were represented by the prestigious New York firms of Betts, Betts, Shef-

One of two vehicles built in 1907 by the Electric Vehicle Company and the Association of Licensed Automobile Manufacturers to test the feasibility of George B. Selden's 1877 road carriage design, patented in 1895 (courtesy of the Henry Ford Museum, Dearborn, Michigan)

field and Betts, and Redding, Greely and Austin. The firm of Fish, Richardson, Herrick and Neave assisted in the preparation of briefs for the case. George Raines served as Selden's personal counsel. Detroit attorney Ralzemond A. Parker of the firm of Parker and Burton, assisted by the firm of Cardoza and Nathan and Elliot J. Stoddard, filed for the defense. The opposing counsel tended to reflect the images of the combatants. The New York lawyers were dapper and polished, suitable for representing a powerful syndicate. Conversely, Parker was a brash midwesterner who wore rumpled clothes, a wide-brimmed hat, and an unkempt white beard, a perfect defender of the little guy.

The strategy of the defense was to attack the patent's validity by showing there was more than enough "prior art" to invalidate the claims of the Selden forces. Parker also took every opportunity to attack the Electric Vehicle Company and the ALAM on monopolistic grounds. At a time of extreme pub-

lic feeling against the forces of monopoly, the strategy gained public favor and bolstered Ford's image.

Patent litigation, then and now, is an extremely slow process, costly and complicated. Few had knowledge enough to understand the technical elements of the Selden case, so much time was spent explaining the claim in the context of automotive history. Furthermore, testimony was taken from witnesses scattered all over the United States. Parker began his case on July 20, 1904, with Ford as his first witness. He then moved to Reading, Pennsylvania, to examine Charles Duryea. The case then took him to Boston, Massachusetts; Providence, Rhode Island; and Pittsburgh, Pennsylvania; before he examined Ransom Olds in Lansing, Michigan. Then he went to Ithaca, New York, where a professor of experimental engineering clearly defined the differences between the Brayton 2-stroke engine (which Selden employed in his design) and the Otto 4-stroke (which the vast majority of American automakers used). Parker concluded in July 1905.

The New York counsel began taking testimony for the complainants on April 11, 1904, and completed their case in June 1905. They emphasized the originality of Selden's combination of features, not that Selden had actually invented any of the components of internal combustion automobile technology. The ALAM rebutted the defense by presenting respected British engine authority Dugold Clerk, who supported Selden's claims. He also admitted in cross-examination that if an engine other than the 2-stroke Brayton type Selden employed could power Selden's road carriage, the validity of the patent would have to be reconsidered. The defense later constructed and demonstrated a car driven by a Lenoir engine. The complainants also built two cars, one under the direction of Selden's sons, the other under the direction of the Electric Vehicle Company. Driving tests of the cars were conducted in the spring and summer of 1907.

In 1907 and 1908 Parker examined Selden in what was the highlight of the case. Then the trial hearing began on May 28, 1909, with Judge Charles Merril Haugh presiding. After the hearing, Haugh retired to his summer home to study the 1,500 pages of briefs generated by the testimony. On September 15, 1909, Haugh filed in favor of the Selden interests.

But the tenacious Henry Ford was not through. Ford Motor Company immediately appealed the decision. The case began on November 27, 1910, before the U.S. Circuit Court of Appeals, with Judges Emile Henry Lacombe, Henry Galbraith Ward, and Walter Chadwick Noyes presiding. The appeals court issued its decision on January 9, 1911, holding that the Selden patent was "valid but not infringed" because it stipulated a 2-stroke Brayton engine, not a 4-stroke Otto. Since the patent had only two years of life remaining, the ALAM decided not to appeal. Later in 1911 the association was dissolved. Ford Motor Company and all other American automakers were free to do as they wished.

References:

C. Lyle Cummins, *Internal Fire* (Lake Oswego, Oreg.: Carnot, 1975), pp. 194-195;

James Rood Doolittle, *The Romance of the Auto Industry* (New York: Klebold, 1916);

H. O. Duncan, *The World on Wheels* (Paris: Obalseston, 1926), pp. 914-919;

William Greenleaf, *Monopoly on Wheels: Henry Ford and the Selden Automobile Patent* (Detroit: Wayne State University Press, 1961);

Allan Nevins, *Ford: The Times, the Man, the Company* (New York: Scribners, 1954);

Lawrence H. Seltzer, *A Financial History of the American Automobile* (Boston & New York: Houghton Mifflin, 1928).

Archives:

Material pertaining to the Selden patent case is in the archives of the Motor Vehicle Manufacturers Association, Detroit, Michigan.

Self-Starters

by Northcoate Hamilton

Columbia, South Carolina

The replacement of the hand-cranked engine starter with an electrically powered system was, along with the development of the closed steel body, one of the most important innovations in creating the consumer-driven automobile industry. During the early years of the automobile the unwieldy and dangerous hand crank severely limited women's use of automobiles. Men also reacted negatively to the hand crank, which had the capability of maiming or killing the careless user. In fact, the danger of the crank led directly to the development of a safe, reliable self-starter.

In the summer of 1910 Byron Carter, the manufacturer of the Cartercar, was injured when he stopped to help a woman restart her stalled engine. When cranking the engine, Carter failed to retard the spark, and when the engine caught, it swung the crank into his jaw. Complications arising from the injury led to Carter's death. Henry Leland, Carter's close friend and the head of Cadillac, distressed at Carter's death, became interested in finding a way to prevent such accidents.

Also interested in solving mechanical problems associated with the development of the automobile was Charles F. Kettering, an engineer and researcher at the National Cash Register Company (NCR) in Dayton, Ohio. One of Kettering's friends and coworkers, Earl Howard, had left NCR to become assistant sales manager at Cadillac, and had later persuaded Kettering to develop a new ignition system for the automaker. When Leland expressed his desire to find a new cranking system, Kettering replied that he believed it was possible to develop an electric starting system. Leland promised to support the research and to install any workable system into the next year's models.

Kettering knew that one of the major problems in developing an electric starter was the size of the motor that would be needed. Other researchers had resisted the idea of electric starters because they believed any motor powerful enough to start an engine would be too heavy for the vehicle. Kettering, who had developed a motor small enough to fit into a cash register, thought otherwise. Returning from Detroit to his research laboratory in Dayton, Kettering and his staff worked furiously to assemble a prototype. He succeeded quickly in using a working model and then turned his attention to perfecting a system small enough and powerful enough to be compatible with Cadillac's models. Another engineering goal was to create a power source that would recharge itself. Kettering devised a system in which a generator fed 24 volts from a storage battery into the starter to ignite the engine and then switched to 6 volts to feed back into the battery to recharge it. His work went quickly, and on December 24, 1910, a prototype was fitted to a Cadillac engine and given a successful trial.

Although the prototype worked, it was still larger than Kettering desired. Work recommenced, and a fully installed starter, of a sufficiently small size to fit on a standard engine, was delivered to the Cadillac Motor Company on February 17, 1911. The next day Leland ordered 12,000 starter units to be delivered for use on the 1912 Cadillac.

The importance of the self-starter is that it opened the automobile market to women, a segment that had resisted the automobile because of the physical demands on the driver by the manual starter. As women came to drive more and more, the marketing of automobiles slowly began to focus on them. The development of the self-starter and the resulting new markets enabled this shift and led to the more sophisticated marketing approach of Alfred P. Sloan of General Motors in the 1920s, which made the automobile industry the dominant industrial enterprise of the twentieth century.

References:

T. A. Boyd, *Professional Amateur: The Biography of Charles Franklin Kettering* (New York: Dutton, 1957);

James J. Flink, *The Automobile Age* (Cambridge, Mass.: MIT Press, 1988);

Stuart Leslie, *Boss Kettering* (New York: Columbia University Press, 1983).

Shock Absorbers

by James Wren

Motor Vehicle Manufacturers Association

The term shock absorber describes the many devices used from the earliest days of the automobile to lessen the impact of the constant bouncing and jarring of a vehicle. Pneumatic tires, spring inserts, and springs themselves were randomly indentified as such. With the fitting of leaf springs to vehicles as a suspension to lessen the jouncing of a ride, it soon became obvious that the opposite effect of the spring rebound was as serious a problem as the impact itself.

The solution to the problem was simple: the attachment of a device between the frame or axle of the vehicle and the spring to stabilize spring reaction. Numerous reaction devices were introduced to complement the spring system in aiding tires in absorbing the shocks. They are generally categorized as follows: friction devices, auxiliary springs, snubbers, and pneumatic or hydraulic cylinders.

Auxiliary spring devices used one or more supplemental spiral or coil springs attached to the frame and the axle or spring. These devices were short-lived, however, due to the difference in spring harmonics which limited their effectiveness.

The first true system to meet with notable success was a friction device for bicycles developed in France by J. M. Truffault. The front of the bicycle was suspended on springs, and used a friction device to keep the bike from oscillating. The system was adapted for American cars around 1899 by Edward V. Hartford, a pioneer automobile enthusiast.

The Truffault-Hartford device consisted of two levers, hinged together with a pad of rubber disks. One lever was attached at the frame; the other was bolted to either the leaf spring or the axle. As a vehicle wheel hit an object or road irregularity, the levers moved towards one another and the rubber discs resisted the vibration of the spring in both directions. A bolt placed at the hinge point could be tightened or loosened to increase or decrease the friction for a stiffer or softer ride. The unit was not only the first automatic shock absorber but was also the first *adjustable* shock absorber. The Truffault-Hartford shock became standard equipment on the Pierce-Arrow in 1905. From then on, new shock absorber designs followed quickly and constantly.

The snubber-type shock absorber, promoted and popularized by the Gabriel Company, was basically a leather strap or belt. The strap was attached to, and wrapped around, a small coil or spring inside a housing attached to the vehicle frame and then strapped or looped around the vehicle axle. It was first developed around 1906.

The hydraulic shock absorber was another French development, first used by Maurice Houdaille and introduced on American cars in the late 1910s. The device featured a piston working in a cylinder filled with viscous fluid. The piston forced the fluid through various-sized openings and valves, the action providing a buffer against spring rebound or deflections of the frame. The hydraulic cylinder or reservoir was attached to the spring or axle with the end of the piston attached to the frame.

Pneumatic shock absorbers were similar, but used a cushion of air as the working medium against which the piston controlled both recoil and compression of the vehicle spring. An air valve was built into the cylinder to maintain the air pressure.

Both the hydraulic and pneumatic shock absorbers were double acting; that is, they cushioned both the downward and upward or rebound effects of the vehicle suspension. By the late 1930s, the double-acting hydraulic-type shock was dominant in the industry.

Samuel Latta Smith

(June 28, 1830-May 7, 1917)

by George S. May

Eastern Michigan University

CAREER: Organizer and developer of mining and transportation companies (1859-1897); stockholder, Olds Motor Vehicle Company (1897-1899); principal financial backer, Olds Motor Works (1899-1908).

Samuel Latta Smith was semiretired in the late 1890s, but the investments the wealthy Detroiter made in the automobile industry were one of the major factors making Detroit and southern Michigan the center of that industry. Smith was born on June 28, 1830, in Algonac on the St. Clair River, not far to the northeast of Detroit. His father, John Keyser Smith, a native of Scotland who served in the War of 1812, and his mother, Catherine Mac-Donald Smith, were pioneer settlers of St. Clair County. After attending public school in Algonac, he went on in 1846 to Albion College, where he completed two years of study before returning to his hometown to go into business. He also became active in Democratic politics and represented his county in the lower house of the state legislature in the late 1850s.

In 1859 Smith, like many young men of his day, left southern Michigan to seek his fortune in the booming mining economy of Michigan's Upper Peninsula. He settled in Houghton in the heart of what became known as the Copper Country. Although he started out as a merchant, he was soon involved in the organization and development of at least six copper mining companies, including the Copper Range Mining Company, second in importance only to the great Calumet and Hecla. To facilitate transport of the area's copper, Smith took the lead in securing the financing for the Marquette, Houghton & Ontonagon Railroad, and he supervised some of its construction, which was completed to L'Anse in 1873 and extended to Houghton 15 years later. He also organized the Copper Range Railroad, which provided the Copper

Samuel Latta Smith (courtesy of the Burton Historical Collection)

Country with a link to the St. Paul Railroad system. His major accomplishment, however, was directing the completion in the 1870s of the Portage Lake and Lake Superior Ship Canal, which cut through the Keweenaw Peninsula and opened the interior of the Copper Country to Great Lakes vessels.

In 1865 Smith and Eliza Seager were married in Lansing, Michigan. Although Smith continued his mining activities in the North (he organized a new copper mining company as late as 1897), he moved his residence to Lansing by the 1880s, leaving his brother-in-law, James H. Seager, to keep tabs on their mutual Copper Country business interests. In Lansing, Smith became closely associated with Edward W. Sparrow in real estate and banking concerns. He moved to Detroit in the 1890s but maintained his Lansing contacts. Thus, since Sparrow agreed to help Ransom E. Olds obtain financial support to produce the car Olds had developed, it was not surprising to find Smith listed as one of the stockholders of the Olds Motor Vehicle Company when it was organized on August 21, 1897. Smith's 500 shares, one-tenth of the number issued, equaled the number assigned to Sparrow and two other investors. All told, the stockholders provided a mere $10,000, and Smith may have made his contribution of $1,000 only as a favor to Sparrow. However, his experience in the transportation industry may have kindled a special interest in automobiles, while Ransom Olds's success as a manufacturer of gasoline engines boded well for the success of his new venture.

Smith was not active in the management of the Olds Motor Vehicle Company, which was run by Olds under the supervision of company president Sparrow. But $10,000 was far too little to permit the company to build a factory separate from the Olds engine plant to assemble the cars. Olds was soon looking for additional capital, and in the winter of 1898-1899, after a fruitless trip to New York where a promise of financial aid failed to materialize, Smith agreed to put up an additional $200,000. With that kind of backing it did not take long to fill in the details of a reorganization of the Olds business as the Olds Motor Works, incorporated on May 8, 1899.

Only sketchy information is available regarding those negotiations, but it is evident that whatever Smith's motives may have been in backing the new company, the instincts that had served him well in his past dealings had not been dulled by age. As much as he may have been intrigued by the automobile's potential, he was not risking $200,000 on the Olds car alone. Instead, he insisted that the Olds Gasoline Engine Works become part of the company. The demand for Olds engines was so great that Smith was virtually guaranteed he would not lose money. If Olds automobiles were a success, he could be the beneficiary of a great windfall at a time when profits from his mining investments were leveling off. If the automobile failed to

make it, he could abandon it before it seriously eroded the profits from the engine division. Smith was kindly disposed toward Olds and wanted to help him out, but at the same time he wanted to protect himself.

Olds accepted Smith's help even though it meant giving up the control he had been accustomed to in his earlier companies. Smith held 19,960 of the initial 20,000 shares of Olds Motor Works stock, with the remaining 40 shares divided equally between Olds, Edward Sparrow, James Seager, and Smith's son Frederic. When an additional 15,000 shares were distributed to the stockholders in the Olds Gasoline Engine and Olds Motor Vehicle companies, the proportion held by Smith was considerably reduced and the amount held by Olds greatly increased. However, in spite of the fact that Smith soon sold more than one-third of his stock, he still owned the largest bloc of shares, and those, together with those held by his sons, in-laws, and friends, gave him control of a solid majority of the company stock.

Although the Detroit orientation of the majority owners helps explain the shift of the company's main offices to Detroit, where a factory was built for the production of the cars, Ransom Olds was the one they counted on to direct that production. In May 1899, therefore, he was named general manager and vice-president, with Samuel Smith elected president. In January 1900 the directors moved Olds up to the presidency, shifting Smith to the position of vice-president. By that time the new Detroit factory had been completed, and by the fall Olds, after having experimented without much success with several different models, settled upon a small runabout with a curved dash to be the first car to carry the Oldsmobile name. By the end of 1901, despite a fire that destroyed the Detroit plant in March of that year, the curved-dash Oldsmobile was becoming the most popular car in the country.

It was in 1901, however, at the very time the automobile side of the business began to show a profit, that Olds's managerial control began to slip. In January, Samuel Smith resumed the office of president while Olds, although continuing as general manager, moved back to the vice-president's office. In addition, Smith's son Frederic now began playing a stronger role in managerial decisions. One reason why Samuel Smith may have brought about the organization of the Olds Motor Works was to provide a new business outlet for his two sons, Frederic and

Angus. The latter, the younger of the two, became a substantial stockholder in the company but never seems to have been deeply involved in policy-making. Not so Frederic, whose purchase of stock in the Olds Gasoline Engine Works in 1898 had been an early sign that the aggressive and ambitious Detroiter was not content to be involved only with his father's mining and real estate concerns.

When the Olds Motor Works was formed, Frederic Smith was named secretary-treasurer, and it was not long before he inserted himself into areas that would not normally have been his responsibility. After the fire of March 1901 he took the lead in negotiations that led to the construction of a new plant in Lansing. The Detroit plant was also rebuilt, and when Olds returned to Lansing in 1902 to assume day-to-day direction, Frederic Smith took on the supervision of the Detroit plant. The job seems to have given him increased confidence of his grasp of managerial matters. By the summer of 1902 he was rebuking Olds for not doing enough to quiet the complaints concerning the defects owners found in their Oldsmobile runabouts. And Smith felt that Olds was not moving energetically enough in the development of a larger touring car to go along with the runabout. Olds did not oppose that, but considering the money they were making from runabout sales, he did not feel as strongly as Smith that developing a bigger model was an urgent matter. Outside the company, Fred Smith's assumption of the leadership role at Olds Motor Works was clearly indicated by the fact that it was he, not Olds, who initiated the talks with the Selden patent forces that led to the formation in March 1903 of the Association of Licensed Automobile Manufacturers, with Smith becoming the first president of that powerful trade association. (It was Frederic Smith who rejected the Ford Motor Company's bid to be a member of that association and thereby paved the way for the most celebrated patent infringement case in American history.)

Olds could hardly not have been annoyed at the interference by Smith in the operations of the company, but he seems to have held himself in check until May 1, 1903, when he angrily reacted to Smith's action in establishing an experimental engineering shop in Detroit without getting Olds's authorization: "I am Vice-President and Manager of this company and such things should not be taken up without my consent or the consent of the board. I have had all I want of this treatment." However,

Fred Smith had the votes that were needed to back him up in any confrontation with Olds, and although the two men tried to give an appearance of working together after that time, Olds seems to have realized that his days with the company were numbered. On January 11, 1904, the directors voted to name Fred Smith to succeed Olds as vice-president and general manager. According to a letter Olds wrote to Smith that month, he agreed to the move in return for Smith's help in selling Olds's stock. The last of the stock was sold that spring, and in August Olds severed his final connections with the Olds Motor Works, resigning his directorship to devote his time to his new Reo Motor Car Company. The parting was not an amicable one, with Olds charging that Smith had hindered rather than helped the sale of his stock, while Smith showed his feelings toward Olds by not even mentioning his name in the account he wrote of his automotive activities in his 1928 memoirs.

Under Smith's direction the Olds Motor Works continued to prosper for some time, setting new production records in 1904 and 1905 that kept it among the top volume producers in the industry. The curved-dash runabout continued to account for most of that production, which would be concentrated entirely in Lansing in 1905. The larger models that Olds and his staff had been working on began to appear by 1904, and by 1907 the 4-cylinder and 6-cylinder Oldsmobiles had completely replaced the runabout. The move resulted in a drastic reduction in sales, from more than 6,000 in 1905 to only 1,600 in 1906 and by 1908 to barely 1,000. Ransom Olds must have gloated as he saw the figures and compared them to the sales of his new Reos, which far exceeded the Oldsmobile's beginning in 1906. To keep the Olds company afloat, Samuel Smith had advanced it more than $1 million of his own funds by 1908.

The Olds Motor Works may have been saved by the fact that William C. Durant became interested in acquiring control of it as part of the consolidation he was putting together when he organized the General Motors (GM) holding company in September 1908. In July, as plans to merge Durant's Buick company with Maxwell-Briscoe were coming apart, Durant went to Lansing and roused Olds company officials, who gave him a quick tour of the Olds plant at three in the morning. He gathered from talking with the Smiths that they would be receptive to a takeover bid, and in October, after making Buick the first of the companies the new GM controlled, Durant presented an offer the Smiths accepted in a deal completed on November 12, 1908. In return for GM taking care of Samuel Smith's claims of $1,044,173.89 that were owed to him by the Olds Motor Works, the Olds stockholders received GM stock valued at $3 million in return for the outstanding Olds stock, which had a par value of $2 million but which was sold on the market for half that amount. Only $17,279 in cash was involved in the exchange, which left the Olds Motor Works as a separate company but one in which GM controlled the stock.

Fred Smith later admitted that Olds had acted unwisely in insisting upon receiving GM preferred stock instead of common stock, which would prove to be far more valuable. Smith retained his managerial position at Olds Motor Works, as part of Durant's announced intention to retain the executives of the companies GM took over. However, the progress the Olds company had made under Fred Smith's leadership did not hold out much hope that he could bring about the kind of improvement in sales Durant desired, so on September 2, 1909, it was announced that Fred Smith and also Angus Smith were resigning from the company, with Fred Smith also giving up the seat on the board of directors he had been given when GM gained control of the Olds Motor Works.

Although Fred Smith, together with his brother, was a major stockholder in the short-lived Owen Motor Car Company, which was taken over in October 1910, interestingly enough, by Ransom Olds's Reo organization, and Smith would live until 1954, his automotive career for all practical purposes ended with his resignation, no doubt under pressure, from the Olds Motor Works. For a time during his ten years with the Olds company he had been one of the industry's major figures, but it was his father's money that had made it possible to establish the company and that had assured the son of his executive status. Samuel Smith had stepped down as president of the Olds Motor Works in October 1902 and had played a much less active role in the company thereafter. But those in the know recognized his importance. When he died on May 7, 1917, less than two months shy of his eighty-seventh birthday, the *Detroit Free Press* credited him with being the "father of the motor car industry in Detroit." The trade journal *Automobile* went even further, declaring that Samuel Smith "commercialized the automobile industry when it was in its infancy. He had the courage to spend millions."

References:

George S. May, *A Most Unique Machine: The Michigan Origins of the American Automobile Industry* (Grand Rapids, Mich.: Eerdmans, 1975);

May, *R. E. Olds: Auto Industry Pioneer* (Grand Rapids, Mich.: Eerdmans, 1977);

Frederic Smith, *Motoring Down a Quarter of a Century* (Detroit: Privately published, 1928).

Archives:

Some correspondence and other material relating to the Smiths is in the R. E. Olds Collection in the Historical Collections at the Michigan State University Library, East Lansing, Michigan.

A. O. Smith Corporation

by Frederick T. Olsen

University of Wisconsin–Milwaukee

Charles Jeremiah Smith, an English immigrant, came to Milwaukee in 1843 as a blacksmith and in 1874 opened a small machine shop. He made parts for baby carriages, and by the 1890s for bicycles, as the bicycling fad swept the United States. C. J. Smith & Sons Company, incorporated in 1892 from his partnership with his sons, became one of the nation's, and perhaps the world's, leading bicycle parts makers, exporting to Canada and Europe. In 1899 the American Bicycle Company was formed to acquire 44 of the nation's bicycle makers, including Smith. The older Smith retired, and some of his sons turned to other business interests. One of them, Arthur Oliver Smith, resigned as general manager in Milwaukee for American Bicycle (under the name Automotive & Cycle Parts Company) in 1904 to form the A. O. Smith Company, a Wisconsin corporation producing tubular frames for bicycles and very shortly automobile frames for such car manufacturers as the Studebaker Electric and the Peerless Automobile companies. The firm also produced tubular steel for Pope-Toledo, Cadillac, Packard, Elmore, and Locomobile, but his great coup came with an order from Henry Ford in 1906 for 10,000 automobile frames. This large-scale order, completed in four months, projected A. O. Smith into the forefront of independent automobile suppliers. Using a press built by another Milwaukee-area firm, Allis-Chalmers, Smith is said to have produced the first pressed-steel automobile frames, thus replacing tubular steel frames and the use of commercial channel or angle iron. The company also made pressed-steel rear axle housings for Ford and others, as well as a variety of additional parts and other iron and steel products.

While A. O. Smith thereafter expanded its parts manufacturing through many acquisitions, its emphasis remained on automobile frames. Constantly expanding frame sales led to relocation of its factory from the south side of Milwaukee to the city's growing northwest side in 1910. Five years later planning began for an automated frame plant, which was built in 1919 and successfully opened two years later; flat sheets of steel were fed into machines in a two-block-long plant that produced a frame in eight seconds, 10,000 per day, with a 180-man work force. This system was used until the introduction of welding in 1958. Smith's frame production leaped from 279,150 in 1921 to 1,022,014 two years later, then leveled off. By 1931 its Milwaukee plant was the world's largest devoted to pressed-steel products. At one time Smith provided parts for 39 automobile makers, including Fiat in Italy and Austin in England.

In 1930 Smith opened a research and engineering facility designed by John Welborn Root, which helped to maintain its state-of-the-art automobile frame position and facilitated its entry into diversified products for automobiles, oil and gas field equipment, water treatment, refrigeration, and power generation. Its major innovation was the fusing of glass to steel for water heaters and silos. In 1914 it developed the Smith Motor wheel, a 1-cylinder, 4-cycle gasoline engine and wheel attached to a bicycle; when later introduced on a buckboard, it became the forerunner of the sports car known as the Smith Flyer. More recently it entered data processing, but divested that business in 1986. Diversification based on research permitted Smith's survival during the Depression. In both world wars A. O. Smith converted to the making of bomb and shell casings and other war materiel.

Smith remains the world's largest independent manufacturer of automobile and truck frames, supplying all of the American Big Three. Its production remains concentrated in its older Milwaukee facilities, but an additional frame plant was built in Granite City, Illinois, in 1952, and since then all expansion and diversification has been in the South and Mexico. The 1960s challenge of the integral or unit body frame as well as other changes in style, comfort, space, and safety of passenger cars were met by Smith quality engineering, but the growing acceptance of front-wheel drive and unibody frames by the 1980s, especially by GM, its largest customer, posed a major threat to Smith. Its nearly 50 percent of the truck frame business also came into question. The result has been a total work force reduction for Smith of about half since its high of 8,000 workers in the 1970s.

From its inception in 1904 A. O. Smith had local investors and became a publicly held corpora- tion, shifting its incorporation to New York in 1916 and to Delaware in 1986. Lloyd Raymond Smith continued the tradition of strong family leadership, and only in the 1980s has professional management largely superseded family influence.

References:

Neita O. Friend, "Through Research ... A Better Way—A. O. Smith Corporation," *Creative Wisconsin*, 6 (Winter 1959): 29-52;

Herbert W. Rice, "Charles Jeremiah Smith and His Sons," *Historical Messenger of the Milwaukee County Historical Society*, 3 (March 1956): 6-8.

Spark Plugs

by James Wren

Motor Vehicle Manufacturers Association

A spark plug is a conducting device that is screwed into a cylinder head of an engine and extends into the combustion chamber to ignite the fuel/air mixture. Generally a single spark plug is used for each cylinder, but engines using two plugs per cylinder have been introduced at various times.

Numerous devices were conceived to ignite the gases in early engines. Direct flame tubes heated by internal flames and platinum heated by an electrical current were the more popular means for ignition in the mid 1800s. Noted European pioneers Nicholas Otto and Etienne Lenoir used such devices in their early engines. In 1860 Lenoir devised a high-tension device with contact points that produced a spark when opened. The spark plug used in his system was attached to a cylinder head with an electrode at the point of juncture. Within a year the design was modified to include another electrode arranged within the body of the plug and surrounded by an insulator. The Lenoir plug was also threaded for attachment to the engine. Earlier plugs had used flanges with nuts and studs for attaching. By the 1900s the threaded spark plug was dominant.

The basic spark plug design uses a one- or two-piece steel body with a one-piece shell that supports an insulator surrounding a center electrode and a ground electrode. High voltage enters the plug through a wire or cable attached to a terminal that is screwed into the insulator. Current flows down the center electrode and jumps from the end of the center electrode to the ground electrode. The distance between the electrodes, or the spark gap, varies for different engines. Copper- and asbestos-lined gaskets are used for sealing purposes between the bushing and the shell.

Contemporary spark plugs have incorporated a resistor around the electrode to reduce the current flow and limit radio and television interference. The resistor also helps to control electrode burning. The plugs are usually located in the vicinity of the engine inlet valves, where the mixture is fresh. A standardized thread size of 7/8 inch was adopted by the Association of Licensed Automobile Manufacturers (ALAM) in the early 1900s.

Spark plug fouling was one of the major engine problems in the early days of the automobile, and motorists were constantly changing plugs. Prices usually varied from 50 cents to $3 per spark plug. The major cause of such fouling was poor piston ring design, which resulted in very poor compression and oil leakage that saturated the electrodes.

Insulator materials such as porcelain, mica, glass, and ceramics also presented various problems for the manufacturers and were under continuous development. Glass and porcelain often cracked at high temperatures in aviation engines. However, porcelain was adequate for automobile spark plugs.

Mica handled the higher temperatures because of its low thermal conductivity but posed a problem in keeping the plugs cool and would absorb oil, moisture, and residue from combustion. The mica was also affected by lead compounds, and when tetraethyl lead was added to gasoline the use of mica in spark plugs slowly disappeared.

The ceramic insulator was introduced in the 1920s, and one of the best-known ceramics, porcelain, was improved over the earlier compounds and became the choice of most spark plug manufacturers until replaced by mullite, then alumina.

Stanley Motor Carriage Company

by George S. May

Eastern Michigan University

Although only about 18,000 were manufactured during its quarter-century production life, the Stanley Steamer is the most famous of all steam-powered automobiles. Indeed, it is the only one of many familiar cars of that type that were manufactured in the early years of the industry. It was the creation of a remarkable set of identical twins, Francis E. and Freelan O. Stanley.

The Stanley brothers were born in Kingfield, Maine, on June 1, 1849, the sons of Solomon and Apphia Stanley. Solomon Stanley was a farmer, but it was soon evident that the twins had no desire to continue in their father's line of work. For a time both became schoolteachers, the fact that they had had little formal education being no impediment to entry into the teaching profession of that period. But they left teaching for other activities that provided greater outlets for their diverse creative talents.

They employed their boyhood whittling skills to start up a business manufacturing violins. Freelan in particular maintained an interest in making violins throughout his life, taking visitors to a room in the automobile factory to show the violin he was working on at that time. Francis used his artistic talent to establish a business in Lewiston, Maine, doing crayon portraits. He then took up photography, which led to the brothers' most important achievement, photographic dry plates. In 1885 they patented a machine for coating dry plates, the first successful process of this type. They established the Stanley Dry Plate Company in Lewiston to manufacture the plates, moving the business to Newton, Massachusetts, in 1889. The business was a notable success and was ultimately sold in 1904 to Eastman Kodak at a great profit.

The Stanley brothers also developed and marketed a home gas generator and X-ray equipment, but the sight of the first horseless carriage at the Brockton, Massachusetts, fair in fall 1896 got them started on the product with which their name would forever be linked. They decided that they could build a better steamer than the one they had seen demonstrated, although, one of them would later admit, "We knew but little about steam engines and less about boilers." By fall 1897 they built a steam carriage, but the engine and boiler they had purchased for the carriage were too heavy. They then designed and built their own lightweight, high-pressure boiler and combined it with a lightweight engine built by J. W. Perry & Sons, a Maine company, to come up with a light, 600-pound steamer that began to attract much attention. Francis Stanley drove one at a speed of more than 27 miles per hour to win a race near Cambridge, Massachusetts, in October 1898, and in 1899 Freelan, together with his wife, drove one over unpaved, rocky roads to the top of Mount Washington, the first car to achieve that feat.

The interest generated by these demonstrations of the steamer's speed and its hill-climbing capabilities led the brothers to form the Stanley Brothers Motor Carriage Company in fall 1898 and to set out to produce 100 of the little vehicles in a vacant factory they acquired in Watertown, near Newton. The publicity they received, however, also attracted the attention of John Brisben Walker, the publisher of *Cosmopolitan* magazine, whose enthusi-

Francis and Freelan Stanley in their 1897 steam car (courtesy of the Smithsonian Institution)

asm for automobiles had been demonstrated in 1896 when *Cosmopolitan* sponsored the nation's second major road race, from City Hall Park, New York, to Irvington, on Memorial Day. Now he approached the Stanley brothers, asking to be allowed to invest in their business. The brothers, who were financially well off and did not need outside help, finally told a persistent Walker that they would sell the business for $250,000, about ten times what they had invested. To their astonishment, Walker accepted their offer.

In May 1899 the Stanley company was purchased by Walker and Amzi Lorenzo Barber, who had made a fortune in asphalt paving. The brothers sold the company, their patents, and the Watertown plant; the business was renamed the Locomobile Company of America. The steamers that now appeared under the Locomobile name were the ones the Stanley twins had designed and built. For a short time they continued as the managers of the Locomobile operation. However, the brothers, who found it difficult enough to work with each other, found it impossible to work for someone else, and

by the end of 1899 they were gone, having agreed not to establish a new steam carriage manufacturing company for at least a year. Walker and Barber soon parted company, with Barber retaining Locomobile and Walker establishing the Mobile Company of America and building a new factory in Tarrytown, New York, where he began to produce in 1900 another copy of the original Stanley Steamer.

In 1900 Barber moved the Locomobile operations to a factory in Bridgeport, Connecticut, in order to be closer to the New York City market, and in 1901 he sold the Watertown factory back to the Stanley brothers together with their patents. The brothers now formed the Stanley Motor Carriage Company and quickly reestablished their reputation as the country's best-known builders of steamers. The new Stanley Steamers were improved, bigger versions of the little Stanleys of 1898, but the extra size and weight did not detract from the performance record for which the original Stanleys were noted. Instead, Fred Marriot set a new world record of 127.6 mph driving a specially built Stan-

Stanley "Wogglebug," which ran a measured mile of 127.66 mph at Daytona Beach, Florida, in 1906 (courtesy of the Harry Austin, Jr., Collection, Glen Cove, New York)

ley racer at Ormond Beach. In 1907 Marriot was back at Ormond Beach and had the racer, which resembled an inverted canoe, up to 197 mph when the vehicle became airborne and crashed, sending the boiler shooting down the beach about a mile and Marriot to the hospital with serious injuries. Marriot survived, but the Stanley brothers abandoned any further attempts to establish speed records.

By 1910 the market for steam-powered automobiles was rapidly drying up. Locomobile in 1902 had begun producing gasoline-powered cars in addition to its steamers, and after 1904 the company discontinued all steamers. The White brothers in Cleveland, who had bought some of the Stanley patents and who produced a steamer some consider superior to the Stanley, likewise switched to gasoline engines in 1910. The Stanley brothers, however, went their own way, continually making improvements. One of the most important was the introduction of a condensing system in 1915, which greatly increased the car's driving range by recycling the steam and reducing the number of times necessary to stop to take on more water. Even after the introduction of the self-starter in the 1912 Cadillac, which by eliminating the difficult task of starting a

gasoline car with a crank killed any real hopes for a revival of interest in steamers, the brothers' reputation was such that they could have sold many more cars than they did had they turned to mass production and done more advertising. But the eccentric twins were not interested, insisting on high-quality handworkmanship that kept annual production to a maximum of around 650 cars.

In 1917 the brothers sold the business. Freelan had not been actively involved in the operations for some time, having moved to Colorado for health reasons and established a hotel. Francis Stanley died on July 31, 1918, as a result of an accident when he ran his steamer off the road to avoid two farm wagons occupying both lanes. Freelan died in 1940. Stanley Steamers continued to be produced until the mid 1920s, the last significant survivors of what many in the late 1890s predicted would be the type of car most likely to succeed among the three types seeking to win the public's favor.

References:

Nick Baldwin and others, *The World Guide to Automobile Manufacturers* (New York: Facts on File, 1987);
Ralph Stein, *The Treasury of the Automobile* (New York: Ridge, 1961).

Steam Cars

by James M. Laux

University of Cincinnati

The invention of the steam engine in eighteenth-century England was followed by efforts to use the power source for locomotion on roads. These attempts in Britain and France, and in the United States by Oliver Evans in 1805, always foundered because the vehicles were too heavy to negotiate the poor roads of the time.

Sylvester H. Roper was the first American to produce lightweight steam cars, and from him there are direct links to the greatest days of the American steam automobile. Roper lived in Roxbury, Massachusetts, and made many small steam engines for river and harbor launches. He also fitted these coal-fired power plants to road carriages, some of which weighed no more than 500 pounds. Roper made an estimated ten road steamers between 1860 and 1895. He died in 1896 at age seventy-two while racing a steam bicycle. Two reasons can be advanced for the failure of Roper's machines to excite much interest: the coal-fired boiler required too much attention, and he was slightly ahead of his time, for the bicycle boom that encouraged the taste for individual mechanical transport came only in the mid 1890s.

George Eli Whitney of the Boston area also made small steam engines for launches and yachts. Whitney became acquainted with Roper in the late 1880s and worked in Roper's shop occasionally. Whitney's own establishment in East Boston may have produced several hundred steam engines for marine use and for stationary power on land. Whitney finished his first steam carriage in 1896, the year of Roper's death. It was similar to Roper's design, but Whitney used kerosene to heat the boiler. Whitney sold several steamers in 1896 and 1897 and in the latter year incorporated the Whitney Motor Wagon Company. In that year he also took a steam car on trips to Claremont, New Hampshire, and to Hartford and Middletown, Connecticut, each more than 100 miles from Boston. Whitney's machines weighed about 800 pounds and sold for $1,500 and up. Whitney neither produced many of these cars himself nor succeeded in finding a larger firm to make and sell them in significant numbers. A few were produced by the Stanley Manufacturing Company (operated by Frank F. Stanley, no relation to the Stanley brothers of the Stanley steamer). The cars sometimes went by the name of McKay.

The intermediary role of providing a bridge between inventor and capitalist was filled by the Stanley brothers. Operators of a photographic equipment firm near Boston, they became interested in steam cars and built two light steamers in 1897 and 1898 rather similar to those of Whitney. The Stanleys had little experience with steam power, but this may have been an advantage. Their machines operated at 150-200 pounds of pressure rather than the standard 100 pounds, and they wound their boiler with piano wire to handle the higher pressure. The Stanleys used a gasoline burner and had an engine built that weighed much less than Whitney's. In a demonstration in Boston in October 1898 a Stanley machine, weighing at least 200 pounds less than the Whitney, proved faster and able to climb a steeper grade. Its triumph led the Stanley brothers to begin manufacturing a batch of 100 steamers. They soon sold their enterprise in May 1899 to the capitalists J. B. Walker and A. L. Barber. Each of these men soon built his own factory, in Tarrytown, New York, and Bridgeport, Connecticut, where Walker made some 600 Mobile steam cars through 1903 and Barber some 5,200 Locomobiles through 1904. Most of these steamers sold at $750 or less.

Although the Locomobile steamers were the first American automobiles built in such large numbers, the Stanley design had many imperfections. It was difficult to start the gasoline burner, which sometimes flared out of control and set the car afire or went out if the wind blew from the wrong

Sylvester H. Roper in one of his steam cars, circa 1868 (courtesy of Automobile Quarterly)

quarter. Boilers burned out if drivers were not attentive. The exhaust steam was not condensed and reused, so water consumption was high (about one gallon per mile). A Locomobile in the hands of a skillful driver in good weather on a smooth road did well, but in other situations it could be a frustrating torture. The company did mitigate some of the problems and for a time employed George E. Whitney to help out, but it shifted to gasoline engines for luxury cars beginning in 1902.

In the United States there were more than 100 makers of steam cars derived from or copied from the Stanley-Locomobile design, but most disappeared quickly. Among those that did not were the Stanleys themselves, who returned to making steam cars in 1901 in Watertown, Massachusetts. They gradually improved the design, adding strength and weight, shifting from gasoline to kerosene fuel, and finally adding a steam condenser in 1915. The Stanley company made several hundred cars per year until 1924, when production ceased after a total of some 14,000 had been manufactured.

A better steam car was the White, designed by Rollin H. White of Cleveland along Stanley lines but with a "semi-flash" boiler and a condenser. The White steamer appeared on the market in 1901 and soon was enlarged to touring car size. Working steam pressure gradually increased to 350 pounds and finally to 600 pounds by 1910. Whites became prestige cars, and the largest model in 1910 cost more than a Rolls-Royce. White abandoned steam power in 1911 after producing 9,122 vehicles.

After the White and Stanley companies ceased making steam cars, enthusiasts occasionally revived the idea. The most prominent was Abner Doble, operator of a machine shop in Waltham, Massachusetts. Doble produced a handful of steamers from 1910 to 1914. In 1916 he arranged to have the Chalmers Motor Company of Detroit make steamers on his designs, but only three appeared. Doble stubbornly continued. In the 1920s a company he formed made about 40 steamers in California. A perfectionist, Doble frequently altered his designs. Trying to make his cars' operation as automatic as possible, he filled them with thermostats, electrical switches, and feedback mechanisms that made them extremely complicated and expensive. He never fully solved the problem of generating adequate steam at widely varying rates and in different environmental temperatures, crucial for automobile operation.

After World War II there were two major efforts in the United States by wealthy and experienced industrialists to develop steam cars. Robert P. McCulloch of chain-saw fame tried in the 1950s, and William P. Lear, an avionics expert, a few years later. Lear began his project in 1968, and in 1971 was encouraged enough to predict that "within ten years the internal combustion engine will be a collector's item." After $17 million of Lear's money evaporated in steam experiments he waved the white flag and pulled out of the race in 1974. Both men found the problems intractable.

Steam cars have received adequate attention in the United States. It has always turned out that gaso-

line models of comparable performance could be made, sold, and maintained for less money.

References:

John H. Bacon, *American Steam Car Pioneers* (Exton, Pa.: Newcomen Society, 1984);

Thomas Derr, *The Modern Steam Car* (Los Angeles: Floyd Clymer, 1942);

Lord Montagu and Anthony Bird, *Steam Cars 1770-1970* (New York: St. Martin's, 1971);

L. J. A. Villalon, "The Birth of an Early Automobile Company," *Bulb Horn* (April-June 1981): 11-21;

Villalon, "The Locomobile Company of America," *The Bulb Horn* (July-September 1986): 16-28; (October-December 1986): 12-22;

Villalon and James M. Laux, "Steaming through New England with Locomobile," *Journal of Transport History*, new series 5 (1979): 65-82;

John Ness Walton, *Doble Steam Cars, Buses, Lorries and Railcars* (Loughborough, U.K.: Steam Power, 1966).

F. B. Stearns Company

by George S. May

Eastern Michigan University

The Stearns Company, for the first 30 years of the twentieth century one of the most prominent of the Cleveland auto companies, drew its name from Frank B. Stearns, who was born in Berea, Ohio, on November 6, 1878. As a teenager Stearns's interest in automobiles is said to have been stimulated by a visit to the Chicago World's Columbian Exposition in 1893, although the evidence of horseless carriages on display at the exposition was so slight that it made no impression on most visitors. Stearns attended University School in Cleveland, where the family then resided, and after graduation he attended the Case School of Applied Science. He left college after about a year, however, to pursue his interest in automobiles.

In the mid 1890s young Stearns built a 1-cylinder car. His work is said to have attracted the attention of Ralph R. and Raymond M. Owen, the first in Cleveland to provide a motor delivery service in connection with a carpet-cleaning business they owned. They joined with Stearns to form F. B. Stearns and Company in 1898. Most of the money came from Stearns's father, Frank M. Stearns, a prosperous businessman. Some 50 small

cars were produced over the next two years, using a 1-cylinder engine of the 2-cycle type that would soon become a rarity in the American auto industry.

The Owen brothers did not stay with Stearns for long, but both continued in the auto industry. Raymond Owen had an especially noteworthy career as an automobile salesman. He established Cleveland's first automobile dealership, went on in 1901 to become the Oldsmobile distributor for the New York area, and from 1904 to 1914 held exclusive rights to the sale of Reo automobiles. Frank Stearns, meanwhile, with more financial support from his father and his wealthy father-in-law, Thomas Wilson, reorganized the business as the F. B. Stearns Company in 1902. He was the president and general manager, while his father was vice-president and secretary. The small Stearns models of the early years were replaced by increasingly bigger and more powerful cars priced as high as $7,500 by 1908. Sales were quite modest, but with the addition of a "baby Stearns" in 1909 annual sales by 1910 totaled 1,000, double those of the preceding year and four times the figure for 1908.

Advertisement for the 1902 Stearns Company automobile

In 1910 taxicabs were added to the Stearns line, and from 1911 to 1916 the company also produced trucks, but the big breakthrough came with the 1912 adoption of an engine developed by Charles Y. Knight that used sleeve valves, which operated much more quietly than engines using poppet valves. Stearns studied the use Daimler of Great Britain had been making of the Knight engine since 1909, and his decision to use the engine in his 1912 models marked its first significant appearance in American cars. For the rest of the company's history it used Knight engines in what were then called the Stearns-Knights, although by the 1920s improvements in poppet valve engines killed the industry's interest in the Knight design.

Stearns offered 4-, 6-, and 8-cylinder models by 1916, when annual production was up to 4,000 units. Frank Stearns, however, left the company the next year, reportedly because of a disagreement over engineering policies. He turned to diesel engines, on which he would be awarded 16 patents. He sold one of his diesels to the navy in 1935 and continued to engage in research, some of it for the federal government, up to his death on July 5, 1955.

The company he had founded continued under new management until December 1925, when John North Willys, whose Willys-Knight models had been the most numerous of the Knight-engined cars, acquired control, paying $10 per share and launching a program to expand the company's production. However, Willys soon discovered that the company had been greatly overvalued. The 4-cylinder Stearns-Knight was dropped in 1926, and although a new straight-eight, priced as high as $5,800, was added in 1927, it was not enough to reverse a trend in which sales declined from 3,759 in 1925 to less than 2,000 in 1929. Those figures, combined with the stock market crash in October 1929, sent Stearns stock down to 12.5 cents per share, and on December 30, 1929, the stockholders threw in the towel and dissolved the company.

The Stearns company produced excellent cars, but low volume and an inadequate dealer system ultimately made it impossible to stand up to the larger and better-financed Michigan companies with which it had been competing.

References:

Nick Baldwin and others, *The World Guide to Automobile Manufacturers* (New York: Facts on File, 1987);

Beverly Rae Kimes and Henry Austin Clark, *Standard Catalog of American Cars, 1805-1942* (Iola, Wis.: Krause, 1985);

Richard Wager, *Golden Wheels* (Cleveland: Western Reserve Historical Society, 1975).

Steering

by James Wren

Motor Vehicle Manufacturers Association

Once man had attached wheels to the axles on his cart or wagon, his next problem was to determine how to move the front axle so that the wagon could turn easily in any direction and was not limited to straight-line travel. The solution was quite simple: merely drill a hole through the axle with a king pin or post attached to the wagon. Then the wheels and axle would swing together in an arc with the wheels parallel to each other yet perpendicular to the same radius. Thus in steering a carriage it was only necessary to pull on one of the reins to move the horse to the right or left, and the pivoted axle attached to the wagon shaft would swing with the horse. For normal speeds the system worked well, but at high speeds or in sudden turns, skidding and tipping were common hazards.

With the advent of the motor vehicle and its great potential for speed, the need for change was evident. The early lightweight runabouts used initially the center pivoted axle, merely attaching a tiller to the center post. For lightweight vehicles moving at slow speeds on smooth roads, the arrangement was adequate, but as speeds increased and motor vehicles became heavier, the manufacturers adopted an Ackerman steering system (invented by George Lenkensperger in 1818), which consisted of axially mounting the front wheels on pivoted hubs so that

they could move independently of the axle. Additionally, it was discovered that as the hub was placed closer to the pivot less leverage was needed and a more solid structure resulted.

Eventually, a hand wheel replaced the tiller, a move which allowed for better control and more power to move the linkages which were attached to the wheels. Yet steering remained a difficult chore. With the introduction of pneumatic tires, even more effort was required. The introduction of reduction gearing saved the day. Various arrangements of worm gears with gears, sectors, rollers, and toothed mechanisms were developed. By the mid 1920s, ball bearings and roller bearings used along with the worm gears further eased the task.

The use of a separate power source to assist the driver in steering was demonstrated as early as 1895 when the Sweany Steam Carriage used the steam which was generated to steer the wheels as well. In 1903, the Columbia electric 5-ton truck was equipped with an extra electric motor solely for steering assistance. Additional experiments with power steering were performed in the mid 1920s, the most notable being Francis Davis who developed a fluid-power system for steering a Packard sedan.

James J. Storrow

(January 21, 1864-March 13, 1926)

by Richard P. Scharchburg

GMI Engineering & Management Institute

CAREER: Lawyer, Fish, Richardson and Storrow (1889-1900); partner, Lee, Higginson & Company (1900-1926); president, General Motors Company (1910-1912); chairman, Nash Motors Company (1916-1926).

James Jackson Storrow was born in Boston, Massachusetts, on January 21, 1864, the son of James J. and Annie M. Perry Storrow. Two other children, an older sister, Elizabeth, and a younger brother, Samuel, were born before Annie Storrow died four years after her marriage. James Storrow, Sr., left Boston's Beacon Hill district with the children and resided for eight years in the nearby country town of Longwood. In 1873 he remarried and moved into a house on Beacon Street back in Boston.

Storrow's childhood was spent in a somber and strictly regulated family routine, presided over by his meticulous father, who practiced law. Evenings were often spent silently studying, facing his brother at a table while their father worked at his desk under a green-shaded lamp. Preparation for college followed in a manner befitting a boy in his social position. He graduated from Noble's School in 1881 and entered Harvard that fall with the class of 1885. He received an A.B. in 1885 followed by an LL.B. in 1888.

After graduation from law school Storrow entered the law office where he had clerked the previous summer. A year later he became a member of the newly formed firm of Fish, Richardson and Storrow. Frederick Fish, the senior partner, was an associate of Storrow's father and had been impressed with the young man's ability and potential. Storrow continued as a member of the firm for 11 years, gaining a reputation as a person "who concentrated his will on the result to be attained, the individual and his human frailties were often forgotten."

James J. Storrow (courtesy of the General Motors Institute Alumni Foundation Collection of Industrial History

His biographer, Henry G. Pearson, comments, "That was Storrow throughout his life."

In his law practice Storrow was both professional and diligent; he enjoyed the legal regimen and worked hard and long. The business of the firm grew rapidly and earned him a reputation for thoroughness and sure instinct. He was often called upon to give advice in matters of business as well as law and soon became involved with the organization of the United Shoe Machinery Company, in which he "held his own with marked success against men of experience and prestige." It came as no surprise to the senior member of the law firm when, in 1900, an investment banking partnership, Lee, Higginson & Company, asked Storrow to give up his law practice to become a partner in the firm. After mulling it over for awhile, he finally accepted.

The firm Storrow joined was formed in 1848 by John Clark Lee and George Higginson and enjoyed a solid reputation in the financial world. That never changed even after Storrow introduced changes in the way Lee, Higginson operated. The firm was bound by the traditions of the day. Most business was conducted in "decent privacy" in the "partners' room." The firm's clients were well-known citizens well connected by social and family ties.

Storrow suggested adding investment salesmen to seek investment opportunities for customers who did not always come walking through the front door. He pushed to open affiliates, not only in Chicago and New York but also in London and Paris. Diminishing profit margins from railroad bonds, which constituted 95 percent of the firm's business in 1900, convinced Storrow that it was necessary to look elsewhere for future profits. By 1913, 75 percent of Lee, Higginson's money was in public utilities and industrial bonds. Unquestionably, Storrow's leadership was responsible for the powerful position of the firm in the first decade of the twentieth century.

Into Storrow's well-established and financially conservative world came a troubled General Motors (GM) Company in 1910. Generally aware of the troubles at GM, Storrow studied the situation carefully and patiently watched daily developments. When a New York group consisting of the Central Trust Company of New York, J. & W. Seligman & Company, and Kuhn, Loeb & Company committed themselves to a salvage operation at GM, Lee, Higginson & Company offered its help as well. A loan of $12.75 million was deemed necessary to meet immediate needs. For that amount of cash GM issued $15 million of 6 percent notes secured by a mortgage of all of its Michigan property. In consideration for underwriting the loan, GM was required to deliver from its treasury $4,169,200 in preferred stock and $2 million in common stock, both at par. In total, therefore, the bankers received $8,419,200 in par value stock and discount on notes for a loan that netted the company $12,750,000. Coincident with the loan and the agreed upon "exile" of GM

founder William C. Durant from active management, the bankers took control of the company.

Storrow was elected chairman of the voting trustees who for the next five years were to manage the affairs of General Motors. Storrow's biographer clearly summarizes Storrow's role: "In effect, he became an industrial executive—the head of a corporation that required not only financing but also the creation of a proper organization, the selection of the right personnel, and the adoption of a sound manufacturing and distribution policy."

Even more significant, Storrow set in place a management structure that effected a sensitive balance between centralization and decentralization of authority. He also recruited and developed people such as Charles W. Nash and Walter P. Chrysler and placed them in key positions. As a result of his innovative management structure and personnel placement skills, he achieved an efficiency in production and distribution that enabled the ailing company to recover its competitive edge in the American automobile industry and also pay its debts, which was Storrow's chief concern from the beginning.

When Storrow could see that the worst of the GM crisis was past and that the manufacturing divisions were operating profitably, he began to search for someone to take his place as president and relieve him of the heavy burden of constant travel and stress. Keenly aware of Nash's outstanding progress at Buick, Storrow decided that he was best suited to continue the reorganization, and in 1912 Nash was elected GM president. Storrow's biographer laconically comments on Storrow's contribution: "He had done the job that devolved upon him as a member of Lee, Higginson & Company; that was all."

While Storrow and the bankers were busily involved in reorganization of General Motors, the exiled Durant had been actively establishing an independent industrial empire culminating in the formation of the Chevrolet Motor Company in 1915. Under the management of A. B. C. Hardy, Durant's "workhorse" from his carriage-manufacturing days, Chevrolet began a spectacular rise in the automobile industry that broke all previous records for a newly formed company. Its success left Chevrolet with surplus capital, which Durant had plans to use. As the major stockholder and beneficiary of the company's prosperity, Durant had privately formulated plans to use the profits to buy GM stock to regain control of GM from Storrow and the banker interests. On September 16, 1915, he made public the final phase of his takeover. The certificates of stock establishing control were brought in by the basketload, and at the same meeting a $50 dividend was declared on the common stocks, which helped repay the loans and replenish the Chevrolet treasury. The GM board of directors was completely reorganized in November 1915, establishing Durant men in office and on key committees. In recognition of the part played in assisting Durant, Pierre S. du Pont was elected chairman of the board. Nash continued as president; but he, too, soon would resign.

The banker reign came to an end with the new board appointments, du Pont's election as chairman, and the final repayment of the 1910 loan. The departure of the banker representatives and Storrow and Nash signaled the consolidation of Durant's power base in GM once again.

Following Nash's resignation, Storrow and Nash decided to go shopping for their own automobile business. They even invited Walter Chrysler, by then a vice-president of General Motors and president of Buick, to join them. However, Durant's salary offer of $500,000 was more than Chrysler could resist or Storrow and Nash were willing to pay to get his talents.

Storrow and Nash then negotiated with Henry B. Joy to purchase the Packard Motor Car Company in Detroit. Joy was agreeable, but Packard stockholders were not interested in selling; the negotiations were dropped. Next, Nash was approached by Mack Trucks with a job offer, but he turned it down. Instead, Nash and Storrow settled on the Thomas B. Jeffery Company of Kenosha, Wisconsin, the original producer of the Rambler. Its founder, after whom the company was named, had died in 1910, and his son, Charles T. Jeffery, was willing to sell for the right price—$5 million. The financial end was handled by Lee, Higginson upon the recommendation of Storrow. The company was renamed Nash Motors Company and came into existence on July 29, 1916. Production soon got underway, and 12,179 Jeffery automobiles were sold as 1917 Nash models. Nash was elected president of the new company, and Storrow was named chairman of the board of directors. With all the stress and demands on Storrow's time during his GM tenure, one might question why he would venture into the problems of organizing and financing an entirely new automobile company, especially in a price range already dominated by Ford and Chevrolet.

The answer probably involves the confidence Storrow had in Nash. Also, Storrow, like so many others, had been "bitten by the auto bug." As his biographer observed, "The spell of this new industry had taken a strong hold on Storrow's pioneering spirit, and with the splendid team which he had brought together he was minded to go on." As chairman he gave all the time necessary to provide the assistance the company needed to assure a chance for success. In the post-World War I market, he felt confident that Nash would continue the prosperous beginnings of production, and he intended to do his part. He wrote to Nash in July 1919 giving him a detailed report of the financial affairs of the company. He reported that it "was in very strong and sound financial condition." There was a large cash balance, "which we ought not to be afraid to use." It was exactly the kind of report on which to launch a program to add to the Nash car line and increase production. The next several years saw the addition of new car lines, the opening of plants in Milwaukee and Racine, the acquisition of the Seaman Body Corporation, and the purchase of the LaFayette Motor Company. The LaFayette venture, however, soon was the source of considerable worry for Storrow.

From the fall of 1920 until the summer of 1921 almost all of Storrow's energy was directed toward improving the financial condition of LaFayette, which had been started to produce a luxury car for Nash Motors. Production lagged behind from the beginning, and sales were even worse. As usual, Lee, Higginson & Company had provided the financial backing, and Storrow expended more strength than he could spare in an effort to salvage the venture. In 1924 continuing losses forced the LaFayette company into receivership. To Storrow, competitive businessman that he was, the failure was a personal embarrassment. The experience no doubt depressed him considerably, and with the presence of the cancer that his doctors had discovered was sapping his vitality and ravaging his body, his family and friends feared for his life.

After a short rest the tonic that seemed to help most was work. Storrow plunged back into the affairs of Nash Motors with his usual routine only slightly curtailed. With the LaFayette disaster behind it, the company concentrated on medium-priced cars that were selling well. Storrow's faith in

Nash's management was unshaken, and over the next few years he provided the additional capital required for necessary expansion. Storrow's faith was fully justified, for by November 30, 1925, the net worth of the company was $38,563,350. Nearly all of the original invested capital had been repaid by the retirement of the initial issue of preferred stock. During the ten years of the company's operations, it had earned net profits totaling $83.6 million.

In spite of the physical limitations forced on him by his illness, Storrow continued the business to which he had committed his life in 1900. Even in his final months he attended regularly to business affairs. But now he and his wife traveled frequently to get away from the press of business and to conserve his strength. They preferred travel in the United States, though he also enjoyed short visits to England—one visit there lasted only two days. He loved his home and friends, and he was always anxious to return to familiar surroundings. His beautiful home at Lincoln near Boston was a favorite spot among the several residences and resorts that he owned. He had enjoyed life to the fullest.

Following a brief visit with President Calvin Coolidge in January 1926, Storrow took what proved to be a last and most pleasant trip to North Carolina with his wife and friends. After the Storrows' return, his cancer that attacked his once athletic body made a new advance. Storrow died March 13, 1926, at home in Lincoln, Massachusetts.

References:

Henry G. Pearson, *Son of New England: James Jackson Storrow* (Boston: Todd, 1932);

John B. Rae, *American Automobile Manufacturers: The First Forty Years* (Philadelphia: Chilton, 1959);

Richard P. Scharchburg, *W. C. Durant: the Boss* (Flint, Mich.: GMI Press, 1972);

Lawrence H. Seltzer, *A Financial History of the Automobile Industry* (Boston: Houghton Mifflin, 1928);

U.S. Federal Trade Commission, *Report on the Motor Vehicle Industry* (Washington, D.C.: Government Printing Office, 1939).

Studebaker Corporation

by Donald T. Critchlow

University of Notre Dame

The Studebaker Corporation began as H. & C. Studebaker Company, a small blacksmithing business established by Henry and Clement Studebaker in South Bend, Indiana, in 1852. In 1858 John Mohler Studebaker, the third eldest brother, returned to South Bend from the California goldfields with $10,000 earned from making wheelbarrows for the miners. With this fortune he bought out Henry's interest in the company. The infusion of new capital allowed the company to undertake rapid expansion.

By the 1860s the company was a major wagon manufacturer. The demand for wagons was great from pioneers settling the West as well as those prospering on the rich soil of the Midwest. The Civil War further encouraged growth with orders from the U.S. government for wagons, artillery caissons, and other vehicles. In 1863 another brother, Peter E. Studebaker, joined the firm. As sales agent, he traveled through the West looking for new business. He set up the first of many depositories at St. Joseph, Missouri, in 1870. Here he became acquainted with Brigham Young and supplied the Mormons with wagons. A depository was later established in Salt Lake City with other depositories to follow in New York City, Chicago, Atlanta, Kansas City, Omaha, Dallas, and San Francisco.

In 1868 the brothers decided to incorporate. The Studebaker Brothers Manufacturing Company was formed with $75,000 in capital from Clement, J. M., and Peter, who became president, treasurer, and secretary respectively. Sales at this time were running approximately $350,000 per year. After disastrous fires in 1872 and 1874 growth continued. The youngest of the Studebaker brothers, Jacob, joined the firm full-time in 1875. He was placed in charge of the carriage department. In that year sales reached $1 million.

During this period the Studebakers dabbled in Republican politics. When fellow Hoosier Benjamin

John M. Studebaker

Harrison was elected president several Studebaker carriages were added to the White House stable. Harrison's influence was evidenced when Clement called his Gothic mansion Tippecanoe.

Studebaker Brothers Manufacturing Company emerged by the 1890s as the world's largest producer of wagons and carriages. The company featured one of the most modern factories in the nation, with nearly 30 different types of vehicles manufactured in a plant that covered 95 acres and employed more than 2,000 workers. The company had one of the best distribution systems in the country, with independently incorporated branch offices and dealers located in every region of the country, as well as in many Latin American countries, Canada, Australia, and England.

In late 1891 the new Studebaker Brothers Manufacturing Company was incorporated under New Jersey law. The reorganization was handled by eastern corporate attorney Frederick S. Fish, who had married J. M.'s daughter in 1887. Acting as the new corporate counsel, Fish within a year had to-

tally reorganized the firm along the lines of a modern corporation. Following the depression of 1893, Studebaker turned to J. P. Morgan to increase the company's stock from $1 million to over $2 million. In the process, Morgan acquired approximately one-sixth of the voting stock of the corporation. Thus as the twentieth century approached Studebaker stood ready to enter the next century as a major corporate power. Backed by Morgan interests, operating with the latest technology, and organized along the lines of an efficient, modern corporation, Studebaker looked toward the continued success of the wagon industry. Nonetheless, the new century, whatever its promises, carried a new challenge to the horse-drawn vehicle industry: the automobile.

Even though the automobile was only in its early stages of development Fish urged the Studebakers to look into the emerging industry, at least as a sideline to their wagon business. He did not want the Studebaker Company to be left behind in what promised to be an expanding market. The company moved cautiously. It first contracted with the Electric Vehicle Company for the construction of 100 bodies with running gear for their electric cabs in New York City in 1897.

Clement Studebaker died November 27, 1901, and John M. assumed the presidency of the company. On November 12, 1901, a new board composed of Fish and his supporters, including Clement Studebaker, Jr., had resolved to begin production of electric and gasoline automobiles. Production was limited to electrics for the first two years, manufacturing Victorias, Phaetons, and runabouts, each using an easy-to-charge battery developed by Westinghouse.

The company's full entrance into gasoline automobile production came in 1904 when Studebaker entered into a contract with an Ohio-based manufacturer, the Garford Manufacturing Company, for the purchase of 200 chassis a year to be delivered to the South Bend plant. Garford had been organized in 1904 by Arthur L. Garford, whose entry into autos had been the bicycle industry. In November 1908 the Studebaker Corporation acquired a controlling interest in Garford. That same year Fish announced that a cooperative arrangement had been made which obligated the Studebaker Company to market 600 cars produced by the newly formed Everitt-Metzger-Flanders auto company. The sale of these medium-priced cars supplemented the sales of the higher-priced Studebaker-Garford autos.

The EMF Company was formed in 1908 to build a mass-produced car which would sell at $1,250. By merging the Wayne Automobile Company and the Northern Auto Company, EMF was formed with three plants already existing. The agreement with Studebaker ensured a strong distribution system for their cars. As Clement's son Col. George M. Studebaker declared, "We considered it more advantageous to form an alliance with a group of men . . . possessing factory facilities, experience, and manufacturing ability of a rare order, as well as an intimate knowledge of the problems peculiar to the motor car than to establish separate facilities of our own." In late 1910 Studebaker acquired EMF. In the process, Studebaker hired Walter Flanders, one of the founders of EMF and former production man for Ford, as production manager of the newly merged company.

To finance the purchase of EMF and to expand production, Studebaker Corporation, working with Goldman Sachs and the Lehman Brothers, was recapitalized as a new corporation on February 14, 1911, under Delaware law. Shortly afterward Studebaker sold its interest in Garford to Willys-Overland. By 1912 the new Studebaker Corporation became a major competitor to Willys, Cadillac, and Buick. Henry Ford's Model T stood in a class by itself, but Studebaker had become a major manufacturer. That year, 1912, Studebaker stood as the third largest automobile manufacturer in the country, producing 28,523 automobiles.

The automobile had cut so significantly into their carriage and buggy business that in 1910 Studebaker stopped producing buggies, but continued to produce other horse-drawn vehicles. Only in 1920 would Studebaker finally sell its wagon division to a Kentucky firm. The automobile had brought profound changes to the Studebaker family and the company. In the end the remaining Studebakers were to become only honorary officers in the company.

Albert Russel Erskine carried Studebaker into its expansion period in the 1920s. Erskine was initially introduced to Frederick Fish by Henry Goldman after Erskine had made a name for himself as treasurer of Underwood Typewriter. He came to Studebaker as the treasurer in 1911, and within a year he had reorganized and centralized the accounting and record-keeping division. Four

Studebaker coupe and sedan, 1918

years later, in 1915, Erskine was elected president, replacing Fish, who became chairman of the board. In the 1920s magazines frequently portrayed Erskine as *the* businessman for the New Age. Erskine symbolized the emergence of the new manager, a finance man.

In the 1920s Erskine took the company into a period of rapid expansion. New manufacturing facilities were built in South Bend, and all operations were consolidated there. In the early 1920s when many other automobile companies were faltering, Studebaker hit new highs in production up to a peak in 1923 of 145,167 cars, a company record that would remain unbroken until the 1940s. Much of this success came with the Light Six, which Erskine had commissioned his engineers Max Wollering and Guy Henry to develop during the war. Other models in the line included a Special-Six and a Big-Six in coupe, speedster, touring, and sedan models. In an attempt to penetrate the lower-priced market, the European styled and much advertised *Erskine* was introduced in 1926 but was not priced competitively. The Chevrolet was making great headway in this market, and in 1928 Ford ᶜsuccessfully introduced the Model A. Erskine then turned to the higher end of the market with a new luxurious *President* model. Shortly afterward Studebaker acquired the prestigious Pierce-Arrow company.

With the onset of the Depression, Erskine was convinced that the downturn was only temporary. Large dividends were paid when profits did not warrant it in the early 1930s. In 1931 the company again tried to bring out a model to compete in the lower-priced range, the *Rockne*. In 1932 sales hit bottom.

Nonetheless Erskine maintained a confidence in the future. Erskine's dividend policy cut heavily into the company's reserve capital funds. Desperate to meet the need for cash to pay the debts accrued during the previous decade of expansion, Erskine made a wily attempt to acquire the cash-rich White Motor Company, a truck manufacturer. When a minority of White shareholders blocked the merger, Erskine's last ploy had failed. The end came that spring following the national banking moratorium declared on March 5, 1933. Thirteen days later, on March 18, 1933, Studebaker entered into receivership. Judge Thomas Slick of the U.S. District Court in South Bend appointed Erskine's protégés, Paul G. Hoffman, Harold Vance, and chairman of the board of White Motors, Anton G. Bean, as friendly receivers of the company. Forced to resign, Erskine died that June a broken man.

Studebaker's revival in the 1930s illustrates Hoffman's and Vance's tenacity in keeping the company going. Once out of receivership in 1935, Hoffman and Vance moved to instill loyalty among their work force. As one leading union official, Red Hill, later recalled, in these years, "every Studebaker employee was a salesman of his own product wherever he went and news of this loyalty spread over the nation. . . ." In turn, Hoffman and Vance moved to accommodate organized labor by recognizing United Auto Worker Union Local 5. The introduction of the Champion in 1939 brought new revenues to the cash-hungry company. The optimism generated by healthy sales, however, was put on hold with the outbreak of the war. World War II brought government contracts to the company, but Studebaker in the postwar period confronted new challenges, particularly with organized labor and its relations with government. Hoffman played a central role in making the crucial decisions which allowed Studebaker to develop a stable relationship with labor, while at the same time securing government defense contracts. Hoffman left Studebaker shortly after the war to head the Marshall Plan in Europe. His close associate Harold Vance carried on the work at Studebaker, but after a brief period of high production, sales began to slacken by the early 1950s. In 1954, confronted by poor sales, Studebaker concluded a merger with Packard.

Under new management, Studebaker struggled to compete with the Big Three. While the other major independent, American Motors, decided to gamble with the production of a single model, the *Rambler*, Studebaker management decided to go with a multimodel approach. American Motors survived; Studebaker did not. Although Raymond Lowey's designs for the Studebaker line were touted as "ahead of its time," consumers proved to be more cautious. On Monday, December 9, 1963, Studebaker closed its South Bend plant. To ensure replacement parts for dealers, operations were continued at the company's Canadian plant. In 1966 the last Studebaker rolled off the Canadian line. Thus ended a 114-year history of vehicle production of the company that had carried the Studebaker name.

References:

Michael Beatty, Patrick Furlong, and Loren Pennington, *Studebaker: Less Than They Promised* (South Bend, Ind.: And Books, 1984);

William A. Cannon and Fred K. Fox, *Studebaker: The Complete Story* (Blue Ridge Summit, Pa.: Tab Books, 1981);

Albert R. Erskine, *History of the Studebaker Corporation* (South Bend, Ind.: Studebaker Corporation, 1924);

Asa E. Hall and Richard M. Langworth, *The Studebaker Century* (Contoocook, N.H.: Dragonwyck, 1983);

Maurice D. Hendry, "Studebaker: One Can Do a Lot of Remembering in South Bend," *Automobile Quarterly*, 10, no. 3 (1972): 228-257;

J. D. "Red" Hill, *A Brief History of the Labor Movement of Studebaker Local No. 5* (South Bend, Ind.: Studebaker Local 5, 1953);

Beverly Rae Kimes, "E & M & F . . . & Leroy," *Automobile Quarterly*, 17, no. 4 (1979): 341-359;

Richard M. Langworth, *Studebaker: The Postwar Years* (Osceola, Wis.: Motorbooks International, 1979);

Stephen Longstreet, *A Century on Wheels* (New York: Holt, 1952);

John B. Rae, *American Automobile Manufacturers: The First Forty Years* (New York: Chilton, 1959);

Alan R. Raucher, *Paul G. Hoffman: Architect of Foreign Aid* (Lexington: University of Kentucky Press, 1985);

Kathleen A. Smallzried and Dorothy J. Roberts, *More Than You Promise* (New York: Harper, 1942);

Studebaker Corporation: One Hundred Years on the Road (South Bend, Ind.: Studebaker Corporation, 1952).

Archives:

Material on Studebaker is located in the Paul G. Hoffman papers, Truman Library, Independence, Missouri; the Studebaker Corporation file, Detroit Public Library, Detroit, Michigan; and the Studebaker Corporation papers, Studebaker National Museum, South Bend, Indiana.

Frederick Winslow Taylor

(March 20, 1856-March 21, 1915)

by David Finkelman

St. Mary's College of Maryland

CAREER: Laborer, clerk, machinist, subforeman, machine shop foreman, and chief engineer, Midvale Steel Company (1878-1889); general manager, Manufacturing Investment Company (1890-1893); consultant, Simonds Company (1893, 1897); consultant, Cramp & Sons (1894); consultant, Johnson Company (1896); consultant, Bethlehem Iron Company (1898-1901).

Frederick Winslow Taylor, American engineer and inventor, was best known for his innovations in factory management practices that earned him the title of "father of scientific management" and made him an influential figure in the development of manufacturing practices in the automobile industry.

Taylor was born into a well-to-do Philadelphia family on March 20, 1856. He attended Phillips Exeter Academy in New Hampshire from 1872 to 1874. He had intended to enter Harvard, and passed Harvard's entrance examination, but began to experience serious vision problems and returned to Philadelphia instead. After working as an apprentice machinist and pattern maker at the Enterprise Hydraulic Works, he began his business career at the Midvale Steel Company in 1878. It was at Midvale that he started to develop the ideas that were to make him famous; he reasoned that there should be a way to bring the engineer's scientific perspective to bear on management as well as machines. Taylor rose rapidly at Midvale, eventually to the post of chief engineer. In 1883 Taylor obtained his mechanical engineering degree from the Stevens Institute of Technology under an unusual arrangement in which he took his exams at Stevens

Frederick Winslow Taylor

with the other students but remained in Philadelphia otherwise. Taylor married Louise Spooner on May 3, 1884.

Taylor left Midvale in 1889 and moved to Maine the following year to become the general manager of the Manufacturing Investment Company, a wood pulp and paper manufacturing firm, a post he held until 1893. Over the next few years, Taylor served as a managerial consultant to a number of companies. His last, longest, and most successful consulting position was with the Bethlehem Iron Company (later Bethlehem Steel) from 1898 to 1901. While at Bethlehem, Taylor conducted two studies that he frequently referred to later in his career. The first involved the loading of pig iron onto railroad cars; the other was concerned with the optimum method to be used in shoveling coal. In both cases, Taylor was able to produce dramatic increases in worker efficiency. Bethlehem was also the site of Taylor's most successful and important invention: with Maunsel White, he developed the heat treatment of tool steel that became known as "high speed steel." Despite these and other successes, Taylor was dismissed from his post at Bethlehem in 1901. By this point, he had developed all the ideas that he was later to promote under the name of "scientific management."

In general terms, Taylor saw scientific management as the substitution of scientific knowledge and methods for individual judgment and "rule-of-thumb" methods. The specific methods and techniques he developed are discussed in four parts, although they are all interrelated. The first involves the separation of planning and doing. It was common practice for workers to be told only in general terms how to do their jobs and what tools to use. In Taylor's system, these instructions became the responsibilities of management. This necessitated a separate planning department which oversaw every aspect of production. It also involved the preparation of detailed instruction cards for workers, which specified exactly how each job should be done. The second aspect is called "functional foremanship." Taylor suggested the use of a number of foremen, each of whom had expertise in a specific function. If a worker was assigned a job that called for several different operations, each operation would be taught and supervised by a different foreman. The third aspect is time study. Taylor advocated dividing each worker's job into basic steps or elements, each of which was timed separately. By combining the times, and allowing for rest and other factors, the proper time for completing the job could be calculated. It is perhaps this aspect of Taylor's system—the image of "the man with the stopwatch"—that most captured public attention. Another aspect of scientific management is the differential piece rate. Under this scheme, a worker would be paid a high rate per piece if he produced a certain number of pieces per day and a low rate per piece if he produced fewer.

Eventually Taylor came to view his system as a solution to the "labor problem." He maintained that if labor and management worked together to make production as efficient as possible, profits would become so large that it would be unnecessary to argue about how they should be divided.

After leaving Bethlehem, Taylor retired. He moved back to Philadelphia, bought a large estate, and developed a passion for gardening. Most of his energies, however, still were devoted to the promotion of scientific management. Much of the work in popularizing and implementing his ideas was done by his followers, most notably Frank Gilbreth, Henry L. Gantt, and Samuel Emerson, although each of them adapted Taylor's ideas and added their own in ways Taylor did not approve of. Scientific management, in some form or other, may have been introduced into as many as 180 American factories during the last fifteen years of Taylor's life.

An event that proved important in the spread of Taylor's ideas was the so-called Eastern Rate Case in 1910. Louis D. Brandeis argued in hearings before the Interstate Commerce Commission that a proposed railroad rate increase would be unnecessary if more efficient management methods, such as those advocated by Taylor, were employed. The hearings catapulted Taylor into national prominence and gave wide currency to the term "scientific management." The publication of Taylor's "Principles of Scientific Management," first serialized in the *American Monthly* in the spring of 1911, further enhanced his reputation; he became a public figure almost overnight. In the last few years of his life, he gave many lectures on scientific management in this country and in Europe; he also testified twice before Congressional committees.

The extent to which Taylor's ideas had a direct influence on automobile industry practices is not clear. He never oversaw the installation of his system in an automobile factory, but two of his associates between 1911 and 1914 did introduce "Taylorism" in the Franklin company's plant in Syracuse, New York. A reorganization of work procedures at the Packard company in 1912 and 1913, said to have been based on Taylor's ideas, reduced by nearly one half the number of workers required to produce a car (although Packard still remained far less efficient in this regard that competitors such as Cadillac). In the same period Taylorism won large support among savants and engineers in Europe, including officials at such leading firms as Renault and Panhard et Levassor. As for Taylor's influence on the Ford Motor Company, however, efforts to find a line between Taylor's theories and the development of Ford's mass-production practices have failed to come up with conclusive evidence. Although there are some close parallels between Taylorism and Fordism and although some of the Ford engineers were no doubt familiar with Taylor's work, it appears that the Taylorization that occurred at Ford resulted from staff members working independently of the Philadelphia theorist.

Taylor died of pneumonia on March 21, 1915. Although few of his ideas have survived in original form, the general goals and principles he espoused remain influential in contemporary management theory.

Publications:

A piece-rate system: being a step toward partial solution of the labor problem (N.p., [1895]);

The adjustment of wages to efficiency; three papers . . . (New York: For the American Economic Association by the Macmillan Company, 1896);

A treatise on concrete, plain and reinforced; materials, construction, and design of concrete and reinforced concrete, with chapters by R. Feret, William B. Fuller & Spencer B. Newberry; by Frederick W. Taylor, M. E., and Sanford E. Thompson . . . (New York: Wiley & Sons, 1905);

*On the art of cutting metals: an address made at the open-*ing of the annual meeting in New York, December 1906 (New York: American Society of Mechanical Engineers [1907]);

The principles of scientific management . . . (New York: Harper & Brothers, 1911);

Shop management (New York: Harper & Brothers, 1911);

Concrete costs: tables and recommendations for estimating the time and cost of labor operations in concrete construction and for introducing economical methods of management (New York: Wiley & Sons, 1912);

Two papers on scientific management. A piece-rate system and Notes on belting (London: G. Routledge & Sons, 1919).

References:

Frank Barkley Copley, *Frederick Winslow Taylor*, 2 volumes (New York: Harper, 1923);

David A. Hounhell, *From the American System to Mass Production, 1800-1932: The Development of Manufacturing Technology in the United States* (Baltimore: Johns Hopkins University Press, 1984);

Sudhir Kakar, *Frederick Taylor: A Study in Personality and Innovation* (Cambridge, Mass.: MIT Press, 1970);

James M. Laux and others, *The Automobile Revolution: The Impact of An Industry* (Chapel Hill: University of North Carolina Press, 1982);

Daniel Nelson, *Frederick W. Taylor and the Rise of Scientific Management* (Madison: University of Wisconsin Press, 1980).

Archives:

Taylor's papers are in the library of the Stevens Institute of Technology, Hoboken, New Jersey.

E. R. Thomas Motor Company

by George S. May

Eastern Michigan University

Although the E. R. Thomas Motor Company lasted for only a decade, it is ensured of immortality by the victory of one of its Thomas Flyers in the 1908 New York-to-Paris race, probably the most celebrated road racing event of all time. The company was founded in 1902 by Edwin Ross Thomas, who was born in Webster, Pennsylvania, on November 3, 1850. His father, Joseph B. Thomas, operated a coal mine in Kentucky when the Civil War broke out in 1861. He moved the family to Evansville, Indiana, where his son attended school. Young Thomas then began a 15-year career steamboating on the Ohio and Mississippi rivers. He subsequently was engaged in coal mining at Evansville and as a railroad and steamboat agent in Memphis. In 1895 Thomas moved to Toronto where he managed bicycle production for H. A. Lozier & Company. Later in 1899, when most Canadian bicycle companies were combined in the Canada Cycle & Motor Company, Thomas became vice-president of that firm.

In 1900 Thomas moved across the border to Buffalo, which was his residence for the remainder of his life. At a time when the bicycle boom of the preceding 15 years was collapsing, Thomas was one of many in that industry who decided to switch to motor vehicle production. He had some experience with gasoline engines, and he first produced motorcycles, starting with a 3-wheeler put out by his Thomas Auto-Bi Company. This was a pioneering American manufacturer of motorcycles, but Thomas used it as a stepping stone to automobiles, raising, it is said, $2 million from community investors, including the hotelman E. W. Statler.

Thomas's first cars appeared in 1901 and were lightweight, 1-cylinder runabouts priced from $650 to $800. The following year the E. R. Thomas Motor Company was organized, and Thomas, like that other and ultimately far more important Buffalo automaker, the George N. Pierce Company, moved up in price brackets. By 1904,

when the first Thomas Flyers appeared, the company was producing a 3-cylinder car selling for $2,500. This was succeeded in 1905 by a 4-cylinder, 40-horsepower model carrying a $3,000 price tag. By November 1906 more than 1,000 of these had been produced, and there were orders for 1,500 more. By 1908 6-cylinder models had been added.

The 1908 New York-to-Paris race, which saw George Schuster and Montague Roberts drive a stock Thomas Flyer Model K across North America, and, after being ferried to Siberia, arriving in Paris after 169 days, ahead of the other competitors, was a testimony to the ruggedness of the American car. But its effect on sales was at best only short-term. Sales of 1,036 cars in 1909 set a record for the company, and there was talk of an ultimate production goal of 7,500 cars a year, but Thomas never came close to that mark. Instead sales declined after 1909, in part, at least, because motorists' problems with the 6-cylinder Thomas Flyers badly damaged the good reputation the earlier cars had gained for the company. Late in 1909 William C. Durant unsuccessfully tried to acquire the Thomas company for General Motors. Eventually in 1911 the Buffalo company was one of the last acquisitions of Benjamin Briscoe's United States (U.S.) Motor Company. U.S. Motor's collapse in 1912 led to the downfall of its subsidiaries, including Thomas, but with sales of only 350 cars in 1912 the Thomas Flyer was probably doomed in any event. All production ceased on February 15, 1913.

Sometime before this, Thomas had retired from the company, although the date of his departure varies according to which source is consulted. He lived until September 13, 1936, but his active role in the automobile industry was over. For a brief time he had been one of the industry's more prominent figures, but his most important contributions were not the Thomas Flyers but the encouragement he gave, directly or indirectly, to others who would have a far greater impact. In 1910 John D. Hertz, part owner of a Chicago taxicab operation, purchased nine Thomas Flyers and was inspired to paint them yellow, thereby launching Hertz's Yellow Cab empire. Earlier in 1906 Thomas played a more direct role in the emergence of one of the industry's more important companies when he was persuaded by Roy D. Chapin to provide financial backing to the plan of Chapin and several other Oldsmobile executives to begin making their own cars. Thomas was the president and principal stockholder of the resulting Thomas-Detroit Motor Car Company. It produced a less expensive car than the Thomas Flyer, which was marketed by Thomas's Buffalo company, thereby enabling Thomas to expand the range of his offerings. But he was either

not interested in maintaining control of the company, or he was not able to deal with the younger, aggressive, and ambitious Detroiters, for within two years he had stepped aside. Within another year Chapin and his partners had taken advantage of the opportunity Thomas had provided and had formed the Hudson Motor Car Company, of which they had undisputed control and which would be for 40 years one of the industry's more innovative and respected companies.

References:

Nick Baldwin and others, *The World Guide to Automobile Manufacturers* (New York: Facts on File, 1987);
Beverly Rae Kimes and Henry Austin Clark, *Standard Catalog of American Cars, 1805-1942* (Iola, Wis.: Krause, 1985).

Charles Arthur Tilt

(June 28, 1877-September 19, 1956)

by Genevieve Wren

Motor Vehicle Research Services

CAREER: J. B. Tilt Shoe Company (1896-1903); stock farm manager, Beloit, Wisconsin (1903-1904); sales manager for Charles Y. Knight (1904-1905); president and treasurer (1905-1945), chairman, Diamond T Motor Car Company (1945-1956).

Truck manufacturer Charles Arthur Tilt, best known for his line of Diamond T trucks, was born in Chicago, Illinois, on June 28, 1877, the son of Joseph Edward and Sarah Bowes Thompson Tilt. He received his education at the University School and Chicago Manual Training School in his hometown and also attended school in Dresden, Germany, for a short time. Tilt's first business experience came in his father's J. B. Tilt Shoe Company, which produced a top-of-the-line shoe called the Diamond T. Tilt started as an apprentice in 1896 and worked his way up in the company hierarchy until he assumed the position of general superintendent in 1901 at the age of twenty-four. In 1903 he left his father's employ to manage a stock farm in Beloit, Wisconsin. In 1904 he made his entry into the automobile business, going to work as sales man-

Charles Arthur Tilt

ager for Charles Y. Knight, inventor of a sleeve-valve car engine known as the Silent Knight. Tilt started working on his own designs and produced an automobile chassis in 1905.

Later in 1905 Tilt left Knight's employ to form the Diamond T Motor Car Company, based in Chicago. He took the positions of president and treasurer in the new firm. The company produced the chassis and outfitted it with custom-built bodies. In 1911 Diamond T switched to the exclusive manufacture of a line of heavy-duty trucks, in the early years sold mainly in the Chicago area. Soon business expanded, and Diamond T established branch sales offices throughout the Midwest. In 1915 Tilt incorporated the company, and in 1917 he expanded production facilities. Shortly thereafter Diamond T won a contract from the U.S. War Department to produce several thousand 3-ton and 5-ton trucks.

After World War I production at Diamond T in-

creased moderately until 1928, when a completely new line of 6-cylinder, pneumatic-tire trucks replaced the old fours. The company also took steps to create a nationwide dealer organization and to promote export of its products at that time. It was able to survive the Depression in good shape and won more war contracts as World War II approached. Diamond T produced some 50,000 military vehicles for the Allies.

Tilt moved up to chairman of the board at Diamond T in 1945. He served in that position until his death on September 19, 1956. His wife, Agnes Josephine Morgan, whom he married in 1902, and daughters, Margaret and Mary Agnes, survived him. Diamond T was purchased in 1958 by White Motor Corporation, which continued to turn out trucks under the Diamond T name.

Reference:

James Wren and Genevieve Wren, *Motor Trucks of America* (Ann Arbor: University of Michigan Press, 1979).

Henry H. Timken

(August 16, 1831-March 16, 1909)

by David J. Andrea

University of Michigan

CAREER: Apprentice and journeyman, Casper Schurmeier Company (1847-1855); founder and president, Timken & Heinzelmann (1855-1860; 1864-1887); prospector (1860); captain, Missouri Militia (1861-1864); founder and president, Timken Carriage Company (1894); president, Carriage Builders National Association (1896-1897); president, Timken Roller Bearing Axle Company (1899-1907).

Henry H. Timken, renowned carriage manufacturer and inventor and best remembered for the tapered roller bearing and the company that bears his name, was born on August 16, 1831, in Bremen, Germany, and died in San Diego, California, on March 16, 1909. Born to a prosperous farming family, Timken was one of seven children. When he was four Timken's mother died, and in 1838 his father and family immigrated to the United States. The family established a home in St. Louis, Missouri, but shortly thereafter moved to a large farm in nearby Se-

dilia. On this farm Timken grew up and developed his mechanical skills and interests.

Timken grew tired of farm life and, like many American inventors of the day, wished to move to the city to apply his mechanical aptitude. After finishing school at sixteen, he left the family farm for St. Louis. He took a job at Casper Schurmeier Company, the city's largest carriage and wagon manufacturer. Timken worked his way through the apprentice program and ultimately earned a journeyman's position.

Ambitious and industrious, Timken left Casper Schurmeier in 1855 to establish his own carriage manufacturing company. That year he married Fredericha Heinzelmann. With his carriage business growing rapidly, Timken needed to establish a branch factory closer to his eastern customers. Joining with his father-in-law, Timken founded Timken & Heinzelmann in Belleville, Illinois. Operating as a branch factory to his St. Louis company,

*Henry H. Timken (courtesy of the
Timken Company)*

Timken & Heinzelmann continued Timken's carriage business success.

Always eager to venture into new activities and seek new money-making opportunities, in 1860 Timken's attention turned to gold. This prompted him to leave his carriage manufacturing firm to prospect at Pike's Peak, Colorado. Returning penniless in six months, Timken joined the 13th Regiment of the Missouri Militia. Timken was mustered out of the Union Army in three years as a captain and returned once again to carriage manufacturing. In 1864 the original St. Louis factory was destroyed by fire and not rebuilt until after the Civil War in 1865.

Timken patented 13 inventions–11 directly related to his carriage production. Striving to improve his product, he developed a carriage spring, for passenger comfort. Known as the Timken spring, this 1877 patent made Timken internationally known and produced a large fortune for him. The success of this invention influenced him to stop carriage production and concentrate his resources on spring man-

ufacturing. Now comfortably wealthy, Timken retired in 1887 to San Diego.

Frustrated with retirement, Timken returned to St. Louis and began carriage manufacturing again in 1894. Timken's two sons oversaw the Timken Carriage Company's daily administration. In recognition of his involvement and success in the carriage industry and his leadership skills, the Carriage Builders National Association (CBNA) elected Timken president of the country's oldest and largest trade association. He served as the CBNA's president from 1896 to 1897.

Even in his advanced years Timken stayed active and continued to be intrigued by mechanical devices. He owned and operated the first automobile in San Diego. The automobile, he admitted, would replace the horse-drawn carriage and wagon. Two patents Timken would receive before his death enhanced that prognosis and further increased Timken's wealth.

Affecting essentially every piece of manufactured equipment with load-bearing shafts or axles, Timken's innovation of the tapered roller bearing allowed engineers to reevaluate designs of motor vehicle and railroad car axles. Other machinery benefited as well. First drafted in 1895, Timken's tapered roller design reduced substantially friction loads on axles caused by a turning vehicle's weight shift. Ball bearing designs of the day did not distribute this friction, called thrust load; ball bearings only dealt with rotational friction caused by the vehicle's stationary downward force. Timken's design also reduced friction caused by centrifugal force.

Timken and his two sons began perfecting and building tapered roller bearing prototypes. To demonstrate Timken's design, his sons loaded a wagon supported by axles with their bearings. Hitched to two small mules, the sons drove through St. Louis. A police officer seeing this overloaded wagon arrested the driver for cruelty to animals. Timken successfully testified that his bearing design reduced pulling effort such that the mules were not maliciously treated.

After he had perfected his design, Timken was awarded two patents in 1898. The following year Timken founded the Timken Roller Bearing Axle Company in St. Louis. Managed by Henry Timken, president; William R. Timken, secretary and treasurer; and Henry H. Timken, Sr., vice-president; the company began producing tapered roller bearings, an industrial product Timken's name would become synonymous with, for the carriage and wagon industry.

The Timken family followed the rise of the automobile industry with great interest. With auto factories being built throughout the Cleveland-Detroit-Chicago industrial belt, Timken knew the auto industry would demand his product. Showing great insight, Timken moved the business to Canton, Ohio, in 1902—a location between his steel suppliers in Pittsburgh and customers in Cleveland and Detroit. Early business was difficult. A recession in 1903 and difficulty convincing early automotive engineers of the need for a bearing of greater cost and value placed the company close to bankruptcy. Applying his trait of persistence and good business sense, Timken finally made a major sale of automotive bearings to the Winston Car Company of Cleveland.

With the company on a stronger foundation, Timken retired again to San Diego and passed away in 1909. It is unknown if Timken envisioned how successful his company would become as a major supplier to the rapidly expanding automotive industry. The introduction of the Ford Model T

helped establish the American automotive industry as the major U.S. manufacturing industry and Detroit as its headquarters. Timken's foresight to move the company to Canton was correct. To better serve his Detroit customers, Timken expanded his business to include automotive as well as wagon axles. Establishing the Timken-Detroit Axle Company, axle production moved from Canton to Detroit in 1909. This company subsequently merged with Standard Steel Spring to form Rockwell Spring & Axle Company in 1953. No longer in the axle business, the Timken company became simply the Timken Roller Bearing Company. Headquartered in Canton, the Timken Company (the name shortened further in 1970) is an international company serving the bearing, specialty steel, and petroleum exploration industries. Today the great-grandson of the founder, W. R. Timken, Jr., serves as chairman.

Reference:

"A History of The Timken Company," (Timken Company, 1978), pp. 1-4, 11-12.

Transmissions

by James Wren

Motor Vehicle Manufacturers Association

By the mid 1890s gasoline engine manufacturers were finally able to reduce the size and weight of their engines and adapt them to carriage, bicycle, and wagon designs. Their success initiated a search for a suitable mechanism to reduce the revolutions of the flywheel so that power could be transmitted to the rear wheels without stalling the engine. Transmissions were commonly used on machinery, but their adaptation to vehicles intended to operate on uneven, bumpy roads, steep hills, and deep sand was a new challenge.

The most prevalent transmission system used on early automobiles was the simple friction-type, in which cones or disks were moved into contact with or across the engine flywheel to provide variable speeds. Other systems used driving belts or pulleys. However, the lack of a suitable long-lasting

friction material, the slippage and stretching of belts, exposure to the elements, and the growth of the automobile in size and weight demanded more durable and sophisticated devices.

The friction and belt-type transmissions reappeared during the "high wheeler" period of 1906 to 1910 and even in later adaptations, but by the turn of the century gear-type transmissions dominated the industry. Constant mesh gears were the earliest such transmissions. Their popularity was due to the ease provided in gear changing. As the name suggests, the gears were in constant mesh, either in a planetary fashion, where several small gears revolved around a large central gear, or in other gear arrangements using individual clutches to move gears in and out of mesh.

The planetary gear sets were popular because

of their easily accessible clutch bands, which were used for shifting the gears, and the simplicity of adding a reverse gear. At high speed all gears were locked and revolved as a unit. The Ford Model T was the greatest proponent of planetary gears, and the modern automatic transmission uses a planetary or compound planetary gear set in its system. However, the limitation of the early planetary gear sets was that they only provided two forward speeds. Greater numbers of gear ratios were offered in constant mesh spur gear units, but the use of separate cone clutches in those systems suffered from the lack of adequate friction material. The spur gears were also extremely noisy and hard to engage and disengage.

Several novel transmission systems, including the Sturtevant and the Dey, appeared in the early 1900s. The first step to developing a fully automatic transmission occurred in 1904 when the Sturtevant automobile offered an automatic clutch. The Sturtevant transmission used three multiple-disk clutches, which were connected to a constant mesh gear in an oil-filled flywheel. The system was controlled by vehicle speed. At 250 engine revolutions per minute, spring-loaded centrifugal weights activated the first clutch, and an overrunning gear device brought in the first gear. High speeds activated devices for successive gears. The Dey transmission used hydraulic motors driven by a primary pump and was the earliest attempt at a hydrostatic transmission.

Although there were many attempts to facilitate gear changing, the sliding gear transmission prevailed for many years. The sliding gear transmission consisted of driving gears on parallel shafts connected to the engine by a friction-type clutch. Gears on the main or input shaft were moved into mesh with smaller gears on an output shaft by sliding them with a lever and fork arrangement controlled by the driver. The various sizes of the gears and the number of teeth on each determined the various ratios and the power obtained. For example, twice the number of teeth on the input gear would indicate a 2-to-1 ratio while an equal number would provide a 1-to-1 ratio in high gear. The designation of a 3- or 4-speed transmission indicated the number of gear ratios available. A special reverse gear was also a part of the sliding gear arrangement. Although the sliding gear transmission dominated, other means to ease the task of shifting gears and operating clutches were tried.

During the mid 1910s great interest developed in magnetic gear shifting. In the systems introduced at that time, speed changes were effected through the use of magnetic plates. The magnetic steel plates were placed opposite each other at short distances. Half of the plates were hollow and contained windings through which electricity was passed to magnetize them and attract the opposite plates. By that means, gears were brought in and out of mesh. The driver controlled the selection of gears through push-button switches. But the magnetic systems were of limited success and could not replace the sliding gear transmission.

Wheels

by James Wren

Motor Vehicle Manufacturers Association

Americans had been manufacturing carriage and wagon wheels for more than a century by the time automobiles first rolled into the streets in the 1890s. Consquently, wooden-spoke wagon wheels, or artillery wheels as they were also called, and lightweight wire-spoke bicycle wheels were readily available for use on automobiles.

The wooden wheel was the cheapest and most available choice in the early years of the automobile industry, but the wood spokes tended to dry and become loose and squeaky. They could be soaked with water to make them swell and tighten their fit and were easily replaced, but care and replacement problems eventually outweighed the advantage of the cheaper price. However, the alternative, the wire-spoke bicycle or carriage wheel with two rows of spokes in tension, was not strong enough to support the weight of an automobile body. Another potential alternative, using compressible springs as spokes, was never successful.

Automobile wheelmakers soon turned to a combination of wire and wood. The rims were usually bolted to the felloes, or curved sections, where the spokes were attached. Steel bands were placed around the wheel when it was intended for prolonged use. Shortly after the turn of the century most automobiles were using pneumatic tires and wheels with a clincher-type fixed rim that had flanges on both sides to grip the tire bead. The demountable clincher rim for wooden-spoke wheels was in common use by 1905.

In succeeding years steel-spoke wheels slowly displaced wooden-spoke and wire-spoke wheels, although some manufacturers continued to use wooden wheels made with steel felloes well into the 1920s. An improved wire-spoke wheel with three rows of spokes enjoyed short-lived popularity in the mid 1910s. During World War I wheels made from steel disks bolted to steel felloes gained prominence. A steel-disk wheel with a clincher rim, the future choice, appeared in 1920.

Wheels with wooden spokes and steel felloes on a 1913 Ford Model T

Rollin H. White

(July 11, 1872-September 10, 1962)

by James M. Laux

University of Cincinnati

CAREER: Vice-president, White Company (1906-1914); president (1916-1928); chairman, Cleveland Tractor Company (1928-1944); chairman, Rollin Motors Company (1923-1925).

An inventor and manufacturer of motor vehicles and tractors, Rollin Henry White was one of three brothers who brought the White Sewing Machine Company into the automobile business. After graduating from Cornell University with an engineering degree in 1893, Rollin worked in his father's sewing machine company and traveled in Europe studying the infant automobile industry. Upon his return to Cleveland in the late 1890s he developed a steam car, using a semiflash boiler for speedy warmups and a condenser to allow the reuse of water. The company began to market the White steamer in 1901. In a few years the automobile business was busy enough to require a large new factory and a separate corporate existence, the White Company, founded in 1906. The oldest brother, Windsor T., served as president; Rollin as first vice-president; and the youngest brother, Walter C., as second vice-president.

Large and luxurious, White steamers brought prestige to their owners and profit to their makers. Nevertheless, in 1909 the firm began making gasoline-powered vehicles, and it abandoned steam in 1911. Its large machines could be adapted for trucks, and the company placed more emphasis on that market after 1912. In 1914 the head of the family, Thomas H. White, died, and the automobile firm was reorganized in 1915 as the White Motor Company. Rollin White had been on leave from the company from 1911 or 1912, probably due to disputes and illness, and formally left it after his father's death, just as it was about to achieve greatness with its trucks in World War I.

Recuperating from his illness, Rollin White visited his brother Clarence Greenleaf White's pine-

Rollin H. White

apple plantation on the island of Maui in Hawaii. The brothers designed a small gasoline-powered tractor for farm use. It proved to be impractical, but upon his return to Cleveland, White designed a light crawler tractor similar to the caterpillar type invented by Benjamin Holt in California. He began to make those in a new establishment, the Cleveland Motor Plow Company, renamed the Cleveland Tractor Company in 1917. Its products soon bore the name "Cletrac," and in 1920 they sold in the amount of $12.6 million. That good year was followed by the recession of 1920-1921 and meager sales. To keep the factory occupied and probably for other reasons Rollin White determined to enter the automobile business.

A first effort, planned in conjunction with E. E. Allyne and Fred M. Zeder in 1922, was still-born, but the second resulted in the formation of Rollin Motors Company in 1923. Rollin White served as chairman of the board, with several former Studebaker executives occupying the other top management posts. The company introduced its Rollin cars late in 1923, aiming at the medium price range with several body styles and selling from $895 to $1,275. The Rollin had a 4-cylinder engine, a 112-inch wheelbase, and 4-wheel brakes. Although touted as "a symphony of mechanical perfection," the Rollin was not in harmony with the market. Some 6,100 were turned out in 1924, but production ceased in the following year.

Cleveland tractors continued as a minor factor in the track-laying market, with sales of $4.3 million in 1927 and $7.4 million in 1928, figures one-sixth and one-fifth those of the Caterpillar Tractor Company. In the latter year Rollin White, now fifty-six, became chairman of the board and his son William King White assumed the presidency. The firm suffered severely in the Depression, as sales fell to $2.3 million in 1933. By 1937 it had recovered to $7.8 million in sales and a profit of $117,000, a year in which Caterpillar's sales were $63.3 million

and profit $10.2 million. In 1938 Cleveland Tractor offered ten models, three powered by diesel engines supplied by the Hercules Company and several operating on wheels.

In the boom of World War II, Cleveland Tractor's sales reached a peak of $43.4 million in 1943, but its management resolved to sell out in the following year. The Oliver Farm Equipment Company bought it in October 1944 for common stock worth about $3.65 million. Rollin White retired fully at this point, at age seventy-two. He died 18 years later at his home in Hobe Sound, Florida, on September 10, 1962.

Rollin White held hundreds of patents on mechanical devices, such as an oil and water separator and a gasoline burner for steam cars and a wide variety of improvements for tractors. He married Katherine King of Oswego, New York, in 1896. They had three children: Elizabeth, William King, and Rollin Henry, Jr.

References:

Ella White Ford, *Descendants of Thomas White, Sudbury, Mass.* (Cleveland: Western Reserve Historical Society, 1952);

Richard Wager, *Golden Wheels* (Cleveland: Western Reserve Historical Society, 1975).

Walter C. White

(September 8, 1876-September 29, 1929)

by James M. Laux

University of Cincinnati

CAREER: Vice-president, White Company (1906-1915); vice-president (1915-1921), president, White Motor Company (1921-1929).

Walter Charles White was the youngest of the three White brothers who developed the White steam car early in the twentieth century. Their father, Thomas H. White, operated the White Sewing Machine Company in Cleveland, Ohio. Walter White graduated from Cornell University in 1898 and received a law degree from New York Law School in 1899. After working for a brief period in the legal office of the New York Central Railroad,

he returned to Cleveland in 1900 to join his father's sewing machine firm, especially its infant steam car department. With the company launched in the automobile business in 1901, he set off for London to establish a European sales branch for its steamers. In 1904 he came back to Cleveland and promoted sales by engaging in races and demonstrations such as the Glidden tours.

When the White Company was organized to handle the automobile business, Walter White took the chair of vice-president and sales manager. He retained those positions when the firm was reorganized in 1915 as the White Motor Company. In

Walter C. White

World War I, White gasoline trucks were widely used and highly praised by the French and American armies, and in 1917 he went to France as chairman of a committee to assist the U.S. Army in setting up a repair and maintenance service for motor vehicles. For its wartime service the White Motor Company received the Croix de Guerre from the French government, and Walter White wore the rosette of a Chevalier in the Legion of Honor.

After the war Walter White assumed the presidency of White Motor in 1921, when his older brother Windsor stepped up to chairman. White trucks sold well in the 1920s. White's chief rival, Mack, sold about 1,000 fewer trucks per year than White, but they were larger and more expensive, so Mack's total sales ran $5 million to $8 million more per year. Mack's dividends from 1924 through 1929 of $6 per common share topped White's, which ranged from $4 in 1917 through 1926 to $1 in 1928 and $2 in 1930.

Walter White did not have to confront the Great Depression of the 1930s, for he died on September 29, 1929, of injuries sustained in an automobile collision on a Saturday morning in Shaker Heights, Ohio. His brothers Windsor and Rollin were with him at the end.

White had served on the board of directors of the Coca-Cola Company just as Coca-Cola's president Robert Woodruff sat on the White company board. Upon his death, his close friend Woodruff assumed the presidency of White Motor for a brief interval.

Walter White had a particular interest in dairying, with a large farm, the "Circle W," near Cleveland, and in the sport of polo. His first marriage, to Marianne Laurie of Elizabeth, New Jersey, ended in divorce. His second, to Mary Virginia Saunders of Sumter, South Carolina, was celebrated in September 1919. From that union were born six daughters and two sons.

Reference:

Richard Wager, *Golden Wheels* (Cleveland: Western Reserve Historical Society, 1975).

Windsor T. White

(August 28, 1866-April 9, 1958)

by James M. Laux

University of Cincinnati

CAREER: Treasurer, Cleveland Machine Screw Company (1893-1895); vice-president (1895-1914), president (1914-1917), chairman, White Sewing Machine Company (1921-1923); president, White Company (1906-1915); president (1915-1921), chairman, White Motor Company (1921-1927).

Windsor T. White was the eldest of three brothers who engaged in various business enterprises springing from the White Sewing Machine Company of Cleveland, Ohio, founded by their father, Thomas H. White. Windsor White graduated from Worcester Polytechnic Institute in 1890. After a few years working for White Sewing Machine and Cleveland Machine Screw (one of his father's creations), he became vice-president of White Sewing Machine in 1895. When Thomas H. White died in 1914, Windsor White succeeded his father as president of the firm.

Meanwhile, in 1901 the company had begun to manufacture steam automobiles on the designs of Windsor's brother Rollin H. White. Those cars became so successful that a separate firm, the White Company, was established in 1906 to manage the operation in a new factory in Cleveland, with Windsor White as president. Although White steam cars were successful, the company also began to make gasoline models in 1909 and abandoned steam in 1911. The robust chassis of the White touring cars were adapted to trucks, and those vehicles became a growing proportion of White's output by 1912. After the death of Thomas H. White in 1914, the White Company was reorganized in 1915 as the White Motor Company, retaining Windsor White as president.

World War I brought large orders to White for military trucks, especially from the French and American governments. Sales rose from $18.3 million in 1916 to $39.6 million in 1918. White supplied some 18,000 trucks during the war. The

Windsor T. White

company gave up passenger car manufacturing in 1918 and thereafter specialized in trucks and buses. White trucks had earned a high reputation during the war, and sales remained strong afterward as the firm stood out as one of the leading American truck producers. Its poorest record in the 1920s was in the recession year of 1921, with 6,727 vehicles sold for $30.3 million. Its best year was 1926, when 12,173 units brought in $64.6 million. At age fifty-four Windsor White became White Motor's chairman in 1921, with his brother Walter C. White assuming the presidency. Then in 1927 Windsor retired from White Motor's management.

Windsor White served as president of the White Sewing Machine Company from 1914 to 1917 and then returned as chairman from 1921 to 1923. In 1921 A. S. Rodgers assumed the presidency of White Sewing Machine and expanded its operations. In 1923 it acquired the Theodor Kundtz company, a maker of wooden cabinets for sewing machines and mass-produced school furniture. The next year it obtained the Domestic Sewing Machine Company from Sears, Roebuck, and thereafter White supplied all the Sears Company's sewing machines.

In January 1926 ownership of the White Sewing Machine Company passed out of the hands of the White family, as the current president and vice-president, A. S. Rodgers and Oscar Grothe, took over in a leveraged buyout underwritten by Wall Street investment houses. The Whites received $9 million the new owners obtained from a public offering of $4 million in 6 percent bonds and $5 million in 8 percent convertible preference shares. At that point White Sewing Machine produced about 125,000 machines annually for $12 to $14 million. It employed between 3,000 and 4,000. Windsor White remained on the board of the sewing machine company until 1929.

In retirement Windsor White took several safaris to hunt big game in Africa. He brought specimens back for Cleveland's natural history museum. In 1892 White married Delia B. Holden, daughter of Liberty E. Holden, publisher of the *Cleveland Plain Dealer* and a free-silver advocate. They had three children. White was a Republican and a Unitarian. After he retired he lived another 30 years, until his death, in his ninety-first year, on April 9, 1958.

References:

Ella White Ford, *Descendants of Thomas White, Sudbury, Mass.* (Cleveland: Western Reserve Historical Society, 1952);

Richard Wager, *Golden Wheels* (Cleveland: Western Reserve Historical Society, 1975).

White Motor Company

by James M. Laux

University of Cincinnati

The White Company, maker of steam cars from 1900 to 1911 and of gasoline cars and trucks from 1909, began as an experiment by the White Sewing Machine Company of Cleveland, Ohio. Thomas H. White moved his small sewing machine firm from Massachusetts to Cleveland in 1866. It prospered, although it never challenged the Singer company's leadership of the industry. Thomas White was sympathetic to new ventures, for by the 1890s his firm had also manufactured roller skates, kerosene lamps, phonographs, and bicycles (about 10,000 per year during the boom period of the mid 1890s). In 1891 he founded the Cleveland Machine Screw Company, later named the Cleveland Automatic Machine Company, a major machine-tool maker.

Thomas White's son Rollin, an engineering graduate of Cornell University in 1894, wanted to make motor cars. After college he traveled in Europe studying automobiles. He chose to use steam power. Experimental work began in 1898, and by spring 1900 four small steamers had been finished. Those cars used a semiflash boiler and condensed the steam for reuse. In its first year on the market, 1901, the White company made 193 steamers, far below the output of its major U.S. steam car competitor, Locomobile. The high quality of the White and its condenser, which allowed much longer runs before adding water became necessary, made it a serious challenger to the Locomobile. When the latter abandoned steam cars in 1904, White continued, making large and elaborate touring cars. Its best production year was 1906—output totaled 1,534—when it also began its separate corporate existence. In November 1906 the White Company was established to manage the steam car business. Rollin White's older brother, Windsor T., became president, his younger brother, Walter C., second vice-president, and Rollin first vice-president. The firm also moved into a new factory in Cleveland. Very large, its one story and sawtooth roof design would become the

Mrs. A. H. Elliott driving her 1910 White steam car

standard for factory design for 40 years.

Although White steamers achieved high prestige, by 1908 the company's management decided the market had turned away from steam. To get a fast start in making the shift to gasoline models, it bought a few chassis from the Delahaye company of France as well as 300 high-quality 4-cylinder engines. The blocks for these engines came from the Peugeot foundry in France, with the machining and parts such as pistons, rods, valves, and crankshafts added by Delahaye. White introduced its first gasoline cars in 1909 as 1910 models and sold some 1,200 of them by the end of that model year. One must conclude that the engines of most of them were copied from the Delahaye. The French firm may have supplied all the crankshafts. White also used French-made Claudel carburetors in 1910-1912. Soon the White 4-cylinder engine was altered in its details from the Delahaye, especially for the 1912 model, which changed from right-hand drive to left-hand drive. In that year White also introduced its own 6-cylinder engine. When the Delahaye firm realized what had happened, it sued White for patent infringement in 1914 but dropped the suit when World War I began and the French government began buying large numbers of White

trucks. White also made about 1,200 steam vehicles in 1910 and then closed out that type the next year. The company produced a total of 9,122 steamers.

The White 4- and 6-cylinder cars were strong enough for easy adaptation to truck use. Such trucks found favor with the U.S. Army by 1912 and also the Russian czarist regime. Four truck models were available from 1912 on, with capacities of .75 tons, 1.5 tons, 3 tons, and 5 tons and prices in 1915 ranging from $2,200 to $4,750. In the American civilian economy, White trucks were used primarily for city pickup and delivery work, as demonstrated by the clients who had the largest numbers in service in 1919: Gulf Refining, Standard Oil of New York, Atlantic Refining, the U.S. Post Office, the meat packers Armour and Swift, Coca-Cola, the department stores Altman and Gimbels, and Railway Express. Some of the 477 Whites owned by the Bell telephone companies may have ventured into the countryside, and the 112 White buses operated by the Yellowstone Park Transportation Company certainly did.

In 1914 the patriarch of the family, Thomas Howard White, died at seventy-eight years of age. Rollin White's official departure from the company for health and other reasons followed, and then the firm reorganized in 1915 as the White Motor Company with $16 million capital, compared to $2.9 million for the predecessor firm. By that time White was shifting its focus from cars to trucks and finding a very large military market. World War I marked the coming of age of motor trucks, at least among the Allied Powers, who used tens of thousands of them, generally to good effect. White sold trucks to the Russian, French, and American armies. Its truck production in 1917 amounted to 5,900, and in 1918 to 12,150. All told, White sold some 18,000 trucks to the Allied governments during the war, for about $52 million. The year 1918 marked the last for White's car manufacturing; the company produced 8,927 gasoline automobiles in ten years.

White's decision to abandon the high-price auto market was wise. Dozens of small producers completed in that area in the 1920s, and almost all of them failed. Truck and bus manufacturing continued at White, the latter taking about one-tenth of the output, and occasionally the company received an order for taxicabs. During that decade White dropped chain drive and began to offer 6-cylinder engines, pneumatic tires, and electric lights. In 1928 it offered trucks for payloads from .75 to 7.5 tons. Most trucks still engaged in pickup and delivery service in urban areas or were used on farms, so the demand for large sizes remained small. White's sales rose from $39.6 million in 1918 to a peak of $64.6 million in 1926 on 12,173 units sold, but profits diminished after approaching $7 million in 1923. White's sales as a share of the entire truck market dropped from 18 percent in 1921 to 8.6 percent in 1929. The major car producers had begun to attack the low end of the truck market, and White's larger vehicles were approaching obsolescence.

Then company president Walter C. White died on September 29, 1929, after an automobile accident, and no member of the family stepped forward to carry on. For a short period Robert W. Woodruff, president of Coca-Cola, took White's reins. Before World War I Woodruff had been purchasing agent for his father's coal and ice company in Atlanta. In 1911 he placed an order for White trucks to replace some of the horse-drawn wagons. The story goes that Woodruff's father took a dim view of that decision and discharged his son from the company. In any event, 1913 found young Woodruff as a salesman for White. By 1923 he had become a vice-

president and sat on the board of directors. In that year he left White's management and returned to Atlanta as president of Coca-Cola, although he retained his seat on the White board. When Woodruff's old friend Walter C. White died, he took over as chairman of the board and president.

The White directors soon brought Ashton G. Bean on board as president in 1930. He had managed several small manufacturing companies in Elyria and Cleveland. An unsentimental taskmaster, Bean "never ate lunch and never hired a friend or a relative in business." He and the White company had to confront the Depression. Sales and earnings suffered grievously. In 1932 White sold 3,619 vehicles for $17.1 million, only one-fourth of 1926 revenue. Financial results had gone in the red in 1930 and dropped to a deficit of $3.6 million by 1932. Nevertheless, White still had large reserves of cash. In 1932 it bought an ailing truck firm, Indiana Motors, a pioneer in offering diesel engines, made by Cummins in this case. In October 1932 White's management accepted a buyout offer from the Studebaker Corporation. Albert Erskine of Studebaker was the quintessential "boomer" of the "roaring twenties." In the early 1930s he kept expecting the national economy and the automobile market to turn the corner back to good times. When that failed to happen, Erskine grew desperate for cash to keep Studebaker going. Somehow he persuaded White's management to join Studebaker, offering $39 in cash, bonds, and stock for each share of White, which was selling for $23. A small minority of White's stockholders held out, however, asking for $40 in cash and bringing up an Ohio statute that seemed to forbid a takeover that would cause an Ohio company to lose its working capital. Erskine finally gave up the takeover effort, and Studebaker went into bankruptcy in March 1933. Two of its younger executives, Paul Hoffman and Harold Vance, took over Studebaker and ultimately saved it. Erskine went home and shot himself. When Studebaker emerged from bankruptcy in 1935 the White stock it still held was distributed to its creditors, mostly banks, which soon sold it. The episode cost White some $5 million in working capital. When President Bean resigned and then died in 1935 the White board named Robert F. Black, an experienced truck man, as president. Formerly with the Mack truck company and then president of the Brockway truck company, Black was an outstanding salesman and manager.

Although under Black's leadership the company introduced a more efficient gasoline engine and an innovative door-to-door delivery vehicle using an air-cooled engine (the White Horse), it did not climb back to 1920s levels of prosperity. In 1936 it finally made a profit on sales of $28.8 million. It continued to allow its small Indiana line of trucks to fit Cummins diesel engines if customers ordered them but failed to recognize the diesel as the wave of the future. Caterpillar, Cummins, General Motors, Mack, Dodge, and International Harvester were more aggressive with diesel engines, the first five with their own designs. Perhaps White succumbed to the "not invented here" attitude.

When World War II arrived, White finally boomed again, producing military vehicles for the U.S. Army (half-tracks, scout cars, and tank transporters). In 1943 its sales peaked at $156.4 million on 21,973 vehicles.

White remained profitable after the war, selling between 10,000 and 20,000 vehicles per year, concentrating on the heavier sizes, where its chief rivals were Mack, International, Ford, and General Motors. The market for heavy trucks rose as highways improved, encouraging more intercity freight traffic by truck. White's market share of trucks of more than 19,500 pounds usually came to just under one-fifth of annual sales in the late 1940s and 1950s. Gradually diesel engines equipped those heavyweights, especially those engaged in long-distance work. White obtained its diesels from Cummins or General Motors. In the 1950s White began buying up its smaller competitors in the heavy truck market, Sterling of Milwaukee in 1951; Autocar of Ardmore, Pennsylvania, in 1953 (which was installed in a new factory in Exton, Pennsylvania); Reo of Lansing, Michigan, in 1957; and the prize, Diamond T of Chicago in 1958, for $10.4 million. The last was moved to the Reo factory in Lansing. From 1951 White also handled sales and service for Freightliner trucks. That firm, a subsidiary of the trucking company Consolidated Freightways, assembled a growing number of heavy trucks. The acquisitions provided more activity for the White network of service branches and dealers and brought more engineering talent to the parent firm. Primarily, the strategy was one of growing by acquisition rather than through internal expansion.

As Black began to face retirement, he gave way to J. N. Bauman, a longtime White employee on the sales side, as president in 1956 and then chairman in 1959. The acquisition policy seemed to have paid off. Sales in 1959 amounted to $333.1 million on 24,640 vehicles, and the firm employed 10,000 people. White's market share of light-heavy trucks (class 7, 26,000 to 33,000 pounds) and heavy trucks (class 8, more than 33,000 pounds) was 25.2 percent in 1959 compared to 10 percent in 1950. It was competing closely with International Harvester for the lead in those niches of the truck market. Profits were only 3 or 4 percent of sales, not very reassuring.

In the post-1945 years the makers of heavy trucks moved toward custom building; that is, letting larger customers specify the engines, transmissions, brakes, suspensions, and even sun visors on the trucks they ordered. Such deviation from standard types raised costs, but most clients preferred the arrangement. White moved toward custom building and to a considerable degree became an assembler of components made by firms specializing in engines, transmissions, and the like.

After Robert Black left White's active management, J. N. Bauman inaugurated an acquisition policy in a related industry. It carried much greater risk than Bauman realized. White began buying a series of smaller farm equipment manufacturers, all in financial difficulty. It hoped to meld them into a large competitor in the industry. The purchases began in 1960-1961 with the Oliver Corporation, including the Cleveland Tractor Company, the latter founded by Rollin White in 1916. Then came a Canadian producer, Cockshutt, in 1962, and Minneapolis-Moline in 1963. Among some smaller acquisitions, it also bought in 1955 a small Ohio diesel engine maker, Superior of Springfield. It hoped to use the resources of that firm to begin diesel engine production for its trucks. That did not work out, so in 1963 White and Cummins, its major supplier of diesel engines, got together and proposed a merger. The merger would have guaranteed Cummins a market and White a supply of diesel engines, but the U.S. Justice Department believed such a union would lessen competition in heavy trucks and vetoed the idea. White then bought the Hercules Engine Company of Canton, Ohio, in 1966 to obtain more expertise in diesel engines. It also bought Euclid from General Motors in 1968. That firm made off-highway vehicles used primarily in construction projects.

In the late 1960s White made what turned out to be a major error. It began construction of a large and expensive factory near Canton, Ohio, to make its own diesel engines. By that time diesel power was used by about 90 percent of new heavy trucks, and the proportion would rise. White planned to use its diesel engines first in the tractors of its farm equipment division and then it its trucks. Soon serious difficulties emerged. Sales of White's farm equipment machinery declined, and heavy truck sales went into a cyclical downturn in 1970. White's share of the heavy truck market also dropped as the Ford Motor Company became a major factor, using Caterpillar diesel engines. White's financial results turned sour in 1969 and showed deficits in 1970 and 1971. The fluctuations in the national truck market do not appear to have been affected by the war in Vietnam. In those circumstances White's chairman, Bauman, and president, Henry J. Nave, began looking for a partner with which to merge. After negotiations with the Ethyl Corporation broke down in May 1970, talks began with White Consolidated Industries. That firm, also based in Cleveland, had grown out of the White Sewing Machine Company. Led from 1956 by Edward Rettig, a former White Motor executive, White Consolidated had also gone on a hunt for acquisitions and had collected a group of kitchen appliance, machine tool, and machinery makers. The White on White merger failed in February 1971, when the Justice Department threatened to bring suit against it as anticompetitive. White Motor's board of directors had had enough by that time and encouraged chairman Bauman to retire on his seventy-second birthday in March 1971.

In May a new chairman came on board, S. E. (Bunkie) Knudsen, son of William S. Knudsen, who had been one of the greats at General Motors and in the U.S. war production effort of the 1940s. The younger Knudsen had served as an executive vice-president at General Motors and as president of Ford but now was available. Knudsen acted vigorously to restore White's fortunes, winning a large short-term loan from a banking syndicate on the strength of his reputation, selling the money-losing Diamond Reo truck division, and offering the unused diesel engine factory in Canton for sale. The Canadian farm equipment maker Massey-Ferguson finally bought it in 1975 at a figure that brought a large loss to White. Meanwhile, White's president, Henry Nave, left to become president of arch-rival Mack, and many other White executives departed as Knudsen brought in a new high-salaried manage-

ment team. He opened a new truck assembly facility at New River Valley, Virginia (west of Roanoke), in 1975 to replace the 70-year-old plant in Cleveland, which finally ended truck production in March 1978. White's revival led the *Cleveland Plain Dealer* to award Knudsen the title "Businessman of the Year" for 1974, but already the company was sinking back into difficulty. Heavy truck sales nationally and at White went into a disastrous decline in 1975, a year in which White recorded its highest-ever deficit, and Freightliner dealt another major blow when it confidentially warned White that in 1976 it would terminate its agreement for White to sell and service its trucks. In recent years Freightliners had accounted for nearly half of White's truck sales and most of its profits. White actually continued to sell Freightliners through 1977. That bad news led Knudsen to scurry about for a merger partner. He found that White Consolidated was still willing, and a bargain was struck that would make White Motor a wholly owned subsidiary of White Consolidated. The Justice Department raised no objection this time, commenting that "White Motor appears to be a failing company." But once again the deal failed at the last minute, when in May 1976 White Consolidated's chairman, Edward Rettig, fell seriously ill and could not negotiate a satisfactory arrangement with White Motor's creditors.

At this juncture the only option left to White Motor's Knudsen was to raise cash by selling off more assets. Those set loose included various machinery subsidiaries not directly involved in truck assembly and also the Euclid division, bought in 1977 by the German car and truck maker, Daimler-Benz.

The major European heavy truck producers began to enter the U.S. market in the 1970s, as overcapacity and vigorous competition in Europe sliced their profits there. In addition, these firms' years of research and development in fuel economy made their engines more efficient than American engines. At White, Knudsen was willing to sell the core truck business. After unsuccessful negotiations with the French firm Renault, which went on to buy control of Mack, it appeared that the German truck builder MAN (Machinenfabrik Augsburg-Nurnberg) would gradually take over White. That effort collapsed in June 1979. Soon after, Cruse Moss, former president of the truck and bus subsidiary of American Motors, joined White as president. Moss moved the White headquarters to Farmington Hills, Michigan, a Detroit suburb, in September 1979. After three years of relatively good truck sales and modest profits, 1977-1979, another oil price crisis and a recession hit White especially hard in 1980. That year it sold only 7,664 trucks, compared with 12,512 a year earlier. Moss continued the sale of assets by disposing of its plant in Exton, Pennsylvania, in 1980. The operations to assemble Autocar trucks there were moved to a small factory in Ogden, Utah.

After nine years at the wheel Bunkie Knudsen retired as chairman in April 1980. Although he had enjoyed some early success, after 1976 White had lost market share annually. Knudsen had failed to bring White back to financial stability. Moss became chairman and in the face of declining sales and mounting losses had to seek refuge from White creditors by filing for Chapter 11 bankruptcy in September 1980. That gave management some time to sell more assets and wait for either better truck sales or a buyer. In November it disposed of the farm equipment division at a big loss to a Dallas investment group. Consolidated Freightways offered to buy White's remaining truck operations, but Chairman Moss turned down the offer. Consolidated, unable to expand its Freightliner production and sales that way, then chose to sell that operation to Daimler-Benz in March 1981. The German firm thereby managed to obtain a large production and distribution operation in North America. At that point Moss was forced out at White by the bankruptcy examiner, and in May 1981 White agreed to a takeover by the Volvo company of Sweden. Freightliner had been distributing Volvo trucks in the United States, but now Volvo's great European rival had taken over that firm. While Daimler-Benz had to pay some $260 million for Freightliner, Volvo paid only $70 million for White's truck operations—assembly plants in Virginia and Utah, a small factory in Orrville, Ohio, and, not least, a strong distribution and dealer network along with the White and Autocar names. But all the uncertainty ruined White's truck sales, which dropped through the floor to just 2,857 in 1981.

Late in 1983 White's creditors received 53 cents on the dollar of claims, while the Volvo-White company headed off toward profitability. The new Swedish management moved its headquarters to Greensboro, North Carolina. Major components for Volvo trucks were imported and assembled in the Virginia plant along with Whites, while Autocars and more Whites were produced in smaller numbers in Utah. Free of heavy debts and money-losing sidelines, Volvo-White began to make a profit in 1984. Its share of the class-8 truck market rose steadily to reach 9.2 percent in 1986, fifth behind Navistar, Paccar (Kenworth and Peterbilt), Freightliner, and Mack. Of Volvo-White's 11,361 heavy trucks sold in 1986, 1,057 were fully assembled Volvos imported from its plant in Belgium. That three of the five largest heavy truck firms in the United States by the mid 1980s were foreign-controlled suggests serious management problems among the American firms. Volvo's share would soon grow larger, for in August 1986 General Motors agreed to join Volvo as the junior partner in a joint venture. GM would close its heavy truck factory, let Volvo assemble those vehicles for it, and put the GM badge on them. In effect GM was phasing out of heavy trucks in Volvo's favor.

The most serious errors White had made that led to its near-collapse and eventual foreign takeover were the decisions to enter the farm equipment business and to build the diesel engine factory. Both required heavy investment financed by loans. Then when the investments did not return a profit, and the truck business had some poor years, the company could not continue alone. If White had developed its own diesel engine in the late 1930s, it might have made a difference, although that did not keep Mack independent, and the Paccar companies have survived without their own engines. Heavier investment in research and development, as was the case with Daimler-Benz, Renault-Berliet, and Volvo, the three largest heavy truck producers in the non-Communist world, might also have changed the story.

References:

Ella White Ford, *The Descendants of Thomas White, Sudbury, Mass, 1638* (Cleveland: Western Reserve Historical Society, 1952);

R. Scoon and J. Small, "White's Relation to Delahaye," *Horseless Carriage Gazette* (January-February 1975): 46-49;

Richard Wager, *Golden Wheels* (Cleveland: Western Reserve Historical Society, 1975);

"White Truck in the Black," *Fortune*, 23 (February 1941): 85-89, 122, 124, 126.

Childe Harold Wills

(June 1, 1878-December 30, 1940)

by George S. May

Eastern Michigan University

CAREER: Chief engineer, Boyer Machine Company (1901-1903); chief engineer and factory manager, Ford Motor Company (1903-1919); president, C. H. Wills & Company (1920-1923); vice-president, Wills-Ste. Claire, Inc. (1923-1926); consulting metallurgist, Chrysler Corporation (1933-1940).

No doubt because he grew tired of being asked about his unusual name—which owed its origins to his parents' fondness for the poetry of George Gordon, Lord Byron—Childe Harold Wills, one of America's foremost automotive engineers, used only the initial C in place of his first name. He was born on June 1, 1878, in Fort Wayne, Indiana, the youngest of three children born to John Carnegie and Mary Engelina Swindell Wills. His paternal grandfather had immigrated to Canada from Forfarshire, Scotland, in 1832. John Wills was a master railroad mechanic who, sometime after his son's birth, moved the family to Detroit, where C. Harold Wills completed his studies in that city's public schools.

Wills followed in his father's footsteps, receiving his first training as a mechanic from his father and then, after completing school, entering an apprenticeship as a toolmaker at the Detroit Lubricating Company. Even as a young man, Wills exhibited all the traits of a workaholic. After working at Detroit Lubricating during the day, he studied engineering, chemistry, and metallurgy at night. After completing his four-year apprenticeship at age twenty-one, he went to work at a machine shop before being employed in 1901 as chief engineer at the Boyer Machine Company, predecessor of the Burroughs Adding Machine Company, which is today's Unisys Corporation.

Sometime during this period Wills became acquainted with Henry Ford, who by 1901 had become well-known in Detroit for his experiments

Childe Harold Wills (courtesy of the National Automotive History Collection, Detroit Public Library)

with automobiles, which led in 1899 to the formation of the Detroit Automobile Company. That company had been dissolved in early 1901 because of Ford's inability to settle upon one car that the company might produce. Others had continued to support his work, however, and in October 1901 Ford received his first significant national attention with the victory of the racing car that he had built and driven in the featured race at Michigan's first automobile races, held in the Detroit suburb of Grosse Pointe. The win encouraged Ford's backers to form the Henry Ford Company, expecting to use his new fame as a selling point for a Ford passenger car. Instead, it only aroused Ford's interest in racing, and when he spent most of his time with the company working on a new racing car, he was fired in early March 1902.

With new backing, Ford continued his work on the racers, and it was at this time that Wills began to work with him, as he would for the next 17 years. Wills may even have done some work for the Henry Ford Company, but after Ford left that company and set up a shop elsewhere, Wills agreed to come in before and after his working day at the Boyer company. Fifteen years younger than Ford, Wills no doubt looked upon this as a chance to gain more experience and also to be associated with something that might offer him greater opportunity in the future than the job at Boyer. He became part of the team of workers that Ford assembled in these early years who worked for him with or without pay. Wills was in the latter category. There is also evidence that he may have contributed some of his own money to help finance the Ford racing venture. In return, either at this time or sometime during the following year, Ford promised Wills a share of the money Ford would eventually make, a promise that Ford kept and that earned Wills a fortune.

Wills and Ford shared the same kind of practical approach to mechanical matters. Both men had a disdain for book learning. "If it's in a book," Wills said when it was suggested that technical information he might need was available in written form, "it's at least four years old and I don't have any use for it." Wills, however, had a better grasp of some of the specifics of mechanics than Ford and was able to take the older man's ideas and make them work.

In spring 1902 he and Ford worked on the design of what was to become not one but two racing cars, the "999," the more famous of the two, and its nearly identical twin, "The Arrow." The shop was not heated, and sometimes at night, when it became too cold for them to hold a pencil or a tool, they would put on boxing gloves and pummel one another to keep warm. During these years Ford was willing to share credit and in 1908 he allowed the *Ford Times* to carry a story that gave Wills an equal part in designing the "999," the victory of which in the second annual Grosse Pointe races in October 1902 solidified Ford's fame as the builder of the day's fastest cars.

Ford in summer 1902 had received the backing of Alexander Y. Malcomson, which ultimately led to the formation of the Ford Motor Company. By October, Ford and Wills had begun to hire workers as the ideas they had been developing for a passenger car took shape. Again, the two men worked together closely, one of the mechanics whom they hired declaring that "Mr. Wills and Mr. Ford got along as well as any engineering couple I've run across in my life, and I've run across a lot of them." Of the two, Wills was the taskmaster, insisting that the staff drive themselves as hard as he drove himself. He earned a reputation for being a tough man to work for, but for Ford that was an asset. "In order to get along with Mr. Ford," one associate later declared, "you had to have a little mean streak in your system. You had to be tough and mean; Mr. Ford enjoyed that."

By spring 1903 an acceptable car had finally been developed, more because of Wills's efforts than Ford's, and plans could go ahead to convert the agreement Ford and Malcomson had made into the company that was formed in June of that year. At the outset Ford was the vice-president of the Ford Motor Company and was in charge of the production side of the business. Wills was hired to serve as Ford's "right-hand man," in the words of William Adams Simonds, author of a laudatory and at least semiofficial biography of Ford. Wills's position was listed as chief engineer and either manufacturing or factory manager. As Ford gained more control of the company he disliked the use of formal job titles, preferring the freedom to be able to use the members of his staff as he chose without the restraints imposed by the establishment of a bureaucratic organization. However, Ford did not object to the *Ford Times*, the company publication, describing Wills in one issue as directing "the entire working of the manufacturing department."

During his 16 years at Ford, Wills did not have the high visibility of some other Ford executives, such as James Couzens, or did not go on to the later great achievements of men such as Charles E. Sorensen or William S. Knudsen that have caused so much attention to be given to their activities at Ford in these early years. But none of them played a more important role in the development of the cars the company produced in that period than Wills. As Ford biographer Allan Nevins has observed, "It was fitting that Wills should be responsible for the style of the name FORD" that appears on all of those cars to the present day. When there was dissatisfaction with the look of the word as the company first used it in its advertising, Wills, who had earned extra money as a teenager making calling cards, dug out his old printing set and created the distinctive flowing lettering familiar to car buyers ever since.

As for the Ford cars from 1903 through 1919, the question of to what extent individual staff members were responsible for the development of the cars and how much credit should be given to Henry Ford remains a much-debated subject. There is no doubt that Henry Ford, as the one with the ultimate control, had to give his approval to what was done. He was a man of vision who came up with many of the basic ideas used in those cars, but implementing those ideas remained the task of his staff. And Wills was the most important member of that staff. The Ford Model A, the first car the company produced after its founding in 1903, may very well have been primarily Wills's work, and Ford continued to rely upon Wills as they worked together on the development of subsequent models, culminating in the Model T, introduced in fall 1908. The concept of that legendary car was unquestionably Ford's, but it was Wills and those whom he had working with him who made that idea a reality. One of the most famous innovations of the Model T was the use of vanadium steel, a lighter steel than automakers had been using, to reduce the weight of the car without reducing its durability. Ford had become aware of this new steel and had recognized its advantages, but it was Wills, for the first time demonstrating the talents that would lead to his being regarded as the country's foremost practical metallurgist, who handled the technical details involved in adapting the metal for the car.

Not only was Wills vitally important to Ford because of the talents he had to design an automobile, but his toolmaking talents enabled him to contribute through machine tool design to the improvements in the production methods for which Ford became famous. Ford recognized the importance of Wills's contributions, but the closeness that had existed between the two men when they were spending those cold evenings in Ford's shop in 1902 working on the "999" was already fading within a few years after the founding of the Ford Motor Company. With success Ford began to dislike sharing the spotlight with others. Although this did not create quite the same problems with Wills

that it did with Ford's business manager, James Couzens, who finally quit the company, Wills nevertheless chafed under the increasingly restrictive atmosphere in the company. In 1912, while Ford was absent for some time, Wills prepared a prototype of a new and improved Model T, incorporating some of the design changes that had appeared in the industry since the debut of the original model in 1908. When Ford returned he was furious and took the prototype outside and personally destroyed it.

It was Henry Ford's authoritarian management style, and his refusal to accept the advice of aides such as Wills that the company's products should be updated, that led to Wills's departure from the company on March 15, 1919. He was the first of numerous top executives that left Ford during that period, but unlike most of the others, Wills seems to have left of his own accord. His departure can, in a sense, be linked with the action Ford took in the first half of 1919 to buy out all the other stockholders in the company. Wills owned no Ford stock, but, in accordance with the promise Ford had made him in 1902 and 1903, he had been receiving, in addition to a very substantial salary, a percentage of the dividends that Ford received on his stockholdings, which constituted a majority of all the stock from 1906 on. On August 6, 1919, Wills received a final payment from Ford of $1,592,128.

Wills left the Ford Motor Company, therefore, under very comfortable financial circumstances. He had come to enjoy the good life—yachting, tennis, hunting, and fishing. A tall, handsome man who was well aware of his good looks and dressed accordingly, Wills had an active social life. He became famous for his love of precious stones, not only wearing them on stickpins, cuff links, and other jewelry, but carrying loose stones around in his pockets. He sometimes surprised associates with a gift from his collection, once presenting a diamond ring to an astonished Charles Sorensen. Wills was also a ladies' man who was married twice, his first marriage ending in divorce around the time he hired Evangeline Côté, an attractive nineteen-year-old, to be his personal secretary in 1912. His action served to introduce the girl to Henry Ford, who was frequently in Wills's office. Ford made no effort to hide his infatuation with Miss Côté, which led to a long-standing relationship between the two.

Wills had one daughter by his first marriage and two sons by his second marriage, to Mary

Coyne, in 1914. Although he had all the money he needed to enjoy himself and his family, Wills's work ethic would not allow him to retire in 1919. Out from under Ford's control, Wills now set about designing the kind of car that Ford's obsession with the Model T had prevented him from producing at the Ford Motor Company. But Wills, who had been the practical one in the Ford-Wills team, now showed that he too had a visionary streak. He acquired 4,250 acres along the St. Clair River, near Port Huron, Michigan, which was the site of the factory that produced his car and also of the model town he built for his workers. Wills hired John R. Lee, who had been in charge of Ford's progressive social programs for workers, to supervise the construction of the village, which was named Marysville, after Wills's second wife, and, on which he spent some $3.5 million before production began.

In 1920 Wills formed C. H. Wills & Company, and in August of that year his car, the Wills-Sainte Claire, was announced. As would be expected, it contained numerous advanced features, including 4-wheeled brakes and the introduction of molybdenum steel, which he adapted for use throughout the car, as he had vanadium steel in the Model T. But August 1920 was an inopportune time to introduce a new car, as the postwar boom turned into a postwar depression. Automobile sales plunged, and when Wills finally began production in March 1921, only 1,532 vehicles were produced that year, not the 10,000 that had been planned. Things picked up somewhat in 1922, with sales exceeding 3,000 for the year, but that was the high-water mark. The company made no profits on the cars that were sold, and by the end of 1922 it was

$8 million in debt. It went into receivership in 1923 and was reorganized as Wills-Sainte Claire, Inc., with Wills demoted to the office of vice-president. Sales did not improve, however, and the company was liquidated in 1926.

The Wills-Sainte Claire is fondly remembered as one of the great cars in a decade of great cars, but its failure resulted from Wills's failing as a manufacturer. He spent too much time and money on the car's development and made too many changes in design to make it possible to produce at a profit. With the collapse of the company, he was saddled with a debt of some $4 million. In 1929 he was involved with the formation of New Era Motors, Inc., which came out with the Ruxton. But that car was also poorly timed, making its debut in 1930 in the midst of the Depression. The company met a quick death. Wills was able to recover from his financial losses and in 1933 returned to a field in which he was most qualified, serving as consulting metallurgist to the Chrysler Corporation. He continued in this position until his death in Detroit's Henry Ford Hospital on December 30, 1940.

References:

Nick Baldwin and others, *The World Guide to Automobile Manufacturers* (New York: Facts On File, 1987);

Allan Nevins, *Ford: The Times, the Man, the Company* (New York: Scribners, 1954);

William Adams Simonds, *Henry Ford: His Life, His Work, His Genius* (Indianapolis: Bobbs-Merrill, 1943).

Archives:

Extensive material on Wills may be found in the Ford Archives at the Henry Ford Museum, Dearborn, Michigan.

John North Willys

(October 25, 1873-August 26, 1935)

by George S. May

Eastern Michigan University

CAREER: Salesman and owner of several businesses (1888-1908); president (1908-1928, 1935), chairman (1928-1935), receiver, Willys-Overland Company (1933-1935); head of Willys Corporation (1917-1921); ambassador to Poland (1930-1932).

Among his contemporaries in the automobile industry, probably only William C. Durant could be said to have rivaled John North Willys in his penchant for spreading his business talents over an ever-widening range of interests, with consequences that proved nearly as fatal to the success of Willys' business activities as it did to Durant's.

Willys was born in Canandaigua, New York, on October 25, 1873. He was one of three children and the only son born to Lydia North and David Smith Willys. Willys attended Canandaigua Academy but left school when he was fifteen to set up a laundry with another teenager in Seneca Falls. After a year they sold the business and split a profit of $200. For a time Willys studied law in the office of a Canandaigua attorney, but upon his father's death he abandoned the law in favor of his first love—business. From 1896 to 1898 he was a traveling salesman for the Boston Woven Hose & Rubber Company. Earlier, however, he had a shop that sold and repaired bicycles, and in 1898, at the peak of the nation's bicycle boom, he invested $500 and bought the Elmira Arms Company, a sporting goods store in Elmira, New York. Under Willys the store specialized in bicycles and soon became a wholesaler. By 1900 the business had annual sales of $500,000, agencies throughout the area, and was handling the entire production of one bicycle manufacturer, experience that was very useful in his later automotive career.

Willys first began to be interested in automobiles around the turn of the century when a Winton appeared in Elmira. When an Elmira doctor in 1901 purchased a Pierce Motorette, Willys traveled

John North Willys

to Buffalo to seek to become the agent for the manufacturer, the George N. Pierce Company. Willys was already familiar with the company since it was an important manufacturer of bicycles. Pierce told Willys that the 1-cylinder Motorette was little more than an experimental vehicle that he was using to test the automobile market, but Willys still wanted to sell the car. By 1903 he had sold only 20 of the cars, for $650 each. But even this modest level of sales was enough to encourage Willys to turn his main attention to this new field. Before long he had taken on the Rambler, produced by another former bicycle manufacturer, Thomas B. Jeffery, and the American, an expensive car produced in Indianapolis beginning in 1906.

Willys, in fact, organized the American Motor Car Sales Company of Elmira in 1906 in order to handle the marketing of the American. At the same time he contracted to sell the entire output of another Indianapolis company, the Overland Auto Company, formed that year by David M. Parry, a carriage manufacturer, and Claude E. Cox, who had designed an earlier Overland car, a few of which had been built in the years 1903 through 1905 by the Standard Wheel Company of Terre Haute, Indiana. Only 47 Overlands were produced in 1906, but Willys, apparently believing that the company was capable of bigger things, contracted to sell 500 of the 2- and 4-cylinder cars in 1907, putting down a deposit of $10,000 to seal the deal.

Few Overlands were produced in 1907, a result of a combination of bad management and the economic problems that beset all automobile companies because of the panic of 1907. Concerned at the failure of the company to deliver the cars he had contracted to sell, Willys went to Indianapolis in November 1907 and discovered that Overland was about to be forced into bankruptcy. The company was $80,000 in debt, had virtually no automobile parts in stock, and no money to pay its dwindling staff of employees. Willys convinced the company's officials to authorize him to take charge and do whatever he could to save the business. In a celebrated and dazzling display of entrepreneurial skills, Willys was able to deposit enough money in the bank to meet the next payroll and borrow enough money to enable him to offer the creditors 10 percent of their bills, with the remainder of what they were owed to be paid in installments or in company stock. He then persuaded the suppliers who accepted this offer to furnish parts on a 90-day term basis.

Having established the grounds for continued operations, Willys in January 1908 carried through the reorganization of the company, which became the Willys-Overland Company, with Willys as president, general manager, and treasurer. David Parry and Claude Cox were forced out. Under Willys' direction, the company in 1908 sold 465 Overlands, paid off the creditors, and ended up with a net profit of more than $50,000. The limited size of the Indianapolis plant forced Willys to assemble some of the cars in a circus tent, and thus he jumped at the chance to buy the vacant plant of the defunct Pope-Toledo car operations for $285,000 in 1909.

Willys then moved the company to Toledo, which was the home of the Willys automotive operations from that time on. He recouped much of the cost of the factory by selling off excess equipment and materials. By 1910 Willys, with these enlarged facilities, had been able to boost output to 15,598 cars, and by 1912 Overlands were second only to Ford in sales. Over the next six years Willys held on to that second place spot, with a peak production of 142,779 in 1916 that was a far cry from the 700,000 plus Model Ts that Ford produced that year, but that was nevertheless an impressive achievement in an industry which had total production in 1916 of only a little more than 1.5 million automobiles.

The turnaround Willys accomplished with the Overland was comparable to the job William Durant had done earlier when he had taken over Buick, another nearly bankrupt firm, and had, within a brief period, built it into one of the two top automakers in the country. But like Durant, who had not been content to continue to manage one successful company but had instead used it as the base on which he established General Motors (GM), Willys's ambitions soon led him to try to expand beyond Willys-Overland into new fields.

In January 1912 Ransom E. Olds stopped in Toledo to confer with Willys, and four days later in New York he noted in his diary that he "went over to see Willys" at Willys's hotel. Unfortunately, since Olds did not indicate in his diary what was discussed, there is no way of knowing for certain what the two executives talked about. However, since 1908 Olds had been trying to sell his Reo company, and by 1911, at least, he was interested in selling his majority stock interest, regardless of what the other stockholders did. It seems almost certain, therefore, that Olds and Willys discussed a takeover of Reo, but if that was the case, Willys, like others whom Olds had approached earlier, must have decided that the money Olds was asking was too much to spend on a company that had production of only about one-third of Willys-Overland's.

In 1913 Willys did buy the Gramm Motor Truck Company of Lima, Ohio, and began to put on the market the first motor vehicle to bear his name, a 1.5 ton truck. Earlier, in 1912, he had acquired control of the Garford Company in Elyria, Ohio, the car production of which had been linked with that of the Studebaker Corporation. Willys shortly abandoned the Garford car and used the

Elyria factory to begin production in 1914 of the best-known of his namesake cars, the Willys-Knight. This model resulted from still another of his acquisitions, the Edwards Motor Company, producer of the Edwards-Knight 4-cylinder car, using the sleeve valve engine developed by Charles Y. Knight. The 1914 Willys-Knight was simply the Edwards-Knight under a new name. Beginning in 1915 the car was assembled at the Willys-Overland plant in Toledo, and the Elyria plant was used only to produce the Knight engines.

In 1915 the growing Willys empire employed 18,000 men at its Toledo operations and 20,000 in other plants in Elyria, Flint, Pontiac, and Buffalo. (The Gramm company in Lima was sold in 1915.) In 1914 Willys acquired control of Toledo's Electric Auto-Lite Company, producer of a generator for automobile lights. During the 1914-1915 period he also gained controlling interests in the Fisk Rubber Company of Chicopee Falls, Massachusetts, the Moline Plow Company, and the Curtiss Aeroplane & Motor Corporation of Buffalo.

In June 1916 Willys came close to pulling off his biggest deal when published reports announced a merger that was about to take place that would involve Willys-Overland, Electric Auto-Lite, the Hudson and Chalmers automobile companies, and United Motors, a combination of five parts manufacturers just put together by William C. Durant. The new company was to be called American Motors, and it is uncertain whether Willys or Durant would have been the dominant figure in the company. Since Durant had just regained control of GM, however, it may be that this merger was intended as an interim step that would have ultimately resulted in a huge new consolidation, but as it turned out the American Motors merger failed to take place, probably because the financing could not be arranged.

Nothing that Willys did in this period was more important than his organizing the Guaranty Securities Company on November 8, 1915. It represented the first major departure from the method by which most cars to this time had been sold, namely, cash on delivery. That method had worked well as long as the demand for cars far exceeded the industry's limited production capacity, but by the second decade of the century concern was beginning to be expressed that the industry could not for long continue to grow on this basis. Henry Ford met the challenge by constantly lowering the price of his mass-produced Model T until by the early 1920s it had dropped below $300. Producers of high-priced cars continued to sell for cash, also, since their customers could afford whatever was being asked. The Overland and the Willys-Knight, however, fell somewhere in between, with price tags several hundred dollars more than the Ford Model T. To attract those who could not or who did not want to pay cash for these cars, Willys offered through the Guaranty Securities Company the opportunity to purchase them through the installment plan. The credit arrangements were modest by modern standards, with the buyer being required to make a substantial down payment with the remainder of the car's price to be paid off, with interest, in a matter of months, not years, but it was a start toward the system of financing upon which car sales would ultimately depend. In April 1916 the company, originally a Toledo firm, was reorganized in New York as the Guaranty Securities Corporation and was financing not only sales of Overlands and Willys-Knights but also Hudson, Maxwell, Reo, Studebaker, Dodge, Ford, and GM cars. Among those whom Willys persuaded to serve on the board of directors was Alfred P. Sloan, Jr., head of the Hyatt Roller Bearing Company, one of the companies that became part of Durant's United Motors consolidation. Sloan became president of that parts company which would later be absorbed by GM. The experience Sloan gained as a director of Guaranty Securities proved useful to him and to GM when that corporation in 1919 formed its own credit agency, General Motors Acceptance Corporation.

In 1917 Willys formed the Willys Corporation as a holding company for his diverse interests. This came in the midst of World War I, which had served to add further to the diversity of these interests. Willys had been in France when the war broke out and had signed military contracts at that time for trucks and ambulances. With the American entry into the war in April 1917, Willys intensified the conversion of his various companies to wartime production. At the same time, however, plans were made for a large-scale resumption of automobile production after the war to take full advantage of the anticipated postwar boom in sales. A new Overland, priced below $500 and intended to compete with the Model T, was in the works. Heavy commitments were also made to suppliers for parts to be delivered after the war, and for the additional plant facilities that would be needed.

For Willys and his business empire, however, the immediate postwar period was an economic nightmare. The industry as a whole was taken by surprise in summer 1920 when the onset of a postwar depression caught the automakers with huge inventories of cars they were no longer able to unload. The debts incurred to finance the production of these cars were also onerous. However, Willys-Overland's troubles had been made even worse by a bitter labor dispute at the Toledo plant, which ended in armed conflict that left two strikers dead and seventy injured. No cars were produced from spring 1919 to nearly the end of the year, a period when other companies were enjoying a great upsurge in sales after the war-imposed slowdown in production. The price of the Overland, when it at last appeared, was not $500 or less, as originally planned, but was $845 as a result of the postwar rise in the cost of materials. Hopes that it would be competitive with Ford's Model T vanished.

When Willys, who had left the management of Willys-Overland in the hands of subordinates while he looked after his other interests, now belatedly sought to take charge, he found the company saddled with debts of more than $50 million. The bankers who had loaned the money were willing to provide additional help to tide the company over this critical period only if someone in whom they had confidence was placed in charge. The man they chose was Walter P. Chrysler, who had left GM in 1919 when he could no longer tolerate Durant's interference in his management of the Buick division. It was Chrysler's outstanding record at Buick, however, that attracted the attention of the bankers and made them willing to accept Chrysler's demand that his annual salary for two years at Willys-Overland be $1 million net. In addition, although Willys retained the title of president while Chrysler served as executive vice-president, Chrysler ran things.

A few days after taking on the job in 1920, Chrysler went into Willys's office in New York. "You never saw another like it," Chrysler declared, "magnificent." Willys was a man who enjoyed his wealth. He had homes at several places, including one in California that he sold to Chrysler for $200,000. He had a $1 million yacht that he turned over to the government during the war, and he built up a substantial collection of the paintings of the old masters, although, he said, always with "an eye to the investment value. I only buy pictures

that I could sell if I wanted to without loss." In keeping with his love of the good life, Willys, Chrysler said, had in his office "a splendid humidor, ornate with gold, a huge affair, stocked with fine cigars. John led me to the table which supported this luxurious chest. He raised the lid and pressed me to have a cigar. . . . Then, when our cigars were burning, I spoke.

'John, I am here to cut your salary.' He was drawing $150,000 a year.

'What's this, Walt?' John looked at me as an actor does when another muffs his lines.

'I'm cutting you to $75,000 a year.'

He gave his head a little toss, and then he laughed. 'I guess we've put our problems in the right man's hands,' he said."

Chrysler's cutting of Willys's salary was symbolic of the cost-cutting approach he took to try to rescue the Willys business empire. Through the contacts he had throughout the industry, Chrysler was able to cut the company's debt by persuading suppliers to cancel some of the overly optimistic contracts Willys-Overland had made earlier. Chrysler argued that for them to insist on enforcing these contract obligations could lead to the company's collapse, whereas by agreeing to cancel the contracts, the suppliers could save the company and look forward to future, much bigger orders when the company's economic stability had been re-established. Action was also taken against certain Willys-Overland officials that "required some executives to restore money which they had, in my opinion," Chrysler said, "squandered."

By 1921 the Willys Corporation had been liquidated, and Electric Auto-Lite, Moline Plow, and some of the other companies the corporation had controlled had resumed their status as independent businesses. Willys's empire had been cut back to his original automotive business. By 1922 conditions at Willys-Overland were looking up. A $16 million bond issue was arranged, and as part of the deal, a new plant in Elizabeth, New Jersey, part of the plant of the Duesenberg Motor Corporation that Willys had purchased in 1919 and then expanded with $14 million in borrowed money, was auctioned off. Working in one section of that plant had been three engineers, Fred M. Zeder, Owen Skelton, and Carl Breer, who had been designing the new cars that Chrysler felt were essential if Willys-Overland was to be restored to the level of prosperity it had enjoyed in the prewar years. But then

Chrysler, while still engaged in the Willys-Overland salvage operation, was asked to rescue the floundering Maxwell and Chalmers companies. In a series of complicated operations, the ethical implications of which could be called into question, Chrysler, who saw in the Maxwell-Chalmers situation an opportunity to gain lasting control of his own company, was able to retain the services of these three engineers and to use one of the cars originally intended for Willys-Overland as the introductory offering of the Chrysler Corporation.

With Willys-Overland out of the woods and John Willys back in command after Chrysler's departure, the Toledo automaker enjoyed a period of prosperity again as the nation's economy pulled out of the postwar depression by 1923. By 1924 the company's financial obligations had been taken care of. Production, which had sagged to 48,000 in 1921 rebounded to 215,000 by 1925. Willys-Overland was the biggest producer of cars using the Knight engine, and in addition to the Willys-Knight, which was probably the least expensive Knight-engined car available, Willys, in December 1925, acquired F. B. Stearns Company, a Cleveland company and the producer of the Stearns-Knight, a far more expensive car. Sales of that car failed to live up to Willys's optimistic expectations, however, and he lost heavily on this investment. The Overland, using a standard engine, remained the mainstay of the company, and in 1926 Willys made another attempt to compete with Ford in the low-priced field, coming out with the Overland Whippet, a 4-cylinder car that sold for $545 in 1927, just less than the price of the new Ford Model A.

In 1928 Willys-Overland had record sales of 314,437, netting $187,233,388. However, Willys may have seen troubles ahead. It was said of him that he was able to make less off of more automobiles "than almost anyone in the business." In any event, in 1929 he sold his 800,000 shares of common stock in Willys-Overland to officials of Electric Auto-Lite for $25 million. He kept his preferred stock but gave up the presidency in favor of the position of chairman of the board. His action was in part dictated by his expectations that he would receive a diplomatic appointment as a result of the large contributions he had made in 1928 on behalf of Herbert Hoover's campaign. On March 1, 1930, Hoover named Willys to be ambassador to Poland. There were reports that the appointment was intended to allow Willys to use his business skills to advise the Poles how to increase the industrial component of an economy that had been traditionally agricultural. However, with the deepening crisis brought on by the Depression, Hoover, according to Willys, asked him in 1932 to resign as "a patriotic duty," so that he might put his talents to better use at home in Toledo.

Willys returned to Toledo after submitting his resignation on April 25, 1932, and resumed active management of the Willys-Overland company. In March 1932 the company had been turned down in its bid for a loan from the Reconstruction Finance Corporation, and by February 1933, it was forced into receivership. Willys, although he was chairman, was also named the receiver. He abandoned all models, including the Willys-Knight, except a new, smaller version of the Whippet that was named the Willys 77. Production was now controlled by the court, and Willys had to apply for permission to produce limited numbers of the car. In January 1935 he resumed the position of president, and sales of the Willys 77, although small, held out hopes that the company would survive this latest crisis. However, the stress of the struggle took its toll on Willys, who died from a cerebral embolism on August 26, 1935. He had been married twice. His first marriage to Isabel Irene Van Wie on December 1, 1897, had ended in divorce in 1934. On July 30, 1934, Willys married Florence Dolan, who survived him, together with a daughter from the first marriage.

Willys was also survived by his company. Sales by 1936 were good enough for the receivership to be brought to an end. The Willys 77, 44,000 of which had been sold, was replaced in 1937 by another small model, the Willys 37, as the company sought to create a niche for itself by offering an alternative to the larger cars that prevailed in the American market. Sales were exceedingly modest, however, and the future of the company would have been much in doubt but for the coming of World War II and the contract Willys-Overland received to build the Jeep. About 361,000 of those sturdy vehicles were produced for the armed forces during the war by the Toledo company, and although the vehicle was also produced by Ford and, in limited numbers, by American Bantam, Willys-Overland was able to identify itself in the public's mind with the Jeep. At the end of the war Charles E. Sorensen, who took over direction of the company after being forced out of Ford, sold the company on the idea of producing a civilian version of the military vehicle, plus a Jeep-based station wagon and the Jeepster. In 1952 Willys followed the lead of Nash and several other small companies and introduced the Willys Aero, a compact car, but although it attracted some buyers, it was the Jeep that kept the Toledo operations going.

In 1953 Kaiser gained control of Willys, and it shortly scrapped the Aero while retaining the money-making Jeep. The vehicle soon became the only motor vehicle being produced by the company that, as Kaiser-Frazer, had made a valiant bid in the postwar years to be the first new automobile company since the 1920s to be able to survive the competition of the bigger companies. In 1970 Ameri-can Motors acquired what was now known as Kaiser Jeep, and Jeep production at the old Willys Toledo complex remained the one bright spot in that troubled company and the main reason why Chrysler purchased American Motors in 1987.

References:
Nick Baldwin and others, *The World Guide to Automobile Manufacturing* (New York: Facts On File, 1987);

Walter P. Chrysler, *Life of An American Workman* (New York: Dodd, Mead, 1950);

Eugene W. Lewis, *Motor Memories: A Saga of Whirling Gears* (Detroit: Alved, 1947);

John B. Rae, *American Automobile Manufacturers. The First Forty Years* (Philadelphia: Chilton, 1959).

Windshields

by James Wren

Motor Vehicle Manufacturers Association

Glass or celluloid screens installed on motor vehicles as shields against wind in front of drivers and passengers were attached on special racers and custom-built vehicles shortly after the automobile was first introduced in Europe in the 1890s. But in the United States, it was not until the early 1900s that windshields began to appear on motor vehicles. What are generally called windshields on today's vehicles were initially called "glass fronts" on early motor vehicles, and they appeared on some models at the turn of the century.

Manufacturers of larger cars such as limousines offered a body on which a "canopy top" extended over the passenger compartment. A large glass panel was framed and fixed between the edge of the top and the dashboard in front of the driver.

Within a few years, open touring models appeared with smaller metal-edged glass panels attached at the top of the dash and extending upward slightly above the occupants' heads. The fabric top was attached to the top of the windshield glass with snaps. Soon two-piece glass panels within a single unit were pivoted at each side for tilting. However, on less-expensive models such as runabouts and small roadsters, windshields were extra equipment. One very distinctive model, the Mercer Roadster, featured a circular windshield in front of the driver and attached to the steering column. With the dominance of the closed car by the early 1920s, windshields became commonplace on most motorcars and were also pivoted to open for interior ventilation.

Alexander Winton

(June 20, 1860-June 21, 1932)

by James M. Laux

University of Cincinnati

CAREER: President, Winton Bicycle Company (1891-1900?); president, Winton Motor Carriage Company (1897-1915); president, Winton Gas Engine & Manufacturing Company (1912-1915); president, Winton Motor Car Company (1915-1924); president (1925-1928), chairman, Winton Engine Company (1928-1930).

Alexander Winton, pioneer automobile manufacturer, was born in Grangemouth, Scotland, the son of Alexander and Helen Fea Winton. He attended elementary school in this town on the Firth of Forth and then labored in shipyards on the Clyde. When he was nineteen he sought a better life in America, encouraged by his brother-in-law Thomas Henderson, a blacksmith in Cleveland, Ohio. After a brief period of employment with the Delamater Iron Works in New York City, and then a few years as assistant engineer on an ocean steamship, he married a Scotswoman, Jeanie Muir McGlashan of Glasgow, in January 1883. Not long afterward the couple settled in Cleveland. He soon found a position as the plant superintendent for a furnace producer, the Phoenix Iron Works.

Meanwhile he tinkered with improvements for bicycles, suddenly popular with young Americans following the introduction of the safety bicycle in 1887 (with wheels of equal size and a chain drive) and pneumatic tires in 1892. Winton established a bicycle repair business in 1890 and introduced a spring-supported saddle, a ball-bearing device, and other refinements. In 1890 or 1891 he began making bicycles for sale and with Thomas Henderson organized the Winton Bicycle Company. In a few years that company thrived, and Winton made several thousand bicycles per year in the mid 1890s. He was not alone. Cleveland boasted several other bicycle producers: Peerless and White (the sewing machine firm) each made up to 10,000 bicycles per year, nearly twice as many as Winton's best year,

Alexander Winton (courtesy of the Motor Vehicle Manufacturers Association)

and the Konigslow and Lozier companies also were major local manufacturers. Nationally, 1896-1897 was the peak of the bicycle boom, when some 300 firms made about one million units. Winton's output of 5,000 to 6,000 made it a rather small factor in the industry. During 1897 the trade suddenly dried up. As a result of the crisis many bicycle firms ultimately shifted to horseless carriages, including all of the Cleveland firms mentioned above. But Winton was the first off the mark and for a few years was the leading gasoline auto producer in the United States.

In 1893, well before the bicycle boom reached its peak, Winton had begun to tinker with the idea of a motorized vehicle. Although he had earlier experience with steam engines, it is interesting that he chose, at this very early date, to work with the gasoline engine. His first effort was a motorized bicycle in 1895. Then in the following year came a 4-wheeled machine with a 1-cylinder engine that might have supplied 8 horsepower. The car held four people in back-to-back seats, was steered by a tiller, and used large pneumatic tires on bicycle-type wheels. Those tires had to be made on a special order by the B. F. Goodrich Company of Akron. Winton had to make most of his own parts or obtain them on a special-order basis from independent shops. That slowed his progress considerably. In October 1896 Winton gave a public demonstration of his car in Cleveland. Apparently it was not ready for the market, for he immediately began work on an improved model. As it was nearing completion and its prospects augured well, the Winton Motor Carriage Company was incorporated on March 1, 1897, with initial capital set at $200,000. Alexander Winton took the title of president, his brother-in-law Thomas Henderson, vice-president, and George H. Brown served as secretary-treasurer. Brown, employed by a Cleveland electric company as a bookkeeper, had ventured some funds in the Winton company.

Winton's new model mounted a 2-cylinder engine that sometimes had to be cooled with ice. It supplied about 10 horsepower. The car's 1,800-pound weight was carried by 3-inch pneumatic tires. In its first public demonstration in early May 1897 he drove it to Elyria and back, 60 miles. Then at the end of that month, on Memorial Day, he drove the machine on a local horse-racing track at a speed exceeding 33 mph. For further publicity Winton and his shop superintendent, William A. Hatcher, set off in the vehicle for New York City on July 28, 1897. Following the "water-level" route through Rochester, but with many difficulties on the disgraceful country roads, this first long-distance automobile trip in the United States ended 800 miles and ten days later in New York with a reported running time of just under 79 hours. Unfortunately, the press paid little attention to the feat. Even the leading motorcar journal of the day, *Horseless Age*, devoted only meager space to the journey.

Back in Cleveland, Winton did receive his first order, for six small buses to carry six passengers each. That job fell through, however, when the first of the machines frightened horses so much that the purchaser, fearful of lawsuits, canceled the contract. The frightened-horse problem, in both town and country, is an often-forgotten difficulty in the first decade or so of automobile history.

Alexander Winton apparently experienced vexations with his 2-cylinder vertical engine, for his new model for 1898 and his first sales success had one cylinder mounted horizontally, supplying 6 horsepower. A mining engineer from Pennsylvania, Robert Allison, eager to buy a gasoline car, had applied at two other gasoline car pioneers, the Duryea shop in Springfield, Massachusetts, and the Haynes-Apperson establishment in Kokomo, Indiana, but neither had one available. On March 24, 1898, Allison appeared at Winton's small factory and after a trial run bought a car, paying $1,000 in cash with a promise of delivery by train in a week. The seventy-one-year-old Allison was satisfied, for he would ultimately buy three later Winton models. Winton went ahead to produce 21 more horseless buggies and eight delivery wagons in 1898. His years of experimentation with gasoline cars and his experience making thousands of bicycles yearly gave him advantages in production and marketing in the late 1890s over the Duryeas, Hayneses, Fords, and other early automobile entrepreneurs.

Sales of Winton cars certainly were aided by the frequent small advertisements placed in the weekly *Scientific American*, for most of the buyers lived far from Cleveland. Even better publicity, and at no cost, came from Winton's second drive from Cleveland to New York City in May 1899. The *Cleveland Plain Dealer* newspaper sponsored the trip, and one of its reporters went along, sending daily articles to his own newspaper and others recounting the vicissitudes of the expedition. In an early history of the automobile industry, J. R. Doolittle characterized the trip as "the first real effort at intelligent publicity with which the new industry has been favored." He estimated that perhaps one million people saw the Winton vehicle as it made its way southward through New York City to the City Hall. As had occurred in France and would soon occur in Britain and Germany, this highly publicized demonstration of an automobile's reliability on ordinary roads broadened the appeal of the car from a coterie of engineers and sportsmen to the public at large. It brought a rush of demand for Winton cars and the few others that were available.

Winton driving his first car, an 1896 "dos-a-dos" (courtesy of the Motor Vehicle Manufacturers Association)

In 1900 Winton took a special racing model to France, the world leader in the young industry, where he entered it in the first of the Gordon Bennett races. Like most of the other entries, the Winton did not finish the 350-mile competition, but as the first American automobile to race in Europe, the Winton generated more favorable publicity. Winton cars also appeared at the earliest automobile shows, in Chicago in September 1900 and New York City in November 1900. Alexander Winton frequently raced his cars in the United States, often winning, but his loss to Henry Ford at the Grosse Pointe racetrack in October 1901 gave the Detroit entrepreneur a vital boost. A year later Winton, driving his new Bullet racing machine, lost to a Ford again on the same track, that Ford car number 999 driven by Barney Oldfield. Winton experienced another failure in May 1901, when he had to give up a projected transcontinental automobile trip in the wastes of Nevada, 11 days out from San Francisco. But two years later a wealthy amateur, Dr. H. N. Jackson, and his chauffeur performed the feat, the first such coast-to-coast journey. Their Winton car was a 2-cylinder, 20-horsepower model

that listed for $2,500. Winton cars now were manufactured in a new factory some four miles west of downtown Cleveland. It comprised seven buildings erected in 1902 and 1903. Some 1200 workers were employed, producing 850 cars in 1903. Alexander Winton was moving to larger and more powerful designs, and more expensive ones, leaving the low-price fields to Olds, Ford, Jeffery, and others. Winton's model introduced in September 1905 cost from $2,500 to $3,500 and had a 6-cylinder engine. The firm would specialize in this size engine thereafter.

Alexander Winton had made large profits in the motorcar business, and he built a large new home in 1903. But in September 1903 the body of his wife of 20 years was found floating in Lake Erie near their home. She left six children. Three years later Winton married La Bell McGlashan, a relative of his first wife.

Although in his early career Winton had tinkered and innovated with bicycles and cars, he did less of that after introducing a compressed-air self-starter on the 1908 models. He was slow to move to left-hand drive, only in 1914, and the electric starter in the same year. The rest of the industry was beginning to pass him by. Winton production in the early 1910s was about 2,250 per year, while in 1913 Ford produced 203,000 cars, Buick 27,000, Cadillac 17,300, and Packard 2,980. One reason for this lag was that Alexander Winton found a new interest, marine engines. In 1911 he designed a 6-cylinder gasoline engine for his yacht and installed three of them in it. The following year he established the Winton Gas Engine & Manufacturing Company to produce them. That firm was merged in 1915 with the auto company under the name Winton Motor Car Company. During the wartime years Winton sold some marine gasoline engines for small naval vessels to the American, Russian, and Italian governments. Sometime after 1912 Alexander Winton began experimenting with marine diesel engines.

August Busch had secured the U.S. patent rights to Rudolf Diesel's compression-ignition engine and had begun to produce them in the United States in 1903. His rights actually expired in 1906, but the general impression in the American engine industry was that they remained valid until 1912. The Busch company did not advise potential competitors of the true state of affairs, so development work by other firms on that type engine began only about 1911. Winton ultimately joined the effort, adapting his gasoline marine engine to the diesel principle. He began supplying a diesel engine during American participation in World War I. He engaged George W. Codrington, an experienced marine engineer, to superintend marine engine manufacture in 1917, and Codrington became general manager of the large-engine operation in 1919.

Automobile production at Winton declined during 1918 as raw materials became scarce and orders for military equipment flowed in. When the war ended Winton resumed normal production. Output for 1920 reached about 2,500, and profits almost touched $3 million. That was the swan song, however, for production during the recession year of 1921 amounted to only 325 cars, and just 690 in the following year. After reducing automobile operations to almost nothing for many months and having refused a possible merger with some other troubled firms making mid- to high-priced cars—Dorris of St. Louis and Haynes of Kokomo—Alexander Winton finally stopped producing automobiles in February 1924.

Winton had not kept up with the changing design of automobiles nor had he expanded production facilities in any major way to achieve economies of scale. Consequently, he was ill-equipped to meet the competition in the middle and upper price ranges in the 1920s, competition from Buick, Oldsmobile, and Cadillac of General Motors, from Studebaker, Packard, Reo, Paige, and other "independent" manufacturers. Sixty years of age in 1920, Alexander Winton preferred neither to turn his auto company over to an energetic younger person nor to invest heavily in new facilities to confront his mass-producing competitors. He let his company falter on in the period from 1921 to 1924, at the cost of millions of dollars from his fortune, and finally shut it down.

The separate engine branch continued operations as the Winton Engine Company, constructing large gasoline and diesel engines. The latter were for marine service. In conjunction with the Electro-Motive Engineering Company of Cleveland, Winton also made gasoline-electric power plants for railcar use. In 1928 he turned over the presidency of the Winton Engine Company to George Codrington, and in 1930 he retired completely. In those years the Winton and Electro-Motive firms considered developing a diesel engine for railway locomotive use, but they could not find the needed capital. Meanwhile, General Motors (GM), led by its director of research Charles F. Kettering, decided to work on small diesels. To get the necessary facilities and experienced technical personnel, GM determined to buy Winton. A GM vice-president, John L. Pratt, argued that "The Winton Engine Company is unquestionably the outstanding Diesel engine manufacturer in the United States." From the Winton company's point of view, the GM connection would bring almost unlimited financial resources. So in 1930 GM acquired Winton for a reported $7 million, and a few months later obtained Electro-Motive as well. The pair, along with Kettering's research group, got GM into the diesel locomotive business in the 1930s. George Codrington stayed on as head of Winton engine, renamed the Cleveland Diesel division in 1938. Alexander Winton did not live to see GM's great success with diesels. He died in 1932 at the age of seventy-two. His second wife, La Bell, had died in 1925. Winton married two more times, in 1927 to Marion Campbell, and, after a divorce, to Mary Ellen Avery in 1930.

Winton left an estate of only $48,868. His real legacy was that of a pioneer in midwestern automobile manufacturing. Design and development appealed to him, not quantity production, mass marketing, or building a large personal fortune. His inclinations and parallel ones by other early Cleveland automobile manufacturers allowed Detroit to take the leadership of the American automobile industry.

Publication:
"Get a Horse," *Saturday Evening Post* (February 8, 1930): 39, 42, 143-144.

References:
William G. Keener, "Ohio's Pioneer Auto Maker: Alexander Winton," *Museum Echoes*, 28 (March 1953): 19-22;
Richard Wager, *Golden Wheels* (Cleveland: Western Reserve Historical Society, 1975).

Winton Motor Carriage Company

by James M. Laux

University of Cincinnati

Winton Motor Carriage Company was the most successful of the early midwestern automobile manufacturers. The bicycle maker Alexander Winton of Cleveland formed the company in 1897 with an authorized capital of $200,000. He had demonstrated his first gasoline-powered car in September 1896, but the first sale did not come until March 1898, a year in which he sold 25 of his 1-cylinder horseless buggies at $1,000 each. Like other very early auto producers, Winton had to fabricate his own parts in his factory two miles east of downtown Cleveland, or make special and expensive arrangements with outside suppliers for small production runs of components. Consequently, the firm made its own spark plugs, radiators, carburetors, brakes, differentials, and transmissions. An outside foundry supplied engine castings, but of poor quality. Winton's pneumatic tires were provided on a special order by B. F. Goodrich of Akron. Nevertheless, Alexander Winton's experience at manufacturing bicycles apparently helped him keep production costs in line, for the company made a $400 profit on each car it sold in 1898.

Winton realized that to create a market he needed publicity. Already in 1897 he had driven a 2-cylinder experimental model over wretched roads from Cleveland to New York City, but except for *Horseless Age* the automotive press hardly noticed the phenomenal achievement, the first long-distance motorcar run in the United States. In 1898 he ran two-inch-column advertisements weekly in *Scientific American* with an illustration of the buggy and touting "no odor," "no vibration," and "all parts inter-

changeable." The ads always referred to the engine as the hydrocarbon type, apparently to sidestep public fears of gasoline explosions. Over five days in May 1899 he again drove a car to New York City, but this time he was wise enough to take a newspaper reporter along. The journalist saw to it that his daily accounts reached nearly three dozen newspapers, whose readers were fascinated. About 100 people bought Winton cars in 1899, now paying $2,000 each. Some of the early buyers would come to the factory in Cleveland, learn how to operate the car, and then ship it home by rail. Others ordered the car by mail sight unseen and either figured out its operation from printed directions or from a factory specialist who would come on the train with the car and stay a few days to instruct the buyer. The company soon established its own sales and service branches in large markets such as New York City, but that was costly, so before long the branches gave way to locally owned automobile dealerships.

In 1900 the Winton company became embroiled in the Selden patent affair. The patent, issued in 1895, could be construed to control all gasoline motor vehicles. It was owned by the Electric Vehicle Company, and in 1900 Electric Vehicle sued the largest producer of gasoline cars in the country, Winton, for infringement. Before the case could be settled, most of the gasoline automakers, including Winton, decided to avoid the expense of extended lawsuits and joined together with Electric Vehicle to establish the Association of Licensed Automobile Manufacturers (ALAM) in 1903. The

The first production Winton automobile, sold in 1898 (courtesy of the Smithsonian Institution)

ALAM attempted to enforce the patent and limit entry to the new industry. Before long the Ford and Jeffery companies and others refused to accept the validity of the Selden patent, and after years of legal maneuvers it was interpreted so narrowly by a federal court in 1911 as to become irrelevant.

In the meantime the Winton company expanded both the output and size of its cars, as their design began to move away from the horseless buggy. In 1901 a wheel replaced the steering tiller. Racing was a common device for winning publicity for cars in the period, and the Winton company entered many races, including the Paris-to-Lyon event in France in 1900 and the subsequent Gordon Bennett races in Europe. In the United States, Winton cars, often with Alexander Winton at the wheel, raced frequently from 1901 through 1905, using special high-powered engines of 2 and 4 cylinders. The company's growing production required larger facilities, and in 1902 it constructed a new factory on the west side of Cleveland near the city limits four miles from downtown. Here it made the 1903 model priced at $2,500, with a 2-cylinder,

20-horsepower plant. That robust and powerful car gained considerable fame when a wealthy Vermont physician, H. Nelson Jackson, and his chauffeur drove one from San Francisco to New York City. This first transcontinental auto trip took 64 days in May, June, and July 1903, much of which was spent negotiating the wilds of Oregon, Idaho, and Wyoming. It took the travelers only six days to complete the last portion, Cleveland to New York. Winton turned out 850 cars in the year but it lost the leadership in gasoline cars. It was surpassed in quantity of output by Oldsmobile, Ford, Cadillac, and Jeffery in the Midwest, and Pope-Hartford in New England, all of which sold at more moderate prices.

Winton continued to aim its cars at the high end of the market, and other Cleveland automakers followed its lead, such as Peerless, Stearns, and the White company with its steam cars. In 1905 the Winton followed French practice by placing its 4-cylinder engine under the hood in front and transmitting its power by shaft to a live rear axle rather than by chains. A new Winton for the following

Alexander Winton driving his 1903 "Bullet No. 2" race car (courtesy of the Smithsonian Institution)

year mounted a 6-cylinder engine. The Winton Six for 1908 cost from $4,500 to $5,500. A compressed air mechanism was used to start the car, and Winton shifted to the electric starting system only after 1914. The firm continued to compete in the high-price range, producing 1,200 in 1909 and 2,339 in 1915, but the founder's interest had turned to marine engines. He established a separate company to make them in 1912. The automobile company changed its name to the Winton Motor Car Company in 1915.

After reducing auto production and making war materiel during World War I, Winton produced about 2,500 cars in 1920, but its expensive machines suffered badly in the postwar recession of 1920-1921. The company never fully recovered,

making only 325 cars in 1921 and 690 in 1922. Unable to compete in the mid- and high-price market with an old-fashioned design, Alexander Winton dissolved his automobile company in February 1924.

The Winton company had pioneered the manufacture of gasoline cars in the Midwest and publicized them vigorously in its early years. Its management's conservative policies for automobiles after 1909, however, condemned it to decline.

References:

William G. Keener, "Ohio's Pioneer Auto Maker: Alexander Winton," *Museum Echoes*, 28 (March 1953): 19-22;

Richard Wager, *Golden Wheels* (Cleveland: Western Reserve Historical Society, 1975).

Contributors

David J. Andrea...*University of Michigan*
Lewis H. Carlson...*Western Michigan University*
Donald T. Critchlow ....*University of Notre Dame*
David Finkelman...*St. Mary's College of Maryland*
James J. Flink...*University of California, Irvine*
Richard B. Folsom...*Henry Ford Estate–Fair Lane*
Ralph D. Gray ....*Indiana University, Indianapolis*
Northcoate Hamilton ....*Columbia, South Carolina*
Louis G. Helverson...*Free Library of Philadelphia*
Charles K. Hyde ....*Wayne State University*
Beverly Rae Kimes ....*New York, New York*
Alec Kirby...*George Washington University*
Robert J. Kothe ....*Atlanta, Georgia*
James M. Laux ....*University of Cincinnati*
George S. May ....*Eastern Michigan University*
Frederick I. Olsen ....*University of Wisconsin–Milwaukee*
John B. Rae...*Harvey Mudd College*
Richard P. Scharchburg ....*GMI Engineering & Management Institute*
Darwin H. Stapleton..*Rockefeller Archive Center*
Bernard A. Weisberger ....*Chatham, New York*
Roger B. White ....*Smithsonian Institution*
Genevieve Wren..*Motor Vehicle Research Services*
James Wren ....*Motor Vehicle Manufacturers Association*

Index